PENNSYLVANIA POWER & LIGHT COMPANY

Single circuit 66KV wood pole transmission line (Lancaster County). This type of transmission line was typically used in the rural electrification of eastern Pennsylvania which took place in the 1920s and 1930s.

Pennsylvania Power & Light Company

A Guide to the Records

By: Michael Nash, John Rumm and Craig Orr

Hagley MUSEUM AND LIBRARY
Wilmington, Delaware

A HAGLEY COLLECTIONS GUIDE

This publication was supported in part by grants from the National Endowment for the Humanities and the Pennsylvania Power & Light Company.

ISBN - 914650-22-X

Contents

Foreword	vii
Preface	ix
PENNSYLVANIA POWER & LIGHT COMPANY: A Brief History	xi
Scope and Content Note.	xvi
Automating the Guide: A Note on Methodology	xxiii
Records of Predecessor Companies	1
Records of Pennsylvania Power & Light and Related Holding Companies	186
Pennsylvania Power & Light Company	186
American Gas & Electric Company	187
Electric Bond and Share Company	187
Lehigh Power Securities Corporation	188
United Gas and Electric Corporation	188
Index	191

Illustrations

Frontispiece

Single circuit 66KV wood pole transmission line (Lancaster County). This type of transmission line was typically used in the rural electrification of eastern Pennsylvania which took place in the 1920s and 1930s.

Following Page 44

Advertising flyers printed on the back of monthly bills by the Edison Electric Company to promote the use of electricity.

Following Page 86

Turbine Room, Hauto Power Plant, Lehigh Navigation Electric Company, 1913.

Rear of Electrical Control Board, Hauto Power Plant, 1913.

Following Page 128

Wallenpaupack Hydro Development, Pennsylvania Power & Light Company, 1926.

Generator Room, Holtwood Hydro Station, Built by Pennsylvania Water & Power Company, 1910.

FOREWORD

The publication of this guide to the Pennsylvania Power & Light Company (PP&L) collection of predecessor and merged companies' records marks both a departure from and a continuation of library tradition at the Hagley Museum and Library. The library department — formerly operating as the Eleutherian Mills Historical Library — has always believed in disseminating detailed information about its manuscript and archives holdings to encourage their use and the advancement of knowledge of business and industry in the Mid-Atlantic states. Consequently, the library published a Guide in 1970 and a Guide Supplement in 1978 under its former name and described 1528 accessions received through 1975.

This guide to the PP&L collection is unique and tradition-breaking, because of its focus on one accession. We feel that the PP&L collection warrants this singular treatment due to its size and importance in telling the story of growing electrical service within a 10,000 square mile region in central eastern Pennsylvania.

Obviously it was part of Hagley's mission to acquire, process, organize, and describe 26 tons of archives made available by Pennsylvania Power & Light Company. George F. Vanderslice, PP&L Vice President and Comptroller, Nicholas G. Foutrakis, Manager of General Accounting, and Eugene A. Wrona, Supervisor of Records Management, cooperated with us to complete this task. The Company also generously supported the printing and distributing of this book. This guide also received very substantial financial support from the Division of Research of the National Endowment for the Humanities. Patricia Shadle of the Endowment staff provided helpful advice on this project.

In the early stages of the undertaking we recognized that we were receiving local history records from the region as well as records on the history of electric power. Thus we and the PP&L Company are cooperating in distributing this guide to historical societies, and public and college libraries within the PP&L service area. Moreover, we plan to cooperate fully with researchers from that region to provide easy access to the information about particular townships, boroughs, cities, and counties.

For three decades Hagley has collected a broad spectrum of historical materials to explain the contributions of the Middle Atlantic states to American economic, business, industrial, and technological history. This institution strives through guides, conferences, and other means to attract an ever widening circle of graduate, postgraduate, and special subject researchers to use its growing store of primary research material. For a wide range of individuals, from school children visiting the museum to advanced research scholars using the library, Hagley is a place of learning. This guide makes a real contribution to Hagley's educational mission, and we are pleased to make it available.

Richmond D. Williams
Deputy Director for Library Administration
Hagley Museum and Library

Preface

On October 11, 1976, when the Pennsylvania Power & Light Company deposited its historical records at Hagley it became the first major supplier of electricity to open its archives for historical research. Three years later we applied for a National Endowment for the Humanities grant to arrange and describe the collection. Professor Thomas Hughes of the University of Pennsylvania strongly endorsed the project, predicting that "within two decades the history of the electrical utilities, along with the history of electrical manufacturers, will be recognized by historians as keys to understanding twentieth century United States history." It is now clear that this 1,000 linear foot collection is an invaluable resource for students of economic, business, technological, political, and social history. The archive consists primarily of the records of the 1,050 companies that merged over a 75-year period (1880-1955) to form the present day Pennsylvania Power & Light Company. The collection describes the industry's tentative beginnings using the Edison system of direct current, the technological innovations which allowed small, inner city utilities to expand beyond their original urban centers, and the consolidation movement that culminated with the formation of a great regional power network. The roles that scientists, engineers, entrepreneurs, workers, politicians, and consumers played in this unfolding drama are well documented.

The primary purpose of this volume is to make the records of the Pennsylvania Power & Light Company available to researchers. There are two series, each of which has been arranged alphabetically: (1) the records of the companies that merged into Pennsylvania Power & Light, (2) the records of Pennsylvania Power & Light and related holding companies. Each entry contains a short company history, while those for operating companies include detailed descriptions of the records along with scope and content notes highlighting material of particular interest. There is a dictionary index with entries for subjects, places, and names (both personal and corporate). Indexed items refer to appropriate collection numbers in the first part of the volume.

In addition to the letters, reports, technical papers, and financial records that form the bulk of the archive, there is a small collection of pictorial material which includes views of electrical apparatus, hydroelectric facilities and street railways. These are stored in the Pictorial Collections and Audio-Visual Services Department, but are described with the appropriate guide entries.

A guide of this kind is always the work of many hands. Our project was financed by a three year National Endowment for the Humanities grant. Dr. Margaret Child, Jeffrey Field, and Pat Shadle worked with us and provided extremely useful advice and encouragement. Dr. Richmond Williams, Hagley's Deputy Director for Library Administration, initiated the project, wrote the grant proposal, and with Hugh Gibb shepherded the undertaking through its early stages. Herman Baron worked with us for almost two years. He edited our manuscript data sheets, constructed the thesaurus, indexes, and the computer program that produced camera-ready page proofs.

Dorothy Jenner and Melissa Croghan were responsible for the editorial work. Their meticulous attention to detail greatly improved the guide. David Gilchrist, Publications Coordinator, helped transform our Manuscript Guide into a book. His professionalism expedited what could have been an extremely difficult process.

Michael Nash
Curator of Manuscripts and Archives
Hagley Museum and Library

Pennsylvania Power & Light Company: A Brief History

Electric supply and manufacture was one of the United States' major growth industries during the early twentieth century. These years saw a rapid shift from the direct use of raw energy (coal and water power) to processed energy (gas and electricity). As Warren Devine[1] has shown in 1900 steam provided 80 percent of America's mechanical drive capacity, and thirty years later electric motors accounted for 78 percent. Electricity was much more efficient than steam, coal, or water power and the increased productivity that it helped generate fueled America's drive toward industrial maturity. This new source of power radically transformed the ways in which most Americans lived and worked. Electric lights, motors, refrigerators, radios, phonographs, and street cars had major impact on all aspects of American life. As Thomas Hughes[2] has pointed out, the great power networks like Pennsylvania Power & Light (PP&L) played a central role in this process. By systematizing and coordinating the distribution of electricity they made it possible to supply power economically to all corners of the continental United States.

Pennsylvania Power & Light had its origins with the various water and gas light companies that began operating in the eastern part of the state during the mid-nineteenth century. Carlisle Gas & Water Company, founded in 1853, was PP&L's first predecessor. During the next twenty-five years scores of other companies began supplying the region's residential and commercial customers. However, in the late 1870s electricity was introduced to the area and started to compete with gas. These first arc lighting systems were used for street lighting. They could not be adapted for domestic use since their lamps were connected in series and when one was turned off the entire system went dark. In the early 1880s Thomas A. Edison began building central stations which were designed to bring power to individual households. In order to allow lamps to be independently controlled Edison designed a series of parallel circuits. However, there were many problems with the early Edison direct current system. It had a one mile distribution radius which limited its practical use to densely populated regions. Beyond these areas there were drastic voltage losses that could only be controlled if large amounts of expensive copper wire were used to conduct electricity. Turning his attention to this problem, Edison developed a three-wire system at his Sunbury, Pennsylvania village station. This reduced the amount of copper wire needed by more than 60 percent and doubled the area in which an electric company could profitably operate. After the Sunbury station was opened on 4 July 1883, Edison and his agent P.B. Shaw of Williamsport began licensing local electric companies to use the system. Within a few years electric utilities were operating in Ashland, Hazleton, Lancaster, Mount Carmel, Pottsville, Shamokin, Harrisburg, Tamaqua, Williamsport and Catasaqua.

The early Edison companies, however, were extremely inefficient. Their direct current generators were small and capacity was usually 25 to 100 kilowatts. They were further weakened by poor load factors and high peaks during evening and weekend hours that left a good deal of unused capacity for most of the working day. Moreover, even after the development of the three-wire system the area to which direct current could be distributed was very limited. In 1885, George Westinghouse, the inventor of the air brake, began to search for a solution. By the fall of the following year he developed an alternating current system which was to revolutionize the electrical industry. Alternating current could be transmitted for long distances at 1000 volts and stepped down to 50 volts at the point of consumption. This vastly increased the area in which a utility could operate and costs were proportionately reduced.

As Forrest McDonald observed in another context, the development of alternating current made it economically feasible to build large hydroelectric plants many miles from the point of consumption. It also facilitated the construction of steam electric generators which "connected the distribution systems of cities together like bulbs on a wire." In short, alternating current made the modern electric utility system possible.[3]

As energy consumption increased, the economic advantages of the Westinghouse method became increasingly significant. By the mid-1890s the Edison companies were unable to compete and faced grave financial difficulties. Dozens of them, including the Sunbury company went bankrupt.[4] Others were forced to purchase modified Westinghouse equipment.

Once the Westinghouse Electric Company began marketing its alternating current equipment entrepreneurs found that they could organize electric light companies with relatively modest investments. As a result, hundreds of small operators entered the business and tried to carve out a portion of the market for themselves. In many areas, three or four companies operated in a single township. After a few years they would often merge, but invariably another competitor soon appeared on the scene. The electrification of anthracite coal mines, street cars and the exploitation of the Susquehanna River intensified the competition. Between 1890 and 1910 many transit and hydroelectric companies began to market their surplus energy at relatively low prices. In rural areas, small factory owners, storekeepers and farmers also installed generating equipment and they soon began distributing electricity.

This was a period of extremely rapid technological development. Improvements were expensive, but if an established company did not make them, a new one would move into its territory and build a more efficient facility. Bitter competition resulted. As rates fell and investment needs increased, the electric companies were often hard pressed to pay interest to bondholders or dividends to stockholders. However, just when it seemed as if the situation would deteriorate into chaos, the technology that made it possible to build regional power networks became available. The development of steam generating turbines and high voltage transmission lines allowed utilities to centralize their generating and distribution facilities. Thus in 1905 when Lehigh Valley Transit Company installed its first modern turbogenerator, it launched a consolidation movement that was to integrate Pennsylvania's young electric industry into a unified system.

During the decade between 1907 and 1917 Scranton Electric, Harwood Electric, Schuylkill Gas & Electric, Lehigh Valley Light and Power, and Lehigh Navigation Electric Companies began installing new turbogenerators and forming large integrated systems. The method of expansion was determined by Pennsylvania public utility law which forbade a company from operating in more than one township. This forced the large electric companies to set up "paper" or non-operating companies to obtain additional franchise rights. The aim was to end destructive competition but in this the industry was only partially successful. By the eve of World War I, Scranton Electric was dominant in the northern anthracite coal field, Harwood Electric controlled a large part of the market in the middle field, which included Luzerne County. Schuylkill Gas & Electric was the largest company in the southern field, while Lehigh Valley Light and Power and Lehigh Navigation Electric Company competed for customers in the Allentown-Bethlehem area. After a decade of merger and consolidation there were still certain areas in which competition was growing increasingly cut-throat. As late as 1917 there were 70 electric companies operating in eastern Pennsylvania. In some localities small companies had certain regional advantages which allowed them to compete effectively. Many of the large utilities were not particularly efficient. In their rush to monopolize the market they often absorbed unprofitable competitors with huge unfunded debts. Not always considering the financial consequences of such consolidations, some companies found that a series of ill-conceived mergers left them only earning one or two percent profit. For example, in 1916, Harwood Electric Company had a net income of only $5,213.13, but was forced to invest more than $500,000 to modernize its plant and equipment.[5]

General Electric Corporation (G.E.) which over the years had provided capital, equipment, and consulting services and in return had acquired a substantial portfolio of utility company securities, found itself in an extremely difficult situation as the financial stability of the electric industry became increasingly precarious. In 1905, in order to resuscitate these companies and convert their stocks and bonds into marketable securities, G.E. organized the Electric Bond and Share Company (EBASCO), a New York holding company. The president of EBASCO, S. Z. Mitchell, who had many years experience reorganizing and managing bankrupt utilities in the Pacific Northwest, was seen by G.E. as being the ideal person to rationalize eastern Pennsylvania's electrical supply system. Under Mitchell's leadership, Bond and Share provided engineering and financial consulting services to utility companies and in return received minority stock ownership. Working through a sub-holding company, Lehigh Power Securities Corporation, EBASCO reorganized the managerial structure of many of the area's electric companies. Most often only 20-25 percent of total capitalization was in common stock, and the holding company was able to exercise control while making modest investments.

Using this approach, EBASCO had quietly become a major presence in eastern Pennsylvania by 1917. In September of that year it acquired a controlling interest in Lehigh Navigation Electric Company and prepared to assume a dominant position in the industry. In 1919 it purchased The Lehigh Valley Light and Power Company and these two giant utilities were soon merged. On 4 June 1920, Pennsylvania Power & Light Company was formed as a result of EBASCO sponsored consolidation of seven operating companies: The Lehigh Valley Light & Power Company, No. 2, Northern Central Gas Company, Northumberland County Gas & Electric, The Harwood Electric Company, The Schuylkill Gas & Electric Company and Pennsylvania Lighting Company. These utilities merged with Pennsylvania Power & Light Company, No. 2, a non-operating company that had been formed several months earlier simply to hold the name.*

The merger agreement succinctly summarized the reasons for this consolidation. It observed that "in order to stabilize production" and reduce costs, most electric companies had "abandoned small, isolated and generally inefficient and unstable privately owned power plants." It now clearly made economic sense to use "large generating stations" which were "interconnected and located near the source of coal supply." Consolidation would allow the industry to "better meet the increasing costs of furnishing service by [introducing] economies in production and distribution." The new regional system was thus organized to eliminate many of the problems caused by the duplication of "plants and equipment" which made the procurement of "capital difficult . . . and costly."[6]

PP&L fulfilled many of the expectations of its founders. By the mid-1920s it was supplying power to almost 400,000 residential and industrial customers in 700 communities. About 40 percent of its energy was sold to the area's anthracite coal mines. Bethlehem Steel consumed another 10 percent with smaller amounts going to the region's slate quarries, textile mills, and cement factories. Most of eastern Pennsylvania, however, was agricultural with no single community having a population of more than 100,000. Bringing these isolated regions into a unified power network was an organizational and technological challenge of considerable magnitude. Fortunately, capital became available as consolidation increased the industry's profitability. During most of the 1920s, PP&L earned about $2,000,000 per year. This represented a 5 or 6 percent return.[7] These profits financed a period of continual growth, modernization, and expansion. In 1923 five additional companies were brought into the system as PP&L extended its territory into the Wilkes-Barre and Williamsport areas. In 1928, thirty-four companies were added to the network which now encompassed all of Schuylkill, Carbon, and Luzerne Counties as well as the state capital at Harrisburg. In 1930, twenty-one more companies were added as PP&L moved into rural Lancaster County. This area became one of the first in the nation to enjoy the benefits of rural electrification. During the 1930s and '40s PP&L installed some 7,600 miles of rural transmission lines that brought electricity to some of the most remote areas of its system.

Pennsylvania Power & Light and Lehigh Power Securities Corporation represented only one branch of the EBASCO system. During the 1920s Electric Bond and Share constructed an elaborate pyramid of holding companies staffed by interlocking directorates. For example, National Power & Light was an EBASCO subsidiary with controlling interests in Lehigh Power Securities Corporation and American Gas and Electric. These companies in turn dominated Pennsylvania Power & Light and The Scranton Electric Company. By 1926 the EBASCO network had total assets of more than 1.8 billion dollars. With 19 million customers it generated 10 percent of the electricity produced in the United States.[8]

*The Scranton Electric Company, which was controlled by another EBASCO sub-holding company, American Gas and Electric, was not formally brought into the PP&L system until the 1950s.

EBASCO's expansion was part of a national trend. During the 1910s and 1920s utility holding companies came to exercise almost total control over the nation's power industry. By 1925, forty-one such companies generated 82 percent of America's electricity.[9] These large networks clearly had many economic advantages as they integrated the entire continental United States into a single system. Their size and ability to raise capital enabled them to invest in the latest technology and rapidly modernize their generating and distribution systems.

Utility holding companies, however, did have their critics who argued that these conglomerates worked systematically to raise prices and profits. A 1928 Federal Trade Commission report accused them of issuing excessively speculative securities, charging high consulting fees, and generally inflating the value of their stock so as to pressure operating companies to increase rates. Furthermore, the F.T.C. charged that utility holding companies were organized in such a way as to permit a few men with relatively small investments to dominate an immensely profitable industry. It often seemed that state and local regulatory agencies were unable to control these giants, and by the late 1920s there was a good deal of public support for breaking up the so-called "power trust."[10]

As attention increasingly focused on General Electric's alleged efforts to monopolize the power industry through Electric Bond and Share, chairman Owen Young sought to separate his company from EBASCO. A 1929 reorganization resulted in the formation of a new Electric Bond and Share which claimed not to be a holding company per se, since it did not have majority control over any of the sub-holding companies it "supervised." Its largest holding was 46.5 percent of National Power and Light stock. The Federal Trade Commission and most state regulatory agencies did not agree with this analysis and proceeded to prosecute EBASCO under the anti-trust laws.

The changed political climate of the 1930s put utility holding companies increasingly on the defensive. President Franklin Roosevelt was convinced that they were keeping the price of electricity at artificially high levels and retarding his recovery program. As a result, he secured the passage of the Public Utility Holding Company Act of 1935. This legislation gave the Securities and Exchange Commission broad powers to regulate utility holding companies, which were in most instances, to be limited to a single tier. Exemptions were to be granted only in cases where it could be proven that simplification would result in the loss of substantial economies. In addition, utility holding companies were now required to register with the S.E.C. and secure its approval before undertaking most financial transactions, including: acquisition of securities, payment of dividends, and reorganization. Electric Bond and Share took the lead in opposing this legislation and refused to register with the S.E.C. until this requirement was upheld by the United States Supreme Court in March 1938. After three years of litigation National Power & Light Company was ordered to dissolve in 1941. Six years later PP&L became an independent utility, and EBASCO was forced to relinquish its control over American Gas & Electric and The Scranton Electric Companies.[11]

Pennsylvania Power & Light, however, continued to expand during the next two decades. In 1947, Mauch Chunk Heat, Power & Electric Light, and Renovo Edison Light, Heat & Power Companies were merged into the system. In 1955, Pennsylvania Water & Power was added and the next year The Scranton Electric Company was brought in. By the mid 1970s PP&L and its various predecessors had absorbed more than 300 operating and 700 non-operating companies. Today, the utility has more than 1,000,000 customers in a 10,000 square mile area of eastern Pennsylvania.

Notes

1. Warren Devine, "From Shafts to Wires," *Journal of Economic History* (June 1983) 347-373.
2. Thomas Hughes, *Networks of Power* (Baltimore: Johns Hopkins University Press, 1983).
3. Forrest McDonald, *Let There Be Light: The Electric Utility Industry In Wisconsin, 1881-1955* (Madison: American History Research Center, 1957).
4. Edison Electric Illuminating Company of Sunbury, Minute Book, February 9, 1891, February 11, 1891, Pennsylvania Power & Light Records (hereafter cited as PP&L).
5. The Harwood Electric Company, Minute Book, February 20, 1917, *PP&L*.
6. The Harwood Electric Company, Minute Book, April 17, 1920, *PP&L*.
7. Pennsylvania Power & Light Company, "Audit Reports" (1925-30), *PP&L*.
8. Federal Trade Commission, *Summary Report on Economic, Financial, and Corporate Phases of Holding and Operating Companies of Electric and Gas Utilities* (Sen. Doc. 92 Pt. 72A 70 Congress, 1st Session, 1953) 1-17.
9. Federal Trade Commission, *Utility Holding Companies* (Sen. Doc. 92, Washington: GPO, 1928-35) 84 volumes; see also Gifford Pinchot, *The Power Monopoly* (Milford, PA, 1928).
10. Pinchot, pp. 1-10.
11. Ellis W. Hawley, *The New Deal and the Problem of Monopoly* (Princeton: University Press, 1966) 325-44.

Scope And Content Note

According to Pennsylvania law electric and gas companies were classified as either "operating" or "non-operating." This distinction was necessary because utilities were state-chartered and allowed to provide service in only one community. If a company desired to extend its area of operation to an adjacent community, it had to incorporate a non-operating or "paper" company to secure franchise rights. The operating company then either merged with or acquired the non-operating company. This operating/non-operating distinction had been applied to all the companies (electric/gas/railway/water) in the collection. This includes those non-utility companies (e.g., real estate firms) which were "non-operating" in the sense that they did not control any property or assets and performed no actual function.

The records of all operating companies in the collection have been grouped into two series: 1) administrative records, and 2) operating records. Administrative records relate to the organization, ownership, capitalization, and management of an operating company. They consist of minute books, annual reports, stock and bond records, legal papers, and correspondence. Operating records refer to a company's daily business activities. They include account books and records pertaining to finances, engineering, construction, production, distribution, sales, personnel, and accounting.

The greatest strength of the PP&L Collection is its diversity. It contains the records of a variety of companies including electric, manufactured and natural gas, steam heating, water supply, street railway, bus and traction, coal mining and coal dredging, real estate, and holding companies. The records document the economic and technical development of these firms in the political and social environment of eastern Pennsylvania.

The earliest companies in the PP&L Collection date back to the 1850s. Among them is Susquehanna Boom Company, which built and operated a logging boom and erected a dam on the Susquehanna River near Williamsport. The company's minute book documents its log-booming and log-running operations and contains annual reports that trace the rise and post-1870s decline of Pennsylvania's lumber industry.

Other records dating back to the 1850s reflect the rapid growth of the urban gas lighting industry in eastern Pennsylvania. Included are the papers of companies located in Carlisle, Mauch Chunk, Milton, Sunbury, Wilkes-Barre, and Williamsport. Minute books of these companies describe the construction and operation of gas works, negotiations with borough and municipal governments for excavation permits and street-lighting contracts, and the shift from coal gas to water gas in the 1870s. Annual reports of gas companies operating in Carlisle, Mauch Chunk, Sunbury, Wilkes-Barre, and Williamsport contain statistical information about the extent of service and the number of types of customers (residential/commercial/institutional). Audit reports and financial statements itemize gas manufacturing and distribution costs. Records of The Carlisle Gas and Water Company also document its construction and operation of a water supply system and illustrate its concern with public health and sanitation in the 1860s and 1870s.

Records of Harrisburg Steam Heat and Power Company, The Hazleton Steam Heating Company, Shenandoah Heat and Power Company, and The Wilkes-Barre Heat, Light and Motor Company, trace the growth of the steam heating industry during the 1870s and 1880s. Minute books of these companies document the installation of central steam heating plants and negotiations with local governments for service to public buildings.

Urban lighting markets were dominated by gas companies until the late 1870s and early 1880s, when the development of arc and incandescent lighting made possible the commercial exploitation of electricity. The introduction of arc lighting is described in detail in correspondence and minute books of Excelsior Electric Company of Harrisburg, which was organized by and installed the system manufactured by Excelsior Electric Company of New York. Minute books of The Wilkes-Barre Electric Light Company trace its organization by another New York arc lighting manufacturer, Arnoux and Hochhausen Electrical Company. Records of Allentown Electric Light and Power Company, The Bethlehem Electric Light Company, and Honesdale Electric Light Heat and Power Company, outline purchases and installation of arc lighting systems manufactured by Thomson-Houston Electric Light, United States Electric Lighting, and American Electric Manufacturing companies. Minute books document competition with gas companies for control of urban lighting markets, contracts with local governments for street lighting, and the development of rate schedules.

Because arc lighting produced an extremely harsh light and burning carbon rods were dangerous, these early systems were used mostly for street lighting and in open-space commercial facilities. The development of incandescent lighting made available a safer, more attractive source of illumination for residential customers. Thomas E. Edison pioneered in the development of a direct current incandescent lighting system in the late 1870s and began commercially exploiting that system in the early 1880s. The records of the Edison companies established in Ashland, Harrisburg, Hazleton, Lancaster, Mount Carmel, Port Clinton, Pottsville, Renovo, Shamokin, Sunbury, Tamaqua, and Williamsport, trace Edison's early involvement in the Pennsylvania electric industry. Minute books document the role of Philip B. Shaw of Williamsport, Pennsylvania agent for The Edison Electric Light Company of New York, who organized and licensed companies to install the Edison system. The minutes also outline the financial relationships between the parent company and its licensees, the installation of Edison central stations, efforts to secure the support of local entrepreneurs, and advertising campaigns to attract customers. Annual reports of The Edison Electric Illuminating Company of Ashland, Penna., contain information furnished to the parent Edison company describing the central station capacity, types of equipment in use, the number of lamps in service, and the company's financial situation.

The electric industry expanded rapidly in eastern Pennsylvania after the mid-1880s. Dozens of new companies were formed to provide arc and incandescent lighting service in communities throughout the region. Minute books and stock records document the beginnings of electric service in localities such as Bloomsburg, Lansford, Lock Haven, Mauch Chunk, Mahonoy City, Scranton, Shamokin, Shenandoah, and Wilkes-Barre. Consumers' records, including lamp sales books of The Bethlehem Electric Light Company, The Edison Electric Illuminating Company of Pottsville, and Honesdale Electric Light Heat and Power Company, and house wiring and meter installation ledgers of Lehigh and Northhampton Light, Heat and Power Company and Trumbauersville Electric Light and Power Company, itemize the number and types of customers and the amount of electricity consumed. Correspondence regarding customers and marketing efforts is found in the files of Excelsior Electric Light, Power and Gas Company, Montgomery and Muncy Electric Light, Heat and Power Company, and Panther Valley Electric Company. Minute books of several companies discuss the question of rate abatements for religious, social, and civic institutions and describe negotiations with local governments for street lighting contracts and permits for erecting poles and stringing wires.

The rapid expansion of the electric industry profoundly affected the gas industry in eastern Pennsylvania. Gas and electric companies competed for control of the residential lighting market. In order to survive, gas companies were forced to implement a variety of strategies: lowering rates, developing new markets, and organizing their own subsidiary electric companies. Minute books of Sunbury Gas Company document rate reductions, agreements with industrial customers for gas heating and fuel service, and progress in obtaining gas heating contracts with residential and commercial customers. Correspondence and working papers of Mauch Chunk Gas Company describe rates, sales of gas appliances, and installations of gas heating equipment.

While gas companies were struggling for survival, the alternating current system developed by the Westinghouse Company in the mid-1880s, facilitated even more rapid expansion of the electric industry. The Edison direct current system was extremely inefficient and limited in its distribution range. The Westinghouse system utilized transformers to step current up to high-voltages for long-distance transmission, and to step down the current for distribution to customers. Westinghouse began marketing this system in 1886. The minute book of Electric Light and Power Company of Carbondale, Pennsylvania, documents the organization and licensing of one of the earliest companies to install an AC system. They also describe the improvements in the company's generating equipment that enabled it to furnish alternating current to an electric street railway.

Alternating current spread rapidly throughout eastern Pennsylvania as its advantages over direct current became increasingly obvious. Minute books of The Bethlehem Electric Light Company, Edison Electric Illuminating companies in Hazleton, Lancaster, Pottsville, and Sunbury, and the minute book and letter book of Renovo Edison Light, Heat and Power Company document the process by which AC replaced DC. Alternating current systems manufactured by Thomson-Houston Electric Light Company and Brush Electric Company were installed by newly-formed companies such as The Mauch Chunk Heat, Power & Electric Light Company and The Minersville Electric Light Company.

The late 1880s and early 1890s witnessed a "battle of the systems" between AC and DC. Records of competing firms in Harrisburg, Lancaster, Shamokin, Sunbury, and Williamsport discuss the effects of this struggle. In Harrisburg, for example, The Harrisburg Electric Light Company competed with Excelsior Electric Company of Harrisburg for control of the city's street and residential lighting markets. The competition forced the Edison-organized electric light company to install an AC system to replace its DC system. Minute books of the two firms also describe their efforts to influence the Harrisburg City Council which granted municipal street lighting contracts.

Because AC and DC systems were not compatible, during the early period there was a haphazard pattern of installation in eastern Pennsylvania. In a given locality one company might furnish AC of 60 cycles, another AC of 25 cycles, and a third might supply DC. Alternating current was initially not adaptable for electric motors, while DC motors were limited to large stationary installations. The development of the universal supply system by Westinghouse in 1893 not only facilitated the standardization of electrical equipment but also made it possible to use both AC and DC to operate electric motors and lights. The system consisted of an AC/DC generator, a transformer, a rotary converter for changing AC into DC and vice versa, and an induction motor. By installing this system, one company could supply both DC and AC for electric lighting and power. Minute books of Allentown Electric Light and Power Company, The Bethlehem Electric Light Company, and West End Electric Light and Power Company, correspondence of Shamokin and Coal Township Light and Power Company, and the voucher register of Paxtang Electric Company, document early installations of this universal supply system.

Advances in hydroelectric power also made an important impact on the industry. During the era when current could not be transmitted over long distances, hydroelectricity could only be used in very limited areas. Minute books of The Citizens Light, Heat and Power Company of Slatington and The Millersburg Electric Light, Heat and Power Company document how difficult it was to distribute hydroelectric power before the mid-1890s. Financial records of the two companies itemize the high costs of copper wiring which had to be installed to cope with voltage losses.

Improvements in transmission made possible by the development of alternating current facilitated the installation of a number of more efficient hydroelectric plants capable of supplying power to wider areas. Minute books of The Lancaster Electric Light, Heat and Power Company describe such an installation.

The successful harnessing of Niagara Falls for power in the late 1890s brought a real stimulus to the development of other large hydroelectric systems. The public attention given to the project, and its immediate financial success, generated a veritable "hydro-mania." Similar projects, however, often failed because they could not secure necessary customers or could not obtain sufficient financial backing. The audit book of Rivers and Streams Company describes an unsuccessful effort by a group of promoters to develop a 10,000 horsepower hydroelectric station on the Delaware River.

A successful hydroelectric project in Pennsylvania is documented in the records of Pennsylvania Water and Power Company and its predecessors. These records trace the efforts of various groups, dating back to the early 1890s, to develop the hydroelectric potential of the lower Susquehanna River. Minute books of McCall Ferry Power Company, and correspondence and memoranda of Susquehanna Canal and Power Company document the bitter and prolonged struggle waged between two groups over the rights to that development. Although McCall Ferry emerged the victor, the rights to that development became the target of a lawsuit brought by the Commonwealth of Pennsylvania. The Commonwealth sought to halt the project because local residents were alarmed at the threat of possible flooding. The effects of this dispute on the company's plans, its construction of a large dam and hydroelectric plant at Holtwood, and the company's bankruptcy during the Panic of 1907, are described in its minute books. The records of its successor, Pennsylvania Water and Power Company (PWP), trace the completion of this project and the operations of the Holtwood facility from 1910 until PWP merged into PP&L in 1955. These records include correspondence and memoranda of chief executive officers, correspondence of its engineering, operating, and test departments, minute books, stock records, contracts, engineering cost papers, and daily logs and diaries describing operations of Holtwood Station and associated substations.

Another impetus to the development of the electric industry in the 1890s came from street railways, with their huge power demands. Until the late 1880s, horses were the main source of power for street railways. These animals were slow, dirty, costly to maintain, and unsuited to long-distance, urban passenger travel. Steam locomotives, while widely used for interurban transport, were too dangerous for use in congested cities. The electrification of traction systems resulted in a street railway construction boom during the twenty-five years before World War I. Minute books, account books, and passenger statistics of Williamsport Passenger Railway Company document the operations of a horsecar railway, experiments with steam power in 1883, and the electrification of the line by 1891. The records of Schuylkill Electric Railway Company trace the efforts of several electrical manufacturers, including Thomson-Houston, Sprague, and The Short Line Railway Company, to promote their electric traction systems.

The growth of street railway service is traced in the records of traction companies in Harrisburg, Lancaster, North Branch, Jersey Shore, and Montoursville. Minute books contain information on routes, construction, acquisition of rolling stock and other equipment, and negotiations with the electric companies which supplied power to the lines. There is also considerable material on earnings and expenses, and the impact of accident and liability claims.

Electric railways provided a ready market for electric companies which were now able to double or quadruple their sales without increasing investment or operating costs. The relationships between traction and electric companies are documented in the minute books and the financial statements of Allentown Electric Light and Power Company and The Edison Electric Illuminating Company of Pottsville. A number of street railways organized their own subsidiary electric companies which sold surplus power to the communities along their lines. Minute books of Schuylkill Light, Heat, and Power Company, Shamokin Electric Light and Power Company, and Sunbury Electric Light and Power Company document this trend.

The power demands created by electric traction were a major impetus for the development of turbo-generating equipment during the 1890s. After the turn of the century, these turbines became larger and more powerful as demand for electricity grew. In 1905 Lehigh Valley Transit Company installed the first modern steam turbo-generator in eastern Pennsylvania in its Allentown plant. Eight years later, Lehigh Navigation Electric Company built its Hauto Steam Generating Station which utilized three 10,000 kw General Electric turbo-generators. At the time of its completion this was the third largest steam turbo-generating plant in the world. Minute books, correspondence, and contract files thoroughly document the project.

The installation of turbo-generators made large amounts of surplus electricity available. Thus, increasingly after the turn of the century, electric companies promoted the electrification of industries in eastern Pennsylvania. Minute books of The Citizens Electric Light and Power Company of Hughesville, Pennsylvania describe the installations of electric motors in grist and woollen mills, furniture factories, and blacksmith shops. Correspondence of Lehigh Navigation Electric Company documents the electrification of cement and steel companies (including Bethlehem Steel), and slate-quarrying operations in the Lehigh Valley. Minute books, construction ledgers, and correspondence of The Harwood Electric Company and its subsidiary, Harwood Coal Company, trace the erection of a large mine-mouth, turbo-generating plant which electrified the area's mines and collieries. Engineering and administrative files in the PWP records document the electrification of the Pennsylvania Railroad's lines in southeast Pennsylvania and northeast Maryland in the 1920s. This project represented the first large-scale effort to electrify the operations of a major railroad company.

Electric companies also promoted the sale of electric appliances to residential customers. Sales of appliances such as fans, vacuum cleaners, irons, and washing machines are documented in the correspondence files of The Citizens Electric Light and Power Company of Hughesville, Pennsylvania, Montgomery and Muncy Electric Light, Heat, and Power Company, and Panther Valley Electric Company, and in the store account ledger of Lehigh and Northampton Light, Heat, and Power Company.

The technological development of the electric industry was expensive, and in a highly competitive environment with relatively low profit margins, entrepreneurs were hard pressed to find the capital necessary to modernize their plant and equipment. Financial statements and minute books document the extremely precarious situation in which many utilities found themselves. The impact of competition on the industry is described in the records of the Edison Electric Illuminating Company of Sunbury and Steelton Light, Heat, and Power Company. Financial records of rival firms in Lancaster, Harrisburg, Shamokin, and Williamsport place the competitive situation in a wider context.

After the Panic of 1893, financially troubled utilities began to look for outside capital in New York and Philadelphia. Records of the Mauch Chunk Heat, Power and Electric Light Company document the process by which a group of Philadelphia investors assumed control. Minute books of the Northumberland Electric Illuminating Company describe how a consortium of Delaware investors led by Pierre and T. Coleman du Pont and John J. Raskob came to dominate the utility companies in Sunbury. Outside investors also worked to consolidate street railway companies in given localities, as is documented in the records of Conestoga Traction Company (Lancaster County), Eastern Pennsylvania Railways Company (Carbon, Columbia, and Schuylkill Counties), and Valley Traction Company (Dauphin and Franklin Counties).

The pace of consolidation and integration of utility companies in eastern Pennsylvania quickened from the late nineteenth into the twentieth century, culminating in the formation of Pennsylvania Power & Light Company in 1920. The archives contain administrative and operating records documenting the history of the seven large companies that formed the original nucleus of PP&L: Columbia and Montour Electric Company, The Harwood Electric Company, The Lehigh Valley Light and Power Company, Northern Central Gas Company, Northumberland County Gas & Electric Company, Pennsylvania Lighting Company, and The Schuylkill Gas and Electric Company. This material describes the organization and financing of these companies and their construction of large generating and distribution systems during the early years of this century. Minute books reveal the managerial strategies and the relationships that these firms had with investment bankers, holding companies, and consulting engineers. The role that Electric Bond and Share Company and its sub-holding company, Lehigh Power Securities Corporation, played in directing the integration of the region's utilities is well-documented. Of particular interest are the minutes of The Lehigh Valley Light and Power Company for 1919-20 which describe the organization of PP&L. Correspondence and agreements of Lehigh Navigation Electric Company outline negotiations between its parent firm, Lehigh Coal and Navigation Company, and Lehigh Power Securities Corporation.

The strategies pursued by PP&L and its parent holding companies, EBASCO and Lehigh Power Securities Corporation, in acquiring utilities in eastern Pennsylvania are documented through correspondence and working papers of PP&L's legal department. Five binders of merger petitions prepared by PP&L lawyers for presentation to the Pennsylvania Public Service Commission, describe the rationale behind the company's expansion. Correspondence files of Anthracite Power Company, East Penn Electric Company, and Edison Electric Company describe the pre-merger negotiations with PP&L.

As PP&L expanded, it also modernized its generating and transmission facilities. Construction ledgers itemize improvements made to stations and substations acquired by the company. Records of Phoenix Utility Company, a wholly-owned subsidiary of EBASCO, document engineering and technical services rendered to PP&L in the construction of Wallenpaupack Steam Electric Station. The joint development by PP&L and The Scranton Electric Company of the 10,000 kw Stanton Steam Station from 1925 to 1927 is described in the records of Stanton Operating Company.

Pennsylvania Water and Power Company, and The Scranton Electric Company also continued to modernize their facilities in the years prior to their acquisition by PP&L. Correspondence and contract files of PWP document its power interconnections with other large electric companies and its participation in the Pennsylvania-New Jersey-Maryland power pool. Files of its test department describe experiments performed on electrical, hydraulic, and communications equipment, while papers of its Holtwood Laboratory document studies of water flow, flood measurement, lightning abatement, and pollution control. Engineering records of The Scranton Electric Company trace its construction and operation of several steam turbo-generators and its interconnections with the transmission facilities of PP&L and other companies.

The increasing technical and economic complexity of the utility industries forced companies to devise new managerial and administrative structures during the early years of the twentieth century. Budgets and correspondence files of the subsidiary companies of Lehigh Power Securities Corporation's "Railways Division" document the administration of the street railway lines it acquired and the managerial strategies developed as competition from automobiles and buses made electric traction increasingly unprofitable. The administrative records of PWP reflect its bureaucratic organization and the division of managerial responsibilities among several departments. Correspondence and memoranda of PWP chief executive officers document their concern with organization, systems operations, interdepartmental relations, and corporate personnel matters. Legal department files of PP&L contain copies of various agreements and contracts with EBASCO for managerial and administrative services which the holding company rendered to its subsidiary.

The new administrative structures developed by large utilities led to a change in the relationship between managers and workers. Payroll records and minute books of utility companies prior to the early 1900s document the more personalized relationship between employers and employees, particularly with regard to wages, employment practices, and job responsibilities which existed in the nineteenth century. Increasingly during the early years of the twentieth century, large utility companies rationalized and formalized their personnel practices. Payroll ledgers and time sheets reflect the standardization of job classifications and rates of pay. Timebooks of Lehigh Navigation Electric Company include observations by supervisory personnel of worker's performances and efficiency. Correspondence files of East Penn Electric Company, Eastern Pennsylvania Railways Company, and PWP refer to personnel matters such as employment procedures, terminations and layoffs, job classifications, salaries of supervisory and clerical workers, safety practices, and welfare work.

As technical, economic, and administrative considerations affected the development of the utility industries in the pre-World War I era, so too political and social considerations shaped their growth during and after the war. Government regulation during the war resulted in a new relationship between the industry and the state. The role of government agencies such as the Federal Fuel Administration and the National Committee on Gas and Electric Service in administering wartime conservation measures is documented in the minute books and correspondence of The Harwood Electric Company, Lehighton Electric Light and Power Company, New Parrysville Consolidated Gas Company, Montoursville Electric Light Company, and Tatamy Light, Heat and Power Company. The War Industries Board's coordination of utility company defense mobilization is described in the records of Lehigh Valley Light and Power Company, The Harwood Electric Company, and The Baltimore Electro Alloys Company. Correspondence and minute books of Eastern Pennsylvania Railways Company document the role played by the National War Labor Board in averting a strike by company employees.

The wartime experiences with government control changed the political and social climate in which the utility companies operated. In the 1920s the remnants of the progressive movement sought to regulate the so-called "power trust." The old Progressives were particularly disturbed by the industry's seeming disinterest in rural electrification. The utilities argued that it was uneconomical to furnish power to these sparsely-populated regions. In Pennsylvania, Governor Gifford Pinchot and his technical assistant Morris L. Cooke, proposed a "Giant Power Board" which would create a state agency to build large mine-mouth electric plants and to require electric companies to furnish low-cost power to rural customers. Industry opposition to this plan is documented in the correspondence of PWP and the minute books of The Scranton Electric Company.

While this controversy was simmering, many small electric companies worked quietly to install rural distribution systems. These efforts are documented in the records of The Citizens Electric Light and Power Company of Hughesville, Pa., The Beach Lake Electric Light Company, Mount Pocono Light and Improvement Company, Strasburg Electric Light, Heat and Power Company, and Winola Electric Company. The correspondence of Aqueduct Mutual Rural Electric Distributing Association traces the formation of a typical unincorporated cooperative and describes the opposition that it encountered when other utility companies challenged its legitimacy.

During the 1930s public concern over the conduct of large utility companies led to the creation of the Federal Power Commission. PP&L's legal department files contain memoranda, exhibits, testimony, and other materials prepared for FPC proceedings, and copies of FPC staff reports relating to the company's activities. Industry opposition to the formation of the FPC and to the enactment of the Public Utility Holding Company Act of 1935 is documented in the minute books of PWP and The Scranton Electric Company. The effect of legal actions brought by the Securities and Exchange Commission against EBASCO is described in the working papers and correspondence of PP&L's legal department.

Defense mobilization during World War II again resulted in increased government involvement in company affairs. Correspondence of PWP and Winola Electric Company document their relationships with the Defense Electric Power Administration. The files of PP&L's sales department contain letters to the War Production Board describing the effect of war mobilization on the company's industrial power contracts. PWP personnel files similarly document the company's involvement with the War Labor Board and with the War Manpower Commission.

The events of the early 1940s set the pattern for the postwar relationship between utility companies and the state. Government regulation was now accepted by the industry, and in this new environment PP&L continued to expand and flourish.

Automating the Guide: A Note on Methodology

From its inception, the Pennsylvania Power & Light Project was conceived of as a vehicle to provide the Hagley staff with an experience in automation. During the planning stages we carefully reviewed the literature on archives and computers with particular attention to the work of Thomas Hickerson and David Bearman. Then, working closely with Professor Philip Bagley of Temple University's Department of Computer Sciences, we constructed sample data sheets and divided them into appropriate fields which were tagged with a single character to identify the computer record. After several months of reviewing the data sheets, we decided to use the following field codes:

a. Collection Number. This number, which is always 1552, the accession number of PP&L.
b. Company Number. Each sub-group, or PP&L company, was given a unique 4-digit number.
c. Sub-group Name. The exact name of the company was entered exactly as shown on PP&L corporate records. No abbreviations or changes of any type were used.
d. Sub-group County. Since all counties are in Pennsylvania, the state name was excluded, and only the county name appears, with the word "County" appended.
e. Sub-group Location. The borough, township or city within the county named in d. above is listed in this field.
f. Title. This refers to the type of archival holdings for PP&L and is always entered as "Records."
g. Inclusive Dates. The years covered by the records were listed in this field.
h. Extent. The linear measurement of the amount of records of each company was entered in this field.
i. Type of Company. This is either "Operating" or "Non-operating."
j. Brief History. A short history of each company is provided.
k. Administrative Records. This includes records such as minute books, stock certificate books, minutes and lease agreements, along with dates.
l. Operating Records. This section includes both description and inclusive dates for financial records, payrolls, audit reports, engineering and construction records.
m. Scope. A general description of the records highlights their importance for historical research.
u. Name Index. Index entries for corporate, personal, and proper noun entries were listed here.
v. Geographic Index. Any location listed on the data sheet was listed as an index entry.
w. Subject Index. The History and Scope sections produced subject entries which were listed in this field.

Philip Bagley and his staff custom-designed a software program written in PL-1 to enter the information from the data sheets using the field codes described above. A unique feature of the software was the creation of an ongoing dictionary or thesaurus for each of the indexes. Most automated guides that have been produced previously have relied on established thesauri and fixed vocabularies. Such an approach, however, has one major draw back — it forces the compilers of a guide to adhere rigidly to a vocabulary which may not always be appropriate to the material being described. Our solution was to construct the thesaurus as we proceeded. This gave us maximum flexibility while still generating a set of index terms for researchers to use to gain access to the collection.

Two computer files were in fact created: a file of the data sheets, and a separate file containing the index terms in the form of a hierarchical dictionary or thesaurus with up to three levels of terms. The link between the two files is a 4-digit number assigned to each term. This number appeared in both the data sheet file and the dictionary file. In the data sheet file, these numbers were listed in the u., v. and w. fields, depending on which index was used. In the dictionary file, a special field was set aside for identifying the specific index.

The production of each index required matching up the index number in the data sheet file with its identical number in the dictionary file. This system allowed us to streamline the keying operation, since each dictionary term had to be inputted only once in the dictionary along with a 4-digit number. This number was then used in the indexing of the data sheets. Each subsequent use of an index term required only keying a 4-digit number, instead of the entire term. This feature was especially helpful in this project since many of the corporate names were very long, and very similar.

A master list of PP&L company names was prepared at the beginning of the project. But as the processing of the records continued, there were additions, deletions, and changes. This caused very few problems, however, since the dictionary of company names was in a separate file and could be easily changed.

The geographical index was originally constructed so that it would be similar to the data sheet fields, i.e., county name, the sub-county. But after reviewing a few sample geographical indexes, it was felt that researchers would have a difficult time finding a township or city since very few would know the county. Therefore, this index was inverted, so that the sub-county level was the primary index term. A separate listing of counties was prepared as a cross-reference tool.

The subject index was created using the natural language of the data sheets, supplemented by generic categories. Although this was the smallest of the three indexes, it could prove to be the most important. Therefore, extra care was taken to add as many terms from the History and Scope sections as possible.

The software produced a host of computer printouts, including data sheet listings and four sets of dictionary listings: alpha by term, numeric by term number, alpha by type of index, and alpha by cross-references alone. The third index printouts — name, geographic and subject — were also made available.

The data were entered by a keyboarder working at home, using a Teletype printing terminal and modem which communicated directly with a Southwest Technical Products multi-user micro-processor system which uses a UNIX-like operating system. Printouts from the terminal were used for proofreading. Every few months the data were transmitted to a large IBM 3033 mainframe for sorting and printing on an IBM 3800 laser printer. The laser printouts are dark and clear on 8-1/2'' x 11'' paper, making it easier to review the printouts.

At a very early stage, sample data were typeset in various formats for review. The software that was used interfaces very well with base-line SYSTEMS Corp., a computer-based service for the publishing industry. After a series of tests, this finding aid was typeset on a III Videocomp computer typesetter. The final typeset product included folios, running heads, and bold and italics. Since the output is graphic-arts quality, the pages were able to go directly to a printer for reproduction.

Herman Baron
Database Consultant
Moylan, Pennsylvania

PENNSYLVANIA POWER & LIGHT COMPANY

PENNSYLVANIA POWER & LIGHT COMPANY

1. **ABINGTON ELECTRIC COMPANY** (Operating).
Lackawanna County, Abington Township.
1911 to 1952, 4 Linear Feet.

History:

The Abington Electric Co. was formed 21 March 1911 through the consolidation and merger of Abington Light, Heat & Power Co., The Dalton Light, Heat & Power Co., and Factoryville Electric Co. It supplied electricity in Dalton Borough and in adjacent townships in Lackawanna County. The firm was controlled by local businessmen until 1927 when Republic Service Corporation, a Delaware based holding company, acquired its stock and began to provide it with managerial and financial assistance. During the late 1920's and 1930's the company was a leader in rural electrification as it extended service to northeastern Pa.'s agricultural communities. In 1952 the Securities and Exchange Commission ordered Republic Service Corporation dissolved. Abington Electric was sold to the Scranton Electric Co.

Administrative Records:

Minute Books, 1911-1952 (4 Volumes)
Memorandum for Public Utility Commission, ca. 1939
Organization Files, 1910-1927
Borough Contracts and Ordinances, 1910-1939
Service Contracts and Agreements, 1910-1928 (2 Volumes)
Service Contracts and Agreements, 1911-1929
Stock Certificate Books, 1911-1950 (3 Volumes)
Stock Transfer Record, 1927

Operating Records:

General Ledgers, 1923-1952 (4 Volumes)
Transfer Ledger, 1945-1952
Journals, 1923-1952 (8 Volumes)
Cash Receipts and Disbursements, 1923-1927
Cashbooks, 1927-1952 (4 Volumes)
Voucher Registers, 1927-1952 (6 Volumes)
Audit Reports, 1930, 1939-1949 (3 Volumes)
Quarterly Reports, 1911-1928
Operating Expenses, 1917

Scope and Content Note:

The records document the company's efforts at rural electrification and provide statistics on the number of customers added. Copies of contracts describe the agreements by which the company supplied power to major industrial customers. There is considerable information describing the company's relationship with the Public Service and Public Utility Commissions which investigated complaints about rates and service. During World War II the company was regulated by the War Production Board. Minute Books describe the operation of the W.P.B. sponsored National Electric Defense Association.

2. **ACCIDENT INSURANCE FUND** (Operating).
Lycoming County, Willamsport City.
1905 to 1924, 8 Linear Inches.

History:

The Accident Insurance Fund was established on 30 September 1905 to serve the Lycoming Improvement Co. group. Its member companies contributed a fixed monthly amount to the fund to cover damage suit claims, accident liabilities, employee sickness funds, casualty insurance premiums, and contractors' liability policies. The fund was closed when the Lycoming Improvement Co. merged into Pennsylvania Power and Light on 25 October 1924.

Operating Records:

Ledger, 1910-1924
Cashbook, 1910-1924
Accrual Record, 1923-1924
Audit Report, Electric Bond and Share Co., 1918-1922

3. **ACQUEDUCT MUTUAL RURAL ELECTRIC DISTRIBUTING ASSOCIATION** (Operating).
Dauphin County, Reed Township.
1924 to 1926, 1 Linear Inch.

History:

Electricity first came to Perry County in 1917 when the newly formed Juniata Public Service Co. began to provide service in the area. Local residents, however, were dissatisfied by the relatively slow pace at which this rural electrification proceeded. In 1924, when the Juniata Co. refused to provide service to Acqueduct Village, a summer resort in Wheatfield Township, they responded by drawing up plans to form the Acqueduct Electric Co. The proposed company was to purchase electricity from a municipally owned power plant operated by Duncannon Borough and distribute it over its own transmission lines. When the Acqueduct Co. attempted to secure a charter from the Public service commission, Juniata Public

Service Co. protested asserting its franchise rights in Perry County. The PSC agreed and refused to issue a charter to the newly organized company. The residents of Acqueduct Village appealed this ruling, citing the extremely slow progress of rural electrification, but their application was again turned down. They then formed the Acqueduct Mutual Rural Electric Distribution Assoc. which functioned as a cooperative and thus did not fall under the jurisdiction of the PSC. This association remained in business until the summer of 1926, when the Juniata Public Service Co. agreed to provide service to its members and purchase its facilities. [The exact spelling of the term "Aqueduct" in this company's name is uncertain. The "Acq" construction was taken from Pennsylvania Power and Light Company records.]

Administrative Records:
Copies of Articles of Association for Charters, 1924-1926
Correspondence, 1924-1926

Scope and Content Note:
The records include Aqueduct Electric Companys's Articles of Association and charter petitions which were filed with the Public Service Commission. The Correspondence File describes Acqueduct Mutual's conflicts with the Juniata Public Service Co. There are also copies of rate schedules and contracts with power suppliers.

4. **AKRON ELECTRIC LIGHT AND POWER COMPANY, NO. 2** (Operating).
Lancaster County, Akron Borough.
1913 to 1918, 1 Linear Foot.

History:
The Akron Electric Light and Power Co. was formed by the consolidation and merger of four non-operating companies on 15 April 1913. Its purpose was to supply electricty in Akron Borough, Lancaster County. In 1917 it merged into the Edison Electric Co., No. 4.

Administrative Records:
Minute Book, 1913-1917
Stock Certificate Book, 1913-1917
Stock Transfer Record, 1916-1917
Stock Ledger, 1913-1917

Operating Records:
General Ledger, 1913-1917
Cashbook, 1916-1918

5. **ALBION ELECTRIC COMPANY** (Non-operating).
Northampton County, Lehigh Township.
1911 to 1913, 1 Linear Inch.

History:
Albion Electric Co. was incorporated 4 April 1911 to supply electricity in Lehigh Township, Northampton County. It merged into Lehigh Navigation Electric Co., No. 2, on 23 December 1912.

6. **ALBURTIS ELECTRIC COMPANY** (Non-operating).
Lehigh County, Alburtis Borough.
1915 to 1916, 1 Linear Inch.

History:
The Alburtis Electric Co. was incorporated 28 December 1915, to supply electricity in Alburtis Borough, Lehigh County. It merged into Lehigh Valley Light and Power Co., No. 2, on 16 September 1916.

7. **ALLEN TOWNSHIP-NORTHAMPTON ELECTRIC COMPANY** (Non-operating).
Northampton County, Allen Township.
1919, 1 Linear Inch.

History:
Allen Township-Northampton Electric Co. was incorporated 14 July 1919 to supply electricity in Allen Township, Northampton County. It merged with six other non-operating companies to form Industrial Power Co. on 25 July 1919.

8. **ALLENTOWN ELECTRIC LIGHT AND POWER COMPANY** (Operating).
Lehigh County, Allentown City.
1883 to 1913, 12 Linear Feet.

History:
The Allentown Electric Light and Power Co. was incorporated 14 March 1883 to supply electricity in Allentown City, Lehigh County. It was the first company to provide electric lighting in eastern Pennsylvania outside of Philadelphia. In 1890, the common stock of the company was acquired by the Allentown and Bethlehem Rapid Transit Co., which held it until 1903 when it went into receivership and was reorganized as the Lehigh Valley Transit Co. The Lehigh Valley Transit Co. held the stock of The Allentown Electric Light and Power Co. until the consolidation of the Allentown company and several other Lehigh Valley companies formed the Lehigh Valley Light and Power Co., No. 3, on 17 March 1913.

Administrative Records:
Minute Books, 1883-1913 (2 Volumes)
STOCK AND BOND RECORDS
Stock Certificate Books—Common, 1884-1908 (2 Volumes)
Stock Certificate Books—Preferred, 1893-1913 (2 Volumes)
Stock Transfer Record—Common, 1886-1893
Stock Transfer Record—Preferred, 1893-1908
Stock Ledger—Common, 1884-1893
Stock Ledger—Preferred, 1893-1913
CORRESPONDENCE
Letterbook, 1909-1912

Operating Records:
General Ledgers, 1884-1913 (5 Volumes)
Journals, 1893-1913 (5 Volumes)
Daybook, 1884-1893
Cashbooks, 1893-1913 (9 Volumes)
Audited Voucher Registers, 1893-1907 (2 Volumes)
Accounts Payable Ledgers, 1900-1913 (2 Volumes)
Expense Ledger, 1905-1908
Distribution of Expenses, 1908-1910
Accrual Record, 1909-1914
Payrolls, 1910-1913
Record of New Customers, Customer Changes, Customers Disconnected, 1907-1911
General Balance Sheet, 1910

Scope and Content Note:
The earliest Minute Book of the company, covering the period 1883-1905, documents operations within Allentown and company purchases of electrical apparatus

from The Thompson Houston Electric Light Co., and The American Electric Lighting and Power Co. Included is correspondence with the Allentown Chief of Police. Other files list repairs to, and replacements of, arc and incandescent street lighting. This documents Allentown's shift from arc lighting to incandescent lighting. Similarly, the records include lists of new customers, customer changes, and customers disconnected (both residential and commercial).

9. ALLISON POWER & LIGHT COMPANY (Non-operating).
Clinton County, Allison Township.
1923, 1 Linear Inch.

History:
Allison Power & Light Co. was incorporated 9 April 1923 to supply electricity in Allison Township, Clinton County. On 27 August 1923 it merged into Pennsylvania Power and Light.

10. AMALGAMATED PARK (Operating).
Lycoming County, Fairfield Township.
1898 to 1902, 1 Linear Inch.

History:
Amalgamated Park was organized in 1898 by Montoursville Passenger Railway Co. as a small amusement park and picnic grounds. It was sold to private interests in 1902, but remained closely associated with the railway.

Operating Records:
Cashbook, 1898-1902

11. AMERICAN ELECTRIC LIGHT AND POWER COMPANY (Non-operating).
Lehigh County, Catasauqua Borough.
1913 to 1914, 1 Linear Inch.

History:
American Electric Light and Power Co. was incorporated 9 May 1913, to supply electricity in Catasauqua Borough, Lehigh County. It merged with Lehigh Valley Light and Power Co., No. 3, on 7 April 1914.

12. AMERICAN ELECTRIC LIGHT COMPANY (Operating).
Columbia County, Bloomsburg Town.
1899 to 1906, 2 Linear Inches.

History:
The American Electric Light Co. was incorporated 25 August 1899, to supply electricity in the Town of Bloomsburg, Columbia County, Pennsylvania.

Administrative Records:
Stock Certificate Book, 1899-1904

Operating Records:
Journal, 1903-1905
Trial Balance, 1906

13. AMERICAN GAS LIGHT COMPANY OF BLOOMSBURG (Operating).
Columbia County, Bloomsburg Town.
1899 to 1906, 1 Linear Inch.

History:
Incorporated 8 August 1899 to manufacture and supply gas for lighting in the town of Bloomsburg, Columbia County. It was controlled by the same interests who formed American Electric Light Co. American gas leased Bloomsburg Gas Company's plant and distribution lines and operated them until 1906 when it was reorganized as the American Gas Light Company of Bloomsburg.

Operating Records:
Trial Balances, 1899-1906

14. ANTHONY-LYCOMING POWER & LIGHT COMPANY (Non-operating).
Lycoming County, Anthony Township.
1928, 1 Linear Inch.

History:
Incorporated 7 May 1928 to supply electricity in Anthony Township, Lycoming County, the Anthony-Lycoming Power & Light Co. merged into Pennsylvania Power and Light on 29 January 1928.

15. ANTHONY-MONTOUR POWER & LIGHT COMPANY (Non-operating).
Montour County, Anthony Township.
1924 to 1925, 1 Linear Inch.

History:
Incorporated 18 August 1924 to supply electricity in Anthony Township, Montour County, the Anthony-Montour Power & Light Co. merged into Pennsylvania Power and Light on 28 October 1924.

16. THE ANTHRACITE ELECTRIC LIGHT AND POWER COMPANY (Operating).
Schuylkill County, Pottsville City.
1883 to 1909, 6 Linear Inches.

History:
The Anthracite Electric Light and Power Co. was incorporated 17 April 1883 to supply electricity in Pottsville, Schuylkill County. In 1896, the Edison Electric Illuminating Co. of Pottsville acquired Anthracite Electric's stock and leased its property. On 20 July 1909 the two companies merged, forming Palo Alto Heat, Light and Power Co.

Administrative Records:
Minute Book, 1883-1909
Stock Certificate Book, 1885-1909
Stock Transfer Record, 1889-1906
Stock Ledger, 1885-1906

Scope and Content Note:
The Minute Book of The Anthracite Electric Light and Power Co. documents the firm's purchase of arc lighting dynamos and other apparatus from the Pennsylvania Diamond Drill Co. Negotiations with Pottsville City Council for street lighting contracts are described in detail.

17. THE ANTHRACITE ELECTRIC LIGHT, HEAT AND POWER COMPANY (Operating).
Luzerne County, Hanover Township.
1905 to 1910, 2 Linear Inches.

History:

Incorporated on 19 July 1905 to supply electricity in Hanover Township, Luzerne County, The Anthracite Electric Light, Heat and Power Co. merged into The Wilkes Barre Co., No. 1, on 28 June 1910.

Administrative Records:

Minute Book, 1905-1910
Stock Certificate Book, 1909-1910

18. ANTHRACITE POWER COMPANY (Operating).
Luzerne County, Butler Township.
1910 to 1933, 3 Linear Feet.

History:

Incorporated on 11 August 1910 as a subsidiary of the Wilkes Barre and Hazleton Railway, the Anthracite Power Co. was chartered in order to supply electricity in the Village of St. John's, Butler Township, Luzerne County, as well as to other points along the railway line. After the railway was abandoned on 21 April 1933, the company was sold to Pennsylvania Power and Light.

Administrative Records:

Minute Book, 1910-1933
STOCK AND BOND RECORDS
Stock Certificate Book, 1915-1933
Stock Transfer Record, 1933
Certificate of Notification in Issue of Capital Stock, 1927
Capital Stock and Corporate Loan Reports, 1918-1930
TAX RECORDS
Capital Stock Tax Returns, 1918-1921, 1926
Income Tax Returns, 1914-1916, 1930-1932
Emergency Profits Tax Reports, 1916-1912
Annual Net Income Returns, 1910-1913
MISCELLANEOUS ADMINISTRATIVE RECORDS
Letters Patent, Receipts, etc., 1910-1933
Application for Charter, 1910
Report Submitted Under the Escheats Act, 1915-1916
Production Reports to the Bureau of Statistics, Pa. Dept. of Labor and Industry, 1915-1920
Annual Reports to the Pa. Division of Public Utilities, 1921-1931
Annual Reports to the Pa. Public Service Commission, 1923-1931
Annual Reports to the Pa. Dept. of Internal Affairs, 1921-1933
Special Reports of Electric Companies to the Federal Trade Commission, 1925-1927
Miscellaneous Agreements and Releases, 1930-1932
CORRESPONDENCE, 1922-1933
"Anthracite Power Co. Correspondence and other Data," 1932-1933 (bound folder)

Operating Records:

General Ledgers, 1910-1933 (2 Volumes)
Journals, 1910-1933 (2 Volumes)
Daybook and Customers Cash Receipts, n.d.
Customers Ledger, 1924-1932
Trial Balances, 1926-1932 (2 Volumes)
Audit Report, PP&L, 1929-1932
Bank Passbook, 1910-1933

Scope and Content Note:

The records of the Anthracite Power Co. consist largely of Administrative Papers. In addition to Stockholders' and Directors' Minutes, the Minute Book contains copies of agreements of mergers and consolidations of several non-operating electric companies with the Anthracite Power Co. Correspondence documents the chartering of these companies as well as the company's relationship with the Governor of Pennsylvania. Included is a map of the territory served by the Anthracite Power Co. Annual Reports, tax returns (1910-1932) and the Certificate of Notification in Issue of Capital Stock (1927) summarize data relating to the company's organization and structure. A correspondence file includes: lists of customers served, types of service rendered, statements of delinquent accounts and reasons for failure to pay. Also included are balance sheets and memoranda relating to Pennsylvania Power and Light's acquisition of the company. Letters and memoranda written in 1932 and 1933 trace the various steps taken by PP&L in assuming control of the company's finances and operations. This documents the method by which PP&L integrated operating electric companies into its structure.

19. ARIEL LIGHT, HEAT AND POWER COMPANY (Operating).
Wayne County, Lake Township.
1923 to 1928, 2 Linear Feet.

History:

Organized 11 July 1923 by the owners of Varden and Lake Ariel Light, Heat and Power Co., in order to extend service from Varden to the neighboring Village of Lake Ariel in the western part of Lake Township, Wayne County, the Ariel Light Heat and Power Co. merged into Pennsylvania Power & Light 28 April 1928.

Administrative Records:

Minute Book, 1923-1928
Stock Certificate Book, 1925-1926
Stock Transfer Record, 1926

Operating Records:

General Ledger, 1926-1928
Journal and Entry Register, 1926-1928
Record of Cash Receipts, 1926-1928
Record of Cash Disbursements, 1926-1928
Summary of Cash, 1926-1928
Audited Voucher Register, 1926-1928
Accounts Payable Ledger, 1926-1928
Detail Ledger, 1926-1928
Trial Balance, 1926-1928
Detail of Cost Study and Fixed Capital, 1926-1927
Expenditure Requisitions, 1926-1928
Summary of Consumers' Accounts Receivable, 1926-1928
Summary of Cashier's Overs and Shorts, 1927-1928
Statements of Consumers' Deposits, 1926-1928
Audit Reports, 1923-1927 (3 Volumes)

20. ARMSTRONG POWER & LIGHT COMPANY (Non-operating).
Lycoming County, Armstrong Township.
1923 to 1924, 1 Linear Inch.

History:

Incorporated 13 November 1923 to supply electricity in Armstrong Township, Lycoming County, the Armstrong Power & Light Co. merged into Pennsylvania Power and Light on 31 March 1924.

21. ASHLAND GAS LIGHT COMPANY (Operating).
Schuylkill County, Ashland Borough.
1924 to 1927, 1 Linear Inch.

History:
Incorporated on 11 August 1874 to furnish natural gas in Ashland Borough and surrounding areas in Schuylkill County, the Ashland Gas Light Co. subsequently erected a 25-kw electric plant and operated an arc lighting system. It sold the electric plant and transmission lines on 25 March 1893 to The Edison Electric Illuminating Co. of Ashland, Pa., but remained in the gas business through 1959.

Operating Records:
Audit Report, PP&L, 1924-1927

Scope and Content Note:
The Company Audit prepared by Pennsylvania Power and Light in 1927 reflects PP&L's interest in taking over independent electric and gas utility companies during the 1920s and 1930s.

22. THE ASHLEY ELECTRIC LIGHT AND POWER COMPANY (Operating).
Luzerne County, Ashley Borough.
1903 to 1904, 1 Linear Inch.

History:
The Ashley Electric Light and Power Co. was incorporated 17 December 1903 to supply electricity in Ashley Borough, Luzerne County. It merged and consolidated with four other companies to form Wilkes Barre Gas and Electric Co. on 22 December 1904.

Administrative Records:
Minute Book, 1903-1904
Stock Certificate Book, 1904

23. ATGLEN ELECTRIC COMPANY (Non-operating).
Chester County, Atglen Borough.
1912, 1 Linear Inch.

History:
Incorporated on 8 May 1912 to supply electricity in Atglen Borough, Chester County, the Atglen Electric Co. consolidated and merged with six other non-operating companies to form Christiana Suburban Electric Co. on 13 May 1912.

24. THE AUBURN ELECTRIC LIGHT, HEAT AND POWER COMPANY (Operating).
Schuylkill County, Auburn Borough.
1911 to 1916, 3 Linear Feet.

History:
Incorporated on 20 December 1910 to supply electricity in Auburn Borough, Schuylkill County, The Auburn Electric Light, Heat and Power Co. merged with Eastern Pennsylvania Light, Heat and Power on 16 August 1916.

Administrative Records:
Minute Book, 1911-1916
Stock Certificate Book, 1911-1916
Stock Transfer Record, 1916
Stock Ledger, 1911-1916
Correspondence, 1911-1916

Operating Records:
General Ledgers, 1911-1916 (2 Volumes)
Journal, 1911-1914
Cashbooks, 1911-1916 (2 Volumes)
Voucher Record, 1916
Accounts Payable Ledger, 1916
Distribution Record, 1916
Invoices, 1911-1916

Scope and Content Note:
The Minute Book contains directors' minutes pertaining to the company's dealings with Auburn Borough. Correspondence includes contracts with Westinghouse Electric & Manufacturing Co. for electrical apparatus. Letters of Charles E. Berger, attorney, to the Auburn Co. interpreting Pa. state laws regulating the sale of electricity beyond the company's franchise in Auburn Borough.

25. AVIS POWER & LIGHT COMPANY (Non-operating).
Clinton County, Avis Borough.
1923 to 1924, 1 Linear Inch.

History:
Incorporated on 13 November 1923 to supply electricity in Avis Borough, Clinton County, Avis Power & Light Co. merged into Pennsylvania Power and Light 31 March 1924.

26. THE BALTIMORE ELECTRO ALLOYS COMPANY (Operating).
Baltimore (Maryland), Baltimore (Maryland).
1919 to 1934, 6 Linear Inches.

History:
The Shawnigan Electro Products Co. was incorporated 12 May 1915 to produce, purchase, and sell metals and gases manufactured through the operation of its electric furnaces. The company moved to Baltimore in 1919 and changed its name to The Baltimore Electro Alloys Co. In 1931 it merged with the Pennsylvania Water & Power Co.

Administrative Records:
Minute Books, 1919-1934 (2 Volumes)
Stock Certificate Book, 1919-1933
Stock Transfer Book, 1919

27. BANKS TOWNSHIP ELECTRIC COMPANY (Non-operating).
Carbon County, Banks Township.
1911 to 1912, 1 Linear Inch.

History:
Banks Township Electric Co. was incorporated 6 February 1911 to supply electricity in Banks Township, Carbon County. It consolidated and merged with three operating and eight non-operating companies to form The Harwood Electric Co. 23 February 1912.

28. BARRETT POWER & LIGHT COMPANY (Non-operating).
Monroe County, Barrett Township.
1923 to 1924, 1 Linear Inch.

History:
Incorporated on 1 May 1923 to supply electricity in Barrett Township, Monroe County, the Barrett Power & Light Co. consolidated and merged with 31 other non-operating companies to form Paupack Power & Light Co., No. 2, on 29 January 1924.

29. BARRY ELECTRIC COMPANY (Non-operating).
Schuylkill County, Barry Township.
1921 to 1922, 1 Linear Inch.

History:
Incorporated on 25 July 1921 to supply electricity in Barry Township, Schuylkill County, the Barry Electric Co. merged into Pennsylvania Power and Light 8 November 1921.

30. BART TOWNSHIP ELECTRIC COMPANY (Non-operating).
Lancaster County, Bart Township.
1928, 1 Linear Inch.

History:
Incorporated on 6 February 1928 to supply electricity in Bart Township, Lancaster County, Bart Township Electric Co. merged into Edison Electric Co., No. 4, on 28 April 1928.

31. BASTRESS-LYCOMING POWER & LIGHT COMPANY (Non-operating).
Lycoming County, Bastress Township.
1928, 1 Linear Inch.

History:
Incorporated on 19 November 1928 to supply electricity in Bastress Township, Lycoming County, Bastress-Lycoming Power & Light Co. merged into Pennsylvania Power and Light 29 December 1928.

32. THE BEACH LAKE ELECTRIC LIGHT COMPANY (Operating).
Wayne County, Berlin Township.
1922 to 1928, 2 Linear Feet.

History:
The Beach Lake Electric Light Co. was incorporated 26 June 1922 to supply electricity in Berlin Township, Wayne County. Company stock was acquired by Lehigh Power Securites Corp. which on 28 May 1928 merged into Pennsylvania Power and Light.

Administrative Records:
Minute Book, 1922-1928
Stock Certificate Book, 1922-1924
Stock Transfer Record, 1924
Stock Ledger, 1922-1928

Operating Records:
General Ledger, 1924-1928
Journal and Entry Register, 1924-1928
Cash Received, 1924-1925
Check Register, 1924-1925
Record of Cash Receipts, 1925-1928
Record of Cash Disbursements, 1925-1928
Summary of Cash, 1925-1928
Audited Voucher Register, 1924-1928
Accounts Payable, 1924-1928
Accounts Receivable, 1924-1928
Detail Ledger, 1924-1928
Accrual Record, 1924-1928
Expenditure Requisitions, 1924-1928
Detail of Cost Study and Fixed Capital, 1925-1927
Summary of Consumers' Accounts Receivable, 1924-1928
Summary of Consumers' Deposits, 1926-1928
Audit Reports, 1922-1927 (3 Volumes)

Scope and Content Note:
The Minute Book provides a vivid portrait of the operations of a small rural electric company and documents its efforts at rural electrification. The records describe the firm's merger with PP&L.

33. BEACON ELECTRIC COMPANY (Non-operating).
Lycoming County, Clinton Township.
1913, 1 Linear Inch.

History:
Incorporated to supply electricity in Clinton Township, Lycoming County, 5 April 1913, Beacon Electric Co. merged into Northumberland County Gas & Electric Co. 28 April 1913.

34. BEAR CREEK POWER & LIGHT COMPANY (Non-operating).
Luzerne County, Bear Creek Township.
1923 to 1924, 1 Linear Inch.

History:
Incorporated on 23 April 1923 to supply electricity in Bear Creek Township, Luzerne County, Bear Creek Power & Light consolidated and merged with 31 other non-operating companies to form Paupack Power & Light Co., No. 2, on 29 January 1924.

35. BEAVER-COLUMBIA POWER & LIGHT COMPANY (Non-operating).
Columbia County, Beaver Township.
1928 to 1929, 1 Linear Inch.

History:
Incorporated 30 April 1928 to supply electricity in Beaver Township, Columbia County, Beaver-Columbia Power & Light Co. merged with 12 other non-operating companies into PP&L on 29 June 1928.

36. BEAVER MEADOW ELECTRIC COMPANY (Operating).
Carbon County, Beaver Meadow Borough.
1911 to 1912, 4 Linear Inches.

History:
Incorporated on 16 June 1911 to supply electricity in the Borough of Beaver Meadow, Carbon County, Beaver Meadow Electric Co. consolidated and merged with Harwood Electric Co. and ten non-operating companies to form The Harwood Electric Co. on 23 February 1912.

Administrative Records:
Stock Certificate Book, 1911-1912

Operating Records:
General Ledger, 1911-1912
Journal, 1911-1912
Audited Voucher Register and Invoice Record, 1911-1912
Monthly Balance Sheets and Loss and Gain Account, 1911-1912

37. BEAVERTOWN ELECTRIC LIGHT COMPANY (Operating).
Snyder County, Beavertown Borough.
1907-1915, 1 Linear Inch.

History:
Formed 9 December 1907 to supply electricity in Beavertown Borough, Snyder County, Beavertown

Electric Light Co. never secured a charter of incorporation. Nevertheless, it erected and operated an electric generating station until 1915, when when it went out of business, after Middleburg Light, Heat and Power Co. began supplying service in the borough.

Administrative Records:
Minute Book, 1907-1915
Stock Subscription Ledger, 1907-1910

Operating Records:
Daybook, 1907-1915

Scope and Content Note:
The Minute Book describes the company's rate schedules, negotiations with Beavertown Borough Board of Supervisors for street lighting contracts and efforts at rural electrification. There is considerable material documenting the efforts to raise operating capital through various civic and social activities.

38. BEECHWOOD ELECTRIC COMPANY
(Non-operating).
Northampton County, Palmer Township.
1911 to 1913, 1 Linear Inch.

History:
Incorporated to supply electricity in Palmer Township, Northampton County on 4 April 1911, Beechwood Electric Co. consolidated and merged with 37 other non-operating companies to form Lehigh Navigation Electric Co., No. 2, on 23 December 1912.

39. BENSALEM TOWNSHIP ELECTRIC COMPANY
(Non-operating).
Bucks County, Bensalem Township.
1913 to 1935, 1 Linear Foot.

History:
Although its charter stated that the purpose of the Bensalem Township Electric Co. was to supply electricity in Bensalem Township, Bucks County, the real purpose was to block Philadelphia Electric Co. extension into that township. Control rested with the officials of Lehigh Valley Light and Power Co., No. 3. This company dissolved on 9 September 1935 without ever having been active. At that time, 97 of the 100 shares of stock were held by Pennsylvania Power and Light.

40. BENTON-COLUMBIA POWER & LIGHT COMPANY (Non-operating).
Columbia County, Benton Township.
1924 to 1925, 1 Linear Inch.

History:
Incorporated on 18 August 1924 to supply electricity in Benton Township, Columbia County, Benton-Columbia Power & Light Co. merged along with 12 other non-operating companies into Pennsylvania Power and Light 19 January 1925.

41. BENTON HYDRO-ELECTRIC COMPANY
(Operating).
Columbia County, Benton Borough.
1916 to 1928, 4 Linear Feet.

History:
Benton Hydro-Electric Co. was the product of a series of reorganizations. Fishing Creek Valley Milling Co. first rendered electrical service to Benton Borough, Columbia County, from 1905 to 1907. In 1907 it sold its electrical apparatus to Benton Electric Light, Heat and Power Co., which went bankrupt in 1913 and was reorganized as Benton Electric Co. When that concern also went into bankruptcy in 1916, it was sold and reorganized as Benton Hydro-Electric Co. In 1924, Lehigh Power Securities Corp. acquired the company's stock and controlled it until the company was merged into PP&L, in 1928.

Administrative Records:
Minute Book, 1916-1928
Stock Certificate Book, 1916-1924
Stock Transfer Record, 1924
Stock Ledger, 1916-1928

Operating Records:
FINANCIAL RECORDS
General Ledgers, 1919-1928 (3 Volumes)
Journal, 1919-1924
Cashbook, 1919-1924
Cash Received, 1924-1925
Check Register, 1924-1925
Record of Cash Receipts, 1925-1928
Record of Cash Disbursements, 1925-1928
Summary of Cash, 1925-1928
Audited Voucher Register, 1924-1928
Invoice Record, 1924-1928
Accounts Payable, 1924-1928
Accounts Receivable, 1924-1928
Detail Ledger—Fixed Capital, 1922-1924
Detail Ledger—Income, 1922-1924
Detail Ledger—General, 1924-1928
Accrual Record, 1924-1928
PERSONNEL RECORDS
Payroll Distribution Sheets, 1924
Detail of Cost Study and Fixed Capital, 1925-1927
Expenditure Requisitions, 1924-1928
Workmen's Compensation Insurance Accrual Statements, 1924-1928
Automobile Cost Reports, 1926
CONSUMER RECORDS
Consumers' Ledger, 1918-1924
Summary of Consumers' Accounts Receivable, 1924-1928
AUDIT REPORTS
Audit Reports, Electric Bond and Share Co., 1926-1927 (2 Volumes)
Audit Reports, PP&L, 1921-1924 (2 Volumes)

42. BERKSHIRE ELECTRIC COMPANY (Operating).
Lancaster County, Lancaster City.
1915 to 1930, 6 Linear Feet.

History:
Berkshire Electric Co. was organized through the consolidation and merger of Sinking Spring Electric Light, Heat and Power Co. and three non-operating companies on 16 November 1915. With offices located in Lancaster and Berks County, it supplied electricity to the Borough of Sinking Spring and to adjoining boroughs, villages and townships in Berks County. In 1922 the company purchased Womelsdorf Electric Co., thereby acquiring a franchise in the Borough of Womelsdorf. The company was merged into Edison Electric Co., No. 4, on 30 June 1925.

Administrative Records:
Minute Books, 1915-1925 (2 Volumes)
Stock Certificate Book, 1915-1925
Stock Transfer Record, 1915-1924
Stock Ledger, 1915-1924
Correspondence File, 1916-1930

Operating Records:
General Ledgers, 1915-1926 (2 Volumes)
Journals, 1915-1926 (2 Volumes)
Cashbooks, 1915-1924 (3 Volumes)
Cashbook and Cash Receipts, 1924-1926
Audited Voucher Registers, 1915-1926 (3 Volumes)
Accounts Payable Ledger, 1923-1926
Notes Payable Ledger, 1922-1924
Analysis of Closed Jobs, 1915-1926
Financial Reports, 1923-1926 (3 Volumes)
Balance Sheets and Income Statements, 1916-1923
Balance Sheets and Income Statements, pencil drafts, 1918-1923
Statistical Reports of Monthly Operations—Electric Dept., 1923-1926
Time Book, Sinking Spring Plant, 1917-1924
Audit Reports, Electric Bond and Share Co., 1921-1925 (2 Volumes)
Audit Reports, PP&L, 1923-1925

Scope and Content Note:
Although the company's Minute Books contain some material pertaining to customer relations, they mainly consist of information about bonds and mortgages. Correspondence, 1916-30, documents company finances, while statement of President S.R. Zimmerman (1921) defends additions and improvements to company equipment and a valuation of property. Also included are some letters pertaining to the Berkshire Division of Edison Electric Co., No. 4.

43. BERRYSBURG ELECTRIC COMPANY
(Non-operating).
Dauphin County, Berrysburg Borough.
1919, 1 Linear Inch.

History:
Berrysburg Electric Co. was incorporated 7 June 1916 to supply electricity in Berrysburg Borough, Dauphin County. It consolidated and merged with five other non-operating companies to form The Citizens Electric Co. (Valley View), 30 October 1919.

44. BERRYSBURG ELECTRIC SERVICE COMPANY
(Non-operating).
Dauphin County, Berrysburg Borough.
1924, 1 Linear Inch.

History:
Berrysburg Electric Service Co., incorporated 4 February 1924 to supply electricity in Berrysburg Borough, Dauphin County, was merged into Middleburg Light, Heat and Power Co., 7 March 1924.

45. THE BERWICK ELECTRIC LIGHT COMPANY
(Operating).
Columbia County, Berwick Borough.
1892 to 1911, 1 Linear Foot.

History:
The Berwick Electric Light Co. was incorporated 4 August 1892 to supply electricity in Berwick Borough, Columbia County. It consolidated and merged with Irondale Electric Light, Heat and Power Co., West Berwick Light, Heat and Power Co., United Gas and Electric Co. of Bloomsburg, Standard Electric Light Co., Standard Gas Co., and 16 non-operating companies to form Columbia Gas and Electric Co., 7 February 1911.

Administrative Records:
Stock Certificate Book, 1892-1909

Operating Records:
General Ledger, 1909-1911
Journal, 1909-1911
Cashbook, 1901-1905
Daybook—goods received, 1900-1910
Invoice Registers, 1893-1896, 1904-1909 (2 Volumes)
Profit and Loss Account Reports, 1892-1895
Balance Sheets, 1892-1893 (2 Volumes)
Income and Operating Expenses, 1909-1911

46. BERWICK GAS COMPANY (Operating).
Luzerne County, Berwick Borough.
1924 to 1927, 1 Linear Inch.

History:
Between 1924 and 1927, Berwick Gas Co. supplied Berwick and Nescopeck Boroughs and Salem and Briar Creek Townships (Luzerne County) with heating gas. The company had its origins as Berwick Consolidated Gas Co. which was formed in 1903.

Operating Records:
Audit Report, PP&L, 1924-1927

47. BETHANY POWER & LIGHT COMPANY
(Non-operating).
Wayne County, Bethany Borough.
1924, 1 Linear Inch.

History:
Bethany Power & Light Co., incorporated 18 February 1924 to supply electricity in Bethany Borough, Wayne County, merged into Honesdale Consolidated Light, Heat and Power Co. along with three other non-operating companies, 12 May 1924.

48. BETHEL-LEBANON POWER & LIGHT COMPANY
(Non-operating).
Lebanon County, Bethel Township.
1927, 1 Linear Inch.

History:
Bethel-Lebanon Power & Light Co. was incorporated 11 July 1927 to supply electricity in a narrow portion of Bethel Township, Lebanon County. It merged with five other non-operating companies into Harrisburg Light and Power Co., No. 2, 16 September 1927.

49. THE BETHLEHEM ELECTRIC LIGHT COMPANY
(Operating).
Northampton County, Bethlehem Borough.
1883 to 1924, 7 Linear Feet.

History:
The Bethlehem Electric Light Company, one of the first electric companies organized in Eastern Pennsylvania,

was incorporated in Bethlehem Borough, Northampton County, 17 September 1883. A group of local businessmen headed by Mr. George Davies, a partner in the steam engine manufacturing firm of Davies & Thomas in Catasauqua Borough, was responsible for organizing the electric company. Initially the directors sought to install an arc lighting system manufactured by Arnoux and Hochhausen Electrical Company of New York, but they soon abandoned that system in favor of the one manufactured by Thomson-Houston Electric Company. By late November 1883 the company's arc lighting apparatus had been put into place and it began securing lighting contracts with local merchants. It also sought unsuccessfully to obtain a street-lighting contract from the Bethlehem Borough Council until March 1885, when a public referendum showed overwhelming public support for the idea. In 1886 the company began providing incandescent lighting service using the storage battery system manufactured by Electrical Accumulator Company of New York, but it encountered such difficulty with the batteries that it abandoned the scheme and instead installed the Westinghouse system of alternating current for incandescent lighting. By 1896 the company had extended its service to the adjacent boroughs of West Bethlehem and South Bethlehem, as well as to neighboring townships in Northampton County. In 1900 its property and franchises were acquired by Lehigh Valley Transit Company and its plant was leased to The Allentown Electric Light and Power Company. The Bethlehem company remained an inactive company until 1924 when it merged into Pennsylvania Power & Light Company.

Administrative Records:

Minute Books, 1893-1923 (3 Volumes)
Stock Certificate Books, 1893-1924 (4 Volumes)
Stock Transfer Record, 1916-1924
Stock Ledger, 1888-1924
List of Dividend Checks, 1919-1924

Operating Records:

General Ledgers, 1900-1924 (4 Volumes)
Cashbooks, 1900-1902 (3 Volumes)
Cash Receipts and Cash Disbursements, 1918-1919
Cashbook and Petty Cash Account, 1914-1919
Income Register, 1914-1918
Detail Ledger of Revenue and Expenses, 1920-1921
Cashier's Report of Electric Light Co. Deposits, 1919-1920
Customers' Deposit Ledger, 1907-1919
Results of Operations, 1907-1909
Expenditure Requisitions, 1917-1924
Retirement Authorities, 1920-1924
Voucher Registers, 1910-1918 (6 Volumes)
Accrual Record, 1909-1918
Detail Repair and Construction Ledger, 1918-1920
Statements of Incompleted Improvements and Special Work Chargeable to Capital, 1918-1920

Scope and Content Note:

Minute Books for the years 1883-1900 contain technical information about equipment purchased by the company from Davies & Thomas (steam engine manufacturers) and Thomson-Houston and Westinghouse (electrical equipment manufacturers). Minute Books also document the negotiations between the Company and Bethlehem Borough which set the terms upon which arc and incandescent street lighting were installed. Also included are company circulars, borough notices, newspaper clippings and other items which trace the progress of electrification in Bethlehem Borough and the results of the campaign by Bethlehem Electric against proposed state legislation regulating electric rates. Customers' Deposit Ledger lists customers served by the company. Monthly "Results of Operations" provide summaries of sales of incandescent lamps to residential and commercial customers.

50. BETHLEHEM TOWNSHIP ELECTRIC LIGHT AND POWER COMPANY (Non-operating).
Northampton County, Bethlehem Township.
1914 to 1915, 2 Linear Inches.

History:

Bethlehem Township Electric Light and Power Co. was incorporated 8 July 1914 to supply electricity in Bethlehem Township, Northampton County. It was merged along with two other non-operating companies into Lehigh Valley Light and Power Co., No. 3, 6 February 1915.

51. BIG SPRING ELECTRIC COMPANY (Operating).
Cumberland County, Newville Borough.
1908 to 1928, 2 Linear Feet.

History:

Big Spring Electric Co. was incorporated to supply electricity in Newville Borough, Cumberland County, 21 April 1908. It changed its name to Big Spring Light and Power Co., 11 June 1926.

Administrative Records:

Minute Book, 1908-1928
Stock Certificate Book, 1908-1928
Bonds and Miscellaneous Investments File, 1920-1926
Bond and Coupon Record, 1908-1926

Operating Records:

General Ledgers, 1912-1926 (2 Volumes)
Journals, 1908-1926 (2 Volumes)
Cashbooks, 1908-1926 (5 Volumes)
Financial Statements, 1916-1926
Employees' Time Cards, 1923-1926
State Workmen's Compensation Insurance Fund File, 1916-1936
Audit Reports, 1923-1926 (5 Volumes)

Scope and Content Note:

The Workmen's Compensation Insurance Fund File contains correspondence, pamphlets, and payroll statements relating to the Pennsylvania Workmen's Compensation Act of 1915. Another file contains correspondence and statements about bonds issued by the company, including lists of bondholders. Employees' Time Cards provide information on wage rates and job classifications.

52. BIG SPRING LIGHT AND POWER COMPANY (Operating).
Cumberland County, Newville Borough.
1908 to 1932, 5 Linear Feet.

History:
Big Spring Light and Power Co. which was incorporated in 1926, had its origin as Big Spring Electric Co. On 2 July 1928 Big Spring Light and Power merged into Pennsylvania Power and Light Co.

Administrative Records:
Minute Book, 1908-1928
Bonds and Miscellaneous Investments File, 1926-1932

Operating Records:
FINANCIAL RECORDS
General Ledgers, 1926-1928 (2 Volumes)
Journal, 1926
Journal Entry Register, 1927-1928
Cashbooks, 1926 (2 Volumes)
Record of Cash Receipts, 1926-1928
Record of Cash Disbursements, 1927-1928
Summary of Cash, 1927-1928
Audited Voucher Register, 1927-1928
Accounts Payable Ledger, 1927-1928
Detail Ledger, 1927-1928
Accrual Record, 1927-1928
Expenditure Requisitions, 1926-1930
Retirement Authorities, 1927-1928
Financial Statements, 1916-1926
Bonds and Miscellaneous Investments File, 1926
Connected Load Report, 1927-1928
Comparative Income Account, 1927-1928
Electricity Used in Operations, 1926
CONSUMER RECORDS
Summary of Consumers' Accounts Receivable, 1926-1928
Summary of Miscellaneous Accounts Receivable, 1926-1928
Power & Lighting Sales Report, 1927-1928
Electricity Supplied Free to Municipalities, 1926
Detail of Other Charges, 1926
Consumers' Deposits, 1926
PERSONNEL RECORDS
Employees' Time Cards, 1926
Payrolls—General, 1926-1928 (2 Volumes)
Distribution of Payroll, 1926
AUDIT REPORTS, 1922-1927 (3 Volumes)

Scope and Content Note:
Time Cards and Payrolls document job classifications, employee hours and wage rates. Information on bonds and investments including lists of bondholders is in the "Bond and Miscellaneous Investment" file. Operating records and Financial Statements, 1916-26, contain statistical data documenting the amount of electricity sold to and used by residential and commercial customers. Also included are lists of customers, inventories of electric supplies and tables of electric rates.

53. BLACK CREEK TOWNSHIP ELECTRIC COMPANY (Non-operating).
Luzerne County, Black Creek Township.
1909, 1 Linear Inch.

History:
Black Creek Township Electric Co. was incorporated 16 June 1909 to supply electricity in Black Creek Township, Luzerne County. It was consolidated and merged with three other operating and eight other non-operating companies to form Harwood Electric Co., 23 June 1909.

54. BLACKSTONE ELECTRIC COMPANY (Non-operating).
Monroe County, Stroud Township.
1911 to 1913, 2 Linear Inches.

History:
Blackstone Electric Co. was incorporated 27 June 1911 to supply electricity in Stroud Township, Monroe County. It consolidated and merged with 37 other non-operating companies to form Lehigh Navigation Electric Co., No. 2, 23 December 1912.

55. BLAKELY ELECTRIC COMPANY (Non-operating).
Lackawanna County, Blakely Borough.
1905 to 1910, 2 Linear Inches.

History:
Blakely Electric Co., incorporated 23 December 1905 to supply electricity in Blakely Borough, Lackawanna County, was sold to Scranton Electric Co. in January 1910.

56. BLOOMING GROVE POWER & LIGHT COMPANY (Non-operating).
Pike County, Blooming Grove Township.
1923 to 1924, 1 Linear Inch.

History:
Blooming Grove Power & Light Co., incorporated 23 April 1923 to supply electricity in Blooming Grove Township, Pike County, was consolidated and merged with 31 other non-operating companies to form Paupack Power & Light Co., No. 2, 20 July 1923.

57. BLOOMSBURG ELECTRIC LIGHT AND POWER COMPANY (Operating).
Columbia County, Bloomsburg Town.
1896 to 1899, 6 Linear Inches.

History:
Bloomsburg Electric Light and Power Co., incorporated 11 December 1889 to supply electricity in the Town of Bloomsburg, Columbia County, was merged into Columbia and Montour Electric Co., 20 May 1913.

Operating Records:
General Ledger, 1896-1899
Journal, 1896-1899
Accounts Payable Statements, 1896-1897
Comparative Income Statements, 1896-1897
Trial Balance, 1896-1897

58. BRADY POWER & LIGHT COMPANY (Non-operating).
Lycoming County, Brady Township.
1922 to 1923, 1 Linear Inch.

History:
Brady Power & Light Co., incorporated 19 February 1923 to supply electricity in Brady Township, Lycoming County, was merged into Pennsylvania Power and Light Co., No. 2, on 17 May 1923.

59. BRIDGETON TOWNSHIP ELECTRIC COMPANY (Non-operating).
Bucks County, Bridgeton Township.
1913 to 1936, 3 Linear Inches.

History:
Bridgeton Township Electric Co. apparently represented an effort by Lehigh Navigation Electric Co., No. 2, to block the expansion of Philadelphia Electric Co. into Bucks County. Incorporated 30 December 1913 to supply electricity in Bridgeton Township, the company was never active. At the time of its dissolution in 1935, Pennsylvania Power & Light controlled 97 of the company's 100 shares of stock.

60. BRISTOL TOWNSHIP ELECTRIC COMPANY (Non-operating).
Bucks County, Bristol Township.
1913 to 1935, 8 Linear Inches.

History:
Bristol Township Electric Co. represented an effort by Lehigh Navigation Electric Co., No. 2, to block the expansion of Philadelphia Electric Co. into Bucks County. Incorporated 30 December 1913 to supply electricity in Bristol Township, Bucks County, the company was never active. At the time of its dissolution in 1935, Pennsylvania Power and Light Co. controlled 97 of the company's 100 shares of stock.

61. BROWNSTONE ELECTRIC LIGHT & POWER COMPANY (Operating).
Lancaster County, West Earl Township.
1925 to 1926, 1 Linear Inch.

History:
Brownstone Electric Light and Power Co. was formed by local businessmen in Brownstone Village, West Earl Township, Lancaster County, in 1922. The company was never incorporated. On 1 August 1925 Edison Electric Co., No. 4, purchased the property of Brownstone Electric Light & Power Co., but the Public Service Commission did not approve the purchase until 8 February 1926.

Operating Records:
Audit Reports, 1925-1926 (2 Volumes)

Scope and Content Note:
Since the history of this long-lived non-operating company does not appear in Pennsylvania Power and Light Company's official corporate history, its Minute Book and other records are valuable in tracing its relationship to those companies which controlled its stock. Audit Reports covering this and other "inactive companies," prepared by Electric Bond and Share Co., summarize financial affairs.

62. BROWNTOWN ELECTRIC COMPANY (Operating).
Wayne County, Clinton Township.
1913 to 1918, 3 Linear Inches.

History:
Browntown Electric Co., incorporated 15 October 1913 to supply electricity in Clinton Township, Wayne County, was merged into Scranton Electric Co., 31 May 1918.

Administrative Records:
Minute Book, 1913-1918

Operating Records:
General Ledger, 1913-1918
Journal, 1913-1918
Cashbook, 1913-1918

63. THE BUCK MOUNTAIN LIGHT, HEAT AND POWER COMPANY (Operating).
Schuylkill County, Mahanoy Township.
1907 to 1917, 2 Linear Inches.

History:
The Buck Mountain Light, Heat and Power Co. was incorporated 6 July 1904 to supply electricity in Mahanoy Township, Schuylkill County. It was merged into The Schuylkill Gas & Electric Co., 10 January 1917.

Administrative Records:
Minute Book, 1907-1917
Stock Certificate Book, 1917
Stock Certificates, 1907
Stock Transfer Record, 1917

64. BUCK POWER & LIGHT COMPANY (Non-operating).
Luzerne County, Buck Township.
1923 to 1924, 1 Linear Inch.

History:
Buck Power & Light Co., incorporated 23 April 1923 to supply electricity in Buck Township, Luzerne County, was consolidated and merged with 31 other non-operating companies to form Paupack Power & Light Co., No. 2, 20 July 1923.

65. BUCKS COUNTY ELECTRIC COMPANY (Operating).
Bucks County, Doylestown City.
1922, 1 Linear Inch.

History:
Bucks County Electric Co. was incorporated to supply electricity in the Boroughs of Doylestown and Newtown, Bucks County. It was consolidated and merged 31 May 1916 with the Doylestown Electric Co. to form the Pennsylvania-New Jersey Power & Light Co. On 14 May 1917 this company changed its name back to the Bucks County Electric Co., which maintained electric generating stations in both Doylestown and Newtown, but usually purchased its electricity from the Pennsylvania-New Jersey Railway Company's Yardley power plant. The company supplied street lighting in these two boroughs until July 1923, when it was consolidated and merged with six other companies to form the Philadelphia Suburban Gas & Electric Co.

Operating Records:
Audit Report, Pennsylvania Power and Light Co., 1922

Scope and Content Note:
The Audit Report for this company reflects Pennsylvania Power and Light Company's interest in taking over small utilities during the 1920's and 1930's. The report contains a memorandum on employees' wages. It also contains financial statistics for Eureka Power Co., a small electric company associated with Bucks County Electric Co., which operated along the line of the Trenton and Princeton Traction Co. in New Jersey.

66. BUFFALO-UNION POWER & LIGHT COMPANY (Non-operating).
Union County, Buffalo Township.
1930, 1 Linear Inch.

History:
Buffalo-Union Power & Light Co., incorporated 14 July 1930 to supply electricity to a portion of Buffalo Township, Union County, was merged into Pennsylvania Power and Light Co. along with East Buffalo-Union Power and Light Co., 8 August 1930.

67. BUTLER LIGHT COMPANY (Non-operating).
Schuylkill County, Butler Township.
1912, 1 Linear Inch.

History:
Butler Light Co., incorporated 29 November 1912 to supply electricity in Butler Township, Schuylkill County, was consolidated and merged with four operating and eight non-operating companies to form Hazelton Electric Co., 16 December. 1912.

68. BUTLER TOWNSHIP ELECTRIC COMPANY (Non-operating).
Luzerne County, Butler Township.
1909, 1 Linear Inch.

History:
Butler Township Electric Co., incorporated 16 June 1909 to supply electricity in Butler Township, Luzerne County, was consolidated and merged with three operating and eight non-operating companies to form Harwood Electric Co., 23 June 1909.

69. BUTLER TOWNSHIP POWER COMPANY (Non-operating).
Schuylkill County, Butler Township.
1910 to 1912, 1 Linear Inch.

History:
Butler Township Power Co., incorporated 26 January 1911 to supply electricity in Butler Township, Schuylkill County, was consolidated and merged with three operating and eight non-operating companies to form The Schuylkill Gas & Electric Co., 12 November 1912.

70. CAERNARVON ELECTRIC COMPANY (Non-operating).
Lancaster County, Caernarvon Township.
1914, 1 Linear Inch.

History:
Caernarvon Electric Co., incorporated 16 September 1914 to supply electricity in Caernarvon Township, Lancaster County, was consolidated and merged with two other non-operating companies and with Edison Electric Co., No. 3, to form Edison Electric Co., No. 4, 29 October 1914.

71. CAERNARVON ELECTRIC LIGHT AND POWER COMPANY (Non-operating).
Berks County, Caernarvon Township.
1915, 1 Linear Inch.

History:
Caernarvon Electric Light and Power Co., incorporated 20 January 1915 to supply electricity in Caernarvon Township, Berks County, was consolidated and merged with five other non-operating companies to form Tri-County Electric Co., 4 February 1915.

72. CAERNARVON TOWNSHIP ELECTRIC COMPANY (Non-operating).
Lancaster County, Caernarvon Township.
1915, 1 Linear Inch.

History:
Caernarvon Township Electric Co., incorporated 20 January 1915 to supply electricity in Caernarvon Township, Lancaster County, was consolidated and merged with five other non-operating companies to form Tri-County Electric Co., 4 February. 1915.

73. CAMERON ELECTRIC COMPANY (Non-operating).
Northumberland County, West Cameron Township.
1921 to 1922, 1 Linear inch.

History:
Cameron Electric Co., incorporated 6 June 1921 to supply electricity in West Cameron Township, Northumberland County, was merged into Pennsylvania Power and Light Co., 3 November 1922.

74. CAMP HILL AND HARRISBURG PASSENGER RAILWAY COMPANY (Operating).
Franklin County, Chambersburg Borough.
1901 to 1904, 1 Linear Inch.

History:
Camp Hill and Harrisburg Passenger Railway Co. was incorporated 18 June 1901, with offices at Chambersburg, Franklin County. It held directors' meetings through 1904 but after that became inactive. As of 1941 it was listed by Pennsylvania Power and Light Co. as virtually out of existence, since it was still recorded on the books of the Secretary of the Commonwealth, but it had failed to use its franchise, pay taxes, or make necessary reports.

Administrative Records:
Minute Book, 1901-1904
Stock Certificate, 1901

75. CAMP HILL TURNPIKE ROAD COMPANY (Operating).
Cumberland County, Philadelphia City.
1903 to 1904, 1 Linear Inch.

History:
Camp Hill Turnpike Road Co. was incorporated 10 December 1903 to build a stone turnpike through Cumberland County. Its offices were located in Philadelphia. Cumberland Valley Railroad Co. acquired the company in 1904 in order to gain right-of-way for a planned trolley line.

Administrative Records:
Minutes of Meetings, 1904
Assignments of Stock, 1904
Charter Application, 1903

76. CANAAN ELECTRIC COMPANY (Non-operating).
Wayne County, Canaan Township.
1916 to 1918, 2 Linear Inches.

History:
Canaan Electric Co., incorporated 28 March 1916 to supply electricity in Canaan Township, Wayne County, was merged into Scranton Electric Co., 16 July 1918.

77. CARBON TRANSIT COMPANY (Operating).
Carbon County, Mauch Chunk Borough.
1924 to 1926, 1 Linear Inch.

History:
Carbon Transit Co. was incorporated 27 July 1908 to provide trolley service in the Borough of Mauch Chunk, Carbon County. It was reorganized as Mauch Chunk & Lehighton Transit Co., 13 March 1919. The successor company continued to experience financial difficulties and finally went bankrupt in 1925.

Administrative Records:
Correspondence, 1924-1926

Scope and Content Note:
Correspondence relates to outstanding bonds of the company in the case of Mauch Chunk Trust Co. vs. Mauch Chunk & Lehighton Transit Co. and Carbon Transit Co. Other correspondence relating to Carbon Transit Co. is found in the files of Eastern Pennsylvania Railways Co.

78. CARBONDALE ELECTRIC COMPANY
(Non-operating).
Lackawanna County, Carbondale City.
1910 to 1912, 1 Linear inch.

History:
Carbondale Electric Co., incorporated 5 May 1910 to supply electricity to the city of Carbondale, Lackawanna County, was merged into Scranton Electric Co., 25 November 1912.

79. CARBONDALE TOWNSHIP ELECTRIC COMPANY (Non-operating).
Lackawanna County, Carbondale Township.
1922 to 1928, 6 Linear Inches.

History:
Carbondale Township Electric Co., incorporated 5 December 1922 to supply electricity in Carbondale Township, Lackawanna County, was consolidated and merged with Scranton Electric Co. and 7 other companies to form The Scranton Electric Co., 3 February 1928.

80. CARLISLE AND MECHANICSBURG STREET RAILWAY COMPANY (Operating).
Franklin County, Chambersburg Borough.
1904 to 1913, 2 Linear Inches.

History:
Carlisle and Mechanicsburg Street Railway Co. was incorporated 11 August 1904 to operate an electric passenger railway in the Boroughs of Carlisle and Mechanicsburg and vicinity, Franklin County. Its offices were located in the Borough of Chambersburg. It was consolidated and merged with five other street railway companies to form Harrisburg and Mechanicsburg Electric Railway Co., 20 January 1913.

Administrative Records:
Minute Book, 1904-1913
Stock Certificates, 1904

81. THE CARLISLE GAS AND WATER COMPANY
(Operating).
Cumberland County, Carlisle Borough.
1853 to 1935, 12 Linear Feet.

History:
Incorporated in 1853 by a special act of the Pennsylvania legislature, The Carlisle Gas & Water Co. was Pennsylvania Power & Light's oldest predecessor. The borough of Carlisle, Cumberland County was one of the company's major stockholders and represented on the Board of Managers. In 1855, the firm constructed a gas plant and distribution system and negotiated a street lighting contract with the borough. Within a few years its residential lighting business was flourshing and the company used its surplus capital to build a dam and hydroelectric plant on Conodoquinet Creek.
The introduction of incandescent electric light posed a serious threat. In an attempt to meet this challenge, in 1878 the company installed a water gas plant which enabled it to manufacture gas more economically. By the next decade it became obvious that gas would never be able to compete with electricity and Carlisle Gas was thus forced to diversify. In 1887, it erected an electric generating station which utilized two Thomson-Houston arc dynamos. After the company introduced an alternating current system in 1895 business grew rapidly. In 1912 it built a modern hydroelectric plant and formed a wholly owned subsidiary Carlisle Light, Heat and Power Company which managed the firm's electric generating and distribution system. In 1925 Lehigh Power Securities Corp. acquired the Carlisle companies and merged them into Pennsylvania Power & Light.

Administrative Records:
Minute Books, 1853-1935 (7 Volumes)
Special Meetings of Board of Managers, 1887-1913
Secretary's Papers of Meetings, 1927-1933
President's Annual Reports to Board of Managers, 1884, 1890, 1892-1899, 1901, 1919
President's Annual Reports to Stockholders, 1857, 1863, 1871, 1873-1874, 1876, 1880-1882, 1896-1912, 1915-1916, 1920-1924
Treasurer's Annual Reports to Board of Managers, and Supporting Accounts and Statements, 1883-1891, 1893-1894, 1896-1917
Quarterly Reports and Statements to Board of Managers (includes President's, Treasurer's, Superintendent's Reports), 1884, 1890-1919
Committee Reports to Board of Managers, 1869, 1889, 1900
Reservoir Water Tests and Analyses Presented to Board of Managers, 1909, 1912-1916
Agreements and Permits, 1900-1902
Agreements and Dealings with Mooreland Land Co., Carlisle, 1910-1916
Borough Council, Carlisle—Correspondence, Notices, 1888-1912
Correspondence, 1878-1913
STOCK AND BOND RECORDS
Stock Subscription Books, 1853 (2 Volumes)
Stock Scrip Receipt Stub Books, 1857-1862
Stock Certificate Books, 1857-1930 (2 Volumes)
Stock Transfer Records, 1854-1930 (2 Volumes)
Stock Ledger, 1853-1930
Bond Stub Book, 1896-1903
Bonds—Lists, Subscriptions, etc., 1882-1920
Note Register, 1905-1925
Dividend Book, 1894-1925

Operating Records:
FINANCIAL RECORDS
General Ledgers, 1870-1875, 1919-1935 (3 Volumes)
Day Book of Materials, 1873-1879
Journal, 1869-1876
Journal Entry Registers, 1926-1935 (2 Volumes)
Cashbooks, 1853-1888, 1909-1911 (3 Volumes)
Summary of Cash, 1927-1935 (2 Volumes)
Record of Cash Disbursements, 1926-1935
Audited Voucher Registers, 1888-1935 (7 Volumes)
Audited Voucher Registers, Gas Dept., 1911-1920 (4 Volumes)
Detail and Construction Ledgers, 1919-1935 (3 Volumes)
Ledger, Fixed Capital and Depreciation, 1917-1926
Ledger, Construction Work in Progress, 1919-1926
Ledger, Depreciation, 1921-1926
Operating Expenses, 1926-1935
Statement of Meter, Coal and Coke Used, 1856-1881 (2 Volumes)
Water Used for Building Purposes, 1884-1896
Quarterly Gas Ledger, 1856-1858
Accrual Record, 1926-1935
Profit and Loss Statements, 1920-1926
PERSONNEL RECORDS
Pay Roll Ledger, 1920
Payrolls, General, 1927-1928
Payrolls, 1855, 1917, 1925
Ledger, Materials and Supplies, 1920-1929 (2 Volumes)
Accounts Payable Ledger, A to Z, 1919-1935 (3 Volumes)
Accounts Payable Ledger, Affiliated Companies, 1929-1935
CONSUMERS RECORDS
Bill Register and Accounts Receivable, 1928-1935
Balance Sheets, 1927-1928
Trial Balances, 1927-1928
New Business, 1927-1928
Compensation Reports, 1929-1935
Record of Meter Installations and Charges, 1923-1927
Summaries of Consumers' Accounts Receivable, 1927, 1929-1935
Summaries of Miscellaneous Accounts Receivable, 1926-1935
Statement of Water Consumers as to Revenue Classification, 1929
Statement of Service Billed in Advance, 1929
Contract Sales—House Wiring, 1929
Summary of Consumers' Deposits, 1929-1934
Statement of Company Rents and Leases, 1929-1934
AUDIT REPORTS, 1926-1935 (6 Volumes)

Scope and Content Note:
The records of Carlisle Gas & Water describe all aspects of company affairs. There is a good deal of technical data documenting the operations of coal, gas and hydroelectric plants. Annual reports tabulate customers served in both residential and commercial settings. These statistics trace the process by which electricity and gas were introduced to the borough. Minutes and correspondence describe the relationship between the company and local government. There is also considerable material documenting the utility's public health concerns. In the 1890's an extensive series of water tests and analyses convinced the company to install a water filtration system in order to control the spread of bacteria and disease. Records document the company's experience with government regulation during World War I as well as its involvement in civic and community affairs.
The records of the company after 1926 reflect the acquisition of a majority of its stock by Lehigh Power Securities Corp. Much of the post-1926 material consists of financial and operating records. The various Audit Reports prepared by Electric Bond and Share Co. and Pennsylvania Power and Light Co., 1926-1935, provide a detailed analysis of company operations during those years.

82. CARLISLE LIGHT, HEAT AND POWER COMPANY (Operating).
Cumberland County, Carlisle Borough.
1912 to 1920, 1 Linear Foot.

History:
Carlisle Light, Heat and Power Co. was incorporated 2 October 1911 by the Board of Managers of the Carlisle Gas and Water Co. to supply electricity in the Borough of Carlisle, after the officials of the latter company concluded that its charter did not cover electric service. The two companies shared the same directors. In 1920 Carlisle Light, Heat and Power Co. was merged into the Carlisle Gas and Water Co.

Administrative Records:
Minute Book, 1912-1920
Secretary's Papers of Meetings, 1912-1920
President's Quarterly Reports to the Board of Managers, 1914, 1916-1918
Treasurer's Quarterly Reports to the Board of Managers, 1914-1919
Stock Certificate Book, 1912-1913

Scope and Content Note:
The Reports of the President and the Treasurer to the Board of Managers document the construction and operation of company gas works, water supply systems and electrical generating equipment. The papers also depict the relationship between the company and the Carlisle Borough Council.

83. CARLISLE-NORTH DICKINSON ELECTRIC COMPANY (Non-operating).
Cumberland County, Dickinson Township.
1927, 1 Linear Inch.

History:
Carlisle-North Dickinson Electric Co., incorporated 14 March 1927 to supply electricity in Dickinson Township, Cumberland County, was merged into The Carlisle Gas and Water Co., 30 April 1927.

84. CARLISLE WATER SUPPLY COMPANY (Non-operating).
Cumberland County, Carlisle Borough.
1928 to 1935, 3 Linear Feet.

History:
Carlisle Water Supply Co. was incorporated 21 June 1928 for the purpose of acquiring the water supply property of The Carlisle Gas and Water Co., after the latter company's stock had been acquired by Pennsylvania Power and Light. The property was never transferred to the new company, however, and in 1931 The Carlisle Gas and Water Co. transferred its water

works and system to the Borough of Carlisle. Subsequently, Carlisle Water Supply Co. became inactive.

85. CASTANEA ELECTRIC LIGHT COMPANY (Non-operating).
Clinton County, Castanea Township.
1916 to 1923, 1 Linear Inch.

History:
Castanea Electric Light Co., incorporated 30 October 1916 to supply electricity in Castanea Township, Clinton County, was consolidated and merged with one operating and five non-operating companies to form Lock Haven Electric Light and Power Co., 23 August 1923.

86. CATASAUQUA ELECTRIC LIGHT AND POWER COMPANY (Operating).
Lehigh County, Catasauqua Borough.
1891 to 1913, 1 Linear Inch.

History:
Catasauqua Electric Light and Power Co., incorporated in 1890 to supply electricity in the vicinity of Catasauqua Borough, Lehigh County, was reorganized in 1893. Lehigh County Electric Co. acquired its franchises and property, 26 May 1900.

Administrative Records:
Stock Certificate Book, 1891-1893

Operating Records:
Journal, 1898-1904
Audit Report, Lybrand, Ross Bros. & Montgomery, 1913

Scope and Content Note:
The Audit Report, an examination of the accounts of Lehigh and Northampton Light, Heat and Power Co., contains a brief synopsis of the history of Catasauqua Electric Light and Power Co.

87. CATASAUQUA GAS COMPANY (Operating).
Lehigh County, Catasauqua Borough.
1897 to 1913, 1 Linear Inch.

History:
Catasauqua Gas Co., incorporated 18 April 1856 to supply gas in Catasauqua Borough, Lehigh County, was merged into People's Gas Co. of Lehigh County, 25 May 1900.

Operating Records:
Balance Sheets, 1897-1901
Trial Balances, 1897-1901
Profit and Loss Statements, 1897-1901
Audit Report, Lybrand, Ross Bros. & Montgomery, 1913

Scope and Content Note:
The Audit Report of Lehigh and Northampton Light, Heat and Power Co., contains a brief synopsis of the history of Catasauqua Gas Co.

88. CATAWISSA-COLUMBIA POWER & LIGHT COMPANY (Non-operating).
Columbia County, Catawissa Township.
1928, 1 Linear Inch.

History:
Catawissa-Columbia Power & Light Co., incorporated 30 April 1928 to supply electricity in Catawissa Township, Columbia County, was merged with 12 other non-operating companies into Pennsylvania Power and Light, 29 June 1928.

89. CEMENTON ELECTRIC LIGHT AND POWER COMPANY (Operating).
Lehigh County, Whitehall Township.
1900 to 1915, 1 Linear Foot.

History:
Cementon Electric Light and Power Co. was incorporated 19 June 1900 to supply electricity in the Townships of Whitehall and North Whitehall, Lehigh County. Its common stock was soon purchased by Lehigh County Electric Co., which operated the company in its own name until 1906, when Lehigh and Northampton Light, Heat and Power Co. acquired it. Finally, on 6 February 1915, Cementon Electric Light and Power's stock was sold to Lehigh Valley Light and Power Co., No. 3.

Administrative Records:
Minute Books, 1900-1915 (2 Volumes)
Installment Receipts on Subscription to Capital Stock, 1900-1913

Operating Records:
Audit Report, Lybrand, Ross Bros. & Montgomery, 1913

Scope and Content Note:
The Audit Report, covering the accounts of Lehigh and Northampton Light, Heat and Power Co., traces the relationship between that company and Cementon Electric Light and Power Co. The operating records of Lehigh and Northampton Light, Heat and Power Co. include records documenting the operations of Cementon Electric Light and Power Co.

90. CENTRAL RIVER COAL AND SUPPLY COMPANY (Operating).
Dauphin County, Harrisburg city.
1917 to 1935, 2 Linear Feet.

History:
Central River Coal and Supply Co. was incorporated 11 June 1917 to dredge river coal in central Pennsylvania. The company which sold coal to a number of industrial customers in the area was owned by United Gas & Engineering Corp., a New York based holding company. Despite continuing support from its parent firm, Central River's financial condition steadily deteriorated and in 1926 it went into receivership. In 1928, Lehigh Power Securities Corp. acquired its stock and turned it over to Pennsylvania Power & Light Company which operated it as a subsidiary. In 1935 the company was dissolved.

Administrative Records:
Minute Books, 1917-1934 (2 Volumes)
Secretary's Papers of Meetings, 1927-1934
Stock Certificate Book, 1917-1933
Stock Transfer Record, 1933
Stock Ledger, 1917-1934
Correspondence, 1918-1928

Operating Records:
General Ledgers, 1917-1934 (2 Volumes)
Journal, 1917-1930
Journal Entry Register, 1929-1934
Cashbooks, 1917-1926 (2 Volumes)
Record of Cash Receipts, 1929-1934
Record of Cash Disbursements, 1929-1935

Summary of Cash, 1928-1935 (2 Volumes)
Audited Voucher Register, 1929-1934
Accounts Payable, 1929-1934
Accounts Payable—Affiliated Companies, 1928-1934
Accounts Receivable, 1924-1934
Bill Register, 1929-1935 condition and its acquisition by PP&L.
Accrual Record, 1929-1934
Sales Record Book, 1918-1924
Statement on Sale of Aqueduct Electric Co., 1924-1928
Statement of Real Estate, Leases and Rentals, 1932-1934
Audit Reports, 1921-1931 (3 Volumes)

Scope and Content Note:
The records contain copies of contracts and accounts which document the relationship between Central River Coal & Supply Co. and its parent holding company. Memoranda document the company's poor financial condition.

91. CENTRE AND WEST END PASSENGER RAILWAY COMPANY (Operating).
Lycoming County, Williamsport City.
1892 to 1894, 1 Linear Inch.

History:
Centre and West End Passenger Railway Co. was incorporated in April 1892 to construct and operate a street railway in the western part of the City of Williamsport, Lycoming County. It merged and consolidated with three other street railway companies to form Vallamont Traction Co., 15 May 1894.

Administrative Records:
Minute Book, 1892-1894

92. CENTRE TOWNSHIP ELECTRIC SERVICE COMPANY (Non-operating).
Snyder County, Centre Township.
1924, 1 Linear Inch.

History:
Centre Township Electric Service Co., incorporated 7 July 1924 to supply electricity in Centre Township, Snyder County, merged into Middleburg Light, Heat and Power Co., 9 August 1924.

93. CENTRE VALLEY ELECTRIC LIGHT AND POWER COMPANY (Non-operating).
Lehigh County, Upper Saucon Township.
1913 to 1916, 1 Linear Inch.

History:
Centre Valley Electric Light and Power Co., incorporated 29 May 1913 to supply electricity in Upper Saucon Township, Lehigh County, was merged with five other non-operating companies into Lehigh Valley Light and Power Co., No. 3, 26 February 1916.

94. CHANCEFORD WATER AND POWER COMPANY (Non-operating).
York County, Chanceford Township.
1902, 1 Linear Inch.

History:
Chanceford Water and Power Co., incorporated 23 May 1902 to supply hydroelectricity in Chanceford Township, York County, was consolidated and merged with three other companies to form Susquehanna Storage Lake and Power Co., 14 August 1902.

95. CHAPMAN ELECTRIC LIGHT COMPANY (Non-operating).
Clinton County, Chapman Township.
1915 to 1916, 1 Linear Inch.

History:
Chapman Electric Light Co. was incorporated 12 April 1915 to supply electricity in Chapman Township, Clinton County, It purchased generating equipment from a private individual who had previously supplied the township with electricity. The company consolidated and merged with three other companies to form Renovo Edison Light, Heat and Power Co., No. 2, 19 July 1916.

96. CHAPMAN ELECTRIC SERVICE COMPANY (Non-operating).
Snyder County, Chapman Township.
1923, 1 Linear Inch.

History:
Chapman Electric Service Co., incorporated 8 October 1923 to supply electricity in Chapman Township, Snyder County, was merged with four other companies into Middleburg Light, Heat and Power Co., 21 November 1923.

97. CHERRY RIDGE LIGHT COMPANY (Operating).
Wayne County, Cherry Ridge Township.
1924, 1 Linear Inch.

History:
Cherry Ridge Light Co. was organized in July 1921 as a partnership for supplying electricity to Cherry Ridge Township, Wayne County. The company was never incorporated.

Operating Records:
Audit Report, Pennsylvania Power and Light Co., 1924

Scope and Content Note:
The Audit Report describing the company's operations and history documents Pennsylvania Power and Light Company's determination to take over small utility companies during the 1920s.

98. CHERRY RIDGE POWER AND LIGHT COMPANY (Non-operating).
Wayne County, Cherry Ridge Township.
1924, 1 Linear Inch.

History:
Cherry Ridge Power and Light Co., incorporated 18 February 1924 to supply electricity in Cherry Ridge Township, Wayne County, was merged with three other non-operating companies into Honesdale Consolidated Light, Heat and Power Co., 12 May 1924.

99. CHESTNUTHILL POWER & LIGHT COMPANY (Non-operating).
Monroe County, Chestnuthill Township.
1923 to 1924, 1 Linear Inch.

History:
Chestnuthill Power & Light Co., incorporated 23 April 1923 to supply electricity in Chestnuthill Township, Monroe County, was consolidated and merged with 31 other non-operating companies to form Paupack Power & Light Co., No. 2, 20 July 1923.

100. CHRISTIANA ELECTRIC COMPANY
(Non-operating).
Lancaster County, Christiana Borough.
1912, 1 Linear Inch.

History:
Christiana Electric Co., incorporated 25 April 1912 to supply electricity in the Borough of Christiana, Lancaster County, consolidated and merged with six other non-operating companies to form Christiana Suburban Electric Co., 15 May 1912.

101. CHRISTIANA SUBURBAN ELECTRIC COMPANY
(Non-operating).
Lancaster County, Christiana Borough.
1912, 1 Linear Inch.

History:
Christiana Suburban Electric Co. was organized on 13 May 1912 as part of the consolidation and merger of seven non-operating companies with franchises in Lancaster and Chester Counties. It merged with Edison Electric Co., No. 1, to form Edison Electric Co., No. 2, on 3 June 1912.

102. CITIZENS ELECTRIC COMPANY (WILLIAMSPORT) (Operating).
Lycoming County, Williamsport City.
1895 to 1925, 2 Linear Feet.

History:
Citizens Electric Company (Williamsport) was incorporated 17 September 1895 by local businessmen to supply electricity in the City of Williamsport and in the Borough of South Williamsport, Lycoming County. Although the early history of the company is uncertain, it appears that the company was never in healthy financial condition, due to the severe competition it encountered from Lycoming Electric Co. The company apparently went into receivership about 1915 and was reorganized and granted new Letters Patent. In 1922, when it was audited by Pennsylvania Power & Light Co., the company's indebtedness was in excess of $70,000. About this time the company's steam generating station in Williamsport, equipped with a 2300-volt General Electric turbogenerator and two smaller alternating current generators, was sold to Abraham Fischer. Its distribution system remained under the control of Carl W. Herdic, Liquidating Trustee of the firm's assets. PP&L purchased the distribution system in November 1925 and acquired the steam electric station from Fischer in January 1926.

Administrative Records:
Minute Book, 1905-1924
Stock Certificate Books, 1908-1924 (2 Volumes)
Stock Transfer Record, 1924
Stock Ledger, 1908-1925

Operating Records:
General Ledger, 1924-1925
Journal Entry Register, 1924-1925
Cash Receipts, 1923-1924
Cash Received, 1924-1925
Check Register, 1924-1925
Record of Cash Receipts, 1925
Record of Cash Disbursements, 1925
Summary of Cash, 1925
Audited Voucher Register, 1924-1925
Accounts Payable, 1924-1925
Accounts Receivable, 1924-1925
Detail Ledger, 1924-1925
Retirement Authority Detail Ledger, 1924
Accrual Record, 1924-1925
Bills, 1924
Audit Report, Pennsylvania Power and Light Co., 1921-1924

Scope and Content Note:
The records document the company's ongoing financial crisis. The Minute Book describes the process by which the company bid for street light contracts (1914), an equity case involving Lycoming Electric Co. (1911) and the final liquidation of the Citizen's Electric Co. (Williamsport).

103. THE CITIZENS ELECTRIC COMPANY (VALLEY VIEW) (Operating).
Schuylkill County, Hegins Township.
1919 to 1930, 4 Linear Feet.

History:
The Citizens Electric Co. (Valley View) was formed 31 October 1919 through the consolidation and merger of six non-operating companies. It rendered electric service in the Village of Valley View, Hegins Township, and in neighboring townships in Schuylkill and Dauphin Counties. The company merged into Pennsylvania Power and Light Co., 31 December 1930.

Administrative Records:
Minute Books, 1919-1930 (2 Volumes)
Stock Certificate Book, 1920-1930
Stock Ledger, 1920-1930
Stock Subscription Ledger, 1919-1920
Ballots, Proxies of Stockholders' Meetings, 1923-1928
Correspondence, 1919-1922
"Rate Schedules, Rules and Regulations for the Supply of Electric Service by The Citizens Electric Co.," 1926

Operating Records:
FINANCIAL RECORDS
General Ledgers, 1919-1930 (2 Volumes)
Journal, 1919-1926
Journal Entry Register, 1928-1930
Record of Cash Receipts and Payments, 1925-1927
Cashbook, 1919-1926
Record of Cash Receipts, 1928-1930
Record of Cash Disbursements, 1928-1930
Summary of Cash, 1928-1930 (2 Volumes)
Accounts Payable, 1928-1930
Accounts Receivable, 1928-1930
Bills, 1927-1928
Invoices, 1920, 1923-1928
Accrual Record, 1928-1930
Financial Reports, 1923, 1925-1926
Gross Receipts Tax Receipts, 1919-1928
Expenditure Requisitions, 1928-1930
Retirement Authorities, 1928-1930
Repair Authorities, 1924
PERSONNEL RECORDS
Time Sheets, 1927-1928
Workmen's Compensation Insurance Accrual Statements, 1928-1930

CONSUMER RECORDS
Summary of Consumers' Accounts Receivable, 1928-1930
Summary of Miscellaneous Accounts Receivable, 1928-1930
Summary of Cashier's Overs and Shorts, 1928-1930
Summary of Consumers' Deposits, 1929-1930
AUDIT REPORTS, 1923-1929 (2 Volumes)

Scope and Content Note:
The records document all aspects of company operations including its formation, extension of service, rate setting, contracts with electric equipment manufacturers, and finally its consolidation and merger into Pennsylvania Power and Light.

104. CITIZENS ELECTRIC ILLUMINATING COMPANY (PITTSTON) (Operating).
Luzerne County, Pittston City.
1903 to 1916, 6 Linear Inches.

History:
Citizens Electric Illuminating Co., which supplied electricity to Pittston City, Luzerne County, was organized about 1900. It merged into Scranton Electric Co., 28 August 1916.

Administrative Records:
Minute Books, 1903-1916 (2 Volumes)
Stock Certificates, 1913-1915

Operating Records:
General Ledgers, 1915-1916 (2 Volumes)
Cashbook, 1916

Scope and Content Note:
The Minute Books document various aspects of company operations, including installation of arc street lighting for Pittston, efforts of other electric companies to encroach upon Citizens Electric Illuminating Company's territory, donations of electric service and lights to various Pittston religious and civic organizations, and injury claims submitted to the company by residents and employees.

105. THE CITIZENS ELECTRIC LIGHT AND POWER COMPANY OF HUGHESVILLE, PA. (Operating).
Lycoming County, Hughesville Borough.
1895 to 1928, 6 Linear Feet.

History:
The Citizens Electric Light and Power Co. of Hughesville, Pa. was formed in 1895 by local businessmen in Hughesville Borough, Lycoming County. The Company installed a generator in The Rishel Furniture Company's factory and constructed a local distribution system. During the late 1890s the company prospered and increased its generating capacity several times. However, water power in the area was insufficient to run a hydroelectric plant and by 1906 the company was forced to start purchasing power from the Eaglesmere Light Co. This Arrangement worked for 13 years until problems developed in the Eaglesmere Company's hydroelectric plant. This led to an increase in rates and continual customer resentment. Several customers protested and began using coal oil lamps. In 1923, the beleagured company was sold to Lehigh Power Securities Corp., which five years later merged it into the PP&L system.

Administrative Records:
Minute Books, 1895-1928 (3 Volumes)
Papers of Stockholders' Meetings and Elections, 1906-1917
Reports of Managing Director, 1903
Petition Concerning Method of Rating Incandescent Lamp Efficiency and Candlepower, n.d.
STOCK AND BOND RECORDS
Stock Certificate Book, 1895-1925
Stock Transfer Records, 1895-1925 (2 Volumes)
Stock Ledger, 1895
Stock Register, 1895-1921
Bond Register, 1917-1922
Dividend Book, 1909-1922
CORRESPONDENCE, 1909-1917

Operating Records:
FINANCIAL RECORDS
General Ledgers, 1895-1928 (6 Volumes)
Journals, 1895-1923 (5 Volumes)
Journal Entry Register, 1924-1928
Cashbooks, 1895-1924 (7 Volumes)
Cash Received, 1924-1925
Summary of Cash, 1925
Audited Voucher Register, 1924-1928
Detail Ledger, 1924-1928
Accounts Payable, 1924-1928
Detail of Cost Study and Fixed Capital, 1925-1927
Light Record Books, 1897-1923 (4 Volumes)
Day Books, 1895-1905, 1918-1924 (5 Volumes)
Record of Purchases for Line Dept., 1895
Material Used in Shop, 1913-1919
Order Books, 1923
Order Book Stubs, 1910-1921
Bills, 1924-1928
Inventory Records, 1911-1919, 1923 (2 Volumes)
Inventories, 1906-1910
Statements of Light and Power, 1907-1919
Reports and Appraisements of Capital Stock, 1895-1906
Report of Corporate Loans, 1896-1906
Gross Receipts Reports, 1895-1906
Insurance and Comparative Revenue Reports, 1910-1911
Trial Balances, 1907-1922
Quarterly Financial Statements, 1901-1922
PERSONNEL RECORDS
Payroll and Wage Reports, 1921-1923
Reports to National Electric Light Assoc. re: Workmen's Compensation, Public Liability Insurance, 1922
Public Liability Insurance Folder, 1921-1922
Workmen's Compensation Insurance Accrual Statements, 1924
Workmen's Compensation Insurance and Public Liability Insurance Accrual Statements, 1925-1928
CONSUMER RECORDS
Summary of Consumers' Accounts Receivable, 1924-1928
Summary of Miscellaneous Accounts Receivable, 1924-1928
Summary of Consumers' Deposits, 1925-1928
AUDIT REPORTS, 1925-1927 (2 Volumes)

Scope and Content Note:
The Minute Books prior to 1925 (when the company's stock was acquired by Lehigh Power Securities Corp.)

document all aspects of company operations. Of particular interest are materials on: rates charged to commercial, residential, civic and religious organizations. There is a file of customer complaints. Negotiations with the Borough Councils of Hughesville and Picture Rocks which awarded street lighting contracts and sought to establish a municipally owned-utility are described in detail. Correspondence documents sales of electrical appliances particularly washing machines and vacuum cleaners. Letters to the National Electric Light Association discuss membership meetings, standardization, technical developments and legislation affecting utility interests. Light Record Books, 1904-16, list customers, breaking them down by number and type of lights used, candlepower, monthly and quarterly rates. Special lists detail those customers supplied with all-night electric service. A petition of unknown authorship discusses the need for new techniques for rating the efficiency of incandescent lamps.

106. THE CITIZENS ELECTRIC LIGHT COMPANY OF SHENANDOAH, PA. (Operating).
Schuylkill County, Shenandoah Borough.
1887 to 1913, 1 Linear Foot.

History:
The Citizens Electric Light Co. of Shenandoah, Pa. was incorporated 18 March 1887 to supply electricity in Shenandoah Borough, Schuylkill County. It was formed by Shenandoah Gas Light Co. in order to gain entry into the electric lighting business in the borough. Thomson-Houston Electric Co. built the plant, consisting of two arc and one incandescent dynamos, and had a representative on the company's board of directors for several years. After 1890, The Shenandoah Electric Illuminating Co. of Shenandoah, Pa., began supplying customers in the borough. The two companies informally divided the market, with the Citizens Company primarily serving commercial customers and the Illuminating Company serving residential customers. This relationship continued for several years, despite the opposition of an "Anti-Trust Association" in the Borough Council. In 1904 a third firm, The Peoples Light, Heat and Power Co. of Shenandoah and Mahanoy City, Schuylkill County, Pa., also began supplying electricity in the borough. The Citizens Company cancelled its informal agreement with the Illuminating Company, upgraded its facilities and began soliciting new customers. Several years of bitter competition followed during which the Shenandoah companies almost went bankrupt. In 1911 Calvin Pardee and his associates, looking to market the surplus power being generated by their Harwood Plant, bought both companies, merging them with ten others to form the Schuylkill Gas and Electric Co.

Administrative Records:
Minute Book, 1887-1910
Stock Certificate Book, 1887-1908
Stock Certificates, 1908-1912

Operating Records:
Journal, 1912-1913
Cashbook and Check Register, 1912-1913
Audited Voucher Register, 1912
Monthly Reports, 1912
Audit Reports, Lawrence E. Brown & Co., 1912 (2 Volumes)

Scope and Content Note:
The Minute Book provides a detailed overview of company operating including the purchase of electric apparatus and arc-lighting equipment from Thomson-Houston Electric Co. Negotiations for street lighting contracts are well documented. There is considerable information describing the competitive situation in the borough and the impact that it had on all aspects of company operations.

107. THE CITIZENS ELECTRIC LIGHT, HEAT AND POWER COMPANY OF LANCASTER, PA.
(Operating).
Lancaster County, Lancaster City.
1893 to 1895, 1 Linear Inch.

History:
The Citizens Electric Light, Heat and Power Co. of Lancaster, Pa. was formed in 1893 by local businessmen in the City of Lancaster. The firm had close ties with Westinghouse Electric & Manufacturing Co., and built a generating plant outside the city housing an alternating current dynamo of 6,000-16 candlepower incandescent capacity. The plant also contained two Western Electric arc lighting dynamos. From the beginning the company competed with The Edison Electric Illuminating Co. of Lancaster, Pa., and underbid it in order to secure municipal street lighting contracts. Faced with the prospect of losing more customers, and reluctant to install additional equipment, the Edison Illuminating Co. bought out the Citizens Co. in 1895.

Administrative Records:
Minute Book, 1895
Certificate Book, 1893-1895

108. THE CITIZENS ELECTRIC LIGHT, HEATING AND POWER COMPANY (SLATINGTON)
(Operating).
Lehigh County, Slatington Borough.
1889 to 1913, 2 Linear Feet.

History:
The Citizens Electric Light, Heating and Power Co. was formed in March 1889 by a group of prominent residents of Slatington Borough, Lehigh County. The organizers erected a 20-kw capacity steam electric power plant on the grounds of Horlacher Brewing Company and offered both incandescent and arc lighting service. Because this was direct current, however, the company could serve only those customers in close proximity to the brewery. In 1890 it built a hydroelectric plant, containing a 60 light dynamo, on the canal of Lehigh Coal and Navigation Co. in the village of Walnutport across the Lehigh River from Slatington. Again, owing to the fact that this plant generated direct current, the company experienced considerable difficulty with voltage losses in transmission. Nevertheless, it continued to expand, installing additional arc and incandescent lighting dynamos, as more customers were added. In 1900 the company's plant and distribution system were leased to a competitor, Slating Power Co., which continued to provide service in Slatington. About 1913 Lehigh Valley Transit Co. acquired the stocks of both concerns, dissolved Slatington Power Co., and consolidated and merged the Citizens Co. with ten others to form Lehigh Valley Light and Power Co., No. 2.

Administrative Records:
Minute Books, Board of Directors, 1889-1912 (2 Volumes)
Minute Book, Stockholders' Meetings, 1891-1912
Stock Certificate Book, 1889-1912
Stock Ledger, 1889-1910
Bank Passbook, 1910-1912

Operating Records:
General Ledgers, 1891-1913 (3 Volumes)
Journals, 1898-1913 (2 Volumes)
Voucher Distribution, 1907-1910
Voucher Register, 1910-1913
Accrual Record, 1909-1914
Distribution of Expenses, 1910-1913

Scope and Content Note:
The Directors' Minute Books provie information on company operations, including purchases of, and improvements to, electrical apparatus, rates for incandescent lighting, relations with the Borough Council of Slatington, and relations with Lehigh Coal and Navigation Co. and Slatington Power Co.

109. CITIZENS GAS & ELECTRIC COMPANY (STROUDSBURG) (Operating).
Monroe County, Stroudsburg Borough.
1915, 1 Linear Inch.

History:
The Citizens Gas & Electric Co. was organized about 1906 after it acquired the property of the Stroudsburg Electric Light and Power Co., No. 1. It rendered electric and gas service to the Boroughs of Stroudsburg and East Stroudsburg, Monroe County. The company discontinued electric service about 1915 and became Citizens Gas Co. of Stroudsburg.

Operating Records:
Appraisal, Stone & Webster, 1915

110. CITIZENS GAS COMPANY (STROUDSBURG) (Operating).
Monroe County, Stroudsburg Borough.
1921 to 1924, 1 Linear Inch.

History:
Citizens Gas Co. was formed in July 1922 through the consolidation and merger of Citizens Gas Co. of Stroudsburg and Stroud Realty Co. It supplied gas in the Boroughs of Stroudsburg and East Stroudsburg, and in Stroud Township, Monroe County.

Operating Records:
Audit Report, Pennsylvania Power & Light Co., 1921-1924

111. CITIZENS GAS COMPANY OF MINERSVILLE, PENNSYLVANIA (Non-operating).
Schuylkill County, Minersville Borough.
1904 to 1910, 2 Linear Inches.

History:
Citizens Gas Co. of Minersville, Pa. was incorporated 20 October 1904 to supply gas for lighting in the Borough of Minersville, Schuylkill County. After the company obtained permission from the Minersville Borough Council to lay gas lines, and engaged a consulting engineer to build a gasworks, its stock was acquired by The Minersville Electric Light Co., No. 1, in 1905. Thereafter, the company was non-operating. It consolidated and merged with the Minersville Electric Light Co., No. 1, and The Minersville Fuel Gas Co., 7 April 1909, to form The Minersville electric Light Co., No. 2.

112. CITIZENS GAS LIGHT COMPANY OF TAMAQUA (Operating).
Schuylkill County, Tamaqua Borough.
1894 to 1909, 6 Linear Inches.

History:
Citizens Gas Light Co. of Tamaqua was the successor to Tamaqua Gas Co. which went bankrupt in 1866. It operated the manufactured gas plant and distribution system which had been constructed by the Tamaqua Co. From 1885 onward it competed with the Edison Electric Illuminating Co. of Tamaqua, Pa., No. 1. In 1896 the Citizens Co. was underbid by its rival and lost the contract for municipal street lighting. On 10 July 1900 the Edison Co. acquired the stock of the Citizens Co. and operated it as a subsidiary until 7 April 1909 when they consolidated to form Edison Electric Illuminating Co. of Tamaqua, Pa., No. 2.

Administrative Records:
Minute Book, 1894-1908
Stock Certificate Book, 1893-1909

Operating Records:
General Ledger, 1906-1909
Audited Voucher Register, 1906-1909
Accounts Payable Ledgers, 1906-1908 (2 Volumes)
Statement of Charges to Local Construction, 1908
Earnings, Operating Expenses, and Balance Sheets, 1905-1908
Monthly Reports, 1906-1909

Scope and Content Note:
The Minute Book documents two decades of competition between Tamaqua's Citizens and Edison companies. There is a good deal of information about operations, finances, and negotiations for street lighting contracts.

113. CITIZENS PASSENGER RAILWAY COMPANY (Operating).
Lycoming County, Williamsport City.
1892 to 1894, 1 Linear Inch.

History:
Citizens Passenger Railway Co. was incorporated 27 May 1892 to build and operate a street railway in the City of Williamsport, Lycoming County. It consolidated and merged with three other street railway companies to form Vallamont Traction Co., 15 May 1894.

Administrative Records:
Minute Book, 1892-1894

Scope and Content Note:
The Minute Book gives operating details about the railway, including the construction and extension of its line, and its dealings with the Williamsport municipal government.

114. CLEVELAND TOWNSHIP ELECTRIC COMPANY (Non-operating).
Columbia County, Cleveland Township.
1916 to 1917, 1 Linear Inch.

History:
Cleveland Township Electric Co., incorporated 18 July 1916 to supply electricity in Cleveland Township, Columbia County, merged into The Harwood Electric Co., 20 June 1917.

115. CLIFFORD-SUSQUEHANNA POWER & LIGHT COMPANY (Non-operating).
Susquehanna County, Clifford Township.
1927 to 1928, 1 Linear Inch.

History:
Clifford-Susquehanna Power & Light Co., incorporated 12 December 1927 to supply electricity in Clifford Township, Susquehanna County, merged into Pennsylvania Power & Light Co., 3 January 1928.

116. CLIFFORD TOWNSHIP ELECTRIC CORPORATION (Non-operating).
Susquehanna County, Clifford Township.
1923 to 1928, 2 Linear Inches.

History:
Clifford Township Electric Corp., incorporated 29 June 1923 to supply electricity in Clifford Township, Susquehanna County, consolidated and merged with eight companies to form The Scranton Electric Co., 3 February 1928.

117. CLIFTON POWER & LIGHT COMPANY (Non-operating).
Lackawanna County, Clifton Township.
1923 to 1924, 1 Linear Inch.

History:
Clifton Power & Light Co., incorporated 7 May 1923 to supply electricity in Clifton Township, Lackawanna County, consolidated and merged with 31 companies to form Paupack Power & Light Co., No. 2, 21 January 1924.

118. THE CLYMER POWER COMPANY (Operating).
Northampton County, Williams Township.
1905 to 1928, 3 Linear Feet.

History:
The Clymer Power Co., incorporated 27 February 1908 to supply electricity in Williams Township, Northampton County, merged into Pennsylvania Power & Light Co., 28 May 1928.

Administrative Records:
Minute Book, 1907-1928
Stock Certificate Book, 1908-1926
Stock Transfer Record, 1926
Stock Ledger, 1908-1928
Agreement, Lee S. Clymer, and Delaware Division Canal Co. and Lehigh Coal and Navigation Co., 1906

Operating Records:
General Ledgers, 1905-1928
Journals, 1905-1926 (2 Volumes)
Journal Entry Register, 1926-1928
Checkbook, 1908-1926
Record of Cash Receipts, 1926-1928
Record of Cash Disbursements, 1926-1928
Summary of Cash, 1926-1928
Audited Voucher Register, 1926-1928
Accounts Payable, 1926-1928
Accounts Receivable, 1926-1928
Detail Ledger, 1926-1928
Accrual Record, 1926-1928
Expenditure Requisitions, 1926-1930
Retirement Authorities, 1930
Detail of Cost Study and Fixed Capital, 1926-1927
Bills and Balance Sheets, 1905-1925 (2 Volumes)
Workmen's Compensation Insurance Accrual Statements, 1926-1928
Bills, 1926-1927
Summary of Consumers' Accounts Receivable, 1926-1928
Audit Reports, 1921-1927 (5 Volumes)

Scope and Content Note:
The records of The Clymer Power Co. represent a continuation of the records of Clymer Power Co., an unincorporated concern that operated a small hydroelectric plant which was taken over when The Clymer Power Co. was organized. The Minute Book contains some information on company operations and finances but consists mainly of stockholders' meetings.

119. COAL CASTLE ELECTRIC RAILWAY COMPANY (Operating).
Schuylkill County, Schuylkill Township.
1899 to 1923, 1 Linear Inch.

History:
Coal Castle Electric Railway Co. was incorporated 6 March 1899 to construct and operate a street railway in Schuylkill County. Shortly after construction of the railway was completed in August 1899, the road was leased to the Pottsville Union Traction Co. Coal Castle Electric Railway Co., seven other street railway companies, Pottsville Union Traction Co. and Eastern Pennsylvania Light, Heat and Power Co. consolidated and merged 25 January 1923 to form Eastern Pennsylvania Power and Railway Co.

Administrative Records:
Minute Book, 1899-1923
Stock Certificate Book, 1899-1923
Stock Transfer Record, 1915-1919

Operating Records:
Audit Report, Haskins and Sells, 1923

Scope and Content Note:
The Minute Book contains information on the railway's right-of-way agreements and construction.

120. COAL LIGHT COMPANY (Non-operating).
Northumberland County, Coal Township.
1912, 1 Linear Inch.

History:
Coal Light Co., incorporated 29 November 1912 to supply electricity in Coal Township, Northumberland County, consolidated and merged with 12 companies to form Hazleton Electric Co., 6 January 1913.

121. COAL TOWNSHIP ELECTRIC COMPANY (Non-operating).
Northumberland County, Coal Township.
1911 to 1913, 1 Linear Inch.

History:
Coal Township Electric Co., incorporated 26 January 1911 to supply electricity in Coal Township, Northumberland County, consolidated and merged with eleven companies to form The Schuylkill Gas & Electric Co., 6 January 1913.

122. COAL TOWNSHIP LIGHT, HEAT AND POWER COMPANY (Non-operating).
Northumberland County, Coal Township.
1910, 1 Linear Inch.

History:
Coal Township Light, Heat and Power Co., incorporated 2 May 1910 to supply electricity in Coal Township, Northumberland County, consolidated and merged with five companies to form Pennsylvania Lighting Co., 22 June 1910.

123. COALDALE ELECTRIC COMPANY (Non-operating).
Schuylkill County, Coaldale Borough.
1914, 1 Linear Inch.

History:
Coaldale Electric Co., incorporated 29 June 1914 to supply electricity in the Borough of Coaldale, Schuylkill County, consolidated and merged with The Panther Valley Electric Light, Heat and Power Co. to form Panther Valley Electric Co., 25 November 1914.

124. COLEBROOK-CLINTON POWER & LIGHT COMPANY (Non-operating).
Clinton County, Colebrook Township.
1929, 1 Linear Inch.

History:
Colebrook-Clinton Power & Light Co., incorporated 3 October 1929 to supply electricity in Colebrook Township, Clinton County, merged into Pennsylvania Power & Light Co., 24 October 1929.

125. COLUMBIA AND MONTOUR ELECTRIC COMPANY (Operating).
Columbia County, Bloomsburg Town.
1909 to 1923, 8 Linear Feet.

History:
Columbia and Montour Electric Co., incorporated 7 November 1912 to supply electricity in the Town of Bloomsburg, Columbia County, consolidated and merged with seven other companies to form Pennsylvania Power & Light Co., 4 June 1920.

Administrative Records:
Portfolio (Historical Narrative), Columbia and Montour Electric Co., 1915
Minute Books, 1912-1920 (2 Volumes)
STOCK AND BOND RECORDS
Stock Certificate Book (Common), 1913-1919
Stock Certificate Book (First Preferred), 1913-1917
Stock Certificate Book (Second Preferred), 1913
Stock Certificate Book (Second Preferred), 1913-1918
Stock Certificate Book (Preferred), 1916-1918

Operating Records:
FINANCIAL RECORDS
General Ledger, 1912-1917
General Ledgers and Detail Ledgers, 1913-1920 (4 Volumes)
Journal, 1912-1917
Journal—Detail Ledger Entries, 1913-1920 (5 Volumes)
Distribution of Cash Receipts, 1913-1921
Cashbook, 1919-1920
Supplementary Cashbooks, 1919-1920 (2 Volumes)
Bank Reconcilement Books, 1913-1919 (2 Volumes)
Bank Account Registers, 1913-1919 (4 Volumes)
Cashier's Report—Bloomsburg, 1919
Cashier's Report—Berwick, 1919
Cashier's Report—Danville, 1919
Accounts Payable, 1913-1919 (2 Volumes)
Balances of Accounts Payable, 1914-1920 (2 Volumes)
Insurance Record, 1912-1919
Expenses Paid in Advance—Rentals, 1914-1917
Accrual Records, 1918-1920 (2 Volumes)
Notes and Bills Payable, Predecessor Companies, 1909-1911
Treasurer's Reports, 1917-1919 (2 Volumes)
Monthly Reports, 1913-1918
CONSUMER RECORDS
Accounts Receivable, 1924-1920 (2 Volumes)
Statements of Accounts Receivable, 1913-1920 (2 Volumes)
Report of Electric Sales, 1913-1920
Report of Gas Sales, 1913-1919
Report of Electric and Gas Sales, 1914-1920
Merchandise Sales Reports, 1919-1920
PERSONNEL RECORDS
Payrolls—Bloomsburg and Danville District, 1914
Payrolls—Berwick District, 1915-1917
Payrolls—Bloomsburg District, 1916-1917 (2 Volumes)
Payrolls—All Districts, 1919-1920
Payroll Distributions, 1918-1919
Electric Distribution Check Roll—Bloomsburg District, 1915
Electric Distribution Check Roll—Danville District, 1915-1916
Electric Distribution Check Roll—Danville District and Transmission Dept., 1917-1918
Electric Distribution Check Roll—Bloomsburg and Berwick Districts, 1918 (2 Volumes)
General Construction Corp., General Reports of Work Done for Company, 1914-1917
Audit Report, F.E. Taylor, 1913-1915

Scope and Content Note:
The Historical Narrative consists of copies of legal documents including: charters of some of the companies absorbed by Columbia and Montour Electric, ordinances, franchises and contracts, brief company histories, sample stock and bond certificates, and digests of mortgages.

The Minute book contains some operating information including records documenting the acquisition of other companies, expenditures for construction and the payment on bonds and mortgages. There is also a copy of the original merger agreement that formed PP&L.

126. COLUMBIA AND MONTOUR ELECTRIC RAILWAY COMPANY (Operating).
Columbia County, Bloomsburg Town.
1901 to 1915, 2 Linear Feet.

History:

Columbia and Montour Electric Railway Co. originated 1 November 1879 through the consolidation and merger of Bloomsburg and Berwick Electric Railway Co. and North Susquehanna Transit Co. It operated a street railway from the Borough of Danville, Montour County, to the Borough of Berwick, Columbia County, by way of the Town of Bloomsburg. The company consolidated and merged with Danville & Bloomsburg Street Railway Co. to form Columbia and Montour Electric Railway Co., 7 February 1911, changing its name in December 1913 to North Branch Transit Co.

Administrative Records:
Portfolio (Historical Narrative), North Branch Transit Co., 1915
Minute Book, 1911-1913
Stock Certificate Book, 1911-1913

Operating Records:
General Ledgers, 1901-1913 (3 Volumes)
Journal, 1901-1908
Cashbooks, 1901-1909
Accounts Payable Ledger, 1909-1913
Detail Ledger, 1912-1913
Inventory, 1913
Monthly Statements, 1901-1910

Scope and Content Note:

The Historical Portfolio contains copies of, and extracts from, various legal documents from Columbia and Montour Electric Railway Co. and its successor firms. Included are digests of corporate charters, franchises and agreements, deeds, mortgages, stock and bond certificates.

127. COLUMBIA COUNTY GAS COMPANY (Non-operating).
Columbia County, Bloomsburg Town.
1913, 1 Linear Inch.

History:

Columbia County Gas Co., incorporated 21 April 1913 to supply gas in parts of Columbia County, was merged into Northern Central Gas Co., 26 December 1913.

128. THE COLUMBIA ELECTRIC LIGHT AND POWER COMPANY (Operating).
Lancaster County, Columbia Borough.
1885 to 1907, 2 Linear Feet.

History:

The Columbia Electric Light and Power Co. was incorporated 6 March 1885 to supply electricity in the Borough of Columbia, Lancaster County. It merged with Columbia Electric Light, Heat and Power Co. 29 April 1905 but did not lose its corporate existence until 1907. From 1901 until 1907 its property and assets were controlled by The Lancaster County Railway & Light Co., a holding company.

Administrative Records:
Minute Book, 1901-1907
Lancaster County Railway and Light Co., Executive Committee Minute Book, 1903-1907
Stock Certificate Book, 1885-1907

Operating Records:
General Ledger, 1901-1907
Cashbook, 1901-1907
Cash Disbursements, 1901-1907
Audited Voucher Register, 1901-1907
Accounts Payable, 1902-1907
Statement of Receipts and Expenditures, 1903-1907
Monthly Statements, 1901-1904

Scope and Content Note:

The Minute Book of The Columbia Electric Light and Power Co. and the Executive Committee Minute Book of Lancaster County Railway and Light Co. contain operating information, including purchases of equipment for, and additions to, the power plant. Dealings with other Lancaster County companies, with the Pennsylvania Railroad, lighting contracts with the Borough of Columbia, and company finances are documented. The Minute Books also clarify the relationship between The Columbia Electric Light and Power Co. and Lancaster County Railway and Light Co., which acted as a holding company.

129. COLUMBIA ELECTRIC LIGHT, HEAT AND POWER COMPANY (Operating).
Lancaster County, Columbia Borough.
1905 to 1914, 3 Linear Feet.

History:

Columbia Electric Light, Heat and Power Co. was incorporated 17 January 1905 to supply electricity in the Borough of Columbia, Lancaster County. It was controlled by a holding company, Lancaster County Railway and Light Co., until 1911, when it consolidated and merged with 17 other companies to form Edison Electric Co., No. 1.

Administrative Records:
Minute Book, 1905-1911
Minute Book, Lancaster County Railway and Light Co., Executive Committee, 1905-1910
Stock ledger, 1905
Bond Register, 1909-1914

Operating Records:
General Ledgers, 1905-1911 (3 Volumes)
Journals, 1905-1911 (2 Volumes)
Cashbook, 1907-1911
Accounts Payable, 1907-1911
Audited Voucher Registers, 1907-1911 (2 Volumes)
Financial Statements, 1905-1909 (3 Volumes)
Statement of Earnings and Expenses, 1906-1907
Bills Payable, 1905-1906
Audit Reports, 1921-1925 (2 Volumes)

Scope and Content Note:

Minute Books document the negotiations leading to the acquisition of the company by Lancaster County. Included is information on bonds, mortgages and finances. The creation of an employee pension planion is described. Executive Committee Minute Book contains some operating information regarding finances and construction. Audit Reports of Edison Electric Co., No. 4, contain histories of Columbia Electric Light, Heat and Power Co. and list bonds and mortgages outstanding.

130. **COLUMBIA GAS AND ELECTRIC COMPANY** (Operating).
Columbia County, Bloomsburg Town.
1911 to 1913, 1 Linear Foot.

History:
Columbia Gas and Electric Co. was formed through the consolidation and merger of 22 companies, 7 February 1911. It supplied gas and electricity to a number of towns and boroughs in the Counties of Columbia, Luzerne, Montour, and Northumberland, with operations centered in the Town of Bloomsburg, Columbia County. The company merged with Columbia and Montour Electric Co., 22 March 1913.

Administrative Records:
Stock Certificate Book, 1911-1913

Operating Records:
General Ledger, 1911-1913
Journal, 1911-1913
Trial Balance, 1911-1913
Voucher Register—Electric Dept., 1911-1913
Voucher Register—Gas Dept., 1911-1913
Income and Operating Expenses—Electric and Gas Depts., 1911-1913
Operating and Construction Ledger—Electric Dept., 1911-1913
Operating and Construction Ledger—Gas Dept., 1911-1913

Scope and Content Note:
Information concerning the company's corporate charter, franchises, and history is contained in the "Portfolio (Historical Narrative)" of Columbia and Montour Electric Co.

131. **COLUMBIA GAS COMPANY** (Operating).
Lancaster County, Columbia Borough.
1929 to 1933, 1 Linear Foot.

History:
Columbia Gas Co. was the successor to The Columbia Gas Co., organized in 1851. It merged with Pennsylvania Power & Light Co., 21 November 1935.

Administrative Records:
Minutes, 1933-1935
Stock Transfer Record, 1934

Operating Records:
Cash Deposits and Withdrawals, 1927-1934
Summary of Cash, 1934-1935
Accounts Receivable Ledger, 1929-1935
Payrolls, 1927-1933
Audit Reports, 1929-1932 (2 Volumes)

Scope and Content Note:
The Minutes contain some information on income and operating expenses. Audit Reports provide a complete record of company operations.

132. **THE COLUMBIA GAS COMPANY** (Operating).
Lancaster County, Columbia Borough.
1911 to 1935, 1 Linear Foot.

History:
The Columbia Gas Co. was incorporated 20 November 1852 to manufacture and supply gas for lighting in the Borough of Columbia, Lancaster County. Its stock was acquired about 1913 by The Lancaster County Railway & Light Co., a New Jersey holding company, which in turn was acquired by Lehigh Power Securities Corp. in 1926. The Columbia Gas Co. was reorganized in 1930, changing its name to Columbia Gas Co.

Administrative Records:
Minute Book, Executive Committee, 1915

Operating Records:
Cash Deposits and Withdrawals, 1927-1934
Accounts Receivable Ledger, 1929-1935
Bills Payable, 1911
Automobile Reports, 1926-1929
Payrolls, 1927-1933
Time Books, 1919-1927 (3 Volumes)
Audit Reports, 1921-1925 (2 Volumes)

Scope and Content Note:
The Minute Book of the Executive Committee of Lancaster County Railway and Light Co. traces the relationship between that holding company and The Columbia Gas Co.
The Audit Reports provide a detailed overview of all aspects of company finances and operations.
Information on employees' wage rates and occupations appears in the Time Books.

133. **COLUMBIA POWER, LIGHT AND RAILWAYS COMPANY** (Operating).
Columbia County, Bloomsburg Town.
1909 to 1914, 2 1/2 Linear Feet.

History:
Columbia Power, Light and Railways Co., a holding company, was incorporated 23 November 1908 in the State of Delaware, with offices located in the Town of Bloomsburg, Columbia County, Pennsylvania. By purchasing stock in various light, transportation, heat, and power companies, the company planned to serve the area between Berwick and Danville in the counties of Columbia, Luzerne and Montour. In order to secure the necessary franchise rights it formed two non-operating companies: Columbia and Montour Electric Co. and Columbia and Montour Electric Railway Co.

Administrative Records:
First Annual Report of Directors, 1910
Stock Certificate Books—Common, 1909-1913 (2 Volumes)
Stock Certificate Books—Preferred, 1909-1914 (2 Volumes)
Stock Ledger—Common, 1909-1913
Stock Ledger—Preferred, 1909-1913

Operating Records:
General Ledgers, 1909-1913 (2 Volumes)
Journal, 1909-1913
Cashbooks, 1909-1913 (2 Volumes)
Cash Disbursements, 1909-1910
Accounts Payable Ledger, 1909-1910
Notes and Bills Payable, 1909-1912
Record of Vouchers Payable for Accounts of Affiliated Companies, 1909

Monthly Operating Statements, 1910-1913
Statement of Earnings of Affiliated Companies, 1909
Voucher Registers, 1909-1913 (2 Volumes)
Income and Operating Expenses, 1912-1913
Audit Report, W.H. Sponsler, 1909

Scope and Content Note:
The Annual Report for 1910 summarizes the history and purpose of the company. Acquisition of stock control in various companies is reflected in the Stock Ledgers. Other operating records trace the relationship between this company and its affiliated companies, including Columbia Gas and Electric Co. and Columbia and Montour Electric Railway Co. The "Portfolio (Historical Narrative)" of Columbia and Montour Electric Co. recapitulates the charters and franchises of those companies acquired under the auspices of Columbia Power, Light and Railways Co.

134. COLUMBUS COLLIERY COMPANY (Operating).
Lackawanna County, Scranton City.
1897 to 1907, 2 Linear Inches.

History:
Columbus Colliery Co. was organized about 1897 to mine anthracite coal in the City of Scranton, Lackawanna County. It remained in operation until about 1899, when it was acquired by Electric Co. of America, a New Jersey holding company. It ceased operations prior to the formation of Scranton Electric Co. in 1907.

Operating Records:
General Ledger, 1901-1907
Cashbook and Expense Journal, 1897-1902
Cashbook, 1903-1907

135. CONESTOGA REALTY COMPANY (Operating).
Lancaster County, Lancaster City.
1908 to 1926, 1 Linear Inch.

History:
Conestoga Realty Co. was organized 18 March 1908 to acquire real estate in the City of Lancaster, Lancaster County. Its assets were leased in 1908 to Conestoga Traction Co. and were sold to that company in 1922. As of 1925, Conestoga Realty Co. was listed as inactive.

Administrative Records:
Lease Agreement, Conestoga Realty Co. and Conestoga Traction Co., 1908

Operating Records:
Audit Reports, 1925-1926 (2 Volumes)

136. CONESTOGA TERMINAL COMPANY (Operating).
Lancaster County, Lancaster City.
1914 to 1935, 4 Linear Feet.

History:
Conestoga Terminal Co. was incorporated 5 February 1914 for the purpose of handling real estate in the City of Lancaster, Lancaster County. It merged into Pennsylvania Power & Light Co. in August 1934. It was formally dissolved in November 1935.

Administrative Records:
Minute Books, 1914-1935 (2 Volumes)
Stock Certificate Book, 1914-1930
Minutes, 1935

Operating Records:
FINANCIAL RECORDS
General Ledgers, 1914-1934 (2 Volumes)
Journal, 1914-1926
Journal Entry Register, 1926-1935
Cashbook, 1914-1926
Cash Disbursements, 1926-1927
Record of Cash Receipts, 1926-1934
Record of Cash Disbursements, 1934-1935
Summary of Cash, 1934-1935
Audited Voucher Registers, 1924-1935 (2 Volumes)
Detail Ledger, 1926-1934
Accounts Payable, 1926
Accounts Payable—Affiliated Companies, 1933-1935
Accounts Receivable, 1926-1934
Accrual Record, 1926
PERSONNEL RECORDS
Pay Roll Distribution, 1931-1933
Statement of Accrual, Workmen's Compensation Insurance, 1934
Payrolls, 1928-1934
AUDIT REPORTS
Audit Report, Electric Bond & Share Co., 1923-1925
Audit Report, Electric Bond & Share Co., 1929-1931
Audit Report, Electric Bond & Share Co., 1931-1932
Audit Report, Pennsylvania Power & Light Co., 1923-1925
Audit Report, Pennsylvania Power & Light Co., 1930
Preliminary Audit Report, Electric Bond & Share Co., 1925
Report on Audit, Electric Bond & Share Co., 1926-1927
Report on Audit, Electric Bond & Share Co., 1927-1929

Scope and Content Note:
The Minute Books reflect the company's involvement in real estate affairs in the City of Lancaster. The Audit Reports provide an overview of the company's finances.

137. CONESTOGA TOWNSHIP ELECTRIC COMPANY (Non-operating).
Lancaster County, Conestoga Township.
1912, 1 Linear Inch.

History:
Conestoga Township Electric Co. was incorporated 7 November 1912 to supply electricity in Conestoga Township, Lancaster County. It consolidated and merged with 17 companies to form Edison Electric Co., No. 3, on 9 December 1912.

138. CONESTOGA TRACTION COMPANY (Operating).
Lancaster County, Lancaster City.
1901 to 1932, 2 1/2 Linear Feet.

History:
Conestoga Traction Co. was organized on 16 January 1900 by the Lancaster County Railway and Light Co., a New Jersey holding company which was attempting to consolidate Lancaster County (Pennsylvania) street railways under its control. Conestoga Traction initially controlled 16 of the county's largest street railways, and in 1918 it merged with its six remaining competitors to form a new Conestoga Traction Co. In 1926, Lehigh Power & Securities acquired the company and five years later merged it into the Conestoga Transporation Co.,

which now monopolized all bus and transportation service in Lancaster County. In 1931 it sold its electrical distribution facilities to Pennsylvania Power and Light.

Administrative Records:
Minute Books, 1903-1931 (2 Volumes)
Correspondence & Reports, 1925-1931
Bond Register, 1906
Photographs (Library, Pictorial Collection)

Operating Records:
FINANCIAL RECORDS
Status of Car Trust Notes, 1918-1926
Bills Payable, 1901-1931
Material and Supplies Reports, 1926-1930
Material and Supplies Analysis, 1926-1930
Material and Supplies Inventory, 1926-1930
Railway Dept. Monthly Statistics, 1911-1926
PERSONNEL RECORDS
Payrolls—Office, 1925-1926
Payrolls—Distribution, 1931
Payrolls—Treasurer's, 1927-1932
Payroll Sheets—General, 1929
Payroll Charges and Workmen's Compensation Insurance, 1929-1930
AUDIT REPORTS, 1921-1925 (4 Volumes)

Scope and Content Note:
The Correspondence file documents many aspects of company operations including budgets, rate policies; accidents; construction; and post-1929 reorganization plans. The Audit Reports provide extensive financial data for the 1921-25 period, with details concerning capitalization and operating expenditures. The Office Payrolls list individuals and their salaries, along with deductions for relief funds. Photographs contain pictures of company rolling stock.

139. CONESTOGA TRANSMISSION COMPANY
(Operating).
Lancaster County, Lancaster City.
1912 to 1938, 2 1/2 Linear Feet.

History:
Created by Edison Electric Co., No. 2, Conestoga Transmission Co. was incorporated 29 November 1912, for the purpose of building, operating, and maintaining lines for the transmission of electricity in Lancaster County. In 1913, it erected a transmission line from Holtwood Dam in Martic Township to the City of Lancaster, which supplied all the power needs of Edison Electric Co. and of Conestoga Traction Co. Pennsylvania Power & Light Co. purchased the company, 20 October 1937.

Administrative Records:
Minute Book, 1912-1937
Papers in connection with Annual Stockholders' Meetings, 1932-1937
Stock Certificate Books, 1913-1938 (5 Volumes)
Stock Transfer Records, 1913-1927
Stock Transfer Records, 1927-1938

Operating Records:
General Ledger, 1913-1938 (2 Volumes)
Journals, 1913-1938 (2 Volumes)
Cash Books, 1912-1938 (2 Volumes)
Audited Voucher Register, 1912-1920
Time Book, 1913
Audit Report, Pennsylvania Power & Light Co., 1923-1925

Scope and Content Note:
The Minute Book contains a copy of the 1913 agreement leasing Conestoga Transmission Company's property to Edison Electric Co. Also included is a list of Company Stockholders, 1913-1938.

140. CONESTOGA TRANSPORTATION COMPANY
(Operating).
Lancaster County, Lancaster City.
1926 to 1930, 4 Linear Inches.

History:
Conestoga Transportation Co. was incorporated 5 December 1922 in order to operate street railways and bus lines in Lancaster County. All its stock was owned by the Conestoga Traction Co.

Administrative Records:
Correspondence, 1926-1930

Operating Records:
Automobile Reports, 1926-1929
Audit Reports, 1926 (2 Volumes)

Scope and Content Note:
The Audit Reports document the company's history, capitalization, and financial status. Additional information about this company appears in the files of the Conestoga Traction Co.

141. CONESTOGA VALLEY ELECTRIC COMPANY
(Operating).
Lancaster County, Ephrata Borough.
1901 to 1930, 2 1/2 Linear Feet.

History:
Conestoga Valley Electric Co. was incorporated 26 December 1916 in order to supply electricity to a number of rural communities in the northeastern part of Lancaster County. It was merged into Pennsylvania Power and Light Co. on 31 December 1930.

Administrative Records:
Minute Book, 1926-1930
Minutes relating to Stockholders' Meetings, 1930
Stock Certificate Book, 1917-1930
Stock Ledger, 1917-1926

Operating Records:
General Ledger, 1926-1930 (2 Volumes)
Journal, 1926
Journal Entry Register, 1926-1930
Miscellaneous Receipts, 1901-1926 (2 Volumes)
Cash Disbursements, 1926-1927
Cash Deposits and Withdrawals, 1927-1930
Cash Receipts, 1926-1930
Audited Voucher Register, 1926-1930
Invoices, 1921-1925
Detail Ledger, 1926-1930
Accounts Receivable, 1926-1930
Accounts Payable, 1926-1930
Fixed Capital, 1926-1930
Accrual Record, 1926-1930
Construction, 1926-1930

Materials & Supplies, 1926-1928 (2 Volumes)
Automobile Services & Costs, 1926-1928
Automobile Reports, 1926-1929
Expenditure Requisitions, 1930
Payrolls, 1927-1928
Audit Reports, 1921-1930 (5 Volumes)

142. CONESTOGA WATER AND POWER COMPANY (Non-operating).
Dauphin County, Harrisburg City.
1902, 1 Linear Inch.

History:
Conestoga Water and Power Co. was incorporated 23 May 1902 for the purpose of supplying water power for commercial purposes in Conestoga Township. On 14 August 1902, it merged and consolidated with three other water and power companies to form Susquehanna Storage-Lake and Power Co.

143. CONEWAGO-DAUPHIN POWER & LIGHT COMPANY (Non-operating).
Dauphin County, Conewago Township.
1930, 1 Linear Inch.

History:
Conewago-Dauphin Power & Light Co. was incorporated 12 September 1930 to supply electricity in Conewago Township, Dauphin County. It was merged into Pennsylvania Power & Light Co. on 20 October 1920.

144. CONEWAGO-YORK POWER & LIGHT COMPANY (Non-operating).
York County, Conewago Township.
1959 to 1960, 1 Linear Inch.

History:
Conewago-York Power & Light Co. was incorporated in October 1959 to supply electricity in Conewago Township, York County. It was merged into Pennsylvania Power & Light Co. in March 1960.

145. CONOY TOWNSHIP ELECTRIC COMPANY (Non-operating).
Lancaster County, Conoy Township.
1912, 1 Linear Inch.

History:
Conoy Township Electric Co. was incorporated 13 November 1912 to supply electricity in Conoy Township, Lancaster County. On 27 November 1912, it was consolidated and merged with thirteen other companies to form Edison Electric Co., No. 3.

146. CONSUMERS ELECTRIC COMPANY OF FREELAND (Non-operating).
Luzerne County, Freeland Borough.
1908 to 1909, 1 Linear Inch.

History:
Consumers Electric Co. of Freeland was incorporated 4 March 1908 to supply electricity in the Borough of Freeland, Luzerne County. It was consolidated and merged with eleven other companies on 23 June 1909 to form Harwood Electric Co.

147. CONSUMERS ELECTRIC COMPANY OF HUGHESTOWN (Operating).
Luzerne County, Hughestown Borough.
1913 to 1918, 1 Linear Inch.

History:
Consumers Electric Co. of Hughestown was incorporated 12 May 1912 for the purpose of supplying electricity in the Borough of Hughestown, Luzerne County. It was merged into Scranton Electric Co. on 16 July 1918.

Administrative Records:
Minute Book, 1913-1918

Scope and Content Note:
The Minute Book shows that Consumers Electric Co. was technically an operating company, in that it submitted proposals for the erection of power lines. However, there is no evidence that any lines were erected by it. The company appears to have been acquired by The Scranton Electric Co., with American Gas and Electric Co. as the major stockholder.

148. CONSUMERS ELECTRIC COMPANY OF THE BOROUGH OF EXETER (Non-operating).
Luzerne County, Exeter Borough.
1912 to 1918, 1 Linear Inch.

History:
Consumers Electric Co. of the Borough of Exeter was incorporated 18 January 1912 to supply electricity to the Borough of Exeter, Luzerne County. It was merged into the Scranton Electric Co. 16 July 1918.

149. CONSUMERS ELECTRIC COMPANY OF THE BOROUGH OF WEST PITTSTON (Non-operating).
Luzerne County, West Pittston Borough.
1912 to 1918, 1 Linear Inch.

History:
Consumers Electric Co. of the Borough of West Pittston was incorporated 18 January 1912 for the purpose of supplying electricity to the Borough of West Pittston, Luzerne County. It was merged into Scranton Electric Co. on 16 July 1918.

150. CONSUMERS ELECTRIC COMPANY OF THE CITY OF PITTSTON (Non-operating).
Luzerne County, Pittston City.
1912 to 1918, 1 Linear Inch.

History:
Consumers Electric Co. of the City of Pittston was incorporated in 1912 to supply electricity to the City of Pittston, Luzerne County. It was merged into Scranton Electric Co. 16 July 1918.

151. CONSUMERS ELECTRIC LIGHT AND POWER COMPANY OF HAZLETON, PA. (Operating).
Luzerne County, Hazleton City.
1906 to 1909, 1 1/2 Linear Feet.

History:
Consumers Electric Light and Power Co. of Hazleton, Pa. was incorporated 17 February 1906 for the purpose of supplying electricity in the City of Hazleton, Luzerne County. On 23 June 1909 it merged and consolidated with eleven other companies to form Harwood Electric Co.

Administrative Records:
Minute Books, 1906-1909 (3 Volumes)
Stock Certificate Book, 1906-1909

Operating Records:
General Ledger, 1907-1909
Journal, 1906-1909
Cashbook, 1906-1909
Audited Voucher Register, 1907-1909
Payrolls, 1907-1909
Balance Sheets, 1907-1909

Scope and Content Note:
The monthly Payrolls of the Consumers Electric Light and Power Co. of Hazleton, Pa., list individuals by name, occupation and salary. The Balance Sheets give complete financial data, showing monthly accounts of assets, liabilities, earnings, and expenditures.

152. THE CONSUMERS GAS COMPANY OF DANVILLE, PENNA. (Operating).
Montour County, Danville Borough.
1889 to 1898, 1/2 Linear Foot.

History:
The Consumers Gas Co. of Danville, Penna., was incorporated 8 November 1882 in Montour County to operate the gas plant of the Danville Gas Co. (incorporated 1854). In 1884, The Consumers Gas Co. built an electric generating station which supplied electricity to the Borough of Danville. In 1889, the company's gas properties were leased by Standard Gas Co., and ten years later Standard Electric Light Co. bought the electric generating station. On 20 May 1913 The Consumers Gas Co. of Danville merged into Columbia and Montour Electric Co.

Operating Records:
Invoices, 1889-1893
Invoices, 1894-1898

Scope and Content Note:
The Invoices of The Consumers Gas Co. of Danville, Penna., provide a detailed look at material and shipping costs incurred by a typical gas company in the 1890's.

153. THE CONSUMERS GAS COMPANY OF WILKES-BARRE (Operating).
Luzerne County, Wilkes-Barre City.
1892 to 1904, 2 Linear Feet.

History:
The Consumers Gas Co. of Wilkes-Barre was incorporated 11 May 1892 to provide gas service, and by 1895 was serving over 500 customers. In 1898 the company was leased by The Gas Co. of Luzerne County. On 22 December 1904 it was consolidated and merged with four other companies to form Wilkes Barre Gas and Electric Co.

Administrative Records:
Minute Books, 1892-1904 (2 Volumes)

Operating Records:
General Ledger, 1892-1898
Journal, 1894-1898
Cashbook, 1892-1898

Scope and Content Note:
The Cashbook of The Consumers Gas Co. of Wilkes-Barre lists expenditures on accounts, while the General Ledger documents fuel expenditures, shipping charges, expense accounts, and office personnel salaries. The Minute Books document capitalization and stock distribution.

154. CONYNGHAM LIGHT COMPANY (Non-operating).
Columbia County, Conyngham Township.
1912, 1 Linear Inch.

History:
Conyngham Light Co. was incorporated 29 November 1912 to supply electricity in the Township of Conyngham, Columbia County. It was consolidated and merged with twelve other companies on 16 December 1912 to form Hazleton Electric Co.

155. CONYNGHAM POWER & LIGHT COMPANY (Non-operating).
Luzerne County, Conyngham Borough.
1922 to 1923, 2 Linear Inches.

History:
Conyngham Power & Light Co. was incorporated 23 August 1922 to supply electricity in the Borough of Conyngham, Luzerne County. It was merged into Pennsylvania Power & Light Co. along with two other companies on 18 November 1922.

156. CONYNGHAM TOWNSHIP ELECTRIC COMPANY (Non-operating).
Columbia County, Conyngham Township.
1911 to 1913, 1 Linear Inch.

History:
Conyngham Township Electric Co. was incorporated 26 January 1911 to supply electricity in the Township of Conyngham, Columbia County. It was consolidated and merged with eleven other companies on 12 November 1912 to form The Schuylkill Gas & Electric Co.

157. THE COOPERSBURG ELECTRIC LIGHT, HEAT AND POWER COMPANY (Operating).
Lehigh County, Coopersburg Borough.
1911 to 1928, 3 1/2 Linear Feet.

History:
The Coopersburg Electric Light, Heat and Power Co. was incorporated 7 June 1911 to supply electricity in the Borough of Coopersburg, Lehigh County. In 1923 the stock of the company was acquired by Lehigh Power Securities Corp. On 28 May 1928 The Coopersburg Electric Light, Heat and Power Co. was merged into Pennsylvania Power & Light Co.

Administrative Records:
Minute Book, 1911-1928
Stock Certificate Book, 1911-1923
Stock Transfer Record, 1923
Stock Ledger, 1911-1923

Operating Records:
FINANCIAL RECORDS
General Ledgers, 1923-1928 (2 Volumes)
Journal Entry Register, 1923
Cash Received, 1923-1925
Cash Register, 1923-1925
Record of Cash Receipts, 1925-1928
Record of Cash Disbursements, 1925-1928
Summary of Cash, 1925-1928
Audited Voucher Register, 1923-1928
Detail Ledger, 1923

Accounts Receivable, 1924-1928
Accounts Payable, 1923-1928
Detail of Cost Study and Fixed Capital, 1925
Expenditure Requisitions, 1923-1927
Retirement Authorities, 1924-1928
Repair Authorities, 1924
Summary of Accounts Receivable, 1926-1928
Summary of Consumers' Deposits, 1926-1928
Summary of Cashiers' Overs and Shorts, 1926-1928
Recapitulation of Jobbing Work, 1928
AUDIT REPORTS, 1919-1927 (3 Volumes)

Scope and Content Note:
The Minute Book of The Coopersburg Electric Light, Heat and Power Co. records the cash receipts and disbursements of the company, but does not always agree with the Cash Disbursements Ledger. The Audit Reports give capitalization and liability figures as well as monthly statements showing profit and loss.

158. COVINGTON POWER & LIGHT COMPANY (Non-operating).
Tioga County, Covington Borough.
1923, 1 Linear Inch.

History:
Covington Power & Light Co. was a "paper company" that Pennsylvania Power & Light organized on 15 March 1923 in order to extend its area of operations into Tioga County. This effort evidently failed and the company was dissolved in October of 1923.

159. CRAWFORD-CLINTON POWER & LIGHT COMPANY (Non-operating).
Clinton County, Crawford Township.
1928 to 1929, 1 Linear Inch.

History:
Crawford-Clinton Power & Light Co. was incorporated 3 October 1929 to supply electricity in the Township of Crawford, Clinton County. It was merged into Pennsylvania Power & Light Co. on 24 October 1929 along with six other companies.

160. THE CRESCENT ELECTRIC COMPANY (Non-operating).
Lackawanna County, Scranton City.
1902 to 1910, 1 Linear Inch.

History:
The Crescent Electric Co. was incorporated prior to 1902 to provide electricity in the City of Scranton, Lackawanna County. On 10 January 1910 it was merged into American Gas & Electric Co.

161. THE CUMBERLAND LIGHT HEAT, AND POWER COMPANY (Operating).
Cumberland County, Mechanicsburg Borough.
1894 to 1905, 1 Linear Inch.

History:
The Cumberland Light, Heat, and Power Co. was incorporated 21 September 1894 to supply electricity in the Borough of Mechanicsburg, Cumberland County. It served several small communities and townships in northeastern Cumberland County. On 21 February 1903 the company was consolidated and merged with seven non-operating companies to form The United Electric Co.

Administrative Records:
Minute Book, 1894-1903
Stock Certificate Book, 1894-1905

Scope and Content Note:
The Minute Book of The Cumberland Light, Heat, and Power Co. includes the company's by-laws, notes on stockholders' meetings, receipts and expenditures, and a brief account of the company's formation.

162. CUMBERLAND RAILWAY COMPANY (Operating).
Cumberland County, Carlisle Borough.
1908 to 1911, 1 Linear Inch.

History:
Cumberland Railway Co. was incorporated 8 October 1908 for the purpose of constructing and operating an electric railway in and around the Borough of Carlisle, Cumberland County. Early in 1909, it made an agreement with Mount Holly Light, Heat and Power Co. to purchase that company's stock. The 1917 Pennsylvania Annual Report of the Bureau of Railways, Dept. of Internal Affairs, lists the company as still being in existence in 1917.

Administrative Records:
Minute Book, 1908-1911

Scope and Content Note:
The Minute Book of Cumberland Railway Co. documents routine business matters and gives a detailed description of the routes covered by the company. Loose minutes in the back of the Minute Book discuss renovation and repair to the line and give a complete list of stockholders.

163. THE CUMBERLAND VALLEY ELECTRIC PASSENGER RAILWAY COMPANY (Operating).
Cumberland County, Carlisle Borough.
1897 to 1904, 1 Linear Inch.

History:
The Cumberland Valley Electric Passenger Railway Co. was incorporated 11 September 1893 to operate an electric railway in and around the Boroughs of Carlisle and Mechanicsburg, Cumberland County. It was sold 25 June 1904 and was subsequently reorganized with Cumberland Valley Traction Co. to form Carlisle and Mechanicsburg Street Railway Co.

Administrative Records:
Minute Book, 1897-1904
Stock Book, no date

Scope and Content Note:
The Minute Book of Cumberland Valley Electric Passenger Railway Co. deals with routine stockholders' and directors' meetings, includes copies of the ordinance establishing the company, and gives a detailed description of the route covered by the company.

164. CUMBERLAND VALLEY TRACTION COMPANY (Operating).
Cumberland County, Carlisle Borough.
1894 to 1895, 1 Linear Inch.

History:
Cumberland Valley Traction Co. was incorporated 18 December 1893 to operate an electric railway in the

Borough of Carlisle, Cumberland County. The company, a lessee of Cumberland Valley Electric Passenger Railway Co., was no longer in existence by 1904.

Operating Records:
Preferred Stock Book, 1894-1895
Common Stock Book, 1894-1895

165. CUMRU TOWNSHIP ELECTRIC LIGHT, HEAT AND POWER COMPANY (Non-operating).
Berks County, Cumru Township.
1906 to 1915, 1 Linear Inch.

History:
Cumru Township Electric Light, Heat and Power Co. was incorporated 24 August 1905 to supply electricity in the Township of Cumru, Berks County. It was consolidated and merged with three other companies 14 August 1915 to form Berkshire Electric Co.

166. DALMATIA LIGHT COMPANY (Operating).
Northumberland County, Dalmatia Village.
1919 to 1923, 1 1/2 Linear Feet.

History:
Dalmatia Light Co. was incorporated 17 July 1919 to supply electricity in the Village of Dalmatia, Northumberland County. It was merged along with four other companies into Middleburg Light, Heat and Power Co. on 21 November 1923.

Administrative Records:
Minute Books, 1919-1923 (3 Volumes)
Stock Certificate Book, 1919-1923
Stock Subscription Ledger, 1919
Letters and Correspondence, 1921-1923

Operating Records:
General Ledger, 1920-1923
Journals, 1919-1923 (2 Volumes)
Bills, 1921-1923
Consumers Ledger, 1919-1923 (2 Volumes)

Scope and Content Note:
The Minute Books of the Dalmatia Light Co. give a good account of the growth and development of a very small electric company during this period. The Ledgers and Journals detail operating expenses, and several payroll sheets are included among the letters and correspondence.

167. DAMASCUS-WAYNE POWER & LIGHT COMPANY (Non-operating).
Wayne County, Damascus Township.
1927 to 1928, 1 Linear Inch.

History:
Damascus-Wayne Power & Light Co. was incorporated 22 March 1928 to supply electricity in the Township of Damascus, Wayne County. On 31 March 1928 it was merged into Pennsylvania Power & Light.

168. DANVILLE & BLOOMSBURG STREET RAILWAY COMPANY (Operating).
Montour County, Danville Borough.
1904 to 1909, 1/2 Linear Foot.

History:
Incorporated on 7 September 1903 to operate an electric railway between the Borough of Danville, Montour County, and the Town of Bloomsburg, Columbia County, Danville & Bloomsburg Street Railway Co. was consolidated and merged with another electric railway company 26 May 1911 to form Columbia and Montour Electric Railway Co.

Operating Records:
Cash Books, 1904-1909 (2 Volumes)
Receipts and Disbursements, 1904-1905

Scope and Content Note:
The operating records of Danville & Bloomsburg Street Railway Co. document routine business expenses.

169. DANVILLE BOROUGH ELECTRIC COMPANY (Non-operating).
Montour County, Danville Borough.
1919 to 1920, 1/2 Linear Foot.

History:
Danville Borough Electric Co. was incorporated 6 November 1919 to supply electricity in the Borough of Danville, Montour County. It was merged along with eight other non-operating companies into Lehigh Industrial Power Co. on 28 April 1920.

170. DAUPHIN BOROUGH POWER & LIGHT COMPANY (Non-operating).
Dauphin County, Dauphin Borough.
1913 to 1914, 1 Linear Inch.

History:
Dauphin Borough Power & Light Co. was incorporated 24 December 1913 to supply electricity in the Borough of Dauphin, Dauphin County. It was merged along with six other non-operating companies into Harrisburg Light and Power Co., No. 2, on 27 December 1913.

171. DELANO LIGHT COMPANY (Non-operating).
Schuylkill County, Delano Township.
1912, 1 Linear Inch.

History:
Delano Light Co. was incorporated 29 November 1912 to supply electricity in the Township of Delano, Schuylkill County. It was consolidated and merged along with twelve other companies 16 December 1912 to form Hazleton Electric Co.

172. DELANO TOWNSHIP ELECTRIC COMPANY (Non-operating).
Schuylkill County, Delano Township.
1910 to 1912, 1 Linear Inch.

History:
Delano Township Electric Co. was incorporated 26 January 1911 to supply electricity in the Township of Delano, Schuylkill County. On 12 November 1912, it was consolidated and merged with eleven other companies to form The Schuylkill Gas & Electric Co.

173. DELAWARE TOWNSHIP ELECTRIC COMPANY (Non-operating).
Northumberland County, Delaware Township.
1913, 1 Linear Inch.

History:
Delaware Township Electric Co. was incorporated 5 April 1913 to supply electricity in the Township of Delaware, Northumberland County. On 28 April 1913, it

was merged into Northumberland County Gas & Electric Co.

174. DENISON ELECTRIC COMPANY (Non-operating).
Luzerne County, Denison Township.
1925 to 1928, 2 Linear Inches.

History:
Denison Electric Co. was incorporated 25 January 1924 to supply electricity in the Township of Denison, Luzerne County. It was merged into Pennsylvania Power & Light Co. 28 May 1928.

175. DENISON POWER & LIGHT COMPANY (Non-operating).
Luzerne County, Denison Township.
1923 to 1924, 2 Linear Inches.

History:
Denison Power & Light Co. was incorporated 25 January 1924 to supply electricity in the Township of Denison, Luzerne County. It was merged into Pennsylvania Power & Light Co., 22 May 1924.

176. DENVER AND EPHRATA RAILWAY COMPANY (Non-operating).
Lancaster County, Lancaster City.
1925 to 1926, 1 Linear Inch.

History:
Denver and Ephrata Railway Co. was incorporated 21 November 1916 to construct an electric railway between the Boroughs of Ephrata and Denver, Lancaster County. The line was planned and the right-of-way acquired, but the line was never constructed and the company remained inactive. On 13 October 1925 the company was merged into Conestoga Traction Co.

177. DERRY POWER & LIGHT COMPANY (Non-operating).
Montour County, Derry Township.
1923 to 1924, 1 Linear Inch.

History:
Derry Power & Light Co. was incorporated 21 November 1923 to supply electricity to the Township of Derry, Montour County. On 16 May 1924 it was merged into Pennsylvania Power & Light Co.

178. DIAMOND ELECTRIC COMPANY OF WASHINGTON TOWNSHIP (Non-operating).
Lehigh County, Washington Township.
1911 to 1913, 1 Linear Inch.

History:
Diamond Electric Co. of Washington Township was incorporated 4 April 1911 to supply electricity in the Township of Washington, Lehigh County. On 23 December it was consolidated and merged with 37 other non-operating companies to form Lehigh Navigation Electric Co., No. 2.

179. DONEGAL GAS COMPANY (Operating).
Lancaster County, Mount Joy Township.
1927 to 1930, 1 Linear Inch.

History:
Donegal Gas Co. was incorporated 12 November 1908 and shortly thereafter acquired control of the Mount Joy Gas Co., which had, during the 1880's, built the original system for manufacturing and distributing natural gas in Mount Joy Township. In 1927, United Gas and Electric Co., which at the time was attempting to consolidate its control over eastern Pennsylvania's natural gas distribution system, purchased Donegal Gas. Three years later this company merged into Pennsylvania Power & Light.

Operating Records:
Bills Payable, 1927
Payrolls, 1930

Scope and Content Note:
The semimonthly Payrolls of Donegal Gas Co. list the name, occupation, pay rate, and wages earned for employees of the company, while the Bills Payable detail various operating expenses.

180. DORRANCE TOWNSHIP ELECTRIC COMPANY (Non-operating).
Luzerne County, Dorrance Township.
1911 to 1912, 1 Linear Inch.

History:
Dorrance Township Electric Co. was incorporated 6 February 1911 to supply electricity in the Township of Dorrance, Luzerne County. On 23 February 1912 it was consolidated and merged with eleven other companies to form The Harwood Electric Co.

181. DOYLESTOWN ELECTRIC LIGHT AND POWER COMPANY (Non-operating).
Bucks County, Doylestown Township.
1913 to 1914, 1 Linear Inch.

History:
Doylestown Electric Light and Power Co. was incorporated 8 December 1913 to supply electricity in the Township of Doylestown, Bucks County. It was merged along with six other non-operating companies into Lehigh Valley Light and Power Co., No. 3, on 29 December 1913.

182. DREHER POWER & LIGHT COMPANY (Non-operating).
Wayne County, Dreher Township.
1923 to 1924, 1 Linear Inch.

History:
Dreher Power & Light Co. was incorporated 1 May 1923 to supply electricity in the Township of Dreher, Wayne County. On 20 July 1923 it was consolidated and merged with 31 other non-operating companies to form Paupack Power & Light Co., No. 2.

183. DU BOISTOWN POWER & LIGHT COMPANY (Non-operating).
Lycoming County, Du Boistown Borough.
1923 to 1924, 1 Linear Inch.

History:
Du Boistown Power & Light Co. was incorporated 9 May 1924 to supply electricity in the Borough of Du Boistown, Lycoming County. It was merged into Pennsylvania Power & Light Co., 30 July 1924.

184. DUNMORE ELECTRIC LIGHT, HEAT AND POWER COMPANY (Operating).
Lackawanna County, Dunmore Borough.
1896 to 1907, 1 Linear Inch.

History:
Dunmore Electric Light, Heat and Power Co. was incorporated 14 September 1896 to supply electricity in the Borough of Dunmore, Lackawanna County. On 21 March 1907 the company was consolidated and merged with four other electric companies to form Scranton Electric Co.

Administrative Records:
Minute Book, 1896-1907

Operating Records:
General Ledger, 1899-1907

Scope and Content Note:
The Minute Book of Dunmore Electric Light, Heat and Power Co. gives a good account of the growth and development of one of the pioneer electric companies in the Scranton area, while the General Ledger provides details on the company's operating expenses.

185. THE DUNMORE STREET RAILWAY COMPANY (Operating).
Lackawanna County, Dunmore Borough.
1896, 1 Linear Inch.

History:
The Dunmore Street Railway Co. was incorporated 2 November 1895 to construct and operate an electric railway in the Borough of Dunmore, Lackawanna County. On 18 December 1896 the company was consolidated and merged with four other companies to form Scranton Railway Co.

Administrative Records:
Minute Book, 1896

Scope and Content Note:
The Minute Book of The Dunmore Street Railway Co. records the proceedings of stockholder and directors' meetings.

186. DUNNSTABLE ELECTRIC LIGHT COMPANY (Non-operating).
Clinton County, Dunnstable Township.
1917, 1 Linear Inch.

History:
Dunnstable Electric Light Co. was incorporated 6 November 1916 to supply electricity in the Township of Dunnstable, Clinton County. It was consolidated and merged with six other companies on 7 May 1917 to form Lock Haven Electric Light and Power Co.

187. DUPONT ELECTRIC COMPANY (Non-operating).
Luzerne County, Dupont Township.
1910 to 1913, 1 Linear Inch.

History:
Dupont Electric Co. was incorporated 7 September 1910 to supply electricity in the Township of Dupont, Luzerne County. It was consolidated and merged with four other electric companies on 8 July 1913 to form Citizens Electric Illuminating Co.

188. DURHAM TOWNSHIP ELECTRIC COMPANY (Non-operating).
Bucks County, Durham Township.
1913 to 1935, 1 1/2 Linear Feet.

History:
Durham Township Electric Co. was incorporated 30 December 1913 to supply electricity in the Township of Durham, Bucks County. In 1917 Lehigh Navigation Electric Co., No. 2, acquired a controlling interest in the company, and three years later sold its stock to Pennsylvania Power & Light.

189. DURYEA BOROUGH-LUZERNE POWER & LIGHT COMPANY (Non-operating).
Luzerne County, Duryea Borough.
1926 to 1927, 1 Linear Inch.

History:
Duryea Borough-Luzerne Power & Light Co. was a "paper company" formed by Pennsylvania Power & Light Co. 9 March 1926 in an effort to expand the company's holdings in northeastern Luzerne County. The company was not incorporated, however, and was ultimately dissolved 27 January 1927.

190. DURYEA ELECTRIC COMPANY (Non-operating).
Luzerne County, Duryea Township.
1910 to 1913, 1 Linear Inch.

History:
Duryea Electric Co. was incorporated 26 October 1909 to supply electricity in the Township of Duryea, Luzerne County. It was consolidated and merged with four other electric companies on 8 July 1913 to form Citizens Electric Illuminating Co.

191. DYBERRY POWER & LIGHT COMPANY (Non-operating).
Wayne County, Dyberry Township.
1923 to 1924, 1 Linear Inch.

History:
Dyberry Power & Light Co. was incorporated 20 February 1924 to supply electricity in the Township of Dyberry, Wayne County. It was merged into Honesdale Consolidated Light, Heat and Power Co. along with three other non-operating companies 12 May 1924.

192. EAGLES MERE LIGHT COMPANY (Operating).
Sullivan County, Eagles Mere Borough.
1921 to 1923, 1 Linear Inch.

History:
Eagles Mere Light Co. was incorporated 7 September 1900 to supply electricity to the Borough of Eagles Mere, Sullivan County. It also sold power to, and was closely associated with, Citizens Electric Light and Power Co. of Hughesville, Pa. On 6 June 1923 it merged into Pennsylvannia Power & Light Co.

Operating Records:
Audit Report, Pennsylvania Power & Light Co., 1921-1923

Scope and Content Note:
The Audit Report documents Pennsylvania Power & Light Company's interest in acquiring control of small rural electric companies during the 1920s in an effort to integrate its sytems in eastern Pennsylvnania.

193. EARL TOWNSHIP ELECTRIC COMPANY (Non-operating).
Lancaster County, Earl Township.
1912, 1 Linear Inch.

History:
Earl Township Electric Co., incorporated 13 November 1912 to supply electricity in Earl Township, Lancaster County, consolidated and merged with 13 companies to form Edison Electric Co., No. 4, 9 December 1912.

194. EAST ALLEN ELECTRIC COMPANY
(Non-operating).
Northampton County, East Allen Township.
1911 to 1913, 1 Linear Inch.

History:
East Allen Electric Co., incorporated 4 April 1911 to supply electricity in East Allen Township, Northampton County, consolidated and merged with 37 companies to form Lehigh Navigation Electric Co., No. 2, on 6 January 1913.

195. EAST BRUNSWICK TOWNSHIP ELECTRIC COMPANY (Non-operating).
Schuylkill County, East Brunswick Township.
1924, 1 Linear Inch.

History:
East Brunswick Township Electric Co., incorporated 4 August 1924 to supply electricity in East Brunswick Township, Schuylkill County, merged into East Penn Electric Co., No. 2, 28 August 1924.

196. EAST BUFFALO-UNION LIGHT & POWER COMPANY (Non-operating).
Union County, East Buffalo Township.
1961, 1 Linear Inch.

History:
East Buffalo-Union Light & Power Co. was incorporated in April 1961 by Pennsylvania Power & Light Co. in order to secure right-of-way in East Buffalo Township, Union County.

197. EAST BUFFALO-UNION POWER & LIGHT COMPANY (Non-operating).
Union County, East Buffalo Township.
1930, 1 Linear Inch.

History:
East Buffalo-Union Power & Light Co., incorporated 14 July 1930 to supply electricity in East Buffalo Township, Union County, merged into Pennsylvania Power & Light Co., 8 August 1930.

198. EAST CAMERON ELECTRIC COMPANY
(Non-operating).
Northumberland County, East Cameron Township.
1921 to 1923, 1 Linear Inch.

History:
East Cameron Electric Co., incorporated 18 January 1922 to supply electricity in East Cameron Township, Northumberland County, merged into Pennsylvania Power & Light Co., 10 April 1922.

199. EAST CHILLISQUAQUE TOWNSHIP NORTHUMBERLAND ELECTRIC COMPANY
(Non-operating).
Northumberland County, East Chillisquaque Township.
1919 to 1920, 1 Linear Inch.

History:
East Chillisquaque Township Northumberland Electric Co., incorporated 6 November 1919 to supply electricity in East Chillisquaque Township, Northumberland County, merged into Lehigh Industrial Power Co., 28 April 1920.

200. EAST DONEGAL TOWNSHIP ELECTRIC LIGHT COMPANY (Non-operating).
Lancaster County, East Donegal Township.
1911, 1 Linear Inch.

History:
East Donegal Township Electric Light Co., incorporated 10 August 1911 to supply electricity in East Donegal Township, Lancaster County, consolidated and merged with 13 companies to form Edison Electric Co., No. 3, 9 December 1912.

201. EAST EARL ELECTRIC COMPANY
(Non-operating).
Lancaster County, East Earl Township.
1914, 1 Linear Inch.

History:
East Earl Electric Co., incorporated 2 October 1914 to supply electricity in East Earl Township, Lancaster County, merged with three companies to form Edison Electric Co., No. 4, 16 December 1914.

202. EAST EARL ELECTRIC LIGHT AND POWER COMPANY (Non-operating).
Lancaster County, East Earl Township.
1915, 1 Linear Inch.

History:
East Earl Electric Light and Power Co., incorporated 27 January 1915 to supply electricity in East Earl Township, Lancaster County, consolidated and merged with five companies to form Tri-County Electric Co., 8 June 1915.

203. EAST END PASSENGER RAILWAY COMPANY
(Operating).
Lycoming County, Williamsport City.
1892 to 1927, 3 Linear Feet.

History:
East End Passenger Railway Co., incorporated in 1892, operated a 3-mile electric street railway line in the City of Williamsport and adjoining Loyalsock Township, Lycoming County. Lehigh Power Securities Corp. acquired control of its stock in 1923. It consolidated and merged with three other railway companies to form Williamsport Railways Co., 21 January 1927.

Administrative Records:
Minute Books, 1892-1913, 1922-1926 (2 Volumes)

Operating Records:
General Ledgers, 1894-1926 (2 Volumes)
Journals, 1904-1923 (2 Volumes)
Cashbooks, 1894-1927 (4 Volumes)
Indexes to Vouchers, 1894-1921 (2 Volumes)
Voucher and Journal Entry Record, 1923-1926
Expenses and Earnings, 1896-1905 (2 Volumes)
Statements of Earnings, Expenses, and Profit and Loss, 1905-1923 (2 Volumes)
Operating Expenses Detail Ledger, 1923-1926
Federal Income Tax Schedule, 1926
Audit Reports, 1905-1926 (4 Volumes)

Scope and Content Note:
The Minute Books document the construction of the railway line, right-of-way, lease agreements, and finances. Audit Reports provide brief histories and summaries of finances and operations.

204. EAST HANOVER-LEBANON LIGHT & POWER COMPANY (Non-operating).
Lebanon County, East Hanover Township.
1940 to 1942, 1 Linear Inch.

History:
East Hanover-Lebanon Light & Power Co., incorporated 24 October 1940 to supply electricity in East Hanover Township, Lebanon County, merged into Pennsylvania Power & Light Co., 15 January 1942.

205. EAST HANOVER-LEBANON POWER & LIGHT COMPANY (Non-operating).
Lebanon County, East Hanover Township.
1927, 1 Linear Inch.

History:
East Hanover-Lebanon Power & Light Co., incorporated 11 July 1927 to supply electricity in East Hanover Township, Lebanon County, merged into Pennsylvania Power & Light Co., 11 October 1927.

206. EAST HEMPFIELD TOWNSHIP ELECTRIC COMPANY (Non-operating).
Lancaster County, East Hempfield Township.
1911, 1 Linear Inch.

History:
East Hempfield Township Electric Co., incorporated 10 August 1911 to supply electricity in East Hempfield Township, Lancaster County, consolidated and merged with 17 companies to form Edison Electric Co., No. 1, 2 October 1911.

207. EAST LAMPETER ELECTRIC LIGHT, HEAT AND POWER COMPANY (Non-operating).
Lancaster County, East Lampeter Township.
1913, 1 Linear Inch.

History:
East Lampeter Electric Light, Heat and Power Co., incorporated 28 February 1913 to supply electricity in East Lampeter Township, Lancaster County, consolidated and merged with four companies to form Strasburg Electric Light, Heat and Power Co., No. 3, 24 May 1913.

208. EAST LAMPETER TOWNSHIP ELECTRIC COMPANY (Non-operating).
Lancaster County, East Lampeter Township.
1911, 1 Linear Inch.

History:
East Lampeter Township Electric Co., incorporated 14 August 1911 to supply electricity in East Lampeter Township, Lancaster County, consolidated and merged with 17 companies to form Edison Electric Co., No. 1, 2 October 1911.

209. EAST MANCHESTER-YORK POWER & LIGHT COMPANY (Non-operating).
York County, East Manchester Township.
1959 to 1960, 1 Linear Inch.

History:
East Manchester-York Power & Light Co., incorporated in October 1959 to supply electricity in East Manchester Township, York County, merged with Pennsylvania Power & Light Co., 24 February 1960.

210. EAST PENN ELECTRIC COMPANY, NO. 2 (Operating).
Schuylkill County, Pottsville City.
1912 to 1931, 13 Linear Feet.

History:
East Penn Electric Co., No. 2, was organized 3 August 1922 through the consolidation and merger of East Penn Electric Co., No. 1, and 13 other non-operating companies. In November 1923 it acquired Eastern Pennsylvania Power and Railway Co., thereby completing a major step in the efforts of J. G. White & Co. to integrate the electric power and railway companies in Pennsylvania's southern anthracite field into a unified system. The company acquired additional operating and non-operating companies from 1923 to 1928. By 1928 it provided electric service to the City of Pottsville, and to boroughs and townships in Cumberland, Perry, Dauphin, Snyder, Juniata, and Lycoming Counties, and gas service in the Borough of Tamaqua, Schuylkill County, serving in all some 200,000 people. The company's Railway Division also provided electric railway and traction service through much of this territory. Pennsylvania Power & Light Co. acquired control of East Penn Electrc Co., No. 2, in 1925.

Administrative Records:
Minute Books, 1922-1928 (2 Volumes)
STOCK AND BOND RECORDS
Stock Certificate Books—Common, 1922-1925 (5 Volumes)
Stock Certificate Books—First Preferred, 1922-1925 (6 Volumes)
Stock Certificate Books—Second Preferred, 1922-1925 (2 Volumes)
Stock Certificate Deposit Receipts—All Classes, 1925
Preferred Stock (First and Second) Dividend Record, 1923-1928
Stock Transfer Record—Common, 1922-1928
Stock Transfer Record—First Preferred, 1922-1928
Stock Transfer Record—Second Preferred, 1922-1928
Stock Ledger—Common, 1922-1925
Stock Ledger—First Preferred, 1922-1928
Stock Ledger—Second Preferred, 1922-1928
Notices from General Managers, 1918-1925
CORRESPONDENCE
Correspondence—J. G. White and Co., 1922-1923
Correspondence—Railways Div., 1924-1931 (4 Boxes)

Operating Records:
FINANCIAL RECORDS
General Ledgers, 1922-1928 (3 Volumes)
Journal, 1922-1923
Journal Entry Registers, 1924-1928 (4 Volumes)
Cashbooks, 1922-1923 (2 Voluems)
Cash Disbursements—Eastern Penna. Power and Railways Co., 1923-1924
Cash Receipts—Railway Div., 1925-1928
Recapitulation of Cash, 1925-1928

Cash Receipts and Disbursements, 1925
Daily Cash Statements, 1924-1926
Summary of Cash (Bank Accounts), 1925-1928
Record of Cash Receipts, 1928
Record of Cash Disbursements, 1925-1928 (2 Volumes)
Accounts Payable Vouchers, 1922-1925
Accounts Payable Ledgers, 1925-1928 (2 Volumes)
Accounts Payable—Railway Div., 1924-1928
Accounts Receivable, 1923-1928 (3 Volumes)
Record of Insurance, 1919-1926
Accrual Record—Rents, Taxes and Insurance, 1925-1928
Accrual Record—Other, 1925-1928
Indices to Work Orders, 1921-1928 (2 Volumes)
Work Orders, 1923-1925
Work Orders—Railway Div., 1924-1926
Operating Expenses—Production and Transmission, 1925-1928
Operating Expenses—Expenditure Requisitions, 1925-1928
Operating Expenses—Gas and Railway, 1925-1928
Revenue and Expenses by Divisions—Railway Div., 1926-1927
Revenue and Expenses by Divisions—Working Papers, 1926-1927
Records of Railway Fares, 1928
Railway Receipts, 1925-1927
Railway Receipts, Fares and Ticket Earnings, 1925-1926
Claim Register—Railway Dept., 1926-1932
PERSONNEL RECORDS
Workmen's Compensation Insurance, 1926-1927
Workmen's Compensation Insurance—Accrual Statements, 1928
Time Book, 1925
MISCELLANEOUS REPORTS
Analysis of Electric Railway Operations, 1925-1928
Operating Reports—Pine Grove, 1925-1926
Automobile Reports, 1927-1928
Automobile Cost Reports, 1925-1926
Merchandise Sales, 1913-1917
Daily Mileage and Earnings Reports, 1925
Monthly Reports to Directors, J.G. White & Co., 1923-1925
Report on Railway Div., Pennsylvania Power & Light Co., 1925
Miscellaneous Reports, Statements and Correspondence, 1924-1928
Construction Ledgers—Electric Railways (4 Volumes)
Construction Ledger—Gas
Retirement Ledgers (3 Volumes)
J. G. White & Co. Orders—Predecessor Companies, 1912-1925 (2 Volumes)
CONSUMER RECORDS
Summary of Accounts Receivable—Consumers, 1925-1928
Summary of Accounts Receivable—Miscellaneous, 1925-1928
Statement of Rents Receivable, 1926-1928
Line Extension Deposit Account, 1927-1928
Summary of Consumers' Deposits, 1927-1928
Summary of Cashiers' Overs and Shorts, 1927-1928
AUDIT REPORTS

Scope and Content Note:
The records of this company include an extremely large collection of correspondence. The letters of the Railway Division document a variety of subjects including: construction and extension of service; public relations, accident and insurance claims; budgets; acquisition of equipment, labor relations, and legal and political matters.

The Minute Books primarily deal with stock and bond transactions. There are also a few references to employee relations and company welfare work. Notices from the General Manager's office describe organizational and administrative changes, safety, work rules and wage rates.

211. EAST PENN ELECTRIC COMPANY OF BARRY TOWNSHIP (Non-operating).
Schuylkill County, Barry Township.
1922, 1 Linear Inch.

History:
East Penn Electric Co. of Barry Township, incorporated 29 June 1922 to supply electricity in Barry Township, Schuylkill County, consolidated and merged with 13 companies to form East Penn Electric Co., No. 2, 3 August 1922.

212. EAST PENN ELECTRIC COMPANY OF BRANCH TOWNSHIP (Non-operating).
Schuylkill County, Branch Township.
1922, 1 Linear Inch.

History:
East Penn Electric Co. of Branch Township, incorporated 29 June 1922 to supply electricity in Branch Township, Schuylkill County, consolidated and merged with 13 companies to form East Penn Electric Co., No. 2, 3 August 1922.

213. EAST PENN ELECTRIC COMPANY OF CASS TOWNSHIP (Non-operating).
Schuylkill County, Cass Township.
1922, 1 Linear Inch.

History:
East Penn Electric Co. of Cass Township, incorporated 29 June 1922 to supply electricity in Cass Township, Schuylkill County, consolidated and merged with 13 companies to form East Penn Electric Co., No. 2, 3 August 1922.

214. EAST PENN ELECTRIC COMPANY OF FOSTER TOWNSHIP (Non-operating).
Schuylkill County, Foster Township.
1922, 1 Linear Inch.

History:
East Penn Electric Co. of Foster Township, incorporated 29 June 1922 to supply electricity in Foster Township, Schuylkill County, consolidated and merged with 13 companies to form East Penn Electric Co., No. 2, 3 August 1922.

215. EAST PENN ELECTRIC COMPANY OF FRAILEY TOWNSHIP (Non-operating).
Schuylkill County, Frailey Township.
1922, 1 Linear Inch.

History:
East Penn Electric Co. of Frailey Township, incorporated 29 June 1922 to supply electricity in Frailey Township, Schuylkill County, consolidated and merged with 13 companies to form East Penn Electric Co., No. 2, 3 August 1922.

216. **EAST PENN ELECTRIC COMPANY OF NEW CASTLE TOWNSHIP** (Non-operating).
Schuylkill County, New Castle Township.
1922, 1 Linear Inch.

History:
East Penn Electric Co. of New Castle Township, incorporated 29 June 1922 to supply electricity in New Castle Township, Schuylkill County, consolidated and merged with 13 companies to form East Penn Electric Co., No. 2, 3 August 1922.

217. **EAST PENN ELECTRIC COMPANY OF NORTH MANHEIM TOWNSHIP** (Non-operating).
Schuylkill County, North Manheim Township.
1922, 1 Linear Inch.

History:
East Penn Electric Co. of North Manheim Township, incorporated 29 June 1922 to supply electricity in North Manheim Township, Schuylkill County, consolidated and merged with 13 companies to form East Penn Electric Co., No. 2, 3 August 1922.

218. **EAST PENN ELECTRIC COMPANY OF REILLY TOWNSHIP** (Non-operating).
Schuylkill County, Reilly Township.
1922, 1 Linear Inch.

History:
East Penn Electric Co. of Reilly Township, incorporated 29 June 1922 to supply electricity in Reilly Township, Schuylkill County, consolidated and merged with 13 companies to form East Penn Electric Co., No. 2, 3 August 1922.

219. **EAST PENN ELECTRIC COMPANY OF SOUTH MANHEIM TOWNSHIP** (Non-operating).
Schuylkill County, South Manheim Township.
1922, 1 Linear Inch.

History:
East Penn Electric Co. of South Manheim Township, incorporated 29 June 1922 to supply electricity in South Manheim Township, Schuylkill County, consolidated and merged with 13 companies to form East Penn Electric Co., No. 2, 3 August 1922.

220. **EAST PENN ELECTRIC COMPANY OF TREMONT TOWNSHIP** (Non-operating).
Schuylkill County, Tremont Township.
1922, 1 Linear Inch.

History:
East Penn Electric Co. of Tremont Township, incorporated 29 June 1922 to supply electricity in Tremont Township, Schuylkill County, consolidated and merged with 13 companies to form East Penn Electric Co., No. 2, 3 August 1922.

221. **EAST PENN ELECTRIC COMPANY OF WASHINGTON TOWNSHIP** (Non-operating).
Schuylkill County, Washington Township.
1922, 1 Linear Inch.

History:
East Penn Electric Co. of Washington Township, incorporated 29 June 1922 to supply electricity in Washington Township, Schuylkill County, consolidated and merged with 13 companies to form East Penn Electric Co., No. 2, 3 August 1922.

222. **EAST PENN ELECTRIC COMPANY OF WAYNE TOWNSHIP** (Non-operating).
Schuylkill County, Wayne Township.
1922, 1 Linear Inch.

History:
East Penn Electric Co. of Wayne Township, incorporated 29 June 1922 to supply electricity in Wayne Township, Schuylkill County, consolidated and merged with 13 companies to form East Penn Electric Co., No. 2, 3 August 1922.

223. **EAST PENN ELECTRIC COMPANY OF WEST BRUNSWICK TOWNSHIP** (Non-operating).
Schuylkill County, West Brunswick Township.
1922, 1 Linear Inch.

History:
East Penn Electric Co. of West Brunswick Township, incorporated 29 June 1922 to supply electricity in West Brunswick Township, Schuylkill County, consolidated and merged with 13 companies to form East Penn Electric Co., No. 2, 3 August 1922.

224. **EAST PENNSYLVANIA GAS & ELECTRIC COMPANY** (Operating).
Bucks County, Bristol Borough.
1922, 1 Linear Inch.

History:
East Pennsylvania Gas & Electric Co. was formed 31 July 1912 through the consolidation and merger of a number of small companies, to provide gas and electric service in the Borough of Bristol, Bucks County, and surrounding communities. It consolidated and merged with six companies to form Philadelphia Suburban Gas and Electric Co., 3 July 1923.

Operating Records:
Audit Report, Pennsylvania Power & Light Co., 1922

225. **EAST PENN TOWNSHIP CARBON ELECTRIC COMPANY** (Non-operating).
Carbon County, East Penn Township.
1919, 1 Linear Inch.

History:
East Penn Township Carbon Electric Co., incorporated 17 July 1919 to supply electricity in East Penn Township, Carbon County, consolidated and merged with six companies to form Industrial Power Co., 11 September 1919.

226. **EAST PENN TRACTION COMPANY** (Operating).
Schuylkill County, Pottsville City.
1923 to 1933, 9 Linear Feet.

History:

East Penn Traction Co. was incorporated 21 May 1928 by officials of Lehigh Power Securities Corp. who were seeking to operate the electric railway properties of East Penn Electric Co., No. 2. East Penn Electric Co. No. 2 acquired all of East Penn Traction Company's stock, and then sold it to Pennsylvania Power & Light Co. East Penn Traction Co. went out of business in 1932 and its franchises were bought by the newly organized East Penn Transportation Co., which operated the old railway lines as motor coach routes.

Administrative Records:

Minute Books, 1928-1932 (2 Volumes)
Stock Certificate Book (Common), 1928-1930
Stock Certificate Book (Preferred), 1928
Stock Transfer Record (Common and Preferred), 1928
Stock Ledger (Common and Preferred), 1928-1930
CORRESPONDENCE
Correspondence and Reports, American Electric Railway Assoc., 1924-1931
Newspaper Clippings, 1928-1930

Operating Records:

FINANCIAL RECORDS
General Ledger, 1928-1932
Journal Entry Register, 1928-1932
Record of Cash Receipts and Disbursements, 1928-1932
Daily Cash Receipts, 1929-1930
Railway Receipts by Divisions, 1927-1931
Accounts Payable Ledger, 1928-1932
Accounts Receivable—Miscellaneous, 1925-1928
Detail Ledger—Charges and Credits, 1925-1927
Detail Ledger—Assets and Liabilities, 1928-1932
Detail Ledger—Operating Revenues, 1928-1932
Detail Ledger—Operating Expenses, 1928-1932
Memoranda and Correspondence—Operating Entries, 1928-1930
Report, Reproduction Costs, 1930
Cash Control and Conservation Reports, 1932
Analysis of Electric Railway Operations, 1924-1931
Monthly Reports by Division, 1925-1932
Manager's Daily Reports, 1930-1931
Revenue and Traffic Statistics, 1931-1932 (2 Volumes)
Daily Reports of Cars in Regular Service, 1930, 1932
Daily Report of Cars in Regular Service, 1931
Car Mileage, 1932
Steel Ties and Concrete Tamping Machines Construction Operations, 1930
Construction Detail Ledger, 1928-1932
PERSONNEL RECORDS
Summary of Payroll Distribution, 1928-1932
Office Payrolls, 1928-1932
Office Pay Checks, 1928-1930
Wage Roll Pay Checks, 1929-1933
Payroll Authority, 1926-1929
Payroll Authority—Pottsville and Lansford, 1930-1932
Workmen's Compensation Insurance Accrual Statements, 1928

Scope and Content Note:

The records of this company represent a continuation of the records of the Railway Div. of East Penn Electric Co., No. 2. They document a broad range of topics, including construction, extension and discontinuance of service; advertising and public relations; accounting and office procedures; legal matters; local politics; and labor relations. A separate run of correspondence between the company and the American Electric Railway Assoc. contains data on revenues, expenses, passengers carried, employee wage rates, and circulars from the A.E.R.A. describing its services as a statistical clearinghouse for the U.S. Dept. of Commerce.

Newspaper clippings document the operations of the company's trolley lines in various communities, including Pottsville, Mauch Chunk, and New Philadelphia. Supplementing these are Manager's Daily Reports describing cars in service, passengers carried, and accidents.

Payroll Authorities list wage rate changes, layoffs and dismissals, and transfers of employees, along with the reasons for such changes. A number of these sheets relate to a prolonged strike in 1928 (also documented in the correspondence). Office Payroll Sheets list the salaries of office, managerial, clerical, and supervisory personnel.

227. EAST PENN TRANSPORTATION COMPANY (Operating).
Schuylkill County, Pottsville City.
1928 to 1939, 2 Linear Feet.

History:

East Penn Transportation Co. was incorporated 6 July 1928 by officials of East Penn Traction Co. in order to operate the bus franchises acquired when East Penn Electric Co. No. 2 merged into Pennsylvania Power & Light. After East Penn Traction Co. discontinued electric railway service in Schuylkill and Carbon Counties, East Penn Transportation Co. provided bus service to the affected areas. Its assets were controlled by Pennsylvania Realty & Investment Co., a subsidiary of PP&L. When PP&L decided to abondon its motor coach operations in 1939, East Penn Transportation Co. was sold.

Administrative Records:

Minute Book, 1928-1939
Correspondence, 1928-1932 (4 Boxes)
Newspaper Clippings, 1928-1932

Operating Records:

Expenditure Requisitions, 1929-1931
Payrolls—Bus Labor, 1933
Payrolls—Office, 1933
Audit Report, Electric Bond and Share Co., 1931-1932

Scope and Content Note:

Correspondence, 1928-32, documents company organization, labor relations, and service complaints. Newspaper clippings describe the company's relations with local government.

228. EAST PROSPECT BOROUGH LIGHT, HEAT & POWER COMPANY (Non-operating).
York County, East Prospect Borough.
1922 to 1923, 1 Linear Inch.

History:

East Prospect Borough Light, Heat & Power Co., incorporated 7 August 1922 to supply electricity in East Prospect Borough, York County, merged into Wrightsville Light and Power Co., 12 March 1923.

229. EAST ROCK HILL ELECTRIC LIGHT AND POWER COMPANY (Non-operating).
Bucks County, East Rock Hill Township.
1913, 1 Linear Inch.

History:
East Rock Hill Electric Light and Power Co., incorporated 8 December 1913 to supply electricity in East Rock Hill Township, Bucks County, merged into Lehigh Valley Light and Power Co., No. 3, 29 December 1913.

230. EAST ROCK HILL TOWNSHIP ELECTRIC LIGHT AND POWER COMPANY (Non-operating).
Bucks County, East Rock Hill Township.
1921 to 1922, 1 Linear Inch.

History:
East Rock Hill Township Electric Light and Power Co., incorporated 21 December 1921 to supply electricity in East Rock Hill Township, Bucks County, consolidated and merged with two companies to form Excelsior Electric Light, Power and Gas Co., No. 3, 2 October 1922.

231. EAST SIDE-CARBON POWER & LIGHT COMPANY (Non-operating).
Carbon County, East Side Borough.
1927, 1 Linear Inch.

History:
East Side-Carbon Power & Light Co., incorporated 3 February 1927 to supply electricity in East Side Borough, Carbon County, merged into White Haven Light, Heat & Power Co., 25 July 1927.

232. EAST UNION LIGHT COMPANY (Non-operating).
Schuylkill County, East Union Township.
1912 to 1913, 1 Linear Inch.

History:
East Union Light Co., incorporated 29 November 1912 to supply electricity in East Union Township, Schuylkill County, consolidated and merged with 12 companies to form Hazleton Electric Co., 6 January 1913.

233. EAST UNION TOWNSHIP ELECTRIC COMPANY (Non-operating).
Schuylkill County, East Union Township.
1911 to 1913, 1 Linear Inch.

History:
East Union Township Electric Co., incorporated 26 January 1911 to supply electricity in East Union Township, Schuylkill County, consolidated and merged with 11 companies to form The Schuylkill Gas and Electric Co., 6 January 1913.

234. EASTERN PENNSYLVANIA GAS COMPANY OF RAHN TOWNSHIP (Non-operating).
Schuylkill County, Rahn Township.
1916 to 1923, 1 Linear Inch.

History:
Eastern Pennsylvania Gas Co. of Rahn Township, incorporated 11 December 1916 to manufacture gas in Rahn Township, Schuylkill County, merged into Eastern Pennsylvania Light, Heat and Power Co., 4 December 1922.

235. EASTERN PENNSYLVANIA LIGHT, HEAT AND POWER COMPANY (Operating).
Schuylkill County, Palo Alto Borough.
1908 to 1925, 7 Linear Feet.

History:
Eastern Pennsylvania Light, Heat and Power Co. was a subsidiary of Eastern Pennsylvania Railways Co. In 1906, John G. White & Co., an engineering firm that was trying to consolidate the electric and street railway systems of Schuylkill and Columbia Counties, purchased the Eastern Pennsylvania Railways Co. in order to gain control of its electric generating and distribution facilities. Between 1909 and 1922 the company acquired the franchises and properties of nearly 40 operating and non-operating companies. On 26 March 1923, it joined with eight other street railway companies to form Eastern Pennsylvania Power and Railways Co.

Administrative Records:
Minute Books, 1909-1923 (2 volumes)
Stock Certificate Book, 1909-1923
Stock Transfer Record, 1916-1919
Rules, Regulations and Rate Schedules, 1909-1922 (2 Volumes)

Operating Records:
General Ledgers, 1909-1923 (3 Volumes)
Journal, 1918-1923
Cashbooks, 1909-1925 (3 Volumes)
Cashbook—Orwigsburg, 1916-1923
Cashbook—Minersville, 1916-1923
Cash Receipt Record, 1917
Prepaid Insurance Book, 1908-1911
Miscellaneous Accrued Liabilities, 1915-1922
Rental Books, 1919-1925 (2 Volumes)
Operating Expenses, 1909-1913
Earnings, Operating Expenses, and Balance Sheets, 1908-1911
Earnings and Balance Sheets, 1910-1911
Distribution Record, 1909-1920
Reconstruction, Extension, and Addition Ledger, 1916-1917
Power Statement and Bill Records, 1917-1923 (7 Volumes)
Operating Statistics, 1909-1910
Monthly Reports—Gas Dept., 1908-1911
Details of Estimate of Cost, 1923
Voucher Register, 1913-1920
Voucher Records, 1909-1923 (3 Volumes)
Audit Reports, 1916-1923 (16 Volumes)

Scope and Content Note:
The Minute Books document the company's effort to gain control of the electric generating and distribution system in Schuylkill and Columbia Counties. The minutes also depict the way the company used a network of interlocking directorates to regulate its various subsidiaries.

Also documented are agreements that Eastern Pennsylvania Power and Railways Co. negotiated with the borough and town councils that granted franchises for street lighting.

Company flyers and circulars detail rate schedules and rules for providing electric service, while Public Service Commission circulars outline rules governing utilities and procedures for initiating rate changes. The "Power Statement and Bill Record" includes the names of commercial and residential customers, amount of power furnished to each, statements of maximum peak demand, surcharges and meter readings.

236. EASTERN PENNSYLVANIA LIGHT, HEAT AND POWER COMPANY OF BARRY TOWNSHIP (Non-operating).
Schuylkill County, Barry Township.
1916 to 1923, 1 Linear Inch.

History:
Eastern Pennsylvania Light, Heat and Power Co. of Barry Township, incorporated 18 October 1916 to supply electricity in Barry Township, Schuylkill County, merged into Eastern Pennsylvania Light, Heat and Power Co., 4 December 1922.

237. EASTERN PENNSYLVANIA LIGHT, HEAT AND POWER COMPANY OF BRANCH TOWNSHIP (Non-operating).
Schuylkill County, Branch Township.
1913, 1 Linear Inch.

History:
Eastern Pennsylvania Light, Heat and Power Co. of Branch Township, incorporated 31 July 1913 to supply electricity in Branch Township, Schuylkill County, merged into Eastern Pennsylvania Light, Heat and Power Co., 10 November 1913.

238. EASTERN PENNSYLVANIA LIGHT, HEAT AND POWER COMPANY OF BUTLER TOWNSHIP (Non-operating).
Schuylkill County, Butler Township.
1913, 1 Linear Inch.

History:
Eastern Pennsylvania Light, Heat and Power Co. of Butler Township, incorporated 29 September 1913 to supply electricity in Butler Township, Schuylkill County, merged into Eastern Pennsylvania Light, Heat and Power Co., 10 November 1913.

239. EASTERN PENNSYLVANIA LIGHT, HEAT AND POWER COMPANY OF CASS TOWNSHIP (Non-operating).
Schuylkill County, Cass Township.
1915 to 1916, 1 Linear Inch.

History:
Eastern Pennsylvania Light, Heat and Power Co. of Cass Township, incorporated 20 October 1915 to supply electricity in Cass Township, Schuylkill County, merged into Eastern Pennsylvania Light, Heat and Power Co., 16 August 1916.

240. EASTERN PENNSYLVANIA LIGHT, HEAT AND POWER COMPANY OF CENTRALIA (Non-operating).
Columbia County, Centralia Borough.
1913, 1 Linear Inch.

History:
Eastern Pennsylvania Light, Heat and Power Co. of Centralia, incorporated 29 September 1913 to supply electricity in Centralia Borough, Columbia County, merged into Eastern Pennsylvania Light, Heat and Power Co., 10 November 1913.

241. EASTERN PENNSYLVANIA LIGHT, HEAT AND POWER COMPANY OF CONYNGHAM TOWNSHIP (Non-operating).
Columbia County, Conyngham Township.
1913, 1 Linear Inch.

History:
Eastern Pennsylvania Light, Heat and Power Co. of Conyngham Township, incorporated 29 September 1913 to supply electricity in Conyngham Township, Columbia County, merged into Eastern Pennsylvania Light, Heat and Power Co., 10 November 1913.

242. EASTERN PENNSYLVANIA LIGHT, HEAT AND POWER COMPANY OF CRESSONA (Non-operating).
Schuylkill County, Cressona Township.
1911 to 1913, 1 Linear Inch.

History:
Eastern Pennsylvania Light, Heat and Power Co. of Cressona, incorporated 26 May 1911 to supply electricity in Cressona Borough, Schuylkill County, merged into Eastern Pennsylvania Light, Heat and Power Co., 26 June 1913.

243. EASTERN PENNSYLVANIA LIGHT, HEAT AND POWER COMPANY OF EAST NORWEGIAN TOWNSHIP (Non-operating).
Schuylkill County, East Norwegian Township.
1915 to 1916, 1 Linear Inch.

History:
Eastern Pennsylvania Light, Heat and Power Co. of East Norwegian Township, Schuylkill County, incorporated 31 December 1915 to supply electricity in East Norwegian Township, Schuylkill County, merged into Eastern Pennsylvania Light, Heat and Power Co., 16 August 1916.

244. EASTERN PENNSYLVANIA LIGHT, HEAT AND POWER COMPANY OF FOSTER TOWNSHIP (Non-operating).
Schuylkill County, Foster Township.
1915 to 1916, 1 Linear Inch.

History:
Eastern Pennsylvania Light, Heat and Power Co. of Foster Township, incorporated 20 October 1915 to supply electricity in Foster Township, Schuylkill County, merged into Eastern Pennsylvania Light, Heat and Power Co., 16 August 1916.

245. EASTERN PENNSYLVANIA LIGHT, HEAT AND POWER COMPANY OF GILBERTON (Non-operating).
Schuylkill County, Gilberton Borough.
1913, 1 Linear Inch.

History:
Eastern Pennsylvania Light, Heat and Power Co. of Gilberton, incorporated 29 September 1913 to supply electricity in Gilberton Borough, Schuylkill County, merged into Eastern Pennsylvania Light, Heat and Power Co., 10 November 1913.

246. EASTERN PENNSYLVANIA LIGHT, HEAT AND POWER COMPANY OF GIRARDSVILLE

(Non-operating).
Schuylkill County, Girardsville Borough.
1913, 1 Linear Inch.

History:
Eastern Pennsylvania Light, Heat and Power Co. of Girardsville, incorporated 29 September 1913 to supply electricity in Girardsville Borough, Schuylkill County, merged into Eastern Pennsylvania Light, Heat and Power Co., 10 November 1913.

247. EASTERN PENNSYLVANIA LIGHT, HEAT AND POWER COMPANY OF GORDON (Non-operating).
Schuylkill County, Gordon Borough.
1915 to 1916, 1 Linear Inch.

History:
Eastern Pennsylvania Light, Heat and Power Co. of Gordon, incorporated 18 August 1915 to supply electricity in Gordon Borough, Schuylkill County, merged into Eastern Pennsylvania Light, Heat and Power Co., 18 July 1916.

248. EASTERN PENNSYLVANIA LIGHT, HEAT AND POWER COMPANY OF HEGINS TOWNSHIP
(Non-operating).
Schuylkill County, Hegins Township.
1921 to 1922, 1 Linear Inch.

History:
Eastern Pennsylvania Light, Heat and Power Co. of Hegins Township, incorporated 3 November 1921 to supply electricity in Hegins Township, Schuylkill County, merged into Eastern Pennsylvania Light, Heat and Power Co., 4 December 1922.

249. EASTERN PENNSYLVANIA LIGHT, HEAT AND POWER COMPANY OF LANDINGVILLE
(Non-operating).
Schuylkill County, Landingville Borough.
1915 to 1916, 1 Linear Inch.

History:
Eastern Pennsylvania Light, Heat and Power Co. of Landingville, incorporated 18 August 1915 to supply electricity in Landingville Borough, Schuylkill County, merged into Eastern Pennsylvania Light, Heat and Power Co., 18 July 1916.

250. EASTERN PENNSYLVANIA LIGHT, HEAT AND POWER COMPANY OF NEW CASTLE TOWNSHIP
(Non-operating).
Schuylkill County, New Castle Township.
1912 to 1913, 1 Linear Inch.

History:
Eastern Pennsylvania Light, Heat and Power Co. of New Castle Township, incorporated 14 October 1912 to supply electricity in New Castle Township, Schuylkill County, merged into Eastern Pennsylvania Light, Heat and Power Co., 26 June 1913.

251. EASTERN PENNSYLVANIA LIGHT, HEAT AND POWER COMPANY OF NORWEGIAN TOWNSHIP
(Non-operating).
Schuylkill County, Norwegian Township.
1912 to 1913, 1 Linear Inch.

History:
Eastern Pennsylvania Light, Heat and Power Co. of Norwegian Township, incorporated 14 October 1912 to supply electricity in Norwegian Township, Schuylkill County, merged into Eastern Pennsylvania Light, Heat and Power Co., 26 June 1913.

252. EASTERN PENNSYLVANIA LIGHT, HEAT AND POWER COMPANY OF PINE GROVE TOWNSHIP
(Non-operating).
Schuylkill County, Pine Grove Township.
1916, 1 Linear Inch.

History:
Eastern Pennsylvania Light, Heat and Power Co. of Pine Grove Township, incorporated 24 April 1916 to supply electricity in Pine Grove Township, Schuylkill County, merged with Eastern Pennsylvania Light, Heat and Power Co., 16 August 1916.

253. EASTERN PENNSYLVANIA LIGHT, HEAT AND POWER COMPANY OF PORTER TOWNSHIP
(Non-operating).
Schuylkill County, Porter Township.
1921 to 1922, 1 Linear Inch.

History:
Eastern Pennsylvania Light, Heat and Power Co. of Porter Township, incorporated 5 May 1921 to supply electricity in Porter Township, Schuylkill County, merged into Eastern Pennsylvania Light, Heat and Power Co., 4 December 1922.

254. EASTERN PENNSYLVANIA LIGHT, HEAT AND POWER COMPANY OF RAHN TOWNSHIP
(Non-operating).
Schuylkill County, Rahn Township.
1916, 1 Linear Inch.

History:
Eastern Pennsylvania Light, Heat and Power Co. of Rahn Township, incorporated 22 May 1916 to supply electricity in Rahn Township, Schuylkill County, merged into Eastern Pennsylvania Light, Heat and Power Co., 16 August 1916.

255. EASTERN PENNSYLVANIA LIGHT, HEAT AND POWER COMPANY OF REILLY TOWNSHIP
(Non-operating).
Schuylkill County, Reilly Township.
1915 to 1916, 1 Linear Inch.

History:
Eastern Pennsylvania Light, Heat and Power Co. of Reilly Township, incorporated 31 December 1915 to supply electricity in Reilly Township, Schuylkill County, merged into Eastern Pennsylvania Light, Heat and Power Co., 16 August 1916.

256. EASTERN PENNSYLVANIA LIGHT, HEAT AND POWER COMPANY OF RYAN TOWNSHIP
(Non-operating).
Schuylkill County, Ryan Township.
1913, 1 Linear Inch.

History:
Eastern Pennsylvania Light, Heat and Power Co. of Ryan Township, incorporated 29 September 1913 to

supply electricity in Ryan Township, Schuylkill County, merged into Eastern Pennsylvania Light, Heat and Power Co., 10 November 1913.

257. EASTERN PENNSYLVANIA LIGHT, HEAT AND POWER COMPANY OF TREMONT TOWNSHIP (Non-operating).
Schuylkill County, Tremont Township.
1915 to 1916, 1 Linear Inch.

History:
Eastern Pennsylvania Light, Heat and Power Co. of Tremont Township, incorporated 31 December 1915 to supply electricity in Tremont Township, Schuylkill County, merged into Eastern Pennsylvania Light, Heat and Power Co., 16 August 1916.

258. EASTERN PENNSYLVANIA LIGHT, HEAT AND POWER COMPANY OF WAYNE TOWNSHIP (Non-operating).
Schuylkill County, Wayne Township.
1915 to 1916, 1 Linear Inch.

History:
Eastern Pennsylvania Light, Heat and Power Co. of Wayne Township, incorporated 31 December 1915 to supply electricity in Wayne Township, Schuylkill County, merged into Eastern Pennsylvania Light, Heat and Power Co., 16 August 1916.

259. EASTERN PENNSYLVANIA LIGHT, HEAT AND POWER COMPANY OF WEST MAHANOY TOWNSHIP (Non-operating).
Schuylkill County, West Mahanoy Township.
1913, 1 Linear Inch.

History:
Eastern Pennsylvania Light, Heat and Power Co. of West Mahanoy Township, incorporated 29 September 1913 to supply electricity in West Mahanoy Township, Schuylkill County, merged into Eastern Pennsylvania Light, Heat and Power Co., 10 November 1913.

260. EASTERN PENNSYLVANIA POWER AND RAILWAYS COMPANY (Operating).
Schuylkill County, Pottsville City.
1922 to 1924, 6 Linear Inches.

History:
Eastern Pennsylvania Power and Railways Co. was organized 26 March 1923 through the consolidation and merger of Eastern Pennsylvania Light, Heat and Power Co., Pottsville Union Traction Co., and eight other street railway companies. It merged with East Penn Electric Co., No. 2, 15 November 1923, thereby completing the efforts of organizers of Eastern Pennsylvania Railways Co. to integrate the electric and railway companies of Schuylkill and Columbia Counties into a unified system.

Administrative Records:
Stock Certificate Book (Common), 1923-1924
Stock Certificate Book (Preferred), 1923-1924

Operating Records:
General Ledger, 1923
Journal, 1923
Power Bills Statements, 1922-1923 (2 Volumes)
Daily Cash Statements, 1923
Monthly Report, April 1923
Audit Report, Haskins & Sells, 1923

Scope and Content Note:
The Power Bills Statements contain information on the names of residential and commercial customers served, amounts of power supplied to them, statements of maximum peak demand, surcharges, and meter readings.

261. EASTERN PENNSYLVANIA RAILWAYS COMPANY (Operating).
Schuylkill County, Palo Alto Borough.
1883 to 1927, 13 Linear Feet.

History:
Eastern Pennsylvania Railways Co. was the successor to Tamaqua & Lansford Street Railway Co., which was organized in 1891. The name change came in 1906 after the Tamaqua company was acquired by John G. White and Co., engineers and contractors. Shortly thereafter, the company assumed control of Tumbling Run Park Association and eight street railways, all of which were owned or leased by Pottsville Union Traction Co. Palo Alto Borough, in Schuylkill County, served as the center of operations for this consolidated system, with some 70 miles of track in Schuylkill, Carbon, and Columbia Counties. Electric power to operate the lines was provided by Eastern Pennsylvania Light, Heat and Power Co. Acquired by Lehigh Power Securities Corp. in 1921, Eastern Pennsylvania Railways Co. consolidated and merged with Eastern Pennsylvania Light, Heat and Power Co., 26 March 1923, to form Eastern Pennsylvania Power and Railways Co. When that company merged into East Penn Electric Co., No. 2, later in 1923, the railway properties formerly owned by Eastern Pennsylvania Railways Co., became the "Railways Division" of East Penn Electric Co. No. 2.

Administrative Records:
Minute Books, 1906-1923 (8 Volumes)
STOCK AND BOND RECORDS
Stock Certificate Books (Common), 1906-1923 (8 Volumes)
Stock Certificate Books (Preferred), 1906-1923 (5 Volumes)
Stock Scrip Books (Common), 1908-1922 (2 Volumes)
Stock Scrip Books (Preferred), 1908-1923 (2 Volumes)
Stock Registers (Common), 1908-1924 (2 Volumes)
Stock Registers (Preferred), 1908-1923 (3 Volumes)
Stock Ledgers (Common), 1906-1923 (2 Volumes)
Stock Ledger (Preferred), 1906-1922
Bond Register Books, 1907-1923 (2 Volumes)
Bond Certificate Book, 1908-1923
MISCELLANEOUS ADMINISTRATIVE RECORDS
Sales of Liberty Bonds, 1918
Document Index, 1883-1908
Index to Records, 1921-1928
Directors' Monthly Reports, 1917-1919
Monthly Reports to Directors, 1920-1922
Testimony Before the Public Service Commission, United Mine Workers of America vs. Eastern Pennsylvania Railways Co., 1919
Operating Bulletins, 1907-1921
CORRESPONDENCE, 1908-1910

Operating Records:
FINANCIAL RECORDS
General Ledgers, 1906-1923 (4 Volumes)

Journals, 1909-1923 (2 Volumes)
Cashbooks, 1906-1908, 1911-1923 (5 Volumes)
Cash Receipts and Disbursements, 1906-1911 (2 Volumes)
Bank Check Stubs, 1910-1912
Audited Voucher Registers, 1906-1923 (3 Volumes)
Accounts Payable Ledgers, 1906-1918 (5 Volumes)
Accounts Receivable Ledgers, 1906-1925 (5 Volumes)
Accounts Receivable Ledger Ticket Sales, 1918-1923
Notes Payable Ledger, 1920-1925
Petty Cash, 1917-1920
Report of Construction Expenditures, 1906-1907
Reconstruction Ledger, 1908-1912
Statement of Charges to Local Construction, 1908
Details of Organization Expenses, 1908
Work Orders Index Book, 1921-1924
Construction Specifications, 1925
Operating Statistics, 1907-1908
Operating Reports, 1907-1910
Operating Statements, Working Papers, and Memoranda, 1917-1919
Power Bills, 1922-1923
Record of Passes Issued, 1910-1926
PERSONNEL RECORDS
Payrolls and Employees' Receipts—Office, 1906-1913
Payrolls and Employees' Receipts—Office, 1913-1917
Payrolls and Employees' Receipts—Office, 1918-1919
Payrolls—General, 1916-1919
Employees' Record Book, 1899-1923
Auditors' Private Record of Employees, 1899-1923
Comparative Statements of Payrolls, 1917-1919
Semimonthly Payroll Reports, 1905-1908 (2 Volumes)
Distribution of Payrolls, 1909-1912
Distribution of Track Force Payrolls, 1912-1913
East Penn Club, Minute Book and Papers, 1912-1917
AUDIT REPORTS, 1916-1923 (12 Volumes)

Scope and Content Note:

The Minute Books, several of which are topically indexed, document a broad range of subjects including: labor relations, lobbying efforts of the Pennsylvania Electric Association, and local government ordinances and regulations. They also depict the ways in which the company and its employees worked with the War Labor Board to prevent strikes and promote the sale of Liberty Bonds during World War I.

Circulars describe work rules, sales of uniforms to employees, and organizational charts. Operating Bulletins contain instructions and directives to trainmen, while operating reports document general business and labor conditions.

A substantial amount of correspondence relates to personnel matters; hiring, layoffs, injuries and wage rates are thoroughly described. The personnel folders for office and clerical staff are particularly detailed. Finally, testimony in the case of United Mine Workers of America vs. Eastern Pennsylvania Railways Co. (1919) documents working conditions and general railroad operations.

262. EAST GREENVILLE ELECTRIC LIGHT, HEAT AND POWER COMPANY (Non-operating).
Montgomery County, East Greenville Borough.
1911 to 1923, 1 Linear Inch.

History:

The history of this non-operating company is rather unusual. Organized on 10 December 1910 by citizens of East Greenville Borough, Montgomery County, the company spent three years constructing electrical generating equipment. After 1913, it in effect became non-operating, existing solely as a legal entity by which the Borough of Greenville could purchase power from the Light Commission of Pennsburg. This arrangement was necessary because Pennsylvania state law forbade one borough from selling power to another. In December of 1923 Pennsylvania Power & Light purchased the company from East Greenville Borough.

263. EAST HANOVER-DAUPHIN POWER & LIGHT COMPANY (Non-operating).
Dauphin County, East Hanover Township.
1927, 1 Linear Inch.

History:

East Hanover-Dauphin Power & Light Co., incorporated 11 July 1927 to supply electricity in East Hanover Township, Dauphin County, merged with five other non-operating companies into Pennsylvania Power & Light Co., 11 October 1927.

264. ECONOMY LIGHT, HEAT & POWER COMPANY (Operating).
Lackawanna County, Scranton City.
1894 to 1913, 6 Linear Inches.

History:

Economy Light, Heat & Power Co., incorporated 4 September 1893 to supply steam heat in the City of Scranton and vicinity, merged with Scranton Electric Co., 22 May 1913.

Administrative Records:
Stock Ledger, 1894-1905
Stock Certificate Book, 1894-1908

Operating Records:
General Ledger, 1905-1913

265. EDEN ELECTRIC LIGHT, HEAT AND POWER COMPANY (Non-operating).
Lancaster County, Eden Township.
1913, 1 Linear Inch.

History:

Eden Electric Light, Heat and Power Co., incorporated 2 January 1913 to supply electricity in Eden Township, Lancaster County, consolidated and merged with four companies to form Strasburg Electric Light, Heat and Power Co., No. 2, 17 March 1913.

266. EDEN TOWNSHIP ELECTRIC COMPANY (Non-operating).
Lancaster County, Eden Township.
1912, 1 Linear Inch.

History:

Eden Township Electric Co., incorporated 13 November 1912 to supply electricity in Eden Township, Lancaster County, consolidated and merged with 13 companies to form Edison Electric Co. No. 3, 9 December 1912.

267. EDISON ELECTRIC COMPANY. NO. 1 (Operating).
Lancaster County, Lancaster City.
1911 to 1912, 1 Linear Inch.

History:
Edison Electric Co., No. 1, was organized 2 October 1911 through the consolidation and merger of four operating and non-operating companies which supplied electricity in the City of Lancaster, Lancaster County, and vicinity. It was organized by the owners of United Gas and Electric Co.,, a New York holding company, that was integrating public utilities in Lancaster County under its control. Edison Electric Co., No. 1, consolidated and merged with Christiana Suburban Electric Co., 17 June 1912, to form Edison Electric Co. No. 2.

Administrative Records:
See Inventory for Edison Electric Co. No. 4

268. EDISON ELECTRIC COMPANY. NO. 2 (Operating).
Lancaster County, Lancaster City.
1912, 1 Linear Inch.

History:
Edison Electric Co., No. 2, was organized 17 June 1912 through the consolidation of Edison Electric Co., No. 1, and Christiana Suburban Electric Co. It merged with 13 companies to form Edison Electric Co. No. 3, 9 December 1912.

Administrative Records:
See Inventory for Edison Electric Co., No. 4

269. EDISON ELECTRIC COMPANY. NO. 3 (Operating).
Lancaster County, Lancaster City.
1912 to 1914, 1 Linear Inch.

History:
Edison Electric Co., No. 3, organized 9 December 1912 through the consolidation of Edison Electric Co., No. 2, and three other companies, merged with three non-operating companies to form Edison Electric Co., No. 4, 16 December 1914.

Administrative Records:
See Inventory for Edison Electric Co., No. 4

270. EDISON ELECTRIC COMPANY, NO. 4 (Operating).
Lancaster County, Lancaster City.
1901 to 1934, 18 Linear Feet.

History:
Edison Electric Co. No. 4 was organized 16 December 1914 through the consolidation and merger of Edison Electric Co., No. 3, and three non-operating companies, thereby completing a major step in the efforts of the owners of United Gas and Electric Co., a New York holding company, to integrate public utilities in Lancaster County into a unified system. Following its organization, Edison Electric Co., No. 4, continued to acquire electric companies (operating and non-operating), so that by 1930 it rendered service to all of Lancaster County and to portions of Bucks and Chester Counties. Lehigh Power Securities Corp. acquired its capital stock in 1926. The company merged with Pennsylvania Power & Light Co., 31 December 1930.

Administrative Records:
Minute Books, 1911-1930 (3 Volumes)
Minute Book—Executive Committee, 1915-1925
Secretary's Papers of Meetings, 1928-1930
Stock Certificate Book, 1911-1930
First and Refunding Five Per Cent Gold Mortgage, Edison Electric Co. to Lancaster Trust Co., 1913-1925

Operating Records:
FINANCIAL RECORDS
General Ledgers, 1911-1930 (5 Volumes)
Journals, 1915-1926 (2 Volumes)
Journal Entry Register, 1926-1930
Cashbooks, 1911-1926 (2 Volumes)
Audited Voucher Registers, 1911-1930 (10 Volumes)
Accounts Payable Ledgers, 1912-1930 (6 Volumes)
Accounts Receivable Ledger, 1926-1930
Assets and Liabilities Detail Ledger, 1926-1930
Accrual Record, 1926-1930
Operating and Non-Operating Revenues and Expenses, 1926-1930 (4 Volumes)
Accounts Receivable—Miscellaneous, 1928-1930
Materials and Supplies, 1926-1930 (11 Volumes)
Automobile Reports—Monthly, 1926-1930 (2 Volumes)
Analysis of Closed Jobs, 1916-1926 (2 Volumes)
Construction Work in Progress, 1926-1930 (7 Volumes)
Fixed Capital, 1926-1930
Construction Work Sheets—Miscellaneous, 1926-1933
Fixed Capital Working Papers, 1926-1930
Property Retired as of February 1931—Detail, 1927-1931 (2 Volumes)
Property Disposal Reports, 1927-1930 (3 Boxes)
Financial Reports—Annual, 1911-1926 (16 Volumes)
Financial Reports and Balance Sheets, 1923-1928 (2 Volumes)
Estimates of Cash Receipts and Requirements, 1927-1929
Consolidated Income—All Companies, 1926-1930
Operation of Engelside Power Plant, 1911-1924
Inter-Company Transactions—All Companies, 1931-1933
Reconcilement of Accounts Payable—All Companies, 1920-1923
Balance Sheets and Income Statements—All Companies, 1923-1926
Budget, 1930
Miscellaneous Working Papers, 1926
Cashier's Reports on Earnings, 1913-1926
Analysis of Merchandise Sales—Working Papers, 1924-1926
Analysis of Consumers' Ledgers—Working Papers, 1926
Installation—Sinking Spring—Working Papers, 1926
Electrical Dept.—Statistical Reports, 1910-1926
PERSONNEL RECORDS
Payroll and Workmen's Compensation Distribution, 1927-1930 (3 Volumes)
Payroll Charges—Detail, 1927-1930
Workmen's Compensation Insurance, 1927-1930
Payrolls—Office, 1925-1930
Time Books—Edison Electric Co., 1901-1907 (10 Volumes)
Time Books—Overhead Dept., 1907-1912 (4 Volumes)
Time Books—Overhead Dept., 1912-1933 (24 Volumes)
Time Books—Conestoga Traction and Edison Electric

Illuminating Co., 1904
Weekly Time Books—Substation Dept., 1938-1943 (2 Volumes)
Weekly Time Books—Overhead Dept., 1921-1926 (6 Volumes)
Time Book—Substation Dept., 1917-1920
Time Book—Rock Hill and Slackwater, 1911-1917
Payroll, 1927-1930 (2 Volumes)
Payroll—Treasurer's, 1927-1930
New Employees on Payroll, 1931
Audit Reports, 1918-1930 (9 Volumes)

Scope and Content Note:

The Minute Books consist primarily of stockholders' minutes, although they do contain some information on company finances and operations. A great deal of financial and operating data also appears in the Audit and Financial Reports, which contain itemized descriptions of construction work in progress, including changes in load capacity and service extensions.

Payroll sheets and Time Books contain information on monthly and weekly earnings and changes in wage rates.

The Electrical Dept. Statistical Reports present tables on various aspects of company operations, including numbers of lamps and motors connected, and interruptions to service.

Included among the Miscellaneous Working Papers are memoranda on company accounting methods, billing procedures, employees receiving current at reduced rates, maps of territory served, and lists of industrial customers.

271. THE EDISON ELECTRIC ILLUMINATING COMPANY OF ASHLAND PENNSYLVANIA (Operating).
Schuylkill County, Ashland Borough.
1885 to 1913, 1 1/2 Linear Feet.

History:

The Edison Electric Illuminating Co. of Ashland Pa., incorporated 17 April 1884 to supply electricity in Ashland Borough, Schuylkill County, was among the earliest electric companies in eastern Pennsylvania. Shortly after its organization, its founders entered into a contract with The Edison Electric Light Co. of New York for the use of Thomas A. Edison's incandescent lighting system. The company expanded service through Schuylkill County prior to its merger with Eastern Pennsylvania Light, Heat and Power Co., 26 June 1913.

Administrative Records:
Minute Books, 1895-1903
Stock Certificate Books, 1885-1913 (3 Volumes)

Operating Records:
General Ledgers, 1885-1913 (3 Volumes)
Daybook, 1896-1912
Reports to The Edison Electric Light Co., 1887-1891 (8 Volumes)

Scope and Content Note:

The Minute Book documents a broad range of company operations including: rate setting, abatements for churches and fraternal organizations, labor relations, customer relations, and agreements with Schuylkill Telephone Co. governing the use of electric lines for telephone services. Annual Reports to The Edison Electric Light Co. provide data on electric station capacity, types of dynamos in use, number of lamps connected, and details of income and expenses.

272. THE EDISON ELECTRIC ILLUMINATING COMPANY OF HAZLETON (Operating).
Luzerne County, Hazleton City.
1883 to 1912, 1 Linear Foot.

History:

The Edison Electric Illuminating Co. of Hazleton, incorporated 13 November 1883 to supply electricity in the City of Hazleton, Luzerne County, was among the earliest electric companies in eastern Pennsylvania to employ Thomas A. Edison's system of direct current and incandescent lighting. The company provided incandescent street and commercial lighting service to a number of customers in Hazleton, using facilities licensed from Edison Electric Light Co. of New York. In 1899 The Edison Electric Illuminating Co. of Hazleton leased its property to Hazleton Electric Light and Power Co; both companies consolidated and merged with 11 companies to form Hazleton Electric Co., 6 January 1913.

Administrative Records:
Minute Books, 1883-1912 (2 Volumes)
Stock Certificate Book, 1884-1912

Operating Records:
General Ledgers, 1883-1899 (2 Volumes)
Customer Ledger, 1889-1892
Invoices, 1898-1899

Scope and Content Note:

The company's first Minute Book (1883-1896) is one of the earliest in the collection and is a valuable source for information on the industry's formative years. It documents Edison Electric Light Company's early promotional efforts, its relationship with the Hazleton Borough Council, and the negotiations which led to its receiving the contract to replace gas street lighting with an incandescent system. Also documented is the installation of the Edison system of direct current, lamp sale statistics, company rules and regulations governing customer service, labor relations and job descriptions. The minutes also trace the changing relationship between the company and its parent concern, The Edison Electric Light Co.

273. THE EDISON ELECTRIC ILLUMINATING COMPANY OF LANCASTER, PA. (Operating).
Lancaster County, Lancaster City.
1886 to 1921, 2 Linear Feet.

History:

The Edison Electric Illuminating Co. of Lancaster, Pa., incorporated 1 March 1886 to supply electricity in the City of Lancaster, Lancaster County, provided the first electric service in that community. The company contracted with The Edison Electric Light Co. of New York to install the Edison system of direct current generation and incandescent lighting. Between 1890 and 1910 the company acquired the franchises and properties of several competitor companies, thereby extending its service through most of Lancaster County. It consolidated and merged with 17 companies to form Edison Electric Co., No. 1, 2 October 1911.

Administrative Records:
Minute Books, 1886-1911 (2 Volumes)
Minute Book—Executive Committee, 1903-1910

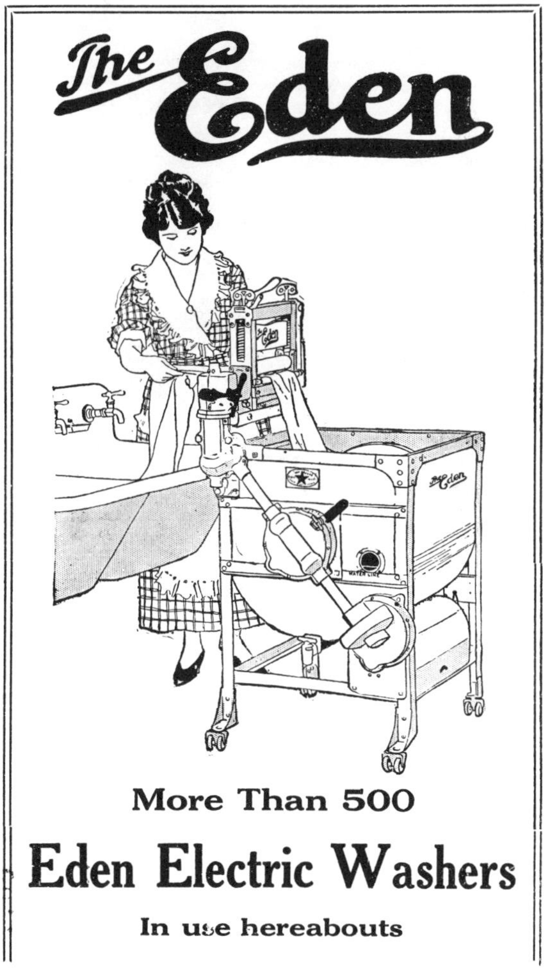

Advertising flyers printed on the back of monthly bills by the Edison Electric Company to promote the use of electricity.

Perfect Coffee
by a
Perfect Method

Stock Certificate Book—Common, 1886-1895
Stock Certificate Book—Preferred, 1907
Bond Register, 1921

Operating Records:
General Ledgers, 1892-1911 (4 Volumes)
Journals, 1892-1911 (4 Volumes)
Cash Receipts and Disbursements, 1895-1900
Miscellaneous Receipts, 1901
Cash Disbursements, 1901-1907
Cashbooks, 1902-1911 (2 Volumes)
Audited Voucher Registers, 1901-1909 (4 Volumes)
Accounts Payable, 1902-1912 (2 Volumes)
Bills Receivable, 1909-1910
Bills Payable, 1902-1911
Statement of Receipts and Expenditures, 1902-1907
Statement of Earnings, Expenditures and Statistics, 1906-1907
Real Estate, Equipment, Lines, Etc., 1901
Monthly Financial Reports, 1901-1909 (5 Volumes)
Annual Report, 1908
Auditor's Report to Directors, 1896

Scope and Content Note:
The Minute Books document all aspects of company operations including: the role of Edison Electric Co. of New York and its Pennsylvania agent, P.B. Shaw, in organizing Edison Electric Co., No. 1; rate setting for residential and commercial customers; and the installation of the Edison system for arc and incandescent lighting. Also documented are the company's attempt to provide power at reduced rates for churches and other social organizations, its relationship with the Lancaster municipal government and its many complicated lawsuits.

274. THE EDISON ELECTRIC ILLUMINATING COMPANY OF MOUNT CARMEL (Operating).
Northumberland County, Mount Carmel Borough.
1883 to 1920, 1 1/2 Linear Feet.

History:
The Edison Electric Illuminating Co. of Mount Carmel was organized on 17 November 1883 by P.B. Shaw, Pennsylvania agent for Edison Electric Light Co. of New York. It was among the earliest companies to install the Edison system of direct current and incandescent lighting. Providing electricity to Mount Carmel in Northumberland County, it subsequently extended service to adjacent localities in the county prior to its merger with Pennsylvania Power & Light on 11 May 1920.

Administrative Records:
Minute Books, 1883-1920 (3 Volumes)
Stock Certificate Book, 1910-1920
Stock Ledger, 1886-1917

Operating Records:
General Ledgers, 1884-1918 (2 Volumes)
Journals, 1884-1920 (2 Volumes)
Cashbooks, 1915-1920 (2 Voluems)
Purchase Book, 1912-1917
Audited Voucher Register, 1917-1920
Expense Statements, 1909-1914
Financial Statements, 1917-1920
Audit Report, Electric Bond and Share Co., 1917-1919

Scope and Content Note:
The Minute Book for the 1883-1910 period provides a complete record of company operations including: organization by officials of Edison Electric Light Co. of New York; the installation of the Edison system for arc and incandescent lighting; regulations governing electric service; rate setting; and negotiations with the Mount Carmel Borough Council.

275. THE EDISON ELECTRIC ILLUMINATING COMPANY OF POTTSVILLE (Operating).
Schuylkill County, Pottsville City.
1889-1909, 6 1/2 Linear Feet.

History:
The Edison Electric Illuminating Co. of Pottsville was incorporated 27 June 1889 to supply electricity in Pottsville City, Schuylkill County. Under a July 1889 agreement with The Edison Electric Light Co. of New York, the Pottsville firm installed the Edison incandescent lighting system in Pottsville and neighboring localities. Between 1889 and 1909 the company expanded its area of operations to include most of Schuylkill County. Finally, on 20 July 1909 it merged with Palo Alto Heat, Light and Power Co.

Administrative Records:
Minute Books—Board of Directors, 1889-1906 (4 Volumes)
Minute Books—Stockholders, 1889-1905 (2 Volumes)
Minute Book—Board of Directors and Stockholders, 1907-1909
Stock Certificate Book, 1889-1909
Stock Transfer Record, 1897-1906
Stock Ledger, 1889-1906
Ballots re: Sale to Palo Alto Heat, Light and Power Co., 1909
Annual Reports of President to Stockholders, 1893-1905

Operating Records:
General Ledgers, 1901-1906 (4 Volumes)
Cashbooks, 1904-1909 (3 Volumes)
Cash Receipts—Sales and Supplies, 1906-1907
Cash Receipts—Consumers, 1907-1909 (3 Volumes)
Audited Voucher Register, 1906-1909
Accounts Payable, 1906-1908 (3 Volumes)
Accounts Receivable, 1907
Statement of Charges to Construction, 1908
Record of Work Orders Issued, 1907-1909
Consumers Ledgers, 1906-1907 (2 Volumes)
Sales Book, 1905-1908
Earning Statements, 1906-1909
Operating Statistics, 1909-1910
Earnings, Operating Expenses, and Balance Sheets, 1905-1908
Audit Reports, 1892-1906 (15 Volumes)

Scope and Content Note:
The Annual Reports of the President to the Stockholders (1893-1905) provide an overview of the company's yearly operations. In particular, they present statistics documenting the number of incandescent and arc lights, and electric motors in use; descriptions of electric generating equipment; and lists of delinquent customers. They also trace the company's efforts to make agreements with, and acquire the franchises of, other

electric companies.

Supplementing the Annual Reports are the Minute Books, which fully describe every aspect of company affairs. These records document the organization of the company by Edison Electric Light Co. of New York; negotiations with Pottsville Borough Council for street lighting franchises and the installation of the Edison system; rate setting, taxation, and the company's relationship with the Association of Edison Illuminating Companies.

Several account volumes give information on customers and service rendered. Consumers' Ledgers list customers, the type of service, and amount of power used. The Sales Book records sales of electric lights and electric supplies to residential, commercial, social, and religious customers. Together, these records provide an excellent means for tracing the installation of arc and incandescent lighting in Schuylkill County.

276. EDISON ELECTRIC ILLUMINATING COMPANY OF SHAMOKIN (Operating).
Northumberland County, Shamokin Borough.
1883 to 1900, 2 Linear Inches.

History:

Edison Electric Illuminating Co. of Shamokin, incorporated 29 November 1882 to supply electricity in the Borough of Shamokin, Northumberland County, was one of the earliest concerns to be licensed by Edison Electric Light Co. of New York. On 29 January 1909 the company consolidated and merged with five other companies to form the Shamokin and Coal Township Light, Heat and Power Co.

Administrative Records:

Stock Certificate Book, 1883-1899
Papers re: Election for Increase of Capital Stock, 1884

Operating Records:

Consumers Ledger, 1887-1900

277. THE EDISON ELECTRIC ILLUMINATING COMPANY OF SUNBURY, PA., NO. 1 (Operating).
Northumberland County, Sunbury Borough.
1883 to 1907, 3 Linear Inches.

History:

The Edison Electric Illuminating Co. of Sunbury, Pa., No. 1, incorporated 30 April 1883 to supply electricity in the Borough of Sunbury, Northumberland County, operated the first commercial three-wire incandescent electric generating plant in the United States. This plant was built under a licensing agreement arranged by P.B. Shaw, Pennsylvania agent for The Edison Electric Light Co., and the generating facility was installed under the supervision of Thomas A. Edison. The principles of the Edison System and operation at the Sunbury plant were based upon several patents issued to Edison including: (1) the Edison Direct current bipolar generator, (2) the Edison three-wire system for electric distribution, (3) the Edison tube for underground wire, and (4) the incandescent lamp. Designed for a 500-light capacity, the Sunbury plant soon experienced problems as customer demand overloaded the system. After 1885, the company was forced to make several improvements which increased its generating capacity. In 1889 the company reorganized as The Edison Electric Illuminating Co. of Sunbury, Pa., No. 2.

Administrative Records:

Minute Book, 1883-1890 (Photostatic Copies)
History, 1907

Operating Records:

General and Consumers Ledger, 1886-1890

Scope and Content Note:

The Minute Book documents the negotiations which took place between Thomas A. Edison and the company, which led to the establishment of the Sunbury plant. Also documented are the problems that had to be overcome during the installation of the three-wire system and the company's effort to raise capital needed for its 1885 expansion. The records also describe rates that were charged, electric meters used, candlepower generated, and expenses and bills.

278. THE EDISON ELECTRIC ILLUMINATING COMPANY OF SUNBURY, PA., NO. 2 (Operating).
Northumberland County, Sunbury Borough.
1890 to 1891, 1 Linear Inch.

History:

The Edison Electric Illuminating Co. of Sunbury, Pa., No. 2, was the successor to The Edison Electric Illuminating Co. of Sunbury, No. 1, which changed its name and received new Letters Patent on 14 February 1890. On 11 February 1891 the company went bankrupt and its assets were eventually sold at a sheriff's sale.

Administrative Records:

Minute Book, 1890-1891

279. THE EDISON ELECTRIC ILLUMINATING COMPANY OF SUNBURY, PA., NO. 3 (Operating).
Northumberland County, Sunbury Borough.
1891 to 1911, 2 Linear Feet.

History:

The Edison Electric Illuminating Co. of Sunbury, Pa., No. 3, was the reorganized company formed after its predecessor, The Edison Electric Illuminating Co. of Sunbury, Pa., No. 2, was sold at sheriff's sale in February 1891. Following its reorganization, the company increased its plant capacity and installed an alternating current generating and distribution system, which it operated along with its original Edison system of direct current generation. The company consolidated and merged with four companies to form The Edison Electric Illuminating Co. of Sunbury, Pa., No. 4, 2 October 1911.

Administrative Records:

Minute Books, 1891-1911 (2 Volumes)
Stock Certificate Book, 1891-1911
Annual Reports and Statements, 1891-1903

Operating Records:

Ledgers, 1891-1903 (2 Volumes)
General Ledgers, 1895-1911 (2 Volumes)
Journals, 1891-1895, 1903-1911 (3 Volumes)
Audited Voucher Register, 1908-1911 (2 Volumes)
Payroll Book, 1907-1912
Financial Statements, 1908-1911

Scope and Content Note:

The Annual Reports fully document most of the important aspects of the company's history including: (1) customer relations, (2) technological improvements in electric generating and distribution facilities, (3) relations with Sunbury Borough Council and negotiations for street lighting contracts, (4) efforts to meet the competitive challenge presented by other electric and gas companies, and (5) company response to the depression of the 1890s. The Minute Book documents routine matters: installation of arc lighting, billing procedures, and wages paid to salaried employees.

280. THE EDISON ELECTRIC ILLUMINATING COMPANY OF TAMAQUA, PA., NO. 1 (Operating).
Schuylkill County, Tamaqua Borough.
1874 to 1909, 2 Linear Feet.

History:
The Edison Electric Illuminating Co. of Tamaqua, Pa., No. 1, was incorporated 8 July 1885 to supply electricity in the Borough of Tamaqua. It was one of several companies licensed by Edison Electric Light Co. of New York to install Thomas A. Edison's direct current and incandescent lighting system. In 1889 the company received new letters patent in the name of The Edison Electric Illuminating Co. Under this name it operated for 20 years. In 1906 the New York engineering firm of J.G. White & Co. acquired control of the firm and operated its property until 1909, when it consolidated and merged with Citizens Gas Light Co. of Tamaqua to form The Edison Electric Illuminating Co. of Tamaqua, Pa., No. 2.

Administrative Records:
Minute Book, 1874-1908
Stock Certificate Book, 1886-1909

Operating Records:
General Ledgers, 1906-1909 (2 Volumes)
Customers' Ledger and Cash Account (2 Volumes)
Cashbook, 1906-1907
Accounts Payable, 1906-1908 (2 Volumes)
Earnings and Expenses, 1907-1908
Record of Work Orders, 1907-1909
Statement of Charges to Local Construction, 1908
Operating Statistics, 1909-1910
Monthly Reports, 1906-1909
Earnings, Operating Expenses, and Balance Sheets, 1905-1908

Scope and Content Note:
The first 57 pages of the company's Minute Book contain the minutes of The Tamaqua Boot and Shoe Manufacturing Co. (1874-77). The rest of the Minute Book consists of minutes of The Edison Illuminating Co. of Tamaqua, Pa., No. 1. These pages document the operations of the company in considerable detail. Of particular interest are: the notes referring to the company's licensing agreement with The Edison Electric Light Co. of New York, and copies of contracts with Southwork Foundry, Edison Machine Works, and General Electric Co., which provided apparatus used to generate electricity. Also documented are relations with customers and local civic and religious organizations, the attempt to standardize rates by installing electric meters, and negotiations with the Tamaqua Borough Council for street lighting contracts.

281. THE EDISON ELECTRIC ILLUMINATING COMPANY OF TAMAQUA, PA., NO. 2 (Operating).
Schuylkill County, Tamaqua Borough.
1909, 1 Linear Inch.

History:
The Edison Electric Illuminating Co. of Tamaqua, Pa., No. 2, was formed through the consolidation and merger of The Edison Electric Illuminating Co. of Tamaqua, Pa., No. 1, and Citizens Gas Light Co. of Tamaqua, 14 May 1909. The company merged into Palo Alto Heat, Light and Power Co., 20 July 1909.

Administrative Records:
Minute Book, 1909
Agreement with Eastern Pennsylvania Railways Co., 1909

282. THE EDISON ELECTRIC ILLUMINATING COMPANY OF WILLIAMSPORT (Operating).
Lycoming County, Williamsport City.
1882 to 1911, 3 Linear Feet.

History:
The Edison Electric Illuminating Co. of Williamsport, incorporated 5 May 1882, was the first Pennsylvania electric company licensed by The Edison Electric Light Co. of New York to install the Edison system of direct current generation and incandescent lighting. P.B. Shaw of Williamsport, the Pennsylvania agent for The Edison Electric Light Co. of New York, organized the Edison Electric Illuminating Co. of Williamsport and several other similar companies in southeastern Pennsylvania during the 1880s. The Williamsport Co., although organized before The Edison Electric Illuminating Co. of Sunbury, did not actually begin operations until a few months after the Sunbury plant had become the first commercial user of the Edison system. Despite this delayed start, the Williamsport plant soon proved very satisfactory, and according to the company's 1884 Annual Report, experts associated with The Edison Electric Light Co. of New York declared that it was "the most substantial and perfect one ever yet installed anywhere in this country or in the world." The company installed arc light dynamos in 1887 and thereafter offered both arc and incandescent lighting service. In 1911, the company consolidated and merged with Lycoming Electric Co. to form Lycoming-Edison Co.

Administrative Records:
Report to Board of Directors, 1888-1890
Minute Books, 1882-1900, 1908-1911 (2 Volumes)
Stock Certificate Books, 1884-1910 (2 Volumes)
Stock Ledger, 1884-1911

Operating Records:
General Ledgers, 1884-1897 (2 Volumes)
Journals, 1884-1911 (7 Volumes)
Cashbooks, 1884-1886, 1900-1907 (8 Volumes)
Treasurer's Account Books, 1890-1907 (3 Volumes)
Consumers' Ledgers, 1885-1888, 1900-1907 (2 Volumes)

Scope and Content Note:
The Minute Books fully document all apsects of company operations during the 1880s and 1890s including: (1) the company's organization by and relationship with The Edison Electric Light Co. of New York, (2) negotiations with Thomas A. Edison that led to the installation of the Edison system, (3) customer and public relations, and (4) job descriptions for salaried employees. The collection also depicts the processes by

which houses were wired, rates were determined, and generating capacity increased. Of particular interest are the minutes describing the legislative lobbying campaign waged by the electric utility companies and the negotiations that led to the issuing of Williamsport's street lighting contracts.

283. THE EDISON ILLUMINATING COMPANY OF EASTON (Operating).
Northumberland County, Easton City.
1907 to 1946, 3 Linear Inches.

History:
The history of The Edison Illuminating Co. of Easton, which supplied electricity in the City of Easton, Northumberland County, is rather complex. The original firm was incorporated in 1888 as Edison Electric Illuminating Co. of Easton, Pa. Stock ownership of the company passed through several holding companies. Furthermore, the company in 1900 leased its properties to Easton Power Co. for 99 years. In 1913 several events occurred which affected the company. First, its parent holding company, Easton Consolidated Electric Co., was acquired by Lehigh Valley Transit Co. Second, a New Jersey holding company, Pennsylvania Utilities Co., acquired Easton Power Co., including the aforementioned lease. Finally, Edison Electric Illuminating Co. of Easton, Pa. was re-incorporated as The Edison Illuminating Co. of Easton. During the next three decades the company became a key link between two giant electric companies: National Power & Light Co. (formed in 1921), which controlled Lehigh Power Securities Corp. and through it Pennsylvania Power & Light Co.; and Metropolitan Edison Co., the New York-based holding company which was the successor to Pennsylvania Utilities Co. When Lehigh Power Securities Corp. was dissolved in 1939 and its assets were transferred to National Power & Light Co., the Securities and Exchange Commission began proceedings against the latter concern. An SEC order of 23 August 1941 directed National Power & Light to dissolve, while a related order directed PP&L to simplify its holdings. The Edison Illuminating Co. of Easton played a large role in these reorganizations, with National Power & Light transferring its outstanding shares of common stock to PP&L late in 1945. In June 1946 PP&L, in turn, sold the Easton company to Metropolitan Edison Co.

Administrative Records:
Stock Transfer Book, 1919-1926
Dividend Obligation Book, 1907
Check Stub Book, 1919-1927

Operating Records:
Summary of Cash, 1938-1946

Scope and Content Note:
Most of the records of The Edison Illuminating Co. of Easton were transferred to the Metropolitan Edison Co. in 1946. The records that were retained are useful for tracing the pattern of interlocking stock ownership that characterized the relationship between Lehigh Power Securities Corp. and its subsidiaries. The records also describe the cash flow between Pennsylvania Power & Light Co., its subsidiaries, and The Edison Illuminating Co. of Easton.

284. EGYPT ELECTRIC LIGHT & POWER COMPANY (Operating).
Lehigh County, Whitehall Township.
1912 to 1917, 1 Linear Inch.

History:
Egypt Electric Light & Power Co., incorporated 22 July 1912 to supply electricity in the Village of Egypt, Whitehall Township, Lehigh County, merged into Lehigh Valley Light and Power Co., No. 3, 17 December 1917.

Administrative Records:
Minute Book, 1912-1917

Scope and Content Note:
The Minute Book describes the contract under which Egypt Electric Light & Power Co. obtained power from Lehigh-Northampton Light, Heat & Power Co. Also documented is the process by which the company negotiated with the Whitehall Township Board of Commissioners for a street lighting contract.

285. ELDON ELECTRIC COMPANY (Non-operating).
Schuylkill County, Rahn Township.
1911 to 1913, 1 Linear Inch.

History:
Eldon Electric Co., incorporated 27 June 1911 to supply electricity in Rahn Township, Schuylkill County, consolidated and merged with 37 companies to form Lehigh Navigation Electric Co., No. 2, 6 January 1913.

286. ELDRED ELECTRIC COMPANY (Non-operating).
Schuylkill County, Eldred Township.
1921 to 1922, 1 Linear Inch.

History:
Eldred Electric Co., incorporated 10 August 1921 to supply electricity in Eldred Township, Schuylkill County, merged with Pennsylvania Power & Light Co., 24 January 1922.

287. ELDRED-LYCOMING POWER & LIGHT COMPANY (Non-operating).
Lycoming County, Eldred Township.
1928, 1 Linear Inch.

History:
Eldred-Lycoming Power & Light Co., incorporated 14 May 1928 to supply electricity in Eldred Township, Lycoming County, merged with Pennsylvania Power & Light Co., 1 August 1928.

288. ELDRED POWER & LIGHT COMPANY (Non-operating).
Monroe County, Eldred Township.
1923 to 1924, 1 Linear Inch.

History:
Eldred Power & Light Co., incorporated 1 May 1923 to supply electricity in Eldred Township, Monroe County, consolidated and merged with 31 companies to form Paupack Power & Light Co., No. 2, 29 January 1924.

289. ELECTRIC COMPANY OF EXETER (Non-operating).
Luzerne County, Exeter Township.
1911 to 1918, 1 Linear Inch.

History:
Electric Co. of Exeter, incorporated 27 November 1911 to supply electricity in Exeter Township, Luzerne County, merged with Scranton Electric Co., 16 July 1918.

290. ELECTRIC LIGHT AND POWER COMPANY OF CARBONDALE, PENNSYLVANIA (Operating).
Lackawanna County, Carbondale City.
1886 to 1908, 2 Linear Inches.

History:
Excelsior Electric Company of Harrisburg was organized in November 1887 by Excelsior Electric Company of Brooklyn, an arc lighting manufacturer, to supply electricity for lighting in the city of Harrisburg. The company built a station containing four thirty-light Excelsior arc lighting dynamos, and began supplying arc lighting service in Harrisburg early in 1888. From the start it competed with The Harrisburg Electric Light Company, which had been supplying incandescent and arc lighting in Harrisburg since 1884. The two companies attempted to work out a market-sharing agreement in the city, but the Excelsior company balked at its rival's demand that it be paid $20,000 before such an agreement could be signed, and the negotiations collapsed. In the face of the competition, the Excelsior company encountered severe financial problems and nearly went into receivership by the summer of 1888. At that point, the parent Excelsior company, which hitherto had provided little financial assistance to its licensee, took over control of the firm. "Our neighbor haveing (sic) a large Incandescent and Arc plant, and good paying Contracts," the company's president told the Board of Directors, "the only plan that suggested itself to keep this company in existance and enable us to compete . . . was to increase our capacity and adopt such means for cheapening our power which would enable us to compete successfully." The new plan contained two elements to achieve that goal: the installation of the newly-developed Westinghouse system of alternating current for incandescent lighting, and the construction of a 200-horsepower hydroelectric plant. By 1890 this plant contained dynamos for 5000 incandescent lamps and 380 arc lights, and a hydro capacity of four 100-horsepower water turbines. The new facilities enabled the company to compete actively with the Harrisburg company for commercial and industrial lighting and power markets, and to enter the domestic lighting market unopposed (the Harrisburg company had previously rejected this as unprofitable, given the technical problems inherent in the Edison DC system).

In 1891 the parent Excelsior company, along with several other small arc lighting manufacturers, were taken over by Thomson-Houston Electric Company as a means of gaining a monopoly in that industry. Charles A. Coffin, the treasurer of Thomson-Houston, thereupon entered into negotiations with Harrisburg Electric Light Company aimed at getting control of the business in that city. The two parties reached agreement in December 1891 whereby Thomson-Houston turned over control of the stock of the Harrisburg Excelsior company to Harrisbur Electric Light Company, in exchange for a commitment by the Harrisburg company to merge and consolidate the two firms and to grant Thomson-Houston and its allied arc lighting companies exclusive manufacturing and marketing rights in the city. The agreement resulted in the formation of The Harrisburg Electric Company in April 1892.

Administrative Records:
Minute Books, 1886-1895, 1899-1908 (2 Volumes)

Scope and Content Note:
The Minute Book covering the 1886-1895 period provides a complete record of company operations. Of particular interest are entries pertaining to the company's organization by the firm of Westinghouse, Church, Kerr & Co., and the Westinghouse Electric & Manufacturing Co. Also documented are: (1) the installation of the Westinghouse system of alternating current, arc and incandescent lighting; (2) negotiations with Carbondale City Council for street lighting contracts; and (3) wages and salaries of company employees.

291. ELIZABETHTOWN ELECTRIC COMPANY (Non-operating).
Lancaster County, Elizabethtown Borough.
1912, 1 Linear Inch.

History:
Elizabethtown Electric Co., incorporated 7 November 1912 to supply electricity in Elizabethtown Borough, Lancaster County, consolidated and merged with 13 companies to form Edison Electric Co., No. 3, 9 December 1912.

292. ELMHURST ELECTRIC COMPANY (Non-operating).
Lackawanna County, Elmhurst Borough.
1922, 1 Linear Inch.

History:
Elmhurst Electric Co., incorporated 25 July 1922 to supply electricity in Elmhurst Borough, Lackawanna County, consolidated and merged with three companies to form Moscow Electric Co., 23 November 1923.

293. ELVERSON ELECTRIC COMPANY (Non-operating).
Chester County, Elverson Borough.
1915, 1 Linear Inch.

History:
Elverson Electric Co., incorporated 27 January 1915 to supply electricity in Elverson Borough, Chester County, consolidated and merged with five companies to form Tri-County Electric Co., 4 February 1915.

294. THE EMANS LIGHT AND POWER COMPANY (Non-operating).
Lehigh County, Emans Borough.
1910 to 1913, 1 Linear Inch.

History:
The Emans Light and Power Co., incorporated 18 January 1910 to supply electricity in Emans Borough, Lehigh County, consolidated and merged with 10 companies to form Lehigh Valley Light and Power Co., No. 2, 2 January 1913.

295. EMPIRE ELECTRIC LIGHT AND POWER COMPANY (Non-operating).
Lehigh County, Coplay Borough.
1913-1918, 1 Linear Inch.

History:
The history of this non-operating firm, Empire Electric Light and Power Co., is interesting in that the company was never actually incorporated nor, for that matter, did it ever actually exist. Officials of Lehigh Valley Transit Co. met in December 1913 to form the company in order to acquire a franchise in Coplay Borough, Lehigh County, and the firm's Letters Patent were secured in June 1914—some six months after this meeting. In the meantime, however, Lehigh County Electric Co., which was controlled by a New Jersey holding company and which had no specified franchise, was sold to Lehigh Valley Transit Co. In May 1914 Lehigh County Electric Co. filed a certificate, approved by the Public Service Commission, specifying Coplay Borough as the district for the subsequent operations. The need for Lehigh Valley Trust Co. to charter Empire Electric Light and Power Co. was obviated by that transaction.

296. EPHRATA TOWNSHIP ELECTRIC COMPANY (Non-operating).
Lancaster County, Ephrata Township.
1912, 1 Linear Inch.

History:
Ephrata Township Electric Co., incorporated 13 November 1912 to supply electricity in Ephrata Township, Lancaster County, consolidated and merged with 13 companies to form Edison Electric Co., No. 3, 9 December 1912.

297. EQUITABLE ELECTRIC COMPANY OF WHITEHALL TOWNSHIP (Non-operating).
Lehigh County, Whitehall Township.
1911 to 1913, 1 Linear Inch.

History:
Equitable Electric Co. of Whitehall Township, incorporated 4 April 1911 to supply electricity in Whitehall Township, Lehigh County, consolidated and merged with 37 companies to form Lehigh Navigation Electric Co., No. 2, 6 January 1913.

298. EXCELSIOR ELECTRIC COMPANY OF HARRISBURG (Operating).
Dauphin County, Harrisburg City.
1887 to 1899, 2 Linear Feet.

History:
Excelsior Electric Co. of Harrisburg was acquired in 1887 by officials of Excelsior Electric Co. of Brooklyn, who sought to introduce the Excelsior system of arc street lighting into Harrisburg. When it entered the incandescent lighting market the next year, the company encountered stiff competition from The Harrisburg Electric Light Co. Fearing a prolonged and costly struggle, the two firms merged in 1892. Then the Excelsior Electric Co. of Harrisburg changed its name to The Harrisburg Electric Co.

Administrative Records:
Minute Book, 1887-1892
Stock Certificate Books, 1887-1890 (2 Volumes)
Stock Ledger, 1887-1891
Orders Drawn on Secretary, 1899
Correspondence, 1888-1892

Operating Records:
General Ledger, 1887-1892
Journal, 1887-1892
Cashbook, 1887-1892
Accounts Payable and Invoices, 1887-1892 (2 Volumes)
Accounts Payable, 1891-1892
Statement of Purchase and Sale of Plant, 1888-1892

Scope and Content Note:
The Minute Book documents the organization of the Excelsior Electric Co. of Harrisburg by the Excelsior Electric Co. of Brooklyn. Also documented is the process by which contracts were negotiated with the Westinghouse Electric Co., which installed the incandescent lighting plant that put the Excelsior company into direct competition with The Harrisburg Electric Light Co. The Correspondence File refers to negotiations with The Thomson-Houston Electric Co., a large manufacturer of electrical equipment that purchased the Excelsior Company's generating plant in 1892.

299. EXCELSIOR ELECTRIC COMPANY OF PLAINFIELD TOWNSHIP (Non-operating).
Northampton County, Plainfield Township.
1911 to 1913, 1 Linear Inch.

History:
Excelsior Electric Co. of Plainfield Township, incorporated 4 April 1911 to supply electricity in Plainfield Township, Northampton County, consolidated and merged with 37 companies to form Lehigh Navigation Electric Co., No. 2, 6 January 1913.

300. EXCELSIOR ELECTRIC LIGHT AND POWER COMPANY (Operating).
Bucks County, Sellersville Borough.
1922 to 1923, 3 Linear Feet.

History:
Excelsior Electric Light and Power Co. was organized 27 July 1922 through the consolidation and merger of three companies. The company supplied electricity to Sellersville Borough and surrounding localities in Bucks County, serving about 2,000 customers. It merged into Pennsylvania Power & Light Co., 23 August 1923.

Administrative Records:
Minute Book, 1922-1923
Stock Certificate Book, 1922-1923
Stock Transfer Record, 1923
Stock Ledger, 1923

Operating Records:
General Ledgers, 1922-1923 (2 Volumes)
Journals, 1922-1923 (2 Volumes)
Cashbook, 1922
Cash Received, 1923
Check Register, 1923
Audited Voucher Register, 1923

Accrual Record, 1923
Detail Ledger, 1923
Expenditure Requisitions, 1923
Retirement Authorities, 1923
Voucher Register, 1922
Bills, 1923
Audit Report, Pennsylvania Power & Light Co., 1922

301. EXCELSIOR ELECTRIC LIGHT, POWER AND GAS COMPANY, NO. 1 (Operating).
Bucks County, Sellersville Borough.
1909 to 1913, 4 Linear Feet.

History:
Excelsior Electric Light, Power and Gas Company No. 1, organized 4 October 1909 through the consolidation merger of three companies, supplied electricity to Sellersville Borough and adjacent territories in Bucks and Montgomery Counties. The company organized several non-operating companies to acquire additional franchise rights late in 1913, merging with these companies to form Excelsior Electric Light, Power and Gas Co., No. 2, 18 December 1913.

Administrative Records:
See Inventory of Excelsior Electric Light, Power and Gas Company, No. 3

302. EXCELSIOR ELECTRIC LIGHT, POWER AND GAS COMPANY, NO. 2 (Operating).
Bucks County, Sellersville Borough.
1913 to 1918, 4 Linear Feet.

History:
Excelsior Electric Light, Power and Gas Co., No. 1, which served Sellersville Borough and adjacent territories in Bucks and Montgomery Counties, organized, consolidated, and merged with three non-operating companies to extend its franchise rights. This action resulted in the formation of Excelsior Electric Light, Power and Gas Company, No., 2, 18 December 1913. In September 1918, through a similar process involving three additional non-operating companies, Excelsior Electric Light, Power and Gas Co., No. 3, was formed.

Administrative Records:
See Excelsior Electric Light, Power and Gas Company, No. 3

303. EXCELSIOR ELECTRIC LIGHT, POWER AND GAS COMPANY, NO. 3 (Operating).
Bucks County, Sellersville Borough.
1906 to 1923, 4 Linear Feet.

History:
Formed 24 September 1918 through the consolidation and merger of Excelsior Electric Light, Power and Gas Co., No. 2 with three non-operating companies, Excelsior Electric Light, Power and Gas Company, No. 3 supplied electricity in Sellersville Borough and surrounding communities in Bucks and Montgomery Counties. In October 1922 the company again consolidated and merged with two non-operating companies to form Excelsior Electric Light and Power Co.

Administrative Records:
Minute Book, 1909-1922
Stock Certificate Book
Correspondence, 1909-1923 (6 Boxes)

Operating Records:
General Ledgers, 1911-1922 (2 vols.)
Journal, 1909-1922
Cashbooks, 1906-1922 (5 vols.)
Accounts Payable, 1911-1922 (2 vols.)

Scope and Content Note:
The correspondence of this company and its two predecessors document (1909-1923) virtually every aspect of their business operations including: customer relations, sales of electrical appliances and market surveys that were conducted in the Sellersville area. There is a good deal of correspondence with other Pennsylvania utility companies including Lehigh Valley Transit Co. and Pennsylvania Power & Light concerning operations, negotiations for franchises and mergers. The correspondence provides considerable information about living and working conditions in rural and small town eastern Pennsylvania during the early decades of the twentieth century.

304. EXETER BOROUGH-LUZERNE POWER AND LIGHT COMPANY (Non-operating).
Luzerne County, Exeter Borough.
1927, 1 Linear Inch.

History:
Exeter Borough-Luzerne Power and Light Co., incorporated 24 January 1927 to supply electricity in Exeter Borough, Luzerne County, merged into Pennsylvania Power & Light Co., 7 March 1927.

305. EXETER ELECTRIC COMPANY (Non-operating).
Luzerne County, Pittston Borough.
1911 to 1919, 1 Linear Inch.

History:
Exeter Electric Co., incorporated 6 September 1911 to supply electricity in Pittston Borough, Luzerne County, was never an operating company, and was formally dissolved in October 1919.

306. EXETER-LUZERNE POWER AND LIGHT COMPANY (Non-operating).
Luzerne County, Exeter Township.
1927, 1 Linear Inch.

History:
Exeter-Luzerne Power and Light Co., incorporated 24 January 1927 to supply electricity in Exeter Township, Luzerne County, merged into Pennsylvania Power & Light Co., 7 March 1927.

307. EXETER POWER COMPANY (Operating).
Luzerne County, Pittston City.
1925 to 1932, 1 Linear Foot.

History:
Exeter Power Co. was formed in May 1925 by Pennsylvania Power & Light Co. and Scranton Electric Co. to undertake the construction of a 100,000-kw capacity steam electric generating station along the Susquehanna River in Pittston, Luzerne County. Construction was completed in 1927.

Operating Records:
Accounts Payable Ledgers, 1925-1927 (2 vols.)
Cashbook, 1925-1929
The Foundation Co., Contract - Improvement, Extra

Work, Materials and Supplies, 1926-1929
Improvement Requisition, 1925-1926
Accrual Records, 1925-1932
Payroll Report - Duplicate Distribution of The Foundation Co. 1925-1927
Payroll Report - Exeter Power Company, 1927

308. EXETER POWER CORPORATION (Operating).
Luzerne County, Exeter Township.
1925 to 1932, 1 Linear Foot.

History:
As construction of the 100,000-kw Stanton Steam Electric Station in Pittston neared completion in 1927, Exeter Power Co. (formed in 1925) was reorganized as Exeter Power Corp. Controlled by a holding company, American Gas and Electric, the new corporation was formed to secure a franchise for generating electricity in Exeter township, and to raise capital for the Stanton Steam Electric Station. In November 1927, Exeter Power Corp. changed its name to Scranton Electric Co., No. 1.

Administrative Records:
Minute Book, 1927
Stock Certificate Book, 1927

Operating Records:
Cashbook, 1925-1929
Accounts Payable Ledger, 1927
Unit Cost Record—Operating Expenses, 1927—1928
Payroll Report, 1927
The Foundation Co. Contract—Improvement, Extra Work, Material, and Supplies, 1926-1929
Accrual Records, 1925-1932

309. FAIRFIELD POWER & LIGHT COMPANY (Non-operating).
Lycoming County, Fairfield Township.
1924, 2 Linear Inches.

History:
Incorporated on 31 March 1924 to supply electricity in the Township of Fairfield, Lycoming County, Fairfield Power & Light Co. merged into Pennsylvania Power & Light Co. on 30 July 1924.

310. FAIRVIEW & RIVERTON PASSENGER RAILWAY COMPANY (Operating).
Cumberland County, West Fairview Borough.
1893 to 1912, 1 Linear Inch.

History:
Incorporated on 16 February 1893 to construct and operate an electric railway in the Township of East Pennsboro, Cumberland County, Fairview & Riverton Passenger Railway Co. was consolidated and merged with five other companies on 10 January 1913 to form Harrisburg and Mechanicsburg Railway Co.

Administrative Records:
Minute Book, 1893-1912

311. FAIRVIEW TOWNSHIP ELECTRIC COMPANY (Non-operating).
Luzerne County, Fairview Township.
1911 to 1912, 1 Linear Inch.

History:
Incorporated on 26 January 1911 to supply electricity in the Township of Fairview, Luzerne County, Fairview Township Electric Co. was consolidated and merged with eleven other companies to form The Harwood Electric Co. on 23 February 1912.

312. FALLS TOWNSHIP ELECTRIC COMPANY (Non-operating).
Bucks County, Falls Township.
1913 to 1935, 1 Linear Foot.

History:
Falls Township Electric Co. was incorporated 30 December 1913 to supply electricity in the Township of Falls, Bucks County. A majority of the company's stock was acquired by Pennsylvania Power & Light Co. from The Lehigh Valley Light and Power Co. late in 1920. The company was dissolved on 30 September 1935.

313. FARMERS ELECTRIC COMPANY (Operating).
Lancaster County, Lancaster City.
1916 to 1930, 2 1/2 Linear Feet.

History:
Formed through the consolidation and merger of five non-operating companies, Farmers Electric Co. was incorporated on 18 May 1916 to supply electricity in a number of townships adjacent to the City of Lancaster. In 1925, United Gas and Electric Co. acquired the company and the next year sold it to Lehigh Power Securities Corp. On 31 December 1930 Farmers Electric Co. merged into Pennsylvania Power & Light Co.

Administrative Records:
Minute Book, 1916-1930
Secretary's Papers of Meetings, 1930
Stock Certificate Book, 1916-1930

Operating Records:
General Ledgers, 1923-1930 (2 vols.)
Journal, 1923-1926
Journal Entry Register, 1926-1930
Cashbook, 1923-1926
Cash Receipts, 1926-1930
Cash Disbursements, 1926-1927
Audited Voucher Register, 1923-1930 (3 vols.)
Accounts Payable, 1926-1930
Accounts Receivable, 1926-1930
Detail Ledger, 1926-1930
Accrual Record, 1926-1930
Fixed Capital, 1926-1930
Construction Ledger, 1926-1930
Analysis of Closed Jobs, 1926-1930
Automobile Services, 1926-1930
Automobile Reports, 1926-1929
Material and Supplies, 1926-1927
Expenditure Requisitions, 1930
Audit Reports 1923-1929 (7 vols.)

Scope and Content Note:
The Minute Book of Farmers Electric Co. documents routine stockholder and directors' meetings. The operating records describe in detail the costs of various goods and services purchased. The Detail Ledger breaks expenses down into various categories: metered commercial lighting, domestic lighting, range and water heating, and farm power. Similarly, Automobile Reports detail routine expenses for maintenance, while the Construction Ledger documents the cost of various construction projects.

314. FARMERS ELECTRIC COMPANY OF CONESTOGA TOWNSHIP (Non-operating).
Lancaster County, Conestoga Township.
1917 to 1930, 1 Linear Inch.

History:
Incorporated on 23 October 1917 to supply electricity in the Township of Conestoga, Lancaster County, Farmers Electric Co. of Conestoga Township merged into Pennsylvania Power & Light Co. on 31 December 1930.

315. FARMERS ELECTRIC COMPANY OF EAST LAMPETER TOWNSHIP (Non-operating).
Lancaster County, East Lampeter Township.
1916, 1 Linear Inch.

History:
Incorporated on 31 December 1915 to supply electricity in the Township of East Lampeter, Lancaster County, Farmers Electric Co. of East Lampeter Township was consolidated and merged with four other non-operating companies on 11 March 1916 to form Farmers Electric Co.

316. FARMERS ELECTRIC COMPANY OF MANHEIM TOWNSHIP (Non-operating).
Lancaster County, Manheim Township.
1916, 1 Linear Inch.

History:
Incorporated on 31 December 1915 to supply electricity in the Township of Manheim, Lancaster County, Farmers Electric Co. of Manheim Township was consolidated and merged with four other non-operating companies on 11 March 1916 to form Farmers Electric Co.

317. FARMERS ELECTRIC COMPANY OF MANOR TOWNSHIP (Non-operating).
Lancaster County, Manor Township.
1919 to 1930, 1 Linear Inch.

History:
Incorporated on 26 November 1919 to supply electricity in the Township of Manor, Lancaster County, Farmers Electric Co. of Manor Township merged into Pennsylvania Power & Light Co. on 31 December 1930.

318. FARMERS ELECTRIC COMPANY OF MARTIC TOWNSHIP (Non-operating).
Lancaster County, Martic Township.
1917 to 1930, 1 Linear Inch.

History:
Incorporated on 23 October 1917 to supply electricity in the Township of Martic, Lancaster County, Farmers Electric Co. of Martic Township merged into Pennsylvania Power & Light Co. on 31 December 1930.

319. FARMERS ELECTRIC COMPANY OF NORTH LANCASTER COUNTY (Operating).
Lancaster County, Clay Township.
1916 to 1936, 1 Linear Foot.

History:
Incorporated on 4 November 1915 to supply electricity in the Township of Clay, Lancaster Township, Farmers Electric Co. of North Lancaster County was merged into Edison Electric Co., No. 4 on 24 November 1917.

Administrative Records:
Minute Book, 1918-1925

Operating Records:
General Ledger, 1916-1926
Journal, 1916-1926
Cash Books, 1917-1926 (2 vols.)
Audit Reports, 1923-1925 (3 vols.)

Scope and Content Note:
The Minute Book of Farmers Electric Co. of North Lancaster County documents routine stockholder and directors' meetings, while the Audit Reports describe expenses, assets and liabilities.

320. FARMERS ELECTRIC COMPANY OF PENN TOWNSHIP (Non-operating).
Lancaster County, Penn Township.
1915 to 1916, 1 Linear Inch.

History:
Incorporated on 17 September 1915 to supply electricity in the Township of Penn, Lancaster County, Farmers Electric Co. of Penn Township was consolidated and merged with four other non-operating companies on 11 March 1916 to form Farmers Electric Co.

321. FARMERS ELECTRIC COMPANY OF PEQUEA TOWNSHIP (Non-operating).
Lancaster County, Pequea Township.
1917 to 1930, 1 Linear Inch.

History:
Incorporated on 23 October 1917 to supply electricity in the Township of Pequea, Lancaster County, Farmers Electric Co. of Pequea Township merged into Pennsylvania Power & Light Co. on 31 December 1930.

322. FARMERS ELECTRIC COMPANY OF UPPER LEACOCK TOWNSHIP (Non-operating).
Lancaster County, Upper Leacock Township.
1916, 1 Linear Inch.

History:
Incorporated on 31 December 1915 to supply electricity in the Township of Upper Leacock, Lancaster County, Farmers Electric Co. of Upper Leacock Township was consolidated and merged with four other non-operating companies on 22 March 1916 to form Farmers Electric Co.

323. FARMERS ELECTRIC COMPANY OF WARWICK TOWNSHIP (Non-operating).
Lancaster County, Warwick Township.
1915 to 1916, 1 Linear Inch.

History:
Incorporated on 17 September 1915 to supply electricity in the Township of Warwick, Lancaster County, Farmers Electric Co. of Warwick Township was consolidated and merged with four other non-operating companies on 11 March 1916 to form Farmers Electric Co.

324. FARMERS ELECTRIC COMPANY OF WASHINGTON BOROUGH (Non-operating).
Lancaster County, Washington Borough.
1919 to 1926, 1 Linear Inch.

History:
Incorporated on 26 November 1919 to supply electricity in the Borough of Washington, Lancaster County, Farmers Electric Co. of Washington Borough was merged into Edison Electric Co., No. 4, on 30 June 1925.

325. FARMERS ELECTRIC COMPANY OF WEST HEMPFIELD TOWNSHIP (Non-operating).
Lancaster County, West Hempfield Township.
1919 to 1930, 2 Linear Inches.

History:
Incorporated on 26 November 1919 to supply electricity in the Township of West Hempfield, Lancaster County, Farmers Electric Co. of West Hempfield Township merged into Pennsylvania Power & Light Co. on 31 December 1930.

326. FAYETTE TOWNSHIP POWER COMPANY (Non-operating).
Juniata County, Fayette Township.
1925 to 1926, 1 Linear Inch.

History:
Incorporated on 21 January 1926 to supply electricity in the Township of Fayette, Juniata County, Fayette Township Power Co. merged into Juniata Public Service Co. on 8 July 1926.

327. FEARNE ELECTRIC COMPANY (Non-operating).
Schuylkill County, Schuylkill Township.
1911 to 1913, 1 Linear Inch.

History:
Incorporated on 27 June 1911 to supply electricity in the Township of Schuylkill, Schuylkill County, Fearne Electric Co. was consolidated and merged with 37 other non-operating companies on 23 December 1912 to form Lehigh Navigation Electric Co., No. 2.

328. FELL ELECTRIC COMPANY (Non-operating).
Lackawanna County, Fell Township.
1910 to 1912, 1/2 Linear Foot.

History:
Incorporated on 5 May 1910 to supply electricity in the Township of Fell, Lackawanna County, Fell Electric Co. was merged 25 November 1912 into Scranton Electric Co.

329. FISHING CREEK-COLUMBIA POWER & LIGHT COMPANY (Non-operating).
Columbia, Fishing Creek Township.
1924 to 1925, 1/2 Linear Foot.

History:
Incorporated on 28 August 1924 to supply electricity in the Township of Fishing Creek, Columbia County, Fishing Creek-Columbia Power & Light Co. merged into Pennsylvania Power & Light Co. along with twelve other non-operating companies on 28 October 1924.

330. FOREST CITY ELECTRIC LIGHT, HEAT & POWER COMPANY (Operating).
Susquehanna County, Forest City.
1896 to 1910, 1/2 Linear Foot.

History:
Incorporated in 1896 to supply electricity in Forest City, Susquehanna County, Forest City Electric Light, Heat & Power Co. merged into Scranton Electric Co. on 20 January 1910.

Administrative Records:
Minute Books, 1896-1910 (2 vols.)

Operating Records:
General Ledger, 1909
Cashbook, 1909-1910

Scope and Content Note:
The Minute Books of Forest City Electric Light, Heat & Power Co. document routine stockholder and directors' meetings, while the General Ledger and Cashbook detail the company's operating expenses.

331. FOSTER TOWNSHIP ELECTRIC COMPANY (Non-operating).
Luzerne County, Foster Township.
1909, 1 Linear Inch.

History:
Incorporated on 16 June 1909 to supply electricity in the Township of Foster, Luzerne County, Foster Township Electric Co. was consolidated and merged with eleven other companies on 23 June 1909 to form Harwood Electric Co.

332. FOUNTAIN HILL ELECTRIC LIGHT, HEAT AND POWER COMPANY (Non-operating).
Lehigh County, Fountain Hill Borough.
1912 to 1914, 1 Linear Inch.

History:
Incorporated on 4 August 1911 to supply electricity in the Borough of Fountain Hill, Lehigh County, Fountain Hill Light, Heat and Power Co. was consolidated and merged with Halcyon Electric Light and Power Co., No. 1 on 23 December 1913 to form Halcyon Electric Light and Power Co., No. 2.

333. THE FOUR CONSOLIDATED ELECTRIC COMPANY (Operating).
Schuylkill County, Middleport Borough.
1910 to 1916, 1/2 Linear Foot.

History:
Incorporated on 5 April 1911, the Four Consolidated Electric Co. purchased power from Eastern Pennsylvania Railways Co. and supplied electricity to several small communities in the vicinity of Middleport, Schuylkill County. On 18 July 1916 the company merged into Eastern Pennsylvania Light, Heat and Power Company.

Administrative Records:
Minute Book, 1911-1916
Stock Certificate Book, 1911

Operating Records:
General Ledger, 1915
Cash Books, 1910-1916 (3 vols.)
Audited Voucher Register, 1915-1916
Accounts Payable, 1910-1916 (2 vols.)
Expenses and Receipts, 1910-1915

Scope and Content Note:
The Minute Book of The Four Consolidated Electric Co. is a routine account of stockholder and directors' meetings, while the Expense and Receipts book compares receipts from lighting with expenditures on a yearly basis. The Accounts Payable book is a record of individuals detailing the amount they owed each month for utility services.

334. THE FRACKVILLE AND GILBERTON LIGHT, HEAT AND POWER COMPANY (Operating).
Schuylkill County, Frackville Borough.
1890 to 1923, 3 Linear Feet.

History:

The Frackville and Gilberton Light, Heat and Power Co. was incorporated 25 August 1890 to supply electricity in the Borough of Frackville, Schuylkill County, and was the first company to supply electricity there. In 1894, the company extended its services to the Borough of Gilberton, and the next year expanded into the Borough of Girardville. In 1902, it began providing service to Mahonoy Plane Village. In 1906, the stock of the company was acquired by Eastern Pennsylvania Railways Co., and on 20 July 1909 Frackville and Gilberton Light, Heat and Power merged along with seven other companies into Palo Alto Heat, Light and Power Co.

Administrative Records:

Minute Books, 1890-1909 (3 vols.)
Stock Certificate Books, 1893-1909 (2 vols.)

Operating Records:

Cashbook, 1906-1907
Accounts Payable, 1906-1908 (2 vols.)
Statement of Charges to Local Construction, 1908
Report of Earnings, 1908-1909
Record of Sales—Work Orders Issued, 1907-1909
Operating Statistics, 1909-1910
Balance Sheets, 1907-1909
Earnings, Operating Expenses and Balance Sheets, 1907-1908
Bank Check Book (Stubs), 1906-1912

Scope and Content Note:

The Minute Books of The Frackville and Gilberton Light, Heat and Power Company document the early years of operations in Schuylkill County. The company's relationship with the Thomson-Houston Electric Light Company is described in considerable detail. The minutes also document the firm's financial problems and attempt to raise capital by securing loans from local businessmen. The process by which it solicited customers and extended service to local social organizations and churches is also described. There is considerable information documenting competition with Schuylkill Light, Heat and Power Company.

335. FRAILEY-SCHUYLKILL POWER & LIGHT COMPANY (Non-operating).
Schuylkill County, Frailey Township.
1925 to 1926, 2 Linear Inches.

History:

Incorporated on 26 March 1926 to supply electricity in a portion of the Township of Frailey, Schuylkill County, Frailey-Schuylkill Power & Light Co. merged into Pennsylvania Power & Light Co. on 14 April 1926.

336. THE FRAILEY TOWNSHIP ELECTRIC COMPANY (Non-operating).
Schuylkill County, Frailey Township.
1913 to 1916, 2 Linear Inches.

History:

Incorporated on 16 December 1913 to supply electricity in the Township of Frailey, Schuylkill County, The Frailey Township Electric Co. was merged along with 15 other companies into Eastern Pennsylvania Light, Heat and Power Co. on 18 July 1916.

337. FRANCONIA ELECTRIC LIGHT AND POWER COMPANY (Non-operating).
Montgomery County, Franconia Township.
1915, 1 Linear Inch.

History:

Incorporated on 19 March 1918 to supply electricity in the Township of Franconia, Montgomery County, Franconia Electric Light and Power Co. was consolidated and merged with three other companies on 10 April 1918 to form Excelsior Electric Light, Power and Gas Co., No. 3.

338. FRANCONIA TOWNSHIP ELECTRIC LIGHT AND POWER COMPANY (Non-operating).
Montomery County, Franconia Township.
1914 to 1916, 1 Linear Inch.

History:

Incorporated on 13 January 1915 to supply electricity in the Township of Franconia, Montgomery County, Franconia Township Electric Light and Power Co. merged along with five other non-operating companies into Lehigh Valley Light and Power Co., No. 3 on 26 February 1916.

339. FRANKLIN-LYCOMING POWER & LIGHT COMPANY (Non-operating).
Lycoming County, Franklin Township.
1924, 2 Linear Inches.

History:

Incorporated on 28 August 1924 to supply electricity in the Township of Franklin, Lycoming County, Franklin-Lycoming Power & Light Co. merged along with four other non-operating companies into The Citizens Electric Light and Power Co. of Hughesville, Pa., on 6 October 1924.

340. FRANKLIN POWER & LIGHT COMPANY (Non-operating).
Carbon County, Franklin Township.
1923, 1 Linear Inch.

History:

Franklin Power & Light, chartered on 15 March 1923, was a "paper company" that Pennsylvania Power & Light created so that it could extend its operations into Franklin Township, Carbon County.

341. FRANKLIN TOWNSHIP CARBON ELECTRIC COMPANY (Operating).
Carbon County, Franklin Township.
1924 to 1928, 1 Linear Foot.

History:

Franklin Township Carbon Electric Co. was incorporated 23 December 1923 by James I. Blakslee in order to extend his individually-operated electric system from the Borough of Weissport into Franklin Township (Carbon County). Affiliated with Lehighton Electric Light & Power Co. until 1926, when it merged with Lehigh Power Securities Corp., the company merged into Pennsylvania Power & Light Co. on 28 May 1928.

Administrative Records:

Minute Book, 1924-1928
Stock Certificate Book, 1924-1927
Stock Transfer Record, 1927
Stock Ledger, 1924-1928

Operating Records:
General Ledger, 1927-1929
Detail of Cost Study and Fixed Capital, 1927
Expenditure Requisitions, 1927-1928
Audit Reports, 1924-1927 (4 vols.)

Scope and Content Note:
The Audit Reports document the company's assets and liabilities while detailing its financial relationship with Lehighton Electric Light & Power Co. Expenditure Requisitions document the costs of construction work such as pole line extensions and installation of new generators.

342. FRANKLIN TOWNSHIP ELECTRIC COMPANY (Non-operating).
Columbia County, Franklin Township.
1916 to 1917, 1/2 Linear Foot.

History:
Incorporated on 3 August 1916 to supply electricity in the Township of Franklin, Columbia County, Franklin Township Electric Co. merged with three other non-operating companies into The Harwood Electric Co. on 20 June 1917.

343. FREEBURG POWER & LIGHT COMPANY (Non-operating).
Snyder County, Freeburg Borough.
1922 to 1923, 1 Linear Foot.

History:
Incorporated on 8 February 1923 to supply electricity in the Borough of Freeburg, Snyder County, Freeburg Power & Light Co. merged into Pennsylvania Power & Light Co. on 5 April 1923.

344. FREELAND ELECTRIC LIGHT HEAT AND POWER COMPANY (Operating).
Luzerne County, Freeland Borough.
1893 to 1912, 1 1/2 Linear Feet.

History:
Incorporated on 21 November 1893 to supply electricity in the Borough of Freeland, Luzerne County, Freeland Electric Light Heat and Power Co. leased its franchises and property to Hazleton Electric Light and Power Co. in 1899. This lease was terminated in 1912 when Freeland Electric Light Heat and Power Co. merged with twelve other companies to form Hazleton Electric Co.

Administrative Records:
Minute Book, 1893-1912
Stock Certificate Books, 1893-1912 (2 vols.)

Operating Records:
General Ledger, 1893-1900
Journal, 1894-1900
Monthly Receipts, 1896-1899
Audited Voucher Register, 1894-1900

Scope and Content Note:
The Minute Book provides an executive-level overview of the growth and development of Freeland Electric Light Heat and Power Co., while the General Ledger is a record of invoices to various accounts. The Journal documents expenses for parts, supplies, and leased energy.

345. FREEMANSBURG ELECTRIC LIGHT AND POWER COMPANY (Non-operating).
Northampton County, Freemansburg Borough.
1914 to 1917, 1 Linear Inch.

History:
Incorporated originally on 27 July 1914 to supply electricity in the Borough of Freemansburg, Northampton County, Freemansburg Electric Light and Power Co. merged along with four other non-operating companies into Lehigh Valley Light and Power Co., No. 3 on 16 September 1916.

346. GALLAGHER-CLINTON POWER & LIGHT COMPANY (Non-operating).
Clinton County, Gallagher Township.
1929, 2 Linear Inches.

History:
Incorporated 3 October 1929 to supply electricity in the Township of Gallagher, Clinton County, Gallagher-Clinton Power & Light Co. was merged with six other companies into Pennsylvania Power & Light Co. on 24 October 1929.

347. GARFIELD COAL COMPANY (Operating).
New Castle County (Delaware), Wilmington City (Delaware).
1918 to 1919, 1 Linear Foot.

History:
Incorporated on 1 August 1918 in Wilmington, Delaware, for the purpose of recovering and processing coal and culm, Garfield Coal Co. changed its name to Glamos Coal Co. on 19 August 1918. The company leased a tract of land on Shamokin Creek near Keefer's Station, east of Sunbury in Northumberland County, Pennsylvania, and took some initial steps to develop the property. On 15 February 1919 Glamos Coal Co. sold its assets, stock, and leases to the Shamokin Valley Coal Co., which owned property at nearby Diebler. Shamokin Valley Coal Co. sold the property to Industrial Fuel Co. on 8 January 1920. By 1925 both Glamos Coal Co. and Shamokin Valley Coal Co. were out of business.

Administrative Records:
Minute Book, 1918-1919

348. THE GAS COMPANY OF LUZERNE COUNTY (Operating).
Luzerne County, Wilkes-Barre City.
1896-1904, 1 Linear Foot.

History:
The Gas Co. of Luzerne County was incorporated 8 January 1897. Seeking to gain market control, it leased the franchises of its two major competitors: The Consumers Gas Co. of Wilkes-Barre and Wilkes-Barre Gas Co. When these leases terminated on 22 December 1904, the three companies merged to form Wilkes-Barre Gas and Electric Co.

Administrative Records:
Minute Books, 1896-1904, (2 vols.)
Stock Certificate Book, 1898-1904
Stock Transfer Record, 1898-1904
Stock Ledger, 1898-1904

Scope and Content Note:
The Minute Books of The Gas Co. of Luzerne County document routine stockholders' and directors' meetings, and the company's 1904 consolidation and merger into Wilkes-Barre Gas and Electric Co.

349. GAS COMPANY OF NORTHUMBERLAND (Operating).
Northumberland County, Northumberland Borough.
1915 to 1930, 3 Linear Feet.

History:
Incorporated on 2 February 1910, Northumberland Gas Co. became Northumberland County's first supplier of gas lighting. In 1913, the company ran into financial difficulties and was sold to a bond holders committee. Reorganized in 1916 as the Gas Co. of Northumberland, it merged with the North Point Gas Co. in 1922. In 1929, the company's stock was acquired by Lehigh Power Securitiies Corp. and the next year it merged into Pennsylvania Power & Light.

Administrative Records:
Minute Book, 1915-1930
Stock Certificate Books, 1916-1930 (2 vols.)
Common Stock Transfer Record, 1929-1930
Preferred Stock Transfer Record, 1929-1930
Stock Ledger, Common, 1918-1930
Stock Ledger, Preferred, 1918-1930

Operating Records:
General Ledger, 1929-1930
Journal, 1918-1929
Journal Entry Register, 1929-1930
Cashbooks, 1920-1929 (3 vols.)
Record of Cash Disbursements, 1929-1930
Audited Voucher Register, 1929-1930
Accounts Payable, 1929-1930
Accounts Receivable, 1929-1930
Detail Ledger, 1929-1930
Accrual Ledger, 1929-1930
Gas Survey and Excavating Permits, 1928-1930
Expenditure Requisitions, 1929-1930
Bills, 1929-1930
Bank Check Book, 1917-1929
Summary of Accounts Receivable, 1929-1930
Summary of Miscellaneous Accounts, 1929
Summary of Cashiers' Overs and Shorts, 1929-1930
Summary of Consumer's Deposits, 1929-1930
Audit Reports, 1924-1929 (3 vols.)

Scope and Content Note:
The Minute Book of Gas Co. of Northumberland contains routine notes on stockholder's and directors' meetings, including accounts of the company's reorganization, and its purchase of North Point Gas Co. The Audit Reports are a record of the company's organization and capitalization, assets and liabilitites. The Gas Survey sheets are mainly blank, but several compare net monthly bills and yearly increases or decreases according to present proposed rates. The Excavation Permits give the location of repair work in the Borough of Northumberland, along with the names of abutting owners. The Expenditure Requisitions give yearly cost estimates for gas main extensions, meter installations, and miscellaneous improvements. The Detail Ledger is a complete account of the company's operating expenses, while the Journal is a record of cash receipts and cash disbursements.

350. GIBSON ELECTRIC COMPANY (Non-operating).
Schuylkill County, Ryan Township.
1911 to 1913, 2 Linear Inches.

History:
Incorporated on 27 June 1911 to supply electricity in the Township of Ryan, Schuylkill County, Gibson Electric Co. was consolidated and merged with 37 other non-operating companies on 23 December 1912 to form Lehigh Navigation Electric Co. No. 2.

351. GOULDSBOROUGH-LACKAWANNA POWER & LIGHT COMPANY (Non-operating).
Lackawanna County, Gouldsborough Borough.
1935 to 1936, 1 Linear Inch.

History:
Incorporated 10 December 1935 to supply electricity in the Borough of Gouldsborough, Lackawanna County, Gouldsborough-Lackawanna Power & Light Co. was merged along with three other non-operating companies into Pennsylvania Power & Light Co. on 24 January 1936.

352. GRATZ ELECTRIC COMPANY (Non-operating).
Dauphin County, Gratz Borough.
1919, 1 Linear Inch.

History:
Incorporated on 2 January 1917 to supply electricity in the Borough of Gratz, Dauphin County, Gratz Electric Co. was consolidated and merged with five other non-operating companies on 30 October 1919 to form The Citizens Electric Co.

353. GRATZ LIGHT AND POWER COMPANY (Operating).
Dauphin County, Gratz Borough.
1921 to 1925, 1 Linear Foot.

History:
Incorporated on 8 February 1922, Gratz Light and Power Co. was the first company to supply electricity in the Borough of Gratz, Dauphin County. On 22 September 1924 the company merged into East Penn Electric Co., No. 2.

Administrative Records:
Minute Book, 1921-1924
Stock Certificate Book, 1922-1924
Stock Register, 1922
Monthly Reports to Directors, 1924

Operating Records:
General Ledger, 1922-1924
Cashbook, 1924
Audited Voucher Register, 1924
Check Book, 1921-1925

Scope and Content Note:
The Minute Books of Gratz Light and Power Co. document stockholders' and directors' meetings, including reports of receipts and expenditures. The Monthly Reports to the Directors contain statements on earnings, operating expenses, assets and liabilities.

354. GREENE-CLINTON POWER & LIGHT COMPANY (Non-operating).
Clinton County, Greene Township.
1928 to 1929, 1 Linear Foot.

History:
Incorporated on 3 October 1929 to supply electricity in the Township of Greene, Clinton County, Greene-Clinton Power & Light Co. was merged along with six other non-operating companies into Pennsylvnia Power & Light Co. on 24 October 1929.

355. GREENE POWER & LIGHT COMPANY (Non-operating).
Pike County, Greene Township.
1923 to 1924, 1 Linear Foot.

History:
Incorporated on 1 May 1923 to supply electricity in the Township of Greene, Pike County, Greene Power & Light Co. was consolidated and merged with 31 other non-operating companies on 20 July 1923 to form Paupack Power & Light Co., No. 2.

356. GREENFIELD TOWNSHIP ELECTRIC CORPORATION (Non-operating).
Lackawanna County, Greenfield Township.
1923 to 1928, 1 Linear Foot.

History:
Incorporated on 11 September 1923 to supply electricity in the Township of Greenfield, Lackawanna County, Greenfield Township Electric Corp. was consolidated and merged with eight other companies on 3 February 1928 to form The Scranton Electric Co.

357. GREENWOOD ELECTRIC COMPANY (Non-operating).
Northampton County, Forks Township.
1911 to 1913, 2 Linear Inches.

History:
Incorporated on 4 April 1911 to supply electricity in the Township of Forks, Northampton County, Greenwood Electric Co. was consolidated and merged with 37 other non-operating companies on 23 December 1912 to form Lehigh Navigation Electric Co., No. 2.

358. GREENWOOD POWER & LIGHT COMPANY (Non-operating).
Columbia County, Greenwood Township.
1923 to 1924, 2 Linear Inches.

History:
Incorporated on 21 November 1923 to supply electricity in the Township of Greenwood, Columbia County, Greenwood Power & Light Co. was merged along with nine other non-operating companies into Pennsylvania Power & Light Co. on 31 March 1924.

359. GREGG POWER & LIGHT COMPANY (Non-operating).
Union County, Gregg Township.
1922 to 1923, 2 Linear Inches.

History:
Incorporated on 23 February 1923 to supply electricity in the Township of Gregg, Union County, Gregg Power & Light Co. was merged along with three other non-operating companies into Pennsylvania Power & Light Co. on 17 May 1923.

360. GRUGAN-CLINTON POWER & LIGHT COMPANY (Non-operating).
Clinton County, Grugan Township.
1929, 1 Linear Inch.

History:
Incorporated on 3 October 1929 to supply electricity in the Township of Grugan, Clinton County, Grugan-Clinton Power & Light Co. was merged with six other non-operating companies into Pennsylvania Power & Light Co. on 24 October 1929.

361. GWYNEDD-FARMERS ELECTRIC LIGHT & POWER COMPANY (Non-operating).
Montgomery County, Upper Gwynedd Township.
1917 to 1919, 1 Linear Inch.

History:
Incorporated 6 February 1917, Gwynedd-Farmers Electric Light & Power Co. was a 'paper company' set up by Lehigh Valley Transit Co. to extend its operations into the Township of Upper Gwynedd, Montgomery County. In 1919, the company merged with Lehigh Valley Transit Co.

362. HAGERSTOWN LIGHT & HEAT COMPANY OF WASHINGTON COUNTY (Operating).
Washington County (Maryland), Hagerstown City (Maryland).
1912 to 1927, 1 Linear Foot.

History:
Hagerstown Light & Heat Co. was incorporated 17 March 1891 to supply gas lighting in the City of Hagerstown, Washington County, Maryland. It used the facilities of Hagerstown Gas Light Co. which it acquired on 29 April 1891. In 1913, the company was bought by Northern Central Gas which five years later sold it to Lehigh Power Securities. In 1920, Pennsylvania Power & Light acquired the company and held it until 1928, when it sold it to the Central Gas and Electric Co.

Administrative Records:
Minute Book, 1912-1927
Stock Transfer Record, 1926

Operating Records:
Analysis of Accounts Receivable, Consumers, 1924
Analysis of Accounts Receivable, Miscellaneous, 1924
Analysis of Bad Debts, 1924
Analysis of Consumers Deposits, 1924
Detail of Cost Study and Fixed Capital, 1922-1927
Expenditure Requisitions, 1919-1927
Retirement Authorities, 1919-1926
Repair Authorities, 1919-1923
Working Papers of Audit, 1924
Audit Reports, 1923-1926 (3 vols.)

Scope and Content Note:
The Minute Book of Hagerstown Light & Heat Co. documents routine stockholders' and directors' meetings. The Expenditure Requisitions detail operating expenses such as boiler replacements, steam pump installations, and automobile purchases. Accounts Receivable list customers, their addresses, and their charges for service, while the Analysis of Bad Debts lists customers in arrears.

363. HALCYON ELECTRIC LIGHT AND POWER COMPANY, NO. 1 (Operating).
Northampton County, South Bethlehem Borough.
1902 to 1913, 1 Linear Foot.

History:

Incorporated 30 January 1902, Halcyon Electric Light and Power Co., No. 1, used an abandoned generator located in the Halcyon Knitting Mills to generate electricity. In the Borough of South Bethlehem its major competitor was The Allentown Electric Light and Power Co. To meet the challenge while reducing costs, the company sought alternative sources of power. In 1910 it turned to the New Jersey Zinc Co. and the next year to Bethlehem Steel. In 1912, Halcyon Electric Light and Power Co., No. 1, was acquired by Lehigh Valley Transit Co. which reorganized it as Halcyon Electric Light and Power Co., No. 2.

Administrative Records:

Minute Books, 1902-1913 (2 vols.)
Stock Certificate Books, 1904-1913 (2 vols.)
Stock Transfer Record, 1904-1909
Stock Ledger, 1909-1912

Scope and Content Note:

The Minute Books of Halcyon Electric Light and Power Co., No. 1 document routine stockholders' and directors' meetings, and contain lists of stockholders. The Stock Ledger, however, gives a more detailed list of stockholders and the number of shares they owned.

364. HALCYON ELECTRIC LIGHT AND POWER COMPANY, NO. 2 (Operating).
Northampton County, South Bethlehem.
1910 to 1918, 2 1/2 Linear Feet.

History:

Halcyon Electric Light and Power Co., No. 2, was incorporated 30 December 1913 following the consolidation and merger of Halcyon Electric Light and Power Co., No. 1, with a non-operating company. This reorganization enabled the company to expand its operations into the Borough of Fountain Hill, Lehigh County. On September 16, 1916, the company was merged into Lehigh Valley Light and Power Co., No. 2.

Administrative Records:

Minute Book, 1914-1916
Stock Certificate Books, 1913-1915 (2 vols.)
Correspondence, 1911-1912

Operating Records:

Day Books, 1911-1912 (2 vols.)
Accounts Payable, 1911-1916 (2 vols.)
Audited Voucher Register, 1914-1916
Sundry Accounts Receivable Ledger, 1911-1912
Accrual Record, 1913-1918
Record of Lamp Sales, 1912
Record of Stores Material, 1911-1912
Consumers' Deposit Ledger, 1912-1916
Payroll Vouchers, 1914-1916
Bank Passbook-Dividend Account, 1910-1012

Scope and Content Note:

The Minute Book of Halcyon Electric Light and Power Co., No. 2, is a routine account of stockholder and directors' meetings. The Daybooks document sales of lamps and other equipment (customers and price are listed). The Consumers Deposit Ledger is a complete listing of customers. The correspondence documents the company's relationship with General Electric, from which it appears to have purchased most of its generating equipment.

365. HALFPENNY AND GROVE, INCORPORATED (Operating).
Union County, Lewis Township.
1926 to 1930, 1 Linear Foot.

History:

In 1903, J.L. Halfpenny and A.E. Grove began using their water-powered grist mill to supply electricity to the Borough of Mifflinburg, Union County. After twenty-three years of successful operations they sought to expand into Lewis Township, and on 17 December 1926 they incorporated for that purpose. In 1929, the company's stock was acquired by Lehigh Power Securities Corp., and the next year it was merged into Pennsylvania Power & Light Co.

Administrative Records:

Minute Book, 1929-1930
Stock Certificate Book, 1928-1930
Stock Transfer Record, 1929-1930
Stock Ledger, 1928-1930

Operating Records:

General Ledgers, 1926-1930 (2 vols.)
Journal, 1926-1929
Journal Entry Register, 1929-1930
Record of Cash Disbursements, 1929-1930
Audited Voucher Register, 1929-1930
Accounts Payable, 1929-1930
Accounts Receivable, 1929-1930
Detail Ledger, 1929-1930
Accrual Records, 1929-1930 (2 vols.)
Expenditure Requisitions, 1929-1931
Retirement Authorities, 1930-1931
Workmen's Compensation Insurance Accrual Statements, 1929-1930
Bills, 1929-1930
Statement of Rents, 1929-1930
Summary of Accounts Receivable—Consumers, 1929-1930
Summary of Accounts Receivable—Miscellaneous, 1929-1930
Audit Reports, 1927-1930 (4 vols)

Scope and Content Note:

The Minute Book of Halfpenny and Grove, Inc. deals with routine stockholders' and directors' meetings, while the General Ledgers detail operating expenses and revenue. The Expenditure Requisitions give estimated costs for electrical construction work, such as short pole line extensions and erection of new lines. The Retirement Authorities give a description and value of items to be scrapped, such as transformers, pipes, and filters. The Accrual Record documents tax and insurance payments.

366. HAMILTON-MONROE POWER & LIGHT COMPANY (Non-operating).
Monroe County, Hamilton Township.
1925, 1 Linear Inch.

History:
Incorporated 7 April 1925 to supply electricity in the Township of Hamilton, Monroe County, Hamilton-Monroe Power & Light Co. was merged with three other non-operating companies into Pennsylvania Power & Light Co. on 8 May 1925.

367. HANOVER ELECTRIC LIGHT AND POWER COMPANY (Non-operating).
Lehigh County, Hanover Township.
191 to 11913, 2 Linear Inches.

History:
Incorporated 10 November 1911 to supply electricity in the Township of Hanover, Lehigh County, Hanover Electric Light and Power Co. was consolidated and merged with ten other companies on 6 December 1912 to form Lehigh Valley Light and Power Co., No. 2.

368. HANOVER TOWNSHIP ELECTRIC COMPANY (Non-operating).
Luzerne County, Hanover Township.
1910 to 1912, 1 Linear Inch.

History:
Incorporated on 26 January 1911 to supply electricity in the Township of Hanover, Luzerne County, Hanover Township Electric Co. was consolidated and merged with eleven other companies on 23 February 1912 to form The Harwood Electric Co.

369. HANOVER TOWNSHIP LEHIGH ELECTRIC COMPANY (Non-operating).
Lehigh County, Hanover Township.
1919, 1 Linear Inch.

History:
Incorporated on 17 July 1919 to supply electricity in the Township of Hanover, Lehigh County, Hanover Township Lehigh Electric Co. was consolidated and merged with six other non-operating companies on 25 July 1919 to form Industrial Power Co.

370. HARRISBURG AND CUMBERLAND VALLEY RAILWAY COMPANY (Non-operating).
Cumberland County, Lower Allen Township.
1895 to 1904, 1 Linear Inch.

History:
Incorporated on 21 February 1895 to operate an electric railway in the Townships of Lower Allen and East Pennsboro, Cumberland County, Harrisburg and Cumberland Valley Railway Co. merged into Harrisburg and Mechanicsburg Electric Railway Co. on 7 August 1895.

371. HARRISBURG AND MECHANICSBURG ELECTRIC RAILWAY COMPANY (Operating).
Franklin County, Chambersburg Borough.
1892 to 1929, 1 Linear Foot.

History:
Harrisburg and Mechanicsburg Electric Railway Co. was incorporated 17 May 1892. In July of 1898, Cumberland Valley Railroad Co. secured a controlling interest in the company, and in 1904 leased it to the Valley Traction Co. In January of 1913, the Valley Traction Co. merged into the Electric Railways Co., taking its lease of Harrisburg and Mechanicsburg Electric Railway Co. with it.

Administrative Records:
Minute Books, 1892-1929 (4 Volumes)
Stock Certificate Books, 1892-1929 (2 Volumes)
Papers, Tally Sheets and other Supporting Papers for Annual and Special Meetings of Stockholders, 1919-1929

Operating Records:
Cash and Time Book, 1901-1904
Materials and Supplies Ledger, 1902-1904

Scope and Content Note:
The Minute Books document routine stockholders' and directors' meetings with the earlier ones containing treasurer's reports. Also included are copies of the 1913 consolidation and merger agreement that describe the company's various landholdings and street railway routes. The Time and Cash Book is a monthly record of daily operations listing individual conductors, motormen, cars, and number of passengers carried on each route.

372. THE HARRISBURG AND RIVERTON STREET RAILWAY COMPANY (Non-operating).
Franklin County, Chambersburg Borough.
1903 to 1912, 2 Linear Inches.

History:
Although incorporated 15 July 1903 for the purpose of constructing and operating an electric railway from the City of Harrisburg to the power house of the Cumberland Light, Heat & Power Company in Riverton, Cumberland County, The Harrisburg and Riverton Street Railway Co. does not appear to have actually been an operating company. Late in 1904, the company's stock was bought by Valley Traction Syndicate, which then conveyed it to Valley Traction Co. On 10 January 1913, The Harrisburg and Riverton Street Railway Co. was consolidated and merged with five other companies to form Harrisburg and Mechanicsburg Electric Railway Co.

373. HARRISBURG ELECTRIC COMPANY (Operating).
Dauphin County, Harrisburg City.
1892 to 1899, 1 1/2 Linear Feet.

History:
Excelsior Electric Co. of Harrisburg was incorporated to supply electricity in the City of Harrisburg on 23 February 1887. In 1888 it ran into financial difficulties and almost went into receivership, but its Brooklyn based parent company took control and began to expand the company's facilities. Early in 1892, the company's stock was acquired by its chief competitor, The Harrisburg Electric Light Co., which then merged into The Excelsior Electric Co. on 12 April 1892. Two days later, the company was re-incorporated as Harrisburg Electric Co. Finally, on 30 September 1899 this company merged into The Harrisburg Light Heat and Power Co.

Administrative Records:
Minute Books, 1892-1899 (2 Volumes)
Stock Certificate Books, 1892-1899 (2 Volumes)

Operating Records:
General Ledger, 1892-1899
Cashbooks, 1892-1899 (3 Volumes)
Daily Cashbooks and Day Books, 1892-1899 (3 Volumes)
Payroll Ledger, 1892-1899

Scope and Content Note:
The Minute Books of Harrisburg Electric Co. document routine directors' meetings. They include monthly accounts of expenditures and earnings, and annual reports. The 1893-1899 volume includes information on the company's contract to light the State Capitol Buildings in Harrisburg, as well as a list of customers disconnected and retained in Steelton.

374. THE HARRISBURG ELECTRIC LIGHT COMPANY (Operating).
Dauphin County, Harrisburg City.
1884 to 1892, 1 Linear foot.

History:
The Harrisburg Electric Light Company was organized in April 1884 by Edison Electric Light Company of New York to supply electricity for lighting and power in the city of Harrisburg. The parent Edison company licensed the Harrisburg company to install an Edison central station for direct current incandescent lighting and supplied it with skilled electricians to construct and operate the station. When the central station commenced operations in May 1885, it was already providing service for over 3200 sixteen-candlepower incandescent lamps to commercial and industrial customers in the city, and was one of few stations in the United States to provide 24-hour electric service. In 1886 the licensing agreement with the parent Edison company was modified to enable the Harrisburg company to furnish electric power for motors produced by Sprague Electric Railway and Motor Company. The installation of a three-horsepower motor to drive the printing press of the Harrisburg Evening Star in November 1886 was one of the earliest such installations of a Sprague DC motor for industrial purposes in this country. Also in 1886, the Harrisburg company obtained permission from the parent Edison company to install Thomson-Houston arc lighting equipment to meet a growing demand for such service from commercial and government customers in the city.

History:
Until late 1887 the company enjoyed a monopoly in Harrisburg. From that point on, however, the company faced what its president termed "harassing warfare" from a new firm, Excelsior Electric Company of Harrisburg, organized by Excelsior Electric Company of Brooklyn. Initial efforts to resolve the rivalry between the two companies turned into a classic example of what electrical historian Thomas P. Hughes has called the "battle of the systems". The Excelsior firm installed the Westinghouse system of alternating current for incandescent lighting and erected a hydroelectric plant to furnish cheaper electric power that that provided by the Harrisburg company. The Harrisburg company retaliated by slashing its rates, upgrading the capacity of its DC central station, and redoubling its efforts to secure industrial, commercial, and governmental customers. In 1891 a syndicate formed by Thomas-Houston Electric Light Company and several other arc lighting manufacturers, acquired control of the Excelsior Electric Company of Harrisburg and began negotiations with the Harrisburg company to resolve the situation in the city. Under an agreement reached in December 1891, the Harrisburg company acquied the stock controlled by the Thomson-Houston syndicate, and in turn consolidated and merged with the Excelsior company. This action, consummated in April 1892, led to the formation of The Harrisburg Electric Company.

Administrative Records:
Minute Books, 1884-1892
Stock Certificate Book, 1885-1892

Operating Records:
General Ledger, 1884-1892
Journal, 1885-1892
Cashbook, 1884-1892
Daily Cashbook and Daybook, 1891-1892
Invoices - Scrapbook Form, 1884-1887

Scope and Content Note:
The Minute Book of The Harrisburg Electric Company is a rich source furnishing detailed information on all aspects of the company's organization and operations. The licensing agreements between the company and Edison Electric Light Company of New York, and between it and Sprague Electric Railway and Motor Company are summarized and reproduced. Entries fully document the stock exchanges, and the supply of technical expertise and Edison electrical equipment to the Harrisburg company, which took place under the terms of the licensing agreements. Annual reports contained in the Minute Book describe the extension of electric service to commercial establishments, factories, and government offices, and the installations of Sprague electric motors and Thomson-Houston arc lighting equipment. Annual financial statements accompanying the annual reports trace the impact of the competition from Excelsior Electric Company of Harrisburg upon the Harrisburg company's profits from 1883 to 1891, while the minutes document the responses by company management to the challenge posed by their rival. A separate minute book, "Minutes of meetings of syndicate in the matter of purchase of plant of the Excelsior Electric Company of Harrisburg." covering the period 1891-1892, summarizes negotiations between the Harrisburg company and the Thomson-Houston syndicate which controlled the Excelsior company. The book also contains copies of letters between the Harrisburg company and Samuel Insull, second vice-president of Edison General Electric Company, regarding these negotiations.

375. HARRISBURG ELECTRIC SERVICE COMPANY (Non-operating).
Dauphin County, Harrisburg City.
1911 to 1913, 1/2 Linear Foot.

History:
Incorporated 24 July 1911 to supply electricity in the City of Harrisburg, Dauphin County, Harrisburg Electric Service Co. was consolidated and merged with another company on 30 June 1913 to form Harrisburg Light and Power Co., No.2.

376. HARRISBURG LIGHT AND POWER COMPANY, NO. 1 (Operating).
Dauphin County, Harrisburg City.
1912 to 1913, 1/2 Linear Foot.

History:
Harrisburg Light and Power Co., No. 1, was incorporated 22 July 1912 to supply electricity to the City of Harrisburg. As part of its effort to control this market, the company soon acquired The Harrisburg Light Heat and Power Co., and the Harrisburg Steam Heat and Power Co. Finally, on 13 June 1913 it consolidated and merged with Harrisburg Electric Service Co. to form Harrisburg Light and Power Co., No. 2.

Administrative Records:
Stock Certificate Books, 1912-1913 (3 Volumes)

377. HARRISBURG LIGHT AND POWER COMPANY, NO. 2 (Operating).
Dauphin County, Harrisburg City.
1911 to 1931, 18 Linear Feet.

History:
Harrisburg Light and Power Co., No. 2, was incorporated 23 October 1913 following the consolidation and merger of Harrisburg Light and Power Co., No. 1, with Harrisburg Electric Service Co. The new company supplied electricity and steam heat to the City of Harrisburg and surrounding communities. Between 1913 and 1928 it extended its area of operation to the Townships of Lower Paxtang, Lower Swarta, Middle Paxtang, West Hanover, and Susquehanna (all in Dauphin County). In 1926, the company's stock was acquired by Lehigh Power Securities Corp., which in 1928 merged it into Pennsylvania Power & Light Co.

Administrative Records:
Minute Books, 1913-1928 (7 Volumes)
Stock Certificate Book—Common, 1913-1926
Stock Certificate Books—Preferred, 1913-1915
Holders of Preferred Capital Stock, 1917-1928
Transfers of Preferred Capital Stock, 1916-1928
Redeemed and Cancelled Gold Notes, 1918-1923
Redeemed and Cancelled Sinking Fund Gold Notes, 1921-1924
Annual Reports By Vice-President & General Manager, 1915-1925
Elmira Stock Purchase Data, Mortgage, Indenture & Franchises, 1912-1918

Operating Records:
FINANCIAL RECORDS
General Ledgers, 1915-1928 (2 Volumes)
Journals, 1912-1925 (3 Volumes)
Journal Entry Register, 1925-1927
Cashbooks, 1912-1927 (2 Volumes)
Record of Cash Receipts, 1927-1928
Record of Cash Disbursements, 1927-1928
Daily Cash Receipts, 1915-1926
Summary of Cash, 1927-1928
Audited Voucher Registers, 1912-1928 (14 Volumes)
Indexes to Audited Vouchers, 1912-1914 (2 Volumes)
Accounts Payable, 1927-1928
Accounts Receivable, 1926-1928
Accounts Receivable - Miscellaneous, 1927-1928
Detail Ledgers, 1915-1928 (3 Volumes)
Detail Ledger - Materials & Supplies, 1915-1924
Materials & Supplies , 1916-1927 (8 Volumes)
Accrual Record, 1913-1919
Financial Reports - Monthly, 1911-1912
Financial Reports - Yearly, 1913-1926 (14 Volumes)
Expenditure Requisitions Ledger, 1918-1927 (3 Volumes)
CONSTRUCTION RECORDS
Construction Data, 1912-1927 (6 Volumes)
Construction and Bond Sales, 1912-1927 (4 Volumes)
Construction Costs - Steam Department, 1914-1918
Report on Actual Cost of Steam Heating System, 1923
Statistical Reports - Electric, 1913-1926
Statistical Reports - Steam, 1915-1925
Record of Increase of Indebtedness, 1913-1928
Analysis of Plant & Expenses for Operating Penn Harris Hotel Steam Plant, 1912-1925
Additions to Plant, 1912-1915
Report of Work Done At Steelton Office, 1927
Inter-Company Eliminations on Comparative Income Account, 1928
Analysis of General Ledger Accounts, 1913-1926
Reports of Construction Made to Fidelity Trust Co., N.Y., 1927-1928
PERSONNEL RECORDS
Payroll Statements in Connection with Public Liabilities Insurance, 1927
Payrolls - Special, 1926-1927 (2 Volumes)
Payrolls - General, 1926-1928 (11 Volumes)
Audit Reports, 1916-1925 (12 Volumes)

Scope and Content Note:
The Minute Books of Harrisburg Light and Power Co. are a record of directors' and stockholders' meetings. They document the large number of mergers that took place during the company's period of expansion. The Correspondence File traces the company's relationship with the Pennsylvania Public Service Commission. Annual Reports review routine operations providing details about construction projects. Special Payrolls record the salaries of executives and office personnel while Construction Data includes cost summaries, blueprints and expenditure authorization forms.

378. THE HARRISBURG LIGHT, HEAT AND POWER COMPANY (Operating).
Dauphin County, Harrisburg City.
1899 to 1912, 4 1/2 Linear Feet.

History:
The Harrisburg Light, Heat and Power Co. was incorporated 14 July 1899 to supply electricity in Harrisburg. After a period of expansion, in 1911 its stock was sold to the New York-based United Gas and Electric Co. which proceeded to organize Harrisburg Electric Service Co. as a holding company for it. On August 6, 1912 the company merged into Harrisburg Light and Power Co., No. 1.

Administrative Records:
Minute Books, 1899-1912 (2 Volumes)
Stock Certificate Books, 1899-1912 (4 Volumes)

Operating Records:
General Ledgers, 1899-1912 (3 Volumes)
Journal, 1899-1912
Cashbooks, 1899-1909 (3 Volumes)
Daily Cashbooks and Daybooks, 1900-1910 (11 Volumes)
Daily Cash Receipts, 1910-1912 (2 Volumes)
Payroll Ledger, 1901-1911 (2 Volumes)
Memo of Inspection, S.J. Dill, 1911
Report on Harrisburg Situation, Lamar Lyndon, 1912

Scope and Content Note:
The Minute Books of The Harrisburg Light, Heat and Power Co. document directors' meetings and contain financial reports. S.J. Dill's "Memo of Inspection," a survey of Harrisburg undertaken for United Gas & Electric Co., compares the finances and facilities of The Harrisburg Light, Heat and Power Co. with those of its major competitor, Paxtang Electric Co. As part of his report, Dill described Harrisburg's major social and economic institutions: businesses, churches, schools, and secret societies. Lamar Lyndon's Auditor's Report analyzed Harrisburg's electric generating and distribution system, and developed a rationale for merger and consolidation.

379. THE HARRISBURG STEAM HEAT AND POWER COMPANY (Operating).
Dauphin County, Harrisburg City.
1886 to 1922, 3 1/2 Linear Feet.

History:
Harrisburg Steam Heat and Power Co. was incorporated 13 October 1886 to supply steam heating in the City of Harrisburg. In 1887 the company received the contract to heat the State Capitol Buildings. In 1912 it purchased its own fleet of dredges and barges and began to supply itself with river coal. On 15 February 1913 the company merged into Harrisburg Light and Power Co., No. 1.

Administrative Records:
Minute Books, 1886-1913(2 Volumes)
Stock Certificate Books, 1887-1913 (2 Volumes)
History of the Company, T.M. Zeiders, c. 1922

Operating Records:
General Ledgers, 1886-1913 (4 Volumes)
Journals, 1886-1913 (4 Volumes)
Cashbooks, 1886-1913 (6 Volumes)
Financial Reports, 1897-1913 (2 Volumes)
Financial Report Data—Miscellaneous, 1905-1913

Scope and Content Note:
The Minute Books of Harrisburg Steam Heat and Power Co. document the development of the company's generating and distribution systems. Financial Reports detail net value, liabilities, assets, earnings, and expenditures, while the "History" provides an overview of the company's three decades of expansion and extension of service.

380. HARRISBURG TERMINAL COMPANY
(Operating).
Dauphin County, Harrisburg City.
1916 to 1934, 3 Linear Feet.

History:
Harrisburg Terminal Co. was incorporated 1 May 1918 for the purpose of acquiring property to construct a railway terminal building, which was never built. The company's stock was owned by Valley Railways until February 1926 when it was acquired by Lehigh Power Securities Corp., which in turn sold it to Pennsylvania Realty & Investment Co. in November of 1933. The company was dissolved on 19 December 1934.

Administrative Records:
Minute Books, 1918-1934 (2 Volumes)
Secretary's Papers of Meetings, 1927-1934
Stock Certificate Book, 1918-1933
Stock Ledger, 1926

Operating Records:
General Ledgers, 1921-1934 (2 Volumes)
Journal, 1921-1926
Journal Entry Register, 1926-1934
Record of Cash Receipts, 1927-1934
Record of Cash Disbursements, 1927-1934
Summary of Cash, 1927-1934
Audited Voucher Register, 1927-1934
Accounts Payable, 1927-1934
Bill Register, 1928-1929
Detail Ledger, 1926-1934
Expenditure Requisitions, 1927-1930
Detailed Cost of Construction, 1927-1930
Analysis of Charges to Expenditure Requisitions, 1927-1930
Agreements, 1927-1931
Sale of Real Estate, 1930
Fixed Capital, Operating Revenue & Expenses, 1916-1929
Comparative Income Account—Trial Balance & Balance Sheets, 1926-1928
Bills, 1928-1929
Audit Reports, 1921-1932 (6 Volumes)

Scope and Content Note:
The Minute Books detail routine stockholder's and directors' meetings, while the Secretary's Papers document elections to the Board of Directors. The Stock Certificate Book gives useful information about stock transactions. The Audit Report contains standard financial data on capitalization, assets and liabilities. Detailed Cost of Construction documents expenditure requisitions and describes the company's real estate transactions.

381. HARTLETON POWER AND LIGHT COMPANY
(Non-operating).
Union County, Hartleton Borough.
1925 to 1930, 1 1/2 Linear Feet.

History:
Incorporated 12 January 1926 to supply electricity in the Borough of Hartleton, Union County, Hartleton Power and Light Co. was leased to Laurel Park Power and Light Co. on 7 September 1929. This lease was terminated on 31 December 1930, when both the lessor and lessee were merged into Pennsylvania Power & Light Co.

382. HARWOOD COAL COMPANY (Operating).
Lehigh County, Allentown City.
1902 to 1932, 13 Linear Feet.

History:
Harwood Coal Co. was incorporated 2 February 1907 as the successor to Calvin Pardee and Co. Its main office was in Allentown, from which the company operated its anthracite coal mines and culm banks. It also leased coal basins from Lehigh Valley Coal Co. On 25 May 1907 the company's stock was acquired by Harwood Electric

Power Co. Two years later, control passed to The Harwood Electric Co. Under a 1 May 1917 contract the Harwood Coal Co. became a joint concern with the Cranberry Creek Coal Co. (a subsidiary of Lehigh Coal and Navigation Co.), with Cranberry Creek managing its operations and selling its products. In 1920, The Harwood Electric Co. merged into Pennsylvania Power & Light and brought the Harwood Coal Co. with it. The Harwood Coal Co., however, soon began to feel the financial impact of having to sell its coal to The Harwood Electric Co. at discount prices. After a decade of decline, the company was dissolved in 1932.

Administrative Records:
Minute Books, 1906-1932 (3 Volumes)
Stock Certificate Book, 1907-1931
Stock Transfer Record, 1917-1931
Stock Ledger, 1907-1931
Annual Reports, 1917-1926 (2 Volumes)

Operating Records:
FINANCIAL RECORDS
General Ledgers, 1902-1932 (6 Volumes)
Journals, 1902-1928 (6 Volumes)
Cashbooks, 1902-1920 (4 Volumes)
Cashbook—Supplementary, 1914-1917
Cashbooks—Auxiliary, 1914-1916 (2 Volumes)
Summaries of Cash, 1925-1932 (2 Volumes)
Cash Receipts, 1910-1924 (4 Volumes)
Cash Received, 1924-1925
Record of Cash Disbursements, 1925-1932
CONSUMER RECORDS
Statement of Unpaid Vouchers, 1914-1916
Invoice Records. 1908-1914 (2 Volumes)
Accounts Receivable, 1913-1932 (3 Volumes)
Summary of Accounts Receivable—Miscellaneous, 1928-1931 (2 Volumes)
List of Bills, 1922
Statements of Bills Rendered, 1916-1928
Detail Ledger, 1917-1928
Expenditure Requisitions and Retirements, 1915-1916
Detail of Cost Study and Fixed Capital, 1926-1927
Consumers Ledger, 1907-1908
COAL PRODUCTION RECORDS
of Mining Coal, 1902-1916 (2 Volumes)
Cost of Coal Production—Assembling Sheets, 1915-1927 (2 Volumes)
Summary of Stock Account, 1926
Fresh Mined Coal Account, 1920-1924
Allocation of Coal Cost and Size, 1915-1927
Sales, Tonnage and Average Price, 1926-1928
Miscellaneous Coal Accounts, 1926
Allocation by Sizes of Coal Produced Reports, 1916-1917
Coal Stock Account Reports, 1915-1930 (3 Volumes)
Cost of Coal Production Reports, 1914-1927 (5 Volumes)
Statements Showing Tonnage of Coal on Hand, Purchased, & Mined, 1926-1928
Manufacturing Cost of Harwood Plant, 1919
Statement of Annual Earnings, 1921
Summary of Financial Situation, 1917
PERSONNEL RECORDS
Compensation Payrolls, 1916-1928 (3 Volumes)
Payroll Summaries and Vouchers, 1914-1925
Retroactive Payroll, 1920
Payrolls, Private, 1911-1920 (2 Volumes)
Payroll Distribution, 1927-1927
Workmen's Compensation Insurance, Voucher Report, 1916-1917
Time Sheet—Special Payrolls, 1924-1928
Inside Timebooks, 1927-1928 (7 Volumes)
Workmen's Compensation Insurance Accrual Statements, 1928-1929 (2 Volumes)
Voucher Record, 1914-1921 D06E
Distribution of Bills Rendered, 1916 D06E
Payrolls, 1916-1927 (4 Volumes)
Subscription to U.S. Liberty Loans, 1919
Liberty Loan Stubs, 1919
AUDIT REPORTS,

Scope and Content Note:
The Minute Books of the Harwood Coal Co. document stockholders' and directors' meetings. Annual Reports describe company operations: maintenance, repairs, accidents, labor relations and strikes. Special Payrolls record the wages of foremen and inspectors, while Private Payrolls record wages of engineering and offfice staff. The Retroactive Payroll documents back wages that were due to employees as a result of the award of the Anthracite Coal Strike Commission (1902). The Workmen's Compensation Insurance Voucher Report records payments to the doctors and the hospitals that provided miners with medical care, while the Compensation Payrolls document pensions that were paid to miners' widows and orphaned children.

383. THE HARWOOD COMPANY (Non-operating).
Luzrne County, Hazle Township.
1912, 2 Linear Inches.

History:
Incorporated on 6 February 1912 to supply electricity in the Township of Hazle, Luzerne County, The Harwood Co. was consolidated and merged with eleven other companies on 23 February 1912 to form The Harwood Electric Co.

384. HARWOOD ELECTRIC COMPANY (Operating).
Luzerne County, Hazle Township.
1909 to 1912, 2 Linear Feet.

History:
Harwood Electric Co. was formed by the consolidation and merger of Harwood Electric Power Co., Consumers Electric Light and Power Co. of Hazelton, and McAdoo Electric Co. with nine non-operating companies on 23 June 1909. Under that agreement, Harwood Electric Co. supplied electricity to the Township of Hazle, the City of Hazleton,the Boroughs of McAdoo and Freeland, and eight other Townships in the Counties of Schuylkill and Luzerne. On 23 February 1912, the company was consolidated and merged with Beaver Electric Co. and ten non-operating companies to form The Harwood Electric Co.

Administrative Records:
Minute Book, 1909-1912
Stock Certificate Book—Common, 1909-1912
Stock Certificate Book—Preferred, 1909-1911
Stock Ledger, 1909
Bond Record, 1909-1910

Operating Records:
FINANCIAL RECORDS
General Ledgers, 1909-1912
Journal, 1909-1912
Cashbook, 1909-1911
Cash Received and Check Register, 1910-1911
Daybook, 1909-1911
Voucher Registers, 1910-1911 (3 Volumes)
Balance Sheets, 1910-1911
Miscellaneous Financial Statements, 1909-1911
Monthly Reports and Preliminaries, 1909-1911
Audit Reports, 1909-1910 (4 Volumes)
PERSONNEL RECORDS
Summary of Payrolls, 1909-1911
Payrolls, 1909-1912
Payroll Distribution, 1909-1912
Time Sheets, 1909-1912 (8 Volumes)

Scope and Content Note:
The Minute Book contains a copy of the agreement under which the company was formed, its bylaws, minutes of directors' meetings, and a copy of the 1912 consolidation and merger agreement. The records also document the company's contractual relationships under which it supplied power to various local concerns such as the Lehigh Valley Coal Co. Additional information on this company will be found in The "Historical Report of The Harwood Electric Co. and Its Antcedent and Allied Companies," filed with The records of the Harwood Electric Co.

385. THE HARWOOD ELECTRIC COMPANY
(Operating).
Luzerne County, Hazleton City.
1907 to 1929, 20 Linear Feet.

History:
The Harwood Electric Co., which supplied electricity to much of Eastern Pennsylvania's anthracite region, was formed as a result of the 23 February 1912 merger of Harwood Electric Co., Beaver Meadow Electric Co. and ten non-operating companies. On March 25, 1913 the company acquired the franchises and properties of the Hazleton Electric Co. and thus greatly expanded its area of operations. Later that year, Lehigh Navigation Electric Co. acquired a controlling interest in The Harwood Electric Co. Thereafter, although the two companies kept separate identities they were run by the same management which carefully coordinated their operations. In 1915, The Harwood Electric Co. constructed a transmission line from its Harwood plant to the Lehigh Navigation Electric Company's main power facility at Hauto. This completed the integration of the two systems. The Harwood Electric Co. continued to expand its area of operations during 1917 and 1918, as it acquired charter rights in Montour, Columbia, Northcumberland and Schuylkill Counties. Despite this growth, The Harwood Electric Co. continued to concentrate on the development and enlargement of its Harwood power plant while simultaneously phasing out subsidiary company power plants. As a result, by 1918 the Harwood plant had a capacity of 33,000-kw. On 4 June 1920, The Harwood Electric Co. was consolidated and merged with seven other companies to form Pennsylvania Power & Light.

Administrative Records:
Minute Books, 1912-1920 (2 Volumes)
Annual Stockholders Reports, 1912-1916 (5 Volumes)
Corporate History
STOCK AND BOND RECORDS
Stock Capitalization Book—Common, 1912-1920 (5 Volumes)
Stock Capitalization Book—Preferred, 1912-1920 (4 Volumes)
Stock Transfer Record—Common, 1913-1920 (3 Volumes)
Stock Transfer Record—Preferred, 1913-1920
Stock Ledger—Common, 1912-1922
Stock Ledger—Preferred, 1912-1920
Stock Ledger of Subsidiary Companies, 1907-1929
Securities Owned, 1912-1914
CORRESPONDENCE, 1913-1919

Operating Records:
FINANCIAL RECORDS
General Ledgers, 1912-1920 (3 Volumes)
Journal, 1912-1920 (3 Volumes)
Cashbooks, 1914-1920 (2 Volumes)
Cashbook and Check Register, 1912-1914
Cashbooks—Auxiliary, 1914-1916 (2 Volumes)
Cashbooks—Supplementary, 1914-1919 (2 Volumes)
Cashbook—Daily, 1914-1918
Cashbook—Daily Cash Receipts, 1914-1915
Accounts Payable, 1914-1920 (3 Volumes)
Balance of Accounts Payable, 1919
Construction Contract Information Sheets, 1917-1918
Cost of Plant 1918
Statements of Charges to Capital, 1918-1920 (2 Volumes)
Accrual Records, 1914-1920 (2 Volumes)
Balance and Taxes Accrued, 1918
Compensation Register, 1916
Accident Register, 1916-1917
Fire Insurance Register, 1915-1917
Coal Received, Consumed and Wasted, 1912-1918
Monthly Returns of Supplies on Hand, 1917
Notes and Bills Payable and Receivable, 1913-1917
Notes Receivable Register, 1913-1919
Statement of Accounts Payable and Journal Entry for Rents Accrued, 1919-1920
Accounts Receivable Ledger, 1916-1918
Merchandise Sales Reports, 1919-1920
Daily Operating Data, 1918-1919
Kilowatt Hours Statistics, 1912-1917
Rate Increase Statement, 1917
Statement of Consumers Ledger Accounts, 1912-1919
Statement of Bad Accounts, 1914-1916
Report of Outstanding Accounts, 1916
MISCELLANEOUS REPORTS
Working Papers of Calvin Pardee Case, 1916-1917
Bills, 1917-1920 (7 Volumes)
Data for Poor's Manual, 1917
Account of Wilmot Engineering Co., 1913-1916
Agreement with Shenandoah Light, Heat and Power Co., 1912
Balance Sheets, 1914-1920 (2 Volumes)
Statement of Income and Profit & Loss, 1913-1918
Monthly Reports, 1915-1918 (2 Volumes)
Financial Reports, 1917-1919

Commercial Reports, 1915-1920
Income Tax Reports, 191301916
PERSONNEL RECORDS
Payrolls, 1912-1920 (3 Volumes)
Payrolls and Distribution, 1912-1919 (2 Volumes)
Payrolls—Workmen's Compensation, 1916-1920 (2 Volumes)
Workmen's Compensation Vouchers, 1916-1917
Statement of Office Salaries, 1916
Earnings of Employees for Income Tax, 1914-1919 (2 Volumes)
Time Sheets, 1912-1919 (3 Volumes)
Audit Reports, 1912-1920 (17 Volumes)

Scope and Content Note:

The Minute Books of The Harwood Electric Co. (1912-1920) contain minutes of directors' meetings, a copy of the consolidation agreement by which the company was formed, annual reports, a copy of the company's regulations and rate schedule, listings of the number of shares of subsidiary companies owned, and a copy of the consolidation agreement which formed Pennsylvania Power & Light. Also included are copies of agreements and contracts for the purchase of electrical equipment. Correspondence of Edward Hughes, purchasing agent, relates to equipment ordered and documents various maintenance problems. There are some schematics attached to these letters. The correspondence of J.S. Wise, general manager (1916-1921), concerns fuel supplies that were largely drawn from the mines of the Harwood Coal Co. A map of these holdings is included.

Other files also document the concern over dwindling coal reserves. The Working Papers of Calvin Pardee Case clearly show that the Pardee family, which had founded the original Harwood Electric Co., felt that they had been shortchanged by the 1912 merger agreement. Finally, the "Historical Report of The Harwood Electric Co. and Its Antecedent and Allied Companies" provides a good overview of the relationship that the company had with its subsidiaries.

386. HARWOOD ELECTRIC POWER COMPANY (Operating).
Luzerne County, Hazleton City.
1906 to 1909, 1 1/2 Linear Feet.

History:

Harwood Electric Power Co. was incorporated 10 January 1907, to supply electricity in Hazle Township, Luzerne County. It was organized by Calvin Pardee, an independent coal operator who wanted to obtain low cost electricity for his extensive mining operations in the Hazleton area. The company's generating plant was set up on property acquired from Mr. Pardee, adjacent to his Harwood Coal Co. Taking over a temporary generating plant, he soon boosted its capacity to 1100-kw. The plant supplied electricity to the Harwood Coal Co., and electric lines were erected to connect the plant with the surrounding communities of McAdoo, Hazleton, and Lattimer. In 1907, the company acquired the stock of both the Harwood Coal Co. and the Harwood Store Co. Harwood Electric Power Co. was consolidated and merged on 23 June 1909 with Consumers Electric Light and Power Co. of Hazleton, Pa., McAdoo Electric Co., and nine non-operating companies to form Harwood Electric Co.

Administrative Records:
Minute Book, 1906-1909
Stock Certificate Book, 1907-1909

Operating Records:
General Ledger, 1907-1909
Journal, 1907-1909
Cashbook, 1907-1909
Accounts Payable, 1906-1907
Payrolls, 1907-1909
Summary of Payrolls, 1907-1909
Statement from Girard National Bank, 1909
Voucher Register, 1907-1909
Time Sheets, 1907-1909

Scope and Content Note:

The Minute Book of Harwood Electric Power Co. documents the Pardee family holdings and interests in the company, and also contains routine minutes of directors' meetings, the company's bylaws, and information on the 1909 consolidation and merger. Also mentioned are the company's purchase of lands near the City of Hazleton and the supplying of electricity to Consumers Electric Co. Additional information on this company will be found in the "Historical Report of The Harwood Electric Co. and Its Antecendet and Allied Companies," filed with the records of The Harwood Electric Co.

387. HARWOOD STORE COMPANY (Operating).
Luzerne County, Hazleton City.
1907 to 1936, 9 Linear Feet.

History:

Harwood Store Co. was a company store owned and operated by Harwood Coal Co., serving coal miners living in Harwood Village near Hazleton. It was incorporated 23 May 1907 by Calvin Pardee, and retained all the assets and property of an earlier store, operated at the same location by the Pardee family since 1875. Two years later, all the stock of the company was transferred to Harwood Electric Co., which continued to operate the store.

Administrative Records:
Minute Books, 1907-1932 (3 Volumes)
Stock Certificate Book, 1907-1931
Stock Transfer Record, 1917-1931
Stock Ledger, 1907-1931
Annual Reports, 1914-1926 (2 Volumes)

Operating Records:
FINANCIAL RECORDS
General Ledgers, 1907-1932 (4 Volumes)
Journal, 1907-1936 (7 Volumes)
Cashbook, 1907-1919 (3 Volumes)
Cashbooks - Auxiliary, 1914-1916 (2 Volumes)
Cashbooks - Supplementary, 1917-1919 (2 Volumes)
Cash Received and Check Register, 1912-1916
Check Register, 1919-1923
Record of Cash Disbursements, 1925-1932
Cash Received, 1919-1935 (2 Volumes)
Notes Payable, 1916-1917
Accounts Payable, 1914-1930 (4 Volumes)
Summary of Cash, 1925-1928
Accrual Record, 1914-1932 (3 Volumes)

Workmen's Compensation Insurance and Tax, 1918-1922
Statement of Bad Accounts, 1915-1917
Accounts Receivable, 1919-1930 (2 Volumes)
Sales and Collection Register, 1924
Sales, 1915
Balance Sheets, 1907-1918
Construction Ledger, 1916-1917
AUDIT REPORTS, 1913-1931 (13 Volumes)

Scope and Content Note:
The Minute Books of the Harwood Store Co. deal almost entirely with routine matters such as stockholders' and directors' meetings. They do, however, clearly establish the interests of the Pardee family in this company. The Sales and Collection Register is an alphabetical list showing the amount of money that was deducted from employee paychecks for company store purchases.

388. HATFIELD ELECTRIC LIGHT AND POWER COMPANY (Non-operating).
Montgomery County, Hatfield Borough.
1913, 1 Linear Inch.

History:
Hatfield Electric Light and Power Co. was incorporated 6 November 1913 to supply electricity in the Borough of Hatfield, Montgomery County. It was consolidated and merged with three other companies on 24 November 1913 to form Excelsior Electric Light, Power and Gas Co., No. 2.

389. HATFIELD ELECTRIC LIGHT AND POWER COMPANY (Non-operating).
Montgomery County, Hatfield Township.
1913 to 1914, 1 Linear Inch.

History:
Hatfield Electric Light and Power Co. was incorporated 8 December 1913 to supply electricity in the Township of Hatfield, Montgomery County. It was merged into Lehigh Valley Light and Power Co., No. 3, on 29 December 1913.

390. HATFIELD TOWNSHIP ELECTRIC LIGHT AND POWER COMPANY (Non-operating).
Montgomery County, Hatfield Township.
1918, 1 Linear Inch.

History:
Hatfield Township Electric Light and Power Co. was incorporated 19 March 1918 to supply electricity in the Township of Hatfield, Montgomery County. On 10 April 1918 it was merged and consolidated with three other companies to form Excelsior Electric Light, Power and Gas Co., No. 3.

391. HAYCOCK-BUCKS POWER & LIGHT COMPANY (Non-operating).
Bucks County, Haycock Township.
1927 to 1928, 2 Linear Inches.

History:
Incorporated on 30 November 1927 to supply electricity in the Township of Haycock, Bucks County, Haycock-Bucks Power & Light Co. was merged into Pennsylvania Power & Light Co. on 10 December 1927.

392. HAZARD ELECTRIC COMPANY (Non-operating).
Lehigh County, Hanover Township.
1911 to 1913, 1 Linear Inch.

History:
Incorporated on 4 April 1911 to supply electricity in the Township of Hanover, Lehigh County, Hazard Electric Co. was merged and consolidated with 37 other non-operating companies on 23 December 1912 to form Lehigh Navigation Electric Co., No.2.

393. HAZLE TOWNSHIP WATER COMPANY (Operating).
Luzerne County, Hazle Township.
1910 to 1951, 3 1/2 Linear Feet.

History:
Hazle Township Water Co. was incorporated 3 February 1910 to supply water in the Township of Hazle, Luzerne County. The company obtained water from Wyoming Valley Water Supply Co. which it then sold to its two main customers, Harwood Coal Co. and Harwood Electric Co. In 1912 Harwood Electric Co. acquired a majority of the company's stock. On 31 October 1913 Hazle Township Water Co. bought a tract of land with water rights from The Milnesville Water Co. This tract also included pumps, motor transformers, wells, various buildings, a pump house, and a reservoir. In exchange for this property, Hazle Township Water Co. took over The Milnesville Water Company's debts to Harwood Coal Co. and The Harwood Electric Co. In 1920, Pennsylvania Power & Light Co. gained control of Hazle Township Water Co.

Administrative Records:
Annual Meeting of Stockholders, 1944-1949 (3 Volumes)
Stock Ledger, Harwood Electric Co.- Subsidiary Companies, 1910-1936
Secretary's Papers of Director's Meetings, 1943-1949 (7 Volumes)
Bylaws, 1940

Operating Records:
FINANCIAL RECORDS
Journals, 1910-1921 (2 Volumes)
Journal Entries, 1914-1918
Cash Receipts and Check Register, 1910-1923 (2 Volumes)
Cashbook, 1914-1919
Cash Received, 1919-1922
Record of Cash Receipts and Disbursements, 1925-1951
Summary of Cash, 1925-1948 (2 Volumes)
Audited Voucher Register, 1914-1918
Voucher Register, 1910-1918
List of Unpaid Vouchers, 1914-1916
Expense Ledger Sheets, 1910-1914
Detail of Cost Study and Fixed Capital, 1926-1927
Statement of Books, 1910-1914
Balance Sheets, 1912-1917
Balance Sheets and Summary of Earnings, 1917-1920
Financial Reports, 1917-1919
Financial and Operating Reports, 1946-1951
Reconcilement of Bank Balances, 1920-1922
Expenditure Requisitions, 1929-1950 (2 Volumes)
Bill Register, 1919-1920

Construction Detail Ledger, 1929-1950
Bills, 1919-1951 (4 Volumes)
CONSUMER RECORDS
Summary of Accounts Receivable—Consumers, 1929-1951 (7 Volumes)
Summary of Accounts Receivable—Miscellaneous, 1926-1933 (5 Volumes)
Summary of Consumers' Deposits, 1936-1951
AUDIT REPORTS, 1913-1932 (9 Volumes)
Construction Budget, 1949

Scope and Content Note:
The records of Hazle Township Water Co. consist mainly of routine financial accounts kept during the company's long existence. Additional information concerning this company may be found in the "Historical Report of The Harwood Electric Co. and Its Antecedent and Allied Companies," filed with the records of The Harwood Electric Co.

394. HAZLETON ELECTRIC COMPANY
(Non-operating).
Luzerne County, Hazleton City.
1913, 1/2 Linear Foot.

History:
Following the consolidation and merger of nine non-operating and four operating companies, Hazleton Electric Co. was incorporated 6 January 1913, for the purpose of supplying electricity to communities in the counties of Columbia, Northumberland, Schuylkill, and Luzerne. On 25 March 1913 the company was merged into The Harwood Electric Co.

395. HAZLETON ELECTRIC LIGHT AND POWER COMPANY (Operating).
Luzerne County, Hazleton City.
1899 to 1912, 4 Linear Feet.

History:
Hazleton Electric Light and Power Co. was incorporated 13 June 1899 to supply electricity in the City of Hazleton, Luzerne County. The company owned no property of its own; instead, it acquired the stock of The Edison Electric Illuminating Co. of Hazleton, Freeland Electric Light Heat and Power Co., and West End Electric Light and Power Co. of Hazleton, and leased the franchises of these companies. Hazleton Electric Light and Power Co. consolidated properties of these three companies and operated them until 6 June 1912, when they were conveyed to the Harwood Electric Co. On 16 December 1912 they merged with Hazleton Electric Light and Power Co. to form Hazleton Electric Co. On 25 March 1913 Hazleton Electric Co. was formally merged into The Harwood Electric Co.

Administrative Records:
Minute Book, 1899-1912
Stock Certificate Book, 1899-1912
Stock Ledger, 1899-1912
Correspondence, 1911-1912

Operating Records:
General Ledgers, 1899-1912 (4 Volumes)
Journals, 1899-1912 (3 Volumes)
Cashbook, 1899-1900
Cashbook and Check Register, 1911-1912
Distribution of Accounts, 1899-1911 (7 Volumes)
Payrolls, 1912
Expenditures, 1911-1912
Monthly Reports, 1911-1912

Scope and Content Note:
The Minute Book of the Hazleton Electric Co. records routine minutes of stockholders' and directors' meetings, and details the company's relationship with its lessee companies. Correspondence documents the acquisition of Hazleton Electric Light and Power Co. by The Harwood Electric Co. Also included in this file are company bylaws; copies of mortgage agreements; lists of investors; and a 1911 report describing the company's organization, franchises, leases, contracts, and stock issues. There is also some payroll information, lists of customers and rate schedules. Additional information can be found in the "Historical Report of The Harwood Electric Co. and Its Antecedent and Allied Companies," filed with the records of The Harwood Electric Co.

396. THE HAZLETON STEAM HEATING COMPANY
(Operating).
Luzerne County, Hazleton City.
1888 to 1924, 9 Linear Feet.

History:
The Hazleton Steam Heating Co. was incorporated 30 August 1886 to supply steam heating in the City of Hazleton, Luzerne County. From about 1907, the company began to experience serious problems with its facilities and was constantly repairing and replacing equipment. This doubtlessly contributed to its financial losses ($3,500) in 1908. The majority of the company's stock was acquired by The Harwood Electric Co. in 1912, but by 1914 it had become clear its plant and equipment were in a dilapidated condition and the company was unprofitable. It was finally dissolved on 31 May 1920.

Administrative Records:
Minute Books, 1889-1920 (5 Volumes)
Stock Certificate Book, 1888-1920
Stock Transfer Record, 1917-1920
Stock Ledgers, 1888-1920 (2 Volumes)
Correspondence, 1912-1914
Report on Steam Heating System, 1914
Annual Report of Secretary, 1910

Operating Records:
FINANCIAL RECORDS
General Ledgers, 1887-1912 (3 Volumes)
General Ledger and Detail, 1911-1920
Journals, 1911-1920 (2 Volumes)
Daybooks, 1902-1911 (3 Volumes)
Cashbooks, 1897-1912 (5 Volumes)
Cash Received and Check Registers, 1911-1923 (5 Volumes)
Accounts Payable, 1914-1921
Accounts Receivable, 1917-1920
Accrual Records, 1915-1920 (3 Volumes)
Accrual Records, 1920
Preliminary Survey and Investigation, 1919
Charges to Capital, 1918-1920 (2 Volumes)
Consumers Ledgers, 1901-1914 (2 Volumes)
Statement of Bad Accounts, 1914-1916
Statement of Earnings, Expenses and Fixed Capital, 1919

General Ledger Balance, 1919
Balance of Accounts Payable, 1919
Net Divisible Income, 1919
Balance Sheets & Summaries of Earnings, 1917-1920
Condensed Statement of Income Account and Profit & Loss, 1914-1917
Monthly Reports, 1911-1919 (2 Volumes)
Repair and Construction Detail Ledger, 1915-1920
Statement of Incompleted Improvement and Special Work, 1916-1919
PERSONNEL RECORDS
Accident Register, 1916-1917
Compensation Register, 1916
Payroll Ledger, 1918-1919 (2 Volumes)
Payrolls, 1915-1919 (2 Volumes)
Subscriptions to U.S. Liberty Loans, 1918-1919
Time Sheets, 1915-1920
AUDIT REPORTS, 1907-1916 (4 Volumes)

Scope and Content Note:
The Minute Books of The Hazleton Steam Heating Co. document the effort to maintain the company's steam heating system. Included are accounts of operating expenses, reports on the company's financial status, discussions of meetings on rates, as well as routine minutes of directors' and stockholders' meetings. The Minute Book lists the various persons and businesses to whom steam heating was supplied. Also included is a 1912 assesment made by a representative of the American District Steam Co. showing why the Hazleton plant was losing money (mainly due to the advanced age of the system, and excessive transmission losses). The Correspondence File deals mainly with the effort to construct a substation for The Harwood Electric Company's Hazleton plant. The Accident Register lists names and addresses of injured employees, date of accident and amount of time lost. The Payroll Ledger and Payrolls are alphabetical listings of employees with occupation, number of hours worked and pay rate.

397. HEGINS-SCHUYLKILL POWER & LIGHT COMPANY (Non-operating).
Schuylkill County, Hegins Township.
1925 to 1926, 1/2 Linear Foot.

History:
Incorporated on 26 March 1926 to supply electricity in the Township of Hegins, Schuylkill County, Hegins-Schuylkill Power & Light Co. was merged along with four other non-operating companies into Pennsylvania Power & Light Co. on 14 April 1926.

398. HEGINS TOWNSHIP ELECTRIC COMPANY (Non-operating).
Schuylkill County, Hegins Township.
1919, 1 Linear Inch.

History:
Incorporated on 14 June 1916 to supply electricity in the Township of Hegins, Schuylkill County, Hegins Township Electric Co. was merged and consolidated with five other non-operating companies on 30 October 1919 to form The Citizens Electric Co.

399. HEIDELBERG POWER & LIGHT COMPANY (Non-operating).
Lehigh County, Heidelberg Township.
1922 to 1923, 2 Linear Inches.

History:
Heidelberg Power & Light was incorporated 15 November 1922 to supply electricity in the Township of Heidelberg, Lehigh County. It was merged into Pennsylvania Power & Light Co. on 19 January 1923.

400. HELLAM-YORK POWER & LIGHT COMPANY (Non-operating).
York County, Hellam Township.
1935 to 1936, 1/2 Linear Foot.

History:
Hellam-York Power & Light Co. was incorporated 10 December 1935 to supply electricity in part of the Township of Hellam, York County. On 24 January 1936, it was merged into Pennsylvania Power & Light Co.

401. HELLERTOWN ELECTRIC LIGHT AND POWER COMPANY (Non-operating).
Northampton County, Hellertown Borough.
1914 to 1917, 2 Linear Inches.

History:
Originally incorporated 27 July 1914 to supply electricity in the Borough of Hellertown, Northampton County, Hellertown Electric Light and Power Co. was re-incorporated 17 May 1916. On 16 September 1916 the company was merged into Lehigh Valley Light and Power Co., No. 3.

402. HEPBURN-LYCOMING POWER & LIGHT CO. (Non-operating).
Lycoming County, Hepburn Township.
1928 to 1929, 1/2 Linear Foot.

History:
Incorporated on 14 May 1928 to supply electricity in the Township of Hepburn, Lycoming County, Hepburn-Lycoming Power & Light Co. was merged into Pennsylvania Power & Light Co. on 29 June 1928.

403. HERRICK-SUSQUEHANNA POWER & LIGHT COMPANY (Non-operating).
Susquehanna County, Herrick Township.
1927 to 1928, 2 Linear Inches.

History:
Herrick-Susquehanna Power & Light Co. was incorporated 20 December 1927 to supply electricity in the Township of Herrick, Susquehanna County. The company was merged into Pennsylvania Power & Light Co. on 3 January 1928.

404. THE HILLSIDE WATER AND POWER COMPANY (Operating).
York County, Lower Chanceford Township.
1902 to 1905, 1 Linear Inch.

History:
Hillside Water and Power Co. was incorporated on 2 September 1902 for the purpose of supplying water power in the Township of Lower Chanceford, York County. It merged and consolidated with Susquehanna Water and Power Co. on 1 April 1905 to form McCall Ferry Power Co.

Administrative Records:
Minute Book, 1902-1905

405. HILLTOWN ELECTRIC LIGHT AND POWER COMPANY, NO. 1 (Non-operating).
Bucks County, Hilltown Township.
1913 to 1914, 1 Linear Inch.

History:

Hilltown Electric Light and Power Co., No. 1, was incorporated 8 December 1913 to supply electricity in the Township of Hilltown, Bucks County. It was merged into Lehigh Valley Light and Power Co., No. 3, on 29 December 1913.

406. HILLTOWN ELECTRIC LIGHT AND POWER COMPANY, NO. 2 (Non-operating).
Bucks County, Hilltown Township.
1918, 1 Linear Inch.

History:

Hilltown Electric Light and Power Co., No. 2, was incorporated 19 March 1918 to supply electricity in the Township of Hilltown, Bucks County. It was merged and consolidated with three other companies on 10 April 1918 to form Excelsior Electric Light, Power and Gas Co., No. 3.

407. HOLLENBACK-LUZERNE POWER & LIGHT COMPANY (Non-operating).
Luzerne County, Hollenback Township.
1924 to 1925, 2 Linear Inches.

History:

Hollenback-Luzerne Power & Light Co. was incorporated 2 October 1924 to supply electricity in the Township of Hollenback, Luzerne County. It was merged into Pennsylvania Power & Light Co. on 26 December 1924.

408. HOLTWOOD COAL COMPANY (Operating).
Lancaster County, Holtwood Borough.
1920 to 1957, 1 Linear Foot.

History:

Holtwood Coal Co. was incorporated in November 1920 by Pennsylvania Water & Power Co. for the purpose of recovering, processing, and selling anthracite coal which had been carried down the Susquehanna River and deposited in the reservoir formed by the Water & Power company's dam at Holtwood. According to a 24 January 1921 note in the parent company's minute book, these operations were to be conducted "slowly and in a conservative manner," Holtwood Coal Co. continued to operate in this leisurely fashion until 1955, when it became inactive. The company was dissolved on 31 December 1957.

Administrative Records:
Stock Certificate Book, 1920-1955

Operating Records:
General Ledger, 1928-1941
Journal, 1920-1942
Financial & Operating Reports, 1955-1957

Scope and Content Note:

The majority of the records of the Holtwood Coal Co. deal with financial matters. Both the Journal and the Ledger give details of operating expenses, such as maintenance expenses, coal costs, costs of dredging equipment, and show profit and loss accounts. The Financial and Operating Reports are balance sheets showing assets and liabilities in the years immediately prior to the company's dissolution.

409. HOLTWOOD POWER COMPANY (Operating).
Lancaster County, Holtwood Borough.
1924 to 1928, 1/2 Linear Foot.

History:

Holtwood Power Co. was incorporated 9 August 1924 to supply electricity in the Township of Martic, Lancaster County. The company built and operated a steam electric generating plant at Holtwood on the Susquehanna River in order to supplement the available hydro power generated by the Pennsylvania Water & Power Company's dam there. The company exchanged its capital stock for a tract of land adjacent to the Susquehanna River which was owned by Pennsylvania Water & Power Co. This deal gave Holtwood Power Co. the right to use all of Pennsylvania Water & Power Company's facilities. This enabled the company to erect a 30,000-horsepower generating plant. On 24 October 1928 the company was sold outright to Pennsylvania Water & Power Co.

Administrative Records:
Minute Book, 1924-1927
Stock Certificate Book, 1924-1927
Stock Transfer Record, 1924-1928

Scope and Content Note:

The Minute Book of the Holtwood Power Co. consists mainly of routine administrative records, such as minutes of stockholders' and directors' meetings, along with details of stock and bond issuances. It does, however, document the company's relationship with the Pennsylvania Water & Power Co.

410. HOLTWOOD REAL ESTATE COMPANY (Operating).
Lancaster County, Holtwood Borough.
1948 to 1957, 1 Linear Foot.

History:

Holtwood Real Estate Co. was incorporated 1 July 1948 by Pennsylvania Water & Power Co. to buy and improve real estate for the company's use, and in order to assist the company's employees in acquiring homes. It also leased homes on land owned by the Water company to its employees. In February 1949, the company purchased a building in the City of Lancaster so that Pennsylvania Water & Power Co. would have additional office space there when needed. Holtwood Real Estate Co. was dissolved on 31 December 1957.

Administrative Records:
Stock Certificate Book, 1948-1955

Operating Records:
General Ledger, 1948-1958
Voucher & Journal Entry Register, 1948-1957
Trial Balance, 1948-1956
Monthly Report on Lease of Properties, 1948-1957
Bills, 1955-1957
Check Stub Book, 1948-1949
Financial & Operating Reports, 1955

Scope and Content Note:
The majority of the records of the Holtwood Real Estate Co. are routine bookkeeping accounts. The Financial and Operating Reports, for example, are balance sheets showing the company's assets and liabilities in the years immediately prior to its dissolution. The Monthly Report on Leased Properties lists some of the company's employees and indicates which properties they were renting from the company.

411. HONESDALE CONSOLIDATED LIGHT, HEAT AND POWER COMPANY (Operating).
Wayne County, Honesdale Borough.
1902 to 1928, 7 1/2 Linear Feet.

History:
Honesdale Consolidated Light, Heat and Power Co. was formed for the purpose of supplying electricity in Wayne County following the 12 December 1902 consolidation and merger of Honesdale Electric Light, Heat and Power Co. and Honesdale Gas Co. The latter company had been in operation since 1854, while the electric company had been in operation since 1887. In 1908, due to an increasing number of customers, Honesdale Consolidated Light, Heat and Power Co. found it necessary to construct a new electric plant, with a capacity of 275-kw. Part of this plant was destroyed by a fire in December 1918, but it was rebuilt and expanded, so that by 1922 its total capacity was 900-kw. From 1916 to 1923 the company steadily expanded its electric service to various small communities in Wayne Couny, and further extended its charter rights in the county on 12 May 1924 when it absorbed four non-operating companies. In 1923 the company's stock was acquired by Lehigh Power Securities Corp. and thereafter it was operated as a part of the Pennsylvania Power & Light Co. system. On 28 May 1928 the company was merged into Pennsylvania Power & Light Co.

Administrative Records:
Minute Books, 1903-1928 (3 Volumes)
Stock Certificate Book, 1903-1924
Stock Transfer Record, 1903-1924 (2 Volumes)
Stock Ledger, 1920-1928

Operating Records:
FINANCIAL RECORDS
General Ledgers, 1920-1928 (2 Volumes)
Journal, 1921-1923
Journal Entry Register, 1923-1926
Journal—Electrical Department, 1902-1924 (10 Volumes)
Journal—Gas Department, 1919-1924 (2 Volumes)
Journal—Gas & Electric Deptartments, 1924
Cashbooks, 1903-1923 (3 Volumes)
Cashbooks—Electric Department, 1904-1923
Cashbooks—Gas Dept., 1904-1923
Cash Deposits, 1911-1923 (2 Volumes)
Petty Cash, 1915-1923 (2 Volumes)
Cash Received, 1923-1925
Cash Register, 1923-1925
Daybooks, 1903-1927
Daybooks—Expenditures, 1903-1917 (3 Volumes)
Daybooks—Electrical Dept., 1914-1918 (3 Volumes)
Record of Cash Receipts, 1925-1928
Record of Cash Disbursements, 1925-1928
Summary of Cash 1925-1928
Audited Voucher Register, 1926-1928
Detail Ledgers, 1917-1928 (5 Volumes)
Sales Ledger, 1912-1921
Accrual Record, 1924-1928
Detail of Cost Study and Fixed Capital, 1925-1927
PERSONNEL RECORDS
Workmen's Compensation Insurance Accrual Statements, 1924-1928
Payroll—Time Keeping & Cost Distribution, 1919-1921
Expense Account Ledger, 1913-1917
CONSUMER RECORDS
Accounts Receivable Ledgers, 1903-1923 (6 Volumes)
Sales Ledger, 1912-1921
Summary of Accounts Receivable—Consumers, 1923-1928
Summary of Accounts Receivable—Miscellaneous, 1923-1928
Summary of Consumer's Deposits, 1925-1928
Rent Statements, 1927-1928
Accounts Payable, 1903-1920 (2 Volumes)
Watt Meter Readings, 1916-1917
Meter Books, 1903-1921 (11 Volumes)
Consumers Ledgers, 1903-1919 (8 Volumes)
Consumers Ledgers—Electrical Dept., 1921-1923 (5 Volumes)
Consumers Ledgers—Gas Dept., 1921-1923
Power Sale Balances, 1903-1919 (4 Volumes)
Material Receipt Books, 1914-1921 (5 Volumes)
Meters Received, 1916-1917
Meter Tests, 1916-1917
Customers' Complaint Book, 1914-1922
Material Charged Against Electrical Dept., 1908-1919
Material Charged Against Gas Dept., 1920
Gas Merchandise Sales, 1921
AUDIT REPORTS, 1921-1926 (4 Volumes)

Scope and Content Note:
The Minute Books of the Honesdale Consolidated Light, Heat and Power Co. contain routine minutes of stockholders' and directors' meetings, a copy of the company's rules and regulations, details of operating expenses, and some correspondence relating to mortgages and the supply of electricity to the Borough of Honesdale. The Payroll lists employees and the number of hours each worked. The Meter Books (1903-1921) list the occupants of each apartment or house served by the company, while the Accounts Receivable Ledgers record the dates during which service was provided. The Customers' Complaint Book is a listing of complaints, mainly about gas bills that were thought to be too high.

412. HONESDALE ELECTRIC LIGHT HEAT AND POWER COMPANY (Operating).
Wayne County, Honesdale Borough.
1884 to 1908, 3 1/2 Linear Feet.

History:
Honesdale Electric Light Heat and Power Co. was incorporated 6 September 1886 to supply electricity in the Borough of Honesdale, Wayne County. It rendered the first electric service in this borough when it began operations in 1887. The company installed a 25-light dynamo for arc lighting in the plant of the Honesdale Iron

Works, which was owned by Mr. Martin B. Allen, one of the principal organizers of the Electric Co. Unfortunately, this dynamo burned out the first time it was turned on. After a good deal of argument with the dynamo's manufacturers, a new, specially-made dynamo with a capacity of 480-60 cp lamps was installed in 1888. Due to a change in Pennsylvania law, the company had to give up its old Letters Patent in 1889 and was re-incorporated 10 December of that year. Also in 1889, the company built a new power plant at the foot of 11th Street in Honesdale, and installed a 500 incandescent light capacity Edison generator in it. By 1892, the capacity of this plant had been boosted to 125-kw and the plant at the Iron Works phased out. On 12 December 1902 the company was consolidated and merged with Honesdale Gas Co. to form Honesdale Light, Heat and Power Co.

Administrative Records:
Minute Books, 1886-1904 (3 Volumes)
Stock Certificate Book - Common, 1887-1903
Stock Certificate Book - Preferred, 1901
Copies of Property Deeds, 1804-1891
Copies of Electric Light Deeds, 1886-1896
List of Original Stockholders & Subsequent Disposition of Stock, 1903

Operating Records:
Journal, 1887-1908
Accounts Receivable Ledgers, 1888-1902 (5 Volumes)
Cashbooks, 1893-1903 (3 Volumes)
Daybooks—Receipts, 1888-1902 (3 Volumes)
Meter Books, 1894-1898 (2 Volumes)
Lamp Records, 1888-1896 (3 Volumes)
Accounts Receivable—Installations, 1896-1899
Consumers Record—Incandescent Lamps, 1888-1891
Monthly Supplement—Electric Light Bills, 1896-1899
Power Plant Daily Record, 1897-1898
Accounts Payable Ledgers, 1884-1903 (3 Volumes)
Order Book with Cost Distribution, 1893-1899
Expense Books, 1887-1903 (2 Volumes)

Scope and Content Note:
The Minute Books of Honesdale Electric Light Heat and Power Co. contain minutes of both stockholders' and directors' meetings which trace the growth and development of the company from its organization until its consolidation and merger with Honesdale Gas Co. in 1902. These minutes include statements of operating expenses and a good deal of correspondence relative to the installation of the company's electric generators. These generators caused a great deal of trouble after installation and the correspondence reflects this, being concerned with technical details concerning their maintenance and operation. Additional correspondence in the Minute Books reflects another complicating factor concerning these dynamos: their manufacturer, American Electric Manufacturing Co., was being sued by a rival company for patent infringement, and the Honesdale Co. was reluctant to purchase equipment that might embroil it in a lawsuit.

Other records of this company include copies of deeds, dating back to 1804, for the property upon which the Honesdale company ultimately built its power plant , and copies of electric light deeds, dating back to 1888, giving the company the right to supply electricity on the same property. The Consumers Record of Incandescent Lamps shows when lamps were installed, and the annual costs of the lamps.

413. HONEY BROOK TOWNSHIP ELECTRIC COMPANY (Non-operating).
Chester County, Honey Brook Township.
1915, 1 Linear Inch.

History:
Honey Brook Township Electric Co. was incorporated 27 January 1915 to supply electricity in the Township of Honey Brook, Chester County. It was consolidated and merged with five other non-operating companies on 2 June 1915 to form Tri-County Electric Co.

414. HOUSEHOLD ELECTRIC LIGHT, HEAT & POWER COMPANY (Operating).
Lackawanna County, Jermyn Borough.
1907 to 1911, 1/2 Linear Foot.

History:
Household Electric Light, Heat & Power Co. No. 1 was organized sometime prior to September 1903 to supply electricity in the Boroughs of Jermyn and Mayfield, Lackawanna County. On 10 September 1903 it was consolidated and merged with Independent Electric Light, Heat & Power Co. to form Household Electric Light, Heat & Power Co., No. 2. American Gas and Electric Co. gained control of the company's stock in June 1910, and on 18 May 1911 it was sold to Scranton Electric Co.

Administrative Records:
Minute Book, 1907-1911

Operating Records:
General Ledger, 1910-1911
Cashbook, 1910-1911

Scope and Content Note:
The Minute Book of the Household Electric Light, Heat & Power Co. contains minutes of stockholders' and directors' meetings, lists of stockholders, and a description of the company's property and franchise rights in the Borough of Jermyn, Lackawanna County. Also in the Minute Book are details of the company's operating expenses.

415. HUBLEY ELECTRIC COMPANY (Operating).
Schuylkill County, Hubley Township.
1923 to 1930, 3 Linear Feet.

History:
Hubley Electric Co. was incorporated 11 July 1923 to supply electricity in the Township of Hubley, Schuylkill County. The company built an electric distribution system to supply the Villages of Sacramento and Spring Glen in Hubley Township, and constructed a line to connect with The Citizens Electric Company's lines in Valley View, so that it could buy power. In 1928, the company's stock was acquired by Lehigh Power Securities Corp., which thereafter operated it as a part of the Pennsylvania Power & Light Company's system. On 31 December 1930, it was merged into Pennsylvania Power & Light Co.

Administrative Records:
Minute Book, 1923-1930
Stock Certificate Book, 1923-1920
Stock Register, 1923-1930

Operating Records:
General Ledgers, 1923-1928 (2 Volumes)
Journal, 1923-1928
Record of Cash Receipts, 1928-1920
Record of Cash Disbursements, 1928-1930
Summary of Cash, 1928-1930 (2 Volumes)
Audited Voucher Register, 1928-1930
Accounts Payable, 1928-1930
Accounts Receivable, 1928-1930
Detail Ledger, 1928-1930
Accrual Record, 1928-1930
Expenditure Requisitions, 1928-1930
Retirement Authorities, 1928-1930
Summary of Accounts Receivble, 1928-1930
Summary of Consumers' Deposits, 1930
Audit Reports, 1924-1929 (2 Volumes)

Scope and Content Note:
The Minute Book of Hubley Electric Co. provides good insight into the day-to-day operation of a small, locally-organized electric company whose directors were supplying electricity to their friends and neighbors as they worked to modernize their community. The Minute Book illustrates the relationship between this local company and Citizens Electric Co. who supplied it with power. The records also document the manner in which small electric companies were absorbed by Pennsylvania Power & Light Co. Most of the records are financial in nature and detail the company's operating expenses and financial condition.

416. HUBLEY TOWNSHIP ELECTRIC COMPANY (Non-operating).
Schuylkill County, Hubley Township.
1919, 1 Linear Inch.

History:
Hubley Township Electric Co. was incorporated 14 June 1916 to supply electricity in the Township of Hubley, Schuylkill County. It was consolidated and merged with five other non-operating companies on 30 October 1919 to form The Citizens Electric Co.

417. HUGHESTOWN BOROUGH-LUZERNE POWER & LIGHT COMPANY (Non-operating).
Lehigh County, Allentown City.
1926 to 1927, 1 Linear Inch.

History:
Hughestown Borough-Luzerne Power & Light Co. was organized on 9 March 1926 by Pennsylvania Power & Light Co. in an attempt to extend its franchises into the Borough of Hughestown, Luzerne County. The company was never incorporated and was dissolved on 25 January 1927.

418. HUGHESTOWN ELECTRIC COMPANY (Non-operating).
Luzerne County, Pittston Borough.
1910 to 1913, 1 Linear Inch.

History:
Hughestown Electric Co. was incorporated 7 September 1910 to supply electricity in the Borough of Pittston, Luzerne County. It was consolidated and merged on 8 July 1913 with four other companies to form Citizens Electric Illuminating Co.

419. THE HUMMELSTOWN CONSOLIDATED WATER COMPANY (Operating).
Dauphin County, Hummelstown Borough.
1906 to 1920, 1 Linear Foot.

History:
Incorporated on 26 September 1887 as The Hummelstown Water Co., this company supplied power to The Hummelstown Electric Light Heat and Power Co., which had been organized by the same interests that controlled the Water Co. On 31 March 1906, the Water Co. acquired the Electric Co. Shortly thereafter, the name of the Water Co. was changed to The Hummelstown Consolidated Water Co. In 1908, the generating capacity of the electric plant was boosted to 560-kw by the installation of new generators and additional steam power facilities. In May 1920, after having defaulted on its mortgage, the company was sold to Mr. Harry C. Ross, who purchased it on behalf of the bondholders. The company was then reorganized as Hummelstown Water & Power Co.

Administrative Records:
Minute Book, 1906-1916

Operating Records:
Detail Ledgers, 1916-1920 (2 Volumes)
Financial Distribution and Capital Account, 1906-1918
Trial Balance, 1915-1916

Scope and Content Note:
The Minute Book of The Hummelstown Consolidated Water Co. contains a great deal of information, including minutes of stockholders' and directors' meetings; lists of stockholders; statements of the company's financial condition, showing assets and liabilities; a mortgage indenture which describes the company's real estate holdings; and a 1915 copy of the company's "Rules, Rates and Regulations Governing the Distribution of Light and Water." Also included is information about the construction of the company's waterworks, the installation of water mains throughout the Borough of Hummelstown, and the company's dealings with the Borough Council concerning the provision of water and hydrants for fire protection and the provision of water and electric service to the municipal buildings. The Minute Book also includes copies of contracts concerning the purchase and renovation of the Union Deposit Mill property in Hummelstown, construction of a pump house and water filtration plant, and renovations to the company's boiler house. The other records of this company are financial in nature and provide details of operating expenses and finances.

420. HUMMELSTOWN WATER & POWER COMPANY (Operating).
Dauphin County, Hummelstown Borough.
1920 to 1932, 4 Linear Feet.

History:
Having failed to meet the interest payments on its mortgage, Hummelstown Consolidated Water Co. was sold to Henry C. Ross and his associates, who purchased it on behalf of the bondholders. The company was then reorganized as Hummelstown Water & Power Co. The stock of the new company was acquired by Harrisburg

Light and Power Co. (Mr. Ross was a vice-president of this company.) The reorganized company continued to supply Hummelstown with water and electricity. In 1921 an 11-kw power line was constructed to bring additional power from the Harrisburg Light and Power Company's Harrisburg plant. The next year, a fire completely destroyed its generating and pumping station. However, these were quickly rebuilt. Early in 1924, the company extended its electric service to the Townships of Derry and South Hannover (both in Dauphin County). In 1928, the company sold all its property to the publicly owned Hummelstown Water Supply Co., and then merged into Pennsylvania Power & Light.

Administrative Records:
Minute Book, 1920-1928
Stock Certificate Book, 1920-1926

Operating Records:
General Ledgers, 1920-1928 (2 Volumes)
Journal, 1920-1927
Journal Entry Register, 1927-1928
Record of Cash Receipts, 1927-1928
Record of Cash Disbursements, 1927-1928
Summary of Cash, 1927-1928
Cash Receipts, 1922-1926
Audited Voucher Register, 1921-1928 (2 Volumes)
Accounts Payable, 1927-1928
Accounts Receivable, 1927-1928
Accounts Receivable—Miscellaneous, 1929-1930
Summary of Accounts Receivable—Miscellaneous, 1927-1928
Summary of Accounts Receivable—Consumers, 1927-1928
Inter-Company Bills, Statements, Etc., 1921-1926
Detail Ledgers, 1920-1928 (2 Volumes)
Accrual Record, 1922-1928 (2 Volumes)
Comparative Income Account, Trial Balance & Balance Sheets, 1927-1928
Operation, Maintanance and Distribution Ledger, 1920-1921
Expenditure Requisitions, 1927-1932
Retirement Authorities, 1927
Financial Reports, 1921-1928
Working Papers, 1924
Audit Reports, 1920-1927 (4 Volumes)

Scope and Content Note:
The Minute Book of Hummelstown Water & Power Co. is a record of the company's growth, and documents its effort to extend its area of operation and service. Also included are Monthly Financial Statements and Construction Records. These documents list both business and residential customers. The "Working Papers" consist of pricing sheets for electric and water property, price quotations on equipment, field notes concerning overhead lines, a report on the company's valuation, and a prospectus which was used in constructing a dam and pumping station.

421. HUMMELSTOWN WATER SUPPLY COMPANY
(Operating).
Dauphin County, Hummelstown Borough.
1928 to 1942, 1 1/2 Linear Feet.

History:
Hummelstown Water Supply Co. was incorporated 22 May 1928 for the purpose of supplying water to the public in the Borough of Hummeltown. Three days later, the company bought all of the property formerly used by Hummelstown Water & Power Co., in return for the Water Supply company's stock. When Pennsylvania Power & Light Co. acquired Hummelstown Water & Power Co. on 25 May 1928, it also acquired control of Hummelstown Water Supply Co.

Administrative Records:
Minute Book, 1928-1942

Operating Records:
Summary of Cash, 1928-1942 (4 Volumes)
Repair Authorities, 1930-1933
Expenditure Requisitions, 1938-1939
Audit Reports, 1928-1932 (3 Volumes)
Summary of Accounts Receivable—Miscellaneous, 1928-1934 (3 Volumes)
Summary of Consumers' Deposits, 1929-1935
Summary of Cashier's Overs and Shorts, 1928-1931
Statements of Real Estate Leases & Rentals, 1932-1934
Statement of Service Billed in Advance, 1930-1935

Scope and Content Note:
The Minute Book of the Hummelstown Water Supply Co. contains routine administrative records, such as minutes of stockholders' and directors' meetings, a copy of the company's bylaws, and information relating to stock issuances. The Repair Authorities give details of construction work undertaken by the company. The Statements of Real Estate Leases and Rentals provide the names of tenants and the location and description of the property or building they were leasing from the company, together with the amount paid in rent.

422. INDUSTRIAL ELECTRIC LIGHT AND POWER COMPANY OF UPPER MACUNGIE
(Non-operating).
Lehigh County, Allentown City.
1917 to 1919, 1 Linear Inch.

History:
Industrial Electric Light and Power Co. of Upper Macungie was organized on 28 April 1917 by Lehigh Valley Light & Power Co. as part of its effort to extend its area of operations in Lehigh County. The company never received a charter and was dissolved in January of 1919.

423. INDUSTRIAL ELECTRIC LIGHT AND POWER COMPANY OF UPPER MILFORD (Non-operating).
Lehigh County, Upper Milford Township.
1917 to 1919, 1/2 Linear Foot.

History:
Industrial Electric Light and Power Co. of Upper Milford was incorporated 14 November 1917 to supply electricity in the Township of Upper Milford, Lehigh County. Two months later the company changed its name to Pennsylvania Power & Light Co., No. 1.

424. INDUSTRIAL FUEL COMPANY (Operating).
Northumberland County, Milton Borough.
1918 to 1935, 3 1/2 Linear Feet.

History:

This company was originally organized in the Borough of Shamokin on 26 June 1918 as Industrial Coal Co., for the purpose of reclaiming anthracite coal from the Shamokin Creek near Sunbury, Pennslvania. It purchased a site on the creek and an already existing coal washery. On 22 August 1918, the company changed its name to Industrial Fuel Co. and was incorporated as such on 24 September 1918. On 8 January 1920 it leased two tracts of land in Upper Augusta Township from Shamokin Valley Coal Co. From these, Industrial Fuel Co. removed coal, culm, and refuse matter. On 12 January 1920 the company moved its main offices from Shamokin to the Borough of Milton. The company's stock was acquired in 1922 by The Milton Maufacturing Co., producers of bar iron, steel casings, and nuts. On 6 December 1929 Pennsylvania Power & Light Co. acquired the stock from the Milton company.

Administrative Records:

Minute Books, 1918-1934 (2 Volumes)
Stock Certificate Book, 1919-1929
Stock Transfer Record Record, 1929
Stock Ledger, 1924-1929

Operating Records:

General Ledgers, 1918-1934 (2 Volumes)
Journals, 1920-1928 (2 Volumes)
Journal Entry Register, 1928-1934
Cashbooks, 1918-1928 (2 Volumes)
Record of Cash Receipts, 1928-1934
Record of Cash Disbursements, 1928-1935
Summary of Cash, 1928-1935 (2 Volumes)
Audited Voucher Register, 1928-1934
Accounts Receivable, 1928-1934
Accrual Record, 1928-1934
Trial Balance, 1930-1934
Bill Register, 1928-1934
Bills, 1928-1932
Retirement Authorities, 1931
Statement of Rents, 1928-1934
Audit Reports, 1925-1931

Scope and Content Note:

The Minute Books of the Industrial Fuel Co. contain routine administrative records such as minutes of stockholders' and directors' meetings, company by-laws and statements of operating expenses. Most of the other records are financial in nature. The Rent Statements are of particular interest as they provide the name of the tenant, location and description of property rented from the company and amount of rent paid.

425. **INDUSTRIAL POWER COMPANY** (Non-operating).
Lehigh County, Allentown City.
1919, 1/2 Linear Foot.

History:

Industrial Power Co. was incorporated 11 September 1919 as a result of the consolidation and merger of seven non-operating companies. On 1 October 1919 the company was consolidated and merged with The Stroudsburg Electric Light and Power Co., No. 2, to form Lehigh Industrial Power Co.

426. **INTERCOURSE ELECTRIC COMPANY**
(Operating).
Lancaster County, Intercourse Village.
1921 to 1930, 3 1/2 Linear Feet.

History:

Intercourse Electric Co. was formed by the 13 January 1921 consolidation and merger of Intercourse Electric Light, Heat and Power Co. with three non-operating companies. After its formation, the company extended its electric distribution system from the Township of Leacock into the Townships of Paradise, East Lampeter, and Salisbury, all in Lancaster County. In 1925 United Gas and Electric Co. gained control of the company's stock, and in 1926 Lehigh Power Securities Corp. acquired it from United Gas and Electric Co. Intercourse Electric Co. was merged into Pennsylvania Power & Light Co. on 31 December 1930.

Administrative Records:

Minute Books, 1924-1930 (2 Volumes)
Secretary's Papers of Meetings, 1930
Stock Certificate Book, 1921-1930
Correspondence, 1921-1925

Operating Records:

General Ledgers, 1923-1930 (3 Volumes)
Journal Entry Register, 1926-1930
Cash Deposits and Withdrawls, 1927-1930
Accounts Receivable, 1926-1930
Detail Ledger, 1926-1930
Construction Ledger, 1926-1930
Analysis of Closed Jobs, 1926
Accrual Record, 1926-1930
Material & Supplies, 1926-1928 (2 Volumes)
Automobile Reports, 1926-1929
Payroll Distribution Sheets - Daily, 1925-1927
Expenditure Requisitions, 1930
Payrolls, 1927-1928
Financial Reports, 1926 (2 Volumes)
Audit Reports, 1921-1930 (6 Volumes)

Scope and Content Note:

The Minute Books of Intercourse Electric Co. contain routine administrative records, including financial statements, showing income and operating expenses, and minutes of stockholders' and directors' meetings. The "Secretary's Papers of Meetings" are extra minutes of several stockholders' meetings. The Daily Payroll Distribution Sheets indicate what kind of work each employee was doing, how many hours it took him to do it, and how much he was paid. Correspondence with the National Electric Light Association describes utility industry advertising strategies. Also included is a 1925 Pennsylvania Public Service Commission general order mandating rural electrification.

427. **INTERCOURSE ELECTRIC LIGHT, HEAT AND POWER COMPANY** (Operating).
Lancaster County, Intercourse Village.
1909 to 1921, 1 Linear Foot.

History:

Intercourse Electric Light, Heat and Power Co. was incorporated 16 September 1909 to supply electricity in the Township of Leacock, Lancaster County. On 13

January 1921 it was consolidated and merged with three non-operating companies to form Intercourse Electric Co.

Administrative Records:
Minute Book, 1909-1916
Stockholders Record, 1918-1921
Correspondence, 1917-1921

Scope and Content Note:
The Minute Book of the Intercourse Electric Light, Heat and Power Co. documents the company's purchase of electricity from Conestoga Traction Co., the construction of electric lines, and the installation of street lighting in Intercourse. Correspondence includes letters about the installation of pumps at Leaman Place, consumers' complaints, letters about the cost of materials, and letters with the State Workmen's Insurance Fund concerning a fatal accident. The Stockholders Record is an alphabetical listing of the company's stockholders, their addresses, and the number of shares of stock controlled.

428. IRONDALE ELECTRIC LIGHT, HEAT AND POWER COMPANY (Operating).
Columbia County, Bloomsburg Town.
1902 to 1911, 1 Linear Foot.

History:
Irondale Electric Light, Heat and Power Co. was incorporated 7 April 1902 to supply electricity in the Town of Bloomsburg, Columbia County. In order to meet the competitive challenge presented by the American Electric Light Co., which had been operating in Bloomsburg since 1899, the company built a 180-kw capacity hydroelectric generating station on Fishing Creek, just outside of town. On 7 February 1911, Irondale Light, Heat and Power Co. was consolidated and merged with American Electric Light and 20 other companies to form Columbia Gas and Electric Co.

Administrative Records:
Stock Certificate Book, 1902-1909

Operating Records:
General Ledger, 1909-1911
Cashbooks, 1903-1906 (2 Volumes)
Cash Receipts, 1906-1909
Accounts Payable, 1906-1909
Bills Receivable, 1904-1907

429. JACKSON-COLUMBIA POWER & LIGHT COMPANY (Non-operating).
Columbia County, Jackson Township.
1924 to 1925, 1/2 Linear Foot.

History:
Incorporated on 28 August 1924 to supply electricity in the Township of Jackson, Columbia County, Jackson-Columbia Power & Light Co. was merged into Pennsylvania Power & Light Co. on 28 October 1924.

430. JACKSON-HERNDON ELECTRIC COMPANY
(Non-operating).
Northumberland County, Jackson Township.
1923, 1 Linear Inch.

History:
Incorporated on 16 October 1923 to supply electricity in the Township of Jackson, Northumberland County, Jackson-Herndon Electric Co. was merged into Middleburg Light Heat and Power Co. on 21 November 1923.

431. JACKSON POWER & LIGHT COMPANY
(Non-operating).
Monroe County, Jackson Township.
1923 to 1924, 2 Linear Inches.

History:
Jackson Power & Light Co. was incorporated 1 May 1923 to supply electricity in the Township of Jackson, Monroe County. It was consolidated and merged with 31 other non-operating companies on 20 July 1923 to form Paupack Power & Light Co., No. 2.

432. JACKSON-SNYDER POWER & LIGHT COMPANY
(Non-operating).
Snyder County, Jackson Township.
1928 to 1929, 2 Linear Inches.

History:
Incorporated on 12 September 1928 to supply electricity in the Township of Jackson, Snyder County, Jackson-Snyder Power & Light Co. was merged into Pennsylvania Power & Light Co. on 29 September 1928.

433. JACKSON TOWNSHIP ELECTRIC COMPANY
(Non-operating).
Dauphin County, Jackson Township.
1924, 2 Linear Inches.

History:
Jackson Township Electric Co. was incorporated 13 August 1924 to supply electricity in the Township of Jackson, Dauphin County. It was merged into the East Penn Electric Co., No. 2, on 28 August 1924.

434. JAMESTOWN ELECTRIC COMPANY (Operating).
Carbon County, Mahoning Township.
1924-1928, 1 Linear Foot.

History:
In 1905 James I. Blakslee, who was operating an electric system in the Borough of Lehighton, Carbon County, extended his distribution lines to serve the Village of Jamestown in neighboring Mahoning Township. Since under Pennsylvania law a single distributor could not provide electricity to more than one township, Blakslee was forced to organize Jamestown Electric Co., which was incorporated 21 December 1923. Three years later the company's stock was acquired by Lehigh Power Securities Corp. which operated it as part of the Pennsylvania Power & Light system. On 28 May 1928 Jamestown Electric Co. was merged into Pennsylvania Power & Light Co.

Administrative Records:
Minute Book, 1924-1928
Stock Certificate Book, 1924-1927
Stock Transfer Record, 1927
Stock Ledger, 1924-1928

Operating Records:
General Ledger, 1927-1928
Journal Entry Register, 1927-1928
Detail of Cost Study and Fixed Capital, 1927
Retirement Authorities, 1928
Expenditure Requisitions, 1927-1928
Audit Reports, 1924-1927 (4 Volumes)

Scope and Content Note:
The Minute Book of the Jamestown Electric Co. contains routine administrative records, primarily minutes of stockholders' and directors' meetings. Most of the records in this collection are financial in nature and provide details of the company's operating expenses. The Audit Reports give information on the company's organization and financial condition.

435. JEDDO-LUZERNE POWER & LIGHT COMPANY (Non-operating).
Luzerne County, Jeddo Borough.
1924 to 1926, 2 Linear Inches.

History:
Jeddo-Luzerne Power & Light Co. was incorporated 26 March 1926 to supply electricity in the Borough of Jeddo, Luzerne County. It was merged into Pennsylvania Power & Light Co. on 14 April 1926.

436. JEFFERSON POWER & LIGHT COMPANY (Non-operating).
Lackawanna County, Jefferson Township.
1923 to 1924, 2 Linear Inches.

History:
Jefferson Power & Light Co. was incorporated 21 May 1923 to supply electricity in the Township of Jefferson, Lackawanna County. It was consolidated and merged with 31 other non-operating companies on 20 July 1923 to form Paupack Power & Light Co., No. 2.

437. JEFFERSON TOWNSHIP ELECTRIC CORPORATION (Non-operating).
Dauphin County, Jefferson Township.
1924, 1 Linear Inch.

History:
Jefferson Township Electric Corp. was incorporated 13 August 1924. It was merged into East Penn Electric Co., No. 2, on 28 August 1924.

438. JENKINS-LUZERNE POWER & LIGHT COMPANY (Non-operating).
Luzerne County, Jenkins Township.
1926 to 1927, 2 Linear Inches.

History:
Jenkins-Luzerne Power & Light Co. was incorporated on 3 February 1927 to supply electricity in the Township of Jenkins, Luzerne County. The company was merged into Pennsylvania Power & Light Co. on 10 February 1927.

439. JENKINS TOWNSHIP ELECTRIC LIGHT, HEAT AND POWER COMPANY (Operating).
Luzerne County, Jenkins Township.
1909 to 1918, 1 Linear Inch.

History:
Jenkins Township Electric Light, Heat and Power Co. was incorporated on 21 July 1909 to supply electricity in the Township of Jenkins, Luzerne County. In April 1918 American Gas & Electric Co. gained control of its stock, and on 16 July 1918 it was sold to the Scranton Electric Co.

Administrative Records:
Minute Book, 1918
Stock Certificate Book, 1909-1918

440. JERMYN ELECTRIC LIGHT, HEAT & POWER COMPANY (Operating).
Lackawanna County, Jermyn Borough.
1891 to 1909, 1 Linear Inch.

History:
Jermyn Electric Light, Heat & Power Co. was organized on 13 January 1891 by Moosic Powder Co., which had surplus electrical capacity after it built a generating system for its factory. This operation was so successful that in 1896 the company installed a new 200-h.p. engine to provide additional power. On 5 March 1902, The Moosic Powder Co. sold the Jermyn Electric Light, Heat & Power Co. to Lackawanna Valley Electric Light & Power Supply Co., which six years later sold it to American Gas & Electric Co. Finally, on 20 September 1910, the company was sold to Scranton Electric Co.

Administrative Records:
Minute Book, 1891-1909

Scope and Content Note:
The Minute Book of Jermyn Electric Light, Heat & Power Co. details the company's relationship with The Moosic Powder Co. It also documents its negotiations with the Jermyn Borough Council for street lighting contracts. Additional information about this company can be found in the Minute Books of The Moosic Powder Co., which are part of the Records of the E.I. du Pont de Nemours & Co., at the Hagley Museum and Library.

441. JERSEY SHORE ELECTRIC COMPANY (Operating).
Lycoming County, Williamsport City.
1903 to 1925, 6 1/2 Linear Feet.

History:
After its incorporation on 14 January 1898, Jersey Shore Electric Co. became the first company to supply electricity in the Borough of Jersey Shore, Lycoming County. Together with Jersey Shore Electric Street Railway Co., this company constructed an electric generating station with a 60-kw capacity. It then constructed an electric distribution system to serve the community. Due to a default in payment of bond interest, the company was sold at sheriff's sale on 1 April 1901 to Mr. Samuel Humes, who represented the bondholders. The bondholders ran the company from 1901 to 1904. In 1905, Lycoming Improvement Co. of Williamsport acquired control of Jersey Shore Electric Co. When Lehigh Power Securities Corp. acquired the stock of Lycoming Improvement Co. in 1923, it assumed control of Jersey Shore Electric Company. On 23 August 1923, Jersey Shore Electric Co. was merged into Pennsylvania Power & Light Co.

Administrative Records:
Minute Books, 1903-1923 (2 Volumes)
Stock Certificate Book, 1904-1923
Stock Ledger, 1904-1913

Operating Records:
General Ledgers, 1903-1923 (3 Volumes)
Journals, 1903-1923 (3 Volumes)
Cashbooks, 1905-1923 (11 Volumes)
Cash Receipts and Disbursements, 1917-1918
Automobile Records, 1923

Retirement Authorities, 1923
Expenditure Requisitions, 1923-1924
Working Papers of Audits, 1923-1925
Audit Reports, 1905-1922 (17 Volumes)

Scope and Content Note:
The Minute Books of the Jersey Shore Electric Co. contain the minutes of routine stockholders' and directors' meetings, a copy of the company's bylaws, and a description of the property owned by the company.

442. JERSEY SHORE ELECTRIC STREET RAILWAY COMPANY (Operating).
Lycoming County, Williamsport City.
1901 to 1927, 1 1/2 Linear Feet.

History:
Jersey Shore Electric Street Railway Co. was incorporated 4 April 1901 to operate an electric railway, approximately four miles long, from the Borough of Jersey Shore, Lycoming County, to the Village of Avis, Clinton County, where the New York Central Railroad's car shops were located. The railway company began service in October 1903. In 1905 the company was purchased by the Lycoming Improvement Co., which was the holding company for the Williamsport Power Securities Corp., and merged into the Pennsylvania Power & Light Co. system. In 1927, the company was sold to Messrs. Ernest Brown and L. Edward Scherer, local businessmen who kept it in operation as a family-run firm until 19 May 1920, when it was dissolved, soon after the announcement that the New York Central's Avis shops were to be closed down.

Administrative Records:
Minute Book, 1923-1927

Operating Records:
General Ledger, 1901-1916
Journal, 1901-1916
Cashbook, 1901-1905
Federal Income Tax Schedules, 1926-1927
Audit Reports, 1905-1926 (17 Volumes)

443. JORDAN-LYCOMING POWER & LIGHT COMPANY (Non-operating).
Lycoming County, Jordan Township.
1924 to 1925, 2 Linear Inches.

History:
Incorporated on 28 August 1924 to supply electricity in the Township of Jordan, Lycoming County, Jordan-Lycoming Power & Light Co. was merged into Pennsylvania Power & Light Co. on 28 October 1924.

444. JUNCTION PASSENGER RAILWAY COMPANY (Operating).
Lycoming County, Williamsport City.
1892 to 1894, 1 Linear Inch.

History:
Junction Passenger Railway Co. was incorporated 8 April 1892 to operate an electric street railway in the City of Williamsport, Lycoming County. It was consolidated and merged with three other electric railway companies on 15 May 1894 to form the Vallamont Traction Co.

Administrative Records:
Minute Book, 1892-1894

445. THE JUNIATA COMPANY, NO. 2 (Operating).
Juniata County, Mifflintown Borough.
1902 to 1917, 1 1/2 Linear Feet.

History:
Electric service was first rendered in the Borough of Mifflintown by Mifflintown Electric Light Co., which was incorporated 4 April 1892. This company constructed a steam electric plant in the Borough of Patterson (present-day Mifflin) as well as a distribution system supplying Mifflintown and Patterson with both arc and incandescent lighting. The property and assets of Mifflintown Electric Light were sold at a sheriff's sale on 25 April 1902 to Mr. Carl F. Espenschade on behalf of the company's bondholders. Mr. Espenschade then sold the company to the Juniata Co., No. 1, which had been incorporated 2 April 1902 to supply electricity in the Borough of Mifflintown. On 10 July 1902 The Juniata Co., No. 1, was consolidated and merged with two non-operating companies to form the Juniata Co., No. 2. Shortly after its formation, the new company rebuilt the power plant at Patterson and reconstructed the town's street lighting system. In 1916 the company's stock was purchased by a group of local businessmen who were attempting to integrate the generating and distribution systems of the various electric companies operating in the area. On 24 September 1917 The Juniata Co., No. 2, was consolidated and merged with 16 other companies to form the Juniata Public Service Co.

Administrative Records:
Minute Book, 1902-1916
Stock Certificate Book, 1902-1917
Stock Register and Transfer, 1916-1917
Stock Ledger, 1902-1915

Operating Records:
General Ledger, 1916-1917
Journal, 1916-1917
Cashbook, 1916-1917
Cash Receipts and Disbursements, 1916-1917 (2 Volumes)
Cash Analysis, 1917

Scope and Content Note:
The Minute Book of The Juniata Co., No. 2, documents the problems encountered while constructing the Patterson power plant and electrical distribution system. Operating expenses, revenues, and rate schedules are detailed. The Minute Books also list company stockholders and trace the street lighting contract negotiations with the Borough Council.

446. JUNIATA LAND COMPANY (Operating).
Perry County, Newport Borough.
1924 to 1934, 2 Linear Inches.

History:
Juniata Land Co. was incorporated 12 August 1924 by East Penn Electric Co. to purchase land along the Juniata River near the Borough of Newport, Perry County, upon which the Juniata River Water Power Co. was to construct a hydroelectric dam and power house. In 1928, the company's stock was acquired by the Pennsylvania Power & Light Co. On 28 December 1934 the company's assets were sold to Pennsylvania Realty & Investment Co. Juniata Land Co. was dissolved on 31 December 1934.

Administrative Records:
Minute Books, 1924-1934 (2 Volumes)
Stock Certificate Book, 1924-1926
Stock Transfer Record, 1926
Stock Ledger, 1924-1926

Operating Records:
General Ledger, 1926-1934
Journal Entry Register, 1926
Detail of Cost Study and Fixed Capital, 1926-1927

447. JUNIATA PUBLIC SERVICE COMPANY
(Operating).
Clearfield County, Clearfield City.
1917 to 1930, 4 1/2 Linear Feet.

History:
Juniata Public Service Co. was incorporated 14 November 1917 following the consolidation and merger of the 17 electric companies which served the area adjacent to the Juniata and Susquehanna Rivers north of the City of Harrisburg. The company's main power plant was at the Borough of Millersburg, Dauphin County. In 1918 plant capacity was boosted by the addition of a 750-kw turbogenerator. Shortly after its formation, the company acquired the stock of Middlesburg Light Heat and Power Co. In 1920, the two power systems were interconnected, but the Middleburg company continued to operate independently. In 1922, another 2500-kw generator was added to the Millersburg power plant. From 1918 to 1928 the company steadily expanded its area of service by the acquisition of over a dozen operating and non-operating companies. One of the most important acquisitions was the Acqueduct Mutual Rural Electric Distribution Association, which owned and operated an electric distribution system in the Townships of Penn and Wheatfield, Perry County, and Reed, Dauphin County. In 1927, Juniata Public Service Company's stock was acquired by Lehigh Power Securities Corp., which thereafter operated it as a part of the Pennsylvania Power & Light Company system. The company was merged into Pennsylvania Power & Light Co. on 28 May 1928.

Administrative Records:
Minute Books, 1917-1928 (2 Volumes)
Secretary's Papers of Meetings, 1918-1928
Stock Subscription Certificate Book, 1917
Stock Certificate Book, 1917-1927
Stock Ledger, 1917-1928
Bond Record, 1918-1919

Operating Records:
FINANCIAL RECORDS
General Ledgers, 1917-1928 (3 Volumes)
Journal, 1917-1927
Journal Entry Register, 1927-1928
Cashbooks, 1917-1924 (5 Volumes)
Cash Receipts and Disbursements, 1924-1927
Record of Cash Disbursements, 1927-1928
Summary of Cash, 1927-1928
Audited Voucher Register, 1919-1927
Accounts Payable, 1927-1928
Summary of Accounts Receivable, 1927-1928
Accounts Receivable—Miscellaneous, 1927-1928
Trial Balance and Balance Sheet, 1927-1928
PERSONNEL RECORDS
Payrolls, 1919-1927
Payrolls—Check Sheets, 1927
Payroll Sheets—Individual, 1918-1921
AUDIT REPORTS, 1922-1927 (3 Volumes)

Scope and Content Note:
The Minute Books of the Juniata Public Service Co. document the 1917 consolidation and merger by which the company was formed, its capitalization and organization, and minutes of stockholders' and directors' meetings. Details of the company's operations cover construction of high tension and other pole lines, installation of powerhouse equipment, coal dredging operations, relations with the Borough Councils of Mifflinburg and Marysville, and a copy of the 1926 rate schedule. The Statement of Reports and the Financial Statements include profit and loss statements of subsidiary companies, details of operating expenses, balance sheets, street lighting contract data, a blueprint map of the territory served, lists of stockholders, and correspondence relating to the 1917 merger and subsequent stock issuances. The Individual Payroll Sheets indicate the employee's occupation, number of hours worked, pay rate per hour, and give a detailed account of job descriptions. Other Payrolls include occasional references to occupations.

448. JUNIATA RIVER WATER COMPANY (Operating).
Perry County, Newport Borough.
1923 to 1935, 2 Linear Inches.

History:
Juniata River Water Power Co. was incorporated 7 November 1923 by East Penn electric Co. to supply electricity in the Borough of Newport, Perry County. The company planned the joint construction of a hydroelectric dam and power house on the Juniata River near Newport with the Watts Water and Power Co. Land for this purpose was acquired on 17 September 1924, but the company did not take steps to develop the site. In 1928 the company's stock was acquired by the Pennsylvania Power & Light Co. In November 1935 the stockholders noted that "the company had not been operating for a number of years" and decided to dissolve it. On 31 December 1935, the company's assets were sold to Pennsylvania Realty & Investment Co.

Administrative Records:
Minute Books, 1923-1935 (2 Volumes)
Stock Certificate Book, 1923-1927
Stock Transfer Record, 1926-1927
Stock Ledger, 1923-1926

Operating Records:
General Ledger, 1926-1935
Journal Entry Register, 1926
Detail of Cost Study and Fixed Capital, 1926-1927

449. KELLY TOWNSHIP ELECTRIC COMPANY
(Non-operating).
Union County, Kelly Township.
1910 to 1911, 1 Linear Inch.

History:
Kelly Township Electric Co., incorporated 31 August 1910 to supply electricity in Kelly Township, Union County, merged into United Light and Power Co., 12 June 1911.

450. KENT ELECTRIC COMPANY (Non-operating).
Monroe County, Smithfield Township.
1911 to 1913, 1 Linear Inch.

History:
Kent Electric Co., incorporated 27 June 1911 to supply electricity in Smithfield Township, Monroe County, consolidated and merged with 37 companies to form Lehigh Navigation Electric Co., No. 2, 6 January 1913.

451. KEYSTONE POWER CORPORATION (Operating).
Elk County, Ridgway Borough.
1922, 1 Linear Inch.

History:
Keystone Power Corp. was incorporated 17 February 1922 with no specified franchise rights. In March 1922, it acquired all the franchises and property of Keystone Electric Service Corp., and thus obtained rights to supply electricity in Ridgway Borough, Elk County, and in other territories in Elk and McKean Counties. The company acquired franchises in Centre County through the purchase of State Centre Electric Co. The stock of Keystone Power Corp. was controlled by Keystone Power & Light Co., a holding company located in Delaware.

Operating Records:
Audit Report, Pennsylvania Power & Light Co., 1922

Scope and Content Note:
The Audit Report, which gives a brief history of the company along with a general overview of its operations, reflects Pennsylvania Power & Light Company's interest in acquiring utility companies, in order to obtain franchise rights in areas it did not serve.

452. KIDDER POWER & LIGHT COMPANY
(Non-operating).
Carbon County, Kidder Township.
1923 to 1924, 1 Linear Inch.

History:
Kidder Power & Light Co., incorporated 23 April 1923 to supply electricity in Kidder Township, Carbon County, consolidated and merged with 31 other companies to form Paupack Power & Light Co., No. 2, 29 January 1924.

453. KILLINGER ELECTRIC COMPANY
(Non-operating).
Dauphin County, Halifax Township.
1916 to 1917, 1 Linear Inch.

History:
Killinger Electric Co., incorporated 14 June 1916 to supply electricity in Halifax Township, Dauphin County, consolidated and merged with 16 companies to form Juniata Public Service Co., 14 November 1917.

454. KLINE TOWNSHIP ELECTRIC COMPANY
(Non-operating).
Schuylkill County, Kline Township.
1909, 1 Linear Inch.

History:
Kline Township Electric Co., incorporated 16 June 1909 to supply electricity in Kline Township, Schuylkill County, consolidated and merged with 11 companies to form Harwood Electric Co., 30 June 1909.

455. KREAMER ELECTRIC COMPANY (Non-operating).
Snyder County, Middle Creek Township.
1923, 1 Linear Inch.

History:
Kreamer Electric Co., incorporated 10 April 1923 to supply electricity in Middle Creek Township, Snyder County, merged into Middleburg Light Heat and Power Co., 28 June 1923.

456. KRICK ELECTRIC COMPANY (Non-operating).
Berks County, Spring Township.
1915 to 1926, 1 Linear Inch.

History:
Krick Electric Co., incorporated 10 November 1915 to supply electricity in Spring Township, Berks County, never actually operated. This non-operating company maintained an independent existence for ten years and on 8 February 1926 merged into Edison Electric Co., No. 4.

457. KULPMONT ELECTRIC COMPANY
(Non-operating).
Northumberland County, Kulpmont Borough.
1918 to 1920, 1 Linear Inch.

History:
Kulpmont Electric Co., incorporated 31 October 1918 to supply electricity in Kulpmont Borough, Northumberland County, merged into Pennsylvania Power & Light Co., 4 November 1920.

458. LACKAWANNA-ARCHBALD POWER & LIGHT COMPANY (Non-operating).
Lackawanna County, Archbald Township.
1955 to 1956, 1 Linear Inch.

History:
Lackawanna-Archbald Power & Light Co., incorporated in September 1955 to supply electricity in Archbald Township, Lackawanna County, merged into Pennsylvania Power & Light Co. in March 1956.

459. LACKAWANNA ELECTRIC LIGHT, HEAT & POWER COMPANY (Operating).
Lackawanna County, Taylor Borough.
1897 to 1910, 1 Linear Inch.

History:
Lackawanna Electric Light, Heat & Power Co. was incorporated in 1897 to supply electricity in Taylor Borough, Lackawanna County. In 1897 the company arranged for the construction of a 2000-candlepower incandescent lighting plant near Taylor, in Lackawanna County. The company leased its plant and property for 99 years to Standard Electric Light, Heat and Power Co. of Avoca, Pennsylvania, in 1901. Scranton Electric Co. acquired Lackawanna Electric Light, Heat & Power Co. in January 1910.

Administrative Records:
Minute Book, 1897-1910

Operating Records:
Consumers' Ledger, 1889-1901

Scope and Content Note:
The Minute Book documents the construction of the company's incandescent lighting plant, and its subsequent lease to Standard Electric Light, Heat and Power Co. The

Consumers' Ledger documents the kind of service each customer was receiving, and the amount of power consumed.

460. LACKAWANNA LIGHT COMPANY (Operating).
Lackawanna County, Scranton City.
1905-1936, 1 Linear Foot.

History:
The West Scranton Light, Heat & Power Co., incorporated in 1905 to supply electricity in the city of Scranton, Lackawanna County, changed its name in 1906 to Lackawanna Light Co. Its power plant, containing two Corliss engines of 1000-horsepower each was completed late in 1906, enabling the company to supply electricity to some 100,000 customers in the city of Scranton. The company's capital stock was owned by the Scranton Electric Co., which operated the firm as a subsidiary until 1935. The franchise rights in Scranton held by Lackawanna Light Co. expired in that year, and the company was merged into The Scranton Electric Co.

Administrative Records:
Minute Books, 1905-1935 (2 Volumes)
Stock Certificate Book, 1926-1935

Operating Records:
General Ledgers, 1907-1936 (2 Volumes)
Invoice and Journal Voucher Register, 1907-1920
Cashbooks, 1907-1936 (2 Volumes)
Insurance, Tax, Rent Registers, 1933-1936 (2 Volumes)

461. LACKAWANNA TOWNSHIP ELECTRIC COMPANY (Non-operating).
Lackawanna County, Lackawanna Township.
1913-1918, 1 Linear Inch.

History:
Lackawanna Township Electric Co., incorporated 7 February 1913 to supply electricity in Lackawanna Township, Lackawanna County, merged into Scranton Electric Co., 15 July 1918.

462. LACKAWANNA VALLEY ELECTRIC LIGHT & POWER SUPPLY COMPANY (Operating).
Lackawanna County, Carbondale City.
1899 to 1910, 1 Linear Inch.

History:
Lackawanna Valley Electric Light & Power Supply Co. was formed in March 1899 through the consolidation and merger of Lackawanna Electric Light & Power Co. and Carbondale Electric Light, Heat & Power Co. It supplied electricity in the City of Carbondale, Lackawanna County. Through purchases of Crescent Electric Co. and Jermyn Electric Light Co., it acquired franchises in several other Lackawanna County localities. In 1910, it, in turn, was acquired by Scranton Electric Co.

Administrative Records:
Minute Book, 1899-1910

Scope and Content Note:
The Minute Book contains some information on company operations and expenditures and documents stockholders' and directors' meetings.

463. LACKAWANNA-WINTON POWER & LIGHT COMPANY (Non-operating).
Lackawanna County, Winton Township.
1955 to 1956, 1 Linear Inch.

History:
Lackawanna-Winton Power & Light Co., incorporated in September 1955 to supply electricity in Winton Township, Lackawanna County, merged into Pennsylvania Power & Light Co. in April 1956.

464. LACKAWAXEN POWER & LIGHT COMPANY (Non-operating).
Pike County, Lackawaxen Township.
1923 to 1924, 1 Linear Inch.

History:
Lackawaxen Power & Light Co., incorporated 1 May 1923 to supply electricity in Lackawaxen Township, Pike County, consolidated and merged with 31 companies to form Paupack Power & Light Co., No. 2, 29 January 1924.

465. LAFLIN BOROUGH-LUZERNE POWER & LIGHT COMPANY (Non-operating).
Luzerne County, Laflin Borough.
1926 to 1927, 1 Linear Inch.

History:
Laflin Borough-Luzerne Power & Light Co. was organized in March 1926 by officials of Pennsylvania Power & Light Co. in order to obtain charter rights in Laflin Borough, Luzerne County. The company, however, never received its Letters Patent, and thus was never incorporated.

466. LAFLIN ELECTRIC COMPANY (Non-operating).
Luzerne County, Laflin Borough.
1924 to 1928, 1 Linear Inch.

History:
Laflin Electric Co., incorporated 24 April 1924 to supply electricity in Laflin Borough, Luzerne County, consolidated and merged with eight companies to form The Scranton Electric Co., 3 February 1928.

467. LAKE HALL LAND COMPANY (Non-operating).
Schuylkill County, Pine Grove Borough.
1925 to 1926, 1 Linear inch.

History:
Lake Hall Land Co., incorporated in Delaware during the early 1920s, owned land along the shore of an artificial lake known as Lake Hall. This lake was formed by East Penn Electric Co. when it constructed its hydroelectric power plant at Pine Grove.

468. LAKE POWER & LIGHT COMPANY (Non-operating).
Wayne County, Lake Township.
1923 to 1924, 1 Linear Inch.

History:
Lake Power & Light Co., incorporated 11 July 1923 to supply electricity in Lake Township, Wayne County,consolidated and merged with 31 companies to form Paupack Power & Light Co., No.2, 29 January 1924.

469. LAMAR-CLINTON POWER & LIGHT COMPANY (Non-operating).
Clinton County, Lamar Township.
1947 to 1949, 1 Linear Inch.

History:
Lamar-Clinton Power & Light Co., incorporated in December 1947 to supply electricity in Lamar Township, Clinton County, merged into Pennsylvania Power & Light Co., December 1948.

470. LANCASTER COUNTY RAILWAY AND LIGHT COMPANY (Operating).
Lancaster County, Lancaster City.
1901 to 1934, 5 Linear Feet.

History:
Lancaster County Railway and Light Co. was incorporated in June 1901. This New Jersey-based holding company owned the capital stock of the Conestoga Traction Co., Lancaster Gas Light and Fuel Co., Edison Electric Co., and Lancaster Electric Light, Heat and Power Co. Under this arrangement, it controlled the electric, gas and street railway systems of Lancaster Co. In 1912 the company's stock was acquired by United Gas and Electric Co., which sold it to Lehigh Power Securities Corp. in 1926. Under the direction of Electric Bond and Share, Lehigh Power Securities transferred all the assets and franchises of the company to Pennsylvania Power & Light in December of 1930.

Administrative Records:
Minute Book—Executive Committee, 1903-1909
Minute Book—Board of Directors and Executive Committee, 1917-1934
Minute Book-Board of Directors and Stockholders, 1934-1935
Stock Certificate Books—Common, 1901-1921 (4 Volumes)
Stock Certificate Books—Preferred, 1901-1931 (9 Volumes)
Stock Transfer Records—Common, 1901-1921 (3 Volumes)
Stock Transfer Records—Preferred, 1901-1927 (4 Volumes)
Stock Certificate Ledger—Common, 1901-1916
Stock Ledger and Transfers—Preferred, 1901-1912
Record of 5% Preferred Stock, 1922-1930
Receipts for Payments for Shares in Syndicate, 1901

Operating Records:
General Ledger, 1901
Cashbooks, 1901-1908 (2 Volumes)
Statement of Receipts and Expenditures, 1901-1907
Audited Voucher Register, 1901-1902
Balance Sheet, 1927
Financial Statements, 1901
Monthly Statements, 1905-1906
Income Taxes, 1922-1925
udit Reports, 1910, 1915-1916 (2 Volumes)

Scope and Content Note:
The Executive Committee Minute Book, 1903-1909, documents the various strategies that Lancaster County Railway and Light Co. adopted to oversee and administer the affairs of its subsidiary companies. In particular, the Minute Book details official concern over labor relations (discipline, wages and salaries). Also documented are negotiations with Lancaster County for street lighting and street repair contracts. The Minutes include copies of the lease and purchase agreements through which the Company acquired control of a number of small street railway companies. Finally, the efforts of United Gas and Electric Co. and Lehigh Power Securities Corp. to consolidate and integrate the various properties owned by Lancaster Railway and Light Co. into an integrated system, are documented in the Board of Directors Minute Book, 1917-1934.

471. LANCASTER ELECTRIC LIGHT, HEAT AND POWER COMPANY (Operating).
Lancaster County, Lancaster City.
1897 to 1930, 3 Linear Feet.

History:
Lancaster Electric Light, Heat and Power Co., incorporated in 1897, supplied electricity to the City of Lancaster, Lancaster County. Its generating facilities consisted of three hydroelectric plants, located near Lancaster. In 1902, its distribution system was leased to The Edison Electric Illuminating Co. of Lancaster, Pa., which in 1917 sold its capital stock to the Lancaster County Railway and Light Co. In 1930, Lancaster Electric Light, Heat and Power Co. was merged into the Pennsylvania Power & Light system.

Administrative Records:
Minute Books, 1905-1930 (3 Volumes)
Secretary's Papers of Meetings, 1899-1930
Stock Certificate Book—Common, 1897-1930
Stock Certificate Books—Preferred, 1922-1930 (4 Volumes)
Stock Transfer Record—Preferred, 1923-1927
Stock Ledger and Transfers, 1897-1918
Dividend Book, 1899-1900
Lists of Preferred Stockholders for Dividend Payments, 1922-1930

Operating Records:
General Ledgers, 1917-1930 (2 Volumes)
Journal, 1917-1926
Journal Entry Register, 1926-1930
Cashbooks, 1899-1904, 1918-1926 (3 Volumes)
Records of Cash Receipts, 1926-1930
Records of Cash Disbursements, 1926-1927
Cash Deposits and Withdrawls, 1927-1930
Audited Voucher Registers, 1912-1930 (2 Volumes)
Accounts Payable Ledgers, 1898-1900, 1918-1930 (3 Volumes)
Accounts Receivable, 1926-1930
Detail Ledgers, 1913-1917, 1926-1930 (2 Volumes)
Construction Ledger, 1928-1929
Analysis of Closed Jobs, 1921-1923
Fixed Capital Detail, 1926-1928
Materials and Supplies Reports, 1926-1928
Automobile Reports, 1926-1929
Financial Statements, 1898-1903, 1923-1928
Financial Reports, 1920-1926 (7 Volumes)
Payrolls, 1927-1930
Audit Reports, 1917-1930

Scope and Content Note:
The Minutes for the period 1905-1917 contain brief annual reports of the president, which describe the company's business and detail improvements made to the company's three hydroelectric plants.

472. LANCASTER, EPHRATA AND LEBANON STREET RAILWAY COMPANY (Operating).
Lancaster County, Lancaster City.
1924 to 1925, 1 Linear Inch.

History:
Lancaster, Ephrata and Lebanon Street Railway Co., incorporated 28 January 1924, purchased properties of Ephrata & Lebanon Street Railway Co. and Ephrata and Lebanon Traction Co. The company operated an electric railway between Ephrata in Lancaster, and Lebanon in Lebanon County, a distance of 23 miles, which served Bethlehem Steel Company's Lebanon plant. Although Electric Bond and Share Co. and Pennsylvania Power & Light Co. both prepared audit reports on the company in 1925 with an eye to acquiring it, the company was never brought into the Pennsylvania Power & Light system.

Operating Records:
Audit Reports, 1924-1925 (2 Volumes)

473. LANCASTER GAS LIGHT AND FUEL COMPANY (Operating).
Lacaster County, Lancaster City.
1898 to 1930, 6 Linear Inches.

History:
Lancaster Gas Light and Fuel Co., incorporated in 1876, provided gas service in the City of Lancaster, Lancaster County. It operated as an independent concern until 1901 when Lancaster County Railway and Light Co. acquired its common stock. Following the acquisition of Lancaster County Railway and Light Co. by Lehigh Power Securities Corp. in 1926, Lancaster Gas Light and Fuel Co. merged into Pennsylvania Power & Light Co.

Administrative Records:
Minute Book Lancaster County Railway and Light Co., Executive Committee, 1903-1915

Operating Records:
Gross Receipts Calculations, 1898-1900
Payrolls—Gas Distribution, 1927-1930
Payrolls—Plant, 1927-1930
Operating Reports, Lancaster Group Companies, 1926, 1929, 1930
Delinquent Customers' Notices, 1926
Audit Reports, 1918-1925 (5 Volumes)

Scope and Content Note:
The Minute book provides an overview of company operations furnishing information of fuel supplies and gas lighting contracts. Payrolls list employees, their occupation, hours worked, and itemize deductions for welfare and benevolent societies.

474. LANCASTER TOWNSHIP ELECTRIC COMPANY (Non-operating).
Lancaster County, Lancaster Township.
1911, 1 Linear Foot.

History:
Lancaster Township Electric Co., incorporated 10 August 1911 to supply electricity in Lancaster Township, Lancaster County, consolidated and merged with 17 companies to form Edison Electric Co., No. 1, 2 October 1911.

475. LANDISBURG LIGHT, HEAT AND POWER COMPANY (Non-operating).
Perry County, Landisburg Borough.
1921 to 1922, 1 Linear Inch.

History:
Landisburg Light, Heat and Power Co., incorporated 15 December 1921 to supply electricity in Landisburg Borough, Perry County, consolidated and merged with two companies to form Sherman Valley Electric Light, Heat and Power Co., 25 October 1922.

476. LAUREL PARK POWER & LIGHT COMPANY (Operating).
Union County, Hartleton Borough.
1926 to 1931, 2 Linear Feet.

History:
Laurel Park Power & Light Co. was incorporated 12 January 1926 by L.E. Yagel, owner of a grist mill in Laurel Park Village in the Borough of Hartleton, Union County. The company provided street lighting service in Hartleton and electric service to neighboring rural customers. Lehigh Power Securities Corp., which acquired the company's stock in 1929, merged it into Pennsylvania Power & Light Co., 31 December 1930.

Administrative Records:
Minute Book, 1926-1930
Stock Certificate Book, 1926-1930
Stock Transfer Record, 1929-1930

Operating Records:
General Ledgers, 1926-1930 (2 Volumes)
Journals, 1926-1930 (2 Volumes)
Record of Cash Receipts (2 Volumes)
Record of Cash Disbursements, 1926-1930 (2 Volumes)
Audited Voucher Register, 1929-1930
Accounts Payable and Receivable, Detail, and Accrual Ledger, 1929-1930
Expenditure Requisitions, 1929-1930
Retirement Authorities, 1929-1931
Workmen's Compensation Insurance Accrual Statements, 1929
Bills, 1929-1930
Summary of Accounts Receivable—Consumers, 1929-1930
Summary of Accounts Receivable—Miscellaneous, 1929-1930
Statement of Rents, 1930
Summary of Cashier's Overs and Shorts, 1930
Audit Reports, 1926-1930 (4 Volumes)

477. LAUREL RUN ELECTRIC COMPANY (Non-operating).
Luzerne County, Laurel Run Borough.
1922 to 1923, 1 Linear Inch.

History:
Laurel Run Electric Co., incorporated 30 March 1922 to supply electricity in Laurel Run Borough, Luzerne County, merged into Prospect Rock Electric Light, Heat and Power Co., 9 April 1923.

478. LAUSANNE TOWNSHIP ELECTRIC COMPANY (Non-operating).
Carbon County, Lausanne Township.
1911 to 1912, 1 Linear Inch.

History:
Lausanne Township Electric Co., incorporated 6 February 1911 to supply electricity in Lausanne Township, Carbon County, consolidated and merged with 11 companies to form The Harwood Electric Co., 26 February 1912.

479. LEACOCK TOWNSHIP ELECTRIC COMPANY (Non-operating).
Lancaster County, Leacock Township.
1912, 1 Linear Inch.

History:
Leacock Township Electric Co., incorporated 25 April 1912 to supply electricity in Leacock Township, Lancaster County, consolidated and merged with six companies to form Christiana Electric Co., 15 May 1912.

480. LEBANON VALLEY LIGHT AND POWER COMPANY (Operating).
Lancaster County, Elizabeth Township.
1915 to 1926, 1 Linear Foot.

History:
Elizabeth Township Electric Co., incorporated in November 1915, shortly thereafter changed its name to Lebanon Valley Light and Power Co. The company, which supplied electricity in Elizabeth Township, Lancaster County, merged into Edison Electric Co., No. 4, 8 February 1926.

Administrative Records:
Minute Books, 1915,1918-1925 (3 Volumes)
Stock Certificate Book, 1923
Bond Coupon Book, 1916-1918

Operating Records:
General Ledger, 1915-1926
Journal, 1915-1926
Cashbook, 1915-1924
Audited Voucher Register, 1920-1926
Audit Reports, 1923-1925 (3 Volumes)

481. LEBANON-WAYNE POWER & LIGHT COMPANY (Non-operating).
Wayne County, Lebanon Township.
1928, 1 Linear Inch.

History:
Lebanon-Wayne Power & Light Co., incorporated 27 September 1928 to supply electricity in Lebanon Township, Wayne County, merged into Pennsylvania Power & Light Co., 19 November 1928.

482. LEHIGH AND NORTHAMPTON LIGHT, HEAT AND POWER COMPANY (Operating).
Lehigh County, Catasauqua Borough.
1907 to 1914, 2 Linear Feet.

History:
Lehigh-Northampton Gas and Electric Co. went bankrupt in 1904, and was in receivership for the next two years. In 1906, it was reorganized as Lehigh and Northampton Light, Heat and Power Co. The company operated a 33-kw power plant in the Borough of Catasauqua, and purchased additional power from Lehigh Valley Transit Co. In December 1913, it merged into Lehigh Valley Transit Co.

Operating Records:
General Ledger, 1908-1908
Journals, 1907-1908 (2 Volumes)
Cashbook—Superintendent, 1907-1908
Cashbooks—Accounts Receivable, 1907-1914 (8 Volumes)
Cashbooks—Electric Dept., 1908-1913 (2 Volumes)
Cashbooks—Gas Dept., 1912-1914 (3 Volumes)
Meter Test Record, 1907-1913
Storeroom Account Ledger, 1908-1913
Cost and Time Books, 1906-1907 (2 Volumes)
Audit Report, 1913

Scope and Content Note:
The Meter Test Record (contained in the Superintendent's book) lists customers, and gives statistical data documenting tests on electric and gas meters. Cost and Time Books are construction and repair records listing type of work performed, with the time spent and cost of each job. There are also records c. 1925 documenting sales of appliances, i.e., vacuum cleaners and washing machines.

483. LEHIGH COUNTY ELECTRIC COMPANY (Operating).
Lehigh County, Coplay Borough.
1900 to 1913, 1 Linear Inch.

History:
Lehigh County Electric Co., incorporated 13 March 1900, was owned by Lehigh-Northampton Gas and Electric Co., a holding company, until December 1906, when it was sold to Lehigh and Northampton Light, Heat and Power Co. On 3 March 1915 it merged into Lehigh Valley Light and Power Co., No. 3.

Administrative Records:
Stock Certificate Book, 1900-1913

Operating Records:
Audit Report, 1913

484. LEHIGH INDUSTRIAL POWER COMPANY (Operating).
Monroe County, Stroudsburg Borough.
1919 to 1923, 1 Linear Foot.

History:
Lehigh Industrial Power Co. was formed 6 November 1919 through the consolidation and merger of The Stroudsburg Electric Light and Power Co. and Industrial Power Co. The company supplied electricity in Stroudsburg and East Stroudsburg Boroughs in Monroe County, and held franchises in several townships in Carbon, Northampton, and Lehigh Counties. In 1920 the company acquired nine non-operating companies gaining franchises in Montour and Northumberland Counties. It merged into Pennsylvania Power & Light Co. on 4 February 1921.

Administrative Records:
Minute Book, 1919-1921
Stock Certificate Book, 1919-1921
Stock Transfer Record, 1919-1921
Stock Ledger, 1919-1921

Operating Records:
General Ledgers, 1919-1921
Cash Received and Check Register, 1919-1921
Accounts Payable, 1919-1921
Accounts Receivable, 1919-1921
Accrual Record, 1919-1921
Payroll Statements, 1920
Payrolls, 1919-1921
Automobile Statements, 1919
Statement of Operating Revenue, 1919-1920
Reconcilement of Bank Balances, 1920-1921
Working Papers on Estimated Receipts and Expenditures, 1919-1921
Statement of Charges to Preliminary Survey and Investigation and Capital Account, 1920
Statement of Sales and Allowances to Customers, 1919-1921
Monthly Merchandise and Jobbing Sales Report, 1919-1921
Retirement Authorities, 1920
Expenditure Requisitions, 1921-1923
Bills, 1919-1920

Scope and Content Note:
The Minute Book contains copies of a contract and other items documenting the company's installation of a 10,000-kw turbogenerator, transformers, switching station, and other electrical apparatus at Lehigh Valley Transit Company's Allentown Power House. The minutes also describe additions and improvements to Hauto Steam Electric Station, Harwood Steam Electric Station, Siegfried Substation, and the construction of tie lines between Siegfried and Allentown. Detailed specifications for these projects appear in the Expenditure Requisitions.

485. LEHIGH NAVIGATION ELECTRIC COMPANY, NO.1 (Non-operating).
Carbon County, Mauch Chunk County.
1911 to 1915, 3 Linear Inches.

History:
Lehigh Navigation Electric Co., No. 1, was incorporated 4 April 1911 to supply electricity in Mauch Chunk Township, Carbon County. The company was organized by officials of the Lehigh Coal and Navigation Co. in order to supply power to coal mines in and around Carbon County. The company was technically "non-operating" in that it did not actually produce or supply electricity. It functioned as a legal entity to negotiate contracts for construction of a 20,000-kw power plant near Hauto, Carbon County. The primary contract was negotiated with L.B. Stillwell, a New York-based consulting engineer. As construction of the Hauto plant neared completion in 1912, the company arranged to consolidate with the 37 non-operating township companies which it had organized in 1911 and 1912. This merger, which was finalized on 6 January 1913, resulted in the formation of Lehigh Navigation Electric Co., No.2.

486. LEHIGH NAVIGATION ELECTRIC COMPANY, NO. 2 (Operating).
Carbon County, Mauch Chunk Township.
1911 to 1924, 18 Linear Feet.

History:
Lehigh Navigation Electric Company, No. 2, formed in 1913 through the consolidation and merger of 38 non-operating companies, was one of the largest electric power companies in Pennsylvania prior to the formation of PP&L. It supplied power to Lehigh Coal and Navigation Co., for its collieries in and around Carbon County. It also supplied power to the Lehigh Valley's cement and steel industries, with Bethlehem Steel being one of the largest customers. In order to meet the area's growing demand for energy, the company built a 30,000-kw turbogenerator steam electric station at Hauto in Carbon County, and a 20,000-kw substation at Siegfried, 18 miles north of Allentown. In 1913, the company acquired a controlling interest in The Harwood Electric Co. and two years later the Hauto plant was linked to the Harwood plant by a 66-kw line. In 1918 capacity was increased again. A 22-kw tie-line was built which linked the company's distribution system to the Lehigh Valley Transit Company's Allentown steam electric station. By the end of World War I, output amounted to some 112,000,000-kwh, and the company's territory extended from Berwick on the Susquehanna River, to Bethlehem in the Lehigh Valley. This area included 150,000 customers.

In 1917, Lehigh Power Securities Corp. acquired the stock of Lehigh Navigation Electric Co. A merger with Lehigh Valley Light and Power Co., No. 3, resulted in the formation of The Lehigh Valley Light and Power Co. on 11 September 1919.

Administrative Records:
Minute Book, 1913-1919
Stock Certificate Book, 1913-1917
Stock Transfer Records, 1914-1917 (2 Volumes)
Stock Ledger, 1913-1919
Binder—Copies of Agreements, Mortgages, etc., 1913-1917
Securities Owned, 1913-1917
Capital Stock Outstanding, 1916
Correspondence, 1913-1921
Ordinances and Contracts at Hauto, 1915-1917
Cement Rate Case Data, 1919-1920
Cement Rate Case Working Papers, 1919-1920

Operating Records:
FINANCIAL RECORDS
General Ledger, 1913-1919
General Ledger and Operating Accounts, 1914-1919 (2 Volumes)
Journal and Day Book, 1913-1919
Journals—Operating Dept., 1914-1918 (2 Volumes)
Journal Entries and Trial Balances, 1914-1918
Cashbooks, 1911-1919 (3 Volumes)
Cashbook—Supplementary, 1918-1919
Cash Received and Check Register, 1919
Cashbook—Inside Construction Dept., 1918-1923
Accounts Receivable Ledger, 1917-1919
Bill Registers, 1914-1920 (3 Volumes)
Operating Ledger, 1914-1917
Operating Ledger—Detail, 1920-1922 (2 Volumes)
Operating Ledger—Lehigh Navigation Electric System

Expenses, 1922-1923
Production and Transmission Expenses, 1914-1918
Commercial and General Expense—Detail, 1914-1918
Construction Contracts, 1917
Construction Contracts—Information Sheets, 1917
Estimates on New Construction Lines
Closed Jobs, 1918-1920
Cost of Plant and Property, 1912-1918 (3 Volumes)
Cost of Plant and Property Statements, 1914-1918
Cost of Electric System, 1919-1920
Plant and Property Ledgers, Companies Merged Into Lehigh Navigation Electric Co., No. 2, 1911-1918 (2 Volumes)
New Structural Cost Proofs, 1912-1915
Analyses of Taxes, 1921
Accrual Records, 1914-1919 (3 Volumes)
Operating Department Expenses File, 1917
Cost of Supplies, 1915-1919
Cost of Customers' Mill and Plant Equipment, 1913-1921 (2 Volumes)
Coal Account, 1917-1918
Coal Consumed Account, 1918-1919
Cars and Fuel Tonnage, 1915-1919
Inventory—Operating Dept., 1915-1917
Supplies on Hand—Nazareth, 1914-1918
Supplies on Hand—Hauto, 1913-1918
Supplies on Hand—South Bethlehem, 1917-1918
Suppplies on Hand—Siegfried, 1914-1918 (2 Volumes)
Stock Account—Nazareth, 1919
Storehouse Record—South Bethlehem, 1916-1918
Storehouse Record—Nazareth, 1914-1916
Copies of Orders Issued, 1911
Summary of Stock Account—Nazareth, 1917-1919 (3 Volumes)
Explosives Reports—Nazareth, 1917-1918
Statements—Consolidated Interest, 1918
Statements—Income Accounts, 1914-1917
Statements—Profit and Loss, 1914-1917
Statements—Delinquent Accounts—South Bethlehem, 1914
Statements—Consumers' Ledger—Martins Creek, 1914-1915
Statements—Consumers' Ledger—South Bethlehem, 1915-1918
Statements—General Electric Co., 1921
Lehigh Navigation Electric System Working Papers
Meter Readings—Bangor District, 1917
Estimates of Loads at Generating Plant, 1917
Suspense on Balance Sheets, 1919
Claim for Cement Bags Lost by Lehigh Navigation Railroad Co., 1924
Daily Construction Progress Reports, 1918-1919
Papers of Contracts to Mr. Mitchell, 1913-1919
Abstracts of Contracts and Orders Issued by L.B. Stillwell, 1911
Services and Expenses of Mr. Stillwell, 1913-1916
Income Tax Reports, 1914-1918
Financial Reports, 1917-1919
Balance Sheets, 1913-1916
Balance Sheets—Small Companies, 1914-1917
Balance Sheets—Pencil Copies, 1917-1919
Electric System Charges as Per Pennsylvania Classification, 1920-1923
Consolidated Income Account Reports, 1919
Consolidated Income Account Reports—Small Companies, 1917
Detail Repair and Construction Ledgers, 1914-1920 (4 Volumes)

PERSONNEL RECORDS
Accident Register, 1916-1917
Time Sheets, 1915-1919 (5 Volumes)
Time Books, 1914
Payroll Ledger, 1918-1919
Payrolls, 1916-1919
Payrolls, 1918-1919
Payrolls—Hauto Plant, 1913-1914
Payrolls—Hauto Plant, 1917-1918
Payrolls—Hauto Plant—Extra Work, 1913
Payrolls—Allentown Power House, 1918-1919
Payrolls—Production Dept., 1914-1917
Payrolls—Distribution Dept., 1914-1917
Payrolls—Construction Dept., 1914-1919
Payroll Distribution—Commercial, 1914-1917 (3 Volumes)
Earnings of Employees from Various Departments, 1919
Classification of Payrolls Applying to Public Liability Insurance, 1916-1919
Workmen's Compensation Payroll, 1915-1916 (2 Volumes)
Workmen's Compensation Vouchers, 1916-1919 (2 Volumes)
Subscriptions to U.S. Liberty Loans, 1918-1920
Liberty Loan Payments, 1918-1920

AUDIT REPORTS, 1916-1917 (2 Volumes)

Scope and Content Note:

The records consist largely of operating financial data. Included is a binder of agreements, deeds, and memoranda collected by the lawyers representing Electric Bond and Share who were involved in the negotiations which resulted in the company's acquisition by Lehigh Power Securities Corp.

Correspondence documents the company's ongoing effort to secure new industrial customers. Of particular interest are the records detailing the electrification of local slate quarries which resulted in the replacement of hand operated drills, hoists and hammers with electric tools. Considerable data, including graphs charting peak load curves and customer demand, and rate schedules also appear in the correspondence file.

The Minute Book depicts the company's relationship with The Harwood Electric Co. and the Lehigh Coal and Navigation Co. The plans to integrate all utilities within the anthracite coal region through consolidation and merger are very well documented as are the company's dealings with the Pennsylvania Public Service Commission. L.B. Stillwell's relationship to the company and the central role that his engineering firm played in its expansion are described.

Finally, there are a variety of records pertaining to industrial relations including: Payrolls, Workmen's Compensation Records, Vouchers for Medical Services, Accident Registers, and Time Books which were prepared by foremen to record their evaluations of workers' performance and attendance.

Turbine Room, Hauto Power Plant, Lehigh Navigation Electric Company, 1913.

Rear of Electrical Control Board, Hauto Power Plant, 1913.

487. LEHIGH-NORTHAMPTON GAS AND ELECTRIC COMPANY (Operating).
Northampton County, Northampton Borough.
1901 to 1913, 2 Linear Feet.

History:
Lehigh-Northampton Gas and Electric Co., incorporated 24 April 1900 in New Jersey, received a franchise to supply gas and electricity in Northampton Borough, Northampton County. Its charter also gave it the rights (non-exclusive) to supply gas and electricity elsewhere in Northampton and Lehigh Counties. In June 1900 it acquired the common stock of Lehigh County Electric Co., Northampton County Electric Co., and Cementon Electric Light and Power Co. It operated these companies in its own name until January 1904 when it went into receivership. In 1906, the common stock held by the company was transferred by its bondholders to a new holding company, Lehigh and Northampton Light, Heat and Power Co. Lehigh-Northampton Gas and Electric Co. thereafter constructed a distribution system in the Boroughs of Northampton and North Catasauqua in Northampton County, and in adjacent territory in Northampton and Lehigh Counties, connecting it to the distribution system of Catasauqua Electric Light and Power Co. In January 1909 the company was dissolved by the State of New Jersey for nonpayment of taxes.

Operating Records:
General Ledgers, 1901-1907 (4 Volumes)
Journals, 1901-1907 (3 Volumes)
Cashbooks, 1902-1908 (7 Volumes)
Expenditure Ledger, 1904-1907
Expenditure Reports, 1905-1907
Construction Expenditures, 1905
Trial Balances, 1905-1907
Audit Report, 1913

Scope and Content Note:
The records of this company overlap with those of the companies whose stock it controlled and with those of Catasauqua Electric Light and Power Co., whose records should also be consulted.

488. LEHIGH POWER & LIGHT COMPANY (Operating).
Wayne County, Lehigh Township.
1923 to 1924, 1 Linear Inch.

History:
Lehigh Power & Light Co., incorporated 23 April 1923 to supply electricity in Lehigh Township, Wayne County, consolidated and merged with 31 companies to form Paupack Power & Light Co., No. 2, 29 January 1924.

489. LEHIGH TOWNSHIP ELECTRIC COMPANY (Non-operating).
Carbon County, Lehigh Township.
1911 to 1912, 1 Linear Inch.

History:
Lehigh Township Electric Co., incorporated 6 February 1911 to supply electricity in Lehigh Township, Carbon County, consolidated and merged with 11 companies to form The Harwood Electric Co., 26 February 1912.

490. LEHIGH TOWNSHIP ELECTRIC LIGHT AND POWER COMPANY (Non-operating).
Northampton, Lehigh Township.
1914 to 1915, 1 Linear Inch.

History:
Lehigh Township Electric Light and Power Co., incorporated 2 October 1914 to supply electricity in Lehigh Township, Northampton County, merged into Lehigh Valley Light and Power Co., No. 3, 3 March 1915.

491. LEHIGH TOWNSHIP POWER & LIGHT COMPANY (Non-operating).
Lackawanna, Lehigh Township.
1923 to 1924, 1 Linear Inch.

History:
Lehigh Township Power & Light Co., incorporated 21 May 1923 to supply electricity in Lehigh Township, Lackawanna County, consolidated and merged with 31 companies to form Paupack Power & Light Company, No. 2, 29 January 1924.

492. THE LEHIGH VALLEY LIGHT AND POWER COMPANY (Operating).
Lehigh County, Allentown City.
1918 to 1922, 4 Linear Feet.

History:
The Lehigh Valley Light and Power Co. was formed in September 1919 through the consolidation of Lehigh Navigation Electric Co. and Lehigh Valley Light and Power Co., No. 3. The company supplied electricity in the Lehigh Valley and in the adjacent anthracite coal region, a territory with a population of approximately 234,000 people. Major cities served included Allentown in Lehigh County, and Bethlehem in Lehigh and Northampton Counties. It was one of eight companies that consolidated and merged in June 1920 to form Pennsylvania Power & Light Co.

Administrative Records:
Minute Book, 1919-1920
Stock Certificate Book, 1919
Stock Transfer Record—Common, 1919
Stock Transfer Record—Preferred, 1919
Stock Ledger—Common, 1919-1920
Stock Ledger—Preferred, 1919-1920

Operating Records:
FINANCIAL RECORDS
General Ledger, 1919-1920
Journal Entries, 1919-1920
Cash Received and Check Register, 1919-1920
Cashier's Reports, 1919-1920
Accounts Payable, A-L, 1919-1920
Accounts Payable, M-Z, 1919-1920
Accounts Receivable, 1919-1920
Balance Sheets and Other Financial Records, 1919-1920
Detail Operating Ledger, 1919-1920
Detail Repair and Construction Ledger, 1918-1919
Detail Ledger—Trial Balances, 1920
Statement of Charges to Capital, 1919-1920
Accrual Record, 1919
Cost Analyses of Contracts—U.S. Housing Corp., 1921
PERSONNEL RECORDS
Payroll Ledger, 1919

Payrolls—Production, 1919
Payrolls—Distribution, 1919-1920 (2 Volumes)
Payrolls—Automobile Dept., 1920
Payroll Summary, 1919-1920
Time Sheets—Siegfried Substation, 1919
Time Sheets—Allentown and Hazleton Stations, 1919
CONSUMER RECORDS
Statement of Sales and Allowances, 1919-1920
Monthly Merchandise and Jobbing Reports, 1919-1920
Financial Reports—Working Papers, 1919-1920
Bills, 1919-1920 (4 Boxes)
Daily Time Tickets, 1919

Scope and Content Note:
The Daily Time Tickets, 1919, furnish information on repairs and servicing of electric appliances leased by customers (e.g., washers, toasters, clocks).

493. LEHIGH VALLEY LIGHT AND POWER COMPANY, NO. 1 (Non-operating).
Lehigh County, Whitehall Township.
1911 to 1913, 1 Linear Inch.

History:
Lehigh Valley Light and Power Co., No. 1, incorporated 10 November 1911 to supply electricity in Whitehall Township, Lehigh County, consolidated and merged with 10 companies to form Lehigh Valley Light and Power Co., No. 2, 2 January 1913.

494. LEHIGH VALLEY LIGHT AND POWER COMPANY, NO. 2 (Operating).
Lehigh County, Whitehall Township.
1912 to 1913, 2 Linear Inches.

History:
Lehigh Valley Light and Power Co., No. 2, was formed by officials of Lehigh Valley Transit Co., 2 January 1913, through the consolidation and merger of The Citizens Electric Light, Heating and Power Co., The Slatedale Electric Light, Heat and Power Co., and nine non-operating township companies. Through this organization the company obtained franchises in the Borough of Slatington, Lehigh County, and in neighboring townships in Lehigh and Northampton Counties. The company remained in existence only a few months. Under a second agreement of consolidation and merger, it combined with The Allentown Electric Light and Power Co., 17 March 1913, to form Lehigh Valley Light and Power Co., No. 3.

Administrative Records:
Minute Book, 1912-1913
Agreement of Consolidation and Merger, 1912
Stock Certificate Book, 1913

495. LEHIGH VALLEY LIGHT AND POWER COMPANY, NO. 3 (Operating).
Lehigh County, Allentown City.
1913 to 1931, 8 Linear Feet.

History:
The formation of the Lehigh Valley Light and Power Company system is an example of the role electric street railway companies played in the early development of the electric power industry. In this case, the prime mover was Lehigh Valley Transit Co., organized in 1903, as the successor to several small local street railway lines in and around the City of Allentown, in Lehigh County. Soon after its formation, the company constructed a large generating plant in Allentown, using 4,000-kw of the power capacity for its railway lines, and supplying its excess capacity, 1,500-kw, to industrial and residential customers. Initially much of this power was distributed by The Allentown Electric Light and Power Co., whose stock the transit company owned. As the transit company extended its railway lines, it added a number of substations and increased the capacity of the Allentown plant. It also took over control of several local electric power companies, including Slatington Power Co. and The Citizens Electric Light, Heating and Power Co. From 1910 to 1911 transit company officials also organized a number of township companies in Lehigh and Northampton Counties, with an eye to obtaining franchise rights in those areas, and to integrating the various power companies in the region into one system. Through two agreements of consolidation and merger in 1913, they created first Lehigh Valley Light and Power Company, No. 2 (Lehigh Valley Light and Power Company, No. 1, had been a non-operating township company), and, through the combination of that company with The Allentown Electric Light and Power Co., Lehigh Valley Light and Power Co., No. 3. From 1913 to 1919 the company continued expanding and extending its area of operation. It thus supplied electricity to much of the Lehigh Valley, including the Cities of Allentown and Bethlehem, the Boroughs of Slatington, South Bethlehem, Emmaus, and Catasauqua, and numerous villages and townships in the Counties of Lehigh, Northampton, and Bucks. It continued to upgrade the Allentown plant, using funds advanced by Lehigh Valley Transit Co., and converted several of the transit company's railway substations from 25-cycle current to 60-cycle current enabling them to supply power for electric lighting. Transmission and distribution systems were also extended and improved. In 1917, the newly-formed Lehigh Power Securities Corp. acquired the stock of Lehigh Valley Transit Co. (and, through it, the stock of Lehigh Valley Light and Power Co., No. 3), and Lehigh Navigation Electric Co. In September 1919, Lehigh Valley Light and Power Co., No. 3, and Lehigh Navigation Electric Co. consolidated and merged to form The Lehigh Valley Light and Power Co., thereby divorcing the light and power business in the Lehigh Valley from the electric street railway business of Lehigh Valley Transit Co.

Administrative Records:
Minute Book, 1913-1919
Stock Certificate Books, 1913-1919 (2 Volumes)
Stock Transfer Record, 1917-1919
Bond Records, 1913-1931 (3 Volumes)
Bond Register, 1913-1931
Bond Coupon Account—First Mortgage, 1913-1931
Agreements with Township Companies for Power, 1913-1918
Historical Report, 1914

Operating Records:
FINANCIAL RECORDS
General Ledgers, 1913-1919 (2 Volumes)
Journal, 1913-1919
Cashbooks, 1913-1921 (4 Volumes)

Cashbook—Supplementary, 1918-1919
Cashbook—Voucher Check, 1919-1919
Daily Cash Statements, 1918-1919
Cash Received, 1919
Check Register, 1919
Accounts Payable Ledgers, 1913-1919 (4 Volumes)
Income Register, 1914-1918
Auxiliary Balances, 1917-1918
Accrual Record, 1918-1919
Construction Ledger, 1914-1915
Construction Equipment Ledger, 1914-1918
Repair and Construction Detail Ledger, 1918-1919
Incomplete Improvements and Special Work. Statements Chargeable to Capital, 1919
Incomplete Improvements and Jobbing Work in Progress, 1919
Preliminary Survey and Investigating Charges, 1919
Summary of Earnings and Related Financial Statements, Lehigh Valley Light and Power Co. Group, 1919
Financial Reports, 1918
Financial Returns and Reports, 1919
Notes Receivable, 1912-1919
Notes Payable, 1919
Cash Sales, 1915-1923 (2 Volumes)
PERSONNEL RECORDS
Payrolls—Consolidated , 1914-1918
Payrolls, 1914-1919 (4 Volumes)
Payrolls-Distribution, 1915-1918 (3 Volumes)
Payrolls—Workmen's Compensation Insurance, 1917-1919
Payroll Vouchers, 1914-1918
Payroll Statements—Line Department, 1918
Payroll Statements—Customer Installation Department, 1918
Payroll Statements—Meter Department, 1918
Liberty Bond Receipts, 1918-1919
CONSUMER RECORDS
Sales and Allowances, 1919
Monthly Merchandise and Jobbing Reports, 1919
Installation and Meter Work, 1918-1919
Application for Service, 1915-1918
Consumers' Deposit Ledger, 1913-1919

Scope and Content Note:

The Minute Book of the company contains relatively little information on company operations, being devoted primarily to stock issues, bonds, and mortgages. Some information does appear regarding the company's relationship to Lehigh Valley Transit Co., its dealings with municipal and borough governments in the areas served, and the plans to consolidate with Lehigh Navigation Electric Co. A Historical Report, prepared in 1914, briefly reviews the company's history to that date, referring in particular to the Allentown Power Plant, rates charged, and advertising efforts. The Report also includes information from the 1910 census pertaining to population and per capita income in the areas served. Copies of about 30 agreements and contracts entered into by this company and its predecessors provide details of work performed for industrial, municipal, and borough customers and rates charged. Applications for Service, 1915-1919, consist of lists of customers applying for service from the company. The lists include customers' addresses, notations as to whether they own or lease their property, and credit ratings.

496. LEHIGHTON ELECTRIC LIGHT AND POWER COMPANY (Operating).
Carbon County, Lehighton Borough.
1912 to 1943, 9 Linear Feet.

History:

Lehighton Electric Light and Power Co., incorporated 4 June 1912, supplied electricity in Lehighton Borough, Carbon County, with a 350-kw plant located in Lehighton. After 1917, the company abandoned this plant, instead purchasing power from Mauch Chunk Light, Heat and Power Co. In 1926, the company's stock was acquired by Lehigh Power Securities Corp., and it was operated as part of the Pennsylvania Power & Light Co. system until January 1938 when it merged into PP&L.

Administrative Records:
Minute Book, 1912-1938
Record Book, 1912-1938
Stock Certificate Book, 1912-1928
Correspondence, 1917-1923 (2 Boxes)

Operating Records:
FINANCIAL RECORDS
General Ledger, 1927-1938
Journal, 1926-1927
Daily Cash Receipts, 1918-1920
Daybooks, 1920-1926 (5 Volumes)
Cash Receipts and Disbursements, 1926-1927
Cash Receipts, 1927-1938
Cash Disbursements, 1927-1938
Summary of Cash, 1927-1938 (3 Volumes)
Accounts Payable Ledgers, 1913-1938 (6 Volumes)
Transmittals & Approvals, 1936-1940
Bills Payable and Receivable, 1925-1926
Detail Ledgers, 1926-1938 (2 Volumes)
Accrual Record, 1927-1938
Income Account and Operating Revenue, 1915-1919 (2 Volumes)
Daily Reports, 1918-1927 (3 Boxes)
Fixed Capital and Cost Study, 1927
Cost Study Report, 1927
PERSONNEL RECORDS
Time Book, 1920-1924
Workmen's Compensation Accrual Statements, 1927-1929
CONSUMER RECORDS
Accounts Receivable Detail Ledger, 1927-1938
Record of Meter Readings, 1920-1926 (2 Volumes)
Summary of Accounts Receivable—Consumers, 1927-1938
Summary of Accounts Receivable—Miscellaneous, 1927-1938
Summary of Customers' Overpayments, 1935-1938
Summary of Consumers' Deposits, 1928-1938
AUDIT REPORTS, 1925-1932 (8 Volumes)

Scope and Content Note:

The Minute Book and Record Book contain little information on company activities during the period 1926-1938 when it was operated by Pennsylvania Power & Light. The memoranda relating to the proposed merger of the Company into PP&L and the liquidation of its assets are of some interest. Correspondence, 1917-1923, contains letters between James I. Blakslee, company president and U.S. Postmaster General, and L.B. Horne, company manager. This file documents Blakslee's effort to use his political leverage to influence both the Pennsylvania Public Service Commission and the Lehighton Borough Council, which set rates and awarded street lighting contracts. Other Correspondence, 1914-1919, documents the effect of World War I on the company, and its relations with the Federal Fuel Administration, which was encouraging conservation of fuel supplies. The impact of wartime labor unrest and strikes are also documented. Finally the collection contains copies of customer bills and files of complaints.

497. LEHMAN-PIKE POWER & LIGHT COMPANY (Non-operating).
Pike County, Lehman Township.
1925, 1 Linear Inch.

History:
Lehman-Pike Power & Light Co., incorporated 7 April 1925 to supply electricity in Lehman Township, Pike County, merged into Pennsylvania Power & Light Co., 8 June 1925.

498. LELAND ELECTRIC LIGHT COMPANY (Non-operating).
Lancaster County, Manheim Borough.
1906 to 1907, 1 Linear Inch.

History:
Leland Electric Light Co., incorporated 7 September 1906 to supply electricity in Manheim Borough, Lancaster County, consolidated and merged with Stoever Electric Light Co. to form Manheim and Mount Joy Electric Light Co., 22 March 1907.

499. LEWIS TOWNSHIP ELECTRIC COMPANY (Non-operating).
Northumberland County, Lewis Township.
1914 to 1915, 1 Linear Inch.

History:
Lewis Township Electric Co., incorporated 8 July 1914 to supply electricity in Lewis Township, Northumberland County, merged into Northumberland County Gas & Electric Co., 7 January 1915.

500. LEWISBURG LIGHT & POWER COMPANY (Non-operating).
Union County, Lewisburg Borough.
1961, 1 Linear Inch.

History:
Lewisburg Light & Power Co., incorporated in April 1961 to supply electricity in Lewisburg Borough, Union County, merged into Pennsylvania Power & Light Co., October 1961.

501. LIBERTY TOWNSHIP MONTOUR ELECTRIC COMPANY (Non-operating).
Montour County, Liberty Township.
1919 to 1920, 1 Linear Inch.

History:
Liberty Township Montour Electric Co., incorporated 6 November 1919 to supply electricity in Liberty Township, Montour County, merged into Lehigh Industrial Power Co., 1 June 1920.

502. LIMESTONE-LYCOMING POWER & LIGHT COMPANY (Non-operating).
Lycoming County, Limestone Township.
1928 to 1929, 1 Linear Inch.

History:
Limestone-Lycoming Power & Light Co., incorporated 27 November 1928 to supply electricity in Limestone Township, Lycoming County, merged into Pennsylvania Power & Light Co., 28 January 1929.

503. LIMESTONE-MONTOUR POWER & LIGHT COMPANY (Non-operating).
Montour County, Limestone Township.
1924 to 1925, 1 Linear Inch.

History:
Limestone-Montour Power & Light Co., incorporated 28 August 1924 to supply electricity in Limestone Township, Montour County, merged into Pennsylvania Power & Light Company, 19 January 1925.

504. LIMESTONE TOWNSHIP ELECTRIC SERVICE COMPANY (Non-operating).
Union County, Limestone Township.
1926, 1 Linear Inch.

History:
Limestone Township Electric Service Co., incorporated 21 January 1926 to supply electricity in Limestone Township, Union County, merged into Middleburg Light, Heat and Power Co., 9 August 1926.

505. THE LITITZ ELECTRIC LIGHT, HEAT AND POWER COMPANY (Operating).
Lancaster County, Lititz Borough.
1893 to 1925, 1 Linear Foot.

History:
The Lititz Electric Light, Heat and Power Co. was incorporated in September 1893 to supply electricity in Lititz Borough, Lancaster County. The company built and operated a steam electric generating plant in Lititz until 1909, when it closed the plant and began purchasing power from Conestoga Traction Co. Its stock was acquired in 1911 by Lancaster County Railway and Light Co., which consolidated and merged it with 17 other companies later in 1911 to form Edison Electric Co., No. 1.

Administrative Records:
Minute Books, 1893-1911 (2 Volumes)
Stock Certificate Book, 1894-1911

Operating Records:
Journal, 1911
Cash Receipts, 1911
Audited Voucher Register, 1911
Financial Reports, 1911
Audit Reports, Edison Electric Co., No. 4, 1921-1925 (2 Volumes)

Scope and Content Note:
The Company's Minute Books provide details about the day-to-day operation of the firm and document its community relations. The records describing the construction of the Lititz power plant are unusually complete. Also documented are efforts to secure customers (residential, commercial, industrial and civic),

and the problems that were involved in negotiating street lighting contracts.

506. LITITZ GAS COMPANY (Operating).
Lancaster County, Lititz Borough.
1921 to 1930, 2 Linear Inches.

History:
Lititz Gas Co., which provided gas service in the Boroughs of Lititz and Manheim, Lancaster County, was formed in 1919 as a result of the reorganization of Lititz, Manheim & Ephrata Gas Company. The company operated a gas plant in Lititz, and distribution systems in the boroughs served. Lancaster County Railway and Light Co. acquired the firm's stock in 1926, and then sold it to Lehigh Power Securities Corp. In 1930, the company merged into Pennsylvania Power & Light Co.

Operating Records:
Payrolls—Gas Distribution, 1927-1930
Payrolls-Gas Plant, 1930
Audit Report, Electric Bond and Share Co., 1921-1925
Audit Reports, Pennsylvania Power & Light Co., 1923-1925, 1930 (2 Volumes)

507. LITTLE LEHIGH ELECTRIC COMPANY (Non-operating).
Berks County, Longswamp Township.
1913 to 1916, 1 Linear Inch.

History:
Little Lehigh Electric Co., incorporated 9 January 1913 to supply electricity in Longswamp Township, Berks County, merged into Lehigh Navigation Electric Co., No. 2, 30 October 1916.

508. LITTLE MAHANOY-NORTHUMBERLAND POWER & LIGHT COMPANY (Non-operating).
Northumberland County, Little Mahanoy Township.
1927 to 1928, 1 Linear Inch.

History:
Little Mahanoy-Northumberland Power & Light Co., incorporated 20 December 1927 to supply electricity in Little Mahanoy Township, Northumberland County, merged into Pennsylvania Power & Light Co., 7 February 1928.

509. LIZARD CREEK ELECTRIC COMPANY (Non-operating).
Carbon County, East Penn Township.
1911 to 1913, 1 Linear Inch.

History:
Lizard Creek Electric Co., incorporated 4 April 1911 to supply electricity in East Penn Township, Carbon County, consolidated and merged with 37 companies to form Lehigh Navigation Electric Co., No. 2, 6 January 1913.

510. LOCK HAVEN ELECTRIC LIGHT AND POWER COMPANY (Operating).
Clinton County, Lock Haven City.
1904 to 1923, 2 Linear Feet.

History:
Lock Haven Electric Light and Power Co., which supplied electricity in the city of Lock Haven, Clinton County, was formed in November 1917 through the consolidation and merger of The Lock Haven Electric Light and Power Co. and six other firms. Lehigh Power Securities Corp. acquired the company's stock in 1923 and merged it into Pennsylvania Power & Light Co., 24 September 1923.

Administrative Records:
Minute Book, 1918-1922
Stock Certificate Books, 1919-1922

Operating Records:
General Ledgers, 1904-1923 (3 Volumes)
Journals, 1904-1923 (4 Volumes)
Cashbooks, 1890-1904 (9 Volumes)
Detail Operating Expense Ledger, 1919-1923
Construction Work in Progress, 1923
Financial Statements, 1890-1921
Retirement Authorities, 1923
Expenditure Requisitions, 1922-1923
Audit Report, 1904-1922

511. THE LOCK HAVEN ELECTRIC LIGHT AND POWER COMPANY (Operating).
Clinton County, Lock Haven City.
1890 to 1917, 3 Linear Inches.

History:
The Lock Haven Electric Light and Power Co., which supplied electriCity in the city of Lock Haven, Clinton County, was incorporated in October 1887 by officials of Lock Haven Gas Co. The company operated a generating plant equipped with 2,000-light dynamos and furnished incandescent lighting and Thomson-Houston arc lighting. In November 1917 it consolidated and merged with six companies to form Lock Haven Electric Light and Power Co.

Administrative Records:
Minute Books, 1890-1917 (2 Volumes)
Stock Certificates, 1891-1917

Scope and Content Note:
The company's Minute Books are much more detailed for the earlier years of the company's existence than for the later years. In particular, the minutes refer to the solicitation of customers, the installation of arc and incandescent lighting systems, and improvements to the Lock Haven generating plant to boost its capacity. Other records of the company are listed under Lock Haven Electric Light and Power Co.

512. LOCK HAVEN GAS COMPANY (Operating).
Clinton County, Lock Haven City.
1890 to 1922, 2 Linear Inches.

History:
Lock Haven Gas Co. was originally formed in 1847 as a gas and water company, to serve the City of Lock Haven, Clinton County. When electricity became commercially available in the mid-1880's, the company organized The Lock Haven Electric Light and Power Co. and switched its customers to electric lighting. The two companies remained very closely associated until 1923 when Lock Haven Electric Light and Power Co. (successor to The Lock Haven Electric Light and Power Co.) merged into Pennsylvania Power & Light Co., at which time the gas company was dissolved.

Administrative Records:
Minute Books, 1890-1917 (2 Volumes)

Operating Records:
Audit Report, 1919-1922

513. LOCUST-COLUMBIA POWER AND LIGHT COMPANY (Non-operating).
Columbia County, Locust Township.
1928, 1 Linear Inch.

History:
Locust-Columbia Power & Light Co., incorporated 10 May 1928 to supply electricity in Locust Township, Columbia County, merged into Pennsylvania Power & Light Co., 1 August 1928.

514. LOGAN-CLINTON POWER & LIGHT COMPANY (Non-operating).
Clinton County, Logan Township.
1929, 1 Linear Inch.

History:
Logan-Clinton Power & Light Co., incorporated 3 October 1929 to supply electricity in Logan Township, Clinton County, merged into Pennsylvania Power & Light Co., 25 November 1929.

515. LOGANTON-CLINTON POWER & LIGHT COMPANY (Non-operating).
Clinton County, Loganton Borough.
1929, 1 Linear Inch.

History:
Loganton-Clinton Power & Light Co., incorporated 3 October 1929 to supply electricity in Loganton Borough, Clinton County, merged into Pennsylvania Power & Light Co., 25 November 1929.

516. LONDONDERRY-DAUPHIN POWER & LIGHT COMPANY (Non-operating).
Dauphin County, Londonderry Township.
1952 to 1953, 1 Linear Inch.

History:
Londonderry-Dauphin Power & Light Co., incorporated in November 1952 to supply electricity in Londonderry Township, Dauphin County, merged into Pennsylvania Power & Light Company in November 1953.

517. LOWER AUGUSTA-NORTHUMBERLAND POWER & LIGHT COMPANY (Non-operating).
Northumberland County, Lower Augusta Township.
1928, 1 Linear Inch.

History:
Lower Augusta-Northumberland Power & Light Co., incorporated 5 June 1928 to supply electricity in Lower Augusta Township, Northumberland County, merged into Pennsylvania Power & Light Co., 1 August 1928.

518. LOWER CHANCEFORD TOWNSHIP TRANSMISSION COMPANY (Non-operating).
York County, Lower Chanceford Township.
1909 to 1910, 1 Linear Inch.

History:
Lower Chanceford Township Transmission Co., incorporated in March 1909 to supply electricity in Lower Chanceford Township, York County, consolidated and merged with Peach Bottom Electric Transmission Co. to form Susquehanna Transmission Co. of Pennsylvania in April 1910.

519. LOWER CHANCEFORD WATER AND POWER COMPANY (Non-operating).
York County, Lower Chanceford Township.
1895 to 1958, 1 Linear Inch.

History:
Lower Chanceford Water and Power Co., incorporated in March 1895 to supply water power in Lower Chanceford Township, York County, filed an "out of existence" affidavit in June 1909. It appears that the company remained on the books, however, for a meeting of the board of directors and stockholders was held 29 October 1957 to adopt a plan of liquidation. The action was effected 28 March 1958.

520. LOWER MACUNGIE TOWNSHIP ELECTRIC LIGHT AND POWER COMPANY (Non-operating).
Lehigh County, Lower Macungie Township.
1915 to 1916, 1 Linear Inch.

History:
Lower Macungie Township Electric Light and Power Co., incorporated 13 January 1915 to supply electricity in Lower Macungie Township, Lehigh County, merged into Lehigh Valley Light and Power Co., No. 3, 18 April 1916.

521. LOWER MAHANOY POWER COMPANY (Non-operating).
Northumberland County, Lower Mahanoy Township.
1923 to 1924, 1 Linear Inch.

History:
Lower Mahanoy Power Co., incorporated 19 December 1923 to supply electricity in Lower Mahanoy Township, Northumberland County, merged into Middleburg Light, Heat and Power Co., 26 February 1924.

522. LOWER MAKEFIELD TOWNSHIP ELECTRIC COMPANY (Non-operating).
Bucks County, Lower Makefield Township.
1913 to 1935, 1 Linear Inch.

History:
Lower Makefield Township Electric Co., incorporated 30 December 1913 to supply electricity in Lower Makefield Township, was one of eleven such "paper companies organized by Lehigh Navigation Electric Co., No. 2. The purpose of these companies, appears to have been twofold: to gain franchise rights in Bucks County, and to block the westward expansion of Philadelphia Electric Co. According to a report prepared in 1917 for Electric Bond and Share Co. prior to the acquisition of Lehigh Navigation Electric Co., No. 2, by Lehigh Power Securities Corp., the counsel for Lehigh Navigation "explained that the reason for keeping these companies separate and distinct from the Lehigh Navigation Electric Co. is that they cover outlying territories and it might be preferable to forfeit their charters and abandon them rather than furnish electricity to one or two consumers. This would not be possible if the Lehigh Navigation Electric Co. were operating in such territory." (A copy of this report is filed with the records of Lehigh Navigation Electric Co.) Control of the eleven township companies was transferred to Pennsylvania Power & Light Co. in 1920, and the companies were listed as "inactive" as of 1925. Lower Makefield Township Electric Co. and the ten other other companies were formally dissolved as of 9

September 1935. The histories of these companies do not appear in PP&L's official history.

523. LOWER MILFORD TOWNSHIP ELECTRIC LIGHT AND POWER COMPANY (Non-operating).
Lehigh County, Lower Milford.
1915 to 1916, 1 Linear Inch.

History:
Lower Milford Township Electric Light and Power Co., incorporated 13 January 1915 to supply electricity in Lower Milford Township, Lehigh County, merged into Lehigh Valley Light and Power Co., No. 3, 18 April 1916.

524. LOWER MOUNT BETHEL ELECTRIC COMPANY (Non-operating).
Northampton County, Lower Mount Bethel Township.
1911 to 1913, 1 Linear Inch.

History:
Lower Mount Bethel Electric Co., incorporated 4 April 1911 to supply electricity in Lower Mount Bethel Township, Northampton County, consolidated and merged with 37 companies to form Lehigh navigation Electric Co., No. 2, 6 January 1913.

525. LOWER NAZARETH ELECTRIC COMPANY (Non-operating).
Northampton County, Lower Nazareth Township.
1911 to 1913, 1 Linear Inch.

History:
Lower Nazareth Electric Co., incorporated 4 April 1911 to supply electricity in Lower Nazareth Township, Northampton County, consolidated and merged with 37 companies to form Lehigh Navigation Electric Co., No. 2, 6 January 1913.

526. LOWER SAUCON ELECTRIC COMPANY (Non-operating).
Northampton County, Lower Saucon Township.
1911 to 1913, 1 Linear Inch.

History:
Lower Saucon Electric Co., incorporated 4 April 1911 to supply electricity in Lower Saucon Township, Northampton County, consolidated and merged with 37 companies to form Lehigh Navigation Electric Co., No. 2, 6 January 1913.

527. LOWER TOWAMENSING-CARBON POWER & LIGHT COMPANY (Non-operating).
Carbon County, Lower Towamensing Township.
1948 to 1949, 1 Linear Inch.

History:
Lower Towamensing-Carbon Power & Light Co., incorporated in May 1948 to supply electricity in Lower Towamensing Township, Carbon County, merged into Pennsylvania Power & Light Co., December 1949.

528. LOWER WINDSOR TOWNSHIP PUBLIC SERVICE COMPANY (Non-operating).
York County, Lower Windsor Township.
1922 to 1923, 1 Linear Inch.

History:
Lower Windsor Township Public Service Co., incorporated 23 August 1922 to supply electricity in Lower Windsor Township, York County, merged into Wrightsville Light and Power Co., 12 March 1923.

529. LOWER WINDSOR WATER AND POWER COMPANY (Non-operating).
York County, Lower Windsor Township.
1902, 1 Linear Inch.

History:
Lower Windosr Water and Power Co., incorporated 29 April 1902 to supply water power for electricity in Lower Windsor Township, York County, consolidated and merged with three companies to form Susquehanna Storage-Lake and Power Co., 14 August 1902.

530. LOWER WINSDOR-YORK POWER & LIGHT COMPANY (Non-operating).
York County, Lower Windsor Township.
1935 to 1936, 1 Linear Inch.

History:
Lower Windsor-York Power & Light Co., incorporated 10 December 1935 to supply electricity in Lower Windsor Township, York County, merged into Pennsylvania Power & Light Co., 9 March 1936.

531. LOWHILL POWER & LIGHT COMPANY (Non-operating).
Lehigh County, Lowhill Township.
1922 to 1923, 1 Linear Inch.

History:
Lowhill Power & Light Co., incorporated 13 October 1922 to supply electricity in Lowhill Township, Lehigh County, merged into Pennsylvania Power & Light Co., 12 March 1923.

532. LOYALSOCK POWER & LIGHT COMPANY (Non-operating).
Lycoming County, Loyalsock Towwnship.
1924, 1 Linear Inch.

History:
Loyalsock Power & Light Co., incorporated 9 May 1924 to supply electricity in Loyalsock Township, Lycoming County, merged into Pennsylvania Power & Light Co., 27 August 1924.

533. LYCOMING CONSOLIDATED FUEL GAS COMPANY (Non-operating).
Lycoming County, Montgomery Borough.
1912 to 1914, 1 Linear Inch.

History:
Lycoming Consolidated Fuel Gas Co., incorporated 5 March 1912 to supply fuel gas in Montgomery Borough and adjacent territories in Lycoming County, merged into Northern Central Gas Co., 17 December 1914.

534. LYCOMING CONSOLIDATED GAS COMPANY (Non-operating).
Lycoming County, Montgomery Borough.
1911 to 1914, 1 Linear Inch.

History:
Lycoming Consolidated Gas Co., incorporated 29 December 1911 to manufacture and supply gas for lighting in Montgomery Borough and adjacent territories in Lycoming County, merged into Northern Central Gas Co., 17 December 1914.

535. LYCOMING-EDISON COMPANY (Operating).
Lycoming County, Williamsport City.
1911 to 1923, 2 Linear Feet.

History:
Lycoming-Edison Co. was formed in 1911 through the consolidation and merger of Lycoming Edison Co. with Edison Electric Illuminating Co. of Williamsport, Pa. It supplied electricity in the City of Williamsport and vicinity, serving a population of about 36,000. The company operated a 21,600-kw plant in Williamsport, with distribution lines throughout Lycoming County. Lehigh Power Securities Corp., which acquired the company in 1923, merged it into Pennsylvania Power & Light Co.

Administrative Records:
Minute Book, 1923
Stock Certificate Book, 1911-1923

Operating Records:
General Ledgers, 1911-1923 (3 Volumes)
Journals, 1911-1923 (3 Volumes)
Audited Voucher Registers, 1911-1923 (2 Volumes)
Detail Ledger, 1920-1923
Detail Automobile Expenses, 1916-1923
Petty Cash Disbursements, 1918-1923
Retirement Authorities, 1919-1923
Expenditure Requisitions, 1923
Williamsport Power Station Record, 1923
Audit Reports, 1911-1922 (7 Volumes)

Scope and Content Note:
The Williamsport Power Station Record provides a graphic analysis of power station operations. It documents amount of power being consumed at different periods of the day and during days of the week.

536. LYCOMING ELECTRIC COMPANY (Operating).
Lycoming County, Williamsport City.
1889 to 1922, 2 Linear Feet.

History:
Lycoming Electric Co. was incorporated 30 September 1889 to supply electricity in the city of Williamsport, Lycoming County. It secured the city's street lighting contract and competed with Edison Electric Illuminating Co. of Williamsport Pa. for customers. This competition continued until 1900 when Lycoming Improvement Co., a New Jersey Corp. which had acquired Lycoming Electric Co.'s stock in 1895, purchased the Edison Co. as well. The two electric companies were operated jointly until 30 March 1911, when they were consolidated and merged to form Lycoming-Edison Co.

Administrative Records:
Minute Book, 1889-1911
Stock Certificate Book, 1900-1910
Stock Ledger, 1890-1911
Bond Transfer Record, 1907
Record of Bondholders, 1891-1922

Operating Records:
General Ledger, 1889-1903
Index to General Ledger, 1889-1903
Journals, 1889-1911 (5 Volumes)
Cash Receipts, 1896-1914
Cashbooks, 1890-1914 (8 Volumes)
Audited Voucher Indexes, 1889-1911 (2 Volumes)
Accounts Payable, 1903-1911
Audit Reports, 1905-1922 (6 Volumes)

Scope and Content Note:
The Minute Books document the early years of the company's history in rich detail. The records describe the construction of generating stations for both arc and incandescent lighting. There is considerable discussion in the minutes about the comparative profitability of arc vs. incandescent lighting. Also documented are efforts to meet the competitive challenge presented by the Edison Illuminating Co. of Williamsport, Pa. and the attempt to block Lycoming Electric Co. from entering the residential lighting market. The minutes depict the company's relationship with the Williamsport municipal government and the process by which contracts for street lighting were negotiated.

537. LYCOMING IMPROVEMENT COMPANY
(Operating).
Lycoming County, Williamsport City.
1894 to 1923, 2 Linear Feet.

History:
Lycoming Improvement Co. was incorporated 9 March 1894 in New Jersey, operating as a holding company to control the stocks of utilities serving Williamsport and other localities in Lycoming County. The company controlled five street railway companies, Lycoming-Edison Co., Jersey Shore Electric Co., and a toll bridge company. It also administered the Accident Insurance Fund for the companies forming the Lycoming group. Under the direction of Lycoming Improvement Co., the two electric companies supplied power to the street railway companies. After Lehigh Power Securities Corp. acquired Lycoming Improvement Co. and its holdings in 1923, the electric companies were merged into Pennsylvania Power & Light Co. and the transportation properties fell under the control of Valley Railways.

Administrative Records:
Minute Books, 1894-1923 (4 Volumes)
Stock Certificate Books, 1894-1923 (2 Volumes)
Stock Transfer Record, 1894-1896
Stock Ledger, 1894-1923

Operating Records:
General Ledger, 1894
Journal, 1894
Cashbook, 1916-1924
Accrual Record, 1923-1924
Statement of Rents for Lycoming Apartments, 1903-1915
Audit Reports, 1905-1922 (12 Volumes)

Scope and Content Note:
The Minute Books of the Lycoming Improvement Co. describe the operation of this typical holding company. Annual Reports, stockholder lists, reports filed with state regulatory agencies, and records of stock and bond transactions trace the relationship between the operating companies and the holding company. Rent statements for the Lycoming Apartments, 1903-1915, list the name of each tenant, along with a record of services that the landlord provided for each apartment.

538. LYCOMING TOWNSHIP-LYCOMING COUNTY POWER & LIGHT COMPANY (Non-operating).
Lycoming County, Lycoming Township.
1928, 1 Linear Inch.

History:
Lycoming Township-Lycoming County Power & Light Co., incorporated 14 May 1928 to supply electricity in Lycoming Township, Lycoming County, merged into Pennsylvania Power & Light Co., 1 August 1928.

539. LYKENS TOWNSHIP ELECTRIC COMPANY (Non-operating).
Dauphin County, Lykens Township.
1924, 1 Linear Inch.

History:
Lykens Township Electric Co., incorporated 5 June 1924 to supply electricity in Lykens Township, Dauphin County, merged into East Penn Electric Co. No. 2, 6 October 1924.

540. LYKENS TOWNSHIP ELECTRIC COMPANY (DAUPHIN) (Non-operating).
Dauphin County, Lykens Township.
1916 to 1920, 1 Linear Inch.

History:
Lykens Township Electric Co., incorporated 14 June 1916 to supply electricity in Lykens Township, Dauphin County, consolidated and merged with five companies to form The Citizens Electric Co., 2 January 1920.

541. LYKENS VALLEY LIGHT AND POWER COMPANY (Operating).
Schuylkill County, Tower City Borough.
1915 to 1923, 2 Linear Feet.

History:
As the successor to Sterling Consolidated Electric Co., Lykens Valley Light and Power Co. supplied electricity in Tower City Borough and surrounding localities in Schuylkill and Dauphin Counties. Between 1915 and 1923 the company continually expanded its territory. It acquired Williams Valley Light, Heat and Power Co. along with several non-operating companies. It then increased the capacity of its generating plants in the Village of Reinerton and the Borough of Williamstown. The company merged into East Penn Electric Co. No. 2, 7 January 1924.

Administrative Records:
Minute Book, 1915-1923
Stock Certificate Books, 1916-1924 (2 Volumes)

Operating Records:
General Ledger, 1915-1918
Journals, 1915-1923 (3 Volumes)
Daily Cashbooks, 1915-1919 (3 Volumes)
Cash Receipts, 1915-1924
Cash Expenditures, 1915-1924
Accounts Payable, 1915-1923
Examination of Capital Expenditures, 1921-1922
Deatil Ledger, 1919-1924
Detail Operating Expenses, 1916-1922
Sales Journal, 1917-1921
Consumers Ledger, 1917
Monthly Reports, 1922-1923
Monthly Reports, 1923
Audit Report, 1923

542. THE MACUNGIE ELECTRIC LIGHT, HEAT AND POWER COMPANY (Operating).
Lehigh County, Macungie Borough.
1908 to 1929, 2 Linear Feet.

History:
The Macungie Electric Light, Heat and Power Co. was incorporated 8 October 1908 to supply electricity in the Borough of Macungie, Lehigh County. The company constructed an electric distribution system in the borough and purchased both alternating and direct current from the Lehigh Valley Transit Co. In 1923, the company's stock was acquired by Lehigh Power Securities Corp., and was thereafter operated as part of the Pennsylvania Power & Light Co. system, into which it was merged on 28 May 1928.

Administrative Records:
Minute Books, 1908-1928 (2 Volumes)
Stock Transfer Record, 1909-1923
Stock Ledgers, 1909-1928 (2 Volumes)
Miscellaneous Letters and Papers, 1922-1923

Operating Records:
General Ledgers, 1908-1928 (2 Volumes)
Journal, 1908-1923
Journal Entry Register, 1923-1928
Cashbook, 1908-1923
Cash Received, 1923-1925
Check Register, 1923-1925
Record of Cash Receipts, 1925-1928
Record of Cash Disbursements, 1925-1928
Summary of Cash, 1925-1928
Accounts Receivable, 1923-1928
Detail Ledger, 1923-1928
Accrual Record, 1923-1928
Detail of Cost Study and Fixed Capital, 1926-1927
Expenditure Requisitions, 1923-1929
Retirement Authorities, 1924-1929
Summary of Accounts Receivable, 1923-1928 (2 Volumes)
Audit Reports, Electric Bond & Share Co., 1925-1927 (2 Volumes)

Scope and Content Note:
The Minute Books of The Macungie Electric Light, Heat and Power Co. include, statements of accounts and operating expenses, and of major customers, such as Century Shoe Co. Also included is information on the company's dealings with the Borough Council, equipment purchases, and the purchase of power from the Lehigh Valley Transit Co. and its subsidiary, Allentown Electric Light and Power Co. The miscellaneous letters and papers consist of annual statements of gross receipts; a workmen's compensation payroll report; a 1922 report to the Bureau of Statistics of the Pennsylvania Department of Internal Affairs; and an engineer's report on company equipment.

543. MADISON-COLUMBIA POWER & LIGHT COMPANY (Non-operating).
Columbia County, Madison County.
1924 to 1925, 2 Linear Inches.

History:
Madison-Columbia Power & Light Co. was incorporated 28 August 1924 to supply electricity in the Township of Madison, Columbia County. On 28 October 1924 it was merged into Pennsylvania Power & Light Co. along with twelve other non-operating companies.

544. MADISON-PERRY POWER & LIGHT COMPANY (Non-operating).
Perry County, Madison Township.
1928 to 1929, 1 Linear Inch.

History:
Madison-Perry Power & Light Co. was incorporated 27 February 1929 to supply electricity in the Township of Madison, Perry County. On 27 March 1929 the company was acquired by Sherman Valley Electric Light, Heat and Power Co.

545. MADISON POWER & LIGHT COMPANY (Non-operating).
Lackawanna County, Madison Township.
1923 to 1924, 1 Linear Inch.

History:
Madison Power & Light Co. was incorporated 21 May 1923 to supply electricity in the Township of Madison, Lackawanna County. The company was consolidated and merged along with 31 other non-operating companies on 20 July 1923 to form Paupack Power & Light Co., No. 2.

546. MAHANOY CITY AND TAMAQUA STREET RAILWAY COMPANY (Non-operating).
Schuylkill County, Tamaqua Borough.
1904 to 1907, 1 Linear Inch.

History:
Mahanoy City and Tamaqua Street Railway Co. was organized in November 1904 by Messrs. E. M. B. Shepp, and John F. McGinty to secure a franchise to operate an electric street railway between Tamaqua and Mahanoy City, Schuylkill County. Power to run this railway was to be supplied by the Tamaqua Light, Heat and Power Co., which these same men organized in January 1905. There is no indication, however, that the Mahanoy City and Tamaqua Street Railway Co. ever attempted to exercise its franchise rights, or build a line from Tamaqua to Mahanoy City.

547. MAHANOY CITY GAS COMPANY (Operating).
Schuylkill County, Mahanoy City Borough.
1886 to 1905, 2 Linear Inches.

History:
Mahanoy City Gas Co. was incorporated 21 September 1874 to supply gas lighting in the Borough of Mahanoy City, Schuylkill County. The company was reorganized on 19 July 1911 as The Mahanoy City Gas Co. In 1912 the Schuylkill Gas and Electric Co. acquired control, and by 1920 the company had ceased operations.

Operating Records:
Auditors Report, 1886-1888
Monthly Financial Statements, 1902-1905

Scope and Content Note:
The Monthly Financial Statements document the company's revenues and expenditures. The 1886-88 Auditor's Report is of particular interest. This report recommended that the company attempt to increase its customers by installing gas lines in all new houses. In order to meet the competitive challenge that was being presented by the new electric industry, the auditor suggested that Mahanoy City Gas Co. use a higher quality gas so as to minimize customer complaints.

548. MAHANOY CITY LIGHT, HEAT AND POWER COMPANY (Operating).
Schuylkill County, Mahanoy City Borough.
1887 to 1922, 2 Linear Feet.

History:
Mahanoy City Light, Heat and Power Co. was incorporated 16 December 1887 and was the first company to supply electricity in the Borough of Mahanoy City. The company built a generating station on Birch Street in Mahanoy City in 1888, using five Thomson-Houston 35-light dynamos. This generating station's capacity was boosted in 1894 by the addition of a 100-kw generator. In 1901 its capacity was further increased by the addition of a 3,600-light generator. In 1907 an electric line was constructed to link the company's plant with the distribution system of The Shenandoah Light, Heat and Power Co., which was owned by the same local businessmen who owned Mahanoy City Light, Heat and Power Co. The two companies shared the cost of adding a 500-kw Westinghouse turbogenerator to the Mahanoy City power station. In 1912, the company's stock was acquired by Schuylkill Gas and Electric Co. Shortly after this acquisition the Mahanoy City power plant was shut down, and the company began to purchase power from The Harwood Electric Co. Mahanoy City Light, Heat and Power Co. was dissolved on 29 September 1923.

Administrative Records:
Minute Books, 1887-1922 (2 Volumes)
Stock Certificate Book, 1888-1917
Stock Transfer Record, 1916-1917
Correspondence, 1909-1910

Operating Records:
General Ledgers, 1888-1914 (2 Volumes)
Journals, 1888-1914 (2 Volumes)
Cash Ledgers, 1887-1913 (2 Volumes)
Cashbooks, 1888-1816 (3 Volumes)
Daily Cash Receipts, 1898-1911 (5 Volumes)
Consumers Ledger, 1891-1905
Audit Reports, 1912-1914 (2 Volumes)
Auditor's Report to Directors, 1890-1899
Monthly Financial Statements, 1902-1913

Scope and Content Note:
The Minute Books document the purchase and installation of electric generating equipment. They also document operating expenses such as employee salaries and purchases of coal, oil, lamps, poles and other equipment.

549. MAHANOY LIGHT COMPANY (Non-operating).
Schuylkill County, Mahanoy Township.
1912, 1 Linear Inch.

History:
Mahanoy Light Co. was incorporated 29 November 1912 to supply electricity in the Township of Mahanoy,

Schuylkill County. On 16 December 1912 the company was consolidated and merged with twelve other companies to form Hazleton Electric Co.

550. MAHANOY TOWNSHIP ELECTRIC COMPANY (Non-operating).
Schuylkill County, Mahanoy Township.
1911, 1 Linear Inch.

History:
This company was incorporated 26 January 1911 under the name Schuylkill Gas and Electric Co., for the purpose of supplying electricity in the Township of Mahanoy, Schuylkill County. The company changed its name to the Mahanoy Township Electric Co. in June 1911. The next year it was consolidated and merged with eleven other companies to form The Schuylkill Gas and Electric Co.

551. MAHONING TOWNSHIP CARBON ELECTRIC COMPANY (Non-operating).
Carbon County, Mahoning Township.
1919, 4 Linear Inches.

History:
Mahoning Township Carbon Electric Co. was incorporated 17 July 1919 to supply electricity in the Township of Mahoning, Carbon County. On 25 July 1919 it was consolidated and merged with six other non-operating companies to form Industrial Power Co.

552. MAHONING TOWNSHIP MONTOUR ELECTRIC COMPANY (Non-operating).
Montour County, Mahoning Township.
1919 to 1920, 3 Linear Inches.

History:
Mahoning Township Montour Electric Co. was incorporated 6 November 1919 for the purpose of supplying electricity in the Township of Mahoning, Montour County. The company was acquired by Lehigh Industrial Power Co. 28 April 1920.

553. MAIN-COLUMBIA POWER & LIGHT COMPANY (Non-operating).
Columbia County, Main Township.
1928 to 1929, 1 Linear Inch.

History:
Main-Columbia Power & Light Co., having been incorporated 10 May 1928 to supply electricity in the Township of Main, Columbia County, was acquired by Pennsylvania Power & Light Co. on 29 June 1928.

554. MANNHEIM AND MOUNT JOY ELECTRIC LIGHT COMPANY (Operating).
Lancaster County, Manheim Borough.
1907 to 1911, 2 Linear Inches.

History:
At a foreclosure sale on 10 May 1906, Messrs. Henry V.H. Stoever and C. Taylor Leland purchased from the Lancaster Valley Electric Light Co. a steam electric generating station in the Borough of Manheim and an electric distribution system serving the Boroughs of Manheim and Mount Joy. On 15 March 1907 Messrs. Stoever and Leland formed Manheim and Mount Joy Electric Light Co., which they operated until 1901 when they sold their franchises and facilities to Lancaster County Railway and Light Co. Manheim and Mount Joy Electric Light Co. was merged with a non-operating company to form Manheim Suburban Electric Co., No. 2 on 16 September, 1911.

Administrative Records:
Minute Book, 1907-1911

Operating Records:
General Ledger, 1911
Statement of Assets & Liabilities, 1910-1911
Statement of Operations, 1911

Scope and Content Note:
Most of the records are financial and relatively routine. There are lists of bank deposits, bills, and customers with unpaid balances. The minutes contain a description of the company's property, and the 1911 merger agreement.

555. MANHEIM SUBURBAN ELECTRIC COMPANY, NO. 1 (Non-operating).
Lancaster County, Manheim Borough.
1911, 1 Linear Inch.

History:
Manheim Suburban Electric Co., No. 1, was incorporated 25 August 1911 to supply electricity in the Borough of Manheim, Lancaster County. On 16 September 1911 it was consolidated and merged with the Manheim and Mount Joy Electric Light Co. to form Manheim Suburban Electric Co., No. 2. This company was consolidated and merged with 17 other companies on 29 September 1911 to form Edison Electric Co. No. 1.

556. MANHEIM TOWNSHIP ELECTRIC COMPANY (Non-operating).
Lancaster County, Manheim Township.
1911, 1 Linear Inch.

History:
Manheim Township Electric Co. was incorporated 10 August 1911 to supply electricity in the Township of Manheim, Lancaster County. It was consolidated and merged with 17 other companies on 29 September 1911 to form Edison Electric Co. No. 1.

557. MANOR TOWNSHIP ELECTRIC COMPANY (Non-operating).
Lancaster County, Manor Township.
1911, 1 Linear Inch.

History:
Manor Township Electric Co. was incorporated 10 August 1911 to supply electricity in the Township of Manor, Lancaster County. On 29 September 1911 it was consolidated and merged with 17 other companies to form Edison Electric Co. No. 1.

558. MANOR WATER AND POWER COMPANY (Non-operating).
Lancaster County, Manor Township.
1902, 1 Linear Inch.

History:
Manor Water and Power Co. was incorporated 23 May 1902 to supply water and water power in the Township of Manor, Lancaster County. The company's main offices were in the City of Harrisburg. On 14 August 1902 it was consolidated and merged with three other water companies to form Susquehanna Storage-Lake and Power Co.

559. MARIETTA ELECTRIC COMPANY
(Non-operating).
Lancaster County, Marietta Township.
1912, 1 Linear Inch.

History:
Marietta Electric Co. was incorporated 7 November 1912 to supply electricity in the Township of Marietta, Lancaster County. It was consolidated and merged with 13 other companies on 27 November 1912 to form Edison Electric Co. No. 3.

560. MARION HEIGHTS ELECTRIC COMPANY
(Non-operating).
Northumberland County, Marion Heights Borough.
1918 to 1921, 2 Linear Inches.

History:
Marion Heights Electric Co. was incorporated 31 October 1918 to supply electricity in the Borough of Marion Heights, Northumberland County. It was acquired by Pennsylvania Power & Light Co. on 30 September 1920.

561. MARLBORO POWER & LIGHT COMPANY
(Non-operating).
Montgomery County, Marlborough Township.
1923, 1 Linear Inch.

History:
Marlboro Power & Light Co. was organized by the Pennsylvania Power & Light Co in April 1923, in an unsuccessful attempt to extend its franchises into the Township of Marlborough, Montgomery County. The company's application for a charter was turned down, and Marlboro Power & Light Co. was dissolved on 24 October 1923.

562. MARLBOROUGH-MONTGOMERY POWER & LIGHT COMPANY (Non-operating).
Montgomery County, Marlborough Township.
1927 to 1928, 1 Linear Inch.

History:
Marlborough-Montgomery Power & Light Co. was incorporated 2 September 1927 to supply electricity in a portion of the Township of Marlborough, Montgomery County. It was acquired by Pennsylvania Power & Light Co. on 16 September 1927.

563. MARSHALL ELECTRIC COMPANY
(Non-operating).
Schuylkill County, Blythe Township.
1911 to 1913, 1 Linear Inch.

History:
Marshall Electric Co. was incorporated 27 June 1911 to supply electricity in the Township of Blythe, Schuylkill County. On 23 December 1912 the company was consolidated and merged with 37 other non-operating companies to form Lehigh Navigation Electric Co., No. 2.

564. MARTIC-DRUMORE ELECTRIC LIGHT, HEAT AND POWER COMPANY (Non-operating).
Lancaster County, Martic Township.
1919 to 1921, 2 Linear Inches.

History:
Martic-Drumore Electric Light, Heat and Power Co. was incorporated 19 February 1920 to supply electricity in the Township of Martic, Lancaster County. On 9 October 1920 it was consolidated and merged with five other companies to form The Lancaster County Electric Light, Heat and Power Co.

565. MARTIC TOWNSHIP ELECTRIC COMPANY
(Non-operating).
Lancaster County, Martic Township.
1912, 1 Linear Inch.

History:
Martic Township Electric Co. was incorporated 7 November 1912 to supply electricity in the Township of Martic, Lancaster County. On 27 November 1912 it was consolidated and merged with 13 other companies to form Edison Electric Co. No. 3.

566. MARTIC WATER AND POWER COMPANY
(Operating).
Lancaster County, Lancaster City.
1895 to 1957, 3 Linear Inches.

History:
Martic Water and Power Co. was incorporated 14 March 1895 to supply electricity in the Boroughs of Wrightsville and York (York County), and Columbia (Lancaster County). The company's main offices were in the City of Lancaster. On 28 June 1898 the company purchased a dam on the Susquehanna River at Columbia, owned by Mr. Stephen J. Caldwell. It began building an additional dam and power house at the site, but stopped construction on 2 September 1902 when the property was sold to the Susquehanna Falls Power Co. Martic Water and Power Co. had ceased operations altogether by the time it was acquired by the McCall Ferry Power Co., in June 1905. It was formally declared out of existence on 19 December 1911. McCall Ferry Power Co. was reorganized in January 1910 as the Pennsylvania Water & Power Co.; and on 10 February 1925 this company acquired all the properties of the Susquehanna Falls company, including the dam site at Columbia.

Administrative Records:
Minute Book, 1905-1899
Stock Certificate Book, 1898-1957

Scope and Content Note:
The Minute Book of the Martic Water and Power Co. documents the company's organization, capitalization, and stockholders' and directors' meetings. Additional information concerning this company can be found in the microfilmed records of the Pennsylvania Water & Power Co.

567. THE MARYSVILLE ELECTRIC LIGHT, HEAT AND POWER COMPANY (Operating).
Perry County, Marysville Borough.
1898 to 1917, 3 Linear Inches.

History:
The Marysville Electric Light, Heat and Power Co. was incorporated 30 December 1897, and was the first company to supply electric in the Borough of Marysville, Perry County. In 1898 the company constructed a steam

electric generating station which consisted of two 60-hp horizontal boilers, a 50-hp high speed engine, and a 30-kw direct current generator. The company extended its distribution system to the Village of Perdix, Perry County in 1902. In 1903 its generator was burned out by an overload, reportedly due to the operations of one of its main customers, West Fairview and Marysville Electric Street Railway Co. The Marysville company was forced to switch over to an alternating current system and install new meters. In 1916, the company's stock was acquired by a group of businessmen who were trying to integrate all the electric companies operating along the Juniata and Susquehanna Rivers, north of the City of Harrisburg. On 24 September 1917 it was consolidated and merged with 16 other companies to form Juniata Public Service Co.

Administrative Records:
Minute Book, 1898-1917
Stock Certificate Book, 1898-1915

Scope and Content Note:
The Minute Book of The Marysville Electric Light, Heat and Power Co. contains routine minutes of stockholders' and directors' meetings, statements of revenue and expenditures, and annual treasurer's reports. Also included is information documenting the company's dealings with The United Electric Co. and The Marysville Water Co., as well as correspondence relating to the company's 1917 consolidation and merger into the Juniata Public Service Co.

568. MAUCH CHUNK & LEHIGHTON TRANSIT COMPANY (Operating).
Carbon County, Mauch Chunk Borough.
1922 to 1931, 1 Linear Inch.

History:
Carbon Transit Co., which had operated an electric street railway in the Mauch Chunk Borough area of Lehigh River Valley, ran into financial difficulties after World War I, and was forced to sell its property and franchises at a foreclosure sale on 13 March 1919. The new owners, who had incorporated themselves as Mauch Chunk & Lehighton Transit Co. on 15 February 1919, continued to operate both the electric street railway and the Flagstaff Amusement Park, which they had also purchased from the Carbon Transit Co. However, this new company also went bankrupt and was sold to Lehigh Power Securities Corp. at a foreclosure sale on 30 June 1925. Lehigh Power Securities then reorganized the company on 13 January 1926 as Mauch Chunk Transit Co.

Administrative Records:
Correspondence, 1922-1931

Scope and Content Note:
The correspondence of Mauch Chunk & Lehighton Transit Co. deals mainly with the recall of the company's bonds for the purposes of reorganization, and includes a list of the company's bondholders. Also included are two traffic accident reports and letters referring to state taxes.

569. MAUCH CHUNK-CARBON GAS COMPANY (Non-operating).
Carbon County, Mauch Chunk Borough.
1927 to 1928, 1 Linear Inch.

History:
Mauch Chunk-Carbon Gas Company was incorporated 21 March 1927 to supply gas in the Boroughs of Mauch Chunk and East Mauch Chunk, Carbon County. On 23 December 1927 the company was merged into Mauch Chunk Gas Co.

570. MAUCH CHUNK GAS COMPANY (Operating).
Carbon County, Mauch Chunk Borough.
1854 to 1929, 3 Linear Feet.

History:
Mauch Chunk Gas Co. was incorporated 3 March 1854 by a special act of the Pennsylvania Legislature for the purpose of supplying gas lighting in the Boroughs of Mauch Chunk and East Mauch Chunk, Carbon County. The company received its Letters Patent on 1 August 1855, making it one of the earliest gas suppliers in the state of Pennsylvania. It built a gas plant in Mauch Chunk, but late in 1861 this plant was washed out by a flood of the Lehigh River. It was rebuilt the following year in the same location. Beginning in 1906 the company faced increasingly heavy competition from The Mauch Chunk Heat, Power & Electric Light Co. and lost many of its customers. In 1926 the company's stock was acquired by Lehigh Power Securities Corp. On 21 March 1927 the company organized the Mauch Chunk-Carbon Gas Co. On 23 December 1927 it was merged into the Mauch Chunk Gas Co., which was in turn merged into Pennsylvania Power & Light Co., on 28 February 1929.

Administrative Records:
Minute Book, 1854-1929
Stock Certificate Books, 1856-1929 (2 Volumes)
Stock Transfer Record, 1883-1919
Stock Ledger, 1883-1929
Bond Record, 1904-1926
Bond Register, 1924-1926
Secretary's Miscellaneous Papers, 1917-1929
Correspondence, 1914-1923

Operating Records:
FINANCIAL RECORDS
General Ledgers, 1904-1929 (4 Volumes)
Journals, 1904-1926
Journal Entry Register, 1926-1929
Record of Cash Receipts, 1926-1929
Record of Cash Disbursements, 1926-1929
Cashbooks, 1904-1926 (3 Volumes)
Summary of Cash, 1926-1929 (2 Volumes)
Invoice Record, 1924-1926
Distribution Book, 1913-1924
Audited Voucher Register, 1926-1929
Accounts Receivable, 1926-1929
Accounts Payable, 1926-1929
Detail Ledger, 1926-1929
Record of Expenses, 1886-1904
Accrual Record, 1926-1929
Detail of Cost Study and Fixed Capital, 1926-1927
Working Papers, 1904-1929
Monthly Reports, 1912-1926
Summary of Accounts Receivable—Consumers, 1926-1929
Summary of Accounts Receivable—Miscellaneous, 1927-1929

Summary of Consumers' Deposits, 1928-1929
Summary of Line Extension Deposits, 1927-1929
MISCELLANEOUS REPORTS
Audit Reports, 1923-1927 (4 Volumes)
Appraisal Report, Day & Zimmerman, Engineers, 1912
PERSONNEL RECORDS
Time Cards, 1926
Workmen's Compensation Insurance Accrual Statements, 1926-1929

Scope and Content Note:

The Minute Book documents stockholders' and directors' meetings. Included are annual statements of earnings and expenditures, and annual reports prepared by the general manager documenting sales and improvements to the gas plant and distribution system. The Secretary's Miscellaneous Papers include lists of stockholders and stock transfers. Much of the correspondence deals wih routine business matters such as purchases of raw materials, gas plant equipment, and gas appliances. The letters between the general manager and the superintendent provide an excellent description of day-to-day operations and include information about rates, gas purification, main construction, labor relations, sales of home appliances, and equipment repairs. The "Working Papers" contain a variety of records including: reports on the cost of gas, descriptions of outstanding accounts with explanations of each uncollected debt, statements of gas used and number of customers served, and descriptions of appliance installations (ranges, hot plates, lights). The Monthly Reports document production and construction (mains built, meters installed, and generating equipment repaired).

Finally, the Engineering Appraisal Report is of particular interest as it assessed the financial condition of the company and compared it to its rival The Mauch Chunk Heat, Power & Electric Light Co. This report includes a description of the Boroughs of Mauch Chunk and East Mauch Chunk, with population statistics and information on local industry. Also included is a detailed description of the Mauch Chunk Gas Company's organization, real estate holdings, generating station and equipment. This report lists customers, and contains a statement of earnings and expenses.

571. THE MAUCH CHUNK HEAT, POWER & ELECTRIC LIGHT COMPANY (Operating).
Carbon County, Mauch Chunk Borough.
1889 to 1947, 5 1/2 Linear Feet.

History:

The Mauch Chunk Heat, Power & Electric Light Co. was incorporated 18 February 1889 to supply electricity in the Boroughs of Mauch Chunk and East Mauch Chunk (Carbon County). The company purchased the Pardee Mill at the corner of Broadway and Susquehanna Streets and remodeled it as a power plant, installing a Westinghouse 750-incandescent light dynamo, and a 2000-candlepower 50-arc light dynamo. This plant remained in service until 1895 when the company built a new facility on the banks of the Lehigh Coal & Navigation Company's Mauch Chunk canal. The new plant contained two 200-horsepower McCormick Water Wheels which ran a 150-kw direct current Westinghouse generator. By 1907 it was becoming increasingly difficult to obtain enough water to run the plant, and the company was forced to install a steam generator in its power house. Three years later an alternating current system was set up. In December 1913 this power plant was destroyed by fire, and the company began to purchase power from the Lehigh Navigation Electric Co. In June 1926, the Republic Service Corp., which operated a number of electric companies in Pennsylvania and Virginia, acquired a majority of the company's stock. In 1947, Republic Service Corp. was forced by the Securities and Exchange Commission to sell these holdings.

Administrative Records:
Minute Book, 1889-1944 (3 Volumes)
Stock Certificate Book—Common, 1922-1947
Stock Certificate Book—Preferred, 1895-1947
Stock Transfer Record, 1909-1939 (2 Volumes)
Stock Ledger, 1895-1937 (2 Volumes)
Statement of Books & Records to Stockholders, 1932
Stockholders' Meetings Data 1889-1947
Correspondence Book, 1896-1900 (2 Volumes)
Correspondence, 1918-1947 (3 Volumes)
Annual Reports to Officers & Directors, 1907-1918
Annual Reports to Stockholders, 1928-1933

Operating Records:
FINANCIAL RECORDS
General Ledgers, 1890-1937 (4 Volumes)
Journals, 1890-1947 (7 Volumes)
Cashbooks, 1890-1920 (2 Volumes)
Detail Ledgers, 1897-1927 (5 Volumes)
Plant Account Ledgers, 1889-1947 (3 Volumes)
Revenue Listings and Statistics, 1940-1944
Appraisal Report, Day & Zimmermen, Engineers, 1912
Financial Reports, 1901-1947 (14 Volumes)
Budgets, 1930-1947 (17 Volumes)
Original Cost Data
Bank Books, 1911-1924
Working Papers, 1908-1946
PERSONNEL RECORDS
Payrolls, 1942-1947
Monthly Time Books, 1916-1938 (4 Volumes)
Employee Earnings Records, 1936-1947
CONSUMER RECORDS
Accounts Receivable, 1939-1944
Accounts Receivable—Delinquent, 1940-1944
Tax-Exempt Customers, 1933-1947 (2 Volumes)

Scope and Content Note:

The Minute Books of The Mauch Chunk Heat, Power & Electric Light Co. contain information about the company's operations, its dealings with the Borough Council and other customers, such as the Mauch Chunk Silk Co., the American Hotel, and the Lehigh Valley Railroad Co. Correspondence falls into three groups. The first group, covering the years 1918-1926, between L. F. Lentz, the company's President, and O. O. Jarrad, its Vice-President, provides a wealth of detailed information concerning day-to-day operations. The second group, dated 1928-1934, contains correspondence with Republic Service Corp., Pennsylvania Power & Light Co., the Pennsylvania State Highway Dept., Central Railroad Co. of New Jersey, and Mauch Chunk Borough council. The third group, 1933-1947, is correspondence with the Pennsylvania Treasury Department's Bureau of Internal

Revenue concerning taxes owed by the company. Letter books are a record of the company's outgoing correspondence and are mainly purchase orders for equipment and letters describing machinery malfunctions. Also included are copies of annual reports, giving information on the installation of equipment and the extension of electric services, and annual statements of earnings and expenditures. The Plant Account Ledger of 1889-1896 contains a copy of an 1896 letter describing the advantages gained by adopting water power. The Working Papers consist mainly of old streetlighting contracts, lists of stockholders, insurance papers, bonds, ledger sheets, and data relating to the costs of the electrical plant. The Monthly Time Books indicate the employee's occupation, pay rate, and number of hours worked, while the Payrolls show the number of hours worked, and rate of pay. The record of "Tax-Exempt Customers" is a listing of the major customers, such as schools, churches, and industries, to whom electricity was supplied. Particularly valuable is the Engineering Appraisal Report of 1912, which is an assessment of the financial, physical, and commercial features of this company and its rival, the Mauch Chunk Gas Co., drawn up for Mr. W. O. Lentz, who controlled both. This report includes a good description of the Boroughs of Mauch Chunk and East Mauch Chunk, with population statistics and information on the number and type of industries there; a detailed description of the company's organization, capitalization, real estate holdings, generating plant and equipment; number and type of customers; and statements of the company's earnings and expenses. The report concludes with suggestions on how to increase the number of customers, increase sales, and make the company more efficient.

572. **MAUCH CHUNK TOWNSHIP CARBON ELECTRIC COMPANY** (Non-operating).
Carbon County, Mauch Chunk Township.
1919, 2 Linear Inches.

History:
Mauch Chunk Township Carbon Electric Co. was incorporated 17 July 1919 to supply electricity in the township of Carbon County. It was consolidated and merged on 25 July 1919 with six other non-operating companies to form Industrial Power Co.

573. **MAUCH CHUNK TRANSIT COMPANY** (Operating).
Carbon County, Mauch Chunk Borough.
1924 to 1932, 1/2 Linear Foot.

History:
Mauch Chunk & Lehighton Transit Co., which operated an electric street railway line in the Lehigh River Valley resort area, in and around the Borough of Mauch Chunk, went bankrupt and was sold at a foreclosure sale on 30 June 1925. The new owners, Lehigh Power Securities Corp., reorganized the company on 13 January 1926 as Mauch Chunk Transit Co., and assigned Eastern Pennsylvania Railways Co. to manage the line. Mauch Chunk Transit Co. discontinued operations on 29 October 1931. Its franchises had been taken over in July 1931 by Mauch Chunk Transportation Co., which tried, without success, to switch to bus service.

Administrative Records:
Secretary's Papers of Meetings, 1926-1932
Correspondence, 1926-1932
Stock Transfer Record, 1926
Bond Ledger, 1926-1927

Operating Records:
Estimate of Cash Receipts and Requirements, 1928-1932
Expenditure Requisitions, 1927
Retirement Authorities, 1927
Audit Reports, 1924-1927

574. **MAUCH CHUNK TRANSPORTATION COMPANY** (Operating).
Carbon County, Mauch Chunk Borough.
1931 to 1932, 1 Linear Inch.

History:
Mauch Chunk Transportation Co. was organized in July 1931 to operate a bus line over the route of the former Mauch Chunk Transit Co. The company did not prosper and its property and franchises were ultimately sold in October 1932. The company dissolved shortly thereafter.

Administrative Records:
Correspondence, 1931-1932

Scope and Content Note:
The correspondence of Mauch Chunk Transportation Co. documents the company's organization, and its attempts to institute a bus service in the Borough of Mauch Chunk.

575. **MAYBERRY TOWNSHIP ELECTRICAL COMPANY** (Non-operating).
Montour County, Mayberry Township.
1916-1917, 1/2 Linear Foot.

History:
Mayberry Township Electric Co. was incorporated 3 August 1916 to supply electricity in the Township of Mayberry, Montour County. It was acquired by The Harwood Electric Co. on 20 June 1917.

576. **THE MAYFIELD ELECTRIC LIGHT, HEAT & POWER COMPANY** (Operating).
Lackawanna County, Mayfield Borough.
1900 to 1910, 2 Linear Inches.

History:
The Mayfield Electric Light, Heat & Power Co. was established in October 1900 by The Moosic Powder Co. in order to supply electricity for the company's powder works in Mayfield. On 5 March 1902 Moosic Powder Company sold the Mayfield company to Lackawanna Valley Electric Light & Powder Supply Co. In September 1908 the company was acquired by American Gas & Electric Co. and two years later was sold again, this time to Scranton Electric Co.

Administrative Records:
Minute Books, 1900-1910 (2 Volumes)

Scope and Content Note:
The Minute Books of The Mayfield Electric Light, Heat & Power Co. detail the company's relationship with The Moosic Powder Co., and include information about the installation of incandescent lighting in the Borough of Mayfield. Additional references to this company can be

found in the Minute Books of The Moosic Powder Co., which are part of the E.I. du Pont de Nemours & Co. records at Hagley Museum and Library.

577. MCADOO ELECTRIC COMPANY (Operating).
Schuylkill County, McAdoo Borough.
1908 to 1909, 1/2 Linear Foot.

History:
McAdoo Electric Co. was established on 27 February 1908 by the Harwood Electric Power Co. which was seeking to extend its franchises to the Borough of McAdoo, Schuylkill County. The McAdoo company leased a power plant and distribution system which had been built by the Borough in 1889, but operated it for only six months before shutting it down. After this, the company purchased its power from the Harwood Electric Power Co. On 23 June 1909 this company was consolidated and merged with eleven other companies to form Harwood Electric Co.

Administrative Records:
Minute Book, 1908-1909
Stock Certificate Book, 1908-1909

Operating Records:
General Ledger, 1908-1909
Journal, 1908-1909
Cashbook, 1908-1909
Balance Sheets, 1908-1909

Scope and Content Note:
The Minute Book documents the McAdoo Electric Company's relationship with the Harwood Electric Co. Further information can be found in the "Historical Report of The Harwood Electric Co. and Its Antecedent and Allied Companies," filed with the records of the Harwood Electric Co.

578. THE MCALISTERVILLE ELECTRIC LIGHT COMPANY (Operating).
Juniata County, McAlisterville Village.
1922 to 1926, 3 Linear Inches.

History:
The McAlisterville Electric Light Co. was incorporated 14 September 1920 by a group of local businessmen in the Village of McAlisterville, Juniata County. The company installed a Delco direct current electric generating and distribution system. This facility was abandoned soon after 8 July 1926, when the company was acquired by the Juniata Public Service Co.

Administrative Records:
Minute Book, 1922-1926
Stock Certificate Book, 1920-1925

Operating Records:
General Ledger, 1925-1926
Journal,1925-1926
Cashbook, 1925-1926

579. MCCALL FERRY POWER COMPANY (Operating).
Lancaster County, Holtwood Borough.
1905 to 1909, 4 Linear Inches.

History:
McCall Ferry Power Co. was incorporated 14 April 1905 following the consolidation and merger of The Hillside Water and Power Co. and the Susquehanna Water and Power Co. The company began construction of a dam and power plant at McCall Ferry (present-day Holtwood) on the Susquehanna River in 1905. This dam was to be 2,530 feet long and was to have a generating capacity of 135,000 h.p., to provide power to Philadelphia and or Baltimore. The dam was about 80 percent completed by November 1907, when the company had to suspend construction due to financial difficulties. The company went into receivership; and its property and assets were sold by order of the U.S. Circuit Court on 7 December 1909, to Mr. J.E. Aldred. Aldred reorganized the company as The Pennsylvania Water & Power Co. on 13 January 1910.

Administrative Records:
Minute Books, 1905-1909 (3 Volumes)

Scope and Content Note:
The Minute Books of the McCall Ferry Power Co. contain minutes of stockholders' and executive committee meetings, as well as details concerning the financing and construction of the company's dam. Included are lists of contracts for machinery, with descriptions of materials and prices. Also included is a copy of a mortgage which deliniates the various deeds through which the company obtained its property. The Pennsylvania Attorney General's opposition to the proposed dam is documented, as are his fears that the project would flood adjacent areas. Further references to the McCall Ferry Power Co. may be found in the Records of the Pennsylvania Water & Power Co.

580. THE MCCALL'S FERRY COMPANY (Operating).
Lancaster County, Holtwood Borough.
1910 to 1936, 1 Linear Inch.

History:
The McCall's Ferry Co. was incorporated 14 September 1881 to operate a ferry across the Susquehanna River at the Village of McCall's Ferry (present-day Holtwood), Lancaster County. In May 1910 the company's stock was acquired by the newly-formed Pennsylvania Water & Power Co. The ferry was still in operation as late as 1923, but was probably not run after that date. In February 1936 the company's assets were sold to Pennsylvania Water & Power Co., and the company was dissolved on 24 April 1936.

Administrative Records:
Minute Book, 1910-1936

Scope and Content Note:
The Minute Book of The McCall's Ferry Co. consists of routine minutes of stockholders' and directors' meetings. Additional information concerning this company may be found in the microfilmed records of the Pennsylvania Water & Power Co.

581. MCEWENSVILLE ELECTRIC COMPANY (Non-operating).
Northumberland County, McEwensville Borough.
1914, 1 Linear Inch.

History:
McEwensville Electric Co. was incoporated on 27 July 1914 to supply electricity in the Borough of McEwensville, Northumberland County. On 3 September 1914 the company was acquired by Northumberland County Gas & Electric Co.

582. MIDDLE SMITHFIELD-MONROE POWER & LIGHT COMPANY (Non-operating).
Monroe County, Middle Smithfield Township.
1925, 4 Linear Inches.

History:
Middle Smithfield-Monroe Power & Light Co. was incorporated 7 April 1925 to supply electricity in a portion of the Township of Middle Smithfield, Monroe County. The company was merged into Pennsylvania Power & Light Co. on 8 May 1925.

583. MIDDLE SMITHFIELD TOWNSHIP-MONROE COUNTY POWER & LIGHT COMPANY (Non-operating).
Monroe County, Middle Smithfield Township.
1927 to 1928, 3 Linear Inches.

History:
Middle Smithfield Township-Monroe County Power & Light Co. was incorporated 2 February 1928 to supply electricity in a portion of the Township of Middle Smithfield, Monroe County. It was merged into Pennsylvania Power & Light Co. on 28 February 1928.

584. THE MIDDLEBURG ELECTRIC COMPANY (Non-operating).
Snyder County, Middleburg Borough.
1905 to 1906, 1 Linear Inch.

History:
The Middleburg Electric Co. was incorporated 8 April 1905 for the purpose of supplying electricity in the Borough of Middleburg, Snyder County. The company was consolidated and merged with three other companies on 3 February 1906 to form Middlecreek Electric Co.

585. MIDDLEBURG LIGHT, HEAT AND POWER COMPANY (Operating).
Snyder County, Middleburg Borough.
1909 to 1930, 3 Linear Feet.

History:
Middleburg Light, Heat and Power Co. was incorporated 11 June 1909 by local entrepreneurs, and was the first company to supply electricity in the Borough of Middleburg, Snyder County. The company constructed a steam electric generating station and distribution system in Middleburg. In 1918 the company's stock was acquired by the businessmen who were forming what was to become the Juniata Public Service Co., which would seek to integrate the various electric companies operating along the Juniata and Susquehanna Rivers, north of the City of Harrisburg. In 1920, the company constructed a 22-kw transmission line to the Borough of Liverpool, Perry County, in order to link up with the Juniata Public Service Company's system, and to purchase power from them. From 1918 to 1926, the Middleburg Light, Heat and Power Co. expanded its area operations to nearby communities in the counties of Snyder, Northumberland, and Dauphin, by creating non-operating companies and then merging them into the parent company. By 1925 the company's power plant had become inadequate, and the following year it began to purchase power from Pennsylvania Power & Light. On 28 May it was merged into the Pennsylvania Power & Light system.

Administrative Records:
Minute Books, 1909-1928 (3 Volumes)
Secretary's Papers of Meetings, 1923-1928
Stock Certificate Book, 1909-1927

Operating Records:
FINANCIAL RECORDS
General Ledgers, 1909-1928 (4 Volumes)
Journals, 1918-1927 (2 Volumes)
Journal Entry Register, 1927-1928
Cash Receipts, 1909-1927 (2 Volumes)
Record of Cash Receipts, 1927-1928
Cash Disbursements, 1918-1927 (2 Volumes)
Record of Cash Disbursements, 1927-1928
Summary of Cash, 1927-1928
Notes and Bills Payable, 1919-1926
Audited Voucher Registers, 1920-1928 (2 Volumes)
Accounts Payable, 1928-1928
Accounts Receivable, 1927-1928
Summary of Accounts Receivable—Consumers, 1927-1928
Summary of Accounts Receivable—Miscellaneous, 1927-1928
PERSONNEL RECORDS
Payroll Distribution, 1920-1927 (2 Volumes)
Payroll Sheets, 1919-1921
AUDIT REPORTS, 1922-1927 (4 Volumes)

Scope and Content Note:
The Minute Books document the company's extension of service, absorption of non-operating companies and relationship with the Juniata Public Service Co. They also document earnings and expenses.

586. MIDDLECREEK ELECTRIC COMPANY (Operating).
Northumberland County, Northumberland Borough.
1905 to 1912, 4 Linear Inches.

History:
The Northumberland Electric Light, Heat and Power Co., incorporated in 1903, was the first company to supply electricity in the Borough of Northumberland. It constructed a steam electric generating station and a distribution system. On 3 February 1906 The Northumberland Electric Co. was consolidated and merged with three non-operating companies to form Middlecreek Electric Co. Middlecreek Electric then built a hydroelectric station of 250-kw capacity in the Village of Hummels Wharf, Snyder County, and connected it to the Northumberland plant. Shortly thereafter, the company constructed a 324-kw steam electric generating station in the City of Sunbury. In 1909 this plant's capacity was boosted to 625-kw. Two years later the company was merged into Northumberland County Gas & Electric Co.

Operating Records:
General Ledger, 1907-1911
Cashbook, 1905-1908
Journal, 1909-1912
Cash Receipts and Disbursements, 1905-1911
Record of Lamp Sales, 1908-1909

Scope and Content Note:
The operating records contain routine financial data. Of particular interest is the "Record of Lamp Sales," a list of sales of electric appliances, including lamps, fans, toasters, stoves, and extension cords, with the price of each item.

587. MIDDLESEX ELECTRIC LIGHT, HEAT AND POWER COMPANY (Operating).
Cumberland County, Middlesex Township.
1922 to 1928, 2 Linear Feet.

History:
The Middlesex Electric Light, Heat and Power Co. was incorporated 23 November 1922 by The United Electric Co., which was trying to extend its franchise into the Township of Middlesex, Cumberland County. Middlesex Electric constructed a distribution system to serve approximately 35 customers in the township, and purchased all its power from The United Electric Co. In 1926 Lehigh Power Securities Corp. acquired Middlesex Electric's stock, and on 28 May 1928 it was merged into the Pennsylvania Power & Light Co.

Administrative Records:
Minute Books, 1922-1928 (3 Volumes)
Secretary's Papers of Meetings, 1926-1928
Stock Certificate Book, 1923-1926
Stock Register, 1923-1925
Stock Transfer Record, 1925
Stock Ledgers, 1923-1925 (2 Volumes)

Operating Records:
General Ledgers, 1923-1928 (2 Volumes)
Journal Entry Register, 1926-1928
Record of Cash Receipts, 1926-1928
Record of Cash Disbursements, 1926-1928
Summary of Cash, 1926-1928
Financial Statements, 1925-1926
Working Papers, 1924-1925
Trial Balances, 1926-1928
Expenditure Requisitions, 1928
Retirement Authorities, 1927-1928
Summary of Accounts Receivable—Consumers, 1926-1928
Summary of Accounts Receivable—Miscellaneous, 1926-1928
Audit Reports, 1923-1927 (4 Volumes)

Scope and Content Note:
The Minute Books of the Middlesex Electric Light, Heat and Power Co. contain routine minutes of stockholders' and directors' meetings. The "Secretary's Papers of Meetings" list stockholders, their voting, and proxy sheets records. The "Working Papers" are lists of bills paid, electric equipment and general supplies purchased, stock transfers, and statements of earnings.

588. MIFFLIN ELECTRIC SERVICE COMPANY (Non-operating).
Dauphin County, Mifflin Township.
1924, 1 Linear Inch.

History:
Mifflin Electric Service Co. was incorporated 8 February 1924 to supply electricity in the Township of Mifflin, Dauphin County. On 7 March 1924 the company was merged into Middleburg Light, Heat and Power Co.

589. MIFFLIN-LYCOMING POWER & LIGHT COMPANY (Non-operating).
Lycoming County, Mifflin Township.
1928 to 1929, 1 Linear Inch.

History:
Mifflin-Lycoming Power & Light Co. was incorporated 14 May 1928 to supply electricity in the Township of Mifflin, Lycoming County. It was merged into Pennsylvania Power & Light Co. on 29 June 1928.

590. MIFFLIN TOWNSHIP ELECTRIC COMPANY (Non-operating).
Dauphin County, Mifflin Township.
1919, 1 Linear Inch.

History:
Mifflin Township Electric Co. was incorporated 14 June 1916 to supply electricity in the Township of MIfflin, Dauphin County. On 30 October 1919 it was consolidated and merged with five other non-operating companies to form The Citizens Electric Co.

591. MILES-CENTRE POWER & LIGHT COMPANY (Non-operating).
Centre County, Miles Township.
1947 to 1949, 2 Linear Inches.

History:
Miles-Centre Power & Light Co. was organized on 26 December 1927 by the Pennsylvania Power & Light Co. in an attempt to secure charter rights in the Township of Miles, Centre County. The company never received its charter and was dissolved on 30 December 1948.

592. MILFORD ELECTRIC LIGHT & POWER COMPANY (Non-operating).
Bucks County, Milford Township.
1912, 1 Linear Inch.

History:
Milford Electric Light & Power Co. was organized on 30 April 1912 by the Citizens Electric Light, Heating and Power Co. in an effort to secure charter rights in Milford Township, Bucks County. The company never received its charter and was dissolved on 10 May 1912.

593. MILFORD TOWNSHIP ELECTRIC LIGHT & POWER COMPANY (Non-operating).
Bucks County, Milford Township.
1914 to 1916, 1 Linear Inch.

History:
Milford Township Electric Light & Power Co. was incorporated 13 January 1915 by Lehigh Valley Light and Power Co., No. 2, in an effort to secure charter rights in Milford Township, Bucks County. On 26 February 1916 the company was merged into Lehigh Valley Light and Power Co., No. 3.

594. MILL CREEK-LYCOMING POWER & LIGHT COMPANY (Non-operating).
Lycoming County, Mill Creek Township.
1924 to 1925, 1 Linear Inch.

History:
Mill Creek-Lycoming Power & Light Co. was incorporated 28 August 1924 to supply electricity in Mill Creek Township, Lycoming County. On 28 October 1924 it was merged into Pennsylvania Power & Light Co.

595. THE MILLERSBURG ELECTRIC LIGHT HEAT AND POWER COMPANY (Operating).
Dauphin County, Millersburg Borough.
1891 to 1918, 1 Linear Foot.

History:
The Millersburg Electric Light Heat and Power Co. was incorporated 24 March 1891, and was the first company to supply electricity in Millersburg Borough, Dauphin County. Soon after its formation, the company purchased a water-powered mill on Wiconisco Creek in Millersburg, and converted it into a hydroelectric plant. In 1895 the company added a steam-powered generator to the plant, and purchased dredging equipment to recover river coal from the creek. By 1908 this plant had a total capacity of just under 500—kw. In 1917 the plant was rebuilt, and a 1000kw turbogenerator was installed. In the same year, the company extended its distribution system to the Boroughs of Liverpool, Perry County, and Halifax, Dauphin County. On 24 September 1917 the company was consolidated and merged with 16 other companies to form the Juniata Public Service Co.

Administrative Records:
Minute Book, 1891-1917
Minutes, 1907-1917
Stock Certificate Book, 1894-1916

Operating Records:
General Ledger, 1916-1917
Journal, 1916-1917
Cashbooks, 1916-1918 (2 Volumes)
Cash Receipts and Disbursements, 1917-1918
Cash Analysis, 1917

Scope and Content Note:
The Minutes of the Millersburg Electric Light Heat and Power Co. document routine stockholders' and directors' meetings, as well as operating expenses. Also included is information on mortgages and electric rates.

596. MILLVILLE ELECTRIC LIGHT COMPANY (Operating).
Columbia County, Millville Borough.
1918 to 1928, 2 Linear Feet.

History:
Millville Electric Light Co. was incorporated 24 September 1918 to supply electricity in Millville Borough, Columbia County. The company purchased all of its power from the Millville Silk Co. In 1923 the company's stock was acquired by Lehigh Power Securities Corp. Millville Electric was then operated as a part of the Pennsylvania Power & Light Co. system until 28 May 1928, when it oficially merged with the Pennsylvania Power & Light Co.

Administrative Records:
Minute Books, 1918-1928 (2 Volumes)
Stock Certificate Book, 1921-1923
Stock Transfer record, 1922-1923 (2 Volumes)
Stock Ledger, no date
Stock Register and Transfer Certificates, 1921-1922

Operating Records:
General Ledger, 1923
Journal Entry Register, 1923-1928
Cash Received, 1923-1925
Cash Register, 1923-1925
Record of Cash Receipts, 1925-1928
Record of Cash Disbursements, 1925-1928
Summary of Cash, 1925-1928
Accounts Receivable, 1924-1928
Summary of Accounts Receivable—Consumers, 1923-1928
Detail Ledger, 1923
Detail of Cost Study and Fixed Capital, 1925-1927
Expenditure Requisitions, 1923-1928
Retirement Authorities, 1923-1927
Workmen's Compensation Insurance Statements, 1923-1928
Audit Reports, 1921-1927 (3 Volumes)

Scope and Content Note:
The Minute Books of the Millville Electric Light Co. contain information concerning the company's purchase of power from the Millville Silk Mill and document the company's expansion. Also included are statements of earnings and expenses.

597. THE MILNESVILLE WATER COMPANY (Operating).
Luzerne County, Milnesville Village.
1892 to 1937, 2 Linear Feet.

History:
Milnesville Water Co. was incorporated 8 December 1892 to supply water in Milnesville Village, Luzerne County. In March 1903 the Pardee family gained control of the company's Board of Directors. Pardee Bros. & Co. purchased the company's charter and its water pipeline to Milnesville on 25 April 1903. The company purchased 325 acres of water-bearing land at the Village of Harwood from the Harwood Coal Co. and installed pumps, pump houses and nine wells. On 10 June 1909 the Milnesville Water Company's stock was acquired by Harwood Electric Co. From 1908 to January 1911 the company supplied water at cost to Pardee Bros. & Co., and from January 1910 to April 1912 supplied water to the Harwood Coal Co. and The Harwood Electric Co. It ceased operations in April 1912. On 31 October 1913 it sold its water-bearing lands at Harwood, with the equipment thereon, to Hazle Township Water Co. In September 1917 The Lehigh Valley Light and Power Co. acquired control of the company.

Administrative Records:
Minute Books, 1892-1937 (2 Volumes)
Stock Certificate Books, 1907-1936 (2 Volumes)
Stock Transfer Record, 1907-1909
Stock Ledgers, 1907-1936 (2 Volumes)

Operating Records:
General Ledger, 1919-1937
Journals, 1910-1921 (2 Volumes)
Journal Entry Register, 1926-1937
Cash Received and Check Register, 1909-1913 (2 Volumes)
Check Registers, 1919-1925 (2 Volumes)
Supplementary Cashbook, 1918-1919
Record of Cash Receipts, 1926
Record of Cash Disbursements, 1925-1928
Summary of Cash, 1925-1928

Unpaid Voucher List, 1914-1917
Record of Amount Paid for Plant, 1907-1912
Audited Voucher Register, 1926-1937
Accrual Record, 1926-1933
Detail of Cost Study and Fixed Capital, 1925-1927 (2 Volumes)
Balance Sheets, 1910-1918
Miscellaneous Financial Statements, 1919-1922
Audit Reports, 1914-1931 (4 Volumes)

Scope and Content Note:
The Minute Books of The Milnesville Water Co. consist entirely of routine minutes of stockholders' and directors' meetings. The Record of Amount Paid for Plant documents a settlement between this company and the Harwood Electric Co. for the costs of improvements to the company's plant at Harwood. For additional information about this company, see the "Historical Report of The Harwood Electric Co. and Its Antecedent and Allied Companies," filed with the records of The Harwood Electric Co.

598. MILTON BOROUGH ELECTRIC COMPANY (Non-operating).
Northumberland County, Milton Borough.
1919 to 1920, 3 Linear Inches.

History:
Milton Borough Electric Co. was incorporated 6 November 1919 to supply electricity in Milton Borough, Northumberland County. On 28 April 1920 the company was merged into Lehigh Industrial Power Co.

599. MILTON ELECTRIC LIGHT AND POWER COMPANY (Operating).
Northumberland County, Milton Borough.
1907 to 1908, 1 Linear Inch.

History:
Milton Electric Light and Power Co. was incorporated 8 February 1892 to supply electricity in Milton Borough, Northumberland County. In 1901 the company was acquired by Railways Company General. Soon after this purchase, Milton Electric began to supply power to the Lewisburg, Milton & Watsontown Railway Co., which was also controlled by Railways Company General. On 16 November 1909 Milton Electric purchased The Pennsylvania General Electric Company's electric power station in order to increase its generating capacity. The next year United Light and Power Co. bought all of Milton Electric's property and franchises, except the power house in Milton.

Operating Records:
Financial Reports, 1907-1908

600. MILTON GAS COMPANY (Operating).
Northumberland County, Milton Borough.
1860 to 1912, 1 1/2 Linear Feet.

History:
Milton Gas Co. was incorporated 8 March 1856 to manufacture and supply gas lighting in Milton Borough, Northumberland County. The company constructed its gas plant in Milton in 1860, and began service that same year. A fire damaged this plant in May 1880, but it was quickly repaired. In 1911 the company extended its gas distribution system to the Borough of Montgomery and the Township of Clinton, Lycoming County, and the Townships of Delaware and Turbot in Northumberland County. On 31 August 1912 the company was merged into Northern Central Gas Co.

Administrative Records:
Minute Book, 1860-1912
Stock Certificate Books, 1860-1912 (2 Volumes)
Stock Transfer Record, 1906-1912
Stock Ledger (no date)

Operating Records:
General Ledgers, 1908-1912 (2 Volumes)
Cashbooks, 1894-1912 (2 Volumes)
Accounts Payable Ledger, 1908-1912 (3 Volumes)
Report of Sales and Output of Gas, 1912

Scope and Content Note:
The Minute Book of Milton Gas Co. includes information about the company's dealings with Milton Borough Council concerning street lighting contracts. Included are descriptions of improvements to the company's gas plant, statements of operating expenses, and several discussions of the company's rates for the supply of gas. The Report of Sales and Output of Gas is a seven-month survey of all costs relative to the manufacture and distribution of gas, as well as a review of the plant's total production of gas for the same period.

601. THE MILTON MANUFACTURING COMPANY (Operating).
Northumberland County, Milton Borough.
1915 to 1922, 1 Linear Inch.

History:
The Milton Manufacturing Co., incorporated in 1893, manufactured cold punched nuts, hot pressed nuts, and refined bar iron at its plant in Milton Borough, Northumberland County. From 1915 to 1922 the company constructed a steam electric generating station, with a capacity of 8,000-kw, at its plant on the Susquehanna River. A few years after this generating station was built, Pennsylvania Power & Light Co. began to operate it for The Milton Manufacturing Co. On 28 February 1928, Pennsylvania Power & Light Co. purchased this generating station.

Administrative Records:
Cost of Plant Construction, Ledger, 1915-1922

Scope and Content Note:
The "Cost of Plant Construction Ledger" provides a detailed account of costs of material, labor, fuel, and tools. This ledger was turned over to Pennsylvania Power & Light so that it could estimate the plant's assets and liabilities.

602. MINERS MILLS ELECTRIC COMPANY (Non-operating).
Luzerne County, Miners Mills Borough.
1921 to 1923, 1 Linear Inch.

History:
Miners Mills Electric Co. was incorporated 22 March 1922 to supply electricity in Miners Mills Borough, Luzerne County. It was merged into Pennsylvania Power & Light Co. 27 August 1923.

603. THE MINERSVILLE ELECTRIC LIGHT COMPANY, NO. 1 (Operating).
Schuylkill County, Minersville Borough.
1886 to 1909, 4 Linear Inches.

History:
The Minersville Electric Light Co., No. 1, was incorporated 16 July 1886 to supply electricity in Minersville Borough, Schuylkill County. The company began to provide service in 1889, after the completion of a power plant with a 35-light arc dynamo, and a 600-light Brush incandescent alternating current dynamo. The following year the plant's capacity was boosted when the 600-light dynamo was replaced with two 1,000-light dynamos. In 1899 a 150-kw Warren Electric Co. generator was installed. In 1905 the company gained control of The Minersville Fuel Gas Co., and the Citizens Gas Co. of Minersville, Pa. In 1906 Eastern Pennsylvania Railways Co. acquired control of The Minersville Electric Light Co., No. 1, and merged it with the two gas companies which it controlled to form the The Minersville Electric Light Co., No. 2.

Administrative Records:
Minute Book, 1886-1908
Stock Certificate Book, 1889-1909
Stock Transfer Record, 1890-1906

Scope and Content Note:
The Minute Book of The Minersville Electric Light Co., No. 1, documents the construction of the company's electric plant and distribution system, its purchases of generating equipment, and its dealings with the Minersville Borough Council concerning street lighting contracts. Also included in the Minute Book are statements of operating expenses, and annual reports on the company's financial condition.

604. THE MINERSVILLE ELECTRIC LIGHT COMPANY, NO. 2 (Operating).
Schuylkill County, Minersville Borough.
1906 to 1910, 2 Linear Feet.

History:
The Minersville Electric Light Co., No. 2, was incorporated 14 May 1909, through the consolidation and merger of The Minersville Electric Light Co., No. 1, with the two non-operating gas companies that it controlled: The Minersville Fuel Gas Co. and Citizens Gas Co. of Minersville, Pa. On 20 July 1909 The Minersville Electric Light Co., No. 2, was merged into Palo Alto Heat, Light and Power Co.

Administrative Records:
Minute Book, 1909

Operating Records:
General Ledgers, 1906-1909 (2 Volumes)
Cashbooks, 1906-1909 (2 Volumes)
Accounts Receivable—Miscellaneous, 1906-1908
Accounts Payable Ledger, 1906-1908 (2 Volumes)
Construction Ledger, 1908-1909
Statement of Charges to Local Construction, 1908
Report of Earnings, 1908-1909
Record of Sales—Work Orders Issued, 1907-1910
Consumers' Ledger, 1906
Consumers' Payments Ledgers, 1906-1910 (2 Volumes)
Operating Statistics, 1909-1910
Balance Sheets, 1906-1909
Earnings, Operating Expenses, Balance Sheets, 1907-1908

Scope and Content Note:
The Minutes of The Minersville Electric Co., No. 2 are routine accounts of stockholders' and directors' meetings. The Record of Sales—Work Orders Issued documents electrical work done for individual customers.

605. THE MINERSVILLE FUEL GAS COMPANY (Non-operating).
Schuylkill County, Minersville Borough.
1905 to 1908, 2 Linear Inches.

History:
The Minersville Fuel Gas Co. was incorporated 7 July 1905 to supply gas for all purposes, except lighting, in the Borough of Minersville, Schuylkill County. On 7 April 1909 it was consolidated and merged with The Minersville Electric Light Co., No. 1, and another non-operating company, Citizens Gas Co. of Minersville, to form The Minersville Electric Light Co., No. 2.

606. MINERSVILLE-SCHUYLKILL POWER & LIGHT COMPANY (Non-operating).
Schuylkill County, Minersville Borough.
1927, 1 Linear Inch.

History:
Minersville-Schuylkill Power & Light Co. was incorporated 1 June 1927 to supply electricity in the Borough of Minersville, Schuylkill County. On 18 July 1927 the company was merged into East Penn Electric Co., No. 2.

607. MITCHELL ELECTRIC COMPANY (Non-operating).
Schuylkill County, Mahanoy Township.
1911 to 1913, 2 Linear Inches.

History:
Mitchell Electric Co. was incorporated 27 June 1911 to supply electricity in the Township of Mahanoy , Schuylkill County. On 23 December 1912 it was consolidated and merged with 37 other non-operating companies to form Lehigh Navigation Electric Co., No. 2.

608. MONROE TOWNSHIP LIGHT COMPANY (Non-operating).
Snyder County, Monroe Township.
1914, 1 Linear Inch.

History:
Monroe Township Light Co. was incorporated 16 September 1914 to supply electricity in the Township of Monroe, Snyder County. On 3 October 1914 it was merged into Northumberland County Gas & Electric Co.

609. MONROE TOWNSHIP POWER COMPANY (Non-operating).
Juniata County, Monroe Township.
1925 to 1926, 1 Linear Inch.

History:
Monroe Township Power Co. was incorporated 21 January 1926 to supply electricity in the Township of Monroe, Juniata County. On 8 July 1926 it was merged into Middleburg Light, Heat and Power Co.

610. MONTGOMERY AND MUNCY ELECTRIC LIGHT, HEAT AND POWER COMPANY (Operating).
Lycoming County, Muncy Borough.
1906 to 1928, 8 Linear Feet.

History:

Montgomery and Muncy Electric Light, Heat and Power Co. was incorporated 9 September 1912 to supply electricity in those boroughs of Lycoming County. On 1 October 1912 the company acquired Montgomery Electric Light and Power Co. and The Muncy Electric Light Heat and Power Co., which had been supplying electricity in the Boroughs of Montgomery and Muncy, respectively. Shortly thereafter, the company constructed a transmission line between these boroughs. The power plant in Montgomery was then shut down, and the company contracted with Montgomery Table Works to buy power. In January 1913 the company extended its distribution system to the Townships of Clinton and Muncy Creek, Lycoming County. Subsequently, the company sold its power plant at Montgomery to Stokes Manufacturing Co. In 1917 the Muncy power plant was also sold. In 1923, in order to meet increased customer demand for electricity, the company began to purchase power from the Watsontown Door & Sash Co., located about 10 miles south of Montgomery, in the Borough of Watsontown. A tie line between Watsontown and Montgomery was constructed for this purpose. In 1923 Lehigh Power Securities Corp. acquired the company's stock and began to operate it as a part of the Pennsylvania Power & Light Co. system. On 28 May 1928 the company was merged into Pennsylvania Power & Light Co.

Administrative Records:

Minute Books, 1912-1928 (2 Volumes)
Stock Certificate Book, 1912-1926
Stock Transfer Record, 1924-1926
Correspondence, 1906-1924

Operating Records:

FINANCIAL RECORDS
General Ledgers, 1912-1928 (3 Volumes)
Journals, 1912-1924 (4 Volumes)
Journal Entry Register, 1924-1928
Cashbook, 1914-1918
Cash Received, 1924-1925
Check Register, 1924-1925
Record of Cash Receipts, 1925-1928
Record of Cash Disbursements, 1925-1928
Summary of Cash, 1925-1928
Accounts Payable Ledger, 1925-1928
Accounts Receivable Ledger, 1925-1928
Detail Ledger, 1924-1928
Accrual Record, 1924-1928
Detail of Cost Study and Fixed Capital, 1925-1927
Record of Mortgage, 1912
Monthly Reports, 1915-1918
PERSONNEL RECORDS
Workmen's Compensation Accrual Statements, 1924-1928
Payrolls, 1915-1916
CONSUMER RECORDS
Cash Sales, 1915-1918 (2 Volumes)
Record of Material Sold, 1012-1023 (4 Volumes)
Consumers Ledgers, 1918 (2 Volumes)
Balance on Consumers Ledger, 1918
Delinquent Accounts, 1917-1918
Consumers Cash Book, 1921-1922
Summary of Accounts Receivable—Consumers, 1926-1928 (2 Volumes)
Summary of Accounts Receivable—Miscellaneous, 1926-1928 (2 Volumes)
Summary of Consumers' Deposits, 1925-1928 (2 Volumes)
Summary of Cashier's Overs and Shorts, 1925-1928
Rents from Real Estate, 1926-1928
Audit Reports, 1921-1926 (4 Volumes)

Scope and Content Note:

The Minute Books of Montgomery and Muncy Electric Light, Heat and Power Co. contain information about electric rates, dealings with the Borough Councils of Muncy and Montgomery in reference to the franchise rights, its agreement for the purchase of power from Montgomery Table Works, its sale of the power plant in Montgomery, and its unsuccessful 1920 negotiations with Pennsylvania Power & Light exploring the possible purchase of power from that company. Also included in the Minute Books are financial data, including lists of stockholders, statements of assets, liabilities, and operating expenses. Correspondence includes letters to electrical manufacturers concerning equipment malfunctions, descriptions of electrical parts, and purchase orders for parts and fuels. Customer correspondence includes complaints about high bills and erratic service. There is also a file of correspondence with the Borough Councils of Muncy and Montgomery documenting negotiations for street lighting contracts. The Payrolls indicate what types of jobs were being performed by each employee. The Record of Material Sold Ledgers list the various electric appliances and parts that were sold to customers.

611. MONTGOMERY ELECTRIC LIGHT AND POWER COMPANY (Operating).
Lycoming County, Montgomery Borough.
1898 to 1912, 4 Linear Inches.

History:

Montgomery Electric Light and Power Co., incorporated 6 December 1897, was the first company to supply electricity in the Borough of Montgomery, Lycoming County. The company built a steam electric generating station, and a distribution system in the borough soon after its incorporation. On 1 October 1912 the company was merged into the Montgomery and Muncy Electric Light, Heat and Power Co.

Operating Records:

General Ledgers, 1898-1912 (2 Volumes)
Journals, 1909-1912 (2 Volumes)

612. MONTOUR COUNTY GAS COMPANY (Non-operating).
Columbia County, Bloomsburg Borough.
1913, 1 Linear Inch.

History:

Montour County Gas Co. was incorporated 21 April 1913 to supply gas lighting and heating in all of Montour

County, except the Borough of Danville. The company was merged into the Northern Central Gas Co. 26 December 1913.

613. MONTOURSVILLE ELECTRIC LIGHT COMPANY (Operating).
Lycoming County, Montoursville Borough.
1898 to 1928, 1 Linear Foot.

History:
Montoursville Electric Light Co. was incorporated 6 December 1897 to supply electricity in Montoursville Borough, Lycoming County, where the company constructed a power plant and distribution system which utilized the direct current Edison system. The power plant contained a 100-kw 550-volt direct current railway generator. This was used to supply power to the Montoursville Passenger Railway Co. In 1909 the power plant's capacity was boosted by the addition of a 150-kw, and a 300-kw 550-volt direct current railway generator. The next year, the company extended its area of operations to the Township of Loyalsock, Lycoming County. In 1923 the power plant's capacity was further increased by the installation of a second-hand 100-kw Triumph Electric Co. generator. In 1924 the company's stock was acquired by Lehigh Power Securities Corp. At this time the distribution system was converted to alternating current. On 28 May 1928 the company was merged into Pennsylvania Power & Light Co.

Administrative Records:
Minute Book, 1899-1928
Stock Certificate Book, 1899-1925
Stock Transfer Record, 1924-1925
Correspondence, 1910-1920

Operating Records:
General Ledgers, 1900-1928 (3 Volumes)
Journals, 1900-1924 (2 Volumes)
Journal Entry Register, 1924-1928
Cashbooks, 1900-1924 (3 Volumes)
Cash Received, 1924-1925
Check Register, 1924-1925
Record of Cash Receipts, 1925-1928
Record of Cash Disbursements, 1925-1928
Summary of Cash, 1925-1928
Audited Voucher Register, 1924-1928
Accounts Payable, 1924-1928
Accounts Receivable, 1924-1928
Detail Ledger, 1924-1928
Accrual Record, 1924-1928
Time Book and Payrolls, 1909-1920 (4 Volumes)
Detail of Cost Study and Fixed Capital, 1925-1927
Financial Reports, 1907-1908
Petty Cash Book, 1900-1908
Cash Journal and Consumers Ledger, 1898-1901
Expenditure Requisitions, 1924-1928
Retirement Authorities, 1924-1927
Workmen's Compensation Insurance Accrual Statements, 1924-1928
Summary of Accounts Receivable—Consumers, 1925
Summary of Accounts Receivable—Miscellaneous, 1926-1928
Summary of Cashiers Overs and Shorts, 1926-1928
Summary of Consumers' Deposits, 1926-1928
Audit Reports, 1917-1927 (5 Volumes)

Scope and Content Note:
The Minute Book contains routine accounts of stockholders' and directors' meetings. The Correspondence file documents negotiations with the Montoursville Borough Council for street and bridge lighting contracts. Also included in the file are letters to the Pennsylvania and United States Departments of Revenue concerning taxes owed by the company. There is also correspondence with the National Committee on Gas and Electric Service which documents measures taken to conserve energy during World War I.

Time Books record employees' pay rates, hours worked, and job descriptions. There is also a small collection of photographs in the Hagley Museum and Library's Pictorial Department.

614. MONTOURSVILLE PASSENGER RAILWAY COMPANY (Operating).
Lycoming County, Montoursville Borough.
1897 to 1925, 2 1/2 Linear Feet.

History:
Montoursville Passenger Railway Co. was incorporated 28 June 1897 to operate an electric street railway in and around Montoursville Borough, Lycoming County. It was closely affiliated with Montoursville Electric Light Co., being under the same management, but operated independently. The company carried passengers, freight, and milk cans in Montoursville, and over a four-mile route to the outskirts of Williamsport. In April 1924 the company's stock was acquired by Lehigh Power Securities Corp. On 17 January 1925 the company's real estate holdings were sold to Pennsylvania Realty & Investment Co., and the company itself was dissolved.

Administrative Records:
Minute Book, 1897-1925
Stock Certificate Book, 1897-1925
Stock Transfer Record, 1924
Stock Ledger, 1909-1924
Correspondence, 1910-1920

Operating Records:
General Ledgers, 1900-1924 (2 Volumes)
Journals, 1900-1924 (2 Volumes)
Cashbooks, 1900-1924 (3 Volumes)
Cashbook and Daily Record, 1906-1924 (7 Volumes)
Notes Payable, 1913-1923
Audit Reports, 1917-1924

Scope and Content Note:
The Minute Book documents the company's relationship with the Montoursville Borough Council, with which it negotiated contracts for street lighting and railroad right-of-way. Correspondence with the National Committee on Gas and Electric Service documents the company's efforts to conserve fuel during World War I.

615. MOORE TOWNSHIP ELECTRIC COMPANY (Non-operating).
Northampton County, Moore Township.
1911 to 1913, 2 Linear Inches.

History:
Moore Township Electric Co., incorporated 4 April 1911 for the purpose of supplying electricity in the Township of Moore, Northampton County, was

consolidated and merged with 37 other non-operating companies on 23 December 1912 to form Lehigh Navigation Electric Co., No. 2.

616. MOOSIC ELECTRIC COMPANY (Non-operating).
Lackawanna County, Moosic Borough.
1910 to 1912, 4 Linear Inches.

History:
Moosic Electric Co. was organized 13 September 1911 by Scranton Electric Co. in order to obtain charter rights for the supply of electricity in the Borough of Moosic, Lackawanna County. On 25 November 1912 the company was merged into Scranton Electric Co.

617. MORAVIA ELECTRIC LIGHT, HEAT AND POWER COMPANY (Non-operating).
Northampton County, Bethlehem City.
1912, 1 Linear Inch.

History:
Moravia Electric Light, Heat and Power Co. was organized by Halycon Electric Light and Power Co. during the summer of 1911, in order to secure charter rights to supply electricity in the western suburbs of the City of Bethlehem. In 1912 The Citizens Electric Light, Heat and Power Co. gained control of Halycon Electric, and Moravia Electric's charter rights.

618. MORELAND-LYCOMING POWER & LIGHT COMPANY (Non-operating).
Lycoming County, Moreland Township.
1924 to 1925, 2 Linear Inches.

History:
Moreland-Lycoming Power & Light Co. was incorporated 28 August 1924 to supply electricity in the Township of Moreland, Lycoming County. The company was merged into the Pennsylvania Power & Light Co. on 28 October 1924.

619. MOSCOW AND COVINGTON ELECTRIC COMPANY (Non-operating).
Lackawanna County, Moscow Borough.
1923, 1 Linear Inch.

History:
Moscow and Covington Electric Co. was organized in June or July 1923 by the Moscow Electric Co., No. 1, in order to secure charter rights in the small communities around the Borough of Moscow, Lackawanna County. On 25 October 1923 the company was consolidated and merged with Moscow Electric Co., No. 1, and two non-operating companies to form Moscow Electric Co., No. 2.

620. MOSCOW AND ROARING BROOK ELECTRIC COMPANY (Non-operating).
Lackawanna County, Moscow Borough.
1923, 1 Linear Inch.

History:
Moscow and Roaring Brook Electric Co. was organized in June or July 1923 by the Moscow Electric Co., No. 1, in order to secure charter rights in the small communities around the Borough of Moscow, Lackawanna County. On 25 October 1923 merged with the Moscow Electric Co., No. 1, and two non-operating companies to form the Moscow Electric Co. No. 2.

621. MOSCOW ELECTRIC COMPANY (Operating).
Lackawanna County, Moscow Borough.
1921 to 1926, 2 Linear Feet.

History:
Moscow Electric Co., No. 1 was incorporated in 1921 to supply electricity in the Boroughs of Moscow, and Elmhurst, Lackawanna County. The company built a distribution system, and began to purchase power from the Scranton Electric Co., in January 1922. On 25 October 1923 the company was consolidated and merged with three non-operating companies to form Moscow Electric Co., No. 2. Scranton Electric Co. acquired the company's stock in May 1927 and purchased its property, assets and franchises on 31 October 1934. Moscow Electric Co., No. 2 was dissolved on 27 November 1934.

Administrative Records:
Minute Book, 1921-1935
Stock Certificate Book, 1922-1928 (2 Volumes)

Operating Records:
General Ledgers, 1922-1935 (3 Volumes)
Invoice Register, 1923-1927
Invoice and Journal Registers, 1927-1932 (2 Volumes)
Cashbooks, 1927-1935 (3 Volumes)
Accounts Receivable—Miscellaneous, 1932-1935
Check Registers, 1928-1935 (2 Volumes)
Construction Work in Progress, 1932-1935
Insurance, Tax and Rent Registers, 1933-1936

Scope and Content Note:
The Minute Book of the Moscow Electric Co. contains annual financial reports, a copy of a 1920 Scranton Electric Co. electric rate schedule, and information on the company's own electric rates and the construction of its distribution system. It also documents the company's effort to work with Pennsylvania Power & Light in order to divide the market.

622. MOUNT CARBON ELECTRIC COMPANY (Non-operating).
Schuylkill County, Mount Carbon Borough.
1924, 1 Linear Inch.

History:
Mount Carbon Electric Co. was incorporated 24 April 1924 to supply electricity in Mount Carbon Borough, Schuylkill County. The company was acquired by East Penn Electric Co. No. 2, on 28 August 1924.

623. MOUNT CARMEL CITIZENS GAS COMPANY (Operating).
Northumberland County, Mount Carmel Township.
1924 to 1927, 1 Linear Inch.

History:
Mount Carmel Citizens Gas Co. was incorporated 23 August 1922 to supply gas for lighting and heating in Mount Carmel Township, Northumberland County. On 11 September 1923 this company purchased the property and assets of Mount Carmel Gas Light Co., which had gone into receivership after it was declared bankrupt in 1918.

Operating Records:
Audit Report, Pennsylvania Power & Light Co., 1924-1927

624. MOUNT CARMEL LIGHT COMPANY
(Non-operating).
Northumberland County, Mount Carmel Township.
1912, 1 Linear Inch.

History:
Mount Carmel Light Co. was incorporated 29 November 1912 to supply electricity in the Township of Mount Carmel, Northumberland County. On 6 January 1913 it was consolidated and merged with twelve other companies to form Hazleton Electric Co.

625. MOUNT CARMEL TOWNSHIP ELECTRIC COMPANY, NO.1 (Non-operating).
Northumberland County, Mount Carmel Township.
1910 to 1912, 1 Linear Inch.

History:
Mount Carmel Township Electric Co., No. 1, was incorporated 26 January 1911 by Mr. Calvin Pardee to supply electricity in the Township of Mount Carmel, Northumberland County. Control of the company's stock was acquired by Schuylkill Gas & Electric Co. in September 1911. On 6 January 1913 this company was consolidated and merged with eleven other companies to form The Schuylkill Gas & Electric Co.

626. MOUNT CARMEL TOWNSHIP ELECTRIC COMPANY, NO. 2 (Non-operating).
Northumberland County, Mount Carmel Township.
1918 to 1921, 1 Linear Inch.

History:
Mount Carmel Township Electric Co., No. 2, was incorporated 31 October 1918 to supply electricity in the Township of Mount Carmel, Northumberland County. It was merged into Pennsylvania Power & Light Co. on 30 September 1920.

627. MOUNT HOLLY LIGHT HEAT AND POWER COMPANY (Operating).
Cumberland County, Carlisle Borough.
1910 to 1911, 1 Linear Inch.

History:
Mount Holly Light Heat and Power Co. was incorporated 18 May 1903 to supply electricity in Carlisle Borough, Cumberland County. The company was owned and operated by the Carlisle and Mount Holly Railway Co., and supplied it with power. In 1909 the company's stock was acquired by Cumberland Railway Co.

Administrative Records:
Minute Book, 1910-1911

Scope and Content Note:
The Minute Book of the Mount Holly Light Heat and Power Co. consists of routine minutes of stockholders' and directors' meetings, and documents the company's agreement to furnish electric power to Carlisle and Mount Holly Railway Co.

628. MOUNT JOY TOWNSHIP ELECTRIC LIGHT COMPANY (Non-operating).
Lancaster County, Mount Joy Township.
1911, 1 Linear Inch.

History:
Mount Joy Township Electric Light Co. was incorporated 10 August 1911 to supply electricity in the Township of Mount Joy, Lancaster County. On 29 September 1911 it was consolidated and merged with 17 other companies to form Edison Electric Co. No.1.

629. THE MOUNT NEBO ELECTRIC LIGHT COMPANY (Operating).
Lancaster County, Martic Township.
1921 to 1930, 3 Linear Inches.

History:
Early in 1921, Farmers Electric Co. announced that it would no longer supply electricity to the Mount Nebo Village in Martic Township, Lancaster County. A group of local citizens met on 4 June 1921 and organized the Mount Nebo Light Power and Improvement Co. This company was owned and operated by its customers, who purchased shares and raised enough capital to purchase Farmers Electric Company's electric distribution facilities. Power was purchased from the Pequea Electric Co. On 15 May 1924 the company was incorporated as The Mount Nebo Electric Light Co. In 1930 the company's stock was acquired by Lehigh Power Securities Corp., and on 31 December 1930 it was merged into Pennsylvania Power & Light Co.

Administrative Records:
Minute Books, 1921-1930 (2 Volumes)
Secretary's Papers of Meetings, 1930
Stock Certificate Book, 1924-1930
Stock Transfer Record, 1925-1930

Operating Records:
General Ledger, 1930
Journal Entry Ledger, 1930
Cash Deposits and Withdrawals, 1930
Cash Receipts, 1930
Audited Voucher Register, 1930
Accounts Payable, 1930
Accounts Receivable, 1930
Detail Ledger, 1930
Accrual Record, 1930
Construction Work in Progress, 1930
Fixed Capital, 1930

Scope and Content Note:
The Minute Books and Secretary's Papers of Meetings of The Mount Nebo Electric Light Co. describe routine stockholders' and directors' meetings. They also contain information about the organization and finances of a rural cooperative electric company.

630. MOUNT PLEASANT POWER & LIGHT COMPANY
(Non-operating).
Columbia County, Mount Pleasant Township.
1923 to 1924, 2 Linear Inches.

History:
Mount Pleasant Power & Light Co. was incorporated 21 November 1923 to supply electricity in the Township of Mount Pleasant, Columbia County. On 31 March 1924 the company was merged into Pennsylvania Power & Light Co.

631. MOUNT PLEASANT-WAYNE POWER & LIGHT COMPANY (Non-operating).
Wayne County, Mount Pleasant Township.
1927 to 1928, 2 Linear Inches.

History:
Mount Pleasant-Wayne Power & Light Co. was incorporated 20 December 1927 for the purpose of supplying electricity in Mount Pleasant Township, Wayne County. On 3 January 1928 the company was merged into Pennsylvania Power & Light Co.

632. MOUNT POCONO LIGHT AND IMPROVEMENT COMPANY (Operating).
Monroe County, Mount Pocono Borough.
1919 to 1928, 1 Linear Foot.

History:
Incorporated to supply electricity on 31 July 1919, Mount Pocono Light and Improvement Co. built a hydroelectric generating station on Devils Hole Creek, near the Borough of Mount Pocono, Monroe County, and constructed a distribution system. Due to persistent water shortages caused by high customer demand for electricity, the company had to reduce the operating hours of its plant. This was done as much as possible during the winter months, since Mount Pocono at that time was primarily a summer resort. By 1922 this problem had become acute, and the company was forced to install a 25-hp oil engine, and a 32-kw generator. A larger 50-hp oil engine was installed later in the year. In 1923 the company began to purchase power from the Pocono Manor Association, which operated its own generating station. In 1925, the Mount Pocono Light and Improvement Co. installed a 56.5-kw generator. The following year, 1926, saw the extension of the company's area of operations to include the Village of Tobyhanna, Monroe County. In 1926 Lehigh Power Securities Corp. acquired the company's stock, and began to operate the company as a part of the Pennsylvania Power & Light Co. system. Mount Pocono Light and Improvement Co. was merged into Pennsylvania Power & Light Co., 28 May 1928.

Administrative Records:
Minute Book, 1919-1928
Stock Certificate Book, 1920-1926
Stock Transfer Record, 1925-1926
Stock Ledger, 1920-1928
Correspondence and Miscellaneous Papers, 1919-1926

Operating Records:
General Ledger, 1923-1928
Journal Entry Register, 1926-1928
Cashbooks, 1919-1925 (2 Volumes)
Record of Cash Receipts, 1926-1928
Record of Cash Disbursements, 1926-1928
Summary of Cash, 1926-1928
Audited Voucher Register, 1919-1928
Accounts Payable, 1926-1928
Accounts Receivable, 1926-1928
Accrual Record, 1926-1928
Detail of Cost Study and Fixed Capital, 1926-1927
Expenditure Requisitions, 1926-1928
Retirement Authorities, 1927-1928
Summary of Accounts Receivable—Consumers, 1926-1928
Statement of Accounts Overpaid, 1928
Summary of Consumers Deposits, 1927-1928
Audit Reports, 1923-1927 (4 Volumes)

Scope and Content Note:
The Minute Book of the Mount Pocono Light and Improvement Co. provides information on the company's organization, the construction of its power plant, the purchase of various types of electrical equipment, and the company's electric rates. Correspondence and miscellaneous papers include invoices, receipts, purchase orders, descriptions of electrical equipment, rate schedules, a map showing the company's property on Devils Hole Creek, and information on stockholders' meetings. Also included are letters to the Pennsylvania Public Service Commission describing the progress of rural electrification, customers' complaints, and requests for service.

633. MOUNTVILLE ELECTRIC LIGHT COMPANY (Non-operating).
Lancaster County, Mountville Borough.
1911, 1 Linear Inch.

History:
Mountville Electric Light Co. was incorporated 10 August 1911 to supply electricity in the Borough of Mountville, Lancaster County. On 29 September 1911 it was consolidated and merged with 17 other companies to form Edison Electric Co No. 1.

634. THE MUNCY ELECTRIC LIGHT HEAT AND POWER COMPANY (Operating).
Lycoming County, Muncy Borough.
1895 to 1919, 3 Linear Inches.

History:
The Muncy Electric Light Heat and Power Co. was incorporated 23 October 1893 to supply electricity in the Borough of Muncy, Lycoming County. Soon after its incorporation, the company built an electric generating station and a distribution system in the borough. On 1 October 1912 the company was merged into Montgomery and Muncy Electric Light, Heat and Power Co.

Operating Records:
Treasurer's Account Book, 1895-1907
Consumers Ledger, 1912-1919

635. THE MUNCY TOWNSHIP LYCOMING COUNTY ELECTRIC COMPANY (Non-operating).
Lycoming County, Muncy Township.
1924 to 1925, 2 Linear Inches.

History:
The Muncy Township Lycoming County Electric Co. was incorporated 17 January 1924 for the purpose of supplying electricity. The company was merged into Montgomery and Muncy Electric Light, Heat and Power Co. on 26 December 1924.

636. MYERS ELECTRIC COMPANY (Non-operating).
Berks County, Longswamp Township.
1916 to 1917, 1 Linear Inch.

History:

Myers Electric Co. was incorporated 4 January 1916 to supply electricity in the Township of Longswamp, Berks County. On 16 September 1916 the company was merged into Lehigh Valley Light and Power Co., No. 3.

637. NAOMI PINES ELECTRIC COMPANY (Operating).
Monroe County, Tobyhanna Township.
1922 to 1931, 6 Linear Inches.

History:

Naomi Pines Electric Co. operated a hydroelectric plant on an artificial lake in a resort area of the Pocono Mountains. In 1922 the company extended its area of operation, and began to supply electricity to the villages of Pocono Pines, Pocono and Pocono Lake. In 1930, Lehigh Power Securities Corp. acquired the stock of the company and merged it into Pennsylvania Power & Light Co.

Administrative Records:
Minute Book, 1922-1930
Stock Certificate Book, 1922-1930
Stock Transfer Record, 1928-1920
Stock Ledger, 1922-1930

Operating Records:
General Ledger, 1928-1930
Journal Entry Register, 1928-1930
Record of Cash Receipts, 1928-1930
Record of Cash Disbursements, 1928-1930
Summaries of Cash, 1928-1930 (2 Volumes)
Audited Voucher Register and Accounts Payable and Receivable, 1928-1930
Expenditure Requisitions, 1928-1930
Retirement Authorities, 1928-1931
Summary of Accounts Receivable—Consumers, 1928-1930
Summary of Consumers' Deposits, 1929-1930
Audit Reports, 1923-1929 (4 Volumes)

638. NATIONAL ELECTRIC LIGHT AND POWER COMPANY (Non-operating).
Lehigh County, North Catasauqua Borough.
1915 to 1918, 1 Linear Inch.

History:

National Electric Light and Power Co. was incorporated in March 1913 to supply electricity in North Catasauqua Borough, Lehigh County. The company's attempt to gain a franchise in that borough was protested by Lehigh and Northampton Light, Heat and Power Co., which controlled the stocks of several electric companies operating in Lehigh County, and had constructed a distribution system in North Catasauqua. The company's protest succeeded, and Northampton County Electric Co. was awarded a franchise in North Catasauqua. National Electric Light and Power Co. was dissolved in December 1918.

639. NESCOPECK TOWNSHIP ELECTRIC COMPANY (Non-operating).
Luzerne County, Nescopeck Township.
1909, 1 Linear Inch.

History:

Nescopeck Township Electric Co., incorporated 16 June 1909 to supply electricity in Nescopeck Township, Luzerne County, consolidated and merged with eleven companies to form Harwood Electric Co., 30 June 1909.

640. NESQUEHONING ELECTRIC COMPANY (Non-operating).
Carbon County, Mahoning Township.
1911 to 1913, 1 Linear Inch.

History:

Nesquehoning Electric Co., incorporated 4 April 1911 to supply electricity in Mahoning Township, Carbon County, consolidated and merged with 37 companies to form Lehigh Navigation Electric Co., No. 2, January 1913.

641. NEW BRITAIN ELECTRIC LIGHT AND POWER COMPANY (Non-operating).
Bucks County, New Britain Township.
1913, 1 Linear Inch.

History:

New Britain Electric Light and Power Co., incorporated 8 December 1913 to supply electricity in New Britain Township, Bucks County, merged into Lehigh Valley Light and Power Co., No. 2, 29 December 1913.

642. NEW BUFFALO POWER COMPANY (Non-operating).
Perry County, New Buffalo Township.
1926, 1 Linear Inch.

History:

New Buffalo Power Co., incorporated 21 January 1926 to supply electricity in New Buffalo Township, Perry County, merged into Juniata Public Service Co., 9 August 1926.

643. NEW HANOVER POWER & LIGHT COMPANY (Non-operating).
Montgomery County, New Hanover Township.
1923, 1 Linear Inch.

History:

New Hanover Power & Light Co., was organized in April 1923 by Pennsylvania Power & Light Co. in an effort to gain franchise rights in New Hanover Township, Montgomery County. The Public Service Commission rejected its application for incorporation, and in August the company was dissolved.

644. NEW HOLLAND ELECTRIC COMPANY (Non-operating).
Lancaster County, New Holland Borough.
1914, 1 Linear Inch.

History:

New Holland Electric Co., incorporated 31 July 1914 to supply electricity in the borough of New Holland, Lancaster County, consolidated and merged with three companies to form Edison Electric Co. No. 4, 16 December 1914.

645. NEW KINGSTON ELECTRIC LIGHT, HEAT AND POWER COMPANY (Operating).
Cumberland County, Silver Spring Township.
1912 to 1930, 1 Linear Foot.

History:
New Kingston Electric Light, Heat and Power Co. was incorporated 29 May 1912 to supply electricity in the village of New Kingston, Silver Spring Township, Cumberland County. The company purchased power from The United Electric Co., and constructed a distribution system to serve the village. Lehigh Power Securities Corp. acquired the company's stock in 1928, and merged it into Pennsylvania Power & Light Co., 16 December 1930.

Administrative Records:
Minute Book, 1912-1930
Stock Certificate Book, 1912-1930
Stock Transfer Record, 1928-1930
Stock Ledger, 1912-1930
Stock Transfer Book, 1912-1920

Operating Records:
General Ledger, 1928-1930
Journal Entry Register, 1928-1930
Cashbook and Receipts, 1925-1928
Cash Receipts, 1925-1928
Record of Cash Receipts, 1928-1930
Record of Cash Disbursements, 1928-1930
Summaries of Cash, 1928-1930 (2 Volumes)
Audited Voucher Register, 1928-1930
Accounts Payable and Receivable, 1928-1930
Treasurer's Account Book, 1921-1925
Expenditure Requisitions, 1928-1930
Retirement Authorities, 1928-1930
Bills, 1930
Summary of Accounts Receivable—Consumers, 1928-1938
Summary of Consumers' Deposits, 1929-1930
Audit Reports, 1923-1929 (3 Volumes)

Scope and Content Note:
The Minute Book provides a good overview of the history of a small rural electric company. It documents its early financial difficulties, and its relationship with local village residents who advanced money for working capital. Within a few years the company began to solicit new customers, and finally reached a level of relative financial stability.

646. NEW PARRYVILLE CONSOLIDATED GAS COMPANY (Operating).
Carbon County, Lehighton Borough.
1912 to 1930, 4 Linear Feet.

History:
New Parryville Consolidated Gas Co. was incorporated 25 April 1912 to manufacture and supply gas for light, fuel and power in the Borough of Lehighton, and adjacent communities in Carbon County. The company installed a gas plant and distribution system in Lehighton. Lehigh Power Securities Corp. acquired the company's stock in 1928, and in December 1930 merged it into Pennsylvania Power & Light Co.

Administrative Records:
Minute Book, 1912-1930
Stock Certificate Books, 1912-1930 (5 Volumes)
Stock Transfer Record, 1926-1930
Stock Ledger, 1913-1930
Stockholders' Transfer Record, 1912-1925
Bond Register, 1913-1930
Correspondence, 1917-1927

Operating Records:
FINANCIAL RECORDS
General Ledgers, 1912-1930 (3 Volumes)
Journal, 1912-1926
Journal Entry Register, 1927-1930
Cashbook, 1912-1927
Daily Cash Disbursements, 1914-1927
Record of Cash Receipts, 1927-1930
Record of Cash Disbursements, 1927-1930
Summaries of Cash, 1927-1930 (2 Volumes)
Audited Voucher Register, 1927-1930
Accounts Payable Ledger, 1927-1930
Detail Ledger, 1927-1930
Accrual Record, 1927-1930
PERSONNEL RECORDS
Insurance Accrual Statements—Workmen's Compensation and Public Liability Insurance, 1927-1930
Time Books, 1913-1927 (2 Volumes)
CONSUMER RECORDS
Cash Sales, 1914-1927
Real Estate Rental Statement, Lehighton Office, 1927-1930
Summary of Accounts Receivable—Consumers, 1927-1930
Summary of Accounts Receivable—Miscellaneous, 1927-1930
Statement of Rents, 1927-1930
Summary of Consumers' Deposits, 1928-1930
AUDIT REPORTS, 1923-1929 (4 Volumes)

Scope and Content Note:
The Minute Book documents the company's various construction projects and provides details on the operation of its gas plant. Correspondence Files document relations with customers, and trace the company's efforts to increase appliance sales, while coping with a consumer boycott called to protest a rate increase. There is also a good deal of correspondence with the Federal Fuel Administration which sought to promote conservation during World War I.

647. NEW RINGGOLD BOROUGH ELECTRIC COMPANY (Non-operating).
Schuylkill County, New Ringgold Borough.
1924, 1 Linear Inch.

History:
New Ringgold Borough Electric Co., incorporated 13 August 1924 to supply electricity in New Ringgold Borough, Schuylkill County, merged into East Penn Electric Co. No. 2, 6 October 1924.

648. NEWBERRY BRIDGE COMPANY (Operating).
Lycoming County, Williamsport City.
1892 to 1927, 4 Linear Inches.

History:
Newberry Bridge Co. was incorporated 18 December 1891 to erect and maintain a bridge over Lycoming Creek in the City of Williamsport. The bridge was completed in 1892, and for ten years was used by the Williamsport

Passenger Railway Co. In 1902 the bridge was washed away by a flood, and a replacement bridge was built by the railway company. Lehigh Power Securities Corp. then acquired the stock of the Lycoming Improvement Co., owners of the bridge company. In 1926 the bridge company was dissolved.

Administrative Records:
Minute Books, 1892-1927 (2 Volumes)
Stock Certificate Book, 1893-1924
Stock Ledger, 1893-1927

Operating Records:
General Ledger, 1891-1927
Journal, 1891-1927
Audit Report, 1922, 1926 (2 Volumes)

Scope and Content Note:
The Minute Book for the period 1892 to 1927 contains some details about the 1892 contract for the railroad bridge, but from 1894 to 1910 no minutes were recorded. Information on the company's history after 1894 appears in the Audit Reports

649. NEWBERRY PASSENGER RAILWAY COMPANY (Operating).
Lycoming County, Williamsport City.
1893, 1 Linear Inch.

History:
The Minute Book of Newberry Passenger Railway Co. records that in April 1893 the Company was incorporated to build and operate an electric street railway, approximately two miles in length, through part of Williamsport. The minutes end in May 1893 with the company awaiting word from City Council for consent to build the line. Because several of the company's directors were also directors of Williamsport Passenger Railway Co., it is presumed that the Newberry Passenger Railway Co. was dissolved, and then permission was given to Williamsport Passenger Railway Co. to build the line.

Administrative Records:
Minute Book, 1893

650. NEWBERRY-YORK POWER & LIGHT COMPANY (Non-operating).
York County, Newberry Township.
1959 to 1960, 1 Linear Inch.

History:
Newberry-York Power & Light Co., incorporated October 1959 to supply electricity in Newberry Township, York County, merged into Pennsylvania Power & Light Co. in March 1960.

651. NEWMANSTOWN ELECTRIC LIGHT AND POWER COMPANY NO. 1 (Non-operating).
Lebanon County, Millcreek Township.
1910, 1 Linear Inch.

History:
Newmanstown Electric Light and Power Co. No. 1, incorporated 10 May 1910 to supply electricity in Millcreek Township, Lebanon County, consolidated and merged with two companies to form Newmanstown Electric Light and Power Co. No. 2, 3 August 1910.

652. NEWMANSTOWN ELECTRIC LIGHT AND POWER COMPANY NO. 2 (Operating).
Lebanon County, Millcreek Township.
1910 to 1926, 4 Linear Inches.

History:
Newmanstown Electric Light and Power Co. No. 2 was formed through the consolidation of three non-operating companies, 3 August 1910. It supplied electricity to the townships of Millcreek, Heidelberg, and Richland Borough, all in Lebanon County. It purchased power from Wernersville Electric Light Co., which operated in adjacent Berks County. Lebanon Valley Light and Power Co. acquired the company's stock in 1915, and operated it until 1923, when the stock was acquired by Lancaster County Railway and Light Co. That company in turn operated Newmanstown Electric Light and Power Co. until 1925, when it was merged into Edison Electric Co. No. 4.

Administrative Records:
Minute Books, 1910-1915, 1918-1925 (2 Volumes)
Stock Certificate Book, 1910-1925
Bond and Warrant, 1916
Assignment of Bond and Mortgage, 1911-1921

Operating Records:
General Ledger, 1915-1926
Journal, 1915-1926
Cashbook, 1915-1926
Audited Voucher Register, 1920-1926
Audit Reports, 1923-1925 (3 Volumes)

653. NEWTON TOWNSHIP ELECTRIC CORPORATION (Non-operating).
Lackawanna County, Newton Township.
1923 to 1928, 2 Linear Inches.

History:
Newton Township Electric Corp., incorporated 11 September 1923 to supply electricity in Newton Township, Lackawanna County, consolidated and merged with eight companies to form The Scranton Electric Co., 3 February 1928.

654. NIPPENOSE POWER & LIGHT COMPANY (Non-operating).
Lycoming County, Nippenose Township.
1923, 1 Linear Inch.

History:
Nippenose Power & Light Co., incorporated 23 February 1923 to supply electricity in Nippenose Township, Lycoming County merged into Pennsylvania Power & Light Co., 1 October 1923.

655. NOCKAMIXON TOWNSHIP ELECTRIC COMPANY (Non-operating).
Bucks County, Nockamixon Township.
1913 to 1935, 2 Linear Inches.

History:
Nockamixon Township Electric Co. was one of eleven township companies chartered by officials of Lehigh Navigation Electric Co. in December 1913 to gain franchise rights in Bucks County. The eleven companies were 'paper companies,' in that they were formed solely to obtain franchise rights, and had no revenues or

operating expenses. They were not merged into Lehigh Navigation Electric Co., the idea being that such companies covered outlying territory, and it would be preferable to forfeit their charters and abandon them, rather than provide service to only a few customers. It would have been impossible to forfeit them if Lehigh Navigation Electric Co. were to operate in the territory. As of 1926 this company, like its ten counterparts, was listed as 'inactive'. It was officially dissolved in 1935.

656. NORTH BRANCH DEVELOPMENT COMPANY
(Operating).
Tioga County, Clymer Township.
1930 to 1942, 6 Linear Feet.

History:

North Branch Development Co., a wholly-owned subsidiary of Pennsylvania Power & Light Co., was organized in 1931 to operate several natural gas wells on 27,400 acres of leased land in Tioga County. The gas from the company's wells was piped from the fields to a PP&L plant near Williamsport by another PP&L subsidiary, Susquehanna Gas Co. The gas was then sold to residential and industrial customers in the Williamsport vicinity. When PP&L organized North Branch Development Co., advisors estimated that they would continue to be productive for about 15 years. The gas fields were depleted much more quickly than anticipated, however, and the company was forced to revise its amortization schedules several times during the 1930's. Early in 1940, PP&L decided that natural gas could no longer be profitably extracted from the Tioga fields. It therefore, began to supply manufactured gas to the Williamsport area and in June 1942 North Branch Development Co. was dissolved.

Administrative Records:

Minute Book, 1931-1941
Correspondence—Lease Data, 1931-1940
Correspondence—Surrendered Leases, 1932-1941
Correspondence—Daily Reports—Field Accounts, 1931-1939
Correspondence—North Branch Development Company & Susquehanna Gas Co., 1932-1942
Natural Gas Rate Case—Respondents' Exhibit Number 54, Detail of Leases Held and Surrendered as of October 31, 1931
Natural Gas Rate Case—Respondents' Exhibit Number 11-B, Natural Gas Property as of October 31, 1932
Leases Surrendered and Retired, n.d.
Unsuccessful Leases Retired, n.d.

Operating Records:

General Ledger, 1931-1942
Journal Entry Register, 1936-1942
Record of Cash Receipts and Disbursements, 1931-1942
Summaries of Cash, 1931-1942 (2 Volumes)
Audited Voucher Register, 1931-1935
Accounts Payable, 1931-1942 (3 Volumes)
Accounts Receivable, 1931-1942
Bill Register, 1931-1942
Construction Detail Ledgers, 1930-1942 (8 Volumes)
Accrual Records, 1931-1942 (2 Volumes)
Accrual Records—Prepaid Rents, 1931-1940 (2 Volumes)
Allocation of General Charges, 1931-1942
Bills, 1931-1942
Payroll Authority, 1931-1941
Operating Files and Working Papers—Well Costs, Lease Overheads, Reconcilement By Accounts, Etc., 1930-1942 (27 Folders)
Operating Files and Working Papers—Statements, Accounts, 1930-1942 (9 Folders)
North Branch Development Co. and Susquehanna Gas Co.—Working Papers, 1931-1942
Income Tax Detail, 1931-1940 (10 Volumes)
Supplement to Natural Gas Income Tax Data, 1931-1940 (6 Volumes)
Memorandum re: Computation of Depreciation and Depletion, 1940
Natural Gas Plant Additions and Retirements, 1931-1938
Amortization Reserves, 1931-1938
Expenditure Requisitions, 1931-1941
Retirement Authorities, 1931
Audit Reports, 1931-1932 (3 Volumes)

Scope and Content Note:

Much of the material in this collection consists of working papers and memoranda prepared for a hearing before the Pennsylvania Public Utilities Commission about 1942. Included are papers on accounting practices, natural gas wells, drilling, amortization schedules, depreciation and depletion schedules, production costs, and leases. The Payroll Authority File consists of correspondence about payrolls, wage adjustments and hours of work. Other information on the company appears in PP&L's Legal Department Files.

657. NORTH BRANCH TRANSIT COMPANY
(Operating).
Columbia County, Bloomsburg Town.
1906 to 1926, 1 Linear Foot.

History:

A February 1911 consolidation and merger of Columbia and Montour Electric Railway Co. and Danville & Bloomsburg Street Railway Co. resulted in the formation of Columbia and Montour Electric Company. In December 1913 the company changed its name to North Branch Transit Co. It operated a 27-mile electric street railway line between the Borough of Danville (Montour County), and the Borough of Berwick (Columbia County), by way of Bloomsburg, where its main office was located. Pennsylvania Power & Light owned 90% of the company's stock, and supplied it with power. In 1925 it went bankrupt, and a bus company took over its franchises.

Administrative Records:

Minute Book, 1914-1915
Stock Certificate Book, 1914-1917
Portfolio and Historical Narrative, 1915
Correspondence and Memoranda, 1922-1926

Operating Records:

Annual Estimates, 1915
Meter Record Book, 1909-1911
Valuation of North Branch Transit Co., 1919 (8 Volumes)

Scope and Content Note:

Copies of charters and franchises are found in the Portfolio and Historical Narrative. Included in the

Correspondence and Memoranda file are fare schedules, timetables, an inventory of property and rolling stock, a report on the company prepared for Pennsylvania Power & Light Co. in 1925, and other items relating to electric street railway operations. Of particular note are the Valuation Reports prepared in 1919, which detail costs for equipment and construction. Included are right-of-way maps and photographs depicting properties and structures along the railway line.

658. NORTH LANCASTER COUNTY ELECTRIC COMPANY (Operating).
Lancaster County, Denver Borough.
1912 to 1916, 3 Linear Inches.

History:
North Lancaster County Electric Co., formed in November 1912 through the consolidation and merger of seven non-operating companies, supplied electricity in the Boroughs of Denver and Terre Haute and surrounding townships in Lancaster County. It purchased power from Edison Electric Co. of Lancaster. In 1915 Lancaster County Railway and Light Co. acquired its stock, merging it into Edison Electric Co. No. 4.

Administrative Records:
Minute Book, 1913-1916
Stock Certificate Book, 1912-1915
Stock Transfer Record, 1913-1915
Stock Ledger, 1912-1915

Operating Records:
General Ledger, 1915-1916
Journal, 1915-1916
Cash Receipts and Disbursements, 1915-1916
Audited Voucher Register, 1915-1916
Statements of Receipts and Expenditures, 1913-1915

659. NORTH MANHEIM TOWNSHIP ELECTRIC LIGHT, HEAT AND POWER COMPANY (Non-operating).
Schuylkill County, North Manheim Township.
1907 to 1909, 1 Linear Inch.

History:
North Manheim Township Electric Light, Heat and Power Co., incorporated 27 February 1907 to supply electricity in North Manheim Township, Schuylkill County, merged into Eastern Pennsylvania Light, Heat and Power Co., 20 July 1909.

660. NORTH-POINT GAS COMPANY (Non-operating).
Northumberland County, Northumberland Borough.
1921 to 1922, 1 Linear Inch.

History:
North-Point Gas Co., incorporated in 1921 to supply gas in Northumberland Borough, Northumberland County, merged into Gas Company of Northumberland in June 1922.

661. NORTH UNION TOWNSHIP ELECTRIC COMPANY (Non-operating).
Schuylkill County, North Union Township.
1918, 1 Linear Inch.

History:
North Union Township Electric Co., incorporated in July 1918 in North Union Township, Schuylkill County, merged into The Harwood Electric Co., 31 December 1918.

662. NORTH WHITEHALL ELECTRIC COMPANY (Non-operating).
Lehigh County, North Whitehall Township.
1911 to 1913, 1 Linear Inch.

History:
North Whitehall Electric Co., incorporated 4 April 1911 to supply electricity in North Whitehall Township, Lehigh County, consolidated and merged with 37 companies to form Lehigh Navigation Electric Co. No. 2, 6 January 1913.

663. NORTH WHITEHALL LIGHT AND POWER COMPANY COMPANY (Non-operating).
Lehigh County, North Whitehall Township.
1911 to 1913, 1 Linear Inch.

History:
North Whitehall Light and Power Co., incorporated 26 December 1911 to supply electricity in North Whitehall Township, Lehigh County, consolidated and merged with ten companies to form Lehigh Valley Light and Power Co., No. 2, 2 January 1913.

664. NORTH WHITEHALL TOWNSHIP LEHIGH ELECTRIC COMPANY (Non-operating).
Lehigh County, North Whitehall Township.
1919, 1 Linear Feet.

History:
North Whitehall Township Lehigh Electric Co., incorporated 17 July 1919 to supply electricity in North Whitehall Township, Lehigh County, consolidated and merged with six companies to form Industrial Power Co., 11 September 1919.

665. NORTHAMPTON COUNTY ELECTRIC COMPANY (Operating).
Northampton County, Allen Township.
1900 to 1915, 1 Linear Inch.

History:
Northampton County Electric Co. was formed 22 March 1900 to supply electricity in Northampton County. In April of that year, the company was taken over by Northampton Gas and Electric Co., a New Jersey holding company. On 3 March 1915 it was merged with Lehigh Valley Light and Power Co., No. 3.

Administrative Records:
Minute Book, 1900-1915
Stock Certificate Book, 1900-1913

666. NORTHAMPTON HEIGHTS ELECTRIC LIGHT, HEAT AND POWER COMPANY (Non-operating).
Northampton County, Northampton Heights Borough.
1911 to 1913, 1 Linear Inch.

History:
Northampton Heights Electric Light, Heat and Power Co., incorporated 4 August 1911 to supply electricity in Northampton Heights Borough, Northampton County, consolidated and merged with ten companies to form Lehigh Valley Light and Power Co. No. 2, 2 January 1913.

667. NORTHERN CENTRAL COMPANY (Operating).
New Castle (Del.), Wilmington City (Del.).
1913 to 1916, 7 Linear Inches.

History:

Northern Central Co. was a holding company organized in Delaware in February 1913 by a group of Philadelphia bankers. The company was designed to integrate and consolidate several utilities operating in the vicinity of Sunbury Borough, Northumberland County. Its stock was held by Corporation Trust Co., a New York City banking and investment firm. Soon after its organization, Northern Central Co. acquired the stocks of Northern Central Gas Co., Columbia and Montour Electric Co., and Northumberland County Gas & Electric Co. Those companies proceeded to take over existing utilities in the area, and organized non-operating township companies to secure franchise rights. In 1917 Lehigh Power Securities Corp. purchased Northern Central Co., and in 1920 Northern Central Gas Co., Northumberland County Gas & Electric Co., and Columbia and Montour Electric Co. were consolidated and merged with five other companies to form Pennsylvania Power & Light Company.

Administrative Records:
Minute Book, 1913-1916
Portfolios and Historical Narratives, 1915 (4 Volumes)

668. NORTHERN CENTRAL GAS COMPANY (Operating).
Northumberland County, Milton Borough.
1912 to 1925, 10 Linear Feet.

History:

Southern Fuel Co., incorporated 29 May 1912 to manufacture and supply gas for heat and fuel in Milton Borough and the townships of Turbut, East Chillisquaque, and Chillisquaque, all in Northumberland County, changed its name in July 1912 to Northern Central Gas Co. The company subsequently acquired Milton Gas Co. and Williamsport Gas Co., and eleven non-operating gas companies, giving it franchise rights in the counties of Columbia, Lycoming, Montour, Northumberland, and Union, serving an area of some 133,000 people. Its stock was held by Northern Central Co., which in turn was controlled by a New York investment firm that was attempting to consolidate the electric and gas companies of the Upper Susquehanna Valley. In 1917 Lehigh Power Securities Corp. acquired the Northern Central Co. and the stocks it held, including those of Northern Central Gas Co., which was one of eight companies that consolidated and merged in June 1920 to form Pennsylvania Power & Light Co.

Administrative Records:
Minute Book, 1912-1920
Stock Certificate Books (Common and Preferred), 1912-1919 (3 Volumes)
Portfolio and Historical Narrative, 1915

Operating Records:
Working Papers on Rate Case—Williamsport District, 1920 (1 Package)
FINANCIAL RECORDS
General Ledgers, 1912-1920 (2 Volumes)
Journals, 1912-1918 (2 Volumes)
Journal Detail Ledger Entries, 1912-1917
Bank Account Registers, 1912-1919 (5 Volumes)
Bank Balance Reconcilement Books, 1912-1919 (2 Volumes)
Treasurer's Report on Bank Balances, 1912-1918
Cashier's Reports—Williamsport and Milton Districts, 1913-1919 (4 Volumes)
Cashbook, 1919
Cashbook—Supplementary, 1919
Accounts Payable, 1912-1920 (3 Volumes)
Bills Payable and Receivable, 1919-1925
Accounts Receivable, 1912-1920 (2 Volumes)
Capital Account, 1919-1920
Detail Ledgers, 1912-1920 (3 Volumes)
Accrual Record, 1920
Statement of Bad Accounts, 1919
Material Issued—Summary, 1916
Balance Sheets and Comparative Summary of Earnings, 1919-1920
Financial Reports, 1912-1917 (5 Volumes)
Monthly Reports, 1919-1920
Monthly Statements, 1919-1920
Monthly Statement of Accounts Receivable, 1919-1920
Detail Repair and Construction Ledger, 1919-1920
Payrolls and Payroll Distributions, 1914-1920
Workmen's Compensation Insurance Payroll, 1919-1920

Scope and Content Note:

The Portfolio and Historical Narrative includes copies of charters, franchises, stock certificates, and describes Northern Central Gas Co. and the companies it acquired.

669. NORTHUMBERLAND COUNTY GAS & ELECTRIC COMPANY (Operating).
Northumberland County, Sunbury Borough.
1911 to 1921, 17 Linear Feet.

History:

Northumberland County Gas & Electric Co. was incorporated 20 September 1911 to supply electricity in Sunbury Borough, Northumberland County. The company's organization occurred at a time when several utilities in the Sunbury area were in financial trouble as a result of cut throat competition. A group of Philadelphia bankers headed by Walbridge and Co. formed Northumberland County Gas & Electric Co. in order to integrate and consolidate the utilities in the area. The stock of this company was held by Northern Central Co., a Delaware holding company, organized and controlled by Corporation Trust Co., a New York banking and investment firm. The Northumberland company soon acquired The Edison Electric Illuminating Co. of Sunbury, Pa. No. 4, and Middlecreek Electric Co. From 1912 to 1915 it organized and took over a number of non-operating companies in order to secure franchise rights. Through these transactions the company acquired steam generating plants in Milton Borough and Sunbury Borough, and a gas works in Sunbury. In 1920 the company was one of eight which consolidated and merged to form Pennsylvania Power & Light Co.

Administrative Records:
Minute Books, 1911-1920 (2 Volumes)
Stock Certificate Books (Common and Preferred), 1911-1918 (7 Volumes)
Five Year 5% Gold Notes, 1913-1918
Portfolio and Historical Narrative, 1915

Operating Records:
History, 1913
Statistical Information, 1915-1918
FINANCIAL RECORDS
General Ledgers, 1911-1920 (5 Volumes)
Journals, 1911-1920 (7 Volumes)
Journal—Free Lighting Distribution, 1919
Cashbooks, 1911-1919 (2 Volumes)
Cash Disbursements, 1919
Bank Account Registers, 1913-1919 (7 Volumes)
Bank Account Reconcilement Books, 1913-1919 (3 Volumes)
Cashier's Reports, 1918-1919 (2 Volumes)
Treasurer's Reports, 1916-1919 (2 Volumes)
Accrual Record, 1920
Financial Reports, 1911-1913
Financial Reports, 1912-1917
Accounts Payable Ledgers, 1913-1920 (3 Volumes)
Accounts Payable—Balances, 1914-1918
Manufacturing Expenses and Financial Reports, 1911
Income and Operating Reports, 1912
Annual Estimates, 1915-1917
Proposed Expenditures, 1916-1918
Voucher Register, 1919-1920
Sub Voucher Register, 1913
Bill Register, 1919-1920
Detail Repair and Construction Ledger, 1919-1920
Bills, 1919-1920
CONSUMER RECORDS
Accounts Receivable Ledgers—Sunbury, 1914-1920 (2 Volumes)
Accounts Receivable Ledgers—Milton, 1914-1920
Statement of Sales and Allowances to Consumers, 1914-1920 (3 Volumes)
Statement of Bad Accounts, 1919
Refunds for Bills Paid Twice, 1914-1919
Meter Inventories, 1915-1917
Transformer Inventories, 1915-1917
PERSONNEL RECORDS
Payrolls—Sunbury District, 1913-1919 (2 Volumes)
Payrolls—Milton District, 1914-1919
Payrolls—All Departments, 1917-1920 (2 Volumes)
Payroll Distribution, 1919-1920
Payroll—Workmen's Compensation Insurance, 1919
Time Books, 1912-1921 (3 Volumes)
AUDIT REPORTS, 1913-1914, 1918 (2 Volumes)

Scope and Content Note:
The Minute Book documents routine stockholders' meetings and describes how the company exercised its right of eminent domain in order to erect transmission lines. The History and Portfolio and Historical Narrative contain copies of charters, borough and township ordinances, and other documents pertaining to acquired companies. Statistical Information binders contain monthly inventories, gas manufacturing statements, comparative statements of monthly payrolls, and statements of operating costs.

670. THE NORTHUMBERLAND ELECTRIC ILLUMINATING COMPANY (Operating).
Northumberland County, Northumberland Borough.
1890 to 1911, 1 Linear Inch.

History:
The Northumberland Electric Illuminating Co. was incorporated in March 1889 to supply electricity in Northumberland Borough, Northumberland County. It was formed by officials of The Sunbury and Northumberland Electric Railway Co., which supplied the electric company with its power. In 1899 a group of businessmen, including Pierre S. du Pont, T. Coleman du Pont, and John J. Raskob, acquired the company's stock and became its directors, remaining in that capacity until 1906 when they sold their interests to the Edison Electric Illuminating Co. of Sunbury, Pa., No. 3. In October 1911 both of these firms consolidated and merged with three others to form The Edison Electric Illuminating Co. of Sunbury Pa., No. 4.

Administrative Records:
Minute Book, 1890-1911
History, 1911

Scope and Content Note:
The History and the Minute Book both contain copies of charters, ordinances, and other agreements pertaining to The Northumberland Electric Illuminating Co. The tenure of Pierre du Pont, T. Coleman du Pont, and John J. Raskob as company directors is also documented.

671. THE NORTHUMBERLAND ELECTRIC LIGHT, HEAT AND POWER COMPANY (Operating).
Northumberland County, Northumberland Borough.
1903 to 1906, 2 Linear Inches.

History:
The Northumberland Electric Light, Heat and Power Co. was incorporated 9 December 1903 to supply electricity in Northumberland Borough, Northumberland County. It constructed a steam generating plant and an electric distribution system to serve the Borough. In 1906 the company consolidated and merged with three non-operating companies to form Middlecreek Electric Co.

Administrative Records:
Minute Book, 1903-1906 (in Middlecreek Electric Co. Record Book)

Scope and Content Note:
The minutes describe negotiations with the Northumberland Borough Council which set the terms under which the Company supplied the borough with incandescent lighting.

672. NORTHUMBERLAND GAS COMPANY (Operating).
Northumberland County, Northumberland Borough.
1910 to 1912, 2 Linear Inches.

History:
Northumberland Gas Co., incorporated 2 February 1910, supplied manufactured gas in Northumberland Borough, Northumberland County. It erected a water gas plant, a gasometer, and four miles of high-pressure gas mains. The company's franchises and property were acquired by Northumberland Gas Heat and Fuel Co. in September 1912 under mortgage lien, but the Northumberland County Court of Common Pleas issued a decree of foreclosure, and the property was sold to a bondholders' committee. In April 1916 Northumberland Gas Co. was reorganized as Gas Co. of Northumberland.

Administrative Records:
Minute Book, 1910-1912

673. NORTHUMBERLAND GAS HEAT AND FUEL COMPANY (Operating).
Northumberland County, Northumberland Borough.
1912 to 1934, 3 Linear Inches.

History:
Northumberland Gas Heat and Fuel Co. was incorporated in March 1912 to supply manufactured gas in Northumberland Borough and Point Township, both in Northumberland County. It was organized by Northern Central Gas Co., which controlled Northumberland County Gas & Electric Co. In 1920 Northumberland County Gas & Electric Co. consolidated and merged with seven companies to form Pennsylvania Power & Light.

Administrative Records:
Minute Books, 1912-1934 (3 Volumes)
Stock Certificate Book, 1913-1925
Stock Transfer Record, 1920-1925
Stock Ledger, 1914-1925

Operating Records:
General Ledger, 1932-1934

674. NOYES ELECTRIC LIGHT COMPANY (Non-operating).
Clinton County, Noyes Township.
1916, 1 Linear Inch.

History:
Noyes Electric Light Co., incorporated 13 June 1916 to supply electricity in Noyes Township, Clinton County, merged into Renovo Edison Light, Heat and Power Co., 19 July 1916.

675. NUANGOLA-LUZERNE POWER & LIGHT COMPANY (Non-operating).
Luzerne County, Nuangola Township.
1927, 1 Linear Inch.

History:
Nuangola-Luzerne Power & Light Co., incorporated 15 February 1927 to supply electricity in Nuangola Township, Luzerne County, merged into Pennsylvania Power & Light Co. 30 April 1927.

676. OAKDALE ELECTRIC COMPANY (Non-operating).
Lehigh County, Salisbury Township.
1911 to 1913, 1 Linear Inch.

History:
Oakdale Electric Co., incorporated 4 April 1911 to supply electricity in Salisbury Township, Lehigh County, consolidated and merged with 37 companies to form Lehigh Navigation Electric Co., No. 2, 6 January 1913.

677. OLD LYCOMING POWER & LIGHT COMPANY (Non-operating).
Lycoming County, Old Lycoming Township.
1924, 1 Linear Inch.

History:
Old Lycoming Power & Light Co., incorporated 9 May 1924 to supply electricity in Old Lycoming Township, Lycoming County, merged into Pennsylvania Power & Light Co., 27 August 1924.

678. OLD PORT POWER COMPANY (Non-operating).
Juniata County, Turbett Township.
1923, 1 Linear Inch.

History:
Old Port Power Co., incorporated 21 November 1923 to supply electricity in Turbett Township, Juniata County, merged into Pennsylvania Power & Light Co. 20 December 1923.

679. OLYPHANT AND WINTON TRACTION STREET RAILWAY COMPANY (Operating).
Lackawanna County, Dunmore Borough.
1894 to 1910, 1 Linear Inch.

History:
Olyphant and Winton Traction Street Railway Co. was organized in January 1893 to build and operate a street railway in the Boroughs of Dunmore and Throop (Lackawanna County). Although the company did build the line, it appears to have become inactive by 1900. The company leased its property to Lackawanna Valley Traction Co., and then consolidated and merged with three companies to form Scranton Railway Co.

Administrative Records:
Minute Book, 1894-1910

680. ORANGE-COLUMBIA POWER & LIGHT COMPANY (Non-operating).
Columbia County, Orange Township.
1924 to 1925, 1 Linear Inch.

History:
Orange-Columbia Power & Light Co., incorporated 28 August 1924 to supply electricity in Orange Township, Columbia County, merged into Pennsylvania Power & Light Co., 19 January 1925.

681. ORANGEVILLE-COLUMBIA POWER & LIGHT COMPANY (Operating).
Columbia County, Orangeville Borough.
1924 to 1928, 6 Linear Inches.

History:
Orangeville-Columbia Power & Light Co. was formed in August 1927 by Pennsylvania Power & Light Co. in order to get charter rights in Orangeville Borough, Columbia County, and to acquire a privately-owned hydroelectric generating station, which had served the Borough since 1907. The company merged into PP&L in July 1928.

Administrative Records:
Minute Book, 1927-1928
Stock Certificates and Stock Ledger, 1927-1928
Stock Transfer Record, 1927-1928

Operating Records:
General Ledger, 1927-1928
Record of Cash Receipts and Disbursements, 1927-1928 (4 Volumes)
Summary of Cash, 1927-1928
Accounts Receivable, 1028-1928
Detail of Cost Study and Fixed Capital, 1927
Expenditure Requisitions, 1927-1928
Retirement Authorities, 1928
Bills, 1928
Bank Checkbook, 1927

Summary of Accounts Receivable—Consumers, 1927-1928
Audit Reports, 1924-1927 (3 Volumes)

682. ORCHARD ELECTRIC COMPANY (Non-operating).
Northampton County, Allen Township.
1911 to 1913, 1 Linear Inch.

History:
Orchard Electric Co., incorporated 4 April 1911 to supply electricity in Allen Township, Northampton County, consolidated and merged with 37 companies to form Lehigh Navigation Electric Co., No. 2, 6 January 1913.

683. OREGON-WAYNE POWER & LIGHT COMPANY (Non-operating).
Wayne County, Oregon Township.
1928, 1 Linear Inch.

History:
Oregon-Wayne Power & Light Co., incorporated 27 September 1928 to supply electricity in Oregon Township, Wayne County, merged into Pennsylvania Power & Light Co., 19 November 1928.

684. ORWIGSBURG ELECTRIC LIGHT, HEAT AND POWER COMPANY (Operating).
Schuylkill County, Orwigsburg Borough.
1907 to 1910, 4 Linear Inches.

History:
Orwigsburg Electric Light, Heat and Power Co., incorporated 27 February 1907 to supply electricity in Orwigsburg Borough, Schuylkill County, was a subsidiary of Eastern Pennsylvania Railways Co. It purchased power from Palo Alto Heat Light and Power Co., with which it merged, 20 July 1909.

Administrative Records:
Minute Book, 1907-1909
Stock Certificates, 1907-1909

Operating Records:
General Ledger, 1907-1909
Charges to Local Construction, 1908
Record of Sales, 1908-1910
Operating Statistics, 1909-1910
Balance Sheets, 1907-1909
Earnings, Operating Expenses, and Balance Sheets, 1907-1908

685. PACKER TOWNSHIP ELECTRIC COMPANY (Non-operating).
Carbon County, Packer Township.
1911 to 1912, 1 Linear Inch.

History:
Packer Township Electric Co. was incorporated 6 February 1911 to supply electricity in the Township of Packer, Carbon County. On 23 February 1912 it was consolidated and merged with eleven companies to form The Harwood Electric Co.

686. PALM ELECTRIC LIGHT & POWER COMPANY, LIMITED (Operating).
Montgomery County, Palm Village.
1914 to 1924, 1 Linear Foot.

History:
Palm Electric Light & Power Co., Limited, was a limited partnership association organized by residents of the Village of Palm, Montgomery County on 20 November 1911. The company purchased its power from the Pennsburg Electric Light Commission, and built its own distribution system in Palm. The company began supplying power to the public in March of 1912. In July 1923 Pennsylvania Power & Light Co. gained control of the company's stock, and on 26 November 1923 it purchased its distribution system.

Administrative Records:
Minute Book, 1911-1925
Stock Certificate Book, 1912-1923
Stock Transfer Record, 1923
Stock Ledger, 1912-1923
Correspondence and Miscellaneous Papers, 1911-1923

Operating Records:
General Ledger, 1914-1923
Journal Entry Register, 1923-1924
Bank Check Book, 1923
Cash Received, 1923-1924
Check Register, 1923-1924
Audited Voucher Register, 1923-1924
Accounts Payable, 1923-1924
Accrual Record, 1923
Summary of Accounts Receivable—Consumers, 1923
Audit Report, Pennsylvania Power & Light Co., 1919-1923

Scope and Content Note:
The minute book of Palm Electric Light & Power Co. contains information about the company's electric rates, construction of its electrical system, and statements of profits and losses. Correspondence and miscellaneous papers include income tax returns, dividend sheets, meter test records, and letters with Pennsburg Electric Light Commission concerning electric rates.

687. PALMERTON-CARBON POWER & LIGHT COMPANY (Non-operating).
Carbon County, Palmerton Borough.
1948 to 1949, 1 Linear Inch.

History:
Palmerton-Carbon Power & Light Co. was incorporated 12 May 1948 by the Pennsylvania Power & Light Co. in order to secure charter rights in the Borough of Palmerton, Carbon County. The company was dissolved 17 November 1949.

688. THE PALMERTON COMPANY (Operating).
Carbon County, Palmerton Borough.
1913 to 1914, 1 Linear Inch.

History:
The Palmerton Co. was incorporated in January 1913. The company controlled three different utilities in the Borough of Palmerton, Carbon County: Pennsylvania Lighting Co., which supplied electric lighting, Palmerton Disposal Co., which supplied sewage service, and Palmerton Telephone Co. The company was acquired by Pennsylvania Power & Light Co. in 1948.

Operating Records:
Trial Balances, 1913-1914

689. PALMERTON DISPOSAL COMPANY (Operating).
Carbon County, Palmerton Borough.
1922 to 1948, 1 Linear Foot.

History:

Palmerton Disposal Co. was incorporated in 1922 to operate a sewer line in the Borough of Palmerton, Carbon County. The company was organized by The Palmerton Co., which controlled three different utilities in Palmerton—electric lighting, telephone service, and sewer service. Palmerton Disposal Co. was still in operation in 1947, but its subsequent history is unknown.

Administrative Records:

Minute Books, 1937-1948 (2 Volumes)

Operating Records:

Cashbooks, 1930-1948 (3 Volumes)
Payroll Distribution, 1922-1948
Employee Earning Record, 1947-1948
Payroll Working Papers, 1947-1948

Scope and Content Note:

In addition to routine minutes of stockholders' and directors' meetings, the Minute Books of the Palmerton Disposal Co. contain statements of operating expenses and details of the company's investments.

690. PALMERTON LIGHTING COMPANY (Operating).
Carbon County, Palmerton Borough.
1912 to 1948, 2 Linear Feet.

History:

Palmerton Lighting Co. was incorporated 22 August 1912 by The Palmerton Co. to supply electricity in the Borough of Palmerton, Carbon County. On 26 September 1912 the company purchased an electric lighting system from the Palmerton Land Co. Palmerton Lighting Co. did not own a power plant. Instead, it purchased its power from the New Jersey Zinc Co. Early in 1915 the company extended its system to the Borough of Bowmanstown, Carbon County. In 1948 Pennsylvania Power & Light Co. acquired the company's stock from The Palmerton Co. On 30 September the company was liquidated.

Administrative Records:

Minute Books, 1912-1948 (6 Volumes)

Operating Records:

General Ledgers, 1912-1948 (5 Volumes)
Journals, 1912-1948 (6 Volumes)
Cashbooks, 1912-1948 (4 Volumes)
Detail Ledger, 1944-1948
Trial Balance, 1912-1915
Kilowatt Hours Distribution, 1939-1943
Payroll Distribution, 1921-1948 (4 Volumes)
Payroll Working Papers, 1947-1948
Employee Earning Record, 1947-1948
Audit Report, Pennsylvania Power & Light Co., 1919-1923

Scope and Content Note:

The Minute Books of the Palmerton Lighting Co. consist of routine minutes of stockholders' and directors' meetings. The Kilowatt Hours Distribution Record lists commercial customers, and the number of kilowatts used monthly.

691. PALMERTON TELEPHONE COMPANY (Operating).
Carbon County, Palmerton Borough.
1922 to 1948, 1 Linear Foot.

History:

Palmerton Telephone Co. was incorporated in 1922 to supply telephone service in the Borough of Palmerton, Carbon County. The company was organized and operated by The Palmerton Co., which controlled three different utility services in Palmerton—telephone, electric lighting, and sewage disposal. The company's stock was acquired by Pennsylvania Power & Light Co. in 1948, and it was operated as an affiliate until 1954. The company's history after that date is unknown, but it probably was dissolved.

Operating Records:

Cashbooks, 1930-1948 (3 Volumes)
Payroll Distribution, 1922-1929
Payroll Working Papers, 1947-1948
Financial and Operating Reports, 1948-1954 (4 Volumes)
Employee Earning Record, 1947-1948

Scope and Content Note:

The records of the Palmerton Telephone Co. are listed with the records of the Palmerton Lighting Co., which was also controlled by The Palmerton Co.

692. PALMYRA POWER & LIGHT COMPANY (Non-operating).
Wayne County, Palmyra Township.
1923 to 1924, 1 Linear Inch.

History:

Palmyra Power & Light Co. was incorporated 1 May 1923 to supply electricity in the Township of Palmyra, Wayne County. It was consolidated and merged with 31 other companies 21 July 1923 to form Paupack Power & Light Co., No. 2.

693. PALMYRA TOWNSHIP POWER & LIGHT COMPANY (Non-operating).
Pike County, Palmyra Township.
1923 to 1924, 1 Linear Inch.

History:

Palmyra Township Power & Light Co. was incorporated 1 May 1923 to supply electricity in the Township of Palmyra, Pike County. On 20 July 1923 it was consolidated and merged with 31 other companies to form Paupack Power & Light Co., No. 2.

694. PALO ALTO HEAT, LIGHT AND POWER COMPANY (Operating).
Schuylkill County, Palo Alto Borough.
1906 to 1909, 1 Linear Inch.

History:

Palo Alto Heat, Light and Power Co., was organized 13 September 1906 by Eastern Pennsylvania Railways Co. which needed a source of power for its electric distribution system. Shortly after its organization, Palo Alto Heat, Light and Power leased the Schuylkill Electric Company's power plant, which had a generating capacity of 1,000-kw. By 1908, the company was supplying power to nine railway and electric companies. On 20 July 1909 it acquired the eight principal companies that supplied electricity in Schuylkill County, and changed its name to Eastern Pennsylvania Light, Heat and Power Co.

Administrative Records:
Stock Certificate Book, 1906

Operating Records:
General Ledger, 1907-1909
Charges to Local Construction, 1908
Payroll Distribution, 1909
Report of Earnings, 1908-1909
Operating Statistics, 1909
Balance Sheets, 1907-1909
Earnings & Operating Expenses, 1907-1908
Voucher Record, 1907-1909

695. PANTHER CREEK ELECTRIC COMPANY
(Non-operating).
Carbon County, Packer Township.
1911 to 1913, 1 Linear Inch.

History:
Panther Creek Electric Co. was incorporated 4 April 1911 to supply electricity in the Township of Packer, Carbon County. On 23 December 1912 it was consolidated and merged with 37 other non-operating companies to form Lehigh Navigation Electric Co., No. 2.

696. PANTHER VALLEY ELECTRIC COMPANY
(Operating).
Carbon County, Lansford Borough.
1914 to 1928, 4 1/2 Linear Feet.

History:
Panther Valley Electric Co. was incorporated 25 November 1914 following the consolidation and merger of The Panther Valley Electric Light Heat and Power Co. with the Coaldale Electric Co. The company supplied electricity in the Boroughs of Lansford and Coaldale, Carbon County, and extended its facilities to the Villages of Hauto and New Columbia. In 1914 it began to purchase power from Lehigh Navigation Electric Co. and then from Pennsylvania Power & Light Co. In 1927 Panther Valley Electric's stock was acquired by Lehigh Power Securities Corp., and thereafter it was operated as part of Pennsylvania Power & Light Co. On 28 May 1928 it was merged into Pennsylvania Power & Light Co.

Administrative Records:
Minute Book, 1914-1928
Stock Certificate Books, 1920-1926
Stock Transfer Record, 1914-1926
Stock Ledger, 1923-1928
Bond Record, 1915-1926
Correspondence, 1914-1915

Operating Records:
General Ledgers, 1916-1928
Journal Entry—Detail Ledger, 1921-1926
Journal Entry Register, 1926-1928
Cashbook, 1916-1926
Cash Account and Check Register, 1919-1921
Bank Account Register, 1922-1926
Record of Cash Receipts, 1926-1928
Record of Cash Disbursements, 1926-1928
Summary of Cash, 1926-1928
Audited Voucher Register, 1916-1919
Notes Payable, 1919-1922
Accounts Payable, 1926-1928
Detail Ledger, 1926-1928
Accrual Record, 1926-1928
Time Book, 1915-1917
Detail of Cost Study and Fixed Capital, 1926-1927
Statements of Operations, 1916-1918
Monthly Reports, 1919-1926
Expenditure Requisitions, 1926-1928
Retirement Authorities, 1926-1928
Workmen's Compensation Insurance Accrual Statements, 1926-1928
Bills Receivable, 1926-1928
Summary of Accounts Receivable—Consumers, 1926-1928 (2 Volumes)
Summary of Accounts Receivable—Miscellaneous, 1926-1928
Recapitulation of Jobbing Works, 1926-1928
Summary of Consumers' Deposits, 1926-1928
Summary of Cashiers' Overs and Shorts, 1926-1928
Miscellaneous statements, 1927-1928
Audit Reports, 1916-1927 (25 Volumes)
Property Transfer Report, 1926

Scope and Content Note:
The Minute Book of Panther Valley Electric Co. contains lists of stockholders, and information concerning operating expenses. Also included is information on the company's promotion of the use of electric appliances. For example, it placed stoves in the schools of Lansford for the use of Domestic Science classes. Correspondence consists mainly of purchase orders for various electric components, but it does include information concerning the company's streetlighting contracts with the borough councils of Lansford and Coaldale, as well as information on the company's advertising campaigns for the sale of electric appliances. The Time Book lists the employees involved in various projects, such as repairs to substations and extensions of pole lines, and the number of hours they worked. The Property Transfer Report, prepared for Lehigh Power Securities Corp., describes the company's transmission and distribution systems, substations and other buildings.

697. THE PANTHER VALLEY ELECTRIC LIGHT HEAT AND POWER COMPANY (Operating).
Carbon County, Lansford Borough.
1892 to 1916, 2 Linear Feet.

History:
In 1888 the Lansford Borough council built an electric generating station and distribution system in the borough, in order to supply the town with electric lighting. The Lehigh Coal and Navigation Co. purchased this system in 1892, because it wished to use the power plant to run its coal mining operations in the area. When The Panther Valley Electric Light Heat and Power Co. was incorporated 20 February 1893, it bought the electric light system in Lansford, and contracted to purchase all its power from Lehigh Coal and Navigation. In 1907 the company extended its area of operations to include the Boroughs of Summit Hill and Coaldale, Carbon County. It was consolidated and merged with Coaldale Electric Co. on 17 August 1914 to form Panther Valley Electric Co.

Administrative Records:
Minute Books, 1892-1914 (2 Volumes)
Stock Certificate Book, 1893-1913
Stock Ledger, 1910-1911
List of Bonds, 1896-1903
Record of Bonds, 1900-1906

Operating Records:
Cashbooks, 1892-1916 (4 Volumes)
Accounts Payable Record Book, 1910-1911
List of Outstanding Bills, 1893-1904

Scope and Content Note:
The Minute Books of The Panther Valley Electric Light Heat and Power Co. describe the company's organization and capitalization, electric rates, operating expenses, and its relationship with The Lehigh Coal and Navigation Co. Also documented are the development and expansion of its electric lighting system, purchases of transformers and other electric equipment, and its dealings with Lansford Borough Council in regard to erecting poles, stringing wires, and installing meters, etc., for street lighting.

698. PARADISE ELECTRIC LIGHT, HEAT AND POWER COMPANY (Non-operating).
Lancaster County, Paradise Township.
1913, 1 Linear Inch.

History:
Paradise Electric Light, Heat and Power Co. was incorporated 2 January 1913 to supply electricity in the Township of Paradise, Lancaster County. On 10 January 1913 it was consolidated and merged with four other companies to form Strasburg Electric Light, Heat and Power Co., No. 2.

699. PARADISE POWER & LIGHT COMPANY (Non-operating).
Monroe County, Paradise Township.
1923 to 1924, 1 Linear Inch.

History:
Paradise Power & Light Co. was incorporated 1 May 1923 to supply electricity in the Township of Paradise, Monroe County. On 20 July 1923 it was consolidated and merged with 31 other companies to form Paupack Power & Light Co., No. 2.

700. PARADISE TOWNSHIP ELECTRIC COMPANY (Non-operating).
Lancaster County, Paradise Township.
1912, 1 Linear Inch.

History:
Paradise Township Electric Co. was incorporated 25 April 1912 to supply electricity in the Township of Paradise, Lancaster County. On 13 May 1912 it was consolidated and merged with six other non-operating companies to form Christiana Suburban Electric Co.

701. PARDEE BROTHERS & COMPANY, INCORPORATED (Operating).
Luzerne County, Hazleton Borough.
1902 to 1906, 2 Linear Inches.

History:
Pardee Brothers & Co., Inc. was an independent anthracite coal mining company organized by Calvin Pardee in 1865 to develop the Lattimer coal mines in the Borough of Hazleton. In 1905 the company constructed a power plant and a distribution system to serve the Villages of Lattimer Mines and Milnesville, where The Harwood Coal Co. was located. On 17 July 1929 Pennsylvania Power & Light Co. purchased these facilities. Pardee Brothers remained in business until 1933, when a financial crisis forced it to liquidate.

Operating Records:
Voucher Record, 1902-1904
Invoice Record, 1906

702. PARRYVILLE ELECTRIC COMPANY (Operating).
Carbon County, Parryville Borough.
1924 to 1928, 3 Linear Inches.

History:
Parryville Electric Co. was incorporated 18 December 1923 by Mr. James I. Blakslee, so that his Weissport Electric Co. could supply electricity in the Borough of Parryville, Carbon County. On 4 June 1926 Parryville Electric acquired the distribution system that Mr. Blakslee had built in Parryville. Later that year Lehigh Power Securities Corp. acquired the company's stock, and thereafter it was operated as part of the Pennsylvania Power & Light system. On 28 May 1928 it officially merged into Pennsylvania Power & Light Co.

Administrative Records:
Minute Book, 1924-1928
Stock Certificate Book, 1924-1927
Stock Transfer Record, 1927
Stock Ledger, 1924-1928

Operating Records:
General Ledger, 1927-1928
Detail of Cost Study and Fixed Capital, 1927
Expenditure Requisitions, 1927-1928
Audit Reports, 1924-1927 (4 Volumes)

Scope and Content Note:
The Minute Book of the Parryville Electric Co. consists of routine minutes of directors' and stockholders' meetings. Both the Minute Book and the Audit Reports document the close relationship between this company and Mr. James I. Blakslee's Lehighton Electric Light and Power Co.

703. PAUPACK ELECTRIC COMPANY (Operating).
Wayne County, Hawley Borough.
1918 to 1928, 3 Linear Feet.

History:
Electric service was first supplied in the Borough of Hawley, Wayne County, by The Hawley Electric Light and Power Co., which was incorporated 1 December 1896. In May 1905 the company's generating station was destroyed by fire. The costs of reconstruction placed a severe financial strain on the company, and it was forced to default on the interest payments of its mortgage. The company was sold at a foreclosure sale on 2 March 1906 to a committee representing the bondholders. On 6 April 1906 it was reorganized as Paupack Electric Co. The bondholders' committee conveyed to it the franchises and property of Hawley Electric Light and Power, including the newly-rebuilt hydroelectric plant on Wallenpaupack Creek in Hawley. In 1919 Paupack Electric installed generating equipment in the basement of the Kimble Silk

Mill in Hawley. In 1922 the company was acquired by a group headed by General F. W. Stillwell, which was planning the construction of a large water power project along Wallenpaupack Creek. In 1924 the company's stock was acquired by Lehigh Power Securities Corp. as part of an agreement by which Pennsylvania Power & Light Co. acquired the land upon which Stillwell's group had been planning to build. Thereafter, Paupack Electric was operated as part of Pennsylvania Power & Light Co. and, in fact, supplied part of the power needed for the construction of Pennsylvania Power & Light's Wallenpaupack Creek hydroelectric dam. On 28 May 1928 Paupack Electric Co. was merged into Pennsylvania Power & Light Co.

Administrative Records:
Minute Book, 1918-1928
Stock Certificate Book, 1911-1923

Operating Records:
General Ledger, 1923-1928
Journal Entry Register, 1923-1928
Cash Received, 1923-1925
Check Register, 1923-1925
Record of Cash Receipts, 1925-1928
Record of Cash Disbursements, 1925-1928
Check Book, 1920-1923
Summary of Cash, 1925-1928
Accounts Payable, 1923-1928
Accounts Receivable, 1923-1928
Detail Ledger, 1923-1928
Accrual Record, 1923-1928
Detail of Cost Study and Fixed Capital, 1925-1927 (2 Volumes)
Retirement Authorities, 1924-1928
Expenditure Requisitions, 1923-1928
Transfer Authorities, 1925
Workmen's Compensation Insurance Accrual Statements, 1923-1928
Summary of Accounts Receivable—Consumers, 1923-1926 (2 Volumes)
Summary of Accounts Receivable—Miscellaneous, 1923-1928 (3 Volumes)
Summary of Rents Receivable, 1926-1928
Summary of Consumers' Deposits, 1925-1928
Summary of Cashiers' Overs and Shorts, 1925-1928
Working Papers of Audits, 1923-1925
Audit Reports, 1921-1927 (3 Volumes)

Scope and Content Note:
The Minute Book of Paupack Electric Co. consists of routine minutes of stockholders' and directors' meetings and documents the company's organization and capitalization. The Audit Reports provide some details on the agreement by which the company passed into the control of Lehigh Power Securities Corp., and give an overview of its financial status.

704. PAUPACK POWER & LIGHT COMPANY, NO. 1 (Non-operating).
Wayne County, Paupack Township.
1923 to 1924, 1 Linear Inch.

History:
Paupack Power & Light Co., No. 1, was incorporated 1 May 1923 to supply electricity in the Township of Paupack, Wayne County. On 20 July 1923 it was consolidated and merged with 31 other companies to form Paupack Power & Light Co., No. 2.

705. PAUPACK POWER & LIGHT COMPANY, NO. 2 (Non-operating).
Wayne County, Paupack Township.
1923 to 1924, 3 Linear Inches.

History:
Paupack Power & Light Co. was incorporated 29 January 1924 to supply electricity in the Township of Paupack. On 17 March 1924 the company was merged into the Pennsylvania Power & Light Co.

706. PAXTANG ELECTRIC COMPANY (Operating).
Dauphin County, Harrisburg City.
1903 to 1912, 4 Linear Inches.

History:
Paxtang Electric Co. was incorporated 30 January 1902 to supply electricity in the City of Harrisburg, Dauphin County. In 1903 the company built a steam electric generating station on Cedar Street in Harrisburg. From the first, it competed with The Harrisburg Light Heat and Power Co. for customers and engaged in an almost ruinous rate war with it. But Paxtang Electric Co. persevered, and by 1912 it was supplying electricity to almost 1,500 customers. At that time the company's electric plant contained three Westinghouse generators with a combined generating capacity of 1,300-kw. On 6 August 1912 the company was merged into Harrisburg Light and Power Co., No. 1.

Administrative Records:
Stock Certificate Book, 1903-1912
Stock Certificates, 1903-1912

Operating Records:
Audited Voucher Register, 1903-1912
Miscellaneous Financial Statements, 1911-1912
Audit Report, 1904

Scope and Content Note:
The records of Paxtang Electric Co. are incomplete. The Audit Report contains a brief account of the company's formation, listing the directors and documenting organizational costs. The Miscellaneous Financial Statements include lists of operating expenses, annual statements of earnings and expenses, and statements of kilowatt-hour sales for light and power.

707. PEACH BOTTOM ELECTRIC TRANSMISSION COMPANY (Non-operating).
York County, Peach Bottom Township.
1909 to 1910, 3 Linear Inches.

History:
Peach Bottom Electric Transmission Co. was incorporated 13 November 1908 to supply electricity in the Township of Peach Bottom, York County. The company was consolidated and merged with Lower Chanceford Township Transmission Co., 16 April 1910, to form Susquehanna Transmission Co. of Penna.

708. PEN ARGYL ELECTRIC LIGHT & POWER COMPANY (Operating).
Northampton County, Pen Argyl Township.
1901 to 1907, 2 Linear Inches.

History:

Pen Argyl Light & Power Co. was organized about 1901 by Allentown Electric Light and Power Co. in order to supply electricity in the Township of Pen Argyl, Northampton County. The company was leased from 1903 to 1905 to Lehigh Valley Traction Co., which controlled the stock of Allentown Electric, and operated a number of street railways in the region north of Allentown. The company's history after 1905 is unclear, but evidently it retained its exclusive franchise in Pen Argyl Township. As late as 1939 this township remained outside Pennsylvania Power & Light Company's system.

Operating Records:

General Ledger, 1901-1907
Cashbook, 1901-1904

709. PENN FOREST POWER & LIGHT COMPANY

(Non-operating).
Carbon County, Penn Forest Township.
1923 to 1924, 1 Linear Inch.

History:

Penn Forest Power & Light Co. was incorporated 1 May 1923 to supply electricity in the Township of Penn Forest, Carbon County. On 20 July 1923 it was consolidated and merged with 31 other non-operating companies to form Paupack Power & Light Co., No. 2.

710. PENN-LYCOMING POWER & LIGHT COMPANY

(Non-operating).
Lycoming County, Penn Township.
1924, 1 Linear Inch.

History:

Penn-Lycoming Power & Light Co. was incorporated 28 August 1924 to supply electricity in the Township of Penn, Lycoming County. On 6 October 1924 the company was merged into The Citizens Electric Light Co. of Hughesville, Pa.

711. PENN TOWNSHIP ELECTRIC LIGHT COMPANY

(Non-operating).
Lancaster County, Penn Township.
1911, 1 Linear Inch.

History:

Penn Township Electric Light Co. was incorporated 10 August 1911 to supply electricity in Penn Township, Lancaster County. On 29 September 1911 it was consolidated and merged with 17 other companies to form Edison Electric Co. No. 1.

712. PENN TOWNSHIP LIGHT COMPANY

(Non-operating).
Snyder County, Penn Township.
1914 , 1 Linear Inch.

History:

Penn Township Light Co. was incorporated 16 September 1914 to supply electricity in the Township of Penn, Snyder County. It merged into Northumberland County Gas & Electric Co. on 3 October 1914.

713. PENNS CREEK HYDRO ELECTRIC COMPANY

(Operating).
Union County, New Berlin Borough.
1918 to 1931, 1 Linear Foot.

History:

Penns Creek Hydro Electric Co. was organized in 1919 by Mr. F.Q. Hartman, who owned and operated a silk mill in the Schoch Mill property in the Borough of New Berlin, Union County. Prior to the organization of this company, Mr. Hartman installed a water-powered generator in his mill and, having secured the necessary franchise, built an electric distribution system. After its dam had been washed away by a flood in 1928, the company moved its generator into the Yarnada Mill in New Berlin. This silk mill was also owned by Mr. Hartman, and was Penns Creek's largest customer. To avoid putting strain on the company's generator, the mill machinery was connected an oil engine and operated directly from it. In 1929 the company's stock was acquired by Lehigh Power Securities Corp. In 1930, its plant was shut down, and on 31 December 1930 it was merged into Pennsylvania Power & Light Co.

Administrative Records:

Minute Book, 1919-1930
Stock Certificate Book, 1919-1930
Stock Transfer Record, 1929-1930
Stock Ledger, 1919-1930

Operating Records:

General Ledgers, 1918-1930 (2 Volumes)
Journal, 1918-1929
Journal Entry Register, 1929-1930
Record of Cash Disbursements, 1929-1930
Audited Voucher Register, 1929-1930
Accounts Payable, 1929-1930
Accounts Receivable, 1929-1930
Bill Register, 1929-1930
Detail Ledgers, 1928-1930 (2 Volumes)
Accrual Record, 1929-1930
Expenditure Requisitions, 1929-1930
Retirement Authorities, 1929-1931
Workmen's Compensation Insurance Accrual Statements, 1929
Summary of Accounts Receivable—Consumers, 1929-1930
Audit Reports, 1924-1929 (3 Volumes)

Scope and Content Note:

In addition to routine minutes of stockholders' and directors' meetings, the Minute Book of the Penns Creek Hydro Electric Co. contains information documenting the company's organization and capitalization, its move to the Yarnada Silk Mill in the Borough of New Berlin, and its ultimate sale to Pennsylvania Power & Light Co. The Audit Reports provide information on the company's financial condition, as well as copies of its electric rate schedules.

714. PENNSBURG ELECTRIC LIGHT COMMISSION

(Operating).
Montgomery County, Pennsburg Borough.
1908 to 1923, 3 Linear Inches.

History:

Pennsburg Electric Light Commission was organized by Pennsburg Borough Council in Montgomery County. It built a steam generating plant and an electric distribution system which went into operation in 1907. Power was supplied to Pennsburg and the nearby communities of

Red Hill, Green Lane, Palm, and East Greenville. On 3 November 1923 Pennsylvania Power & Light Co. purchased the power plant and distribution system from the Council in order to secure operating rights in Pennsburg.

Administrative Records:
Correspondence, 1908-1922

Operating Records:
Daybook, 1909-1913
Audit Report, Pennsylvania Power & Light Co., 1921-1923
Contracts, 1910-1923

Scope and Content Note:
Correspondence of Pennsburg Electric Light Commission consists of purchase orders for electrical parts, boiler parts, and fuel. The file also contains information on the company's electric rates and the expansion of its boiler plant. The contracts are for alterations to the boiler plant, incandescent lighting and new transformers.

715. PENNSBURG POWER & LIGHT COMPANY (Non-operating).
Montgomery County, Pennsburg Borough.
1923 to 1924, 2 Linear Inches.

History:
After having purchased the power plant and distribution system built and operated by Pennsburg Borough Electric Light Commission, Pennsylvania Power & Light Co. incorporated Pennsburg Power & Light Co. 17 October 1923, in order to secure a franchise in the Borough of Pennsburg, Montgomery County. On 2 November 1923, Pennsburg Power & Light was merged into Pennsylvania Power & Light Co.

716. PENNSYLVANIA LIGHTING COMPANY (Operating).
Northumberland County, Shamokin Borough.
1910 to 1920, 5 Linear Feet.

History:
Pennsylvania Lighting Co. was incorporated 22 June 1910 as a result of the consolidation and merger of Shamokin and Coal Township Light, Heat and Power Co. with two non-operating companies. The company supplied electricity in the Boroughs of Shamokin and Mount Carmel, and gas lighting in the Borough of Shamokin. Soon after its formation, the company built a new gas plant and extended its gas service to the Townships of Shamokin and Ralpho, Northumberland County. In 1916 the generating capacity of the plant which the company had inherited from the Shamokin and Coal Township company was boosted from 3,400-kw to 4,900-kw. The next year the company acquired the stock of The Edison Electric Illuminating Co. of Mount Carmel, and The Trevorton Electric Light and Power Co. These two operating companies were merged into Pennsylvania Lighting Co. in April 1920. On 12 April 1920 Pennsylvania Lighting Co. was consolidated and merged with seven other companies to form Pennsylvania Power & Light Co.

Administrative Records:
Minute Books, 1910-1920 (2 Volumes)
Stock Certificate Books, 1910 (2 Volumes)
Stock Certificates, 1910-1920
Stock Transfer Ledger, 1910-1913

Operating Records:
Correspondence and Miscellaneous Papers, 1910-1920
FINANCIAL RECORDS
General Ledgers, 1910-1920 (2 Volumes)
Journals, 1910-1920 (2 Volumes)
Cashbooks, 1910-1920 (3 Volumes)
Cash Receipts and Expenditures Monthly Reports, 1919-1920
CONSUMER RECORDS
Accounts Receivable Ledger, 1910-1915 (3 Volumes)
Miscellaneous Sales, 1910-1915 (4 Volumes)
Monthly Statements, Balance Sheets, and Inventories
Comparative Income Statements and General Balance Sheets, 1918-1920
Commercial Report, 1916-1917
PERSONNEL RECORDS
Monthly Time Book, 1910-1915
Payrolls and Payroll Vouchers, 1916-1917
Payrolls and Monthly Statements, 1916
Audit Report, 1917-1919

Scope and Content Note:
The Minute Books of Pennsylvania Lighting Co. contain information regarding the company's gas and electric rates, the construction of its new gas plant in 1910-1911, its street lighting contracts, and the purchase of Liberty Bonds by the company on behalf of its employees. Also included in the Minute Books are a copy of the consolidation and merger agreement by which the company was formed, lists of expenditures for improvements to the company's gas and electric distribution systems, and various financial statements. The Correspondence and Miscellaneous Papers are those of the company's treasurer, and deal mainly with insurance policies and overdue bills, as well as with the financial problems of The Ohio River Electric Railway and Power Co., an Ohio-based power company controlled by Pennsylvania Lighting. The Monthly Time Book lists the company's employees and their pay rates, and occasionally notes their occupation. The Miscellaneous Sales Ledgers list customers and their addresses; various electrical parts purchased, such as globes, tubes, insulators, and wire; and the services performed by the company, such as installing appliances, putting in wiring, and attaching plugs. The Monthly Cash Receipts and Expenditures Reports include inventories of electrical and gas parts and equipment, and lists of total gas and electric sales.

717. PENNSYLVANIA POWER & LIGHT COMPANY, NO. 1 (Non-operating).
Lehigh County, Upper Milford Township.
1918 to 1919, 2 Linear Inches.

History:
Pennsylvania Power & Light Co., No. 1 (so indicated to distinguish this company from the operating company of the same name), was a 'paper company' incorporated by Lehigh Navigation Electric Co., No. 2 on 29 October

1917 in order to establish charter rights in the Township of Upper Milford, Lehigh County. On 16 Octoberit was merged into The Lehigh Valley Light and Power Company.

718. PENNSYLVANIA POWER & LIGHT COMPANY, NO. 2 (Non-operating).
Snyder County, Washington Township.
1919 to 1920, 1 Linear Inch.

History:
Pennsylvania Power & Light Co. was a 'paper company' incorporated 12 August 1919 by The Lehigh Valley Light and Power Co., which at that time was ostensibly attempting to secure charter rights in Washington Township, Snyder County. The Lehigh Valley Light and Power Co., controlled by Electric Bond and Share, however, had a hidden agenda. It was in the process of consolidating its control over eastern Pennsylvania's electrical generating and distribution system. With this end in mind, the company wanted to establish a hold on the name "Pennsylvania Power & Light Co". That is why this small non-operating company was given this name. On 17 April 1920 the planned merger took place. Seven operating companies and this "paper company" were officially consolidated to form Pennsylvania Power & Light Co.

719. PENNSYLVANIA REALTY & INVESTMENT COMPANY (Operating).
Lehigh County, Allentown City.
1923 to 1948, 2 1/2 Linear Feet.

History:
Pennsylvania Realty and Investment Co. was incorporated 13 November 1923 for the purpose of buying and selling real estate in and around Allentown. The company was controlled by Pennsylvania Power & Light Co., which purchased land from it for its Allentown Service Depot. The company was dissolved on 30 April 1951.

Operating Records:
Cash Received, 1923-1925
Check Register, 1923-1925
Record of Cash Receipts, 1923
Record of Cash Disbursements, 1923
Summary of Cash, 1925-1948 (3 Volumes)
Detail of Cost Study and Fixed Capital, 1925-1927
Expenditure Requisitions, 1927-1951
Summary of Accounts Receivable—Miscellaneous, 1913-1938
Statements of Real Estate Leases and Rentals, 1926-1939
Audit Reports, 1925-1932 (6 Volumes)
Bank Check Book, 1923
Bank Passbook, 1923-1925

720. PENNSYLVANIA TRANSMISSION COMPANY (Operating).
Lancaster County, Holtwood Village.
1932 to 1939, 2 Linear Inches.

History:
Pennsylvania Transmission Co. was incorporated 1 April 1932 to build and operate a series of transmission lines between Pennsylvania Water & Power Company's Safe Harbor plant and Baltimore, Maryland. The company was organized by Pennsylvania Water & Power Co., which paid for the construction of the transmission lines.

Administrative Records:
Minute Books, 1932-1939
Stock Certificate Book, 1932-1933
Index to Minutes, 1932-1939

Scope and Content Note:
The Minute Book of Pennsylvania Transmission Co. contains copies of deeds and agreements with Pennsylvania Water & Power Co.

721. PENNSYLVANIA WATER & POWER COMPANY (Operating).
Lancaster County, Martic Township.
1896 to 1955, 54 Linear Feet.

History:
Pennsylvania Water & Power Co. (PW&P) was incorporated in January 1910 to develop water power on the Susquehanna River. Its main facility was in the Village of Holtwood, Martic Township, Lancaster County. PW&P was formed by a group of Boston and New York bankers who raised capital for the construction of a dam and a hydroelectric plant equipped with ten large turbogenerators. The plant generated some 104,000-kw of electricity which was supplemented by another 30,000-kw that was generated by Holtwood Power Co. (a PW&P subsidiary). The backers of this project were determined to construct a hydroelectric facility on the Susquehanna to rival New York State's Niagara Falls. The second phase of their program saw the construction of a dam and a hydroelectric plant at Safe Harbor, eight miles upriver from Holtwood. By the mid-1930's, the Safe Harbor plant consisted of seven generating units which produced 230,000-kw of electricity. Once completed, the PW&P system was integrated with other large power systems that supplied the Chesapeake-Eastern Pennsylvania area. In June 1955, Pennsylvania Water and Power consolidated and merged with Pennsylvania Power & Light Co.

Administrative Records:
Minute Books, 1910-1955 (10 Volumes)
Index to Papers, 1930-1949
STOCK AND BOND RECORDS
Cancelled Stock Certificates, 1910-1955
List of Registered Common Stock Holders, 1955
Lists of Registered Preferred and Common Stock Holders, 1955
Cancelled Bonds and Cancelled Bond List, 1955
Common Stock and Capital Stock Ledgers—Closed Accounts, 1937-1951 (9 Volumes)
Common Stock and Capital Stock Ledgers—Open Accounts, n.d. (9 Volumes)
Common and Preferred Stock Ledger—Open Domestic and Foreign Accounts, A-Z
Common Stock Transfer Sheets, 1946-1951 (5 Volumes)
Preferred Stock Transfer Record, 1933-1951
Voting Trust Certificates—Closed Accounts, A-Z, 1910-1927
List of Stockholders Entitled to Rights, 1924-1933
Capital Stock Ledger, A-Z, 1912-1926
Closed Accounts, 1919-1933 (6 Volumes)
Proxy Lists—Common and Preferred Stockholders, 1951

Wallenpaupack Hydro Development, Pennsylvania Power & Light Company, 1926.

Generator Room, Holtwood Hydro Station, Built by Pennsylvania Water & Power Company, 1910.

(3 Volumes)
Lists of Debited Stock Accounts, 1953-1955
List of Registered Common Stock Holders, 1955

Operating Records:
Detail List of Stockholders as of the Close of Business, 1955
List of Common Stockholders, 1955
Common Stock Transfer Sheets, 1951-1955 (16 Volumes)
Preferred Stock Transfer Sheets, 1951-1954 (2 Volumes)
Affadavit and Bond of Indemnity for Lost Stock Certificate, 1953
MISCELLANEOUS REPORTS
Complete Charter of Pennsylvania Water & Power Co. and Predessors, 1910
Papers and Reports for Directors' and Stockholders' Meetings, 1930-1955
CORRESPONDENCE
Executive Officer Correspondence and Papers, 1923-1955 (27 Boxes)
Washington Contract Negotiations, 1921-1938 (on microfilm)
Correspondence—Baltimore Electro Alloys Co., 1915-1931 (on microfilm)
Correspondence—Operating Department-Penn Water & Power Co., 1914-1942 (on microfilm)
Correspondence—Holtwood Coal Co., 1921-1941 (on microfilm)
Administrative Department Contract Files, 1923-1946 (on microfilm)
Correspondence—Test Department, 1921-1942 (on microfilm)
ENGINEERING AND CONSTRUCTION DATA
Original Cost Files, 1896-1954 (on microfilm)
Correspondence—Baltimore Engineering Department, 1914-1953 (on microfilm)
Fixed Capital Cost Ledgers, 1910-1918 (2 Volumes)
Construction Cost Ledger, 1919-1923
Construction Cost Record, 1924
Construction Job Descriptions and Details, 1910-1938
Construction Job Cost Record, 1927-1936
Job Summary—Holtwood Steam Plant, 1924
Operating Department—Steam Station Turbine Log Sheets, 1925-1934 (on microfilm)
Operating Department—Holtwood Hydro-25 Cycle Diary, 1914-1954 (microfilm)
Operating Department—Holtwood Hydro-60 Cycle Diary, 1925-1954 (on microfilm)
Operating Department—Holtwood Hydro-25 Cycle Log Sheets, 1910-1915 (on microfilm)
Operating Department—Holtwood Hydro-Floormen's Diary, 1914-1954 (on microfilm)
Operating Department—Violet Hill Substation-60 Cycle Diary, 1924-1946 (on microfilm)
Operating Department—Manor Substation-69 kv Log Sheets, 1948-1954 (on microfilm)
Operating Department—Face Rock Substation-69 kv Log Sheets, 1951-1953 (on microfilm)
Operating Department—Holtwood Hydro—25 Cycle Log Sheets, 1916-1922 (on microfilm)
Operating Department—Holtwood Hydro-25 Cycle and 60 Cycle Log Sheets, 1923-1954 (on microfilm)
Operating Department—Violet Hill Substation-60 Cycle Log Sheets, 1923-1946 (on microfilm)
Operating Department—Disturbance Reports, 1910-1954 (on microfilm)
Operating Department—Steam Station Turbine Log Sheets, 1925-1953 (on microfilm)
Operating Department—Boiler Room Log Books, 1937-1947 (on microfilm)
W.H. Ballantyne (Engineer) Files, 1940-1947 (on microfilm)
Test Department Files, 1918-1948 (on microfilm)
Operating Department—Baltimore Office—Load Dispatchers' Diary, 1951-1954 (on microfilm)

Scope and Content Note:
The records of Pennsylvania Water & Power Co are the largest and most comprehensive group of materials in the Pennsylvania Power & Light Co. Collection. The firm's Minute Books fully document the construction of Holtwood Dam and Power Station, the relationship between the company and Safe Harbor Water Power Corp. and other subsidiaries, and rate hearings before the Pennsylvania Public Utilities Commission. Files containing Annual Reports, financial statements, and operating statistics, prepared for directors' and stockholders' meetings from 1930 to 1955, supplement the Minute Books. Executive Officer correspondence for the period 1914-1942 documents general operations, installation of safety equipment, construction, hydraulic testing, corporate organization, budgets, labor relations, and relations with engineering and trade associations. The files for the 1940s and 1950s contain the papers of G. W. Spaulding, engineer and executive vice president, Samuel Sexton III, administrative assistant to the president, and John R. Baker, personnel manager. Spaulding's papers document the electrification of the Pennsylvania Railroad's line between Safe Harbor and Washington, D.C. Sexton's papers document PW&P's relationship with the Federal Power Commission and other regulatroy agencies. John Baker's papers document personnel practices. Included are reports on wages, pensions, and union organizing campaigns. There is also considerable material describing the company's relationship with the National War Labor Board during World War II. Finally, the records of the Test and Engineering Departments document the activities of Holtwood Laboratory which rated the efficiency of turbines and other generating equipment, and was responsible for forecasting floods, conducting hydrology studies and coordinating land acquisitions.

722. **PEOPLES BRIDGE COMPANY** (Operating).
Dauphin County, Harrisburg City.
1924 to 1926, 1 Linear Inch.

History:
Peoples Bridge Co. was incorporated in 1889 to own and operate a toll bridge across the Susquehanna River at Harrisburg. The bridge was built in 1889-1890, and opened in April 1890. Valley Railways, which was controlled by Lehigh Power Securities Corp., leased trackage rights across the bridge for one of its subsidiary street railways.

Operating Records:
Audit Report, 1924-1926

723. THE PEOPLE'S LIGHT, HEAT AND POWER COMPANY OF SHENANDOAH AND MAHANOY CITY, SCHUYLKILL COUNTY, PENNSYLVANIA (Operating).
Schuylkill County, Mahanoy City Borough.
1904 to 1913, 2 Linear Feet.

History:
The People's Light, Heat and Power Co. of Shenandoah and Mahanoy City, Schuylkill County, Penna., was incorporated 9 September 1904 following the consolidation and merger of The People's Electric Light, Heat and Power Co. of Shenandoah, Penna. with Peoples Light, Heat and Power Co. of Mahanoy Township. In 1905 the company constructed a generating station in the Borough of Mahanoy City, and built a distribution system to supply that borough, and the Borough of Shenandoah with electricity. From its first days of operation, the company was faced with competition from the Mahanoy City Light, Heat and Power Co. In 1911, having discovered that its charter gave it a franchise to supply electricity in the Township of Mahanoy but not in Mahanoy City the company formed The United Light, Heat and Power Co. of Mahanoy, City. This company had the requisite charter, and the People's company deeded it the distribution system in Mahanoy City. In 1912, the stocks of both the People's company and the United company were acquired by Mr. Calvin Pardee. They were then consolidated and merged with ten other companies on 12 November 1912 to form The Schuylkill Gas and Electric Co.

Administrative Records:
Minute Book, 1904-1911
Stock Certificate Books, 1904-1912 (2 Volumes)
Stock Ledger, 1904-1911
Record of Bond Sales, 1908-1911
Correspondence, 1911-1912

Operating Records:
General Ledger, 1911-1913
Journal, 1911-1913
Cash Book, 1906-1911
Cash Receipts and Check Register, 1911-1912
Record of Invoices Paid, 1905-1911
Notes and Bills Payable and Receivable, 1908-1909
Notes Payable, 1908-1911
Accounts Payable, 1908-1911
Detail Ledger, 1908-1911
Monthly Reports, 1907-1912 (2 Volumes)
Time Sheets, 1911-1912
Voucher Register, 1911-1912

Scope and Content Note:
The Minute Book of The People's Light, Heat and Power Co. of Shenandoah and Mahanoy City, Schuylkill Counry, Penna. contains information concerning the company's day-to-day activities and its financial status, lists of operating expenses, details concerning the purchase of electrical and boiler equipment, and a copy of the company's bylaws, which states that notices of the annual stockholders' meeting "shall be given to one English and one Lithuanian newspaper of general circulation in Mahanoy City". Correspondence relates mainly to the purchase of the company's stock by Mr. Calvin Pardee on behalf of The Harwood Electric Co. Also included is a 1911 report describing the company's facilities in Mahanoy City and Shenandoah. Time Sheets list employees, the number of hours worked, rate of pay, and occasionally occupation. For additional information concerning this company, see the "Historical Report of The Harwood Electric Co. and Its Antecedent and Allied Companies," filed with the records of The Harwood Electric Co.

724. PEQUEA ELECTRIC COMPANY (Operating).
Lancaster County, Martic Township.
1921 to 1930, 1/2 Linear Foot.

History:
Pequea Electric Co. was incorporated 6 October 1921 to supply electricity in the Township of Martic, Lancaster County. The company, which purchased all its power from the Edison Electric Illuminating Co. of Lancaster, built and operated an electric distribution system to serve the Villages of Pequea, Martic Forge, and Marticville. In 1930 the company's stock was acquired by Lehigh Power Securities Corp., and on 31 December 1930 it was merged into Pennsylvania Power & Light Co.

Administrative Records:
Minute Book, 1930
Stock Certificate Book, 1921-1930

Operating Records:
General Ledger, 1930
Journal Entry Register, 1930
Expenditure Requisitions, 1930
Cash Deposits and Withdrawls, 1930
Audited Voucher Register, 1930
Accounts Payable, 1930
Accounts Receivable, 1930
Construction Ledger, 1930
Fixed Capital, 1930
Detail Ledger, 1930
Accrual Record, 1930
Cash Receipts and Disbursements, 1925-1930 (2 Volumes)

Scope and Content Note:
Most of the records of the Pequea Electric Co. are financial, and document the company's operations following its 1930 acquisition by Lehigh Power Securities Corp.

725. PEQUEA ELECTRIC LIGHT, HEAT AND POWER COMPANY (Non-operating).
Lancaster County, Pequea Township.
1913, 1 Linear Inch.

History:
Pequea Electric Light, Heat and Power Co. was incorporated 28 February 1913 to supply electricity in the Township of Pequea, Lancaster County. It was consolidated and merged with four other companies 20 March 1913 to form Strasburg Electric Light, Heat and Power Co. No. 3.

726. PEQUEA TOWNSHIP ELECTRIC COMPANY (Non-operating).
Lancaster County, Pequea Township.
1912, 1 Linear Inch.

History:
Pequea Township Electric Co. was incorporated 7 November 1912 to supply electricity in the Township of Pequea, Lancaster County. On 27 November 1912 it was consolidated and merged with 13 other companies to form Edison Electric Co. No. 3.

727. PEQUEA WATER AND POWER COMPANY (Non-operating).
Lancaster County, Pequea Township.
1902, 1 Linear Inch.

History:
Pequea Water and Power Co. was incorporated 23 May 1902 to supply hydroelectric power and drinking water in the Township of Martic, Lancaster County. On 14 August 1902 the company was consolidated and merged with Muddy Creek Water and Power Co. to form Susquehanna Falls Power Co.

728. THE PERRY ELECTRIC LIGHT, HEAT AND POWER COMPANY (Operating).
Perry County, Newport Borough.
1898 to 1917, 1 Linear Foot.

History:
The Perry Electric Light, Heat and Power Co. was incorporated 16 August 1898 to supply electricity in northeastern Perry County. The company constructed a steam electric generating station, using a 75-kw generator and a 125-hp engine, in Newport Borough. Electric service to Newport, Bloomfield, and Millerstown began in 1899. In 1904 the company's stock was acquired by Mr. Edward E. Marshall, owner of Juniata Furnace and Foundry Co., and a new generating station was built on the grounds of the foundry. In 1916 Mr. Marshall sold the company's stock to consortium of businessmen who were in the process of forming Juniata Public Service Co., which was attempting to consolidate various electric companies along the Juniata and Susquehanna Rivers, north of Harrisburg. On 24 September 1924 Perry Electric was consolidated and merged with 16 other companies to form Juniata Public Service Co.

Administrative Records:
Minute Book, 1898-1917
Stock Certificate Book, 1898-1916
Stock Ledger, 1898-1916

Operating Records:
General Ledger, 1916-1917
Journal, 1916-1917
Cashbook, 1916-1917
Cash Receipts and Disbursements, 1916-1917 (2 Volumes)
Cash Analysis, 1916-1917

Scope and Content Note:
The Minute Book of The Perry Electric Light, Heat and Power Co. consists of routine minutes of stockholders' and directors' meetings, and provides basic information concerning the company's organization and capitalization, as well as a deed description of the company's property.

729. PHOENIX UTILITY COMPANY (Operating).
Lehigh County, Allentown City.
1919 to 1934, 21 Linear Feet.

History:
Phoenix Utility Co., organized in 1919, was a wholly-owned subsidiary of Electric Bond and Share Co. The company built substations, installed generating equipment, and erected transmission lines. One of its largest projects was the Wallenpaupack hydroelectric dam. In 1934 the company's name was changed to Phoenix Engineering Co.

Operating Records:
General Ledgers, 1919-1933 (6 Volumes)
Audited Voucher Register—Harrisburg Operations, 1927-1928 (2 Volumes)
Audited Voucher Register—Pennsylvania Operations, 1920-1923 (6 Volumes)
Journal Entry Vouchers—Lehigh Operations, 1919-1933 (15 Volumes)
Motor Vehicle Reports, 1922-1933 (40 Volumes)
Audit Reports, 1919-1932 (4 Volumes)
Payroll Sheets, 1929-1932 (3 Volumes)
Wallenpaupack Project Papers, 1925-1934
Final Cost Analysis (91 Volumes)
Comparison of Actual and Estimated Costs—Pennsylvania Operations, 1922
Trial Balances & Itemized Statements, 1920-1933
Balance Sheets & Supporting Schedules, 1920-1932
Acceptance Letters of Pennsylvania Power & Light Co., of Work Done By Phoenix Utility Co., 1923-1933 (2 Volumes)

Scope and Content Note:
The Records of Phoenix Utility Co. document the engineering and construction work that was performed for Pennsylvania Power & Light Co. The various jobs are described in minute detail, with analysis of the cost of labor and materials.

730. PIATT POWER & LIGHT COMPANY (Non-operating).
Lycoming County, Piatt Township.
1923 to 1924, 1 Linear Inch.

History:
Piatt Power & Light Co. was incorporated 21 November 1923 to supply electricity in the Township of Piatt, Lycoming County. On 31 March 1924 it was merged into Pennsylvania Power & Light Co.

731. PICTURE ROCKS POWER & LIGHT COMPANY (Non-operating).
Lycoming County, Picture Rocks Borough.
1924, 1 Linear Inch.

History:
Picture Rocks Power & Light Co. was incorporated 28 August 1924 to supply electricity in the Borough of Picture Rocks, Lycoming County. It was merged into The Citizens Electric Light and Power Co. of Hughesville, Pa. 6 October 1924.

732. PINE-COLUMBIA POWER & LIGHT COMPANY (Non-operating).
Columbia County, Pine Township.
1924 to 1925, 1 Linear Inch.

History:
Pine-Columbia Power & Light Co. was incorporated 28

August 1924 to supply electricity in the Township of Pine, Columbia County. On 28 October 1924 it was merged it into Pennsylvania Power & Light Co.

733. PINE CREEK POWER & LIGHT COMPANY (Non-operating).
Clinton County, Pine Creek Township.
1923 to 1924, 1 Linear Inch.

History:
Pine Creek Power & Light Co. was incorporated 21 November 1923 to supply electricity in the Township of Pine Creek, Clinton County. On 31 March 1924 it was merged into Pennsylvania Power & Light Co.

734. PINE GROVE ELECTRIC LIGHT, HEAT & POWER COMPANY (Operating).
Schuylkill County, Pine Grove Borough.
1912 to 1937, 3 1/2 Linear Feet.

History:
Pine Grove Electric Light, Heat & Power Co. was incorporated 23 October 1912 to supply electricity to Pine Grove Borough. The company purchased its power from Eastern Pennsylvania Light, Heat and Power Co. In 1922 Pine Grove Electric's stock was acquired by East Penn Electric Co., which merged it into Pennsylvania Power & Light Co.

Administrative Records:
Minute Books, 1912-1935 (2 Volumes)
Stock Certificate Books, 1912-1925
Stock Transfer Record, 1922-1925
Stock Ledger, 1922-1925

Operating Records:
FINANCIAL RECORDS
General Ledgers, 1918-1935 (3 Volumes)
Cashbooks, 1918-1925 (2 Volumes)
Record of Cash Receipts, 1925-1935
Record of Cash Disbursements, 1925-1935
Summary of Cash, 1925-1935 (2 Volumes)
Accounts Payable, 1918-1935 (2 Volumes)
Accounts Receivable Detail Ledger, 1925-1935
Construction Ledger, 1924-1925
Detail Ledger, 1925-1935
Detail of Cost Study and Fixed Capital, 1925-1927 (2 Volumes)
CONSUMER RECORDS
Record of Material Sold, 1920-1921
Summary of Accounts Receivable—Consumers, 1925-1935
Summary of Accounts Receivable—Miscllaneous, 1928-1935
Summary of Consumer's Deposits, 1925-1928
Line Extension Deposits, 1926-1928
AUDIT REPORTS, 1920-1932 (9 Volumes)

Scope and Content Note:
The Minute Books of Pine Grove Electric Light, Heat & Power Co. consist of routine minutes of stockholders' and directors' meetings. Monthly Reports list electric sales, costs of power purchased, maintenance costs, and general expenses. The Record of Material Sold is a list of customers who had their homes wired for electricity, and includes an inventory of the company's tools and equipment.

735. PINE GROVE-SCHUYLKILL POWER & LIGHT COMPANY (Non-operating).
Schuylkill County, Pine Grove Township.
1925 to 1926, 1 Linear Inch.

History:
Pine Grove-Schuylkill Power & Light Co. was incorporated 26 March 1926 to supply electricity in a portion of the Township of Pine Grove, Schuylkill County. It was merged into Pennsylvania Power & Light Co. 14 April 1926.

736. PINE GROVE TOWNSHIP-SCHUYLKILL COUNTY POWER & LIGHT COMPANY (Non-operating).
Schuylkill County, Pine Grove Township.
1927 to 1928, 1 Linear Inch.

History:
Pine Grove Township-Schuylkill County Power & Light Co., incorporated 2 September 1927 to supply electricity in a portion of the Township of Pine Grove, Schuylkill County, was merged into Pennsylvania Power & Light Co. 16 September 1927.

737. PIONEER ELECTRIC LIGHT COMPANY (Operating).
Lancaster County, Lancaster City.
1921 to 1930, 1 Linear Foot.

History:
The Lancaster County Electric Light, Heat and Power Co. was incorporated 22 March 1921 after the consolidation and merger of six non-operating companies. On 20 May 1921 this company changed its name to Pioneer Electric Light Co. It supplied electricity in several townships in southwest Lancaster County, purchasing power from Pennsylvania Water & Power Company's generating station at Holtwood on the Susquehanna River. Early in 1927, Pioneer Electric's stock was acquired by United Gas and Electric Co. In August 1927 it was acquired by Lehigh Power Securities Corp. On 31 December 1930 the company was merged into Pennsylvania Power & Light Co.

Administrative Records:
Minute Book, 1927-1930
Secretary's Papers of Meetings, 1930
Stock Certificate Book, 1921-1930
Stock Ledger, undated

Operating Records:
General Ledger, 1927-1930
Journal Entry Register, 1927-1930
Cash Receipts, 1921-1930
Audited Voucher Register, 1927-1930
Accounts Receivable, 1927-1930
Construction Work in Progress, 1927-1930
Detail Ledger, 1927-1930
Accrual Record, 1927-1930
Expenditure Requisitions, 1930
Audit Report, 1927-1929

Scope and Content Note:
The Minute Book and the Secretary's Papers of Meetings of Pioneer Electric Light Co. consist of routine minutes of stockholders' and directors' meetings.

738. PITTSTON CITY ELECTRIC COMPANY
(Non-operating).
Luzerne County, Pittston City.
1910 to 1919, 2 Linear Inches.

History:
Pittston City Electric Co. was incorporated 7 September 1910 to supply electricity in Pittston, Luzerne County. The company was never an operating company, and was formally dissolved on 8 October 1919.

739. PITTSTON ELECTRIC COMPANY (Non-operating).
Luzerne County, Pittston Borough.
1909, 1 Linear Inch.

History:
Pittston Electric Co. was incorporated 11 November 1909 to supply electricity in the Borough of Pittston, Luzerne County. Later that year the company's stock was acquired by American Gas & Electric Co., and it was then merged into Scranton Electric Co.

740. PITTSTON-LUZERNE POWER & LIGHT COMPANY (Non-operating).
Luzerne County, Pittston Borough.
1926 to 1927, 1 Linear Inch.

History:
Pittston-Luzerne Power & Light Co. was organized 16 March 1926 by Pennsylvania Power & Light Co. in order to secure charter rights in the Borough of Pittston, Luzerne County. This attempt was unsuccessful, and the company was dissolved on 25 January 1927.

741. PLAINS ELECTRIC COMPANY (Non-operating).
Luzerne County, Plains Township.
1921 to 1923, 2 Linear Inches.

History:
Plains Electric Co. was incorporated 22 March 1922 to supply electricity in the Township of Plains, Luzerne County. It was merged into Pennsylvania Power & Light Co. on 27 August 1923.

742. PLUMSTEAD TOWNSHIP ELECTRIC COMPANY
(Non-operating).
Bucks County, Plumstead Township.
1913 to 1935, 3 Linear Inches.

History:
Plumstead Township Electric Co. was incorporated 30 December 1913 by Lehigh Navigation Electric Co. in order to secure charter rights in the Township of Plumstead, Bucks County. The company remained inactive throughout its existence. Its stock was conveyed to The Lehigh Valley Light and Power Co. when that company acquired Lehigh Navigation. In 1920, Lehigh Valley Light and Power merged Plumstead Township Electric Co. into Pennsylvania Power & Light Co.

743. POCONO POWER & LIGHT COMPANY
(Non-operating).
Monroe County, Pocono Township.
1923 to 1924, 2 Linear Inches.

History:
Pocono Power & Light Co. was incorporated 1 May 1923 to supply electricity in the Township of Pocono, Monroe County. On 20 July 1923 it was consolidated and merged with 31 other non-operating companies to form Paupack Power & Light Co., No. 2.

744. POINT TOWNSHIP ELECTRIC COMPANY
(Non-operating).
Northumberland County, Point Township.
1912, 1 Linear Inch.

History:
Point Township Electric Co. was incorporated 11 October 1911 to supply electricity in the Township of Point, Northumberland County. On 31 December 1912 it was merged into Northumberland County Gas & Electric Co.

745. POINT TOWNSHIP GAS COMPANY
(Non-operating).
Northumberland County, Point Township.
1911 to 1912, 1 Linear Inch.

History:
Point Township Gas Co. was incorporated 2 February 1910 to manufacture and supply gas for lighting in the Township of Point, Northumberland County. It was merged into Northumberland Gas Heat and Fuel Co. on 20 September 1912.

746. POLK POWER & LIGHT COMPANY
(Non-operating).
Monroe County, Polk Township.
1923 to 1924, 2 Linear Inches.

History:
Polk Power & Light Co. was incorporated 1 May 1923 to supply electricity in the Township of Polk, Monroe County. On 20 July 1923 it was consolidated and merged with 31 other non-operating companies to form Paupack Power & Light Co., No. 2.

747. THE PORT CARBON & MIDDLEPORT ELECTRIC RAILWAY COMPANY (Operating).
Schuylkill County, Pottsville City.
1898 to 1923, 1/2 Linear Foot.

History:
The Port Carbon & Middleport Electric Railway Co. was incoporated in July 1898 to operate an electric street railway between the Boroughs of Port Carbon and Middleport, Schuylkill County. By July 1900 the company had secured a clear right-of-way along its proposed route, and in September 1900 construction was begun. On 15 October 1900 the company leased its property and franchises to Pottsville Union Traction Co. The first cars went into operation on the company's partially completed line in January 1901. In January 1905 the company extended its line to Tamaqua. On 25 January 1923 it was consolidated and merged with Eastern Pennsylvania Light, Heat and Power Co., and Pottsville Union Traction Co., to form Eastern Pennsylvania Power and Railway Co.

Administrative Records:
Minute Books, 1898-1923 (2 Volumes)
Stock Certificate Book, 1898-1923
Stock Transfer Record, 1916-1919

Operating Records:
General Ledger, 1898-1903
Cashbook, 1898-1906

Scope and Content Note:
In addition to routine minutes of stockholders' and directors' meetings, the Minute Books of The Port Carbon & Middleport Electric Railway Co. document the company's relationship with Pottsville Union Traction Co., the construction of its rail system, and rights-of-way.

748. THE PORT CARBON ELECTRIC LIGHT HEAT AND POWER COMPANY (Operating).
Schuylkill County, Port Carbon Borough.
1890 to 1924, 1/2 Linear Foot.

History:
The Port Carbon Electric Light Heat and Power Co. was incorporated 20 March 1890. It was the first company to supply electricity in the Borough of Port Carbon, Schuylkill County, using power plant equipment purchased from United Edison Manufacturing Co. The company's business increased so rapidly that by 1896 it had to replace its original power equipment with two 500-light dynamos, in order to meet customer demands for power. On 11 November 1902 it leased all of its property to The Edison Electric Illuminating Co. of Pottsville. In 1904 a boiler explosion forced the closing of the company's generating station in Port Carbon, and thereafter power was purchased from The Edison Electric Illuminating Company's plant in nearby Pottsville. On 17 November 1924 the company was merged into East Penn Electric Co. No. 2.

Administrative Records:
Minute Books, 1890-1924 (2 Volumes)
Stock Certificate Book, 1890-1924
Correspondence and Miscellaneous Papers, 1895-1907

Operating Records:
Daybook, 1905-1906

Scope and Content Note:
The Minute Books of The Port Carbon Light Heat and Power Co. document the company's organization, capitalization, construction and expansion. There is also information on its rates, as well as statements of earnings and expenses. Correspondence includes letters from suppliers describing the advantages of various electric components.

749. THE PORT CLINTON LIGHT, HEAT AND POWER COMPANY (Operating).
Schuylkill County, Port Clinton Borough.
1916, 1 Linear Inch.

History:
The Port Clinton Light, Heat and Power Co. was incorporated 10 October 1913 by The Auburn Electric Light, Heat and Power Co. to supply electricity in the Borough of Port Clinton, Schuylkill County. The company purchased all of its power from Auburn Electric. On 11 March 1914 the Port Clinton company sold its property and franchises to Auburn Electric, and two years later merged into Eastern Pennsylvania Light, Heat and Power Co.

Administrative Records:
Minute Book, 1916
Stock Transfer Record, 1916

750. PORTER-LYCOMING POWER & LIGHT COMPANY (Non-operating).
Lycoming County, Porter Township.
1923 to 1924, 1 Linear Inch.

History:
Porter-Lycoming Power & Light Co. was incorpoated 21 November 1923 to supply electricity in the Township of Porter, Lycoming County. It was merged into Pennsylvania Power & Light Co. on 31 March 1924.

751. PORTER POWER & LIGHT COMPANY (Non-operating).
Pike County, Porter Township.
1923 to 1924, 1 Linear Inch.

History:
Porter Power & Light Co. was incorporated 13 June 1923 to supply electricity in the Township of Porter, Pike County. On 20 July 1923 it was consolidated and merged with 31 other non-operating companies to form Paupack Power & Light Co., No. 2.

752. POTTSVILLE AND READING RAILWAY COMPANY (Operating).
Schuylkill County, Pottsville City.
1894 to 1923, 3 Linear Inches.

History:
Pottsville and Reading Railway Co. was incorporated in August 1894 to operate an electric street railway between the City of Pottsville, Schuylkill County and the City of Reading, Berks County. On 1 February 1895 the company leased its franchises and property to Schuylkill Electric Railway Co. Later that year, it secured rights to operate an electric railway in the Boroughs of Mount Carbon, Schuylkill Haven, and Cressona, and leased other rights-of-way between Mount Carbon and Reading from the Philadelphia and Reading Reading Railroad Co. On 11 October 1897 the company began to operate railway cars over these lines. The company's lease was transferred on 25 August 1899 to Pottsville Union Traction Co. On 25 January 1923 Pottsville and Reading Railway Co. was consolidated and merged with Eastern Pennsylvania Light, Heat and Power Co. and Pottsville Union Traction Co., to form Eastern Pennsylvania Power and Railway Co.

Administrative Records:
Minute Book, 1894-1923
Stock Certificate Books, 1895-1923 (2 Volumes)
Stock Transfer Record, 1915-1919
Ordinances, 1894-1908

Scope and Content Note:
The Minute Book of Pottsville and Reading Railway Co. documents routine stockholders' and directors' meetings. Also included is information on capitalization, and the company's relationship with Schuylkill Electric Railway Co. and Pottsville Union Traction Company. The ordinances contain contracts between the company and the various boroughs through which its tracks ran.

753. POTTSVILLE & ST. CLAIR ELECTRIC RAILWAY COMPANY (Operating).
Schuylkill County, St. Clair Borough.
1915 to 1923, 3 Linear Inches.

History:
Pottsville & St. Clair Electric Railway Co. was incorporated 13 October 1915 to operate an electric street railway in the Borough of St. Clair, Schuylkill County. In May 1916 the company leased its property and franchises to the Pottsville Union Traction Co. On 25 January 1923 it consolidated and merged with Eastern Pennsylvania Light, Heat and Power Co. and Pottsville Union Traction Co. to form Eastern Pennsylvania Power and Railway Co.

Administrative Records:
Minute Book, 1915-1923
Stock Certificate Book, 1915-1923
Stock Transfer Record, 1915-1919

Operating Records:
General Ledger, 1917-1922
Journal, 1915-1923
Audit Reports, 1916-1923 (3 Volumes)

Scope and Content Note:
In addition to routine minutes of stockholders' and directors' meetings, the Minute Book of the Pottsville & St. Clair Electric Railway Co. contains copies of the following documents: a very detailed trackage and traffic agreement with the Schuylkill County Railway Co., ordinances establishing the company's franchises, a state highway department permit to build its line, a construction contract for the same, and a lease with the Pottsville Union Traction Co.

754. POTTSVILLE GAS COMPANY (Operating).
Schuylkill County, Pottsville City.
1923 to 1926, 1 Linear Inch.

History:
Pottsville Gas Co. was incorporated by a special Act of the Pennsylvania General Assembly in 1850. The company owned and operated a gas plant in Pottsville, utilizing the Lowe Water Gas Process. It supplied gas in Pottsville, and in nearby Port Carbon and Mt. Carbon. Schuylkill County Light & Fuel Co. gained control of the company's stock in 1902, but was forced to relinquish it when its assets were sold at a foreclosure sale in 1920. In 1926, when the company's stock again became available, Pennsylvania Power & Light Co. audited Pottsville Gas in order to determine the advisability of acquiring it. However, no action was taken by Pennsylvania Power & Light Co., and Pottsville Gas was purchased by Central Gas & Electric Co. in 1927. Pottsville Gas Co. was still in operation in 1940, but its history thereafter is unknown.

Operating Records:
Audit Report, 1923-1926
Valuation Reports, 1926 (2 Volumes)

Scope and Content Note:
The Audit Report and Valuation Reports of Pottsville Gas Co. provide an overview of the company's organization, capitalization, and development, as well as an assessment of its financial condition.

755. POTTSVILLE-MAUCH CHUNK BUS LINE
(Operating).
Schuylkill County, Pottsville City.
1928, 1 Linear Inch.

History:
Pottsville-Mauch Chunk Bus Line was briefly controlled by Pennsylvania Power & Light Co. It was operated by Mr. H.F. Dicke, and ran buses between Mauch Chunk Borough, Carbon County, and Pottsville City, Schuylkill County, as well as special excursion trips. Its history after 1928 is unknown.

Operating Records:
Bills, 1928

756. POTTSVILLE UNION TRACTION COMPANY
(Operating).
Schuylkill County, Pottsville City.
1899 to 1925, 4 Linear Feet.

History:
Pottsville Union Traction Co. was incorporated 15 May 1899 for the purpose of consolidating and operating the various electric street railway companies in and around the City of Pottsville, Schuylkill County. On 24 August 1899 the company purchased a controlling interest in the Schuylkill Electric Railway Co. On 15 October 1900 it leased the Port Carbon and Middleport Electric Railway Co., and the next year purchased its stock. In November 1907 the company leased its power plant to the Palo Alto Heat, Light and Power Co. In return, Palo Alto Heat, Light and Power agreed to supply Pottsville Union Traction with electricity at cost. On 25 January 1923 the company consolidated and merged with its major creditor, Eastern Pennsylvania Light, Heat and Power Co., and eight smaller street railway companies to form Eastern Pennsylvania Power and Railway Co.

Administrative Records:
Minute Books, 1899-1923 (2 Volumes)
Stock Certificate Book, 1899-1923
Stock Transfer Records, 1900-1919 (2 Volumes)
Stock Ledger, 1899-1906

Operating Records:
General Ledgers, 1899-1923 (4 Volumes)
Ledger, 1906
Journals, 1899-1923 (2 Volumes)
Cashbooks, 1899-1923 (4 Volumes)
Daily Record, 1904-1905
Distribution Record, 1922-1925
Accounts Payable Ledgers, 1906-1908 (2 Volumes)
Accounts Receivable Ledger, 1906-1908
Detail of Expenditure of Requisitions, 1922-1923
Accrual Record, 1908-1919 (2 Volumes)
Distribution of Payrolls, 1909-1913 (2 Volumes)
Charges to Local Construction, 1908
Construction Ledger, 1908-1912
Construction Account, Audited and Passed, 1920-1925
Operating Statistics, 1909-1910
Operating Statistics Report, 1907-1910
Ticket Sales, 1909-1910
List of Tickets Sold, 1914-1917 (3 Volumes)
List of Car Mileage, 1908
Work Orders, 1913
Balance Sheets, 1907-1910 (2 Volumes)
Audit Reports, 1906-1923 (3 Volumes)

Scope and Content Note:
The Minute Books document Pottsville Union Traction Company's organization and growth. Included are lists of stockholders and reports of the president and treasurer. Also included are copies of lease agreements, mortgages, and accident claims. A letter from a committee of motormen and conductors represented by Division 118 of the Amalgamated Association of Street Railway Employees of America presents the union's demands for recognition, increased pay, and shorter hours.

757. PRICE POWER & LIGHT COMPANY
(Non-operating).
Monroe County, Price Township.
1923 to 1924, 2 Linear Inches.

History:
Price Power & Light Co. was incorporated 1 May 1923 to supply electricity in the Township of Price, Monroe County. On 20 July 1923 it was consolidated and merged with 31 other non-operating companies to form Paupack Power & Light Co., No. 2.

758. PRICEBURG ELECTRIC LIGHT COMPANY
(Operating).
Lackawanna County, Dickson City Borough.
1898 to 1907, 3 Linear Inches.

History:
Priceburg Electric Light Co. was incorporated 5 May 1893 to supply electricity in the Borough of Dickson City. On 21 March 1907 the company was consolidated and merged with four other electric companies to form Scranton Electric Co.

Administrative Records:
Minute Book, 1906-1907

Operating Records:
Consumers Ledger, 1896-1907

Scope and Content Note:
The Minute Book documents routine stockholders' and directors' meetings. Included is a copy of the 1907 agreement which led to the formation of the Scranton Electric Co. The Consumers Ledger lists customers, and documents the work that was done for them, e.g., installation of lights and wiring.

759. PRIMROSE ELECTRIC COMPANY
(Non-operating).
Northampton County, Bethlehem Township.
1911 to 1913, 2 Linear Inches.

History:
Primrose Electric Co. was incorporated 4 April 1911 to supply electricity in the Township of Bethlehem, Northampton County. On 23 December 1912 it was consolidated and merged with 37 other non-operating companies to form Lehigh Navigation Electric Co., No. 2.

760. PROMPTON ELECTRIC COMPANY (Operating).
Wayne County, Prompton Borough.
1922 to 1928, 1 Linear Foot.

History:
Prompton Electric Co., incorporated 30 August 1922, was the first company to supply electricity in the Borough of Prompton, Wayne County. The company built an electric distribution system in Prompton, and constructed a transmission line to the Borough of Honesdale, where it purchased its power from the Honesdale Consolidated Light, Heat and Power Co. The company's stock was acquired by Lehigh Power Securities Corp. in 1924, and it was operated as part of Pennsylvania Power & Light Co. On 28 May 1928 Prompton Electric was merged into Pennsylvania Power & Light Co.

Administrative Records:
Minute Book, 1922-1928
Stock Certificate Book, 1922-1924
Stock Transfer Record, 1922-1924
Stock Ledger, 1922-1928

Operating Records:
General Ledger, 1924-1928
Cash Received, 1924-1925
Check Register, 1924-1925
Record of Cash Receipts, 1925-1928
Record of Cash Disbursements, 1925-1928
Summary of Cash, 1925-1928
Accounts Payable, 1924-1928
Accounts Receivable, 1924-1928
Bill Register, 1924-1928
Detail Ledger, 1924-1928
Accrual Ledger, 1924-1928
Detail of Cost Study and Fixed Capital, 1925-1927 (2 Volumes)
Expenditure Requisitions, 1924-1928
Summary of Accounts Receivable—Consumers, 1924-1928
Summary of Consumers' Deposits, 1927-1928
Audit Reports, 1924-1927 (3 Volumes)

Scope and Content Note:
The Minute Book of the Prompton Electric Co. documents the construction of the company's distribution system, its problems with delinquent customers, and its financial difficulties. Also included are monthly statements of receipts and expenses.

761. PROSPECT ROCK ELECTRIC LIGHT, HEAT AND POWER COMPANY (Operating).
Luzerne County, Wilkes-Barre Township.
1905 to 1928, 1 Linear Foot.

History:
Prospect Rock Electric Light, Heat and Power Co. was incorporated 27 April 1905 to supply electricity in the Township of Wilkes-Barre, Luzerne County. In 1909 the company constructed an electric distribution system to serve the township, and began to purchase its power from Wilkes-Barre Gas and Electric Co. At the same time, it extended its operations into the Borough of Laurel Run, despite having no charter to operate there. In 1923 Prospect Rock Electric created and then absorbed a paper company, Laurel Run Electric Co., in order to obtain the necessary franchise. In 1926 its stock was acquired by Lehigh Power Securities Corp., which operated it as part of Pennsylvania Power & Light Co. On 28 May 1928 Prospect Rock was merged into Pennsylvania Power & Light.

Administrative Records:
Minute Book, 1905-1928
Stock Certificate Book, 1909-1926
Stock Transfer Record, 1926
Stock Ledger, 1909-1928

Operating Records:
General Ledgers, 1924-1928 (2 Volumes)
Cashbook, 1924-1925
Checkbook, 1924-1926
Record of Cash Receipts, 1926-1928
Record of Cash Disbursements, 1926-1928
Summary of Cash, 1926-1928
Audited Voucher Register,1926-1928
Accounts Payable, 1926-1928
Accounts Receivable, 1926-1928
Bill Register, 1926-1928
Detail Ledger, 1926-1928
Accrual Record, 1926-1928
Detail of Cost Study and Fixed Capital, 1926-1927
Expenditure Requisitions, 1926-1928
Retirement Authorities, 1926-1927
Summary of Accounts Receivable, 1926-1928 (2 Volumes)
Summary of Consumers' Deposits, 1927-1928
Audit Reports, 1923-1927 (4 Volumes)

Scope and Content Note:
The Minute Book of Prospect Run Electric Light, Heat and Power Co. documents the company's dealings with the Wilkes-Barre Township commissioners regarding street lighting contracts, the construction of the company's lighting system, its negotiations with Wilkes-Barre Gas and Electric Co. for the purchase of power, and its relationship which Laurel Run Electric Co.

762. PROVIDENCE ELECTRIC LIGHT, HEAT AND POWER COMPANY (Non-operating).
Lancaster County, Providence Township.
1913, 1 Linear Inch.

History:
Providence Electric Light, Heat and Power Co. was incorporated 2 January 1913 to supply electricity in the Township of Providence, Lancaster County. On 10 January 1913 it was consolidated and merged with four other companies to form Strasburg Electric Light, Heat and Power Co., No. 2.

763. PROVIDENCE TOWNSHIP ELECTRIC COMPANY (Non-operating).
Lancaster County, Providence Township.
1912, 1 Linear Inch.

History:
Providence Township Electric Co. was incorporated 7 November 1912 to supply electricity in the Township of Providence, Lancaster County. On 27 November 1912 it was consolidated and merged with 13 other companies to form Edison Electric Co. No. 3.

764. QUARRYVILLE ELECTRIC LIGHT, HEAT AND POWER COMPANY (Non-operating).
Lancaster County, Quarryville Borough.
1913, 1 Linear Inch.

History:
Quarryville Electric Light, Heat and Power Co. was incorporated 28 February 1913 to supply electricity in the Borough of Quarryville, Lancaster County. On 20 March 1913 it was consolidated and merged with four other companies to form Strasburg Electric Light, Heat and Power Co., No. 3.

765. RAHN TOWNSHIP ELECTRIC COMPANY (Non-operating).
Schuylkill County, Rahn Township.
1909, 1 Linear Inch.

History:
Rahn Township Electric Co., incorporated 16 June 1909 to supply electricity in Rahn Township, Schuylkill County, consolidated and merged with eleven companies to form Harwood Electric Co., 30 June 1909.

766. RAILWAY ELECTRIC LIGHT & POWER COMPANY (Non-operating).
Montgomery County, Lower Gwynedd Township.
1917, 1 Linear Inch.

History:
Railway Electric Light & Power Co. was organized in June 1917 in an effort to get charter rights in Lower Gwynedd Township, Montgomery County. For unknown reasons, the company organizers never received approval from the Public Service Commission for its charter application, and thus the company was never incorporated.

767. RALPHO ELECTRIC COMPANY (Non-operating).
Northumberland County, Ralpho Township.
1921 to 1922, 1 Linear Inch.

History:
Ralpho Electric Co., incorporated 10 August 1921 to supply electricity in Ralpho Township, Northumberland County, merged into Pennsylvania Power & Light Co., 24 January 1922.

768. RALPHO TOWNSHIP ELECTRIC LIGHT COMPANY (Non-operating).
Lancaster County, Ralpho Township.
1911, 1 Linear Inch.

History:
Ralpho Township Electric Light Co., incorporated 10 August 1911 to supply electricity in Ralpho Township, Lancaster County, consolidated and merged with 17 companies to form Edison Electric Co. No. 1, 2 October 1911.

769. RANSOM-LACKAWANNA POWER & LIGHT COMPANY (Non-operating).
Lackawanna County, Ransom Township.
1926, 1 Linear Inch.

History:
Ransom-Lackawanna Power & Light Co. was formed in March 1926 by Pennsylvania Power & Light Co. in an effort to gain charter rights in Ransom Township, Lackawanna County. The company's application for a charter was not approved, and the company was never incorporated.

770. RANSOM TOWNSHIP ELECTRIC COMPANY (Non-operating).
Lackawanna County, Ransom Township.
1923 to 1928, 1 Linear Inch.

History:
Ransom Township Electric Co., incorporated in October 1923 to supply electricity in Ransom Township, Lackawanna County, consolidated and merged with eight companies to form The Scranton Electric Co., February 1928.

771. THE RED HILL ELECTRIC LIGHT AND POWER COMPANY, LIMITED (Operating).
Montgomery Township, Red Hill Borough.
1910 to 1923, 8 Linear Inches.

History:
The Red Hill Electric Light and Power Co., Ltd. was a limited partnership association formed by residents of Red Hill Borough, Montgomery County, to construct an electrical distribution system. The company obtained power from a generating plant in Pennsburg Borough, Montgomery County. After Pennsylvania Power & Light Co. acquired the Pennsburg plant in 1923, it formed a non-operating company, Red Hill Power & Light Co., in order to obtain charter rights in Red Hill.

Administrative Records:
Minute Book, 1910-1923
Stock Certificate Book, 1910-1923
Stock Transfer Record, 1923
Correspondence and Agreements, 1910-1923

Operating Records:
Treasurers' Cashbook, 1910-1923
Audit Report, 1921-1923

Scope and Content Note:
The Minute Book documents the erection of the company's distribution system, as well as its relationship to Pennsburg Electric Light Commission.

772. RED HILL POWER & LIGHT COMPANY (Non-operating).
Montgomery County, Red Hill Borough.
1923, 1 Linear Inch.

History:
Red Hill Power & Light Co., incorporated 17 October 1923 to supply electrictiy in Red Hill Borough, Montgomery County, merged into Pennsylvania Power & Light Co., 2 November 1923.

773. REED TOWNSHIP ELECTRIC COMPANY (Non-operating).
Dauphin County, Reed Township.
1925 to 1926, 1 Linear Inch.

History:
Reed Township Electric Co. incorporated 30 June 1925 to supply electricity in Reed Township, Dauphin County, merged into Pennsylvania Power & Light Co., 20 December 1926.

774. RENOVO EDISON LIGHT, HEAT AND POWER COMPANY (Operating).
Clinton County, Renovo Borough.
1886 to 1947, 6 Linear Feet.

History:
Renovo Edison Electric Light, Heat and Power Co. was incorporated in November 1885 to supply electricity in Renovo Borough, Clinton County. The company was organized by P. B. Shaw, Pennsylvania agent for The Edison Electric Light Co., to install the Edison system of direct current and incandescent lighting. It erected a 2,000-light electric plant and a central station in 1887. In October 1915 the company extended its area of operation to South Renovo and several adjoining townships. In 1926 Republic Service Corp. acquired a controlling interest in the Renovo Company, and operated it under a management contract for twenty-one years. In 1947 the Securities and Exchange Commission found that this arrangement violated federal statute, and Republic Service Corp. was ordered to sell the Renovo Co. to Pennsylvania Power & Light Co.

Administrative Records:
Minute Books, 1886-1947 (5 Volumes)
Stock Certificate Book, 1886-1947
Stock Transfer Record and Register Certificate, 1886-1924
Letterbooks, 1892-1894, 1912-1913 (2 Volumes)

Operating Records:
General Ledgers, 1887-1947 (10 Volumes)
Journals, 1901-1947 (10 Volumes)
Cashbooks, 1888-1947 (14 Volumes)
Voucher Registers, 1926-1947 (3 Volumes)
Bills Receivable and Payable Ledger, 1901-1915
Plant Account Ledger, 1937-1947
Accounts Receivable Ledger, 1912-1934
Electric Energy Tax Record, 1933-1943
Insurance Policies, 1934-1940
Working Papers—Taxes, Budgets, Debts, 1942-1944
Financial Statements, 1942-1947
Financial Reports, 1914-1940 (6 Volumes)

Scope and Content Note:
The Minute Books for the period 1886-1926 (prior to the acquisition of the company by Republic Service Corp.) contain some information documenting the organization of the company by P.B. Shaw, and his installation of the Edison system of direct current. Shaw's relationship to Edison Electric Light Co. of New York is well documented. Also included are annual reports, lists of bills paid, and bonds issued. Letterbooks document negotiations with the Renovo Central Labor Union over wages and hours.

775. RENOVO HEATING COMPANY (Operating).
Clinton County, Renovo Borough.
1913 to 1947, 1 Linear Foot.

History:
In 1901 Renovo Edison Light, Heat and Power Co. of Renovo, Pa., constructed a steam-heating system in Renovo Borough. It operated this business until 1912, when it organized Renovo Heating Co., to which it sold the system in exchange for $31,000 of the new company's

capital stock. The electric company furnished steam to the heating company in exchange for one-third of the steam company's annual gross receipts. In 1947, after Pennsylvania Power & Light Co. acquired the electric company, the steam heating equipment distribution system and the stock of Renovo Heating Co. were sold to a private individual.

Operating Records:
General Ledgers, 1913-1941 (3 Volumes)
Journals, 1913-1940 (2 Volumes)
Cashbooks, 1912-1945 (7 Volumes)
Financial Reports, 1914-1926
Financial Statements, 1942-1947
Trial Balance, 1942-1944

776. RICHLAND ELECTRIC LIGHT AND POWER COMPANY (Operating).
Bucks County, Richlandtown Borough.
1912 to 1914, 6 Linear Inches.

History:
Richland Electric Light and Power Co. was incorporated 6 June 1912 to supply electricity in Richlandtown Borough, Bucks County. It was formed by Allentown Electric Light and Power Co. in order to construct a 2,300-volt 3-phase tie-line from Lehigh Valley Transit Company's Quakertown Substation to Richlandtown Borough, and to build a distribution system. Following construction, the company was merged into Lehigh Valley Light and Power Co.,No. 3.

Administrative Records:
Minute Book, 1912-1913
Stock Certificate Book, 1912-1913

Operating Records:
General Ledger, 1912-1914
Journal, 1912-1914
Cashbook, 1912-1914
Voucher Index, 1912-1914
Construction Ledger, 1912-1913

777. RICHLAND TOWNSHIP ELECTRIC LIGHT AND POWER COMPANY (Non-operating).
Bucks County, Richland Township.
1913, 1 Linear Inch.

History:
Richland Township Electric Light And Power Co., incorporated 8 December 1913 to supply electricity in Richland Township, Bucks County, merged into Lehigh Valley Light and Power Co., No. 3, 19 December 1913.

778. RIEGELSVILLE ELECTRIC COMPANY (Non-operating).
Bucks County, Riegelsville Borough.
1916 to 1935, 1 Linear Inch.

History:
Riegelsville Electric Co., incorporated 30 November 1916 to supply electricity in Riegelsville Borough, Bucks County, was one of 13 non-operating 'paper companies' organized by Lehigh Navigation Electric Co. to gain franchise rights. The companies were never merged into Lehigh Navigation, because it was deemed preferable to forfeit their charters rather than furnish electricity to a handful of customers. The charter of Riegelsville Electric Co. was listed as 'inactive' as of 1926.

779. RINGTOWN LIGHT, HEAT AND POWER COMPANY (Operating).
Schuylkill County, Ringtown Borough.
1908 to 1928, 1 Linear Foot.

History:
Ringtown Light, Heat and Power Co. was incorporated in October 1908 to supply electricity in Ringtown Borough, Schuylkill County. The company erected a 50-kw hydroelectric plant to generate power, but an inadequate supply of water forced the company to abandon this plant in favor of a steam electric generating station. In 1914, the company began to buy power from The Schuylkill Gas and Electric Co. Its stock was acquired by Lehigh Power and Securities Corp. in 1926, which two years later merged it into Pennsylvania Power & Light Co.

Administrative Records:
Minute Book, 1908-1928
Stock Certificate Book, 1908-1926
Stock Transfer Record, 1926
Stock Ledger, 1908-1928

Operating Records:
General Ledgers, 1908-1914, 1926-1928 (2 Volumes)
Journal Entry Register, 1926-1928
Record of Cash Receipts, 1920-1928
Record of Cash Disbursements, 1926-1928
Summary of Cash, 1926-1928
Audited Voucher Register, 1926-1928
Analysis of Material Charges, 1927
Detail of Cost Study and Fixed Capital, 1926-1927
Expenditure Requisitons, 1926-1928
Retirement Authorities, 1927-1928
Summary of Accounts Receivable—Consumers, 1926-1928
Summary of Consumers' Deposits, 1926-1928
Summary of Cashier's Overs and Shorts, 1926-1928
Audit Reports, 1923-1927 (4 Volumes)

Scope and Content Note:
The Minute Book documents routine directors' and stockholders meetings. Included is some information on rate setting and negotiations for street lighting contracts. Also documented are company procedures for sending out salesmen to represent it in bidding for contracts.

780. RIVERS AND STREAMS COMPANY (Operating).
Bucks County, Tinicum Township.
1925, 1 Linear Inch.

History:
Rivers and Streams Company was a New Jersey holding company that was formed in the early 1920's to develop a unified hydroelectric power system for the Musconetong, Pehatcong and Delaware Rivers. It formed a small electric company and organized a construction company, but in 1925, when Pennsylvania Power & Light Co. conducted a preliminary audit, it discovered that the project had been stillborn.

Operating Records:
Audit Report, 1925

Scope and Content Note:
The Audit Report contains a brief historical outline of

Rivers and Streams Company, and describes the companies it controlled. Included is a memorandum estimating the cost of developing a 10,000-horsepower hydroelectric plant along the Delaware River at Marshall Island, near Tinicum Township in Bucks County.

781. ROARING BROOK POWER & LIGHT COMPANY (Non-operating).
Lackawanna County, Roaring Brook Township.
1923, 1 Linear Inch.

History:
Roaring Brook Power & Light Co. was organized by Pennsylvania Power & Light Co. in March 1923 in order to get charter rights in Roaring Brook Township, Lackawanna County, but its application was rejected by the Pennsylvania Public Service Commission. The company was never incorporated.

782. ROARING CREEK-COLUMBIA POWER & LIGHT COMPANY (Non-operating).
Columbia County, Roaring Creek Township.
1928, 1 Linear Inch.

History:
Roaring Creek-Columbia Power & Light Co., incorporated 10 May 1928 to supply electricity in Roaring Creek Township, Columbia County, merged into Pennsylvania Power & Light Co., 1 August 1928.

783. ROCKEFELLER-NORTHUMBERLAND POWER & LIGHT COMPANY (Non-operating).
Northumberland County, Rockefeller Township.
1926 to 1927, 1 Linear Inch.

History:
Rockefeller-Northumberland Power & Light Co., incorporated 12 January 1927 to supply electricity in Rockefeller Township, Northumberland County, merged into Pennsylvania Power & Light Co., 25 April 1927.

784. ROCKLAND TOWNSHIP ELECTRIC COMPANY (Non-operating).
Berks County, Rockland Township.
1916, 1 Linear Inch.

History:
Rockland Township Electric Co., incorporated 25 January 1916 to supply electricity in Rockland Township, Berks County, merged into Pennsylvania Power & Light Co., 30 October 1916.

785. ROSS-MONROE POWER & LIGNT COMPANY (Non-operating).
Monroe County, Ross Township.
1925, 1 Linear Inch.

History:
Ross-Monroe Power & Light Co., incorporated 7 April 1925 to supply electricity in Ross Township, Monroe County, merged into Pennsylvania Power & Light Co., 8 June 1925.

786. RUSCOMBMANOR TOWNSHIP ELECTRIC COMPANY (Non-operating).
Berks County, Ruscombmanor Township.
1916, 1 Linear Inch.

History:
Ruscombmanor Township Electric Co., incorporated 25 January 1916 to supply electricity in Ruscombmanor Township, Berks County, merged into Pennsylvania Power & Light Co., 30 October 1916.

787. RUSH TOWNSHIP ELECTRIC COMPANY (DAUPHIN) (Non-operating).
Dauphin County, Rush Township.
1924, 1 Linear Inch.

History:
Rush Township Electric Co., incorporated 13 August 1924 to supply electricity in Rush Township, Dauphin County, merged into Pennsylvania Power & Light Co., 6 October 1924.

788. RUSH TOWNSHIP ELECTRIC COMPANY (NORTHUMBERLAND) (Non-operating).
Northumberland County, Rush Township.
1916 to 1917, 1 Linear Inch.

History:
Rush Township Electric Co., incorporated 3 August 1916 to supply electricity in Rush Township, Northumberland County, merged into Pennsylvania Power & Light Co., 23 July 1917.

789. RUSH TOWNSHIP ELECTRIC COMPANY (SCHUYLKILL) (Non-operating).
Schuylkill County, Rush Township.
1909, 1 Linear Inch.

History:
Rush Township Electric Co., incorporated 16 June 1909 to supply electricity in Rush Township, Schuylkill County, consolidated and merged with eleven companies to form Harwood Electric Co., 30 July 1909.

790. RUSH TOWNSHIP-NORTHUMBERLAND ELECTRIC COMPANY (Non-operating).
Northumberland County, Rush Township.
1919 to 1920, 1 Linear Inch.

History:
Rush Township-Northumberland Electric Co., incorporated 6 November 1919 to supply electricity in Rush Township, Northumberland County, merged into Lehigh Industrial Power Co., 1 June 1920.

791. SADSBURY TOWNSHIP ELECTRIC COMPANY (Non-operating).
Lancaster County, Sadsbury Township.
1912, 1 Linear Inch.

History:
Sadsbury Township Electric Co., incorporated 25 April 1912 to supply electricity in Sadsbury Township, Lancaster County consolidated and merged with six companies to form Christiana Suburban Electric Co., 15 May 1912.

792. SALEM POWER & LIGHT COMPANY (Non-operating).
Wayne County, Salem Township.
1923 to 1924, 1 Linear Inch.

History:
Salem Power & Light Co., incorporated 1 May 1923 to supply electricity in Salem Township, Wayne County,

consolidated and merged with 31 companies to form Paupack Power & Light Co., No. 2, 29 January 1924.

793. SALFORD-MONTGOMERY POWER & LIGHT COMPANY (Non-operating).
Montgomery County, Salford Township.
1927, 1 Linear Inch.

History:
Salford-Montgomery Power & Light Co., incorporated 11 July 1927 to supply electricity in Salford Township, Montgomery County, merged into Pennsylvania Power & Light Co., 11 October 1927.

794. SALISBURY ELECTRIC LIGHT AND POWER COMPANY (Non-operating).
Lehigh County, Salisbury Township.
1911 to 1913, 1 Linear Inch.

History:
Salisbury Electric Light and Power Co., incorporated 10 November 1911 to supply electricity in Salisbury Township. Lehigh County, consolidated and merged with ten companies to form Lehigh Valley Light and Power Co., No. 2, January 1913.

795. SALISBURY TOWNSHIP ELECTRIC COMPANY (Non-operating).
Lancaster County, Salisbury Township.
1912, 1 Linear Inch.

History:
Salisbury Township Electric Co., incorporated 25 April 1912 to supply electricity in Salisbury Township, Lancaster County, consolidated and merged with six companies to form Christiana Suburban Electric Co., 15 May 1912.

796. SALLADSBURG-LYCOMING POWER & LIGHT COMPANY (Non-operating).
Lycoming County, Salladsburg Township.
1928, 1 Linear Inch.

History:
Salladsburg-Lycoming Power & Light Co., incorporated 14 May 1928 to supply electricity in Salladsburg Township, Lycomin County, merged into Pennsylvania Power & Light Co., 29 June 1928.

797. SAMBO ELECTRIC LIGHT AND POWER COMPANY (Non-operating).
Monroe Township, East Stroudsburg Township.
1 1913, 1 Linear Inch.

History:
Sambo Electric Light and Power Co., incorporated 21 April 1913 to supply electricity in East Stroudsburg Township, Monroe County, consolidated and merged with The Stroudsburg Electric Light and Power Co., No. 1, to form The Stroudsburg Electric Light and Power Co., No. 2, 28 July 1913.

798. SAUCONA ELECTRIC LIGHT, HEAT AND POWER COMPANY (Non-operating).
Northampton County, Saucon Township.
1911 to 1913, 1 Linear Inch.

History:
Saucona Electric Light, Heat and Power Co., incorporated 24 July 1911 to supply electricity in Saucon Township, Northampton County, consolidated and merged with ten companies to form Lehigh Valley Light and Power Co., No. 2, 2 January 1913.

799. SCHUYLKILL ELECTRIC COMPANY (Operating).
Schuylkill County, Girardville Borough.
1913 to 1928, 6 Linear Feet.

History:
Schuylkill Electric Co. was formed in December 1913 through the consolidation and merger of Schuylkill Light, Heat and Power Co. and ten non-operating companies. It supplied electricity to several communities in the anthracite regions of Schuylkill and Columbia Counties. Organized by the directors of Schuylkill Railway Co., it used a powerhouse in Girardville and a substation in Mahanoy City to generate power for the railway, and to serve residential and commercial customers in adjacent communities. The company competed with Eastern Pennsylvania Light, Heat and Power Co. To meet this challange it negotiated a contract with The Schuylkill Gas and Electric Co. to purchase power. In 1923, Lehigh Power Securities Corp. acquired the company, and five years later merged it into Pennsylvania Power & Light Co.

Administrative Records:
Minute Books, 1913-1928 (2 Volumes)
Stock Certificate Book, 1913-1924
Stock Transfer Record, 1923-1924
Stock Ledger, 1914-1928
Correspondence and Memoranda, 1918-1926
Tariff and Rate Papers, 1920-1923 (1 Box)

Operating Records:
FINANCIAL RECORDS
General Ledgers, 1913-1928 (5 Volumes)
Journals, 1913-1923 (2 Volumes)
Journal Entry Register, 1923-1928
Cashbooks, 1913-1923 (2 Volumes)
Daily Cash Receipts, 1921-1923
Cash Received, 1923-1925
Cash Register, 1923-1925
Record of Cash Receipts, 1925-1928
Record of Cash Disbursements, 1925-1928
Cashbooks, 1914-1923 (5 Volumes)
Invoice Records, 1919-1923 (3 Volumes)
Accounts Payable, 1922-1928 (2 Volumes)
Bill Register, 1926-1928
Operating Ledger, 1920-1923
Detail Ledger, 1926-1928
Accrual Record, 1923-1928
Detail of Cost Study and Fixed Capital, 1925-1927
Purchase Orders, 1919-1923
Closing Entries, 1921
Annual Financial Reports, 1921-1922
PERSONNEL RECORDS
Labor Analysis Sheets, 1921-1923
Statement of Workmen's Compensation Insurance, 1923
Workmen's Compensation Insurance Accrual Statements, 1924-1928
Payroll and Salary Vouchers, 1919-1922
CONSUMER RECORDS
Recapitulation of Consumers' Ledger, 1920-1923 (6 Volumes)

Bills Rendered, 1921-1923
Current Rendered Bills, 1918-1922
Accounts Receivable, 1924-1928
Summary of Accounts Receivable, 1923-1928
Summary of Accounts Receivable—Miscellaneous, 1923-1927
Statements of House Wiring Contracts, 1926-1927
Summary of Consumers' Deposits, 1925-1928
AUDIT REPORTS, 1923-1926 (3 Volumes)

Scope and Content Note:
The Minute Books document company operations in detail and discuss the merits of various electric railway power systems. Thomson-Houston and Shortline equipment are compared. Company welfare work and contributions to the Young Men's Christian Association are also documented. Records describe accident insurance claims and resulting law suits.

800. SCHUYLKILL ELECTRIC RAILWAY COMPANY (Operating).
Schuylkill County, Pottsville City.
1889 to 1923, 2 Linear Feet.

History:
Schuylkill Electric Railway Co. was incorporated 4 October 1889 to build and operate an electric street railway in Pottsville. In 1899 the company was leased to Pottsville Union Traction Co. which was in the process of consolidating the various street railways in the area under its control. On 25 January 1923 Pottsville Union Traction Co. and Eastern Pennsylvania Light, Heat and Power Co. were consolidated and merged to form Eastern Pennsylvania Power and Railway Co.

Administrative Records:
Minute Books—Directors' Minutes, 1889-1908 (2 Volumes)
Minute Books—Stockholders' Minutes, 1889-1907 (2 Volumes)
Minute Books—Directors' and Stockholders' Minutes, 1908-1923 (2 Volumes)
Stock Certificate Books, 1890-1923 (3 Volumes)
Dividends Paid Book, 1891-1892
Index to Contents of Vault, undated

Operating Records:
General Ledgers, 1889-1899 (4 Volumes)
Journal, 1896-1899
Daybook, 1889-1892
Cashbook, 1889-1898
Storeroom Material Ledger, 1921-1923
Trial Balance, 1891-1892
Inventory, 1891
Audit Reports, 1919-1923 (2 Volumes)

Scope and Content Note:
The Minute Books document the company operations in detail. The debate over the choice of an electric railway system is of particular interest, as the merits of both the Thomson-Houston system, and The Shortline Railway system were discussed and compared. Also documented are the company's charitable contributions to the Young Men's Christian Association, and its welfare work. In addition, the Minute Books record accident insurance claims against the company, and discuss the resulting law suits.

801. SCHUYLKILL GAS AND ELECTRIC COMPANY (Non-operating).
Schuylkill County, Mahanoy Township.
1911 to 1913, 3 Linear Inches.

History:
Originally incorporated 26 January 1911 as Mahanoy Township Electric Co., to supply electricity in Mahanoy Township, Schuylkill County, this company changed its name in June 1911 to Schuylkill Gas and Electric Co. It consolidated and merged with eleven companies to form The Schuylkill Gas and Electric Co., 6 January 1913.

802. THE SCHUYLKILL GAS AND ELECTRIC COMPANY (Operating).
Schuylkill County, Mahanoy City Borough.
1911 to 1920, 5 Linear Feet.

History:
The Schuylkill Gas and Electric Co. was organized 6 January 1913 through the consolidation and merger of 12 small electric companies. It was organized by Calvin Pardee and associates (who had also organized The Harwood Electric Co.), but were seeking a market for the surplus power that was being generated by the Harwood plant. A survey of the electric companies serving the Shenandoah Valley revealed that there were a large number of small utilities operating in a very limited market. The resultant cutthroat competition had forced all of them to the verge of bankruptcy. The Pardee interests therefore bought the stocks of most of these small electric companies, in order to merge them and create a more rational integrated system. This effort culminated in the formation of The Schuylkill Gas and Electric Co. The new company abandoned most of the area's inefficient power plants and constructed a distribution system that tied the region to the Harwood plant. In 1917, Lehigh Power Securities Corp. acquired the stock of The Schuylkill Gas and Electric Co. and three years later consolidated and merged it with six others to form Pennsylvania Power & Light Co.

Administrative Records:
Minute Book, 1912-1920
Stock Certificate Book, 1913-1920
Stock Transfer Record, 1916-1920
Securities Register, 1913-1916
Bond Registers, 1911-1915 (3 Volumes)
Bonds Outstanding, 1915-1916
Interest on Demand Notes, 1912-1914
Correspondence and Memoranda, 1911-1913
Report on Steam Heating System for The Schuylkill Gas and Electric Co., 1914

Operating Records:
FINANCIAL RECORDS
General Ledgers, 1913-1920 (3 Volumes)
Journals, 1913-1920 (2 Volumes)
Cash Received and Check Register, 1913-1914
Cashbook, 1914-1919
Cash Received, 1919-1920
Audited Vouchers, 1914-1916 (2 Volumes)
Daily Cash Receipts, 1914-1915
Supplementary Cashbooks, 1914-1919 (2 Volumes)
Unpaid Vouchers List, 1914-1916

Accounts Payable, 1914-1920
Accounts Payable—Transfer, 1914-1917
Accounts Payable—Balances, 1919-1920
Detail Operating Ledgers, 1913-1920 (2 Volumes)
Accrual Record, 1914-1916
Accrual Registers, 1919-1920 (2 Volumes)
Profit and Loss Accounts, 1914-1916
Monthly Reports, 1919-1920
Financial Reports, 1913-1918
Detail Repair and Construction Ledger, 1918-1920
Repair and Retirement Authority Ledger, 1913-1919
Incomplete Improvements and Special Work Chargeable, 1915-1919
Consumers' Deposits, 1917-1919
Five Year Comparative Statement, 1914-1919
PERSONNEL RECORDS
Accident Register, 1916-1917
Compensation Register, 1916-1917
Payrolls—Workmen's Compensation Insurance, 1918-1919
Payrolls—Private, 1913-1918
Classification of Payrolls Applying to Workmen's Compensation Insurance, 1918-1919
Classification of Payrolls Applying to Public Liability Insurance, 1916-1919
Number of Employees and Earnings, 1914-1917, 1920
Workmen's Compensation Insurance Vouchers, 1916
CONSUMER RECORDS
Sales and Allowances Made to Consumers, 1919-1920
Statement of Bad Accounts, 1913-1916
Merchandise Sales and Expense Reports, 1919-1920
AUDIT REPORTS, 1914-1920 (8 Volumes)

Scope and Content Note:

Correspondence (1911-1913) documents the formation of The Schuylkill Gas and Electric Co. There are details on the organization of the non-operating township companies which were needed to secure charter rights in the area. The letters between Alfred D. Pardee, president and A.W. Drake, vice-president, document stock purchases, bond issues and the company's legal problems. A report on the steam heating system of The Schuylkill Gas and Electric Co.,prepared in 1914, details the company's industrial, commercial and residential customers, and the income derived from each group. Also included are cost estimates and blueprints for new substations.

803. THE SCHUYLKILL HAVEN & ORWIGSBURG STREET RAILWAY COMPANY (Operating).
Schuylkill County, Schuylkill Haven Borough.
1898 to 1923, 3 Linear Inches.

History:

The Schuylkill Haven & Orwigsburg Street Railway Co. was incorporated in March 1898 to build and operate an electric street railway between the boroughs of Schuylkill Haven and Orwigsburg in Schuylkill County. The line, six miles in length, was roughly circular and connected to the line of the Pottsville and Reading Railroad. In order to secure the necessary power the company leased the Schuylkill Electric Railway Co. In January 1923 it merged with seven other railway companies to form Eastern Pennsylvania Power and Railway Co.

Administrative Records:
Minute Books, 1898-1923 (2 Volumes)
Stock Certificate Book, 1895-1922

Operating Records:
General Ledger, 1898-1905
Audit Report, 1923

Scope and Content Note:

The first Minute Book, 1898-1919, documents the construction of the railroad, efforts to secure right-of-way agreements, and the company's leases with Schuylkill Electric Railway Co.

804. SCHUYLKILL LIGHT, HEAT AND POWER COMPANY (Operating).
Schuylkill County, Girardville Borough.
1900 to 1913, 1 Linear Inch.

History:

Schuylkill Light, Heat and Power Co. was incorporated in February 1901 by Schuylkill Railway Co. in order to supply electricity in Girardville Borough, Schuylkill County. The railway company thus directly competed with The Frackville and Gilberton Light, Heat and Power Co. which was the major supplier of incandescent lighting in Girardville. On 19 December, 1913, seeking to extend the electric company's territory, Schuylkill Railway organized ten non-operating companies and merged them to form Schuylkill Electric Co.

Administrative Records:
Minute Book, 1900-9913

Operating Records:
Accounts Payable, 1902-1903

805. SCHUYLKILL SUBWAY COMPANY (Non-operating).
Schuylkill County, Pottsville City.
1902, 1 Linear Inch.

History:

In a June 1902 meeting, officials of The Edison Electric Illuminating Co. explored the possibility of establishing a Schuylkill Subway Co. These plans, however, never went beyond this initial meeting.

806. SCOTT TOWNSHIP ELECTRIC CORPORATION (Non-operating).
Lackawanna County, Scott Township.
1923 to 1928, 1 Linear Inch.

History:

Scott Township Electric Corp., incorporated 11 September 1923 to supply electricity in Scott Township, Lackawanna County, consolidated and merged with eight companies to form The Scranton Electric Co., 3 February 1928.

807. SCRANTON ELECTRIC COMPANY (Operating).
Lackawanna County, Scranton City.
1907 to 1928, 8 Linear Feet.

History:

Scranton Electric Co. was organized in April 1907 through the consolidation and merger of the five electric companies operating in the city of Scranton and adjacent areas of Lackawanna County. The company thus acquired a monopoly over Scranton's electric generating and distribution system. It built three central power substations of 6900-kw capacity to generate the power that it sold to 60,000 residential and commercial customers. It also negotiated street lighting contracts in Scranton and the boroughs of Dunmore, Throop and Dickson. In 1928, it acquired Lackawanna Valley Electric Light & Power Supply Co. of Carbondale, and extended its area of operations to that borough. Scranton Electric Co. was controlled by American Gas & Electric Co. This New Jersey holding company was controlled by Electric Bond and Share Co., which until the late 1920s was controlled by General Electric. Electric Bond and Share also controlled Pennsylvania Power & Light Co.; Scranton Electric Co. and PP&L, therefore, worked together and never competed with each other. In 1927, the two companies built a 50,000-kw hydroelectric generating station in Harding, Pa. As part of this effort they organized Exter Power Corp. In November of 1927, this corporation changed its name to The Scranton Electric Co. No. 1. Three months later Scranton Electric Co. and The Scranton Electric Co. No. 1 merged to form The Scranton Electric Co. No. 2. In 1956 Pennsylvania Power & Light Co. formally acquired The Scranton Electric Co. No. 2.

Administrative Records:
Stock Certificate Books, 1907-1928 (3 Volumes)

Operating Records:
General Ledgers, 1907-1928 (7 Volumes)
Cashbooks, 1913-1928 (9 Volumes)
Accounts Payable Ledgers, 1916-1928 (5 Volumes)
Construction Work in Progress Ledgers, 1909-1928 (14 Volumes)
Insurance Register, 1925-1928
Rent Register, 1925-1928
Invoice and Journal Entry Registers, 1919-1928 (6 Volumes)

Scope and Content Note:
Most of the company's Administrative Records, including its Minute Books, were destroyed in 1939. Operating Records document Scranton Electric Company's many ambitious building projects, and detail the construction of the Harding hydroelectric plant.

808. SCRANTON ELECTRIC COMPANY NO. 2
(Operating).
Lackawanna County, Scranton City.
1921 to 1956, 30 Linear Feet.

History:
The Scranton Electric Co. No. 2 was organized in February 1928 through the consolidation and merger of seven non-operating township companies with Scranton Electric Co. and The Scranton Electric Co. No. 1. The Scranton Electric Co No. 2 supplied electricity to the city of Scranton, Lackawanna County and parts of Wyoming, Susquehanna, and Wayne Counties. This area, which is the heart of Pennsylvania's anthracite coal region, contained more than 80,000 residential and 10,000 commercial customers. In order to meet this demand the company generated power at three large plants: (1) the 50,000-kw Harding plant, (2) the 62,000-kw Suburban Low Pressure Station located in Scranton, built in 1929, and (3) the 25,000-kw Suburban High Pressure Station, also located in Scranton and built in 1948.

History:
American Gas and Electric Co., a New Jersey holding company, controlled The Scranton Electric Co. No. 2 until 1946. After some complicated stock transactions, Pennsylvania Power & Light acquired 91% of the company's stock in July of 1953. In October, the two company's merged. It took almost three years for this agreement to be approved by the Pennsylvania Public Utilities Commission. When it finally was in January of 1956, The Scranton Electric Co. No. 2 was formally designated as Pennsylvania Power & Light Co.'s Scranton Division.

Administrative Records:
Minute Books, 1927-1954 (12 Volumes)
STOCK AND BOND RECORDS
Stock Certificate Book, 1928-1946
Stock Transfer Records, 1920-1955 (7 Volumes)
List of Security Holders, 1954

Operating Records:
FINANCIAL RECORDS
General Ledgers, 1928-1953 (10 Volumes)
General Ledgers—Stanton Station Div., 1937-1952 (3 Volumes)
General Ledger—Construction Dept., 1946-1948, 1952-1954
General Ledger—Investment in Stanton Plant by The Scranton Electric Co. and Pennsylvania Power & Light Co., 1925-1929
Cashbooks, 1928-1955 (12 Volumes)
Cashbooks—Stanton Station Div., 1937-1954 (2 Volumes)
Cashbook—Construction Dept., 1946-1948
Consumers' Deposits Ledger, 1931-1933
Rents Receivable—Associated Companies, 1929-1954
Accounts Receivable—Construction Dept., Suburban Plant, 1946
Accounts Receivable Miscellaneous Ledgers, 1929-1954 (8 Volumes)
Accounts Receivable—Stanton Station Div., 1937-1954
Operating Expense Ledgers, 1929-1953 (17 Volumes)
Operating Expense Ledgers—Stanton Station Division., 1937-1954 (3 Volumes)
Construction Work in Progress Ledgers, 1926-1939 (13 Volumes)
Construction Work in Progress—Stanton Station Unit 3, 1952-1943 (12 Volumes)
Construction Work in Progress—Plant Extensions, 1921-1924 (3 Volumes)
Automotive Maintenance, Construction, Cost Ledgers, 1929-1943 (5 Volumes)
Transportation Expense Clearing Ledger, 1944-1954
Merchandise and Jobbing Expense Ledger, 1929-1954
Merchandise Stock Ledger, 1931-1934
Fuel Ledgers, 1927-1928 (2 Volumes)
Daily Coal Records—Stanton Station Div., 1941-1943, 1952-1955 (4 Volumes)
Daily Coal Records—Stanton Station, Unit Number 3, 1953-1955
Daily Coal Records—Suburban Plant, 1954-1955
Insurance, Tax and Rent Registers, 1929-1947 (19 Volumes)
Rent Registers, 1947-1953 (13 Volumes)

Insurance and Tax Registers—Stanton Station Div., 1937-1953 (13 Volumes)
Trial Balances, 1937-1953 (9 Volumes)
Trial Balances—Stanton Station Div., 1937-1954 (2 Volumes)
Trial Balances—Construction Dept., 1946-1954
Steam Heat Services—Construction Work in Progress, 1954-1955
Automotive Cost Report, 1929-1938
PERSONNEL RECORDS
Confidential Payroll Check Register Sheets, 1951-1956 (11 Volumes)

Scope and Content Note:

The Minute Books of The Scranton Electric Co. No. 2 (1927-1946)) document stock, bond, mortgage transactions, and mergers. The records describe the company's relationships with the American Gas & Electric and Pennsylvania Power & Light Company. There is also some information documenting the company's relationship with the National Industrial Recovery Administration which sought to enforce compliance with the Roosevelt Administration's Codes of Fair Competition during the depression of the 1930s. The Minute Books describe the company's opposition to the Public Utility Holding Co. Act of 1935. There is also considerable documentation on the company's pension and retirement plan which was organized in 1940.

After May 1946, following the company's sale to Irving Trust Co., the Minute Books become much more detailed. Included are revenue, expense, income, and dividend statements, and reports to stockholders. There are full accounts of advertising; sales promotion campaigns; and the company's efforts to improve its community relations, which brought it into contact with the Chamber of Commerce, the Young Men's Christian Association, and the Community Chest. The Minutes also describe construction projects and document rate schedules, as well as the process by which the Pennsylvania Public Utilities Commission set them. There is also a good deal of information on employee relations and the collective bargaining contracts that were negotiated with both the American Federation of Labor and the Congress of Industrial Organizations. The company's effort to establish an Employees' Welfare Association is well described. Finally, statements of uncollected customer bills during the depression of the 1930s provide a good deal of useful information on unemployment and population mobility.

809. SCRANTON ELECTRIC LIGHT AND HEAT COMPANY (Operating).
Lackawanna County, Scranton City.
1894 to 1907, 1 Linear Inch.

History:

Scranton Electric Light was incorporated 12 May 1883 to supply electricity in the city of Scranton, Lackawanna County. At some point prior to 1899, its stock was acquired by Pennsylvania Manufacturing Light & Power Co., a holding company; and then control passed to the Electric Co. of America. The Scranton company was one of five which consolidated and merged in April 1907 to form Scranton Electric Co.

Operating Records:

General Ledger, 1894-1907

810. SELINSGROVE GAS COMPANY (Non-operating).
Snyder County, Selinsgrove Borough.
1912, 1 Linear Inch.

History:

Selinsgrove Gas Co., incorporated 25 January 1912 to manufacture and supply gas for heat and fuel in Selinsgrove Borough, Snyder County, merged into Northumberland County Gas & Electric Co., 31 December 1912.

811. SELINSGROVE GAS LIGHT COMPANY (Non-operating).
Snyder County, Selinsgrove Borough.
1912, 1 Linear Inch.

History:

Selinsgrove Gas Light Co., incorporated 25 January 1912 to supply manufactured gas for lighting in Selinsgrove Borough, merged into Northumberland County Gas & Electric Co., 31 December 1912.

812. SELLERSVILLE POWER & LIGHT COMPANY (Non-operating).
Bucks County, Sellersville Borough.
1923, 1 Linear Inch.

History:

Sellersville Power & Light Co., incorporated 24 April 1923 to supply electricity in Sellersville Borough, Bucks County, merged into Pennsylvania Power & Light Co., 1 October 1923.

813. SHAMOKIN AND COAL TOWNSHIP LIGHT AND POWER COMPANY (Operating).
Northumberland County, Shamokin Borough.
1900 to 1909, 2 Linear Feet.

History:

Shamokin and Coal Township Light and Power Co. was incorporated in September 1900 to supply electricity in Shamokin Borough and Coal Township, Northumberland County. It was organized by local residents who were dissatisfied with the service provided by Shamokin Light, Heat and Power Co. The company built a power plant equipped with 250-kw Westinghouse generators, and installed two Erie City steam engines, representing the latest state of the art, having been exhibited at the Buffalo Pan-American Exposition of 1901. Given the competition prevailing in Shamokin (4 electric companies), it is little wonder that the company experienced considerable difficulties during its eight years of existence. In January 1908 it consolidated and merged with five companies, including its competitors, to form Shamokin and Coal Township Light, Heat and Power Co.

Administrative Records:

Secretary's Papers of Meetings, 1902-1906 (1 Box)
Stock Certificate Book, 1901
Stock Ledger, 1900-1907
Stock Subscription Ledger, 1900-1903
Correspondence, 1901-1907 (1 Box)

Operating Records:

General Ledger, 1907-1909
Journals, 1905-1909 (2 Volumes)
Cashbooks, 1900-1908 (7 Volumes)
Bills Payable and Receivable, 1901-1908

Accounts Payable During Construction, 1907-1908
Time Book, 1901-1908
Consumers Ledger, 1902-1907
Treasurers Monthly Reports, 1901-1908

Scope and Content Note:

Correspondence largely consists of letters from suppliers of electrical apparatus, which document the construction of Shamokin generating station. The correspondence with officials of Erie City Iron Works provides a good picture of general business conditions, and documents the impact that iron and steel strikes had on production.

The papers of the company's Secretary contain minutes of directors' meetings, annual reports, and financial statements. They also document the company's legal problems, efforts to increase its capitalization, and the effects that cutthroat competition had on profitability. Finally, the Superintendent's report of January 1902 evaluates the efficiency of the company's generating and distribution system.

814. SHAMOKIN AND COAL TOWNSHIP LIGHT, HEAT AND POWER COMPANY (Operating).
Northumberland County, Shamokin Borough.
1907 to 1910, 2 Linear Feet.

History:

In 1900, two competing companies, Shamokin Light, Heat and Power Co. and Shamokin and Coal Township Light and Power Co., began distributing electricity in the borough of Shamokin. In 1907, the two companies merged and formed Shamokin and Coal Township Light, Heat and Power Co. In June 1910 this new company consolidated with two non-operating companies to form Pennsylvania Lighting Co.

Administrative Records:
Stockholders' Minutes, 1908
Stock Certificate Books, 1908-1910 (3 Volumes)

Operating Records:
General Ledger, 1908-1909
Journal, 1908-1909
Cashbooks, 1908-1910 (6 Volumes)
Cashbooks—Gas Department, 1907-1910 (3 Volumes)
Purchase and Distribution Ledgers, 1909-1910 (2 Volumes)
Construction Accounts Payable, 1907-1909 (2 Volumes)
Treasurer's Monthly Reports, 1908-1910
Monthly Time Book, 1908-1909

815. THE SHAMOKIN ARC LIGHT COMPANY (Operating).
Northumberland county, Shamokin Borough.
1888 to 1899, 1 Linear Inch.

History:

The Shamokin Arc Light Co. was incorporated in August 1887 by the Edison Electric Illuminating Co. of Shamokin, Pa., in order to obtain a street lighting contract in Shamokin Borough, Northumberland County. In 1899 its stock was acquired by Shamokin Light, Heat and Power Co., a New Jersey holding company. It was one of five firms which consolidated and merged to form Shamokin and Coal Township Light, Heat and Power Co. in January 1908.

Administrative Records:
Stock Certificates, 1888-1899

816. SHAMOKIN ELECTRIC COMPANY (Non-operating).
Northumberland County, Shamokin Township.
1921 to 1922, 1 Linear Inch.

History:

Shamokin Electric Co., incorporated 10 August 1921 to supply electricity in Shamokin Township, Northumberland County, merged into Pennsylvania Power & Light Co., 24 January 1922.

817. SHAMOKIN ELECTRIC LIGHT AND POWER COMPANY (Operating).
Northumberland County, Shamokin Borough.
1891 to 1907, 3 Linear Inches.

History:

Shamokin Electric Light and Power Co. was organized in December 1890 by officials of Shamokin Street Railway Co. The electric company did not become operational until 1896, however, and by then its stock had been acquired by interests which already controlled two other electric companies operating in Shamokin. The company supplied the street railway with power, and joined with Edison Electric Illuminating Co. of Shamokin, Pa. in introducing alternating current to the borough. In 1900, the company's stock was acquired by a New Jersey holding company, Shamokin Light, Heat and Power Co. In December 1907 it consolidated and merged with four companies to form Shamokin and Coal Township Light, Heat and Power Company.

Administrative Records:
Minute Book, 1899-1907
Stock Certificates, 1891-1899

818. SHAMOKIN GAS COMPANY (Non-operating).
Northumberland County, Shamokin Borough.
1907 to 1910, 1 Linear Inch.

History:

Shamokin Gas Co., incorporated 20 August 1907 to supply manufactured gas in Shamokin Borough, Northumberland County, consolidated and merged with two companies to form Pennsylvania Lighting Co., 22 June 1910.

819. THE SHAMOKIN GAS LIGHT COMPANY (Operating).
Northumberland County, Shamokin Borough.
1875 to 1898, 1 Linear Inch.

History:

Incorporated in 1874, The Shamokin Gas Light Co. supplied manufactured gas in Shamokin Borough, Northumberland County. It constructed a coal gas manufacturing plant and distribution system. After 1899 the company's stock was controlled by Shamokin Light, Heat and Power Co. In 1907, it was consolidated and merged with five companies to form Shamokin and Coal Township Light, Heat and Power Co., 29 January 1908.

Administrative Records:
Stock Certificates, 1875-1898

820. SHAMOKIN LIGHT, HEAT AND POWER COMPANY (Operating).
Northumberland County, Shamokin Borough.
1899 to 1902, 1 Linear Inch.

History:
Shamokin Light, Heat and Power Co. was incorporated in New Jersey in November 1899. At that time three electric companies were generating and distributing electricity in Shamokin Borough. The new holding company purchased their stocks and sought to construct an efficient system. In 1900, however, a group of local residents set up a competing company, the Shamokin and Coal Township Light and Power Co. For seven years the two companies operated in the same market before merging to form the Shamokin and Coal Township Light, Heat and Power Co.

Administrative Records:
Agreements, 1899
Stock Ledger, 1899-1902

821. SHARSWOOD ELECTRIC COMPANY
(Non-operating).
Schuylkill County, Rush Township.
1911 to 1913, 1 Linear Inch.

History:
Sharswood Electric Co., incorporated 27 June 1911 to supply electricity in Rush Township, Schuylkill County, consolidated and merged with 37 companies to form Lehigh Navigation Electric Co., 6 January 1913.

822. THE SHAWINIGAN ELECTRO PRODUCTS COMPANY (Operating).
Baltimore (Md), Baltimore City.
1915 to 1919, 3 Linear Inches.

History:
The Shawinigan Electro Products Co. was incorporated in Baltimore, Maryland, 12 May 1915, to produce electro-chemicals. Ferro-Silicon was its main product. The company was controlled by Pennsylvania Water & Power Co. and constructed several hydroelectric furnaces on the banks of the Susquehanna River in Highlandtown, Maryland. In December 1919 the company's name was changed to The Baltimore Electro Alloys Co.

Administrative Records:
Minute Book, 1915-1919
Stock Certificate Book, 1915-1917

823. THE SHENANDOAH ELECTRIC ILLUMINATING COMPANY OF SHENANDOAH, PA. (Operating).
Schuylkill County, Shenandoah Borough.
1886 to 1891, 8 Linear Inches.

History:
Incorporated August 1886 to supply electricity in Shenandoah Borough, Schuylkill County, The Shenandoah Electric Illuminating Co. of Shenandoah, Pa., built an incandescent electric light plant of two Brush arc generators in 1887. In 1899 its stock was acquired by Shenandoah Heat and Power Co., which operated it until 1906.

Administrative Records:
Minute Books, 1886-1890
Stock Certificate Book, 1887-1888

Operating Records:
General Ledger, 1886-1889
Cashbook, 1886-1891

Scope and Content Note:
The company's first Minute Book, 1886-1899, documents the organization and operation of the firm. Of particular interest are accounts of trips taken by company officials to New York City to meet with Thomas A. Edison, and with representatives of Westinghouse, Church, Kerr & Co. to discuss the merits of various electric lighting systems.

824. SHENANDOAH GAS LIGHT COMPANY
(Operating).
Schuylkill County, Shenandoah Borough.
1879 to 1906, 6 Linear Inches.

History:
Shenandoah Gas Light Co. was incorporated in December 1874 to supply gas for lighting in Shenandoah Borough, Schuylkill County. It built a manufactured gas plant in the borough, and operated it until 1899 when Shenandoah Heat and Power Co., a holding company, acquired control of its stock, along with that of The Shenandoah Electric Illuminating Co. of Shenandoah, Pa. The holding company operated both firms until October 1906, when all three were consolidated and merged to form The Shenandoah Light, Heat and Power Co.

Administrative Records:
Stock Certificates, n.d.
Stock Ledger, 1879-1906

Operating Records:
Journal and Expense Ledger, 1889-1906
Customers' Ledger, 1889-1894

825. SHENANDOAH HEAT AND POWER COMPANY
(Operating).
Schuylkill County, Shenandoah Borough.
1889 to 1906, 8 Linear Inches.

History:
Shenandoah Heat and Power Co. was organized in April 1889 to supply steam, heat and power to Shenandoah Borough, Schuylkill County. Formed as a holding company by officials of Shenandoah Gas Light Co. and the Shenandoah Electric Illuminating Co. of Shenandoah, Pa., the firm acquired the stocks of both companies and operated them until October 1906, when all three were consolidated and merged to form the Shenandoah Light, Heat and Power Co.

Administrative Records:
Minute Books, 1889-1906 (2 Volumes)
Stock Certificate Books, 1889-1906 (3 Volumes)

Operating Records:
Journal and Expense Ledger, 1889-1906
Cashbooks, 1889-1906 (3 Volumes)

Scope and Content Note:
Shenandoah Heat and Power Company's Minute Books document all aspects of the operations of the electrical, gas, and steam heating businesses which were conducted by the companies whose stock it controlled. Included is material on (1) rate setting (2) repair work (3) customer relations (4) rebates (5) employee relations and salaries. There is also information on construction contracts and fire protection methods.

826. THE SHENANDOAH LIGHT, HEAT AND POWER COMPANY (Operating).
Schuylkill County, Shenandoah Borough.
1906 to 1935, 7 Linear Feet.

History:
The Shenandoah Light, Heat and Power Co. was formed in October 1906 through the consolidation and merger of a holding company, Shenandoah Heat and Power Co., with two companies whose stock it had controlled: Shenandoah Gas Light Co. and The Shenandoah Electric Illuminating Co. of Shenandoah, Pa. The new company supplied gas, electricity, and steam heat in Shenandoah Borough, Schuylkill County. It operated an electric plant in the borough and constructed a tie line linking the plant to the distribution system of Mahanoy City Light, Heat and Power Co., a firm controlled by the same officials who controlled the Shenandoah company. In April 1913 The Schuylkill Gas and Electric Co. acquired the stock of The Shenandoah Light, Heat and Power Co. as part of a program to integrate utility companies in the territory. The Shenandoah electric plant was then abandoned, and its 1300 customers werhooked up to the Schuylkill Company's Harwood power plant. In 1928 Shenandoah. The lease was continued after The Schuylkill Gas and Electric Co. consolidated and merged with seven companies to form Pennsylvania Power & Light Co. in 1920. In November 1935, The Shenandoah Light, Heat and Power Co. was merged into PP&L, cancelling the lease agreement.

Administrative Records:
Stock Certificate Book, 1906-1934
Stock Transfer Record, 1916-1934
Stock Ledger, 1906-1935
Stock Index, 1910

Operating Records:
FINANCIAL RECORDS
General Ledgers, 1910-1935 (5 Volumes)
Journals, 1912-1921 (2 Volumes)
Journals—Operating Accounts, 1914-1918
Journal Entry Registers, 1923-1935 (2 Volumes)
Cashbooks, 1906-1907, 1909-1914 (3 Volumes)
Daybook, 1911-1924
Daily Cash Collection Book, 1906-1907
Record of Cash Receipts, 1925-1935
Record of Cash Disbursements, 1925-1935
Cash Summary, 1925-1928
Cash Received Summary, 1929-1935
Cash Received and Check Registers, 1913-1935 (5 Volumes)
Audited Voucher Registers, 1914-1918, 1922-1935 (4 Volumes)
Accounts Payable, 1914-1935 (2 Volumes)
Accounts Payable—Affiliated Companies, 1928-1935
Accounts Receivable, 1919-1923
Accounts Receivable—Detail Ledger, 1924-1935
Summaries of Accounts Receivable, 1921-1935
Detail Ledgers, 1910-1917, 1924-1934 (3 Volumes)
Accrual Records, 1919-1935 (2 Volumes)
Materials and Supplies Ledger, 1907-1909
Record of Supplies Sold, 1907-1910
Supplies on Hand, 1917-1918
Comparative Balance Sheets, 1915-1917
PERSONNEL RECORDS
Statement Showing Classification of Payrolls, 1916-1919
Payrolls, 1919-1921
Workmen's Compensation Insurance Accrual Statements, 1922-1935
Accident Register, 1917
MISCELLANEOUS REPORTS
Monthly Financial Reports, 1913-1918
Financial Reports, 1917-1920
Summary of Consumers' Reports, 1925-1935
Miscellaneous Reports, 1935
Audit Reports, 1912-1932 (9 Volumes)

Scope and Content Note:
The company's Minute Book for the period prior to 1913 contains information on various aspects of routine operations, such as: (1) rates for steam-heating and electric service, (2) purchases of electrical apparatus and improvements to the company's electric plant, (3) wage increases for company employees, and (4) stock issues and dividends. The minutes also document the company's negotiations with officials of The Harwood Electric Co. for the sale of The Shenandoah Light, Heat and Power Co., and for the transfer of property and assets to The Schuylkill Gas and Electric Co., 1912-1913.

827. SHENANDOAH-SCHUYLKILL GAS COMPANY (Non-operating).
Schuylkill County, Shenandoah Borough.
1935 to 1936, 1 Linear Inch.

History:
Shenandoah-Schuylkill Gas Co., incorporated 10 December 1935 to supply electricity in Shenandoah Borough, Schuylkill County, merged into Pennsylvania Power & Light Co., 9 March 1936.

828. SHERMAN VALLEY ELECTRIC LIGHT, HEAT AND POWER COMPANY (Operating).
Perry County, Landisburg Borough.
1922 to 1930, 2 Linear Feet.

History:
Sherman Valley Electric Light, Heat and Power Co. was formed in October 1922 through the consolidation and merger of Sherman's Valley Light, Heat and Power Co. and two non-operating companies. It provided service in Landisburg Borough and vicinity, Perry County. In 1928 Lehigh Power Securities Corp. acquired its stock and merged it into Pennsylvania Power & Light Co.

Administrative Records:
Minute Book, 1924-1930
Stock Certificates, 1925-1930
Stock Ledger, 1925-1930

Operating Records:
FINANCIAL RECORDS
General Ledgers, 1926-1930 (2 Volumes)
Journal, 1926-1928
Daybook, 1922-1923
Cashbook, 1923-1924
Checkbook, 1923-1924
Check Stubs, 1927-1928
Cash Receipts and Disbursements, 1926-1927

Record of Cash Receipts, 1928-1930
Record of Cash Disbursements, 1928-1930
Summary of Cash, 1928-1930 (2 Volumes)
Accounts Payable, 1928-1930
Workmen's Compensation Insurance Accrual Statements, 1928-1930
Accounts Receivable, 1929-1930
List of Material Sold, 1924-1928
Consumers' Ledger, 1925-1926
Summaries—Consumers' Accounts Receivable, 1928-1929
Summaries—Miscellaneous Accounts Receivable, 1928-1930
Summaries—Line Extension Deposits, 1929-1930
Summaries—Rents Receivable Statements, 1929-1930
Summaries—House Wiring Contract Sales, 1929
AUDIT REPORTS, 1924-1930 (4 Volumes)

829. SHERMAN'S VALLEY LIGHT, HEAT AND POWER COMPANY (Operating).
Perry County, Tyrone Township.
1910 to 1922, 6 Linear Inches.

History:

Sherman's Valley Light, Heat and Power Co. was incorporated in February 1910 to supply electricity in Tyrone Township, Perry County. It built a 30-kw hydroelectric plant in Loysville which generated power for the local orphanage and grist mill. After the plant expanded, it began to provide service to residential customers. In October 1922 the company consolidated and merged with two non-operating companies to form Sherman Valley Electric Light, Heat and Power Co.

Administrative Records:
Stock Certificates, 1910
Stock Ledger, 1910

Operating Records:
Journals, 1910-1915 (2 Volumes)
Cashbook, 1910-1915
Daybook and Cashbook, 1910-1918
Daybook, 1918-1922
Detail Ledgers, 1910-1922 (2 Volumes)

830. SHOHOLA-PIKE LIGHT & POWER COMPANY (Non-operating).
Pike County, Shohola Township.
1937 to 1938, 1 Linear Inch.

History:

Shohola-Pike Light & Power Co., incorporated 28 September 1937 to supply electricity in Shohola Township, Pike County, merged into Pennsylvania Power & Light Co., 7 June 1938.

831. SHOHOLA POWER COMPANY (Operating).
Pike County, Shohola Township.
1924 to 1938, 6 Linear Inches.

History:

Shohola Power Co. was incorporated in March 1924 to supply electricity in Shohola Township, Pike County. The company built a hydroelectric generating plant and distribution system. Shohola Power Co. was controlled by Rockland Light and Power Co., a New York firm. In 1938, the Shohola Power Company's distribution system was sold to Pennsylvania Power & Light, which formed Shohola-Pike Light & Power Co.

Administrative Records:
Minute Book, 1924-1938

Operating Records:
General Ledgers, and Supporting Details, 1926-1938 (3 Volumes)
Balance Sheet, 1938

Scope and Content Note:

Rate schedules for residential and commercial customers, annual reports, and information on the company's relationship with Rockland Light and Power Co., appear in the Minute Book.

832. SHREWSBURY-LYCOMING POWER & LIGHT COMPANY (Non-operating).
Lycoming County, Shrewsbury Township.
1924, 1 Linear Inch.

History:

Shrewsbury-Lycoming Power & Light Co., incorporated 28 August 1924 to supply electricity in Shrewsbury Township, Lycoming County, merged into The Citizens Electric Light and Power Co. of Hughesville, Pa., 27 October 1924.

833. SILVERDALE ELECTRIC LIGHT AND POWER COMPANY (Non-operating).
Bucks County, Silverdale Borough.
1913, 1 Linear Inch.

History:

Silverdale Electric Light and Power Co., incorporated 6 November 1913 to supply electricity in Silverdale Borough. Bucks County, consolidated and merged with three companies to form Excelsior Electric Light, Power and Gas Co., No. 2, 18 December 1913.

834. SKIDMORE ELECTRIC COMPANY (Non-operating).
Northampton County, Hanover Township.
1911 to 1913, 1 Linear Inch.

History:

Skidmore Electric Co., incorporated 4 April 1911 to supply electricity in Hanover Township, Northampton County, consolidated and merged with 37 companies to form Lehigh Navigation Electric Co., No. 2, 6 January 1913.

835. THE SLATEDALE ELECTRIC LIGHT, HEAT AND POWER COMPANY (Operating).
Lehigh County, Washington Township.
1910 to 1912, 2 Linear Inches.

History:

The Slatedale Electric Light, Heat and Power Co. was incorporated in December 1908 by a group of local businessmen who were seeking to supply electricity in Washington Township, Lehigh County. After erecting distribution lines, the company began to purchase power from The Lehigh Valley Traction Co. In 1912, the Allentown Electric Light and Power Co. acquired the stock of the Slatedale company and merged it with ten other companies to form Lehigh Valley Light and Power Co., No. 2.

Administrative Records:
Minute Book, 1910-1912
Stock Certificate Book, 1910-1912

836. SLATINGTON LIGHT AND POWER COMPANY (Non-operating).
Lehigh County, Slatington Borough.
1909 to 1912, 1 Linear Inch.

History:
Slatington Light and Power Co., incorporated in July 1909 to supply electricity in Slatington Borough, Lehigh County, was formed by interests who controlled Allentown Electric Light and Power Co. It never owned any physical property, however, and it was dissolved by order of The Court of Common Pleas of Lehigh County in March 1912.

837. SLATINGTON POWER COMPANY (Operating).
Lehigh County, Slatington Borough.
1900 to 1912, 1 Linear Inch.

History:
Slatington Power Co. was incorporated 5 March 1900 to supply waterpower to Slatington Borough, Lehigh County. Shortly after its formation, the company leased a hydroelectric plant from The Citizens Electric Co. The plant contained a 60-light dynamo for arc lighting, an 1800-light dynamo for incandescent lighting, and a distribution system. Slatington Power Co. also built a 600-kw steam generating station adjacent to the hydroelectric plant and sold power to Allentown and Slatington Street Railway Co., whose stock it controlled. In 1905, Lehigh Valley Transit Co. acquired the stock of Slatington Power Co. and held it until the company was dissolved on 3 June 1912.

Administrative Records:
Minute Book, 1900-1912
Stock Certificate Book, 1900-1908

838. SLOCUM-LUZERNE POWER & LIGHT COMPANY (Non-operating).
Luzerne County, Slocum Township.
1928, 1 Linear Inch.

History:
Slocum-Luzerne Power & Light Co., incorporated 31 August 1928 to supply electricity in Slocum Township, Luzerne County, merged into Pennsylvania Power & Light Co., 29 October 1928.

839. SNYDERTOWN POWER & LIGHT COMPANY (Non-operating).
Northumberland County, Snydertown Borough.
1922, 1 Linear Inch.

History:
Snydertown Power & Light Co., incorporated 5 October 1922 to supply electricity in Snydertown Borough, Northumberland County, merged into Pennsylvania Power & Light Co., 18 December 1922.

840. SOLEBURY TOWNSHIP ELECTRIC COMPANY (Non-operating).
Bucks County, Solebury Township.
1913 to 1935, 4 Linear Inches.

History:
Solebury Township Electric Co., incorporated 30 December 1913 to supply electricity in Solebury Township, Bucks County, was one of 13 'paper companies' formed by officials of Lehigh Navigation Electric Co. Like the other 12, the Solebury company was non-operating and was kept separate from, and not merged into, Lehigh Navigation Electric Co. because, as the company's attorney explained, "they cover outlying territory and it might be preferable to forfeit their charters and abandon them rather than furnish electricity to one or two customers. This would not be possible if the Lehigh Navigation Electric Co. were operating in such territory." Audit Reports for the 1920s list these companies as "inactive"; they were apparently dissolved in 1935.

841. SOUDERTON ELECTRIC LIGHT AND POWER COMPANY (Non-operating).
Montgomery County, Souderton Borough.
1913, 1 Linear Inch.

History:
Souderton Electric Light and Power Co., incorporated 6 November 1913 to supply electricity in Souderton Borough, Montgomery County, consolidated and merged with three companies to form Excelsior Electric Light, Power and Gas Co. No. 2, 18 December 1913.

842. SOUDERTON POWER & LIGHT COMPANY (Non-operating).
Montgomery County, Souderton Borough.
1929, 1 Linear Inch.

History:
Souderton Power & Light Co., incorporated 15 August 1929 to supply electricity in Souderton Borough, Montgomery County, merged into Pennsylvania Power & Light Co., 10 September 1929.

843. THE SOUTH BETHLEHEM ELECTRIC LIGHT COMPANY (Operating).
Northampton County, South Bethlehem Borough.
1899 to 1918, 2 Linear Inches.

History:
The South Bethlehem Electric Light Co. was incorporated in April 1899 to supply electricity in South Bethlehem Borough, Northampton County. The local businessmen who organized the company intended to purchase electricity which was being generated by a knitting mill, to supply the borough with power for street lighting. The company, however, operated for only three months before it was leased to The Allentown Electric Light and Power Co. The company then began purchasing power from The Bethlehem Electric Light Co. This arrangement lasted until January 1919 when The South Bethlehem Electric Light Co. was merged into Lehigh Valley Light and Power Co., No. 3.

Administrative Records:
Minute Book, 1899-1918
Stock Certificate Book, 1899-1918
Agreements, 1899

Scope and Content Note:
The Minute Book contains the agreement under which The Bethlehem Electric Light Co. furnished power to The Allentown Electric Light and Power Co. Also included are copies of street lighting contracts.

844. SOUTH HANOVER-DAUPHIN POWER & LIGHT COMPANY (Non-operating).
Dauphin County, South Hanover Township.
1927, 1 Linear Inch.

History:
South Hanover-Dauphin Power & Light Co., incorporated 2 September 1927 to supply electricity in South Hanover Township, Dauphin County, merged into Pennsylvania Power & Light Co., 11 October 1927.

845. SOUTH MIDDLETON STREET RAILWAY COMPANY (Non-operating).
Cumberland County, South Middleton Township.
1903 to 1904, 1 Linear Inch.

History:
South Middleton Street Railway Co. was incorporated in June 1903 to operate a street railway in South Middleton Township, Cumberland County. The company was organized by Cumberland Valley Railroad Co., Chambersburg, Pennsylvania. Valley Traction Co., a holding company, acquired the stock of both the South Middleton and Cumberland Valley companies late in 1903. South Middleton Street Railway Co. was dissolved in May 1904 without ever having operated.

846. SOUTH RENOVO ELECTRIC LIGHT COMPANY (Non-operating).
Clinton County, South Renovo Township.
1916 to 1917, 1 Linear Inch.

History:
South Renovo Electric Light Co., incorporated in June 1916 to supply electricity in South Renovo Township, Clinton County, merged into Renovo Edison Light, Heat and Power Co., January 1917.

847. SOUTH SIDE PASSENGER RAILWAY COMPANY (Operating).
Lycoming County, South Williamsport Borough.
1892 to 1927, 2 Linear Feet.

History:
South Side Passenger Railway Co. was organized in March 1892 to operate an electric street railway in South Williamsport Borough and the city of Williamsport, Lycoming County. J. Henry Cochran organized this company and five other street railway companies in Williamsport to compete with Williamsport Passenger Railway Co. After the death of the president of the Williamsport company, Cochran acquired it and formed a holding company, Lycoming Improvement Co., to control its stock and the stocks of his five other street railway companies. In June 1926 all of them were consolidated and merged to form Williamsport Railways Co.

Administrative Records:
Minute Books, 1892-1895, 1911-1913, 1922-1926 (3 Volumes)

Operating Records:
General Ledgers, 1899-1926 (2 Volumes)
Journals, 1895-1923 (4 Volumes)
Journal Entry Record and Voucher Register, 1923-1926
Cashbooks, 1901-1911, 1921-1927 (2 Volumes)
Indexes to Vouchers, 1895-1921 (2 Volumes)
Federal Income Tax Schedules, 1926
Audit Reports, 1918-1922 (2 Volumes)

Scope and Content Note:
The company's Minute Books contain information on the route of the railroad and its construction, repairs to its tracks, and earnings. The minutes also document the relationship between this company, Citizens Passenger Railway Co.; Centre and West End Passenger Railway; and other lines controlled by J. Henry Cochran, a Pennsylvania State Senator.

848. SOUTH WHITEHALL ELECTRIC LIGHT AND POWER COMPANY (Non-operating).
Lehigh County, South Whitehall Township.
1911 to 1913, 1 Linear Inch.

History:
South Whitehall Electric Light and Power Co., incorporated 10 November 1911 to supply electricity in South Whitehall Township, Lehigh County, consolidated and merged with ten companies to form Lehigh Valley Light and Power Co., No. 1, 2 January 1913.

849. SOUTH WHITEHALL ELECTRIC LIGHT COMPANY (Non-operating).
Lehigh County, South Whitehall Township.
1911 to 1913, 1 Linear Inch.

History:
South Whitehall Electric Light Co., incorporated 4 April 1911 to supply electricity in South Whitehall Township, Lehigh County, consolidated and merged with 37 companies to form Lehigh Navigation Electric Co., No. 2, 6 January 1913.

850. SOUTH WILLIAMSPORT POWER & LIGHT COMPANY (Non-operating).
Lycoming County, South Williamsport Borough.
1924, 1 Linear Inch.

History:
South Williamsport Power & Light Co., incorporated 9 May 1924 to supply electricity in South Williamsport Borough, Lycoming County, merged into Pennsylvania Power & Light Co., 27 August 1924.

851. SOUTHERN LIGHT COMPANY (Non-operating).
Northumberland County, Chillisquaque Township.
1912, 1 Linear Inch.

History:
Southern Light Co., incorporated 29 May 1912 to supply manufactured gas for lighting in Chillisquaque Township and East Chillisquaque Township, Northumberland County, merged into Northern Central Gas Co., 31 August 1912.

852. SPRING BROOK POWER & LIGHT COMPANY (Non-operating).
Lackawanna County, Spring Brook Township.
1923 to 1924, 1 Linear Inch.

History:
Spring Brook Power & Light Co., incorporated 21 May 1923 to supply electricity in Spring Brook Township, Lackawanna County, consolidated and merged with 31 companies to form Paupack Power & Light Co. No. 2, 29 January 1924.

853. SPRING TOWNSHIP LIGHT, HEAT AND POWER COMPANY (Non-operating).
Perry County, Spring Township.
1921 to 1922, 1 Linear Inch.

History:
Spring Township Light, Heat and Power Co., incorporated 15 December 1921 to supply electricity in Spring Township, Perry County, consolidated and merged with two companies to form Sherman Valley Electric Light, Heat and Power Co., 25 October 1922.

854. SPRINGFIELD TOWNSHIP ELECTRIC LIGHT AND POWER COMPANY (Non-operating).
Bucks County, Springfield Township.
1913, 1 Linear Inch.

History:
Springfield Township Electric Light and Power Co., incorporated 8 December 1913 to supply electricity in Springfield Township, Bucks County, merged into Lehigh Valley Light and Power Co., No. 3, 29 December 1913.

855. STANDARD CONSTRUCTION COMPANY OF BLOOMSBURG (Operating).
Columbia County, Bloomsburg Town.
1903 to 1904, 1 Linear Inch.

History:
Standard Construction Co. of Bloomsburg was formed in 1903 in order to build a street railway in Bloomsburg, Columbia County. Once the road bed was constructed and the track was laid, the company was dissolved.

Operating Records:
General Ledger, Cashbook, 1903-1904

856. THE STANDARD ELECTRIC COMPANY OF PARSONS, PA. (Operating).
Luzerne County, Parsons Borough.
1898 to 1910, 2 Linear Inches.

History:
The Standard Electric Co. of Parsons, Pa. was incorporated in August 1898 to supply electricity in Parsons Borough, Luzerne County. The company acquired a steam electric generating station and distribution system from Keystone Electric Construction Co. In June 1910 it consolidated and merged with three companies to form The Wilkes-Barre Co., No. 2.

Administrative Records:
Minute Book, 1899-1910 (includes Consumers' Ledger, 1898-1899)
Stock Certificate Books, 1899-1910 (2 Volumes)

Operating Records:
General Ledgers, 1908-1910 (2 Volumes)
Cashbook, 1902-1910

Scope and Content Note:
The Minute Book documents routine operations including the construction of the company's generating station, and purchases of electrical apparatus and supplies. Also included are materials describing the process by which rates were set, and the various systems of arc and incandescent lighting that were installed.

857. STANDARD ELECTRIC COMPANY OF WASHINGTON TOWNSHIP (Non-operating).
Northampton County, Washington Township.
1911 to 1913, 1 Linear Inch.

History:
Standard Electric Co. of Washington Township, incorporated 4 April 1911 to supply electricity in Washington Township, Northampton County, consolidated and merged with 37 companies to form Lehigh Navigation Electric Co., 6 January 1913.

858. STANDARD ELECTRIC COMPANY (Operating).
Montour County, Danville Borough.
1899 to 1911, 3 Linear Inches.

History:
Standard Electric Light Co. was incorporated 26 October 1899 to supply electricity in Danville Borough, Montour County. Shortly after its formation the company leased The Consumers Gas Co. of Danville, Pa.'s steam electric generating station and distribution system. It operated this property until May 1911 when it consolidated and merged with 21 companies to form Columbia Gas and Electric Co.

Administrative Records:
Stock Certificate Book, 1899-1911

Operating Records:
General Ledger, 1899-1909
Cashbook, 1899-1908

859. STANDARD ELECTRIC LIGHT, HEAT AND POWER COMPANY OF AVOCA, PA. (Operating).
Luzerne County, Avoca Borough.
1898 to 1909, 3 Linear Inches.

History:
Standard Electric Light, Heat and Power Co. of Avoca, Pa., was incorporated 15 December 1897 to supply electricity in Avoca Borough, Luzerne County. It operated a generating station in Avoca until 21 January 1910, when it merged into The Scranton Electric Co.

Administrative Records:
Stock Certificate Book, 1898-1909

Operating Records:
General Ledger, 1898-1909
Consumers' Ledgers, 1901-1903, 1907-1908 (2 Volumes)

860. STANDARD GAS COMPANY (Operating).
Montour County, Danville Borough.
1899 to 1911, 3 Linear Inches.

History:
Standard Gas Co. was incorporated in October 1899 to supply manufactured gas for lighting in Danville Borough, Montour County. Shortly after its formation it leased The Consumers Gas Co. of Danville, Pa.'s manufactured gas plant and distribution system. It operated this property until May 1911, when it consolidated and merged with 21 companies to form Columbia Gas and Electric Co.

Administrative Records:
Stock Certificate Book, 1899-1911

Operating Records:
General Ledger, 1899-1909
Cashbook, 1899-1908

861. STANTON OPERATING COMPANY (Operating).
Luzerne County, Exeter Township.
1925 to 1937, 5 Linear Feet.

History:

Stanton Operating Co. was incorporated 19 April 1927 by officials of Pennsylvania Power & Light Co. and The Scranton Electric Co. to "render expert engineering and managerial advice" to the Stanton Electric Station. The 100,000-kw steam-turbine generating station, located on the Susquehanna River in Exeter Township, Luzerne County, had been jointly constructed by the two companies. Each retained 50% ownership. The arrangement continued until May 1937 when PP&L, in response to pressure by the Federal Power and the Pennsylvania Public Utilities Commissions, agreed to transfer control of the station to The Scranton Electric Co. Subsequently, that company operated the station as its Stanton Station Division.

Administrative Records:
Minute Book, 1927-1937

Operating Records:
General Ledgers, 1927-1937 (3 Volumes)
Cashbook, 1928-1937
Records of Cash Receipts and Disbursements, 1927
Accounts Payable Ledger—Stanton Plant, 1928
Accounts Payable Ledgers, 1928-1930 (2 Volumes)
Accounts Payable Ledger—Voucher Proof Sheets, 1931-1934
Accounts Receivable Miscellaneous Ledgers, 1928-1937 (2 Volumes)
Operating Expense Ledgers, 1931-1937 (3 Volumes)
Automotive Cost Report, 1931-1937
Accrual Records, 1925-1937 (2 Volumes)
Bank Passbook, 1927-1928
Bills Supporting Journal Entries, 1931-1933
Bills Supporting Journal Entries, 1934-1936
Audit Report and Examination of Investments in Stanton Station, Pennsylvania Power & Light Co., 1928

Scope and Content Note:

The Minute Book documents the relationship between Pennsylvania Power & Light Co. and The Scranton Electric Co. in the joint operation of Stanton Station. It also contains a copy of the letter sent by PP&L President J.S. Wise, Jr., and The Scranton Electric Co. President George N. Tidd, to Stanton Operating Co., advising of PP&L's decision to turn over complete control of the station to The Scranton Electric Co. A detailed examination of the financial investments of PP&L and The Scranton Electric Co. in building the Stanton Station is found in an Audit Report of 1928. Construction Ledgers and other records documenting the construction of the station from 1925 to 1927, and its operation after 1937, are filed with the records of The Scranton Electric Co.

862. STAR ELECTRIC COMPANY (Non-operating).
Northampton County, Bushkill Township.
1911 to 1913, 1 Linear Inch.

History:

Star Electric Co., incorporated 4 April 1911 to supply electricity in Bushkill Township, Northampton County, consolidated and merged with 37 companies to form Lehigh Navigation Electric Co., 6 January 1913.

863. STEELTON LIGHT, HEAT AND POWER COMPANY (Operating).
Dauphin County, Steelton Borough.
1892 to 1914, 2 Linear Feet.

History:

Steelton Light, Heat and Power Co. was incorporated 15 August 1892 by local residents of Steelton, Dauphin County, to supply electricity in the borough. Among the company's customers was Pennsylvania Steel Co. To meet this demand, the electric company built a steam electric generating plant equipped with dynamos of 1200-light capacity for incandescent lighting, and 110-light capacity for arc lighting. In 1905 a fire destroyed the station, and for the next several years the company purchased power from various nearby electric companies. Eventually, the company experienced such difficulty in obtaining power that in September 1913 its executive committee voted to sell the firm to its main competitor, Harrisburg Light and Power Co.

Administrative Records:
Minute Books, 1890-1913 (2 Volumes)
Minute Book—Executive Committee, 1908-1913
Stock Certificate Books, 1892-1913 (2 Volumes)

Operating Records:
General Ledgers, 1894-1905, 1902-1913 (2 Volumes)
Journal, 1900-1913
Cashbooks, 1903-1914 (5 Volumes)
Audited Voucher Register, 1910-1913
Monthly Statements, 1895-1898
Financial Data, 1911-1912

Scope and Content Note:

The company's Minute Books document routine operations in considerable detail. There is information regarding: (1) the purchase of electrical dynamos, arc and incandescent lights, (2) setting of rates for residential and commercial customers, (3) competition with other electric companies, and (4) wages and hours of employees. A lengthy report describes the 1905 fire and the resultant damage to the company's generating station. Minutes for the period 1906-1913 detail the company's efforts to secure power from other sources. They also describe the company's ongoing financial problems, as well as disputes with auditors about the nature of their profit reports. Also documented is the company's unsuccessful experiment with tungsten arc lights for street lighting. The Minute Book of the Executive Committee describes the decision to sell the company to Harrisburg Light and Power Co. Finally, there is considerable information about social conditions in Steelton during the 1890's and 1900's. The growth of local social and civic organizations are documented in the Minute Books, which describe the company's decision to provide free electrical and other financial assistance to these groups.

864. STERLING CONSOLIDATED ELECTRIC COMPANY (Operating).
Schuylkill County, Tower City Borough.
1909 to 1916, 8 Linear Inches.

History:
Sterling Consolidated Electric Co. was organized in March 1909 through the consolidation and merger of The Sterling Electric Light Heat and Power Co. and five non-operating companies. It supplied electricity to Lykens Borough, Dauphin County, and Tower City Borough, Schuylkill County, as well as to nearby townships. It generated power in its 150-kw plan located in Reinerton. In 1910, the company leased the generating facilities of one of its main competitors, Williams Valley Light, Heat and Power Co. The two distribution systems were merged, and three years later Sterling Consolidated Electric Co. changed its name to Lykens Valley Light and Power Co.

Administrative Records:
Minute Book, 1909-1915
Stock Certificate Book, 1909-1916

Operating Records:
Cashbooks, 1909-1915 (7 Volumes)
Daybook, 1909-1915
Audited Voucher Register, 1913-1915

Scope and Content Note:
The Minute Book documents various aspects of company operations, including: (1) the purchase of electrical apparatus, (2) the building of the company's generating station in Reinerton Village, (3) the installation of its distribution lines in the territory served, (4) rate setting service, and (5) capital stock issues. The Minute Book also contains a 'forword' (sic) which briefly outlines the efforts of other parties to provide electric service in Tower City Borough from 1900 to 1908.

865. STERLING POWER & LIGHT COMPANY (Non-operating).
Wayne County, Sterling Township.
1923 to 1924, 1 Linear Inch.

History:
Sterling Power & Light Co., incorporated 1 May 1923 to supply electricity in Sterling Township, Wayne County, consolidated and merged with 31 companies to form Paupack Power & Light Co. No. 2, 29 January 1924.

866. STILLWATER-COLUMBIA POWER & LIGHT COMPANY (Non-operating).
Columbia County, Stillwater Borough.
1924, 1 Linear Inch.

History:
Stillwater-Columbia Power & Light Co., incorporated 2 October 1924 to supply electricity in Stillwater Borough, Columbia County, merged into Pennsylvania Power & Light Co., 19 January 1925.

867. STOCKERTOWN LIGHT, HEAT AND POWER COMPANY (Non-operating).
Northampton County, Stockertown Borough.
1924 to 1928, 1 Linear Inch.

History:
Stockertown Light, Heat and Power Co., incorporated 9 May 1924 to supply electricity in Stockertown Borough, Northampton County, merged into Pennsylvania Power & Light Co., 2 July 1928.

868. STOEVER ELECTRIC LIGHT COMPANY (Non-operating).
Lancaster County, Mount Joy Borough.
1906 to 1907, 1 Linear Inch.

History:
Stoever Electric Light Co., incorporated 7 September 1906 to supply electricity in Mount Joy Borough, Lancaster County, consolidated and merged with Leland Electric Light Co. to form Manheim and Mount Joy Electric Light Co., 22 March 1907.

869. STORY ELECTRIC COMPANY (Non-operating).
Schuylkill County, Norwegian Township.
1911 to 1913, 1 Linear Inch.

History:
Story Electric Co., incorporated 27 June 1911 to supply electricity in Norwegian Township, Schuylkill County, consolidated and merged with 37 companies to form Lehigh Navigation Electric Co., 6 January 1913.

870. STRASBURG BOROUGH ELECTRIC LIGHT, HEAT AND POWER COMPANY (Non-operating).
Lancaster County, Strasburg Borough.
1913, 1 Linear Inch.

History:
Strasburg Borough Electric Light, Heat and Power Co., incorporated 28 February 1913 to supply electricity in Strasburg Borough, Lancaster County, consolidated and merged with four companies to form Strasburg Electric Light, Heat and Power Co., No. 3, 24 May 1913.

871. STRASBURG ELECTRIC LIGHT, HEAT AND POWER COMPANY, NO. 1 (Operating).
Lancaster County, Strasburg Borough.
1907 to 1913, 1 Linear Foot.

History:
Strasburg Electric Light, Heat and Power Co., No. 1 was incorporated 31 January 1907 to supply electricity in Strasburg Borough, Lancaster County. The company purchased a grist mill which had been outfitted with electrical generators, and used this facility to produce power. In order to supplement this source, it purchased power from The Edison Electric Illuminating Co. of Lancaster, Pa. In 1913, it organized four non-operating companies to secure charter rights in other areas, and consolidated them to form Strasburg Electric Light, Heat and Power Co., No. 2.

Administrative Records:
Minute Books, 1907-1913 (2 Volumes)
Secretary's Papers of Meetings, 1907-1913
Stock Certificate Books, 1907-1913 (2 Volumes)
Stock Transfer Record, 1907-1913
Stock Subscription Record, 1911

Operating Records:
Cashbook, 1907-1913

Scope and Content Note:
The Minute Books of The Strasburg Electric Light, Heat and Power Co., No. 1, provide a detailed account of routine company affairs. Included are records documenting: (1) the purchase of grist mills and electric generating stations at Edisonville and Wheathead, (2) improvements and repairs to mills, generators, water

wheels and mill races, and (3) negotiations with the Strasburg and Quarryville Borough Council for street lighting contracts.

The minutes also document the process by which street lighting systems were converted from carbon arc lighting to tungsten lighting. Finally, there is a good deal of material tracing the progress of rural electrification, and the impact that it had on local farmers, grist millers and stone quarry operators.

872. STRASBURG ELECTRIC LIGHT, HEAT AND POWER COMPANY, NO. 2 (Operating).
Lancaster County, Strasburg Borough.
1913, 4 Linear Inches.

History:
Strasburg Electric Light, Heat and Power Co., No. 2, was formed in March 1913 through the consolidation and merger of Strasburg Electric Light, Heat and Power Co., No. 1 with four non-operating companies. It provided electric service in Strasburg Borough and adjacent townships in Lancaster County. The company operated two power stations, one in Edisonville, and the other in Wheatland Mills, both located in old mill buildings. After its formation, the company increased the capacities of both of these plants, and began to supply its customers with 60-cycle current. In May 1913 it consolidated and merged with four non-operating companies to form Strasburg Electric Light, Heat and Power Co., No. 3.

Administrative Records:
Minute Book, 1913
Stock Certificate Book, 1913
Stock Transfer Record, 1913

Operating Records:
Cashbook, 1913

873. STRASBURG ELECTRIC LIGHT, HEAT AND POWER COMPANY, NO. 3 (Operating).
Lancaster County, Strasburg Borough.
1913 to 1923, 6 Linear Inches.

History:
Strasburg Electric Light, Heat and Power Co. No. 3 was formed in May 1913 through the consolidation and merger of Strasburg Electric Light, Heat and Power Co., No. 2 with four non-operating companies. It provided electric service in Strasburg Borough and surrounding townships in Lancaster County. After its formation, the company purchased a 150-kw generator and other equipment from General Electric Co. to further upgrade the capacity of its Edisonville station. It also rebuilt the hydraulic part of this plant to accommodate new turbines. In March 1923 the company was acquired by, and merged into, Edison Electric Co. No. 4.

Administrative Records:
Minute Book, 1913-1923
Stock Certificate Book, 1913-1915
Stock Transfer Record, 1913

Operating Records:
Cashbooks, 1913-1923 (2 Volumes)
Cash Receipts and Disbursements, 1919-1922

Scope and Content Note:
The Minute Books of The Strasburg Electric Light, Heat and Power Co., No. 3 document all aspects of company operations. There is a good deal of material tracing the progress of rural electrification in Lancaster County, and the impact that it had on farmers, grist millers, lumbermen, and blacksmiths. The minutes also document the process by which the company set rates for residential and commercial customers.

874. STRASBURG TOWNSHIP ELECTRIC COMPANY (Non-operating).
Lancaster County, Strasburg Township.
1912, 1 Linear Inch.

History:
Strasburg Township Electric Co., incorporated 7 November 1912 to supply electricity in Strasburg Township, Lancaster County, consolidated and merged with 13 companies to form Edison Electric Co. No. 3, 9 December 1912.

875. THE STROUDSBURG ELECTRIC LIGHT AND POWER COMPANY, NO. 1 (Operating).
Monroe County, Stroudsburg Borough.
1889 to 1913, 3 Linear Inches.

History:
The Stroudsburg Electric Light and Power Co., No. 1 was incorporated 8 March 1889 to supply electricity in Stroudsburg Borough, Monroe County. Local residents who organized the company erected a small power station in Stroudsburg. In 1906 the entire property was leased to Citizens Gas Co. of Stroudsburg, which operated it until 1913, when the electric company was consolidated and merged with a non-operating company, Sambo Electric Light and Power Co., to form The Stroudsburg Electric Light and Power Co., No. 2.

Administrative Records:
Minute Books, 1889-1906,1913 (2 Volumes)

Scope and Content Note:
The Minute Books of The Stroudsburg Electric Light and Power Co., No. 1 document routine company operations in considerable detail. There is information on contracts with Excelsior Electric Light Co. of Brooklyn, to provide arc lighting, and with Harrisburg Car Co. which manufactured steam generating equipment. Also documented are: (1) the process by which rates were set, (2) negotiations for street lighting contracts, and (3) agreements with Stroudsburg Passenger Railway Co. and Citizens Gas Co. The last few pages of the Minute Books contain statistics on the lengths of incandescent wires laid by the company to serve particular industrial and commercial customers.

876. THE STROUDSBURG ELECTRIC LIGHT AND POWER COMPANY, NO. 2 (Operating).
Monroe County, Stroudsburg Borough.
1913 to 1920, 3 Linear Feet.

History:
The Stroudsburg Electric Light and Power Co., No. 2 was formed through the consolidation and merger of The Stroudsburg Electric Light and Power Co., No. 1 and Sambo Electric Light and Power Co. In 1914, the Citizens Gas & Electric Light and Power Co. purchased a controlling interest in Stroudsburg Electric and abandoned the company's generating plant. In 1919, the company was consolidated and merged with Industrial Power Co. to form Lehigh Industrial Power Co.

Administrative Records:
Minute Book, 1913-1919
Agreement of Consolidation and Merger, 1919
Stock Certificate Book, 1918-1919
Stock Transfer Record, 1916-1919
Historical Report on Organization and Capitalization, 1916

Operating Records:
FINANCIAL RECORDS
General Ledgers, 1916-1919 (3 Volumes)
Journal, 1916-1919 (2 Volumes)
Cashbooks, 1916-1919 (2 Volumes)
Statement of Consumers' Ledger, 1916-1918
Voucher Registers, 1916-1919 (2 Volumes)
Unpaid Vouchers, 1916
Outstanding Vouchers, 1918-1919
Detail Repair and Construction Ledgers, 1916-1920 (2 Volumes)
Accounts Payable, 1916-1919
Cost of Plant and Property, 1916-1918
Accrual Record, 1916
Detail of Operating Expenses, 1916-1918
Monthly Balance Sheets, 1916-1917
PERSONNEL RECORDS
Accident Register, 1916-1917
Payrolls, 1917-1919
Payroll Ledger, 1917
Payrolls—Recapitulation, 1916-1917
Workmen's Compensation Reports, 1917-1919

Scope and Content Note:
The Minute Book of The Stroudsburg Electric Light and Power Co., No. 2 contains some information on property appraisals, rates for street lighting in Stroudsburg Borough, and earning statements. Details of company assets, capitalization, and earnings, and historical synopses of the company's organization, franchises, and agreements will be found in the Historical Report on Organization and Capitalization.

877. THE SUBURBAN ELECTRIC LIGHT COMPANY (Operating).
Lackawanna County, Scranton City.
1901 to 1907, 1 Linear Inch.

History:
The Suburban Electric Light Co. was incorporated 25 October 1887 to supply electricity in Scranton, and in Dunmore Borough, Lackawanna County. It consolidated and merged with four companies to form Scranton Electric Co., 21 March 1907.

Operating Records:
General Ledger, 1901-1907
Index to Consumers' Ledger, n.d.

878. SUGAR LOAF TOWNSHIP ELECTRIC COMPANY (Non-operating).
Luzerne County, Sugar Loaf Township.
1909, 1 Linear Inch.

History:
Sugar Loaf Township Electric Co., incorporated 16 June 1909 to supply electricity in Sugar Loaf Township, Luzerne County, consolidated and merged with 11 companies to form Harwood Electric Co., 30 June 1909.

879. SUGAR VALLEY LIGHT, POWER & HEAT COMPANY (Operating).
Clinton County, Loganton Borough.
1929, 1 Linear Inch.

History:
Sugar Valley Light, Power & Heat Co. was formed in 1926 by Samuel D. Ilgen of Loganton Borough, Clinton County, to supply electricity to the borough's residents. Ilgen built and operated an electric plant of 40-kw capacity and a distribution system. In November 1929 Pennsylvania Power & Light Co. formed a non-operating company, Loganton Clinton Power & Light Co., to gain charter rights in the borough and to acquire Ilgen's equipment. After acquiring the property, PP&L dissolved Ilgen's company, abandoned the generating station, and tied the borough's distribution network into its own system.

Operating Records:
Audit Report, Pennsylvania Power & Light Co., 1929

880. SUGARLOAF-COLUMBIA POWER & LIGHT COMPANY (Non-operating).
Columbia County, Sugarloaf Township.
1924, 1 Linear Inch.

History:
Sugarloaf-Columbia Power & Light Co., incorporated 28 August 1924 to supply electricity in Sugarloaf Township, Columbia County, merged into Pennsylvania Power & Light Co., 19 January 1925.

881. SULLIVAN COUNTY ELECTRIC COMPANY, NO. 1 (Operating).
Sullivan County, Dushore Borough.
1920 to 1923, 1 Linear Inch.

History:
Sullivan County Electric Co., No. 1 was formed in January 1920 through the consolidation and merger of seven companies. It supplied electricity in Dushore Borough, and Laporte Borough, Sullivan County, and New Albany Borough, Bradford County, and adjacent townships in both counties. In March 1923 it consolidated and merged with 12 companies to form Sullivan County Electric Co., No. 2. Although Pennsylvania Power & Light Co. audited the company in 1923 with a view to acquire it, it was never merged into PP&L.

Operating Records:
Rate Schedules, 1920
Audit Report, Pennsylvania Power & Light Co., 1923

882. THE SUNBURY AND NORTHUMBERLAND ELECTRIC RAILWAY COMPANY (Operating).
Northumberland County, Sunbury Borough.
1894 to 1911, 1 Linear Inch.

History:
The Sunbury and Northumberland Electric Railway Co. was formed in 1899 to operate an electric street railway line between Sunbury and Northumberland Borough, Northumberland County. It also provided electricity to the Sunbury Electric Light and Power Co. The electric company operated the railway as a subsidiary. It erected a generating station and leased it to the railroad in exchange for electricity. This arrangement

lasted until 1911, when the electric company merged into The Edison Electric Illuminating Co. of Sunbury, Pa., No. 4. The railway now became an independent company, changing its name to Northumberland County Railway Co.

Administrative Records:
Stock Certificate Book, 1894-1907

Operating Records:
Payrolls, 1907-1911

883. THE SUNBURY ELECTRIC COMPANY (Non-operating).
Northumberland County, Sunbury Borough.
1905 to 1906, 1 Linear Inch.

History:
The Sunbury Electric Co., incorporated 4 May 1905 to supply electricity in Sunbury Borough, Northumberland County, consolidated and merged with three companies to form Middlecreek Electric Co. 6 March 1906.

884. SUNBURY ELECTRIC LIGHT AND POWER COMPANY (Operating).
Northumberland County, Sunbury Borough.
1890 to 1913, 3 Linear Inches.

History:
Sunbury Electric Light and Power Co. was incorporated 3 January 1890 to supply electricity in Sunbury Borough, Northumberland County. It was organized by officials of The Sunbury and Northumberland Electric Co. to compete with The Edison Electric Illuminating Co. of Sunbury, No. 1. After its formation, the electric company acquired the railway company and operated it as a subsidiary, erecting a generating station in Sunbury which it leased to the railway. In return, the railway company agreed to furnish power to the electric company. In 1900 a new group, headed by Pierre S. du Pont and T. Coleman du Pont, formed a syndicate to acquire both the electric company and the railroad, along with The Northumberland Electric Illuminating Co. This syndicate operated the three companies until 1905 when P.B. Shaw, leader of the group controlling The Edison Electric Illuminating Co. of Sunbury, Pa., No. 3, acquired the three companies. In 1907 the Edison group leased the properties held by Sunbury Electric Light and Power Co. The lease agreement terminated when The Edison Electric Illuminating Co. of Sunbury, Pa., No. 3, Sunbury Electric Light and Power Co., The Northumberland Electric Illuminating Co. and two others formed The Edison Electric Illuminating Co. of Sunbury, Pa., No. 4.

Administrative Records:
Minute Book, 1890-1911
History of Northumberland County Gas and Electric Co., 1913
History of Sunbury Electric Light and Power Co., 1907

Operating Records:
Cashbook, 1900-1903

Scope and Content Note:
The Minute Book of Sunbury Electric Light and Power Co. contains little information on company operations. It does, however, trace the involvement of Pierre S. du Pont, T. Coleman du Pont, and John J. Raskob in the company's directorships, and its takeover by P.B. Shaw of The Edison Electric Illuminating Co. of Sunbury, Pa., No. 3, in 1905. Copies of company agreements, borough ordinances, deeds, and other legal records appear in the two company histories.

885. SUNBURY GAS COMPANY, NO. 2 (Operating).
Northumberland County, Sunbury Borough.
1899 to 1905, 6 Linear Inches.

History:
Sunbury Gas Co., No. 2, was incorporated 12 September 1899 to manufacture and supply gas for lighting, in Sunbury Borough, and Upper Augusta Township, all in Northumberland County. Soon after its formation, it acquired the Sunbury Gas and Light Co., and for the next six years operated its gas plant and distribution system. In 1905 it consolidated and merged with Sunbury Gas Fuel and Power Co. to form Sunbury Gas Co., No. 3.

Administrative Records:
Minute Book, 1899-1904
Stock Certificate Book, 1899-1904
Stock Ledger, 1899-1904

Operating Records:
General Ledgers, 1899-1905 (2 Volumes)
Journal, 1900-1905
Payroll Ledger, 1901-1905
Consumers' Ledger, 1899-1901

Scope and Content Note:
The Minute Book of Sunbury Gas Co., No. 2, documents most aspects of company operations. Particularly informative are the secretary's annual reports which describe: (1) improvements and additions to the company's manufactured gas plant and gas distribution system, and (2) customer relations and extensions of service to industrial customers such as the Pennsylvania Railroad shops in Sunbury, Susquehanna Dye Works, and Susquehanna Silk Factory. The reports provide statistics on customers added, appliances sold, and miles of gas lines. They also describe Sunbury's social structure and economic life, including: population, ethnic composition, and prospects for business.

886. SUNBURY GAS COMPANY, NO. 3 (Operating).
Northumberland County, Sunbury Borough.
1905 to 1911, 8 Linear Inches.

History:
Sunbury Gas Co., No. 3, formed in March 1905 through the consolidation and merger of Sunbury Gas Co., No. 2 and Sunbury Gas Fuel and Power Co., supplied manufactured gas for lighting, heat, and power in Sunbury Borough, and Upper Augusta Township, all in Northumberland County. It operated a large manufactured gas plant, serving a number of industrial, commercial, and residential customers. In 1907 The Edison Electric Illuminating Co. of Sunbury, Pa., No. 3 acquired control of Sunbury Gas Co. and operated it until October 1911, when both companies consolidated and merged with three other firms to form Edison Electric Illuminating Co. of Sunbury, Pa., No. 4.

Administrative Records:
Minute Books, 1905-1911 (2 Volumes)
Stock Certificate Book, 1906-1911
Stock Ledger, 1906-1909

Operating Records:
General Ledgers, 1905-1911 (2 Volumes)
Journal, 1905-1911 (2 Volumes)
Audited Voucher Register, 1908-1911
Payroll Ledger, 1905-1912
Commercial Reports, 1911

Scope and Content Note:
The Minute Book contains the Secretary's Annual Reports describing routine business activities and improvements that were made to the company's manufactured gas plant and distribution system. Also documented is the process by which the company extended service to both commercial and industrial customers such as the Susquehanna Silk Factory, and the Susquehanna Dye Works. In addition, the minutes depict the efforts made to retain customers. There is a good deal of information tracing the company's relationship to The Edison Electric Illuminating Co. of Sunbury, Pa., No. 3.

887. SUPERIOR ELECTRIC LIGHT & POWER COMPANY (Non-operating).
Montgomery County, Upper Dublin Township.
1917 to 1918, 1 Linear Inch.

History:
Superior Electric Light & Power Co. was formed in February 1917 by Lehigh Valley Transit Co. to secure charter rights, in order to supply electricity in Upper Dublin Township, Montgomery County. Its charter was never approved, and the company never obtained its Letters Patent.

888. SUSQUEHANNA BOOM COMPANY (Operating).
Lycoming County, Williamsport City.
1862 to 1937, 4 Linear Inches.

History:
Susquehanna Boom Co. was incorporated 26 March 1846 to boom and raft logs in the Susquehanna River at Williamsport City in Lycoming County. It took advantage of the huge expanse of virgin timber which lined the river and employed lumbermen to raft logs, downriver to the company's boom,. The boom which held several million logs was a very profitable operation as it provided wood for thirty sawmills and lumberyards located in the Williamsport area. By the 1900's the area's timber reserves had become depleted, and with business rapidly declining the company was sold to the Lycoming Improvement Co. in 1908. The Improvement Co. reorganized the Susquehanna Boom Co. and used it to maintain the dam across the river. In 1923 Lehigh Power and Securities Corp. acquired control of the Lycoming Improvement Co. The Susquehanna Boom Co. proved to be a valuable asset. It retained river rights at Williamsport and supplied condensing water which was used at various generating plants. As an Audit Report observed, "If the dam was taken out it would tend to make the operation of the Williamsport Power Plant a very difficult matter." By 1925 control of the company had passed to Pennsylvania Power & Light. Susquehanna Boom Co. was listed as "inactive", and was finally dissolved in 1937. PP&L retained control of the Williamsport Dam and Susquehanna River rights.

Administrative Records:
Minute Book, 1862-1937
Minutes, 1937
Stock Certificate Book, 1870-1937
Stock Ledger, 1851-1910

Operating Records:
General Ledger, 1926-1937
Audit Reports, 1924-1931 (6 Volumes)

Scope and Content Note:
The Minute Book of Susquehanna Boom Co. contains both Director's and Stockholders' Minutes. They are quite detailed and record various aspects of company operations including: (1) log-running and log-booming, (2) construction of the dam across the Susquehanna, (3) land purchases and river rights, (4) the company's reactions to legislation governing river tolls and, (5) the use of the river for floating logs. Statistics illustrate the growth of the lumber industry in southeastern Pennsylvania in the nineteenth century, and to its subsequent decline after 1900. Copies of correspondence in the Minute Book trace the company's relationship to Eau Claire Lumber Co., Eau Claire, Wisconsin. Minutes and Audit Reports for the period after 1910 describe repairs to the dam, financial underwriting of the company by Williamsport Passenger Railway Co., and its relation with Lycoming Improvement Co., Lehigh Power Securities Corp., and Pennsylvania Power & Light Co.

889. SUSQUEHANNA CANAL AND POWER COMPANY (Operating).
Lancaster County, Martic Township.
1902 to 1955, 6 Linear Inches.

History:
Susquehanna Canal and Power Co. was incorporated 17 April 1902 in Martic Township, Lancaster County. Company organizers were interested in promoting a threefold plan to: (1) extend the tidewater navigation of the Chesapeake Bay northward on the Susquehanna River to a large storage dam at Columbia, Pa., (2) develop the 200 foot drop of the river so hydroelectric power could be generated and then supplied to Baltimore, Philadelphia and Wilmington, and (3) establish an electric railway along the canal towpath. The promoters organized Tide Water and Susquehanna River Railroad Co. and Susquehanna Falls Power Co. as part of this projected development. In the meantime, opposition arose from a group which had devised its own scheme for developing the hydroelectric potential of the Susquehanna River at McCall's Ferry and which had begun to buy up land along the route of the old Tidewater Canal in Maryland. Beginning in late 1902, the McCall's Ferry group fought unsuccessfully to have legislation passed in the Pennsylvania legislature to repeal the corporate charter of Susquehanna Canal and Power Co., based on the claim that the company's charter limited it to the operation of the canal. The Harrisburg Board of Trade, however, lobbied successfully for the Susquehanna group. In October 1903 the opposing groups signed the "Harrisburg Agreement", which gave the McCall's Ferry interests the

right to build a dam, and waived any damages resulting from flooding of the canal and proposed railroad route caused by its construction. The Susquehanna company balked when it learned that the McCall's Ferry group also planned to build dams and hydroelectric facilities at Peach Bottom in Maryland. The two parties did not resume negotiations until early 1905. They arrived at an agreement under which Susquehanna Canal and Power Co. would construct the dams and hydroelectric facilities on the Susquehanna River. At that point the State of Pennsylvania stepped in. In Pennsylvania vs McCall Ferry Power Co. et al., 1906, the state tried to block the project by saying that Susquehanna Canal and Power Co. could not consent to the possible destruction of its property, and that McCall Ferry Power Co. was seeking to act beyond its specified charter rights. The case was ultimately decided in favor of McCall Ferry Power Co. Susquehanna Canal and Power Co., for its part, maintained that it had ceded to the opposing group only the right to use the waters which it controlled, and that it had not given it any property rights. That point became moot in 1910 when McCall Ferry Power Co. bought out Susquehanna Canal and Power Co. and its subsidiaries. The successor to McCall Ferry Power Co., Pennsylvania Water & Power Co., continued to operate Susquehanna Canal and Power Co. as a subsidiary until it was merged into Pennsylvania Power & Light Co. in 1955. PP&L dissolved the Canal Power Co. in 1958.

Administrative Records:
Stock Certificate Book, 1902-1955
Stock Certificates, Susquehanna Falls Power Co., Susquehanna Storage Lake and Power Co., 1902

Operating Records:
Journal, 1942-1958
Financial and Operating Reports, 1955-1958

Scope and Content Note:
In addition to the few records listed under Susquehanna Canal and Power Co. above, a large body of correspondence, court briefs, affadavits, agreements, and other information relating to the company is indexed in the microfilm records of Pennsylvania Water and Power Co. That material documents the prolonged battle waged by the Susquehanna promoters, and the backers of McCall Ferry Power Co. over the use of the Susquehanna River for hydroelectricity. It also traces the efforts to repeal the charter of Susquehanna Canal and Power Co in the Pennsylvania State Legislature.

890. SUSQUEHANNA COLLIERIES COMPANY (Operating).
Dauphin County, Lykens Borough.
1918 to 1922, 3 Linear Feet.

History:
Susquehanna Collieries Co., formed in 1918, was successor to Susquehanna Coal Co. It operated a number of anthracite coal mines in Lycoming, Northumberland, Dauphin, and Luzerne Counties in Pennsylvania. Following its formation, the company began electrifying its collieries, retaining the services of H.C. Felver, an engineering and contracting firm. H.C. Felver completed this work in 1922, the year in which Susquehanna Collieries Co. was acquired by M.A. Hanna & Co., a holding company. In the late 1920s the companies began divesting itself of the generating plants it had erected to serve its mines since under Pennsylvania law if it did not it could be considered a public utility. Susquehanna Collieries then sold its generating station to Pennsylvania Power & Light Co. In 1942 PP&L gained control of the Lykens Steam Electric Station, Lykens Borough, Dauphin County. This particular station had been erected by Susquehanna Collieries about 1918 to pulverize coal and burn it to feed three turbine generators, with a total capacity of 17,000-kw.

Operating Records:
Materials Cost Registers, 1918-1920 (3 Volumes)
Insurance Record, 1918-1920
Authorities for Expenditures, 1918-1922 (2 Volumes)
Journal Vouchers, 1919-1922
Invoice Transmittal Statements, 1918-1922 (2 Volumes)
Accident and Liability Insurance Payroll Statements, 1918-1922
Superintendent's Cash Reports, 1918-1922
Material Reports, Inventories, Order Registers, 1918-1922
Time Books, 1918-1920
Time Books, 1920-1921

Scope and Content Note:
The records listed under Susquehanna Collieries Co. consist of accounts, expenditure requisitions, time books, and othe materials relating to the operations of H.C. Felfer, engineers and contractors. They are useful both for describing the process of electrification which was undertaken at Susquehanna Collieries's coal mines, and for tracing the business procedures of an engineering and contracting firm.

891. SUSQUEHANNA GAS COMPANY (Operating).
Lycoming County, Williamsport City.
1930 to 1945, 1 Linear Foot.

History:
Susquehanna Gas Co. was incorporated by Pennsylvania Power & Light Co. 14 January 1931 to produce, transport and sell natural gas in areas coincedent with PP&L's manufactured gas territory. PP&L formed the gas company in 1930 after natural gas fields were discovered in Tioga County, near the northwestern section of PP&L's territory. It also formed North Branch Development Co. to operate natural gas drills in the Tioga fields. Susquehanna Gas Co. provided the gas transmission service for PP&L, operating a 14 inch pipeline from the Tioga fields to PP&L's natural gas plant in Williamsport, Lycoming County. It also acquired control of Conestoga Terminal Co. and Columbia Gas Co. By the late 1930s the Tioga fields had become depleted and PP&L began dismantling its gas rigs. As of 1941 Susquehanna Gas Co. had become inactive.

Operating Records:
Summary of Cash, 1931-1945 (2 Volumes)
Transmittals and Approvals, 1936
Repair Authorities, 1933
Expenditure Requisitions, 1931-1941
Work in Progress Transfer Binders, 1931-1944 (4 Volumes)
Fixed Capital Control Ledger, 1930-1940

Amortization of Investment, 1931-1941
Audit Reports, 1931-1932
Payroll Authority, 1931-1941
Payroll Transmittals, 1932-1941

Scope and Content Note:
Considerable information about the operations of Susquehanna Gas Co. appears in the correspondence, memoranda, reports, and Audit Reports listed under North Branch Development Co.

892. SUSQUEHANNA ICE COMPANY (Operating).
Clinton County, Renovo Borough.
1942 to 1946, 2 Linear Inches.

History:
Susquehanna Ice Co. was incorporated about 1936 by interests connected with Renovo Edison Light, Heat and Power Co., No. 2 to manufacture ice in Renovo Borough, Clinton County. The stock of the company was controlled by Republic Service Corp., a Delaware holding company which also controlled Renovo Edison. In February 1943 the Securities and Exchange Commission ordered Republic Service to recapitalize its corporate structure, and to divest itself of most of its assets. In 1946 the Susquehanna Ice Co. was sold to Pennsylvania Power & Light Co. (which also acquired Renovo Edison).

Operating Records:
Financial Statements, 1942-1946

893. SUSQUEHANNA POWER & LIGHT COMPANY (Non-operating).
Lycoming County, Susquehanna Township.
1923, 1 Linear Inch.

History:
Susquehanna Power & Light Co., incorporated 23 February 1923 to supply electricity in Susquehanna Township, Lycoming County, merged into Pennsylvania Power & Light Co., 27 August 1923.

894. SUSQUEHANNA TRANSMISSION COMPANY OF PENNSYLVANIA (Operating).
Lancaster County, Martic Township.
1910 to 1937, 1 Linear Inch.

History:
Susquehanna Transmission Co. of Pa., a wholly owned subsidiary of Pennsylvania Water & Power Co. was incorporated 16 April 1910 to construct and operate electric distribution, transmission, telegraph and telephone lines. The lines extended eight miles from the Holtwood Dam on the Susquehanna River in Martic Township, Lancaster County, into the state of Maryland. At that point they connected to a Baltimore substation. By 1917, Susquehanna Transmission Co. of Pa. had erected two steel tower lines over the company's right-of-way in York County. Each carried three 3-phase aluminum lines of 70,000 volts capacity. Pennsylvania Water & Power Co. operated Susquehanna Transmission Co. of Pa. until 1939, at which point it dissolved the company as a wholly-owned subsidiary and acquired its assets.

Administrative Records:
Minute Books, 1910-1930 (2 Volumes)
Stock Certificate Book, 1911-1937

895. SWATARA-LEBANON POWER & LIGHT COMPANY (Non-operating).
Lebanon County, Swatara Township.
1927, 1 Linear Inch.

History:
Swatara-Lebanon Power & Light Co., incorporated 2 September 1927 to supply electricity in Swatara Township, Lebanon County, merged into Pennsylvania Power & Light Co., 16 September 1927.

896. TAMAQUA & LANSFORD STREET RAILWAY COMPANY (Operating).
Carbon County, Lansford Borough.
1893 to 1907, 3 Linear Feet.

History:
Tamaqua & Lansford Street Railway Co. was incorporated 2 November 1891 to operate an electric street railway between the Boroughs of Tamaqua, Schuylkill County, and Lansford, Carbon County. The company was organized and controlled by Lehigh Coal and Navigation Co. Construction was delayed for several years because the company did not have the consent of the Tamaqua, and Lansford, Borough Councils. However, in 1897 it received the necessary franchises. Construction began in June, and by October the first trains were operating on the line. From 1901 to 1903 service was extended to the Borough of Mauch Chunk. In 1906, the company sold its assets to J.G. White & Co., engineers and contractors. Its name was changed to Eastern Pennsylvania Railways Co.

Administrative Records:
Minute Book, 1893-1906
Stock Certificate Book, 1897-1906
Stock Ledger, 1897-1906

Operating Records:
General Ledger, 1897-1906
Journal, 1897-1906
Record of Bills, 1897-1904
Accounts Payable Ledger, 1906-1907
Inventory—Plant and Property, 1899-1905
Original Income Reports, 1897-1906
Daily Time Book, 1904-1907
Audited Voucher Register, 1905

Scope and Content Note:
The Minute Book documents the company's organization, its relationship to the Lehigh Coal and Navigation Co. and the communities it served. Also included are copies of trackage and traffic agreements, descriptions of routes, financial statements, and a report from a consulting engineer describing electrical equipment installed in the company's power house. The Daily Time Book lists employees, the number of hours they worked per day, and the date when conductors and motormen were placed on a regular route.

897. THE TAMAQUA AND POTTSVILLE ELECTRIC RAILROAD (Operating).
Schuylkill County, Pottsville City.
1896 to 1923, 1/2 Linear Foot.

History:
The Tamaqua and Pottsville Electric Railroad was

incorporated 5 May 1892. It operated an electric street railway between Pottsville, Port Carbon, and St. Clair, Schuylkill County. On 28 July 1896 the company leased its line to the Schuylkill Electric Railway Co., which had financed its construction. The company began service in 1897. On 1 September 1899 Schuylkill Electric Railway Co. leased this company to Pottsville Union Traction Co., which had gained control of all the street railways operating in the vicinity of Pottsville. In January 1905 the company decided to extend its line from St. Clair to the Borough of Shenandoah, and by December of that year it obtained almost all of the necessary rights-of-way. However, nothing was done to construct the line. On 25 January 1923, The Tamaqua and Pottsville Electric Railroad was consolidated and merged with Eastern Pennsylvania Light, Heat and Power Co., and Pottsville Union Traction Co. to form Eastern Pennsylvania Power and Railway Co.

Administrative Records:
Minute Books, 1896-1923 (2 Volumes)
Stock Certificate Books, 1895-1923 (2 Volumes)

Operating Records:
Cashbook, 1905-1906
Audit Report, 1923

Scope and Content Note:
The Minute Book of The Tamaqua and Pottsville Electric Railroad documents the company's organization, its relationships with the Schuylkill Electric Railway Co. and the Pottsville Union Traction Co., and its dealings with the communities it served. Also included are copies of ordinances granting the company rights-of-way, and trackage and traffic agreements.

898. TAMAQUA LIGHT, HEAT AND POWER COMPANY (Operating).
Schuylkill County, Tamaqua Borough.
1905 to 1909, 3 Linear Inches.

History:
Tamaqua Light, Heat and Power Co. was incorporated 24 February 1905 to supply electricity in the Borough of Tamaqua Schuylkill County. The company erected an electric generating plant and secured a contract to provide street lighting in the Borough. It competed fiercely with The Edison Electric Illuminating Co. of Tamaqua, Pa., and repeatedly tried to buy out its rival. In 1908 the company enlarged its power plant by adding two additional generators. Early in 1909 Eastern Pennsylvania Railways Co. gained control of the Tamaqua company's stock, and on 20 July 1909 it was merged into Palo Alto Heat, Light and Power Co.

Administrative Records:
Minute Book, 1905-1909
Stock Certificate Book, 1909
Ballots—Sale to Palo Alto Heat, Light & Power Co., 1909

Operating Records:
General Ledger, 1909
Cashbook, 1909
Operating Statistics, 1909
Balance Sheets, 1909

Scope and Content Note:
The Minute Book of the Tamaqua Light, Heat and Power Co. provides information about the company's purchases of equipment for its power house, and its rivalry with The Edison Electric Illuminating Co. of Tamaqua Pa.

899. TAMAQUA-SCHUYLKILL GAS COMPANY (Non-operating).
Schuylkill County, Tamaqua Borough.
1927 to 1928, 1 Linear Inch.

History:
Tamaqua-Schuylkill Gas Co. was incorporated 31 August 1927 to manufacture and supply gas in the Borough of Tamaqua, Schuylkill County. On 29 October 1927 it was merged into East Penn Electric Co. No. 2.

900. TANEY ELECTRIC COMPANY (Non-operating).
Schuylkill County, East Norwegian Township.
1911 to 1913, 1 Linear Inch.

History:
Taney Electric Co. was incorporated 27 June 1911 to supply electricity in the Township of East Norwegian, Schuylkill County. On 23 December 1912 it was consolidated and merged with 37 non-operating companies to form Lehigh Navigation Electric Co. No. 2.

901. TATAMY LIGHT HEAT AND POWER COMPANY (Operating).
Northampton County, Tatamy Borough.
1907 to 1928, 2 1/2 Linear Feet.

History:
Tatamy Light Heat and Power Co. was incorporated 4 January 1907 by the Messinger family, owners of the Messinger Manufacturing Co., located in the Borough of Tatamy, Northumberland County. Tatamy Light Heat and Power purchased its electricity from the Messinger Manufacturing Co. and built a distribution system to serve the Borough. In 1915 both companies began to purchase their electricity from Lehigh Navigation Electric Co. In 1920 Tatamy Light Heat and Power extended its service to the Tatamy Silk Mill, and in 1924 expanded again to serve the Borough of Stockertown, by incorporating the "paper company", Stockertown Light, Heat & Power Co. In 1925 the Tatamy company's stock was acquired by Lehigh Power Securities Corp., which integrated it into the Pennsylvania Power & Light Co. system. The company was merged into Pennsylvania Power & Light on 28 May 1928.

Administrative Records:
Minute Book, 1907-1928
Stock Certificate Books, 1907-1925 (2 Volumes)
Stock Transfer Record, 1925
Stock Ledger, 1922-1928
Correspondence & Miscellaneous Papers, 1907-1922

Operating Records:
FINANCIAL RECORDS
General Ledgers, 1923-1928 (2 Volumes)
Journal, 1923-1925
Journal Entry Register, 1925-1928

Cashbook, 1924-1925
Record of Cash Receipts, 1925-1928
Record of Cash Disbursements, 1925-1928
Summary of Cash, 1925
etail Ledger, 1925-1928
Detail of Cost Study and Fixed Capital, 1926-1927
CONSUMER RECORDS
Accounts Receivable, 1925-1928
Summary of Accounts Receivable—Consumers, 1925-1928
Summary of Accounts Receivable—Miscellaneous, 1926-1928
Summary of Consumers' Deposits, 1925-1928
AUDIT REPORTS, 1923-1927 (4 Volumes)

Scope and Content Note:
The Minute Book clearly documents the dominant role that the Messinger family played in the company. It also lists operating expenses and electric rates. The Correspondence File describes the company's dealings with the Borough Council of Tatamy, and negotiations for street lighting contracts. There is also some material documenting the United States Fuel Administration's recommendations for coal conservation during World War I.

902. TAYLOR ELECTRIC COMPANY (Operating).
Lackawanna County, Taylor Township.
1911 to 1912, 2 Linear Inches.

History:
Taylor Electric Co. was organized by American Gas & Electric Co. in July 1911 to supply electricity in the Township of Taylor, Lackawanna County. It was serving only three or four customers on a regular basis by the time it was merged into Scranton Electric Co. on 25 November 1912.

Operating Records:
General Ledger, 1911-1912
Journal, 1911-1912
Cashbook, 1911-1912

903. TELFORD POWER & LIGHT COMPANY (Non-operating).
Bucks County, Telford Borough.
1923 to 1924, 1 Linear Inch.

History:
Telford Power & Light Co. was incorporated 21 November 1923 to supply electricity in the Borough of Telford, Bucks County. On 31 March 1924 it was merged into Pennsylvania Power & Light Co.

904. TEXAS POWER & LIGHT COMPANY (Non-operating).
Wayne County, Texas Township.
1923 to 1924, 1 Linear Inch.

History:
Texas Power & Light Co., incorporated 20 February 1924 to supply electricity in the Township of Texas, Wayne County, was merged into Honesdale Consolidated Light, Heat and Power Co. 12 May 1924.

905. TINICUM TOWNSHIP ELECTRIC COMPANY (Non-operating).
Bucks County, Tinicum Township.
1913 to 1935, 2 Linear Inches.

History:
Tinicum Township Electric Co. was one of eleven companies chartered by Lehigh Navigation Electric Co. in December 1913 to obtain franchise rights in the townships along the Delaware Canal, in Bucks County. At this time, Lehigh Navigation Electric Co. was controlled by Lehigh Coal and Navigation Co., which also controlled the Delaware Canal Co. Tinicum Township Electric Co. and its ten counterparts were "paper companies," formed solely to secure franchise rights. They never engaged in active operations. As of 1926, Tinicum Township Electric Co. was listed as 'inactive.' In 1935 it was officially dissolved.

906. TOBYHANNA POWER & LIGHT COMPANY (Non-operating).
Monroe County, Tobyhanna Township.
1923 to 1924, 1 Linear Inch.

History:
Tobyhanna Power & Light Co. was incorporated 1 May 1923 to supply electricity in the Township of Tobyhanna, Monroe County. On 20 July 1923 it was consolidated and merged with 31 other non-operating companies to form Paupack Power & Light Co. No. 2.

907. TOPTON ELECTRIC COMPANY (Non-operating).
Berks County, Topton Borough.
1916 to 1917, 1 Linear Inch.

History:
Topton Electric Co. was incorporated 4 January 1916 to supply electricity in the Borough of Topton, Berks County. On 16 September 1916 the company was merged into Lehigh Valley Light and Power Co. No. 3.

908. TOWAMENCIN-MONTGOMERY POWER & LIGHT COMPANY (Non-operating).
Montgomery County, Towamencin Township.
1927 to 1928, 1 Linear Inch.

History:
Towamencin-Montgomery Power & Light Co. was incorporated 2 September 1927 to supply electricity in a portion of the Township of Towamencin, Montgomery County. On 16 September 1927 the company was merged into Pennsylvania Power & Light Co.

909. TOWAMENSING POWER & LIGHT COMPANY (Non-operating).
Carbon County, Towamensing Township.
1923 to 1924, 1 Linear Inch.

History:
Towamensing Power & Light Co. was incorporated 1 May 1923 to supply electricity in the Township of Towamensing, Carbon County. On 20 July 1923 it was consolidated and merged with 31 non-operating companies to form Paupack Power & Light Co. No. 2.

910. TOWER CITY ELECTRIC COMPANY (Non-operating).
Schuylkill County, Tower City Borough.
1909 to 1910, 1 Linear Inch.

History:
Tower City Electric Co. was incorporated 7 December 1909 to supply electricity in the Borough of Tower City, Schuylkill County. In May 1910 the company was taken over by United Gas & Electric Co.

911. TREMONT & DONALDSON ELECTRIC LIGHT COMPANY (Operating).
Schuylkill County, Tremont Borough.
1916 to 1925, 1 Linear Inch.

History:
Tremont & Donaldson Electric Light Co. was probably incorporated in 1916 to supply electricity in the Borough of Tremont, and the Village of Donaldson, Schuylkill County. It was a subsidiary of Eastern Pennsylvania Railways Co.

Operating Records:
Cashbook, 1916-1925
Comments on Audit, 1920

912. TREMONT AND PINE GROVE ELECTRIC LIGHT HEAT AND POWER COMPANY (Operating).
Schuylkill County, Tremont Borough.
1905 to 1916, 4 Linear Inches.

History:
Tremont and Pine Grove Electric Light Heat and Power Co. was incorporated 18 June 1894 to supply electricity in the Boroughs of Tremont, and Pine Grove, Schuylkill County. The company built an electric generating plant in Tremont, and a distribution system to serve Tremont, and Pine Grove. In 1906 the company extended its service to the Village of Donaldson, Schuylkill County. It merged into Eastern Pennsylvania Light, Heat and Power Co, 18 July 1916.

Administrative Records:
Minute Book, 1905-1916
Stock Certificate Books, 1905-1916 (2 Volumes)
Stock Transfer Record, 1916

Operating Records:
General Ledger, 1916
Cashbook, 1916
Accounts Payable Ledger, 1916

Scope and Content Note:
The Minute Book of Tremont and Pine Grove Electric Light Heat and Power Co. documents routine stockholders' and directors' meetings, while the other records provide infromation regarding the company's financial condition in 1916.

913. TREMONT-SCHUYLKILL POWER & LIGHT COMPANY (Non-operating).
Schuylkill County, Tremont Township.
1925 to 1926, 1 Linear Inch.

History:
Tremont-Schuylkill Power & Light Co. was incorporated 26 March 1926 to supply electricity in a portion of the Township of Tremont, Schuylkill County. On 14 April 1926 the company was merged into Pennsylvania Power & Light Co.

914. THE TREVORTON ELECTRIC LIGHT AND POWER COMPANY (Operating).
Northumberland County, Trevorton Village.
1901 to 1920, 1 Linear Foot.

History:
The Trevorton Electric Light and Power Co. was incorporated 12 August 1901 to supply electricity in the Village of Treverton, Northumberland County. The company built a small steam electric generating station and a distribution system to serve the village. In April 1912 it sold its power plant to the Pennsylvania Lighting Co., which had acquired a majority of its stock. In March 1915 the boiler and generating equipment were sold, and the company began to purchase electricity from Pennsylvania Lighting Co. On 16 April 1920 the company was merged into Pennsylvania Lighting Co.

Administrative Records:
Minute Book, 1906-1920
Stock Certificate Book, 1904-1920

Operating Records:
General Ledger, 1912-1920
Journal, 1912-1920
Cashbook, 1912-1920
Payroll Vouchers and Payrolls, 1916-1917
Trial Balances, 1912-1920
Monthly Statements, 1912-1920
Tax on Capital Stock, 1902-1922
Tax on Gross Receipts, 1901-1911
Audit Report, 1917-1919

Scope and Content Note:
In addition to documenting stockholders' and directors' meetings, the Minute Book of The Trevorton Electric Light and Power Co. includes statements of assets and liabilities, and a 1906 rate schedule which indicates that service was priced according to type of establishment, e.g., saloon, mill or private residence. The company's payrolls list employees, their job descriptions and pay rates. The Monthly Statements show various financial data, such as net earnings, detailed breakdowns of expenses, and assets and liabilities.

915. TRI-COUNTY ELECTRIC COMPANY (Operating).
Lancaster County, Lincoln Borough.
1915 to 1926, 1 Linear Foot.

History:
Tri-County Electric Co. was organized on 4 February 1925 following the consolidation and merger of six non-operating companies. Early in 1915 Tri-County Electric, which had its main offices in the Borough of Lincoln, purchased the distribution system which had been built by Mr. Jacob S. Weaver in the Village of Churchtown. The company then extended this system to several villages and townships in the rural areas of Lancaster, Berks and Chester Counties. It purchased all of its power from Edison Electric Co. No. 4. Tri-County Electric's service was not very efficient, and was plagued by frequent outages due to transformer burn-outs and other accidents. In 1924 the company's stock was acquired by Lancaster County Railway and Light Co. It was merged into Edison Electric Co. on 30 June 1925.

Administrative Records:
Minute Books, 1915-1925 (2 Volumes)
Stock Certificate Book, 1915-1925
Stock Transfer Record, 1916

Operating Records:
General Ledger, 1924-1926
Journal, 1924-1926
Cashbook, 1924-1926

Daybook, 1920-1921
Miscellaneous Financial Statements, 1923-1924
Expenses, 1915-1919
Financial Report, 1924-1926
Expenditure Requisitions, 1924-1926
Audit Reports, 1923-1925 (4 Volumes)

Scope and Content Note:
The Minute Book of the Tri-County Electric Co. contains information on the company's rates, customers, dealings with the Borough Councils of Honey Brook, and Elverson in regard to street lighting contracts. Also included are statements of earnings and operating expenses, lists of stockholders, and a copy of an agreement with Mr. Jacob S. Weaver for the purchase of his distribution system in the Village of Churchtown.

916. TROXELVILLE POWER COMPANY
(Non-operating).
Snyder County, Adams Township.
1923, 1 Linear Inch.

History:
Troxeville Power Co., incorporated 1 November 1923 to supply electricity in the Township of Adams, Snyder County, was merged into Middleburg Light, Heat and Power Co. 21 November 1923.

917. TRUMBAUERSVILLE ELECTRIC LIGHT AND POWER COMPANY (Operating).
Bucks County, Trumbauersville Borough.
1912 to 1919, 1 Linear Foot.

History:
Trumbauersville Electric Light and Power Co. was incorporated 6 June 1912 by the Lehigh Valley Transit Co. The company supplied electricity in the Borough of Trumbauersville, Bucks County, during its short period of operations prior to its merger into Lehigh Valley Light and Power Co. No. 3, 29 December 1913.

Administrative Records:
Stock Certificate Book, 1912-1913

Operating Records:
General Ledger, 1912-1914
Journal, 1912-1914
Cashbook, 1912-1914
Voucher Index, undated
Installations and Meter Work, 1912-1919
Cancelled Checks, 1912-1914
Check Stubs, 1912-1914
Bank Passbook, 1913-1914

Scope and Content Note:
The Installations and Meter Work Account is of particular interest as it documents installation and maintenance work done on meters. Included are inventories of electrical fixtures in residential and commercial property, and demographic data on the occupants. Renters and owners are seperately classified.

918. TUCKAHOE LITHIA WATER COMPANY
(Operating).
Northumberland County, Milton Borough.
1898 to 1908, 1 Linear Inch.

History:
Tuckahoe Lithia Water Co. was incorporated 15 November 1898 to bottle and sell spring water from the Tuckahoe Springs near the Borough of Milton, Northumberland County. The company sold its water under the trade name of "Lithia Water" through company-sponsored agencies in Pennsylvania, New York, and Canada. In April 1908 the company's stock was acquired by the Northumberland County Railway and Light Co., which was in the process of securing monopolies over the supply of water, waterpower, and electricity in Northumberland County. This company already owned the other major producer of Lithia water, Tuckhoe Mineral Springs Co., No. 2. Tuckahoe Lithia Water Co. was probably merged into that company soon after its acquisition by Northumberland County Railway and Light.

Administrative Records:
Minute Book, 1898-1908
Stock Certificate Book, 1899-1908
Application for Incorporation, 1898
Letters Patent, 1898
Certificate of Change of Principal Office, 1908

Scope and Content Note:
The Minute Book of the Tuckahoe Lithia Water Co. documents the company's organization, franchise rights and rivalry with Tuckahoe Mineral Springs Co., No. 2. Also included is a financial report detailing the company's assets and liabilities.

919. TUCKAHOE MINERAL SPRINGS COMPANY, NO. 1 (Operating).
Northumberland County, Milton Borough.
1899 to 1901, 1 Linear Inch.

History:
Tuckahoe Mineral Springs Co., No. 1, was incorporated in 1898. The company bottled and sold spring water from the Tuckahoe Springs near the Borough of Milton, Northumberland County, under the trade name of "Lithia Water." By 1900 the company was selling its water through company-sponsored agencies in New York, Pennsylvania, Canada, Indiana, and Kentucky. In May 1901 the company sold its assets and franchises to the Tuckahoe Mineral Springs Co. of Northumberland, Northumberland County, Pennsylvania, and then dissolved itself 19 July 1901.

Administrative Records:
Minute Book, 1899-1901

920. TUCKAHOE MINERAL SPRINGS COMPANY, NO. 2 (Operating).
Northumberland County, Milton Borough.
1907, 1 Linear Inch.

History:
Tuckahoe Mineral Springs Co., No. 2, was incorporated in the State of Delaware in 1907. The company was organized by the Northumberland County Railway and Light Co., which was in the process of securing monopolies on the supply of water, waterpower, and electricity in the County of Northumberland. Tuckahoe Mineral Springs Co. bottled and sold spring water from the Tuckahoe Springs near the Borough of Milton,

Northumberland County, under the trade name of "Lithia Water". It was controlled by Northumberland County Railway and Light until 1911, when a number of that company's holdings, including Tuckahoe Mineral Springs Co., were acquired by the Northumberland County Gas & Electric Co. The history of the Tuckahoe Mineral Springs Co. thereafter is unknown.

Administrative Records:
Stock Certificate Book, 1907

921. TUCKAHOE MINERAL SPRINGS COMPANY OF NORTHUMBERLAND, NORTHUMBERLAND COUNTY, PENNSYLVANIA (Operating).
Northumberland County, Milton Borough.
1901 to 1906, 1 Linear Inch.

History:
Tuckahoe Mineral Springs Co. of Northumberland, Northumberland County, Pennsylvania, was incorporated in the State of Delaware in May 1901. Shortly after its incorporation, the company purchased the assets and franchises of the Tuckahoe Mineral Springs Co., No. 1. It then began to bottle and sell spring water under the trade name of "Lithia Water". In 1907 the company was acquired by Northumberland County Railway and Light Co., which then used its property and assets to set up Tuckahoe Mineral Springs Co., No. 2.

Administrative Records:
Minute Book, 1901-1906

922. TUMBLING RUN PARK ASSOCIATION (Operating).
Schuylkill County, North Manheim Township.
1902 to 1934, 1 1/2 Linear Feet.

History:
Tumbling Run Lake in North Manheim Township, Schuylkill County, resulted from the construction of two reservoirs in the late 19th century. It was already the site of a hotel, a restaurant, and several boathouses by 1902, when Mr. Robert E. Lee purchased the property. Mr. Lee sold the property to the Tumbling Run Park Association, of which he was the president, shortly after its incorporation 16 May 1902. The Park Association was controlled by the Tamaqua and Lansford Street Railway Co., which also operated an electric railway line to Tumbling Run Park. The Park Association improved the park's grounds, repaired the buildings, and added other attractions. By 1905 the park could boast a hotel, a restaurant, a theatre (at which the Tumbling Run Opera Co. gave performances), a beach with boathouses, baseball fields, and several other attractions common to the amusement parks of the day, such as a photo gallery, a carousel, a penny arcade, a dancing pavilion, a shooting gallerys, a soda fountain, and a bowling alley. The park began to experience financial difficulties in 1908 and became increasingly unprofitable to operate. It closed in 1914. By August 1921, according to its Minute Book, the Park Association felt that "the property was of no further use to the company," and it began to sell parcels of land. On 24 June 1922 the remaining property was sold to the Philadelphia & Reading Coal & Iron Co. At this time there was an effort made to dissolve the company, but a minority of stockholders objected and the idea was dropped. The Park Association finally filed an "out of existence" affidavit on 31 March 1934.

Administrative Records:
Minute Book, 1902-1925
Stock Certificate Book, 1902-1903
Stock Transfer Record, 1916-1919

Operating Records:
General Ledgers, 1902-1934 (4 Volumes)
Daily Cash Receipts, 1907-1910
Cashbooks, 1902-1922
Record of Cash Receipts, 1902-1908
Daybook, 1904-1906
Audited Voucher Registers, 1906-1917 (3 Volumes)
Accounts Payable, 1906-1908 (2 Volumes)
Charges to Local Construction, 1908
Payroll Book, 1902-1906
Earnings & Operating Expenses, 1907-1908
Balance Sheets, 1907-1911
Journal, 1918-1922
Audit Report, 1920-1925

Scope and Content Note:
The Minute Book of the Tumbling Run Park Association documents the company's organization, its relationship with the Tamaqua and Lansford Street Railway Co., and its development of Tumbling Run Park as a popular amusement center. The Payroll Book lists the company's employees and their pay rates, and shows where they worked in the park—at the bar, the carousel, the theatre, the soda fountain, etc. This book can be used to trace the addition of new amusements to the park, and to determine the length of its season. The Daily Cash Receipts show how many people attended each attraction, and occasionally note special events (such as baseball games), or theatre productions (such as "A Night in Old Japan".) Filed with the receipts from Tumbling Run Park, and providing the same information, are daily receipts from Manila Grove Park, another popular amusement park owned by the Tamaqua and Lansford Street Railway Co.

923. TUNKHANNOCK POWER & LIGHT COMPANY (Non-operating).
Monroe County, Tunkhannock Township.
1923 to 1924, 1 Linear Inch.

History:
Tunkhannock Power & Light Co. was incorporated 1 May 1923 to supply electricity in the Township of Tunkhannock, Monroe County. On 20 July 1923 it was consolidated and merged with 31 other non-operating companies to form Paupack Power & Light Co. No.2.

924. TURBOT TOWNSHIP NORTHUMBERLAND ELECTRIC COMPANY (Non-operating).
Northumberland County, Turbot Township.
1919 to 1920, 1 Linear Inch.

History:
Turbot Township Northumberland Electric Co., incorporated 6 November 1919 to supply electricity in the Township of Turbot, Northumberland County, was merged into Lehigh Industrial Power Co. on 28 April 1920.

925. TURBOTVILLE ELECTRIC COMPANY (Non-operating).
Northumberland County, Turbotville Borough.
1914, 1 Linear Inch.

History:
Turbotville Electric Co. was incorporated 27 July 1914 to supply electricity in the Borough of Turbotville, Northumberland County. On 3 September 1914 it was merged into Northumberland County Gas & Electric Co.

926. TURBOT TOWNSHIP ELECTRIC COMPANY (Non-operating).
Northumberland County, Turbot Township.
1912, 1 Linear Inch.

History:
Turbot Township Electric Co. was incorporated 5 January 1912 to supply electricity in the Township of Turbot, Northumberland County. On 31 December 1912 it was merged into Northumberland County Gas & Electric Co.

927. UNION-BUFFALO POWER & LIGHT COMPANY (Non-operating).
Union County, Buffalo Township.
1952 to 1953, 1 Linear Inch.

History:
Union-Buffalo Power & Light Co. was incorporated 17 December 1952 by the Pennsylvania Power & Light Co. to supply electricity in the Township of Buffalo, Union County. It was merged into Pennsylvania Power & Light Co., 12 November 1953.

928. UNION-EAST BUFFALO POWER & LIGHT COMPANY (Non-operating).
Union County, East Buffalo Township.
1952 to 1953, 1 Linear Inch.

History:
Union-East Buffalo Power & Light Co. was incorporated by Pennsylvania Power & Light Co. 17 December 1952 to supply electricity in the Township of East Buffalo, Union County. On 12 November 1953 it was merged into Pennsylvania Power & Light Co.

929. UNION ELECTRIC POWER COMPANY (Non-operating).
Dauphin County, Derry Township.
1923, 1 Linear Inch.

History:
Union Electric Power Co., incorporated 19 June 1912 to supply electricity in the Township of Derry, Dauphin County, was merged into Hummelstown Water & Power Co. on 2 January 1924.

930. UNION-LEBANON LIGHT & POWER COMPANY (Non-operating).
Lebanon County, Union Township.
1940 to 1942, 1 Linear Inch.

History:
Union-Lebanon Light & Power Co. was incorporated 22 November 1940 to supply electricity in a portion of the Township of Union, Lebanon County. On 6 November 1941 its property and assets were sold to Pennsylvania Power & Light Co., and on 5 January 1942 it was officially dissolved.

931. UNION-LEBANON POWER & LIGHT COMPANY (Non-operating).
Lebanon County, Union Township.
1927, 1 Linear Inch.

History:
Union-Lebanon Power & Light Co. was incorporated 2 September 1927 to supply electricity in a portion of the Township of Union, Lebanon County. On 16 September 1927 it was merged into Harrisburg Light and Power Co. No. 2.

932. UNION LIGHT AND POWER COMPANY (Non-operating).
Luzerne County, Parsons Borough.
1909 to 1910, 1 Linear Inch.

History:
Union Light and Power Co. was incorporated 18 March 1909 to supply gas lighting in the Boroughs of Parsons and Miners Mills (later annexed to the City of Wilkes-Barre), Luzerne County. On 17 May 1910 the company was consolidated and merged with four other companies to form The Wilkes-Barre Co. No. 2.

933. UNION LIGHT COMPANY (Non-operating).
Schuylkill County, Union Township.
1912, 1 Linear Inch.

History:
Union Light Co. was incorporated 29 November 1912 to supply electricity in the Township of Union, Schuylkill County. On 16 December 1912 it was consolidated and merged with twelve other companies to form Hazleton Electric Co.

934. UNION PASSENGER RAILWAY COMPANY (Non-operating).
Lycoming County, Williamsport City.
1893, 1 Linear Inch.

History:
Union Passenger Railway Co. was incorporated 3 April 1893 to operate an electric street railway in the City of Williamsport, Lycoming County. The company was organized by the Williamsport Passenger Railway Co. in order to extend its own lines and to block the expansion of rival companies. Union Passenger Railway's proposed route, only 1/3 of a mile long, would have connected the Williamsport company's East 3rd Street route with the route of The East End Passenger Railway Co. However, no steps were taken to construct this route and the company remained inactive.

935. UNION POWER & LIGHT COMPANY (Non-operating).
Union County, Union Township.
1923, 1 Linear Inch.

History:
Union Power & Light Co. was incorporated 9 April 1923 to supply electricity in the Township of Union, Union County. On 17 May 1923 it was merged into Pennsylvania Power & Light Co.

936. UNION POWER COMPANY (Operating).
Union County, Lewisburg Borough.
1910 to 1911, 1 Linear Inch.

History:
Union Power Co. was incorporated 31 August 1910 to supply electricity in the Borough of Lewisburg, Union County. In November 1910 the company received the

contract for street lighting in Lewisburg. The company leased all the lines, equipment, and franchises of The Lewisburg Light, Heat and Power Co. on 9 March 1911. Union Power's stock was acquired by United Light and Power Co. in 1911, and was merged into that company 12 June 1911.

Administrative Records:
Minute Book, 1910-1911

Scope and Content Note:
The Minute Book of Union Power Co. contains minutes of stockholders' and directors' meetings, as well as information regarding the company's efforts to secure control of street lighting in the Borough of Lewisburg.

937. UNION TOWNSHIP POWER & LIGHT COMPANY (Non-operating).
Snyder County, Union Township.
1923, 1 Linear Inch.

History:
Union Township Power & Light Co., incorporated 9 April 1923 to supply electricity in the Township of Union, Snyder County, was merged into Pennsylvania Power & Light Co. on 17 May 1923.

938. UNION TOWNSHIP POWER COMPANY (Non-operating).
Schuylkill County, Union Township.
1910 to 1912, 1 Linear Inch.

History:
Union Township Power Co. was incorporated 26 January 1911 to supply electricity in the Township of Union, Schuylkill County. On 12 November 1912 it was consolidated and merged with eleven other companies to form The Schuylkill Gas and Electric Co.

939. UNIONDALE-SUSQUEHANNA POWER & LIGHT COMPANY (Non-operating).
Susquehanna County, Uniondale Borough.
1927 to 1928, 1 Linear Inch.

History:
Uniondale-Susquehanna Power & Light Co., incorporated 20 December 1927 to supply electricity in the Borough of Uniondale, Susquehanna County, was merged into Pennsylvania Power & Light Co. on 3 January 1928.

940. UNIONTOWN PUBLIC SERVICE CORPORATION (Non-operating).
Dauphin County, Uniontown Borough.
1923, 1 Linear Inch.

History:
Uniontown Public Service Corp. was incorporated 19 December 1923 to supply electricity in the Borough of Uniontown, Dauphin County. On 15 January 1924 it was merged into Middleburg Light, Heat and Power Co.

941. THE UNITED ELECTRIC COMPANY (Operating).
Cumberland County, Lemoyne Borough.
1903 to 1928, 4 Linear Feet.

History:
The United Electric Co. was incorporated March 1903 as the result of the consolidation and merger of The Cumberland Light, Heat and Power Co. with seven non-operating companies. The company had its main offices in the Borough of Lemoyne, and supplied electricity in the County of Cumberland. It was organized and owned by Valley Traction Co., which operated an electric street railway system throughout Cumberland County. Soon after United Electric's formation, the generating capacity of Cumberland Light, Heat and Power's power plant was boosted to 4,600-kw in order to meet the power requirements of both the street railway system and the new electric company. At first United Electric's lines only paralleled the tracks of the street railways, serving the Boroughs of Mechanicsburg, Carlisle, Enola, and New Cumberland, but the company steadily expanded its area of operations to include a number of communities in Cumberland and York Counties. In 1922 United Electric's distribution system and that of Harrisburg Light and Power Co. were interconnected. In 1925 Lehigh Power Securities Corp. acquired the stock of United Electric's parent company, Valley Railways (successor to Valley Traction Co.), and in 1927 its distribution system was interconnected with that of the Pennsylvania Power & Light Co. On 28 May 1928 the company was merged into Pennsylvania Power & Light.

Administrative Records:
Minute Books, 1903-1928 (3 Volumes)

Operating Records:
FINANCIAL RECORDS
General Ledgers, 1905-1928 (4 Volumes)
Journals, 1904-1926 (2 Volumes)
Journal Entry Register, 1926-1928
Cashbook, 1925-1926
Distribution of Receipts 1925-1926
Record of Cash Receipts, 1926-1928
Record of Cash Disbursements, 1926-1928
Summary of Cash, 1926-1928
Audited Voucher Registers, 1925-1926 (4 Volumes)
Accounts Payable Ledger, 1926-1928
Plant Improvement, 1911
Distribution of Expenses, 1922-1924
Income Accounts, 1926
Detail Ledger, 1926-1928
Comparative Statement of Earnings and Expenses, 1906-1925
Financial Reports, 1917-1926
Expenditure Requisitions, 1926-1928
Retirement Authorities, 1926-1928
Connected Load Reports, 1926-1927
Comparative Income Account, 1926-1927
Balance Sheets, 1926-1927
CONSUMER RECORDS
Power Lighting Sales Reports, 1926-1927
Summary of Accounts Receivable, 1926-1928
AUDIT REPORTS, 1921-1927

Scope and Content Note:
The Minute Book documents stockholders' and directors' meetings as well as the company's relationship with Valley Railways and Valley Traction Co. It contains copies of mortgages, bylaws and the 1903 merger agreement by which the company was formed. In addition to analyzing the company's financial status, the Audit Report contains copies of electric rate schedules, a

breakdown of operating expenses and lists of franchises. The Power and Light Sales Report lists commercial and residential customers, the number of kilowatt hours they purchased, and the purposes for which this electricity was used (cooking, street lighting, heating etc.)

942. UNITED ELECTRIC LIGHT & POWER COMPANY (Non-operating).
Northampton County, Allen Township.
1913 to 1918, 1 Linear Inch.

History:
United Electric Light & Power Co. was incorporated 26 March 1913 by Lehigh Valley Transit Co. in order to secure franchise rights in the Township of Allen, Northumberland County. The company never entered into active operations and was dissolved on 17 June 1918.

943. UNITED GAS AND ELECTRIC COMPANY OF BLOOMBURG (Operating).
Columbia County, Bloomsburg Town.
1906 to 1909, 1 Linear Inch.

History:
United Gas and Electric Co. of Bloomsburg, which supplied gas and electricity in the Town of Bloomsburg, Columbia County, resulted from the 27 October 1906 consolidation and merger of the American Gas Light Co. of Bloomsburg, Pa., and the American Electric Light Co. of Bloomsburg, Pa. Both of these earlier companies had run into financial difficulties and had been sold to Mr. E.B. Tustin, who then conveyed them to the new company. United Gas and Electric Co. of Bloomsburg was consolidated and merged 7 February 1911 with 21 other companies to form Columbia Gas and Electric Co.

Administrative Records:
Stock Certificate Books, 1906-1909 (2 Volumes)
Stock Transfer Record, 1907-1908
Stock Ledger, 1907-1908

Operating Records:
Trial Balances, 1907-1909

944. UNITED LIGHT AND POWER COMPANY (Operating).
Northumberland County, Milton Borough.
1909 to 1911, 1/2 Linear Foot.

History:
United Light and Power Co. was incorporated 7 December 1909 to supply electricity in the Borough of Milton, Northumberland County. In November 1909 the company had acquired The Pennsylvania General Electric Company's steam electric generating plant in Milton. Soon after its formation the company extended its distribution system to the Borough of Lewisburg, Union County, leased The Lewisburg Light, Heat and Power Co., and then supplied that company with electricity from its power plant in Milton. On 4 January 1910 United Light and Power purchased the property and equipment of the Milton Electric Light and Power Co. and leased its power plant. Later that year the company built a 1,000-kw steam electric generating station in Milton and a distribution line to Sunbury Borough, Northumberland County. In 1911 service was extended to the Village of West Milton, Union County. United Light and Power Co. was consolidated and merged with four other companies 28 August 1911 to form The Edison Electric Illuminating Co. of Sunbury, Pa., No. 4.

Administrative Records:
Minute Book, 1909-1910

Operating Records:
General Ledger, 1911
Cashbook, 1910-1911
Audited Voucher Register, 1910-1911
Statement of Receipts and Expenditures, 1910-1911

Scope and Content Note:
The Minute Book of the United Light and Power Co. documents routine stockholders' and directors' meetings, and contains copies of the company's charter and bylaws.

945. THE UNITED LIGHT, HEAT AND POWER COMPANY OF MAHANOY CITY, PA. (Operating).
Schuylkill County, Mahanoy City Borough.
1910 to 1913, 4 Linear Inches.

History:
The United Light, Heat and Power Co. of Mahanoy City, Pa. was incorporated 27 June 1911 to supply electricity in the Borough of Mahanoy City, Schuylkill County. It was organized by The People's Electric Light, Heat and Power Co. of Shenandoah & Mahanoy City, Pennsylvania, when that company discovered that its charter did not permit it to supply electricity in the Borough of Mahanoy City, even though it had been doing so since 1904. In 1912 the stock of both companies was acquired by the Pardee family interests. The company was consolidated and merged with eleven other companies 12 November 1912 to form The Schuylkill Gas and Electric Co.

Administrative Records:
Minute Book, 1911

Operating Records:
General Ledger, 1910-1913
Journal, 1911-1913
Cash Received, 1911-1912
Check Register, 1911-1912
Payrolls, 1911-1912
Monthly Reports, 1911-1912
Voucher Register, 1911-1912

Scope and Content Note:
The Monthly Reports of The United Light, Heat and Power Co. of Mahanoy City, Pa. document sales of arc and incandescent lighting to both residential customers and local governments. Payrolls list names and wages of employees. Additional information concerning this company may be found in the "Historical Report of The Harwood Electric Co. and Its Antecedent and Allied Companies," filed with the records of The Harwood Electric Co.

946. UPPER ALSACE TOWNSHIP ELECTRIC COMPANY (Non-operating).
Berks County, Upper Alsace Township.
1915 to 1916, 1 Linear Inch.

History:
Upper Alsace Township Electric Co. was incorporated 21 February 1916 to supply electricity in the Township of Upper Alsace, Berks County. On 27 September 1916 it was merged into Lehigh Navigation Electric Co. No. 2.

947. UPPER AUGUSTA POWER & LIGHT COMPANY (Non-operating).
Northumberland County, Upper Augusta Township.
1922 to 1923, 1 Linear Inch.

History:
Upper Augusta Power & Light Co., incorporated 5 October 1922 to supply electricity in the Township of Upper Augusta, Northumberland County, was merged into Pennsylvania Power & Light Co. on 18 November 1922.

948. UPPER FAIRFIELD-LYCOMING POWER & LIGHT COMPANY (Non-operating).
Lycoming County, Upper Fairfield Township.
1924 to 1925, 1 Linear Inch.

History:
Upper Fairfield-Lycoming Power & Light Co. was incorporated 28 August 1924 to supply electricity in the Township of Upper Fairfield, Lycoming County. On 28 October 1924 it was merged into Pennsylvania Power & Light Co.

949. UPPER HANOVER POWER & LIGHT COMPANY (Non-operating).
Montgomery County, Upper Hanover Township.
1923 to 1924, 1 Linear Inch.

History:
Upper Hanover Power & Light Co. was incorporated 17 October 1923 to supply electricity in the Township of Upper Hanover Montgomery County. On 2 November 1923 it was merged into Pennsylvania Power & Light Co.

950. UPPER LEACOCK TOWNSHIP ELECTRIC COMPANY (Non-operating).
Lancaster County, Upper Leacock Township.
1912, 1 Linear Inch.

History:
Upper Leacock Township Electric Co. was incorporated 13 November 1912 to supply electricity in the Township of Upper Leacock, Lancaster County. On 27 November 1912 it was consolidated and merged with 13 other companies to form Edison Electric Co. No. 3.

951. UPPER MACUNGIE ELECTRIC COMPANY (Non-operating).
Lehigh County, Upper Macungie Township.
1911 to 1913, 1 Linear Inch.

History:
Upper Macungie Electric Co. was incorporated 4 April 1911 to supply electricity in the Township of Upper Macungie, Lehigh County. On 23 December 1912 it was consolidated and merged with 37 other non-operating companies to form Lehigh Navigation Electric Co. No. 2.

952. UPPER MAHANOY-NORTHUMBERLAND POWER & LIGHT COMPANY (Non-operating).
Northumberland County, Upper Mahanoy Township.
1928, 1 Linear Inch.

History:
Upper Mahanoy-Northumberland Power & Light Co. was incorporated 24 July 1928 to supply electricity in the Township of Upper Mahanoy, Northumberland County. On 18 August 1928 the company was merged into Pennsylvania Power & Light Co.

953. UPPER MAHANTONGO TOWNSHIP ELECTRIC COMPANY (Non-operating).
Schuylkill County, Upper Mahantongo Township.
1924, 1 Linear Inch.

History:
Upper Mahantongo Township Electric Co., incorporated 13 August 1924 to supply electricity in the Township of Upper Mahantongo, Schuylkill County, was merged East Penn Electric Co. No. 2, on 28 August 1924.

954. UPPER MAKEFIELD TOWNSHIP ELECTRIC COMPANY (Non-operating).
Bucks County, Upper Makefield Township.
1913 to 1935, 1 Linear Inch.

History:
Upper Makefield Township Electric Co. was one of eleven companies chartered by Lehigh Navigation Electric Co. in December 1913 to obtain franchise rights in the townships along the Delaware Canal in Bucks County. At that time, Lehigh Navigation Electric Co. was controlled by Lehigh Coal and Navigation Co., which also controlled the Delaware Canal Co. Upper Makefield Township Electric Co. and its ten counterparts were "paper companies", formed solely to secure franchise rights. They never entered into active operations. As of 1926 Upper Makefield Township Electric Co. was listed as "inactive." In 1935 it was officially dissolved.

955. UPPER MILFORD ELECTRIC COMPANY (Non-operating).
Lehigh County, Upper Milford Township.
1911 to 1913, 2 Linear Inches.

History:
Upper Milford Electric Co. was incorporated 4 April 1911 to supply electricity in the Township of Upper Milford, Lehigh County. On 23 December 1912 it was consolidated and merged with 37 other non-operating companies to form Lehigh Navigation Electric Co. No. 2.

956. UPPER MOUNT BETHEL ELECTRIC COMPANY (Non-operating).
Northampton County, Upper Mount Bethel Township.
1911 to 1913, 1 Linear Inch.

History:
Upper Mount Bethel Electric Co. was incorporated 4 April 1911 to supply electricity in the Township of Upper Mount Bethel, Northampton County. On 23 December 1912 it was consolidated and merged with 37 other non-operating companies to form Lehigh Navigation Electric Co. No. 2.

957. UPPER NAZARETH ELECTRIC COMPANY (Non-operating).
Northampton County, Upper Nazareth Township.
1911 to 1913, 1 Linear Inch.

History:
Upper Nazareth Electric Co., incorporated 4 April 1911 to supply electricity in the Township of Upper Nazareth, Northampton County, was consolidated and merged with 37 other non-operating companies on 23 December 1912 to form Lehigh Navigation Electric Co. No. 2.

958. UPPER SAUCON ELECTRIC COMPANY
(Non-operating).
Lehigh County, Upper Saucon Township.
1914 to 1916, 1 Linear Inch.

History:
Upper Saucon Electric Co. was incorporated 11 November 1914 to supply electricity in the Township of Upper Saucon, Lehigh County. On 27 September 1916 it was merged into Lehigh Navigation Electric Co. No. 2.

959. UTILITIES CONSTRUCTION COMPANY
(Operating).
Dauphin County, Harrisburg City.
1910 to 1912, 2 Linear Inches.

History:
Utilities Construction Co. was incorporated 12 July 1910 to engage in general contracting work. The company's only project was the construction of a gas plant for Northumberland Gas Co., which was completed in July 1911. In October 1912 the company's stock was acquired by Northumberland Gas, Heat and Fuel Co., as was that of Northumberland Gas Co. After this date Utilities Construction Co. does not seem to have engaged in active operations.

Administrative Records:
Minute Book, 1910-1912

960. UTILITIES SUPPLY COMPANY (Non-operating).
Lackawanna County, Scranton City.
1917 to 1919, 1 Linear Inch.

History:
Utilities Supply Co. was incorporated in January 1917 by the American Gas and Electric Co. It was still in existence in November 1919 but its history thereafter is unknown. It was probably merged into Scranton Electric Co. at some point.

961. VALLAMONT PASSENGER RAILWAY COMPANY
(Operating).
Lycoming County, Williamsport City.
1893 to 1894, 1/2 Linear Foot.

History:
Vallamont Passenger Railway Co. was incorporated in 1892 to operate an electric street railway in the City of Williamsport, Lycoming County. The company was organized by State Senator J. Henry Cochran as part of his efforts to compete with the Williamsport Passenger Railway Co. in the early 1890 s. Vallamont Passenger Railway began operations on 29 July 1893 over a route serving Vallamont Park, and the northern part of Williamsport. On 15 May 1894 the company was consolidated and merged with three other Cochran-controlled companies—Citizens Passenger Railway Co., Centre and West End Passenger Railway Co., and Junction Passenger Railway Co.—to form the Vallamont Traction Co.

Operating Records:
General Ledger, 1893-1894
Journal, 1893-1894

962. VALLAMONT TRACTION COMPANY (Operating).
Lycoming County, Williamsport City.
1894 to 1927, 2 Linear Feet.

History:
Vallamont Traction Co. resulted from the consolidation and merger 15 May 1894 of the Centre and West End Railway Co., the Citizens Passenger Railway Co., the Junction Passenger Railway Co., and the Vallamont Passanger Railway Co. All four of these companies were controlled by state Senator J. Henry Cochran through the Lycoming Improvement Co. In 1923 these companies were acquired by Lehigh Power Securities Corp. which formally merged them to form Williamsport Railways Co.

Administrative Records:
Minute Books, 1911-1926 (92 Volumes)
Stock Certificate Book, 1894

Operating Records:
General Ledgers, 1894-1926 (2 Volumes)
Journals, 1894-1923 (2 Volumes)
Cashbooks, 1894-1927 (4 Volumes)
Index to Vouchers, 1894-1921 (2 Volumes)
Voucher Record, 1923-1927
Federal Income Tax Schedule, 1926
Audited Voucher Record, 1894-1899
Audit Reports, 1918-1926 (2 Volumes)

Scope and Content Note:
The Minute Books of Vallamont Traction Co. document stockholders' and directors' meetings. The Audit Reports provide an overview of the company's financial condition.

963. VALLEY ELECTRIC SERVICE COMPANY
(Operating).
Northumberland County, Herndon Borough.
1912 to 1923, 1 Linear Foot.

History:
Valley Electric Service Co. was incorporated 18 November 1912 to supply electricity in the Borough of Herndon, Northumberland County. It was organized by the owners of the Herndon Spinning Mill, who installed an engine and generator in their silk mill to supply both their own company and the surrounding borough with electricity. On 21 November 1923 the company was merged into Middleburg Light, Heat and Power Co., and thereafter electricity was supplied from that company's 22-kv substation at Dalmatia.

Administrative Records:
Minute Book, 1912-1923
Stock Certificate Book, 1913-1923

Operating Records:
General Ledger, 1923
Journal, 1923
Journal and Cash Ledger, 1912-1923
Daybook, 1923-1924
Trial Balance, 1923

Scope and Content Note:
The Minute Book of Valley Electric Service Co. documents routine stockholders' and directors' meetings, provides information concerning the company's organization, and includes a list of stockholders.

964. VALLEY RAILWAYS (Operating).
Cumberland County, Lemoyne Borough.
1893 to 1941, 30 Linear Feet.

History:

Valley Railways was incorporated 27 July 1912 for the purpose of consolidating a number of electric street railway companies operating in the Harrisburg area. The company's main office was located in the Borough of Lemoyne, Cumberland County. On 20 January 1913 it acquired Valley Traction Co., which in turn controlled United Electric Co. and six other electric street railway companies. On the same day, five of these railways were merged into the sixth, the Harrisburg and Mechanicsburg Electric Railway Co. Valley Railways operated profitably for a number of years but began to experience financial difficulties soon after World War I. In March 1922, the company was forced to reduce its service in the Borough of Carlisle, Cumberland County, because it was operating there at a heavy loss. In January 1926, control of the company passed to Lehigh Power Securities Corp. Electric Bond and Share Co. then began to provide it with supervision and engineering services. On 25 April 1929 the Harrisburg and Mechanicsburg railway company was merged into Valley Railways. In June 1930, the company abandoned its line between Mechanicsburg and Carlisle since traffic over that route had declined substantially. Valley Railways then formed an affiliated firm, Valley Transportation Co., to operate a bus line between Mechanicsburg and Carlisle. By January 1931, traffic on the company's Mechanicsburg, White Hill, and Marysville lines had also declined to the point of unprofitability. The company's streetcar service along these routes was replaced with bus service provided by Valley Transportation. In March 1936, when the Pennsylvania Public Service Commission closed the Peoples Bridge Company's Walnut Street bridge across the Susquehanna River at Harrisburg to all electric trolley car traffic, the company's western routes to Mechanicsburg and Carlisle were severed. On 9 April 1938 the company discontinued all street railway service and began to sell off its property. In April 1938 its car barn in Harrisburg was sold to Valley Transportation Co. The last of the company's property was sold to Pennsylvania Realty & Investment Co. in February 1941. Valley Railways was dissolved 13 November 1941.

Administrative Records:

Minute Books, 1912-1925 (5 Volumes)
Stock Certificates, 1918-1946 (2 Volumes)
Stock Ledger and Transfer Record, 1912-1916
Stock Ledger, 1916-1939
Stock Transfer Record, 1915-1916
Correspondence and Miscellaneous Papers, 1921-1932
Deeds & Ordinances, 1893-1939
Newspaper Clippings, 1928-1932

Operating Records:

FINANCIAL RECORDS
General Ledgers, 1904-1941 (4 Volumes)
Miscellaneous Accounts Ledgers, 1914-1926 (5 Volumes)
Miscellaneous Accounts Ledger—Inactive, 1934
Journals, 1910-1926 (4 Volumes)
Journal Voucher Register, 1926-1941
Accrual Record, 1925-1926
Detail Ledgers, 1926-1941 (2 Volumes)
Accounts Payable Ledgers, 1926-1941 (2 Volumes)
Accounts Receivable Ledgers, 1923-1941 (4 Volumes)
Accounts Receivable & Payable Ledger—Monthly Summary, 1939-1941
Summary of Accounts Receivable—Miscellaneous, 1931-1939
Material Ledger, 1920-1926
Job Ledgers, 1909-1926 (2 Volumes)
Cash Statements, 1925-1926
Final Statements of Accounts, Lemoyne Bottleneck Construction Project, 1929 (4 Volumes)
Bill Register, 1926-1941
Cash Control and Conservation Reports, 1932-1937 (2 Volumes)
Fixed Capital Additions, 1929-1931
Comparative Statements of Earnings and Expenses, 1906-1926
Balance Sheets and Comparative Statements of Earnings, 1926-1928
Comparative Income Accounts, 1926-1940
PERSONNEL RECORDS
Workmen's Compensation Accrual Statements, 1927-1931
Workmen's Compensation and Payroll Detail Ledger, 1927-1932
Payroll Authorities, 1927-1938
Payroll Deposit Accounts, 1925-1926 (2 Volumes)
Payroll Book, 1920-1922
Payrolls, 1926-1938 (12 Volumes)
Cash and Time Books, 1905-1926 (14 Volumes)
Payroll Distribution Sheets, 1928-1930
Time and Material Record—Maintenance Jobs, 1913-1917
OPERATING STATISTICS
Comparative Statements of Passengers Carried and Earnings per Car Mile, 1913-1927
Abstracts of Conductors' Returns and Detail of Passenger and Freight Revenue, 1926-1929
Abstracts of Conductors' Returns, 1932-1934 (3 Volumes)
Passenger Receipts by Division—Daily Reports, 1927-1939 (9 Volumes)
Records of Cash Receipts, 1912-1914
Report on Adjustments to Property and Services Costs, 1931
Stock Inventory Sheets, 1932-1937
Daily Report Sheets, 1936-1937
Divisional Operating Statistics and Daily Earnings Reports, 1930-1937
Daily Revenue Recapitulation Sheets, 1935
Monthly Statistical Reports, 1927-1939
District Cash Book, 1926-1938
District Office Bill Register, 1926-1928
AUDIT REPORTS, 1921-1925 (3 Volumes)
PAPERS OF SUBSIDIARY COMPANIES
Cumberland Valley Traction Co.—Cash and Time Book, 1897-1901
Harrisburg and Mechanicsburg Electric Railway Co.—General Ledger, 1902-1904
Harrisburg and Mechanicsburg Electric Railway Co.—Journal, 1904
Harrisburg and Mechanicsburg Electric Railway Co.—Stock Ledger, 1893-1907
Harrisburg and Mechanicsburg Electric Railway

Co.—Cash and Time Book, 1897-1901
Harrisburg and Mechanicsburg Electric Railway Co.—Record of Receipts, 1902-1903
HARRISBURG TERMINAL CO.—Fixed Capital Additions, 1929-1931
United Electric Co.—Journal, 1926
United Electric Co.—Ledger, Miscellaneous Accounts, 1919
United Electric Co.—Comparative Statements of Earnings & Expenses, 1912-1919 (10 Volumes)
United Electric Co.—Record of Cash Receipts, 1908-1910 (2 Volumes)
United Electric Co.—Record of Cash Receipts—Office, 1921-1925 (3 Volumes)
Valley Traction—General Ledger, 1904-1912
Valley Traction—Journal, 1904-1926 (2 Volumes)
Valley Traction—Cashbook, 1905-1915
Valley Traction—Fixed Capital Additions, 1929-1931
Valley Traction—Cash and Time Books, 1904-1913 (7 Volumes)
Valley Traction—Journals, 1910-1914 (2 Volumes)
Valley Traction—Journal, Miscellaneous Accounts, 1906
Valley Traction—Ledgers, Miscellaneous Accounts, 1902-1913 (15 Volumes)
Valley Traction—Record of Materials Purchased, 1906-1910
Valley Traction—Comparative Statements of Earnings and Income per Car Mile, 1913-1927
Valley Transportation Co.—Stock Inventory Sheets, 1932-1937
Valley Transportation Co.—Daily Abstract of Bus Operators' Returns, 1932-1934 (3 Volumes)
Valley Transportation Co.—Daily Report Sheets, 1936-1937
Valley Transportation Co.—Divisional Operating Statistics & Daily Earning Record, 1930-1937
Valley Transportation Co.—Daily Revenue Recapitulation Sheets, 1935
Valley Transportation Co.—Monthly Statistical Reports, 1927-1939
Valley Transportation Co.—District Cashbooks, 1926-1938
Valley Transportation Co.—District Office Bill Register, 1926-1928

Scope and Content Note:

The Minute Books of Valley Railways document the company's takeover of the Valley Traction Co. and the 1913 consolidation and merger of several street railways into the Harrisburg and Mechanicsburg Electric Railway Co. There are also Financial Statements, which record earnings and expenditures, and other materials documenting the construction of the Harrisburg terminal. An ongoing dispute with Harrisburg City Council over downtown traffic congestion is described. Correspondence Files include accounts of accidents; considerable information about the company's routes, competitive position and advertising campaigns; and describes its relationship with the Pennsylvania Public Service Commission.

965. VALLEY TOWNSHIP MONTOUR ELECTRIC COMPANY (Non-operating).
Montour County, Valley Township.
1919 to 1920, 2 Linear Inches.

History:

Valley Township Montour Electric Co., incorporated 6 November 1919 to supply electricity in Valley Township, Montour County, was merged into Lehigh Industrial Power Co. on 28 April 1920.

966. VALLEY TRACTION COMPANY (Operating).
Franklin County, Chambersburg Borough.
1903 to 1913, 1/2 Linear Foot.

History:

Valley Traction Co. was incorporated 18 November 1903 to acquire and operate several electric street railways which ran westward from Harrisburg, Dauphin County, into the Counties of Cumberland and Perry. The company's main offices were in the Borough of Chambersburg, Franklin County. On 1 January 1904 the company leased Harrisburg & Mechanicsburg Electric Railway Co. Through this lease it also gained control of White Hill & Mechanicsburg Electric Railway, West Fairview & Marysville Electric Railway, Carlisle & Mechanicsburg Street Railway, and Fairview & Riverton Passenger Railway. In December 1904 the company purchased controlling interests in the stocks of these companies, as well as those of The Cumberland Valley Electric Passenger Railway Co., The Cumberland, Heat and Power Co., Camp Hill Turnpike Road Co., South Middleton Street Railway Co., and The United Electric Co. These companies were managed by Valley Traction, but retained their separate identities. Valley Traction purchased some of the electricity needed to run these lines from York Haven Water & Power Co., but found it necessary to maintain a steam electric generating station of its own due to the York Haven plant's generating problems. In July 1909 Valley Traction rebuilt this steam plant, located in the Borough of Lemoyne, in order to free itself from dependence on the York Haven company. In March 1911 the company began to install Westinghouse electric generating equipment. By December 1912 control of Valley Traction Company's stock had been secured by Valley Railways Co. The companies merged on 20 January 1913.

Administrative Records:
Minute Book, 1903-1912
Stock Certificate Books, 1911-1912 (2 Volumes)
Stock Ledger and Transfer Record, 1904-1912

Operating Records:
General Ledger, 1904-1912
Miscellaneous Ledger, 1905-1906
Comparative Statements of Earnings & Expenses, 1906-1912 (7 Volumes)
Materials & Supplies Ledger, 1906-1909
Cash and Time Books, 1904-1913 (7 Volumes)

Scope and Content Note:

The Minute Book of Valley Traction Co. documents stockholders' and directors' meetings and includes annual statements of earnings and expenses. Also included are details of the company's stock acquisitions and information concerning repairs and improvements to the company's railway lines. Cash and Time Books list conductors and motormen, and give statistics, such as mileage, number of passengers carried, and receipts, for each trip run.

967. VALLEY TRANSPORTATION COMPANY (Operating).
Cumberland Borough, Lemoyne Borough.
1930 to 1939, 1 Linear Inch.

History:
Valley Transportation Co. was incorporated 13 June 1930 by Valley Railways Co. With its main offices located in the Borough of Lemoyne, Cumberland County, the company provided regularly scheduled and specially chartered bus service in the Counties of Dauphin, Perry, and Cumberland. On 1 May 1939 the company was sold to a group of local businessmen.

Administrative Records:
Minute Book, 1930-1939

Scope and Content Note:
The Minute Book of the Valley Transportation Co. documents routine stockholders' and directors' meetings as well as it rules and rate schedules.

968. VANDLING ELECTRIC COMPANY (Operating).
Lackawanna County, Vandling Borough.
1913 to 1918, 2 Linear Inches.

History:
Vandling Electric Co. was organized in March 1913 by American Gas and Electric Co. The company supplied electricity to only four or five customers in the Borough of Vandling, Lackawanna County, and purchased its power from Scranton Electric Co. On 31 May 1918 it was merged into Scranton Electric Co.

Operating Records:
General Ledger, 1913-1918
Journal, 1913-1918
Cashbook, 1913-1918

969. VARDEN AND LAKE ARIEL LIGHT, HEAT AND POWER COMPANY (Operating).
Wayne County, South Canaan Township.
1916 to 1928, 1/2 Linear Foot.

History:
The Varden and Lake Ariel Light, Heat and Power Co. was incorporated 22 June 1916 to supply electricity in the Township of South Canaan, Wayne County. It was organized by the Kizer family, owners of a grist mill in the Village of Varden, South Canaan Township, who had installed a 15-kw direct-current generator. The surplus was sold to local residents. In 1926 this company's stock was acquired by Lehigh Power Securities Corp., and it was thereafter operated as part of Pennsylvania Power & Light Co., into which it was merged 28 May 1928.

Administrative Records:
Minute Book, 1916-1928
Stock Transfer Record, 1926
Stock Ledger, 1925-1928

Operating Records:
FINANCIAL RECORDS
General Ledger, 1926-1928
Journal Entry Register, 1926-1928
Record of Cash Receipts, 1926-1928
Record of Cash Disbursements, 1926-1928
Summary of Cash, 1926-1928
Detail of Cost Study and Fixed Capital, 1926-1927
Summary of Accounts Receivable, 1926-1928
Summary of Consumers' Deposits, 1926-1928
Statement of Accounts Overpaid, 1927-1928
AUDIT REPORTS, 1923-1927 (3 Volumes)

Scope and Content Note:
The Minute Book of Varden and Lake Ariel Light, Heat and Power Co. documents routine stockholders' and directors' meetings. The rest of the records are financial in nature and date from the period after the company was acquired by Lehigh Power Securities Corp.

970. WALKER POWER & LIGHT COMPANY (Non-operating).
Schuylkill County, Walker Township.
1923 to 1924, 1 Linear Inch.

History:
Walker Power & Light Co. was incorporated 8 February 1924 to supply electricity in the Township of Walker, Schuylkill County. On 16 May 1924 it was merged into the Pennsylvania Power & Light Co.

971. WALNUTPORT ELECTRIC LIGHT AND POWER COMPANY (Non-operating).
Northampton County, Walnutport Borough.
1914 to 1915, 1 Linear Inch.

History:
Walnutport Electric Light and Power Co. was incorporated 2 October 1914 to supply electricity in the Borough of Walnutport, Northampton County. On 6 February 1915 it was merged into Lehigh Valley Light and Power Co., No. 2.

972. WARWICK TOWNSHIP ELECTRIC COMPANY (Non-operating).
Lancaster County, Warwick Township.
1911, 1 Linear Inch.

History:
Warwick Township Electric Co. was incorporated 10 August 1911 to supply electricity in the Township of Warwick, Lancaster County. On 29 September 1911 it was consolidated and merged with 17 companies to form Edison Electric Co., No. 1.

973. WASHINGTON-LYCOMING POWER & LIGHT COMPANY (Non-operating).
Lycoming County, Washington Township.
1928 to 1929, 1 Linear Inch.

History:
Washington-Lycoming Power & Light Co. was incorporated 27 November 1928 to supply electricity in the Township of Washington, Lycoming County. On 29 December 1928 it was merged into the Pennsylvania Power & Light Co.

974. WASHINGTON-NORTHUMBERLAND POWER & LIGHT COMPANY (Non-operating).
Northumberland County, Washington Township.
1928, 1 Linear Inch.

History:
Washington-Northumberland Power & Light Co. was incorporated 24 July 1928 to supply electricity in the Township of Washington, Northumberland County. On 18 August 1928 it was merged into the Pennsylvania Power & Light Co.

975. WASHINGTON SQUARE ELECTRIC LIGHT & POWER COMPANY (Non-operating).
Montgomery County, Whitpain Township.
1917 to 1919, 1 Linear Inch.

History:
Washington Square Electric Light & Power Co. was organized 6 February 1917 by the Lehigh Valley Light & Power Co. to supply electricity in the Township of Whitpain, Montgomery County. The company failed to secure a charter and it was dissolved 3 January 1919.

976. WASHINGTON TOWNSHIP ELECTRIC LIGHT AND POWER COMPANY (Non-operating).
Lehigh County, Washington Township.
1909 to 1913, 1 Linear Inch.

History:
Washington Township Electric Light and Power Co. was incorporated 26 December 1911 to supply electricity in that township of Lehigh County. It was consolidated and merged 6 December 1912 with ten other companies to form Lehigh Valley Light and Power Co., No. 2.

977. WASHINGTON TOWNSHIP ELECTRIC LIGHT COMPANY (Non-operating).
Snyder County, Washington Township.
1919, 1 Linear Inch.

History:
Washington Township Electric Light Co. was a "paper company" incorporated 12 August 1919 by The Lehigh Valley Light & Power Co., which at that time was ostensibly attempting to secure charter rights in the Township of Washington, Snyder County. The Lehigh Valley Light & Power Co., controlled by Electric Bond & Share, however, had a hidden agenda. It was in the process of consolidating its hold over eastern Pennsylvania's electrical generating and distribution system. The company wanted to establish a hold on the name Pennsylvania Power & Light so Washington Township Electric Light Company's name was changed to Pennsylvania Power & Light Co. On 17 April 1920 the planned merger took place. Seven operating companies and this "paper company" were officially consolidated to form Pennsylvania Power & Light Co.

987. WASHINGTON TOWNSHIP ELECTRIC LIGHT, HEAT AND POWER COMPANY (Non-operating).
Dauphin County, Washington Township.
1922 to 1923, 1 Linear Inch.

History:
Washington Township Electric Light, Heat and Power Co. was incorporated 23 April 1923 to supply electricity in the Township of Washington, Dauphin County. On 30 April 1923 it was merged into East Penn Electric Co., No. 2.

979. WASHINGTON TOWNSHIP LEHIGH ELECTRIC COMPANY (Non-operating).
Lehigh County, Washington Township.
1919, 1 Linear Inch.

History:
Washington Township Lehigh Electric Co. was incorporated 17 July 1919 to supply electricity in the Township of Washington, Lehigh County. On 25 July 1919 it was consolidated and merged with six other non-operating companies to form Industrial Power Co.

980. WASHINGTONVILLE POWER & LIGHT COMPANY (Non-operating).
Montour County, Washingtonville Borough.
1923 to 1924, 1 Linear Inch.

History:
Washingtonville Power & Light Co. was incorporated 30 November 1923 to supply electricity in the Borough of Washingtonville, Montour County. On 16 May 1924 it was merged into the Pennsylvania Power & Light Co.

981. WATSON-LYCOMING POWER & LIGHT COMPANY (Non-operating).
Lycoming County, Watson Township.
1928 to 1929, 1 Linear Inch.

History:
Watson-Lycoming Power & Light Co. was incorporated 14 May 1928 to supply electricity in the Township of Watson, Lycoming County. On 29 June 1928 it was merged into the Pennsylvania Power & Light Co.

982. WATSONTOWN DOOR & SASH COMPANY (Operating).
Northumberland County, Watsontown Borough.
1929 to 1930, 1 Linear Inch.

History:
Watsontown Door & Sash Co. was established in 1866 as a manufacturer of window frames, doors, blinds, cabinets, and millwork. Its plant contained steam electric generating equipment, and the company sold surplus electricity to the Borough of Watsontown, which had constructed an electric distribution system in the community. In June 1929 the company went bankrupt. In August it sold its power generating equipment to the Pennsylvania Power & Light Co., but continued to operate it on that company's behalf. Sometime later, probably in the mid-1930's, the plant was shut down and Pennsylvania Power & Light began supplying electricity directly to the Borough.

Operating Records:
Audit Report, 1929-1930

Scope and Content Note:
The records of the Watsontown Door & Sash Co. consist of a single Audit Report prepared for the Pennsylvania Power & Light Co. after it had purchased this company's electric generating equipment. The Audit Report reviews both the costs of running this plant and the terms of the agreement whereby Watsontown Door & Sash continued to run the plant for Pennsylvania Power & Light after August 1929.

983. WATTS WATER AND POWER COMPANY (Operating).
Perry County, Newport Borough.
1923 to 1935, 3 Linear Inches.

History:
Watts Water and Power Co. was incorporated 7 November 1923. The company was involved jointly with the Juniata River Water Power Co. in the construction of a hydroelectric power station on the Juniata River near the Borough of Newport, Perry County. Land and

flooding rights for this project were obtained from both the East Penn Electric Co. and the Pennsylvania Railroad. In April 1925 the company's stock was acquired by East Penn Electric Co., which three years later sold it to Pennsylvania Power & Light. The company was dissolved 31 December 1935 since according to the Minute Book, it 'had not been operating for a number of years' and had 'no prospect of operating in the future.'

Administrative Records:
Minute Books, 1923-1935 (2 Volumes)
Stock Certificate Book, 1923-1927
Stock Transfer Record, 1926-1927
Stock Ledger, 1926-1927

Operating Records:
Audited Voucher and Journal entry Register, 1926
Detail of Cost Study and Fixed Capital, 1926-1927

Scope and Content Note:
The Minute Book of the Watts Water and Power Co. documents routine stockholders' and directors' meetings, and contains information about the company's organization, capitalization, and acquisition of land and flooding rights from East Penn Electric Co. and the Pennsylvania Railroad Co.

984. WAYMART ELECTRIC COMPANY (Operating).
Wayne County, Waymart Borough.
1916 to 1918, 2 Linear Inches.

History:
Waymart Electric Co. was organized 24 May 1916 by the American Gas and Electric Co. to supply electricity in the Borough of Waymart, Wayne County. The company's main offices were located in the City of Scranton, where it was under the supervision of the Scranton Electric Co. On 31 May 1918 it was merged into the Scranton Electric Co.

Operating Records:
General Ledger, 1916-1918
Journal, 1916-1918
Cashbook, 1916-1918

985. WAYNE POWER & LIGHT COMPANY
(Non-operating).
Clinton County, Wayne Township.
1923 to 1924, 1 Linear Inch.

History:
Wayne Power & Light Co. was incorporated 30 November 1923 to supply electricity in the Township of Wayne, Clinton County. On 31 March 1924 it was merged into the Pennsylvania Power & Light Co.

986. WAYNE TOWNSHIP ELECTRIC CORPORATION
(Non-operating).
Dauphin County, Wayne Township.
1924, 1 Linear Inch.

History:
Wayne Township Electric Corp. was incorporated 13 August 1924 to supply electricity in the Township of Wayne, Dauphin County. On 28 August 1924 it was merged into East Penn Electric Co., No. 2.

987. WEISSPORT ELECTRIC COMPANY (Operating).
Carbon County, Weissport Borough.
1924 to 1928, 1/2 Linear Foot.

History:
Electricity was first supplied in the Borough of Weissport, Carbon County, in 1890 when The Carbon County Improvement Co. built a hydroelectric generating station using the Lehigh Coal and Navigation Company's canal. This plant only supplied electricity to a planing mill and an ice plant located at the site. Electricity was not supplied to the general public until 1893, when additional equipment was installed and a distribution system built. In 1900 James I. Blakslee bought this plant and began operating it. After a flood destroyed the plant in 1902, electricity was supplied to Weissport from the generating station owned by Mr. Blakslee in the Borough of Lehighton. On 21 December 1923 Mr. Blakslee had the Weissport Electric Co. incorporated, having hitherto operated without a charter. Three years later the company's stock was acquired by Lehigh Power Securities Corp., and it was thereafter operated as a part of the Pennsylvania Power & Light Co. system, into which it was merged 28 May 1928.

Administrative Records:
Minute Book, 1924-1928
Stock Certificate Book, 1924-1927
Stock Transfer Ledger, 1927
Stock Ledger, 1924-1928

Operating Records:
Journal Entry Register, 1927-1928
Audited Voucher Register, 1927-1928
Accounts Payable Ledger, 1927-1928
Detail Ledger, 1928
Detail of Cost Study and Fixed Capital, 1927
Expenditure Requisitions, 1927-1928
Audit Reports, 1924-1927 (4 Volumes)

Scope and Content Note:
The Minute Book of Weissport Electric Co. documents the meetings of the company's stockholders and directors, and contains a copy of the ordinance granting the company's franchise to operate in the Borough of Weissport. The Audit Reports describe the company's status as an affiliate of Mr. James I. Blakslee's Lehighton Electric Light and Power Co., and also contains schedules along with rules and regulations which govern the supply of electricity to the public.

988. THE WEST BRUNSWICK TOWNSHIP LIGHT, HEAT AND POWER COMPANY (Non-operating).
Schuylkill County, West Brunswick Township.
1916, 1 Linear Inch.

History:
The West Brunswick Township Light, Heat and Power Co. was incorporated 10 October 1913 to supply electricity in the Township of West Brunswick, Schuylkill County. On 18 July 1916 it was merged into Eastern Pennsylvania Light, Heat and Power Co.

989. WEST BUFFALO-UNION POWER & LIGHT COMPANY (Non-operating).
Union County, West Buffalo Township.
1928 to 1929, 1 Linear Inch.

History:
West Buffalo-Union Power & Light Co. was incorporated 27 November 1928 to supply electricity in

the Township of West Buffalo, Union County. On 29 December 1928 it was merged into the Pennsylvania Power & Light Co.

990. WEST CAMERON-NORTHUNBERLAND POWER & LIGHT COMPANY (Non-operating).
Northumberland County, West Cameron Township.
1926 to 1927, 1 Linear Inch.

History:
West Cameron-Northumberland Power & Light Co. was incorporated 12 January 1927 to supply electricity in the Township of West Cameron, Northumberland County. On 21 February 1927 it was merged into the Pennsylvania Power & Light Co.

991. WEST CHILLISQUAQUE TOWNSHIP ELECTRIC COMPANY (Non-operating).
Northumberland County, West Chillisquaque Township.
1912, 1 Linear Inch.

History:
West Chillisquaque Township Electric Co. was incorporated 11 October 1911 to supply electricity in that Township of Northumberland County. On 31 December 1912 it was merged into Northumberland County Gas & Electric Co.

992. WEST CHILLISQUAQUE TOWNSHIP-NORTHUMBERLAND ELECTRIC COMPANY (Non-operating).
Northumberland County, West Chillisquaque Township.
1919 to 1920, 1 Linear Inch.

History:
West Chillisquaque Township-Northumberland Electric Co. was incorporated 6 November 1919 to supply electricity in that Township of Northumberland County. On 28 April 1920 it was merged into Lehigh Industrial Power Co.

993. WEST COCALICO TOWNSHIP ELECTRIC COMPANY (Non-operating).
Lancaster County, West Cocalico Township.
1918 to 1934, 1 Linear Inch.

History:
West Cocalico Township Electric Co. was incorporated 20 July 1911 to supply electricity in the Township of West Cocalico, Lancaster County. On 21 August 1912 it was consolidated and merged with six other non-operating companies to form the North Lancaster County Electric Co.

994. WEST DONEGAL TOWNSHIP ELECTRIC LIGHT COMPANY (Non-operating).
Lancaster County, West Donegal Township.
1911, 1 Linear Inch.

History:
West Donegal Township Electric Light Co. was incorporated 10 August 1911 to supply electricity in the Township of West Donegal, Lancaster County. On 29 September 1911 it was consolidated and merged with 17 other companies to form Edison Electric Co., No. 1.

995. WEST EARL TOWNSHIP ELECTRIC COMPANY (Non-operating).
Lancaster County, West Earl Township.
1912, 1 Linear Inch.

History:
West Earl Township Electric Co. was incorporated 13 November 1912 to supply electricity in the Township of West Earl, Lancaster County. On 27 November 1912 it was consolidated and merged with 13 other companies to form Edison Electric Co., No. 3.

996. WEST END ELECTRIC LIGHT AND POWER COMPANY (Operating).
Luzerne County, West Hazleton Borough.
1895 to 1912, 1 Linear Foot.

History:
West End Electric Light and Power Co. was incorporated 28 May 1895 to supply electricity in the Borough of West Hazleton, Luzerne County. The company constructed a power plant on Ridge Avenue in the adjoining Village of Green Ridge and installed a 250-kw generator. In 1897 it became the first company to supply electricity to the Hazleton area and shortly thereafter negotiated street lighting contracts with the township. On 30 June 1899 the company leased its property and franchises to Hazleton Electric Light and Power Co., and two years later the West End Power plant was shut down, as electricity could now be supplied more efficiently from the Hazleton generating station. On 6 June 1912 the Harwood Electric Co. acquired a controlling interest in West End Electric Co. In December of that year West End Electric Light and Power Co. was consolidated and merged with twelve other companies to form Hazleton Electric Co.

Administrative Records:
Minute Book, 1895-1912
Stock Certificate Book, 1896-1912

Scope and Content Note:
The Minute Book of West End Electric Co. contains a good deal of information documenting the construction of the company's powerhouse and the installation of its Weston engines, Stanley Alternating Dynamos, and Western Electric Arc Dynamos. Also included are brief descriptions of other companies' powerhouses and electric equipment, compiled in a survey of standard electric utility practices. The company's dealings with the Supervisors of Hazle Township, and the Borough Council of McAdoo in regard to street lighting contracts are referred to in the minutes. Also included are lists of operating expenses and an itemized inventory of the company's tools. Additional information concerning this company may be found in the "Historical Report of The Harwood Electric Co. and Its Antecedent and Allied Companies," filed with the records of The Harwood Electric Co.

997. WEST FAIRVIEW AND MARYSVILLE ELECTRIC STREET RAILWAY COMPANY (Operating).
Cumberland County, East Pennsboro Township.
1901 to 1912, 2 Linear Inches.

History:
West Fairwiew and Marysville Electric Street Railway Co. was incorporated 19 June 1901 to operate an electric street railway between the Town of West Fairview, Cumberland County, and the Borough of Marysville, Perry County. In July 1902 the company entered into an

agreement to link up and share tracks with Harrisburg and Mechanicsburg Electric Railway Co. The next year, the railway extended its lines to East Pennsboro Township, Cumberland County. On 1 January 1904 the company leased its lines to Valley Traction Co., and in December Valley Traction purchased a controlling interest. On 10 January 1913 the company was consolidated and merged with five other electric railways that were also controlled by Valley Railways to form a new Harrisburg and Mechanicsburg Electric Railway Co.

Administrative Records:
Minute Book, 1901-1910
Stock Certificate Book, 1903-1912

Scope and Content Note:
The Minute Book contains information about the construction and development of the company's lines, descriptions of its routes, copies of ordinances granting it franchises to operate in several small communities, right-of-way agreements with property holders, and a copy of the lease of its line to Valley Traction Co.

998. **WEST HEMPFIELD TOWNSHIP ELECTRIC COMPANY** (Non-operating).
Lancaster County, West Hempfield Township.
1911, 1 Linear Inch.

History:
West Hempfield Township Electric Co. was incorporated 10 August 1911 to supply electricity in the Township of West Hempfield, Lancaster County. On 29 September 1911 it was consolidated and merged with 17 other companies to form Edison Electric Co., No. 1.

999. **WEST LAMPETER ELECTRIC LIGHT, HEAT AND POWER COMPANY** (Non-operating).
Lancaster County, West Lampeter Township.
1913, 1 Linear Inch.

History:
West Lampeter Electric Light, Heat and Power Co. was incorporated 2 January 1913 to supply electricity in the Township of West Lampeter, Lancaster County. On 10 January 1913 it was consolidated and merged with four other companies to form Strasburg Electric Light, Heat and Power Co., No. 2.

1000. **WEST LAMPETER TOWNSHIP ELECTRIC COMPANY** (Non-operating).
Lancaster County, West Lampeter Township.
1911, 1 Linear Inch.

History:
West Lampeter Township Electric Co. was incorporated 10 August 1911 to supply electricity in the Township of West Lampeter, Lancaster County. On 29 September 1911 it was consolidated and merged with 17 other companies to form Edison Electric Co., No. 1.

1001. **WEST MAHANOY LIGHT COMPANY** (Non-operating).
Schuylkill County, West Mahanoy Township.
1912, 1 Linear Inch.

History:
West Mahanoy Light Co. was incorporated 29 November 1912 to supply electricity in the Township of West Mahanoy, Schuylkill County. It was consolidated and merged with twelve other companies 16 December 1912 to form Hazleton Electric Co.

1002. **WEST MAHANOY TOWNSHIP ELECTRIC COMPANY** (Non-operating).
Schuylkill County, West Mahanoy Township.
1910 to 1912, 1 Linear Inch.

History:
West Mahanoy Township Electric Co. was incorporated 26 January 1911 to supply electricity in the Township of West Mahanoy, Schuylkill County. On 12 November 1912 it was consolidated and merged with eleven other companies to form The Schuylkill Gas and Electric Co.

1003. **WEST NANTMEAL ELECTRIC COMPANY** (Non-operating).
Chester County, West Nantmeal Township.
1923, 1 Linear Inch.

History:
West Nantmeal Electric Co. was incorporated 23 April 1923 to supply electricity in the Township of West Nantmeal, Chester County. On 16 May 1923 the company was merged into the Tri-County Electric Co.

1004. **WEST PENN TOWNSHIP ELECTRIC COMPANY** (Non-operating).
Schuylkill County, West Penn Township.
1924, 1 Linear Inch.

History:
West Penn Township Electric Co. was incorporated 13 August 1924 to supply electricity in the Township of West Penn, Schuylkill County. On 28 August 1924 it was merged into East Penn Electric Co., No. 2.

1005. **WEST PERRY POWER COMPANY** (Non-operating).
Snyder County, West Perry Township.
1925 to 1926, 1 Linear Inch.

History:
West Perry Power Co. was incorporated 21 January 1926 to supply electricity in the Township of West Perry, Snyder County. On 8 July 1926 it was merged into the Middleburg Light, Heat and Power Co.

1006. **WEST PITTSTON ELECTRIC COMPANY** (Non-operating).
Luzerne County, Pittston Borough.
1910 to 1919, 2 Linear Inches.

History:
West Pittston Electric Co. was incorporated 7 September 1910 to supply electricity in the Borough of Pittston, Luzerne County. It was a 'paper company' formed by the Scranton Electric Co. in order to secure franchise rights in this area. It did not engage in any active operations, and seems to have been dissolved in March 1919.

1007. **WEST PITTSTON-EXETER RAILROAD COMPANY** (Operating).
Luzerne County, Exeter Township.
1925 to 1974, 3 1/2 Linear Feet.

History:
West Pittston-Exeter Railroad Co. was incorporated 16 July 1925 by the American Gas and Electric Co. The

company operated a railroad which carried coal from the Borough of West Pittston to the Pennsylvania Power & Light Company's Exeter generating station. On 11 April 1934 the company's stock was acquired by Pennsylvania Realty & Investment Co., which was controlled by Pennsylvania Power & Light. On 31 January 1956 the railraod's stock was transferred to Pennsylvania Power & Light's control. The West Pittston-Exeter Railroad is still in operation today.

Administrative Records:
Minute Book, 1925-1948
Stock Certificate Book, 1934-1974
Stock Certificates, 1934-1974

Operating Records:
General Ledgers, 1925-1952 (5 Volumes)
Cashbooks, 1925-1944 (2 Volumes)
Accounts Payable Ledger, 1931-1934
Operating Expense Ledgers, 1931-1954 (3 Volumes)
Accounts Receivable Miscellaneous Ledgers, 1927-1955 (2 Volumes)
Accounts Payable Ledgers, 1926-1930 (4 Volumes)
Improvement Requisitions, 1925-1931 (2 Volumes)
Subsidiary Ledger—Investments in Roads and Equipment, 1931-1952
Insurance and Tax Registers, 1925-1953 (4 Volumes)
Trial Balances—General Ledger, 1940-1955 (2 Volumes)
Cash Record, 1929-1930
Payroll Report, 1925-1926
Audit Report, 1928
Financial and Operating Reports, 1925-1962

Scope and Content Note:
The Minute Book of the West Pittston-Exeter Railroad Co. documents the company's organization and capitalization, its appropriations of land for its right-of-way, its adoption of a retirement plan for its employees in 1941, and copies of the Inter-State Commerce Commission's rulings on the company's activities and status. The Payroll Reports list the company's train crews and construction personnel by name, and give their occupations and pay rates.

1008. WEST ROCKHILL TOWNSHIP ELECTRIC LIGHT AND POWER COMPANY, NO. 1 (Non-operating).
Bucks County, West Rockhill Township.
1914 to 1916, 1 Linear Inch.

History:
West Rockhill Township Electric Light and Power Co., No. 1, was incorporated 13 January 1915 to supply electricity in the Township of West Rockhill, Bucks County. It was merged into Lehigh Valley Light and Power Co., No. 3, on 26 February 1916.

1009. WEST ROCKHILL TOWNSHIP ELECTRIC LIGHT AND POWER COMPANY, NO. 2 (Non-operating).
Bucks County, West Rockhill Township.
1921 to 1922, 1 Linear Inch.

History:
West Rockhill Township Electric Light and Power Co., No. 2, was incorporated 15 December 1921 to supply electricity in the Township of West Rockhill, Bucks County. On 27 July 1922 it was consolidated and merged with Excelsior Electric Light, Power and Gas Co., No. 3, and the East Rock Hill Township Electric Light and Power Co. to form Excelsior Electric Light and Power Co.

1010. WEST SADSBURY TOWNSHIP ELECTRIC COMPANY (Non-operating).
Chester County, West Sadsbury Township.
1924 to 1926, 1 Linear Inch.

History:
West Sadsbury Township Electric Co. was incorporated 21 January 1924 to supply electricity in the Township of West Sadsbury, Chester County. On 30 June 1925 the company was merged into Edison Electric Co., No. 4.

1011. THE WEST SCRANTON LIGHT HEAT & POWER COMPANY (Operating).
Lackawanna County, Scranton City.
1905, 1 Linear Inch.

History:
The West Scranton Light Heat & Power Co. was incorporated 3 March 1905 to supply electricity in the City of Scranton, Lackawanna County. On 29 November 1905 the company contracted with the Corporate Organization & Audit Co. for the construction of an electric power plant and distribution system to be built in Scranton. On 5 December 1905 the company changed its name to the Lackawanna Light Co.

Administrative Records:
Minute Book, 1905

1012. WEST TELFORD POWER & LIGHT COMPANY (Non-operating).
Montgomery County, West Telford Borough.
1923, 1 Linear Inch.

History:
West Telford Power & Light Co. was incorporated 24 April 1923 to supply electricity in the Borough of West Telford, Montgomery County. On 27 August 1923 it was merged into the Pennsylvania Power & Light Co.

1013. WESTERN CHESTER COUNTY ELECTRIC COMPANY (Non-operating).
Chester County, Sadsbury Township.
1912, 1 Linear Inch.

History:
Western Chester County Electric Co. was incorporated 8 May 1912 to supply electricity in the Township of Sadsbury, Chester County. On 13 May 1912 it was consolidated and merged with six other non-operating companies to form the Christiana Suburban Electric Co.

1014. WHITE DEER POWER & LIGHT COMPANY (Non-operating).
Union County, White Deer Township.
1922 to 1923, 1 Linear Inch.

History:
White Deer Power & Light Co. was incorporated 23 February 1923 to supply electricity in the Township of White Deer, Union County. On 25 May 1923 it was merged into the Pennsylvania Power & Light Co.

1015. WHITE HAVEN LIGHT, HEAT & POWER COMPANY (Operating).
Luzerne County, White Haven Borough.
1923 to 1934, 2 Linear Feet.

History:
Electricity was first supplied in the Borough of White Haven, Luzerne County, in 1892 when Wilson J. Hauser constructed a hydroelectric station on the Lehigh Coal and Navigation Company's canal, and began operating as the White Haven Electric Illuminating Plant. Mr. Hauser installed street lights and an electric distribution system in White Haven. In 1906 he moved his power plant to a new location on the canal, where he installed generating equipment with a capacity of 125-kw. By 1923 he had boosted this to 400-kw. On 19 June 1923 Mr. Hauser incorporated his operations under the name White Haven Light, Heat & Power Co., and extended his distribution system to the Township of Denison, Luzerne County, and the Borough of East Side, Carbon County. In 1926 Lehigh Power Securities Corp. acquired control of the company's stock, and it was thereafter operated as a part of the Pennsylvania Power & Light Co. system, into which it was merged 28 May 1928.

Administrative Records:
Minute Book, 1923-1928
Stock Certificate Book, 1923-1926
Stock Transfer Record, 1926

Operating Records:
General Ledger, 1926-1928
Journal Entry Register, 1926-1928
Cashbook, 1920-1925
Cash Account and Sales, 1926
Record of Cash Receipts, 1926-1928
Record of Cash Disbursements, 1926-1928
Summary of Cash, 1926-1928
Bill Register, 1926-1928
Detail Ledger, 1926-1928
Detail of Cost Study and Fixed Capital, 1926-1927
Expenditure Requisitions, 1926-1928
Retirement Authorities, 1928
Workmen's Compensation Insurance Accrual Statements, 1926-1928
Summary of Accounts Receivable—Consumers, 1926-1928
Summary of Accounts Receivable—Miscellaneous, 1926-1934
Summary of Cashier's Overs and Shorts, 1926-1928
Summary of Consumer's Reports, 1926-1928
Audit Reports, 1923-1927 (4 Volumes)

Scope and Content Note:
The Minute Book of the White Haven Light, Heat & Power Co. documents routine stockholders' and directors' meetings for the period after the company's incorporation in 1923. The Audit Reports contain rate schedules for the supply of electricity to residential and commercial customers.

1016. WHITE HILL & MECHANICSBURG PASSENGER RAILWAY COMPANY (Operating).
Cumberland County, Mechanicsburg Borough.
1901 to 1912, 1 Linear Inch.

History:
White Hill & Mechanicsburg Passenger Railway Co. was incorporated 8 January 1901 to operate an electric street railway linking the towns of Cumberland County with the City of Harrisburg, Dauphin County. The company's line initially extended from the Borough of Mechanicsburg to the Cumberland Valley Railroad's passenger station at White Hill (from which passengers could travel directly on to Harrisburg). This line was later extended to the boroughs of Camp Hill and Carlisle. On 28 May 1902 the company turned control of its line over to the Harrisburg and Mechanicsburg Electric Railway Co. On 1 January 1904 the Valley Traction Co. leased the Harrisburg and Mechanicsburg line and thus gained control of the White Hill & Mechanicsburg company. In December 1904 Valley Traction purchased a controlling interest in the White Hill & Mechanicsburg Co. On 10 January 1913 it was consolidated and merged with five other railways—all controlled by Valley Traction—to form a new Harrisburg and Mechanicsburg Electric Railway Co.

Administrative Records:
Minute Book, 1901-1912

Scope and Content Note:
The Minute Book of the White Hill and Mechanicsburg Passenger Railway Co. documents the construction and development of the company's lines and its dealings with various borough councils concerning the acquisition of franchise rights. Also included are copies of its bylaws, several ordinances granting franchise rights, and route descriptions.

1017. THE WILKES BARRE COMPANY, NO. 1
(Non-operating).
Luzerne County, Wilkes-Barre City.
1910, 3 Linear Inches.

History:
The Wilkes-Barre Co., No. 1 was incorporated 17 May 1910 to supply electricity in the City of Wilkes Barre, Luzerne County. On 31 May 1910 it negotiated an agreement to merge with The Wilkes Barre Heat, Light and Motor Co. to form The Wilkes Barre Co., No. 2. However, this agreement was never consumated as the No. 1 company merged with the Wilkes Barre Gas and Electric Co. forming The Wilkes Barre Co., No. 3 on 29 June 1910.

1018. THE WILKES BARRE COMPANY, NO. 2
(Non-operating).
Luzerne County, Wilkes-Barre City.
1910 to 1923, 2 Linear Inches.

History:
The Wilkes Barre Co., No. 2 was formed 31 May 1910 when the Wilkes Barre Co., No. 1 negotiated a merger agreement with The Wilkes Barre Heat, Light and Motor Co. This agreement was never finalized, as one month later The Wilkes Barre Co., No. 1 merged with The Wilkes Barre Gas and Electric Co. The No. 2 company existed as a "paper company" until 8 August 1923 when it officially merged into Pennsylvania Power & Light Co.

1019. THE WILKES-BARRE COMPANY, NO. 3
(Operating).
Luzerne County, Wilkes-Barre City.
1910 to 1931, 12 Linear Feet.

History:
The Wilkes-Barre Co., No. 3, was incorporated 29 June 1910 following the consolidation and merger of The

Wilkes Barre Co., No. 1, and the Wilkes Barre Gas and Electric Co. Shortly thereafter, the company acquired the stock and assets of The Standard Electric Co. of Parsons, Penna., and that of The Anthracite Electric Light, Heat and Power Co. The Wilkes-Barre Co., No. 3, supplied gas, electric lighting, and steam heating in the City of Wilkes-Barre, and its business expanded rapidly. In 1915 the United Gas & Electrical Engineering Corp. of New York obtained control of the company. In 1921 Lehigh Power Securities Corp. acquired the company's stock. On 23 August 1923 the company was merged into Pennsylvania Power & Light Co.

Administrative Records:
Minute Books, 1910-1923 (4 Volumes)
Stock Certificate Books, 1910-1923 (9 Volumes)
Stock Ledgers, 1910-1922 (3 Volumes)

Operating Records:
FINANCIAL RECORDS
General Ledgers, 1910-1923 (5 Volumes)
Journals, 1910-1917 (7 Volumes)
Cashbooks, 1910-1922 (3 Volumes)
Voucher Expense Indexes, 1910-1922 (3 Volumes)
Voucher Record, 1922-1923
Detail Ledgers—Expenses, 1910-1922 (5 Volumes)
Construction Work in Progress, 1919-1921
Accrual Record, 1916-1923 (2 Volumes)
Balance Sheets, 1910-1922 (3 Volumes)
MISCELLANEOUS REPORTS
Financial Reports, 1910-1921 (5 Volumes)
Record of Miscellaneous Expenses, 1910-1916 (2 Volumes)
Expenses Ledger of Operating Dept., 1911-1922
Report of Monthly Operations—Steam Dept., 1915-1921
Report of Monthly Operations—Electrical Dept., 1917-1922
Report of Monthly Operations—Gas Dept., 1911-1922
Audit Report, Pennsylvania Power & Light Co., 1922

Scope and Content Note:
The Minute Books contain several detailed reports written by the general manager describing all aspects of company operations. Included are documents which analyze the economic conditions in Wilkes-Barre. Also included are charts documenting rates charged to residential and commercial customers. Financial statements detail earnings and describe property acquired through various mergers. Operating reports for the electric, steam and gas departments provide a wide range of statistical material documenting the number of kilowatt hours generated, quantities of fuel consumed, number of employees working in various departments, lamps serviced, steam meters in use, and amounts of gas being manufactured.

1020. WILKES BARRE ELECTRIC COMPANY (Operating).
Luzerne County, Wilkes-Barre City.
1904, 1 Linear Inch.

History:
Wilkes Barre Electric Co. was incorporated 29 November 1904 after the consolidation and merger of The Wilkes Barre Electric Light Co. and The Wyoming Valley Electric Light, Heat and Power Co. On 22 December 1904 the company was consolidated and merged with four other companies to form Wilkes Barre Gas and Electric Co.

Administrative Records:
Minute Book, 1904

1021. THE WILKES-BARRE ELECTRIC LIGHT COMPANY (Operating).
Luzerne County, Wilkes-Barre City.
1883 to 1904, 1 1/2 Linear Feet.

History:
The Wilkes-Barre Electric Light Co. was incorporated 24 January 1883 to supply electric lighting in the City of Wilkes-Barre, Luzerne County. The company constructed a power plant on Butler Alley to house its Arnoux and Hochhausen arc lighting equipment. In 1885 the company switched to the Edison direct current system for incandescent lighting and installed two 400-light and four 800-light Edison machines. Late in 1886 the company acquired The Excelsior Electric Co. of Wilkes-Barre. It then installed Excelsior Electric's arc lighting equipment. In 1895 another power plant was constucted at Mill Creek. New equipment which boosted generating capacity to 930-kw was installed and the Butler Alley operation was sold. On 16 November 1904 the company was consolidated and merged with Wyoming Valley Electric Light, Heat and Power Co. to form Wilkes Barre Electric Co.

Administrative Records:
Minute Books, 1883-1904 (4 Volumes)
Stock Certificate Books, 1883-1896 (2 Volumes)

Operating Records:
General Ledgers, 1885-1899 (2 Volumes)
Journals, 1887-1899 (3 Volumes)
Trial Balances, 1892-1898

Scope and Content Note:
The Minute Books describe the process by which incandescent lighting was introduced in Wilkes-Barre. There is considerable information on the construction of the local power house and the prices the company charged for lamps and electric hook-ups. The company's relationship with Wilkes-Barre City Council is well documented as are its negotiations for street lighting contracts. Financial statements show earnings, expenses, assets and liabilities.

1022. WILKES BARRE GAS AND ELECTRIC COMPANY (Operating).
Luzerne County, Wilkes-Barre City.
1904 to 1923, 3 Linear Feet.

History:
Wilkes Barre Gas and Electric Co. was incorporated 29 December 1904 following the consolidation and merger of the Wilkes-Barre Gas Co., The Consumers Gas Co. of Wilkes-Barre, The Gas Co. of Luzerne County, the Wilkes Barre Electric Co., and The Ashley Electric Light and Power Co. The new company was formed by a consortium of Philadelphia bankers, headed by Forrest & Co., which was trying to monopolize the gas and electric business in the Wilkes-Barre area. The company consolidated the various properties it had acquired into a single operating unit, making improvements as necessary.

For example, the generating capacity of the Wilkes Barre Electric Company's River Plant was boosted from approximately 1000-kw to 3490-kw. On 7 June 1910 the company was merged with The Wilkes Barre Co., No. 1, to form The Wilkes Barre Co., No. 3.

Administrative Records:
Minute Books, 1904-1923 (9 Volumes)
Stock Certificate Books, 1904-1910 (5 Volumes)
Stock Ledger, 1923

Operating Records:
General Ledgers, 1904-1905
Journal, 1905-1910
Cashbooks, 1904-1910 (4 Volumes)
Construction Expenditures, 1904-1910
Abstract of Operating Expenses, 1907-1910

Scope and Content Note:
The Minute Books contain a great deal of information documenting the company's routine operations and finances. These volumes describe various improvements made to electric and gas plants as well as to the distribution systems. Two 1905 reports from J.G. White & Co., Inc., Engineers, evaluate the efficiency of the gas and electric departments. Several very detailed annual reports describe completed improvements and other aspects of company operations. The minutes also contain Audit Reports, Gas Rate Schedules, and tables documenting fuel consumption. Payrolls list workers, their occupations and pay rates. Finally, there are several files of material describing the relationship of the company to Wilkes-Barre City Council, which determined rates for selling gas and awarded street lighting contracts.

1023. WILKES-BARRE GAS COMPANY (Operating).
Luzerne County, Wilkes-Barre City.
1854 to 1904, 1 Linear Foot.

History:
Wilkes-Barre Gas Co. was incorporated 20 April 1854 by a special act of the Pennsylvania General Assembly. The company used the coal gas process to supply gas lighting in Wilkes-Barre in 1856. The next year it extended its distribution system to the boroughs of Kingston, Wyoming, and West Pittston, and to other suburbs of Wilkes-Barre. The company's gas plant was completed in 1858, but by 1869 demand had grown so much that the company had to install additional equipment. In 1879 it switched from the coal gas process to the Lowe water gas process, necessitating the installation of entirely new apparatus. In 1893 the company was faced with competition for the first time when The Consumers Gas Co. of Wilkes-Barre began operations. This challenge ended on 29 June 1898, when both companies were leased to The Gas Co. of Luzerne County. The latter company had been formed specifically for that purpose by a consortium of Philadelphia bankers headed by Forrest & Co. In 1904 it contracted with J. G. White & Co., Inc. to operate and manage its property. Later that year it was consolidated and merged with four other companies, including The Consumers Gas Co. of Wilkes-Barre, and The Gas Co. of Luzerne County, to form Wilkes Barre Gas and Electric Co.

Administrative Records:
Minute Bolks, 1854-1904 (4 Vooumes)

Operating Records:
General Ledgers, 1864-1898 (2 Volumes)
Journal, 1875-1898
Cashbooks, 1857-1898 (3 Volumes)
Statements & Trial Balances, 1886-1898 (2 Volumes)

Scope and Content Note:
The Minute Books contain routine minutes and include material documenting the construction of gas works and pipe lines. The company's relationship with Wilkes-Barre City Council is described in detail. Negotiations for street lighting contracts and pipe line construction are well documented.

1024. THE WILKES BARRE HEAT, LIGHT AND MOTOR COMPANY (Operating).
Luzerne County, Wilkes-Barre City.
1886 to 1910, 2 1/2 Linear Feet.

History:
The Wilkes Barre Heat, Light and Motor Company was incorporated 28 April 1886 to supply steam heating in Wilkes-Barre, Luzerne County. Shortly after its incorporation it constructed a steam heating plant on the corner of Bennett and North Washington Streets. The company's first major contract was to heat the Court House in Wilkes-Barre. Its distribution system steadily grew and by 1893 business was so good that the company found it necessary to construct another plant, this time on Gildersleeve Street. This plant was destroyed by a fire in 1908, but was quickly rebuilt. On 31 May 1910 the company was consolidated and merged with The Wilkes Barre Co., No. 1, and three other companies to form The Wilkes Barre Co., No. 2.

Administrative Records:
Minute Books, 1886-1910 (2 Volumes)
Stock Certificate Book, 1889-1910
Stock Certificates and Wills, 1886-1910
Stock Ledger, 1886-1910

Operating Records:
General Ledgers, 1886-1910 (4 Volumes)
Journals, 1893-1910 (2 Volumes)
Cashbooks, 1886-1910 (7 Volumes)

Scope and Content Note:
The Minute Books document routine stockholders' and directors' meetings. There is a good deal of information describing the company's relationship with the Luzerne County Commissioners who were responsible for the installation of the court house steam heating system. The Minute Books also contain annual Financial Statements which detail assets, liabilities and operating expenses. Finally, there is a 1909 pamphlet describing consumer rules and regulations.

1025. WILKES-BARRE TOWNSHIP ELECTRIC COMPANY (Non-operating).
Luzerne County, Wilkes-Barre Township.
1910 to 1912, 1 Linear Inch.

History:
Wilkes-Barre Township Electric Co. was incorporated 26 January 1911 to supply electricity in the Township of Wilkes-Barre, Luzerne County. On 23 February 1912 it was consolidated and merged with eleven other companies to form The Harwood Electric Co.

1026. WILLIAMS TOWNSHIP ELECTRIC COMPANY (Non-operating).
Northampton County, Williams Township.
1913 to 1935, 3 Linear Inches.

History:
Williams Township Electric Co. was one of eleven electric companies chartered by the Lehigh Navigation Electric Co. in December 1913 to obtain franchise rights in the townships along the Delaware Canal in Bucks and Northampton Counties. At this time, the Lehigh Navigation Electric Co. was controlled by Lehigh Coal and Navigation Co., which also controlled Delaware Canal Co. Williams Township Electric Co. and its counterparts were "paper companies", formed solely to secure franchise rights. Williams Township Electric Co. was officially declared out of existence 30 September 1935.

1027. WILLIAMS VALLEY LIGHT HEAT AND POWER COMPANY (Operating).
Dauphin County, Williamstown Borough.
1890 to 1922, 3 1/2 Linear Feet.

History:
Williams Valley Light Heat and Power Co. was incorporated 17 September 1890 to supply electricity in the Boroughs of Lykens, Williamstown, and Tower City, and the Village of Wiconisco, all in Dauphin County. The company constructed a power station near Williamstown shortly after its incorporation. On 27 April 1910 it leased all its property to its main competitor, the Sterling Consolidated Electric Co. Five years later the two companies officially merged.

Administrative Records:
Stock Certificate Book, 1890-1915

Operating Records:
General Ledgers, 1901-1910 (2 Volumes)
Journals, 1900-1917 (2 Volumes)
Cashbooks, 1900-1914 (5 Volumes)
Daybooks, 1901-1911 (2 Volumes)
Accounts Payable, 1915
Accounts Receivable, 1915
Consumers' Ledgers, 1891-1912 (6 Volumes)
Light Ledger, 1908-1910
Meter Readings, 1903-1910
Bank Statements, 1915-1922

Scope and Content Note:
The Meter Readings Ledger of the Williams Valley Light Heat and Power Co. lists the company's customers, their addresses, occupations, and shows their monthly meter readings and charges. The company's Light Ledger is an alphabetical listing of its customers and their monthly charges for electricity.

1028. WILLIAMSPORT ELECTRIC COMPANY (Operating).
Lycoming County, Williamsport City.
1901 to 1924, 2 Linear Feet.

History:
Williamsport Electric Co. was formed in 1899 by the Edison Associated Companies. Located in the City of Williamsport, Lycoming County, the company bought and sold electrical parts and supplies, and installed and repaired electrical equipment for the Edison companies in the area. Although it functioned as an independent operating company, it was not incorporated as such until 15 March 1922. The next year Pennsylvania Power & Light gained control of the company. In January 1924 Williamsport Electric ceased operations.

Administrative Records:
Minute Book, 1923-1924
Stock Certificate Book, 1922-1923

Operating Records:
General Ledgers, 1901-1924 (3 Volumes)
Journals, 1906-1923 (4 Volumes)
Journal Entry Register, 1923-1924
Daily Cash Receipts, 1921-1924 (2 Volumes)
Cash Disbursements, 1923-1924 (2 Volumes)
Voucher Indexes, 1910-1923 (3 Volumes)
Bill Register, 1921-1924
Detail Ledger—Revenues, 1923-1924
Working Papers and Financial Reports, 1922-1923
Retirement Authorities, 1924
Audit Reports, 1918-1924
Cash Receipts, 1901-1907

Scope and Content Note:
The Minute Book of the Williamsport Electric Co. contains routine minutes. The Audit Reports include lists of uncollectable accounts and inventories of materials and supplies.

1029. WILLIAMSPORT GAS COMPANY (Operating).
Lycoming County, Williamsport City.
1858 to 1912, 4 Linear Feet.

History:
Williamsport Gas Co. started supplying gas for lighting in April 1853. During the 1860s it began supplying Williamsport with gas for street lights. On 1 November 1875 it leased the property and plant of its leading rival, the Lycoming Gas and Water Co. Shortly before 1900 the company extended its gas lighting system across the Susquehanna River to the Borough of South Williamsport. In 1906 the company was purchased by a New York consortium led by H. D. Walbridge & Co. Six years later it was merged into Northern Central Gas Co.

Administrative Records:
Minute Book, 1870-1912 (6 Volumes)
Stock Certificate Books, 1858-1912 (6 Volumes)
Stock Transfer Record, 1899-1908
Stock Certificate Register, 1899-1910

Operating Records:
FINANCIAL RECORDS
General Ledgers, 1871-1912 (5 Volumes)
Journals, 1870-1912 (5 Volumes)
Cashbooks, 1876-1907 (5 Volumes)
Treasurer's Account Book, 1899-1904
Accounts Payable Ledger, 1906
General Detail Ledger, 1911-1912
Expense Detail Ledger, 1908
PERSONNEL RECORDS
Payrolls, 1912
AUDIT REPORT, 1906-1908

Scope and Content Note:
The Minutes of Stockholders' and Board of Managers meetings contain a great deal of information about the operation of this Pennsylvania gas company. The relationship with Williamsport City Council is well documented as are the negotiations for street lighting contracts. There is also a good deal of material on rate setting procedures and consumer rules and regulations. The company's relationship with its rival, Lycoming Gas and Water Co., is described in detail. Finally, monthly financial status reviews include statements of receipts and expenditures, tables listing the size and location of gas mains, and annual production figures.

1030. WILLIAMSPORT PASSENGER RAILWAY COMPANY (Operating).
Lycoming County, Williamsport City.
1879 to 1930, 4 1/2 Linear Feet.

History:
Williamsport Passenger Railway Co. was incorporated 15 April 1863. It began operations 15 July 1865 with one horse-drawn streetcar running over a two-mile long route. On 1 January 1878 the company was leased to Mr. A.B. Middaugh under somewhat clouded circumstances. The company subsequently sued Middaugh, claiming that 'said lease was a gross fraud upon the stockholders and if continued will end in the ruin of the road and the rights of the Stockholders.' On 27 June 1879 Middaugh surrendered the line. Later that year, control passed to a group of local businessmen headed by Mr. Robert P. Allen. In 1890 Mr. Hiram R. Rhoads became president after his Philadelphia syndicate bought the company. The next year Rhoads introduced Williamsport's first electric street railway cars. In 1892, the company was faced with a competitive challenge when Pennsylvania State Senator J. Henry Cochran organized five new electric street railway companies in Williamsport. After Rhoads died on February 1894, Cochran formed the Lycoming Improvement Co. in order to raise capital to purchase the Williamsport Passenger Railway Co. This deal was consumated on 9 March 1894. Thereafter, the company was operated as part of the Cochran holdings. On 10 June 1894 it was consolidated and merged with three other Cochran companies to form the Williamsport Railways Co.

Administrative Records:
Minute Books, 1879-1926 (3 Volumes)
Bond Transfer Record, 1907-1923

Operating Records:
General Ledgers, 1888-1890 (5 Volumes)
Journals, 1888-1923 (7 Volumes)
Cashbooks, 1888-1926 (6 Volumes)
Indexes to Vouchers, 1891-1930 (6 Volumes)
Voucher Record, 1923-1926
Control Auto Expense, 1923-1926
Automobile Service Ledger, 1923-1926
Monthly Automobile Reports, 1924-1926
Record of Passenger Business, 1892-1921 (5 Volumes)
Miscellaneous Statements, 1915-1925
Federal Income Tax Schedule, 1926
Audit Reports, 1918-1926 (2 Volumes)

Scope and Content Note:
The Minute Books describe the company's transition from horse-drawn, to electric, street railway cars. There is considerable information on fares and car purchases. The Records of Passenger Business include daily statistics on the number of passengers carried, miles travelled, and total ticket sales.

1031. WILLIAMSPORT RAILWAYS COMPANY
(Operating).
Lycoming County, Williamsport City.
1921 to 1933, 5 Linear Feet.

History:
Williamsport Railways Co. was incorporated 21 January 1927 following the consolidation and merger of Vallamont Traction Co., East End Passenger Railway Co., and Williamsport Passenger Railway Co., all of which were owned by Lehigh Power Securities Corp. Following its formation, the company took steps to improve service: new equipment and cars were purchased, a new car barn was built, and the company contracted with Electric Bond and Share Co. to supervise its operations. However, business continued to decline due to competition from automobiles and jitney buses as well as from the ever-increasing costs of maintenance and repair. On 29 January 1931 the company decided to abandon service along its Vallamont Division line. In February 1933 its directors voted to liquidate the company and made arrangements for Williamsport Transportation Co., to operate buses over some of its old routes. The last electric streetcar in Williamsport made its final run on 11 June 1933.

Administrative Records:
Minute Books, 1926-1933 (2 Volumes)
Stock Certificate Books, 1927
Stock Transfer Record, 1927
Stock Ledger, 1927
Correspondence and Miscellaneous Papers, 1921-1933

Operating Records:
FINANCIAL RECORDS
General Ledger, 1927-1934
Journal Entry Register, 1927-1934
Cashbooks, 1927-1933 (2 Volumes)
Detail Ledger, 1927-1933
Detail Ledger—Construction Jobs, 1927-1931
Accrual Record, 1931-1933
Federal Income Tax Schedules, 1927-1931
Construction Ledger, 1921-1924
Balance Sheets, 1927-1932
Operating Revenue and Expenses—Statistics, 1922-1923
Daily Receipts, 1925-1930
Statements of Weekly Passes Honored by Lines, 1928-1933
Maps, n.d.
MISCELLANEOUS REPORTS
Audit Reports, 1927-1932 (2 Volumes)
Annual Reports to Public Service Commission, 1927-1932
Monthly Cash Control Reports, 1932
Quarterly Financial Reports, 1927-1931

Scope and Content Note:
The Minute Books of the Williamsport Railways Co. provide information regarding the company's fare rates and the sale of its old car barn, and include a copy of the 1926 agreement of consolidation and merger by which the company was formed. The Correspondence and Miscellaneous Papers deal with a number of aspects of the company's operations and include information on its equipment purchases, legal transactions, safety procedures, accident reports, streetcar routes, wage rates, personnel, relations with various municipalities, its membership in the Pennsylvania Street Railway Association and the American Electric Railways Association, and its relationship with Electric Bond and Share Co. Also included are construction and maintenance reports, complete with blueprints; narrative reports of the company's operations; and its certificates of public convenience. The Daily Receipts list the amount of money taken in per day and list any special events that occurred on individual days. The Maps of Williamsport show the company's electric street railway routes.

1032. WILLIAMSPORT TRANSPORTATION COMPANY (Operating).
Lycoming County, Williamsport City.
1924 to 1933, 2 Linear Inches.

History:
Williamsport Transportation Co. was incorporated 11 December 1924 by Pennsylvania Power & Light Co. The company operated a largely unsuccessful bus line between the Borough of South Williamsport and Williamsport. In 1931 control of the company's stock was acquired by Williamsport Railways Co., which was also owned by Pennsylvania Power & Light.

Administrative Records:
Minute Book, 1924-1933
Stock Transfer Record, 1925-1926
Correspondence and Miscellaneous Papers, 1924-1933

Operating Records:
Audit Reports, 1926-1932 (2 Volumes)
Cash Control Report, 1932
Operating Revenue and Expenses, 1930-1932
Budget, 1931

Scope and Content Note:
Correspondence and Miscellaneous Papers of Williamsport Transportation Co. document many aspects of the company's operations, including the purchase of buses, legal affairs, fuel records, equipment status, bus routings, accounting procedures, and competition from other companies.

1033. WILLIAMSTOWN GAS COMPANY (Operating).
Dauphin County, Lykens Borough.
1925 to 1927, 1 Linear Inch.

History:
This company was incorporated 14 November 1911 as Gas Co. of Dauphin. It changed its name to Williamstown Gas Co. on 11 June 1926. The company supplied gas for lighting and heating in the Boroughs of Lykens and Williamstown, Dauphin County. On 25 August 1926 it purchased the property and franchises of Lykens Valley Consolidated Gas Co., which operated in the same area. Through the creation of two "paper companies" in February 1927 the company extended its operations to the Borough of Tower City in Dauphin County. In July 1927 Pennsylvania Power & Light Co. audited this company to determine the advisability of purchasing it, but decided not to. The company's subsequent history is unknown.

Operating Records:
Audit Report, Pennsylvania Power & Light Co., 1925-1927

1034. WINOLA ELECTRIC COMPANY (Operating).
Lackawanna County, West Abington Township.
1927 to 1956, 1 Linear Foot.

History:
Winola Electric Co. was incorporated 19 September 1919 to supply electricity in the Township of West Abington, Lackawanna County. The company did not generate any power. Instead, it erected a distribution system and connected it to Abington Electric Co., from which all the electricity was purchased. In May 1956 Pennsylvania Power & Light Co. acquired control of its stock. It was merged into Pennsylvania Power & Light on 27 June 1956.

Administrative Records:
Minute Book, 1927-1956
Stock Certificate Books, 1927-1956
Correspondence and Miscellaneous Papers, 1937-1956

Operating Records:
General Ledger, 1956
Journal, 1956
Detail Ledger—Revenues, 1956
Detail Ledger—Expenses, 1956
Tariffs and Rate Schedules, 1927-1939
List of Customers and Meter Numbers, undated
U.S. Defense Electric Power Administration Data, 1951-1952
Pennsylvania Public Utility Commission General Assessment Reports, 1937-1955
Pennsylvania Public Utility Commission Regulations & Miscellaneous Data, 1928-1951
Federal Power Commission—Power System Statements, 1938-1950
Federal Department of Commerce—Industrial Census Reports, 1932-1937
Bank Check Stubs & Pass Books, 1927-1956
Cashbook, 1947-1956
Cash Disbursements, 1938-1956
Financial & Operating Reports, 1956 (2 Volumes)

Scope and Content Note:
The Minute Book of Winola Electric Co. documents routine stockholders' and directors' meetings, with particular emphasis on those meetings that dealt with the company's 1956 merger into Pennsylvania Power & Light. Correspondence and miscellaneous papers from 1937-1939 deal with complaints made to the Pennsylvania Public Utilities Commission about the company's operations. These provide a picture of the slow progress of electrification in this overwhelmingly rural area. Other records document the company's dealings with various regulatory commissions, such as the United States Defense Electric Power Administration, and the Federal Power Commission, during World War II.

1035. WOLF TOWNSHIP LYCOMING COUNTY ELECTRIC COMPANY (Non-operating).
Lycoming County, Wolf Township.
1924, 1 Linear Inch.

History:
Wolf Township Lycoming County Electric Co. was incorporated 28 August 1924 to supply electricity in the township of Wolf, Lycoming County. On 6 October 1924 it was merged into The Citizens Electric Light and Power Co. of Hughesville Pa.

1036. WOODWARD POWER & LIGHT COMPANY (Non-operating).
Lycoming County, Woodward Township.
1923 to 1924, 1 Linear Inch.

History:
Woodward Power & Light Co. was incorporated 21 November 1923 to supply electricity in the Township of Woodward, Lycoming County. On 31 March 1924 it was merged into Pennsylvania Power & Light Co.

1037. WRIGHT TOWNSHIP ELECTRIC COMPANY (Non-operating).
Luzerne County, Wright Township.
1910 to 1912, 1 Linear Inch.

History:
Wright Township Electric Co. was incorporated 26 January 1911 to supply electricity in the Township of Wright, Luzerne County. On 23 February 1923 the company was consolidated and merged with eleven other companies to form The Harwood Electric Co.

1038. WRIGHTSVILLE LIGHT AND POWER COMPANY (Operating).
York County, Wrightsville Borough.
1902 to 1930, 2 Linear Feet.

History:
Wrightsville Light and Power Co. was incorporated 15 January 1902 to supply electricity in the Borough of Wrightsvile, York County. The company constructed an electric power plant with a generating capacity of 100-kw. This facility was housed in a converted mill building and run primarily by water power. In 1915, after the company began to purchase its electricity from Edison Light and Power Co. of York, Pa., its power plant was shut down. In 1923 the company extended its area of operations to the Township of Lower Windsor and the Borough of East Prospect. Two years later its stock was acquired by United Gas and Electric Co. Shortly thereafter, the stock was acquired by Lehigh Power Securities Corp. On 31 December 1930 it was merged into Pennsylvania Power & Light Co.

Administrative Records:
Minute Books, 1907-1930 (2 Volumes)
Secretary's Papers of Meetings, 1930
Stock Certificate Book, 1902-1930

Operating Records:
General Ledgers, 1908-1930 (3 Volumes)
Journal Entry Register, 1926-1930
Record of Cash Disbursements, 1926-1927
Audited Voucher Registers, 1926-1930 (2 Volumes)
Invoice Record, 1926-1930
Construction Ledger, 1926-1930
Construction Worksheets, 1926
Detail Ledgers, 1926-1929 (2 Volumes)
Transportation Expenses, 1922-1927
Automobile Reports, 1926-1929
Materials and Supplies Reports, 1926-1930
Financial Reports, 1926
Expenditure Requisitions, 1930
Audit Reports, 1921-1929 (5 Volumes)

Scope and Content Note:
In addition to documenting stockholders' and directors' meetings, the Minute Books contain monthly financial statements, showing revenues and operating expenses. Also included is correspondence relating to company bond issues. Materials and Supplies Reports provide the prices of electric parts and appliances such as washers and irons.

1039. WRIGHTSVILLE WATER SUPPLY COMPANY (Operating).
York County, Wrightsville Borough.
1921 to 1942, 2 Linear Feet.

History:
Wrightsville Water Supply Co. was incorporated 16 June 1897 to supply water to the public in the Borough of Wrightsville, York County. The company purchased the necessary franchises and tracts of land, and then constructed a reservoir and water works. On 1 August 1925 American Gas and Electric Co. acquired Wrightsville Water Supply and moved its main offices. In March 1929 Electric Bond and Share Co. contracted to supply the company with supervision, engineering and general services. In December 1933 the company was acquired by Pennsylvania Power & Light Co.

Administrative Records:
Minute Books, 1927-1942 (2 Volumes)

Operating Records:
Summary of Cash, 1938-1942
Cash Receipts Ledger, 1926
Expenditure Requisitions, 1931-1941
Retirement Authorities, 1931
Audit Reports, 1921-1932 (4 Volumes)

Scope and Content Note:
The Minute Books of the Wrightsville Water Supply Co. document routine stockholders' and directors' meetings. The Audit Reports provide information about the company's formation, a description of the Borough of Wrightsville, information about a 1922 dispute over a proposed rate hike, and a description of the company's property and operations.

1040. WYOMING BOROUGH-LUZERNE POWER & LIGHT COMPANY (Non-operating).
Luzerne County, Wyoming Borough.
1927, 1 Linear Inch.

History:
Wyoming Borough-Luzerne Power & Light Co. was incorporated 30 March 1927 to supply electricity in a portion of the Borough of Wyoming, Luzerne County. On 9 April 1927 the company was merged into Pennsylvania Power & Light Co.

1041. **THE WYOMING VALLEY ELECTRIC LIGHT, HEAT AND POWER COMPANY** (Operating).
Luzerne County, Wilkes-Barre City.
1898 to 1904, 1 Linear Foot.

History:

Incorporated 21 October 1898, The Wyoming Valley Light, Heat and Power Co. was formed by a group of Philadelphia bankers, headed by Forrest and Co., in order to acquire a number of gas and electric companies in the Wilkes-Barre area. This group acquired the stock of The Wilkes-Barre Electric Light Co. on 21 October 1898. Operating the Wilkes Barre company's Mill Creek electric generating station, Wyoming Valley supplied electricity for lighting and power to the City of Wilkes-Barre and its environs. On 16 November 1904 it was consolidated and merged with The Wilkes-Barre Electric Light Co. to form Wilkes Barre Electric Co.

Administrative Records:

Minute Book, 1898-1904
Stock Certificate Book, 1898-1904
Stock Transfer Record, 1898-1904
Stock Ledger, 1898-1904
Bonds, 1904

Operating Records:

General Ledgers, 1899-1904 (2 Volumes)
Cashbooks, 1898-1904 (2 Volumes)
Financial Statements, 1898-1904

1042. **YORK COUNTY ELECTRIC COMPANY** (Non-operating).
York County, Fairview Township.
1919 to 1926, 2 Linear Inches.

History:

York County Electric Co. was incorporated 30 January 1920 to supply electricity in the Township of Fairview, York County. On 9 August 1926 the company was merged into The United Electric Co.

1043. **YORK-EAST MANCHESTER POWER & LIGHT COMPANY** (Non-operating).
York County, East Manchester Borough.
1957, 1 Linear Inch.

History:

York-East Manchester Power & Light Co. was incorporated by Pennsylvania Power & Light Co. 13 May 1957 to supply electricity in the Borough of East Manchester, York County. On 5 November 1957 it was merged into Pennsylvania Power & Light Co.

1044. **YORK-YORK HAVEN POWER & LIGHT COMPANY** (Non-operating).
York County, York Haven Borough.
1957, 1 Linear Inch.

History:

York-York Haven Power & Light Co. was incorporated by Pennsylvania Power & Light Co. 13 May 1957 to supply electricity in the Borough of York Haven, York County. On 5 November 1957 it was merged into Pennsylvania Power & Light Co.

1045. **ZERBE ELECTRIC COMPANY** (Non-operating).
Northumberland County, Zerbe Township.
1921 to 1922, 1 Linear Inch.

History:

Zerbe Electric Co. was incorporated 10 August 1921 to supply electricity in the Township of Zerbe, Northumberland County. On 8 November 1921 it was merged into Pennsylvania Power & Light Co.

1046. **PENNSYLVANIA POWER & LIGHT COMPANY** (Operating).
Lehigh County, Allentown City.
1920 to date, 10 Linear Feet.

History:

Pennsylvania Power & Light Co. was formed 4 June 1920 through the consolidation and merger of Pennsylvania Power & Light Co., No. 2 (a non-operating company) and seven operating companies: The Lehigh Valley Light & Power Co., Northern Central Gas Co., Columbia and Montour Electric Co., Northumberland County Gas & Electric Co., The Harwood Electric Co., The Schuylkill Gas and Electric Co., and Pennsylvania Lighting Co. The stocks of all but the last of these companies were controlled by Lehigh Power Securities Corp., a holding company formed in 1917 by Electric Bond and Share Co. EBASCO had entered eastern Pennsylvania in order to integrate the area's utility companies into a unified system. The 1920 consolidation provided the nucleus. During the next decade PP&L continued to expand, with important mergers taking place in 1923 (5 companies), 1928 (31 companies) and 1930 (21 companies). However, a 1938 Securities and Exchange Commission order cited EBASCO for violation of the Public Utilities Holding Company Act. Litigation dragged on for almost a decade, but after the Supreme Court upheld the SEC's position, EBASCO was forced to simplify its structure and PP&L was set up as an independent utility in 1947. PP&L continued to expand during the late 1940s and 1950s. Mauch Chunk Heat Power & Electric Co. and Renovo Edison Light, Heat & Power Companies were added to the system in 1947. Pennsylvania Water & Power was merged into it in 1955 and the next year The Scranton Electric Company joined. By 1982, PP&L was serving over 1,000,000 customers in a 10,000 square mile area of eastern Pennsylvania.

Administrative Records:

Pennsylvania Power & Light Company History, 1939 (3 Volumes)
Merger Petitions, 1920-1939 (5 Volumes)
Historical Chart, 1939
Legal Department, Records, (1920-1943) (12 Volumes)
Legal Department—Records, 1920-1943 (12 Boxes)
Correspondence, 1920-1937
Correspondence—National Defense, 1932-1945 (3 Boxes)
Annual and Regional Stockholders' Meetings, 1948
Pennsylvania Power & Light Co. Vertical File, 1978-present
Indices of Predecessor Company Records, (12 Volumes)
Indices to Records (various) (8 Volumes)

Operating Records:

FINANCIAL RECORDS
Accounts Ledger—Past, Present, Future Accounts, 1946-1947
Accounts Payable Ledgers—Associated Companies, 1920-1941 (2 Volumes)

Accounts Payable Invoice Register, 1928-1930
Accounts Payable—Scranton, 1952
Voucher Registers—Construction Accounts, 1928-1932 (5 Volumes)
Voucher Register—Field Accounts, 1919-1921
Voucher Register—Tie Line Extension, 1920-1921
Delinquent Accounts Analysis, 1922-1933 (4 Volumes)
Financial and Operating Reports, Affiliated Companies, 1946-1966 (9 Volumes)
Plant Reconciliations and Analyses, 1936
Yearly Analyses of Fixed Capital Additions, 1919-1925
Working Papers—Financial and Cost Studies,
PERSONNEL RECORDS
Time Sheets—Harwood Plant, 1920
Time Sheets—Hazleton District, 1920
Time Sheets—Siegfried Plant, 1920-1921
Time Sheets—Harwood Plant and Hazleton District, 1921-1922 (2 Volumes)
Time Sheets—Siegfried Plant and Hazleton,1922
Time Sheets—Hauto Plant, 1921-1922 (2 Volumes)
Payrolls—Harrisburg, Allentown, 1928-1930 (2 Volumes)
Payrolls—Field, 1921
Payrolls—Distribution, Harrisburg District, 1928 (3 Volumes)
AUDIT REPORTS
Pennsylvania Power & Light Co., Traveling Auditors' Reports, 1920-1937
Audit Reports, Electric Bond and Share Co., 1922-1930 (4 Volumes)

Scope and Content Note:

Pennsylvania Power & Light's 1939 Corporate History is essential for an understanding of the company's evolution and development. These three volumes contain historical information on more than 950 predecessor companies. The Merger Petitions (1920-1939) which were presented to the Public Utility Commission are a useful listing of the various merged companies and provide detailed analyses of their operations and finances. Correspondence documentstwo broad areas: (1) Personnel and labor relations, and (2) Sales including contract work done for the government during World War II. The files of the Personnel Department contain information on wages, hours, and job classifications and beneficial societies while Sales Department material documents World War II defense contracts and how shortages of manpower and raw materials affected company operations during this period. The files of the Legal Department document the company's problems with the Securities and Exchange, the Federal Power and the Pennsylvania Public Utilities Commissions during the 1930s and 1940s. These records clearly delineate the relationship of PP&L to Electric Bond and Share and Lehigh Power Securities Corp. and contain a good deal of information on PP&L's organization, capitalization and rate structure.

1047. AMERICAN GAS & ELECTRIC COMPANY
(Operating).
New York State, New York City.
1908 to 1910, 1 Linear Inch.

History:

American Gas & Electric Co. was a holding company incorporated in New York 20 December 1906 by Electric Bond and Share Co. to administer the 25 gas and electric companies acquired from the Electric Co. of America. Among the companies were Scranton Electric Co. and Edison Electric Illuminating Co. of Altoona, Pa. Other were located in Atlantic City, New Jersey; Consholing, West Virginia; Muncie, Indiana; Rockford, Illinois; Canton, Ohio; and Wheeling, West Virginia. In February 1925, EBASCO consolidated and merged American Gas & Electric Co. with Appalachian Service Corp. to form The American Gas and Electric Co.

Operating Records:

Statistical Register, 1908-1910

Scope and Content Note:

The Statiscal Register contains a variety of operating statistics broken down by locality, and, in some cases, by company, for the 25 companies controlled by American Gas & Electric Co. Included are statistics on income and revenue, employees and wages and salaries paid, coal used, connected load, labor costs, administrative expenses, advertising and public relations budgets, and sales of appliances and lamps.

1048. ELECTRIC BOND AND SHARE COMPANY
(Operating).
New York State, New York City.
1923 to 1932, 6 Linear Feet.

History:

Electric Bond and Share Co. was the largest utility holding company in the United States during the 1920's and 1930's. It controlled about 10% of the electricity generated in the country. The company had its origins in the 1890's when General Electric Co. (G.E.) organized Electrical Securities Co. of Boston to assist small utilities who wanted to buy generating equipment. Electrical Securities bought the stocks and bonds that were being issued by these electric companies and used them as collateral in financing the purchases of G.E. products. After the panic of 1893 when large numbers of electric and gas companies went bankrupt, these securities became virtually worthless. Therefore, in 1905, G.E. formed Electric Bond & Share in order to try to convert its portfolio of utility company stocks and bonds into marketable securities. EBASCO's president, S.Z. Mitchell, who had many years' experience in managing and financing small utilities in the Northwest, was seen by G.E. as being well suited to bring order to the utility industry. Under his direction EBASCO helped to revitalize hundreds of small electric companies by making technical, managerial and financial consultants available to them. The goal was to integrate these utilities into a rational generating and distribution system. To this end, EBASCO constructed an elaborate pyramid of holding companies including American Gas & Electric Co., which controlled The Scranton Electric Co., and Lehigh Power Securities Corp., which controlled Pennsylvania Power & Light. Bond & Share 'supervised' these holding companies, staffing them with interlocking directors and officers. Mitchell, for example, while chairman of EBASCO also served as director of Lehigh Power Securities Corp.

History:

As public attention increasingly focused upon General Electric's alleged efforts to monopolize the utility industry, chairman, Owen D. Young, sought to separate his company from EBASCO. In January 1925, G.E. formed Electric Bond & Share Securities Corp. which acquired all of EBASCO's stock. Four years later these two companies merged to form Electric Bond and Share Co. The new EBASCO claimed that it was no longer a holding company since it did not have majority control over any of the companies it "supervised." The Federal Trade and Securities and Exchange Commissions did not agree with this assessment. Late in 1935, following the enactment of the Public Utility Holding Company Act, the SEC brought suit in U.S. District Court, charging EBASCO with failing to register as a holding company. EBASCO fought this action, maintaining that the 1935 law was unconstitutional. It did, however, terminate its service contracts with American Gas & Electric and Lehigh Power Securities Corp. After the Supreme Court ruled that EBASCO had to comply with the law, the SEC moved to break up Bond and Share. As a result Pennsylvania Power & Light was set up as an independent utility in 1947. EBASCO was also forced to give up its control of American Gas & Electric and The Scranton Co.

Administrative Records:

Instructions to Traveling Auditors and Translations of Accounts, 1924 (3 Volumes)

Operating Records:

Personnel Application Form, 1926
Statistical Department—Analyses of Street Railway Operations, 1928-1931
Audit Reports—Ariel Light, Heat and Power Company to Hazle Township Water Company, 1923-1932
Audit Reports—Honesdale Consolidated Light, Heat & Power Company to Paupack Electric Company, 1923-1932
Audit Reports—Penns Creek Hydro Electric Company to Wrightsville Water Supply Company, 1923-1932

Scope and Content Note:

The records document EBASCO's relationship with Pennsylvania Power & Light, Conestoga Traction, Valley Railways and other companies controlled by Lehigh Power Securities Corp. Instructions to Travelling Auditors and the Audit Reports they prepared describe the ways in which EBASCO exercised financial control over its client companies and provided them with engineering and service contracts. Charts prepared by EBASCO's Statistical Department give information on nearly 50 street railway lines supervised by the company.

1049. LEHIGH POWER SECURITIES CORPORATION
(Operating).
New York State, New York City.
1919 to 1939, 1 Linear Foot.

History:

Lehigh Power Securities Corp. was incorporated in Delaware 19 July 1917 as a holding company. Its organizers, Electric Bond and Share Co., created it as part of their program to integrate electric and gas utility companies in eastern Pennsylvania. The corporation acquired the stock of Lehigh Navigation Electric Co. and through this firm the stock of The Harwood Electric Co. and its subsidiaries. It also acquired of Lehigh Valley Transit Co., Lehigh Valley Light & Power Co., and of the companies formerly controlled by Northern Central Co. A 4 June 1920 consolidation formed Pennsylvania Power & Light Co. During the 1920's and early 1930's PP&L continued to expand. Lehigh Power Securities Corp. played an important role in this process, acting as the temporary repository for the stocks of those companies destined for merger. The corporation also continued to hold stock control of several companies which were operated independently of PP&L, including Lancaster County Railway & Light Co., Lehigh Valley Transit Co., Mauch Chunk Transit Co., Wrightsville Light & Power Co., and Wrightsville Water Supply Co. By 1939 the subsidiary companies controlled by Lehigh Power Securities Corp. supplied electricity in over 700 communities.

From 1926 until 1939 Lehigh Power Securities Corp. itself was controlled by National Power & Light Co., which in turn was controlled by Electric Bond and Share Co. In 1938 The Securities and Exchange Commission cited EBASCO for violating the recently enacted Public Utility Holding Company Act. After a protracted lawsuit, EBASCO was forced to dismantle much of the complex hierarchy of sub-holding and holding companies it had created. As a part of this process, Lehigh Power Securities Corp. was liquidated in September 1939 and all of its assets were formally transferred to National Power & Light.

Administrative Records:

Correspondence, 1919-1928
Stock Transfer Record, 1939

Operating Records:

Budgets—Properties, 1930
Budgets—Pennsylvania Transportation Companies, 1928-1931
Property Disposal Records, 1928-1930
Working Papers, ca. 1920-1930

Scope and Content Note:

Correspondence, 1919-1928, is fragmentary but provides some information on Lehigh Power Securities Corporation's acquisition of various utility holding companies. There is also a good deal of material documenting the corporation's involvement in employee welfare work. Working Papers and Budgets provide financial information on subsidiary companies such as Lehigh Valley Transit Co. and Conestoga Traction Co.

1050. UNITED GAS AND ELECTRIC CORPORATION
(Operating).
New York State, New York City.
1918 to 1925, 6 Linear Inches.

History:

United Gas and Electric Corp., formed 20 July 1923 through the consolidation and merger of Berkshire Corp., and United Gas & Electric Corp., was a holding company chartered under Connecticut law to control utility and street railway companies. Its offices were located in New York City. United Gas & Electric Corp., its predecessor, had been formed in 1912 to acquire control of several small utility holding companies including Lancaster County Railway & Light Co. and Harrisburg Light & Power Co. By 1923, when United Gas and Electric Corp., was formed, the parent holding company controlled 11 subsidiary firms including Valley Railways. The new company inherited the substantial debts of its predecessors and found itself in extremely precarious financial condition. It tried to solve this problem by forming United Securities Corp., which consolidated the company's Pennsylvania properties with Lehigh Power Securities Corporation. In exchange for assuming United Gas and Electric Corporation's debt, Lehigh Power Securities Corp. acquired control of the electric generating, distribution and street railway business in Lancaster County and the Harrisburg area. This process was formalized by a 23 January 1926 merger.

Operating Records:

Income Tax Statements—Lancaster County Railway & Light Co., 1922-1924

Reconcilement of Accounts Payable—Lancaster Companies, 1920-1923

Papers in Connection with Federal Income Tax and Excess Profits Tax Returns of Leased and Owned Companies, 1918-1925

INDEX

A

Abington Electric Co.
1, 1034
Abington Light, Heat & Power Co.
1
Abington Township, Lackawanna County
1
Accident Insurance Fund
2, 537
Accidents
claims
2, 104, 210, 426, 427, 756, 800
lawsuits
800
reports
226, 382, 396, 486, 568, 964, 1031
Accounting methods
226, 270, 656, 1032
Acqueduct Mutual Rural Electric Distributing Association
3, 447
Adams Township, Snyder County
916
Advertising
budgets
138, 226, 721, 964, 1047
campaigns
226, 426, 696, 808, 964
Akron Borough, Lancaster County
4
Akron Electric Light and Power Co. No. 2
4
Albion Electric Co.
5
Alburtis Borough, Lehigh County
6
Alburtis Electric Co.
6
Aldred, J.E.
579, 721
Allen, Martin B.
412
Allen, Robert P.
1030
Allen Township, Northampton County
7, 665, 682, 942
Allen Township-Northampton Electric Co.
7
Allentown and Bethlehem Rapid Transit Co.
8
Allentown and Slatington Street Railway Co.
837
Allentown Chiefs of Police
8
Allentown City, Lehigh County
8, 382, 417, 422, 425, 484, 486, 492, 495, 719, 729, 1046
demographic data
495
Allentown Electric Light and Power Co.
8, 49, 363, 494, 495, 542, 708, 776, 835, 836, 843
Allison Power & Light Co.
9
Allison Township, Clinton County
9
Alternating current
49, 107, 272, 273, 275, 277, 279, 290, 298, 567, 571, 603, 613, 817, 996
Alternating current equipment manufacturers
Brush Electric Co.
603
Stanley Electric Manufacturing Co.
996
Westinghouse Electric & Manufacturing Co.
24, 49, 107, 290, 298, 571, 706, 813
Amalgamated Association of Street Railway Employees
757
Amalgamated Park
10
American District Steam Co.
396
American Electric Light and Power Co.
8, 11
American Electric Light Co.
12, 428, 943
American Electric Manufacturing Co.
8, 412
American Electric Railways Association
226, 1031
American Federation of Labor (AFL)
808
The American Gas and Electric Co.
1047
American Gas & Electric Co.
147, 160, 308, 414, 439, 440, 576, 739, 807, 808, 960, 968, 984, 1007, 1039
American Gas Light Co. of Bloomsburg
13, 943
American Hotel
571
American Hydroelectric Pioneers, Inc.
721
American Institute of Electrical Engineers
721
American Society of Mechanical Engineers
721
Amortization schedules
656
Amusement parks
10, 568, 922
Arthur Anderson & Co.
1
Anthony-Lycoming Power & Light Co.
14
Anthony-Montour Power & Light Co.
15
Anthony Township, Lycoming County
14
Anthony Township, Montour County
15
Anthracite coal mining
see Coal mining
Anthracite Coal Strike Commission
382
The Anthracite Electric Light and Power Co.
16
The Anthracite Electric Light, Heat and Power Co.
17, 1019
Anthracite Power Co.
18
Anti-Trust Association
106

Anti-trust litigation
861
Apartment buildings and tenants
411, 421, 424, 496, 537, 646, 917
Appalachian Service Corp.
1047
Appliances
see Electric, and Gas Appliances
Aqueduct Electric Co.
3, 90
Arc lighting
8, 16, 21, 49, 81, 104, 105, 106, 107, 273, 274, 275, 279, 282, 290, 298, 374, 412, 445, 511, 536, 571, 613, 815, 837, 863, 871, 875, 945, 1021
evaluation
856
tungsten lights
863, 871
Arc lighting dynamos
107, 571, 603
Arc lighting equipment manufacturers
American Electric Light Co.
8, 12
American Electric Manufacturing Co.
8, 412
Arnoux and Hochhausen Electrical Co.
1021
Brush Electric Co.
298, 374, 823
Excelsior Electric Co. of Brooklyn
298, 374, 1021
General Electric Co.
280
Thomson-Houston Electric Co.
8, 49, 81, 107, 298, 374
United States Electric Co.
49
Western Electric Co.
107, 996
Weston Electric Light Co.
996
Archbald Township, Lackawanna County
458
Ariel Light, Heat and Power Co.
19
Armstrong Power & Light Co.
20
Armstrong Township, Lycoming County
20
Arnoux and Hochhausen Electrical Co.
1021
Ashland Borough, Schuylkill County
21, 271
Ashland Gas Light Co.
21
The Ashley Electric Light and Power Co.
22, 1022
Ashley Borough, Luzerne County
22
Association of Edison Illuminating Companies
272, 274, 275, 374
Atglen Borough, Chester County
23
Atglen Electric Co.
23
Atlantic City, New Jersey
1047
The Auburn Electric Light, Heat and Power Co.
24, 749
Auburn Borough, Schuylkill County
24
Auditing methods
1048, 1049
Avis Borough, Clinton County
25
Avis Power & Light Co.
25
Avis Village, Clinton County
442
Avoca Borough, Luzerne County
859

B

Bacteriological testing
81
Baker, John R.
721
Ballantyne, W.H.
721
The Baltimore Electro Alloys Co.
26, 721, 822
Baltimore City, Baltimore County, Maryland
26, 720, 822, 894
Baltimore, Md., power supply to
26, 577, 720, 721, 894
Bankrupt companies
8, 41, 90, 102, 105, 112, 278, 441, 445, 482, 487, 554, 567, 568, 573, 579, 623, 657, 672, 703, 754, 943, 982
Banks Township, Carbon County
27
Banks Township Electric Co.
27
Barrett Power & Light Co.
28
Barrett Township, Monroe County
28
Barry Electric Co.
29
Barry Township, Schuylkill County
29, 211, 236
Bart Township Electric Co.
30
Bart Township, Lancaster County
30
Bastress-Lycoming Power & Light Co.
31
Bastress Township, Lycoming County
31
The Beach Lake Electric Light Co.
32
Beacon Electric Co.
33
Bear Creek Power & Light Co.
34
Bear Creek Township, Luzerne County
34
Beaver-Columbia Power & Light Co.
35
Beaver Meadow Borough, Carbon County
36
Beaver Meadow Electric Co.
36, 384, 385
Beaver Township, Columbia County
35
Beavertown Borough Board of Supervisors
37
Beavertown Borough, Snyder County
37
civic and social organizations
37
Beavertown Electric Light Co.
37
Beechwood Electric Co.
38
Benevolent societies
473, 1046
Bensalem Township, Bucks County
39
Bensalem Township Electric Co.
39
Benton Borough, Columbia County
41
Benton-Columbia Power & Light Co.
40, 400
Benton Electric Co.
41
Benton Electric Light, Heat and Power Co.
41
Benton Hydro-Electric Co.
41
Benton Township, Columbia County
40
Berger, Charles E.
24
Berks County
915
Caernarvon Township
71
Cumru Township
165
Longswamp Township
507
Rockland Township
784
Ruscombmanor Township
786
Sinking Springs Borough
42
Spring Township
456
Topton Borough
907
Upper Alsace Township
946
Womelsdorf Borough
42
Berkshire Corp.
1050
Berkshire Electric Co.
42, 165
Berlin Township, Wayne County
32
Berrysburg Borough, Dauphin County
43, 44
Berrysburg Electric Co.
43
Berrysburg Electric Service Co.
44
Berwick Borough, Columbia County
45, 46, 126, 657
Berwick Consolidated Gas Co.
46
The Berwick Electric Light Co.
45

Berwick Gas Co.
46
Berwick Town, Columbia County
133
Bethany Borough, Wayne County
47
Bethany Power & Light Co.
47
Bethel-Lebanon Power & Light Co.
48
Bethel Township, Lebanon County
48
Bethelehem City, Northampton County
492, 495, 617
Bethlehem Borough, Northampton County
49
The Bethlehem Electric Light Co.
49, 843
Bethlehem Steel Co.
363, 472, 486
Bethlehem Township Electric Light and Power Co.
50
Bethlehem Township, Northampton County
50, 759
Big Spring Electric Co.
51, 52
Big Spring Light and Power Co.
51, 52
Black Creek Township Electric Co.
53
Black Creek Township, Luzerne County
53
Black powder
576
Blackstone Electric Co.
54
Blakely Borough, Lackawanna County
55
Blakely Electric Co.
55
Blakslee, James I.
341, 434, 496, 987
Blooming Grove Power & Light Co.
56
Blooming Grove Township, Pike County
56
Bloomsburg and Berwick Electric Railway Co.
126
Bloomsburg Borough, Columbia County
612
Bloomsburg Electric Light and Power Co.
57
Bloomsburg Town, Columbia County
12, 13, 57, 125, 126, 127, 130, 133, 168, 428, 657, 855, 943
Blythe Township, Schuylkill County
563
Boards of Directors
see Interlocking directorates and stock control

Bonds
42, 51, 52, 77, 125, 129, 210, 409, 441, 495, 537, 568, 721, 774, 808, 1048
Bradford County
881
New Albany Borough
881
Brady Power & Light Co.
58
Brady Township, Lycoming County
58
Branch Township, Schuylkill County
212, 237
Briar Creek Township, Luzerne County
46
Bridge companies
557, 648, 722
Bridges, lighting of
613
Bridgeton Township, Bucks County
59
Bridgeton Township Electric Co.
59
Bristol Borough, Bucks County
224
Bristol Township, Bucks County
60
Bristol Township Electric Co.
60
Brown, Ernest
442
Lawrence E. Brown & Co.
106
Brownstone Electric Light & Power Co.
61
Brownstone Village, West Earl Township, Lancaster County
61
Browntown Electric Co.
62
Brush Electric Co.
278, 374, 603, 823
The Buck Mountain Light, Heat and Power Co.
63
Buck Power & Light Co.
64
Buck Township, Luzerne County
64
Bucks County
270, 300, 301, 302, 303, 495, 905, 954, 1026
Bensalem Township
39
Bridgeton Township
59
Bristol Borough
224
Bristol Township
60
Doylestown City
65, 181
Durham Township
188
Falls Township
312
Haycock Township
391
Hilltown Township
405, 406
Lower Makefield Township
522
Milford Township
592, 593
Rock Hill Township
229, 230
Sellersville Borough
300, 301, 302, 303, 812
Silverdale Borough
833
social and economic conditions
303
Solebury Township
840
Springfield Township
854
Telford Borough
903
Tinicum Township
905
Trumbauersville Borough
917
Upper Makefield Township
954
West Rockhill Township
1008, 1009
Bucks County Electric Co.
65
Buffalo-Pan American Exposition of 1901
813
Buffalo Township, Union County
66, 927
Buffalo-Union Power & Light Co.
66
Bus transportation companies
138, 140, 226, 227, 573, 574, 657, 755, 964, 967, 1031, 1032
Bushkill Township, Northampton County
862
Butler Light Co.
67
Butler Township Electric Co.
68
Butler Township, Luzerne County
68
Butler Township Power Co.
69
Butler Township, Schuylkill County
67, 69, 238

C

Caernarvon Electric Co.
70
Caernarvon Electric Light and Power Co.
71
Caernarvon Township, Berks County
71
Caernarvon Township Electric Co.
72
Caernarvon Township, Lancaster County
70, 72
Caldwell, Stephen J.
566
Cameron Electric Co.
73
Camp Hill and Harrisburg Passenger Railway Co.
74

Camp Hill Borough, Cumberland County
1016
Camp Hill Turnpike Road Co.
75, 966
Canaan Electric Co.
76
Canaan Township, Wayne County
76
Canal companies
889
Candlepower, methods of rating
105
Canton, Ohio
1047
Capital, raising of operating
37, 277, 813
Capitalization of companies
140, 153, 157, 277, 566, 728, 748, 752, 754
and local entrepreneurs
8, 49, 61, 271, 273, 274, 275, 277, 282, 385, 386, 412, 415, 645, 835, 843, 864, 879, 901
Carbon County
227, 261, 484, 486, 646
Banks Township
27
Beaver Meadow Borough
36
East Mauch Chunk Borough
569, 570, 571
East Penn Township
225, 509
East Side Borough
231, 1015
Franklin Township
340, 341
Kidder Township
452
Lansford Borough
896
Lausanne Township
478
Lehigh Township
489
Lehighton Borough
496, 987
Lower Towamensing Township
527
Mahanoy Township
551
Mahoning Township
434
Mauch Chunk Borough
77, 485, 568, 569, 570, 571, 573, 574, 755, 896
Mauch Chunk Township
486, 572
Towamensing Township
909
Weissport Borough
341, 987
Carbon County Inprovement Co.
987
Carbon Transit Co.
77, 568
Carbondale Borough, Lackawanna County
807
Carbondale City Council
290
Carbondale City, Lackawanna County
78, 290, 462
Carbondale Electric Co.
78
Carbondale Electric Light, Heat & Power Co.
462
Carbondale Township Electric Co.
79
Carbondale Township, Lackawanna County
79
Carlisle and Mechanicsburg Street Railway Co.
80, 163, 966
Carlisle Borough, Cumberland County
80, 81, 82, 84, 162, 163, 164, 627, 941, 964, 1016
politics
81, 82, 105
social and economic conditions
81
The Carlisle Gas and Water Co.
81, 82, 83, 84
Carlisle Light, Heat and Power Co.
81, 82
Carlisle-North Dickinson Electric Co.
83
Carlisle Water Supply Co.
84
Carpentry shop, electricity generated by
982
Cass Township, Schuylkill County
213, 239
Castanea Electric Light Co.
85
Castanea Township, Clinton County
85
Casualty insurance premiums
2
Catasauqua Borough, Lehigh County
11, 86, 87, 482, 495
Catasauqua Electric Light and Power Co.
86, 487
Catasauqua Gas Co.
87
Catawissa-Columbia Power & Light Co.
88
Catawissa Township, Columbia County
88
Cement plants
electrification of
486
Cementon Electric Light and Power Co.
89, 487
Central Gas and Electric Co.
362
Central Railroad Co. of N.J.
571
Central River Coal and Supply Co.
90
Centralia Borough, Columbia County
240
Centre and West End Passenger Railway Co.
91, 847, 961, 962
Centre County
451
Miles Township
591
Centre Township Electric Service Co.
92
Centre Township, Snyder County
92
Centre Valley Electric Light and Power Co.
93
Century Shoe Co.
542
Chambersburg Borough, Franklin County
74, 80, 371, 372, 966
Chanceford Township, York County
94
Chanceford Water and Power Co.
94
Chapman Electric Light Co.
95
Chapman Electric Service Co.
96
Chapman Township, Clinton County
95
Chapman Township, Snyder County
96
Cherry Ridge Light Co.
97
Cherry Ridge Power and Light Co.
98
Cherry Ridge Township, Wayne County
97, 98
Chesapeake Bay
721, 889
Chesnuthill Power & Light Co.
99
Chesnuthill Township, Monroe County
99
Chester County
270, 915
Atglen Borough
23
Elverson Borough
293
Honey Brook Township
413
West Nantmeal Township
1003
West Sadsbury Township
1010, 1013
Chillisquaque Township, Northumberland County
851
Christiana Borough, Lancaster County
100, 101
Christiana Electric Co.
100
Christiana Suburban Electric Co.
23, 100, 101, 267, 268, 479, 700, 791, 795, 1013
Church, William
290
Churches
and utility rates
273
Harrisburg
378
Lancaster
273

(continued)

Mauch Chunk
571
Pittston
104
Pottsville
275
Renovo
774
Churchtown Village, Lancaster County
915
The Citizens Electric Co.
352
The Citizens Electric Co. (Valley View)
43, 103, 398, 415, 416, 540, 590
Citizens Electric Co. (Williamsport)
102
Citizens Electric Illuminating Co. (Pittston)
104, 187, 190, 418
The Citizens Electric Light and Power Co. of Hughesville, Pa.
105, 339, 710, 731, 832, 1035
The Citizens Electric Light Co. of Shenandoah, Pa.
106
The Citizens Electric Light, Heat and Power Co. of Lancaster, Pa.
107, 617
The Citizens Electric Light, Heating and Power Co. (Slatington)
108, 494, 495, 592, 837
Citizens Gas & Electric Co. (Stroudsburg)
109, 110, 876
Citizens Gas Co. of Minersville, Pa.
111, 603, 604, 605
Citizens Gas Co. (Stroudsburg)
109, 110, 875
Citizens Gas Light Co. of Tamaqua
112, 280, 281
Citizens Passenger Railway Co.
113, 847, 961, 962
Civic organizations and social activities
37, 104, 271, 273, 378, 863
Clader, Will A.
313
Claims for damage suits
2
Clay Township, Lancaster County
319
Clearfield City, Clearfield County
447
Clearfield County
Clearfield City
447
Cleveland Township, Columbia County
114
Cleveland Township Electric Co.
114
Clifford Borough, Susquehanna County
115, 116
Clifford-Susquehanna Power & Light Co.
115
Clifford Township Electric Corp.
116
Clifton Borough, Lackawanna County
117
Clifton Power & Light Co.
117
Clinton County
Allison Township
9
Avis Borough
25
Avis Village
442
Castanea Township
85
Chapman Township
95
Colebrook Township
124
Crawford Township
159
Dunnstable Township
186
Gallagher Township
346
Greene Township
354
Grugan Township
360
Lamar Township
469
Lock Haven City
510, 511, 512
Logan Township
514
Loganton Borough
515, 879
Renovo Borough
892
South Renovo Township
846
Wayne Township
985
Clinton Township, Lycoming County
33, 600, 610
Clinton Township, Wayne County
62
Clymer, Lee S.
118
Clymer Power Co.
118
The Clymer Power Co.
118
Coal
anthracite
808, 890
conservation
496, 646, 721, 901
consumption of
81, 384, 385, 486, 721, 808, 1019, 1022, 1023, 1047
processing and recovery
347, 408, 721, 890
reserves
385
transportation by railroad
1007
Coal Castle Electric Railway Co.
119
Coal dredging companies
90, 105, 379, 424, 447, 595
Coal gas manufacturing plant
819, 1023
Coal Light Co.
120
Coal mining companies
81, 105, 134, 382, 386, 387, 697, 799, 890
medical care for miners
382
miners' working conditions
261
power supply to
382, 485, 492, 697, 701, 890, 1046
strike of 1902
382
strike of 1922
799
Coal Township Electric Co.
121
Coal Township Light, Heat and Power Co.
122
Coal Township, Northumberland County
120, 121, 122, 813
Coaldale Borough, Schuylkill County
123
Coaldale Electric Co.
123, 696, 697
Cochran, J. Henry, State Senator
847, 961, 962, 1030
Coffin, Charles A.
298, 373
Colebrook-Clinton Power & Light Co.
124
Colebrook Township, Clinton County
124
Collective bargaining
721, 756, 774, 808
Collieries
134
electrification of
382, 383, 697, 701, 890
Columbia and Montour Electric Co.
57, 125, 130, 133, 152, 657, 667, 1046
Columbia and Montour Electric Railway Co.
126, 133, 168, 657
Columbia Borough, Lancaster County
128, 129, 131, 132, 566
Columbia County
130, 133, 235, 260, 261, 385, 394, 668, 799
Beaver Township
35
Benton Borough
41
Benton Township
40
Berwick Borough
45, 46, 126, 657
Berwick Town
133
Bloomsburg Borough
612
Bloomsburg Town
12, 13, 57, 125, 126, 127, 130, 133, 168, 428, 657, 855, 943
Catawissa Township
88
Centralia Borough
240
Cleveland Township
114
Conyngham Township
154, 156, 241
Danville Town
133

(continued)

Fishing Creek Township
329
Franklin Township
342
Green Township
358
Jackson Township
429
Locust Township
513
Madison Township
543
Main Township
553
Millville Borough
596
Nescopeck Borough
46
Roaring Creek Township
782
Stillwater Borough
866
Sugarloaf Township
880
Columbia County Gas Co.
127
The Columbia Electric Light and Power Co.
128, 129
Columbia Electric Light, Heat and Power Co.
128, 129
Columbia Gas and Electric Co.
45, 130, 133, 428, 858, 860, 943
Columbia Gas Co.
131, 132, 891
The Columbia Gas Co.
131, 132
Columbia Power, Light and Railways Co.
133
Columbus Colliery Co.
134
Community relations
81, 505, 721, 808, 896, 897
Company housing
382, 385, 387, 410, 424, 721, 890
Company stores
387
Competition
between electric companies
104, 106, 107, 273, 279, 298, 363, 373, 374, 428, 536, 669, 706, 723, 802, 804, 813, 814, 820, 863, 884, 889, 898
between electric companies and gas companies
547, 570, 571
between gas companies
349
Edison companies vs. Westinghouse companies
107, 112, 298, 373
impact of, upon utilities
106, 277, 278, 280, 298, 363, 373, 374, 378, 813, 820, 863
Condensing water supply companies
888
Conestoga Realty Co.
135
Conestoga Terminal Co.
136, 891
Conestoga Township Electric Co.
137
Conestoga Township, Lancaster County
137, 314
Conestoga Traction Co.
135, 138, 139, 140, 176, 270, 427, 470, 505, 1048, 1049
Conestoga Transmission Co.
139
Conestoga Transportation Co.
138, 140
Conestoga Valley Electric Co.
141
Conestoga Water and Power Co.
142
Conewago-Dauphin Power & Light Co.
143
Conewago Township, Dauphin County
143
Conewago Township, York County
144
Conewago-York Power & Light Co.
144
Congress of Industrial Organizations (CIO)
721, 808
Connecticut
1050
Conoy Township Electric Co.
145
Conoy Township, Lancaster County
145, 964
Conservation of fuel supplies
496, 901
World War I
496, 645, 901
World War II
1, 721, 774, 808, 1046
Consholing, West Virginia
1047
Consolidated Gas Electric Light and Power Co. of Baltimore
721
Construction companies
729, 959
Construction costs
210, 365, 536, 686, 807, 808, 825
Consulting engineers
111, 396, 896
H. C. Felver
890
John G. White & Co.
210, 235, 261, 280, 898, 1022, 1023
Stillwell, L. B.
485, 486
Wilmot Engineering Corp.
385
Consulting engineers
EBASCO Services, Inc.
721, 1048
Consumers Electric Co. of Freeland
146
Consumers Electric Co. of Hughestown
147
Consumers Electric Co. of the Borough of Exeter
148
Consumers Electric Co. of the Borough of West Pittston
149
Consumers Electric Co. of the City of Pittston
150
Consumers Electric Light and Power Co. of Hazleton, Pa.
151, 384, 386
The Consumers Gas Co. of Danville, Pennsylvania
152, 858, 860
The Consumers Gas Co. of Wilkes-Barre
153, 348, 1022, 1023
Contractors' liability insurance
2
Conyngham Borough, Luzerne County
155
Conyngham Light Co.
154
Conyngham Power & Light Co.
155
Conyngham Township, Columbia County
154, 156, 241
Conyngham Township Electric Co.
156
Cooperative arrangements for rural electric service
3, 629, 686, 771
The Coopersburg Electric Light, Heat and Power Co.
157
Coplay Borough, Lehigh County
295, 483
Corliss engines
460
Corporate Organization & Audit Co.
1011
Court cases
261, 836
Court of Common Pleas of Lehigh County
836
Covington Borough, Tioga County
158
Covington Power & Light Co.
158
Cranberry Creek Coal Co.
382, 917
Crawford-Clinton Power & Light Co.
159
Crawford Township, Clinton County
159
The Crescent Electric Co.
160, 462
Cressona Township, Schuylkill County
242
Culm
dredging
424
processing and recovery
347, 382
Cumberland County
75, 210, 941, 966, 967, 1016
Camp Hill Borough
1016
Carlisle Borough
80, 81, 82, 84, 162, 163, 164, 627, 941, 964, 1016
Dickinson Township
83
East Pennsboro Township
310, 370, 997

(continued)

Enola Borough
941
Lemoyne Borough
941, 964
Lower Township
370
Mechanicsburg Borough
80, 161, 163, 941, 964, 1016
Middlesex Township
587
New Cumberland Borough
941
Newville Borough
51, 52
Riverton Town
372
South Middleton Township
845
West Fairview Borough
310, 997
White Hill Borough
1016
The Cumberland Light, Heat and Power Co.
161, 941, 966
Cumberland Railway Co.
162, 627
The Cumberland Valley Electric Passenger Railway Co.
163, 164, 966
Cumberland Valley Railroad Co.
75, 371, 845, 1016
Cumberland Valley Traction Co.
163, 164
Cumru Township, Berks County
165
Cumru Township Electric Light, Heat and Power Co.
165
Customers
boycotts
105, 646
commercial
18, 49, 52, 81, 82, 103, 104, 105, 210, 260, 270, 271, 272, 273, 274, 275, 277, 279, 280, 282, 298, 313, 373, 378, 396, 411, 412, 486, 495, 505, 570, 571, 610, 613, 690, 696, 716, 802, 831, 863, 873, 875, 885, 886, 914, 941, 943, 1015, 1019, 1022, 1027, 1034, 1046
complaints
1, 105, 106, 227, 411, 427, 496, 547, 610, 632, 645, 646, 1034
delinquent bill accounts and payments
18, 81, 275, 362, 554, 760, 808, 1028
disconnections of service
8, 49, 226, 373
electricity consumption
690, 917, 941
industrial
1, 270, 298, 373, 542, 571, 713, 721, 799, 802, 863, 901
lists of
8, 18, 81, 105, 334, 362, 364
relations of companies with
42, 271, 272, 279, 280, 282, 303, 486, 496, 570, 571, 646, 825, 885, 915, 1039
residential
8, 18, 49, 52, 81, 82, 103, 104, 105, 106, 210, 235, 270, 271, 272, 273, 274, 275, 277, 279, 280, 282, 303, 313, 333, 334, 349, 362, 364, 373, 385, 395, 411, 412, 426, 427, 482, 495, 505, 570, 571, 604, 610, 613, 697, 716, 734, 758, 799, 802, 825, 831, 863, 873, 875, 885, 886, 941, 943, 945, 1015, 1019, 1021, 1022, 1027, 1034
service to
275, 412, 459, 495, 734, 758
solicitation of
49, 271, 273, 274, 275, 277, 279, 282, 298, 373, 495, 505, 511, 547, 571, 610, 696, 748, 885, 886, 964

D

Dalmatia Light Co.
166
Dalmatia Village, Northumberland County
166, 963
The Dalton Light, Heat & Power Co.
1
Damage suit claims
2
Damascus Township, Wayne County
167
Damascus-Wayne Power & Light Co.
167
Dams
566, 579
construction of
721, 888, 889
Danville & Bloomsburg Street Railway Co.
126, 168, 657
Danville Borough Electric Co.
169
Danville Borough, Montour County
126, 152, 169, 467, 612, 657, 858, 860
Danville Gas Co.
152
Danville Town, Columbia County
133
Dauphin Borough, Dauphin County
170
Dauphin Borough Power & Light Co.
170
Dauphin County
103, 210, 541, 585, 890, 967
Berrysburg Borough
43, 44
Conewago Township
143
Dauphin Borough
170
Derry Township
420, 929
East Hanover Township
263
Gratz Borough
352, 353
Halifax Borough
595
Halifax Township
453
Harrisburg City
90, 142, 298, 373, 374, 375, 376, 377, 378, 379, 380, 447, 558, 585, 706, 722, 728, 959, 964, 966, 1016
Hummelstown Borough
419, 420, 421
Jackson Township
433
Jefferson Township
437
Londonderry Township
516
Lower Paxtang Township
377
Lower Swarata Township
377
Lykens Borough
864, 1027, 1033
Lykens Township
539, 540
Middle Paxtang Township
377
Mifflin Township
588, 590
Millersburg Borough
447, 595
Reed Township
3, 447, 773
Rush Township
787
South Hanover Township
420, 844
Steelton Borough
863
Susquehanna Township
377
Tower City Borough
1027, 1033
Uniontown Borough
940
Upper Paxton Township
1033
Washington Township
987
Wayne Township
986
West Hanover Township
377
Wiconisco Village
1027
Williamstown Borough
541, 1027
Davies & Thomas
49
Day & Zimmerman
570, 571
Defense contracts
1046
Defense Electric Power Administration
1034
Delano Light Co.
171
Delano Township Electric Co.
172
Delano Township, Schuylkill County
171, 172
Delaware Canal Co.
954
Delaware
133, 451, 667, 669, 892, 920, 921, 1049
Delaware Canal
954, 1026
Delaware Canal Co.
905, 1026

Delaware Divison Coal Co.
118
Delaware Township Electric Co.
173
Delaware Township, Northumberland County
173, 600
Delco direct current
578
Demographic data
570, 571, 808, 885, 917
Denison Electric Co.
174
Denison Power & Light Co.
175
Denison Township, Luzerne County
174, 175, 1015
Denver and Ephrata Railway Co.
176
Depressions, economic
1890s
279, 298, 373, 374, 1048
1907
886
1921
799
1930s
721, 808, 1046
Derry Power & Light Co.
177
Derry Township, Dauphin County
420, 929
Derry Township, Montour County
177
Diamond Electric Co. of Washington Township
178
Dicke, H.F.
755
Dickinson Township, Cumberland County
83
Dickson Borough, Lackawanna County
807
Dill, S.J.
378
Direct current
see also The Edison Electric Light Co. of N.Y.
108, 271, 272, 274, 373, 571, 578, 613, 774, 1021
Delco system
578
voltage losses in distribution
108
Discontinuance of service
8, 49, 226, 373
Dividends
see Stockholders, dividends
Donaldson Village, Schuylkill County
912
Donegal Gas Co.
179
Dorrance Township Electric Co.
180
Dorrance Township, Luzerne County
180
Doylestown City, Bucks County
65, 181
Doylestown Electric Light and Power Co.
181
Drake, A.W.
802
Dreher Power & Light Co.
182
Dreher Township, Wayne County
182
Du Boistown Borough, Lycoming County
183
Du Boistown Power & Light Co.
183
Duncannon Borough Council
3
Dunmore Borough, Lackawanna County
184, 185, 679, 807, 877
Dunmore Electric Light, Heat & Power Co.
184
The Dunmore Street Railway Co.
185
Dunnstable Electric Light Co.
186
Dunnstable Township, Clinton County
186
E.I. du Pont de Nemours & Co.
440, 576
Dupont Electric Co.
187
du Pont, Pierre S.
884
du Pont, T. Coleman
884
Dupont Township, Luzerne County
187
Durham Township, Bucks County
188
Durham Township Electric Co.
188
Duryea Borough, Luzerne County
189
Duryea Borough-Luzerne Power & Light Co.
189
Duryea Electric Co.
190
Duryea Township, Luzerne County
190
Dushore Borough, Sullivan County
881
Dyberry Power & Light Co.
191
Dyberry Township, Wayne County
191
Dynamos
271, 412, 511, 548, 571, 603, 748, 837, 863, 996
110-light
863
1200-light
863
1800-light
837
2,000-light
511
60-light
837

E

Eagles Mere Borough, Sullivan County
192
Eagles Mere Light Co.
105, 192
Earl Township Electric Co.
193
Earl Township, Lancaster County
193
East Allen Electric Co.
194
East Allen Township, Northampton County
194
East Brunswick Township Electric Co.
192, 195
East Brunswick Township, Schuylkill County
195
East Buffalo Township, Union County
196, 197, 928
East Buffalo-Union Light & Power Co.
196
East Buffalo-Union Power & Light Co.
66, 197
East Cameron Electric Co.
198
East Cameron Township, Northumberland County
198
East Chillisquaque Township, Northumberland County
199, 668, 851
East Chillisquaque Township Northumberland Electric Co.
199
East Donegal Township Electric Light Co.
200
East Donegal Township, Lancaster County
200
East Earl Electric Co.
201
East Earl Electric Light and Power Co.
202
East Earl Township, Lancaster County
201, 202
East End Passenger Railway Co.
203, 934, 1031
East Greenville Borough, Montgomery County
262, 714
East Greenville Electric Light, Heat and Power Co.
262
East Hanover-Dauphin Power & Light Co.
263
East Hanover-Lebanon Light & Power Co.
204
East Hanover-Lebanon Power & Light Co.
205
East Hanover Township, Dauphin County
263
East Hanover Township, Lebanon County
204, 205

East Hempfield Township Electric Co.
206
East Hempfield Township, Lancaster County
206
East Lampeter Electric Light, Heat and Power Co.
207
East Lampeter Township Electric Co.
208
East Lampeter Township, Lancaster County
207, 208, 315, 426
East Manchester Borough, York County
1043
East Manchester Township, York County
269
East Manchester-York Power & Light Co.
269
East Mauch Chunk Borough, Carbon County
569, 570, 571
East Norwegian Township, Schuylkill County
243, 900
East Penn Electric Co. No. 1
210, 467, 734, 983
East Penn Electric Co. No. 2
195, 210, 211, 212, 213, 214, 215, 216, 217, 218, 219, 220, 221, 222, 223, 226, 227, 260, 261, 353, 433, 437, 446, 448, 539, 541, 606, 622, 647, 748, 899, 953, 986, 987, 1004
East Penn Electric Co. of Barry Township
211
East Penn Electric Co. of Branch Township
212
East Penn Electric Co. of Cass Township
213
East Penn Electric Co. of Foster Township
214
East Penn Electric Co. of Frailey Township
215
East Penn Electric Co. of New Castle Township
216
East Penn Electric Co. of North Manheim Township
217
East Penn Electric Co. of Reilly Township
218
East Penn Electric Co. of South Manheim Township
219
East Penn Electric Co. of Tremont Township
220
East Penn Electric Co. of Washington Township
221
East Penn Electric Co. of Wayne Township
222
East Penn Electric Co. of West Brunswick Township
223
East Penn Township, Carbon County
225, 509
East Penn Township Carbon Electric Co.
225
East Penn Traction Co.
226, 227
East Penn Transportation Co.
226, 227
East Pennsboro Township, Cumberland County
310, 370, 997
East Pennsylvania Gas & Electric Co.
224
East Pittston Borough, Luzerne County
1023
East Prospect Borough Light, Heat & Power Co.
228
East Prospect Borough, York County
228, 1038
East Rock Hill Electric Light and Power Co.
229
East Rock Hill Township Electric Light and Power Co.
230, 1009
East Side Borough, Carbon County
231, 1015
East Side-Carbon Power & Light Co.
231
East Stroudsburg Borough, Monroe County
109, 110, 484
East Stroudsburg Township, Monroe County
797
East Union Light Co.
232
East Union Township Electric Co.
233
East Union Township, Schuylkill County
232, 233
Eastern Pennsylvania Gas Co. of Rahn Township
234
Eastern Pennsylvania Light, Heat and Power Co.
24, 119, 234, 235, 236, 237, 238, 239, 240, 241, 242, 243, 244, 245, 246, 247, 248, 249, 250, 251, 252, 253, 254, 255, 256, 257, 258, 259, 260, 261, 271, 333, 336, 659, 694, 734, 747, 749, 752, 753, 756, 799, 800, 897, 912, 988
Eastern Pennsylvania Light, Heat and Power Co. of Barry Township
236
Eastern Pennsylvania Light, Heat and Power Co. of Branch Township
237
Eastern Pennsylvania Light, Heat and Power Co. of Butler Township
238
Eastern Pennsylvania Light, Heat and Power Co. of Cass Township
239
Eastern Pennsylvania Light, Heat and Power Co. of Centralia
240
Eastern Pennsylvania Light, Heat and Power Co. of Conyngham Township
241
Eastern Pennsylvania Light, Heat and Power Co. of Cressona
242
Eastern Pennsylvania Light, Heat and Power Co. of East Norwegian Township
243
Eastern Pennsylvania Light, Heat and Power Co. of Foster Township
244
Eastern Pennsylvania Light, Heat and Power Co. of Gilberton
245
Eastern Pennsylvania Light, Heat and Power Co. of Girardsville
246
Eastern Pennsylvania Light, Heat and Power Co. of Gordon
247
Eastern Pennsylvania Light, Heat and Power Co. of Hegins Township
248
Eastern Pennsylvania Light, Heat and Power Co. of Landingville
249
Eastern Pennsylvania Light, Heat and Power Co. of New Castle Township
250
Eastern Pennsylvania Light, Heat and Power Co. of Norwegian Township
251
Eastern Pennsylvania Light, Heat and Power Co. of Pine Grove Township
252
Eastern Pennsylvania Light, Heat and Power Co. of Porter Township
253
Eastern Pennsylvania Light, Heat and Power Co. of Rahn Township
254
Eastern Pennsylvania Light, Heat and Power Co. of Reilly Township
255
Eastern Pennsylvania Light, Heat and Power Co. of Ryan Township
256
Eastern Pennsylvania Light, Heat and Power Co. of Tremont Township
257
Eastern Pennsylvania Light, Heat and Power Co. of Wayne Township
258
Eastern Pennsylvania Light, Heat and Power Co. of West Mahanoy Township
259
Eastern Pennsylvania Power and Railway Co.
119, 210, 235, 260, 261, 747, 752, 753, 756, 800, 803, 897
Eastern Pennsylvania Railways Co.
77, 235, 260, 261, 280, 281, 333, 334, 573, 603, 684, 694, 896, 898, 911
Easton City, Northumberland County
283
Easton Consolidated Electric Co.
283

Easton Power Co.
283
Eau Claire Lumber Co.
888
EBASCO Services, Inc.
1048
Eby, A. M.
396
Economy Light, Heat & Power Co.
264
Eden Electric Light, Heat and Power Co.
265
Eden Township Electric Co.
266
Eden Township, Lancaster County
265, 266
Edison Associated Companies
1028
Edison Electric Co. No. 1
101, 129, 206, 208, 267, 268, 273, 470, 474, 505, 555, 556, 557, 628, 633, 711, 768, 972, 994, 998
Edison Electric Co. No. 2
101, 139, 267, 268, 269
Edison Electric Co. No. 3
70, 137, 145, 200, 266, 268, 269, 270, 291, 296, 559, 565, 726, 763, 874, 950, 995
Edison Electric Co. No. 4
4, 30, 42, 61, 70, 129, 193, 201, 269, 270, 319, 324, 456, 480, 644, 652, 658, 873, 915, 1010
The Edison Electric Illuminating Co.
280, 281
Edison Electric Illuminating Co. of Altoona, Pa.
1047
Edison Electric Illuminating Co. of Easton, Pa.
283
The Edison Electric Illuminating Co. of Hazleton
272, 395
The Edison Electric Illuminating Co. of Lancaster, Pa.
107, 273, 471, 658, 724, 871
The Edison Electric Illuminating Co. of Mount Carmel
274, 716
Edison Electric Institute
721
The Edison Electric Illuminating Co. of Pottsville
16, 275, 748, 805
Edison Electric Illuminating Co. of Shamokin, Pa.
276, 815, 817
The Edison Electric Illuminating Co. of Sunbury No. 1
277, 278, 282, 884
The Edison Electric Illuminating Co. of Sunbury, Pa., No. 2
277, 278, 279
The Edison Electric Illuminating Co. of Sunbury, Pa., No. 3
279, 670, 884, 886
The Edison Electric Illuminating Co. of Sunbury, Pa., No. 4
279, 669, 670, 882, 884, 886, 944
The Edison Electric Illuminating Co. of Williamsport
282, 535, 536
The Edison Electric Light Co. of N.Y.
direct current generating system
108, 271, 272, 273, 274, 275, 279, 280, 282, 373, 374, 412, 613, 774, 1021
incandescent lamp
271, 273, 275, 277, 278, 279, 282, 373, 374, 774
licensing arrangements
271, 273, 274, 275, 278, 280, 282, 374, 774
three-wire system
277
tube for underground wire
277
Edison General Electric Co.
412
The Edison Illuminating Co. of Easton
283
Edison Light and Power Co. of York, Pa.
1038
Edison Machine Works
280
Edison, Thomas A.
271, 272, 277, 282, 823
Edisonville Town, Lancaster County
871, 872, 873
Efficiency
arc lighting
856
electric generating and distribution
378, 721, 813, 1022
gas works
1022
incandescent lighting
105, 536
steam heating
396
Egypt Electric Light & Power Co.
284
Egypt Village, Whitehall Township, Lehigh County
284
Eldon Electric Co.
285
Eldred Electric Co.
286
Eldred-Lycoming Power & Light Co.
287
Eldred Power & Light Co.
288
Eldred Township, Lycoming County
287
Eldred Township, Monroe County
288
Eldred Township, Schuylkill County
286
Electric appliances
105, 275, 303, 364, 482, 586, 610, 645, 646, 696, 716, 1019, 1038
repairs and servicing
492
sales
105, 303, 482, 586, 645, 696, 716, 1047
Electric Bond and Share Co.
807, 964, 1031, 1039, 1046, 1047, 1048, 1049
Electric Bond and Share Securities Corp.
1048
Electric Co. of America
134, 809, 1047
Electric Co. of Exeter
289
Electric Investors, Inc.
1048
Electric Light and Power Co. of Carbondale, Pennsylvania
290
Electric meters
81, 235, 260, 261, 275, 277, 280, 313, 411, 482, 495, 669, 686, 917, 1027, 1034
installation and maintenance work
917
Electric motors
275, 298, 374
Electric railways
see Railway companies
Electric Railways Co.
371
Electric rates
see Rate schedules—electric companies
Electric Securities Co. of Boston
1048
Electric service
all-night
49, 105, 373
efficiency
1022
Electric storage battery manufacturers
Electrical Accumulator Co. of N.Y.
49, 412
New York Accumulator Co.
49
Electric transmission companies
139, 518, 707, 720, 894
Electrical Accumulator Co. of N.Y.
49, 412
Electrical generating and distribution systems
construction of
621, 8, 24, 41, 49, 81, 82, 102, 103, 105, 106, 107, 108, 235, 270, 271, 272, 273, 274, 275, 277, 278, 279, 280, 282, 290, 298, 307, 308, 334, 373, 374, 377, 384, 385, 409, 411, 412, 445, 447, 459, 486, 487, 492, 495, 505, 542, 548, 567, 570, 571, 578, 585, 601, 603, 610, 613, 697, 714, 716, 721, 774, 779, 808, 826, 831, 863, 873, 875, 901, 941, 996, 1019, 1021, 1022, 1027, 1038, 1046
Electrical manufacturers' licensing arrangements
The Edison Electric Light Co. of N.Y.
271, 272, 273, 274, 275, 276, 277, 280, 412, 774, 1021
Excelsior Electric Co. of Brooklyn
298
Thomson-Houston Electric Co.
8, 49, 106, 107, 290
Electricity
consumption and sales statistics
8, 49, 52, 81, 105, 125, 235, 260, 270, 275, 313, 333, 373, 374, 385, 411, 412, 486, 492, 690, 706, 716, 721, 734, 941, 945, 1019, 1027
generating and distribution costs
270, 313, 377, 385, 411, 495, 716, 721, 734, 813, 941, 1019, 1022, 1047
Electrification of Pennsylvania Railroad
721

Electrochemicals
manufacture of
26, 721, 822
Elizabeth Township Electric Co.
480
Elizabeth Township, Lancaster County
480
Elizabethtown Borough, Lancaster County
291
Elizabethtown Electric Co.
291
Elk County
451
Ridgway Borough
451
Elmhurst Borough, Lackawanna County
292
Elmhurst Electric Co.
292
Elverson Borough, Chester County
293
Elverson Electric Co.
293
The Emans Light and Power Co.
294
Emans Borough, Lehigh County
294
Emmaus Borough, Northampton County
495
Empire Electric Light and Power Co.
295
Employees
accidents
426, 427
benevolent societies
473, 808, 1046
clerical and office
261
clubs
261, 721
collective bargaining
808
company housing
382, 385, 387, 410, 424, 721, 890
discipline
470
dismissals
226
evaluations of
486, 721
hiring
261
hours worked
52, 863, 896, 1046
injuries to
261
job classifications
51, 52, 132, 1046
job descriptions
272, 585, 613, 914, 1029
labor turnover
721
lay-offs
226, 261
medical services
382, 486, 721
occupations
1022
pension plans
129, 275, 382, 721, 808, 1007
receiving current at reduced rates
270
relations of co. with
808, 825, 1031, 1046
retirement plans
808
salaries
153, 179, 226, 235, 279, 282, 290, 334, 377, 385, 395, 411, 473, 486, 585, 669, 689, 690, 691, 721, 825, 826, 896, 945
salaries, clerical and office
226, 382, 447
salaries, managerial
226
salaries of foremen, engineers and inspectors
382
sickness funds
2, 473, 721, 1046
time cards
51, 52
trade unions
261, 706, 721, 756, 774, 808
transfers
226
wage rates
51, 52, 65, 132, 166, 179, 210, 226, 261, 270, 290, 334, 377, 382, 396, 470, 495, 571, 581, 610, 613, 656, 716, 721, 723, 876, 882, 922, 1022, 1029, 1031, 1046, 1047
welfare assoc.
473, 808, 1049
work rules
210, 261
Energy conservation
World War I
613, 614
World War II
721, 808, 1046
Engineering and service contracts
see also Consulting engineers
1048
Enola Borough, Cumberland County
941
Ephrata & Lebanon Street Railway Co.
472
Ephrata and Lebanon Traction Co.
472
Ephrata Borough, Lancaster County
141, 176, 296, 472
Ephrata Township Electric Co.
296
Equitable Electric Co. of Whitehall Township
297
Erie City Iron Works
813
Espenschade, Carl F.
445
Eureka Power Co.
65
Excelsior Electric Co. of Brooklyn
298, 373, 1021
licensing arrangements
298, 373, 875
Excelsior Electric Co. of Harrisburg
298, 373, 374
Excelsior Electric Co. of Plainfield Township
299
The Excelsior Electric Co. of Wilkes-Barre
1021
Excelsior Electric Light and Power Co.
300, 303, 1009
Excelsior Electric Light, Power and Gas Co. No. 1
301, 302
Excelsior Electric Light, Power and Gas Co. No. 2
301, 302, 303, 388, 833, 841
Excelsior Electric Light, Power and Gas Co. No. 3
230, 302, 303, 337, 390, 406, 1009
Executive officers
salaries
377, 721
Exeter Borough, Luzerne County
148, 304
Exeter Borough-Luzerne Power and Light Co.
304
Exeter Electric Co.
305
Exeter-Luzerne Power and Light Co.
306
Exeter Power Co.
307, 308
Exeter Power Corp.
308, 807
Exeter Township, Luzerne County
289, 306, 308, 861, 1007

F

Factoryville Electric Co.
1
Fairfield Power & Light Co.
309
Fairfield Township, Lycoming County
10, 309
Fairview & Riverton Passenger Railway Co.
310, 966
Fairview Township Electric Co.
311
Fairview Township, Luzerne County
311
Fairview Township, York County
1042
Falls Township, Bucks County
312
Falls Township Electric Co.
312
Farm power
see also Rural electrification
313
Farmers Electric Co.
313, 315, 316, 320, 322, 323
Farmers Electric Co. of Conestoga Township
314
Farmers Electric Co. of East Lampeter Township
315
Farmers Electric Co. of Manheim Township
316
Farmers Electric Co. of Manor Township
317

Farmers Electric Co. of Martic Township
318, 629
Farmers Electric Co. of North Lancaster County
319
Farmers Electric Co. of Penn Township
320
Farmers Electric Co. of Pequea Township
321
Farmers Electric Co. of Upper Leacock Township
322
Farmers Electric Co. of Warwick Township
323
Farmers Electric Co. of Washington Borough
324
Farmers Electric Co. of West Hempfield Township
325
Fayette Township, Juniata County
326
Fayette Township Power Co.
326
Fearne Electric Co.
327
Federal Defense Power Administration
1, 721, 1034
Federal Fuel Admin.
496, 901
Federal Power Commission
721, 861, 1034, 1046
Federal Trade Commission
18, 1048
Fell Electric Co.
328
Fell Township, Lackawanna County
328
Felver, H.C.
890
Ferry companies
580
Fidelity Trust Co.
377
Fire protection methods
81, 419, 825
Fires and explosions
235, 411, 412, 419, 567, 571, 600, 703, 748, 863, 915, 1024
Fishing Creek
428
Fishing Creek-Columbia Power & Light Co.
329
Fishing Creek Township, Columbia County
329
Fishing Creek Valley Milling Co.
41
Flagstaff Amusement Park
568
Flood control
721
Flood forecasting
721
Floods
destruction by
81, 108, 118, 282, 987
Forest City Electric Light, Heat & Power Co.
330
Forest City, Susquehanna County
330
Forks Township, Northampton County
357
Forrest & Co.
1022, 1023, 1041
Forstall, Robinson & Luquerr
570
Foster Township Electric Co.
331
Foster Township, Luzerne County
331
Foster Township, Schuylkill County
214, 244
The Foundation Co.
307, 308
Fountain Hill Borough, Lehigh County
332, 364
Fountain Hill Electric Light, Heat and Power Co.
332
The Four Consolidated Electric Co.
333
The Frackville and Gilberton Light, Heat and Power Co.
334, 804
Frackville Borough, Schuylkill County
334
Frailey-Schuylkill Power & Light Co.
335
The Frailey Township Electric Co.
336
Frailey Township, Schuylkill County
215, 335, 336
Franchises, efforts to acquire
see also 'Paper companies'
3, 24, 42, 59, 60, 104, 125, 126, 158, 189, 210, 262, 303, 334, 348, 361, 377, 395, 411, 462, 485, 495, 546, 585, 592, 638, 643, 681, 761, 781, 896, 945, 954, 997, 1016, 1026, 1033
Franconia Electric Light and Power Co.
337
Franconia Township Electric Light and Power Co.
338
Franconia Township, Montgomery County
337, 338
Franklin County
Chambersburg Borough
74, 80, 371, 372, 966
Franklin-Lycoming Power & Light Co.
339
Franklin Power & Light Co.
340
Franklin Township, Carbon County
340, 341
Franklin Township Carbon Electric Co.
341
Franklin Township, Columbia County
342
Franklin Township Electric Co.
342
Franklin Township, Lycoming County
339
Fraternal organizations
Ashland
271
Beavertown
37
Harrisburg
378
Lancaster
273
Palo Alto
261
Steelton
863
Freeburg Borough, Snyder County
343
Freeburg Power & Light Co.
343
Freeland Borough, Luzerne County
146, 344, 384
Freeland Electric Light Heat and Power Co.
344, 395
Freemansburg Borough, Northampton County
345
Freemansburg Electric Light and Power Co.
345
Freight railways
electric
614, 1007
Fuel
conservation
see Energy conservation
consumption
81, 385, 486, 1019, 1022, 1047
supplies
385, 473
Fuel gas supply companies
533

G

Gallagher-Clinton Power & Light Co.
346
Gallagher Township, Clinton County
346
Gallie, C.H.
51
Garfield Coal Co.
347
Gas
see Natural gas, and Manufactured gas
consumption and sales statistics
81, 125, 349, 473, 570, 600, 1019, 1047
manufacturing and distribution costs
81, 411, 570, 600, 669, 885, 886, 1019, 1022, 1029, 1047
Gas appliances
570, 885, 886
Gas Co. of Dauphin
1033
The Gas Co. of Luzerne County
153, 347, 348, 1022, 1023
Gas Co. of Northumberland
349, 660, 672
Gas companies
competition with electric companies
16, 21, 81, 152, 271, 547, 570, 885, 886
entrance into electric lighting market by
21, 81, 82, 152, 511, 512

Gas heating
46, 570, 885, 886, 1033
Gas lighting
13, 81, 362, 473, 570, 885, 1023, 1029
Gas main construction
570, 1029
Gas meters
349, 482
Gas plant improvements
570
Gas purification
570
Gases, sale of
26, 570
Gasworks
construction of
81, 112, 570, 600, 646, 716, 885, 886, 1023
General Construction Corp.
125
General Electric Co.
280, 363, 364, 412, 807, 873, 944, 1048
Generating and distribution system efficiency
813
Gibson Electric Co.
350
Gilberton Borough, Schuylkill County
245, 334
Girard National Bank
386
Girardville Borough, Schuylkill County
246, 334, 799, 804
Glamos Coal Co.
347
Glen Village, Hubly Township, Schuylkill County
415
Gordon Borough, Schuylkill County
247
Gouldsborough Borough, Lackawanna County
351
Gouldsborough-Lackawanna Power & Light Co.
351
Government defaults
799
Gratz Borough, Dauphin County
352, 353
Gratz Electric Co.
352
Gratz Light and Power Co.
353
Green Ridge Village, Luzerne County
996
Green Township, Columbia County
358
Greene-Clinton Power & Light Co.
354
Greene Power & Light Co.
355
Greene Township, Clinton County
354
Greene Township, Pike County
355
Greenfield Township Electric Corp.
356, 541
Greenfield Township, Lackawanna County
356
Greenwood Electric Co.
357
Greenwood Power & Light Co. (Columbia)
358
Gregg Power & Light Co.
359
Gregg Township, Union County
359
Griest Building
136
Grist mills
electrification
105, 365, 476, 829, 871, 872, 969
Grove, A.E.
365
Grugan-Clinton Power & Light Co.
360
Grugan Township, Clinton County
360
Gwynedd-Farmers Electric Light & Power Co.
361

H

Hagerstown City, Washington County, Maryland
362
Hagerstown Gas Light Co.
362
Hagerstown Light & Heat Co. of Washington County
362, 364
Halcyon Electric Light and Power Co. No., 1
332, 363, 364, 617
Halcyon Electric Light and Power Co., No., 2
332, 363
Halcyon Knitting Mills
363
Halfpenny and Grove, Inc.
365
Halfpenny, J.L.
365
Halifax Borough, Dauphin County
595
Halifax Township, Dauphin County
453
Hamilton-Monroe Power & Light Co.
366
Hamilton Township, Monroe County
366
M.A. Hanna & Co.
890
Hanover Electric Light and Power Co.
367
Hanover Township Electric Co.
368
Hanover Township, Lehigh County
367, 369, 392
Hanover Township Lehigh Electric Co.
369
Hanover Township, Luzerne County
17, 368
Hanover Township, Northampton County
834
Harding City, Lackawanna County
807
Harding Hydroelectric Station
807, 808
Harrisburg Agreement
889
Harrisburg and Cumberland Electric Railway Co.
370
Harrisburg and Mchanicsburg Electric Railway Co., No. 2
997
Harrisburg and Mechanicsburg Electric Railway Co.
80, 310, 370, 371, 372, 964, 966, 997, 1016
The Harrisburg and Riverton Street Railway Co.
372
Harrisburg Board of Trade
889
Harrisburg Car Co.
875
Harrisburg City Council
298, 373, 374, 377, 378, 379, 964, 966
Harrisburg City, Dauphin County
90, 142, 298, 373, 374, 375, 376, 377, 378, 379, 380, 447, 558, 585, 706, 722, 728, 959, 964, 966, 1016
railway terminal construction
964
secret societies in
378
social and economic conditions
298, 373, 374, 378, 964
Harrisburg Electric Co.
298, 373, 374
The Harrisburg Electric Light Co.
298, 373, 374
Harrisburg Electric Service Co.
375, 376, 377, 378
Harrisburg Light and Power Co., No. 1
376, 377, 378, 379, 420, 706, 863, 941
Harrisburg Light and Power Co., No. 2
48, 170, 375, 376, 377, 931
The Harrisburg Light, Heat and Power Co.
373, 376, 378, 706
The Harrisburg Steam Heat and Power Co.
376, 379
Harrisburg Terminal Co.
380
Hartleton Borough, Union County
381
Hartleton Power and Light Co.
381
Harwood Coal Co.
382, 385, 386, 387, 393, 597
The Harwood Co.
383
Harwood Electric Co.
53, 68, 146, 151, 331, 384, 385, 386, 387, 393, 454, 484, 577, 597, 639, 765, 789, 802, 878, 996
The Harwood Electric Co.
27, 36, 114, 180, 311, 342, 368, 382, 383, 384, 385, 393, 394, 395, 396, 478, 486, 489, 548, 575, 577, 597, 661, 685, 701, 723, 802, 826, 945, 996, 1025, 1037, 1046, 1049
Harwood Electric Power Co.
382, 384, 386, 577
Harwood Store Co.
386, 387
Harwood Village, Luzerne County
387

Haskins & Sells
119, 210, 235, 734, 753, 756
Hatfield Borough, Montgomery County
388
Hatfield Electric Light and Power Co. (Borough)
388
Hatfield Electric Light and Power Co. (Township)
389
Hatfield Township Electric Light and Power Co.
390
Hatfield Township, Montgomery County
389, 390
Hauser, William J.
1015
Hauto Steam Electric Station
484, 485, 486
Haycock-Bucks Power & Light Co.
391
Haycock Township, Bucks County
391
Hazard Electric Co.
392
Hazle Township, Luzerne County
383, 384, 386, 393
Hazle Township Supervisors
996
Hazle Township Water Co.
393, 597
Hazleton Borough Council
272
Hazleton City, Luzerne County
151, 272, 384, 385, 386, 387, 394, 395, 396
Hazleton Electric Co.
67, 120, 154, 171, 232, 272, 344, 385, 394, 395, 549, 624, 933, 996, 1001
Hazleton Electric Light and Power Co.
272, 344, 395, 996
The Hazleton Steam Heating Co.
396
Heating gas supply companies
see Gas companies
Heating services
range
313
water
313
Hegins-Schuylkill Power & Light Co.
397
Hegins Township Electric Co.
398
Hegins Township, Schuylkill County
248, 397, 398
Heidelberg Power & Light Co.
399
Heidelberg Township, Lehigh County
399
John Heins & Co.
203, 441, 442
John Heiss & Co.
536, 537
Hellam Township, York County
400
Hellerton Borough, Northampton County
401
Hellertown Electric Light and Power Co.
401
Hepburn-Lycoming Power & Light Co.
402
Hepburn Township, Lycoming County
402
Herndon Borough, Northumberland County
963
Herndon Spinning Mill
963
Herrick-Susquehanna Power & Light Co.
403
Herrick Township, Susquehanna County
403
The Hillside Water and Power Co.
404, 579
Hilltown Electric Light and Power Co. (No. 1)
405
Hilltown Electric Light and Power Co. (No. 2)
406
Hilltown Township, Bucks County
405, 406
Holding companies
see also Interlocking directorates and stock control
42, 45, 90, 128, 129, 132, 133, 134, 138, 267, 270, 283, 470, 483, 487, 537, 665, 667, 669, 780, 807, 808, 809, 815, 817, 820, 824, 825, 826, 847, 890, 892, 1046, 1047, 1048, 1049, 1050
Hollenback-Luzerne Power & Light Co.
407
Hollenback Township, Luzerne County
407
Holtwood Borough, Lancaster County
408, 409, 410, 579, 580
Holtwood Coal Co.
408, 721
Holtwood Dam
721, 894
Holtwood Laboratory
721
Holtwood Power Co.
409, 721
Holtwood Real Estate Co.
410
Holtwood Village, Martic Township, Lancaster County
721
Honesdale Borough, Wayne County
411, 412
Honesdale Consolidated Light, Heat and Power Co.
47, 98, 191, 411, 412, 760, 904
Honesdale Electric Light Heat and Power Co.
411, 412
Honesdale Gas Co.
411, 412
Honesdale Iron Works
412
Honey Brook Township, Chester County
413
Honey Brook Township Electric Co.
413
Horne, L.B.
496
Household Electric Light, Heat & Power Co.
414
Household Electric Light, Heat & Power Co., No. 1
414
Household Electric Light, Heat & Power Co., No. 2
414
Hubley Electric Co.
415
Hubley Township Electric Co.
416
Hubly Township, Schuylkill County
415, 416
Hughes, Edward
385
Hughestown Borough, Luzerne County
147, 417
Hughestown Borough-Luzerne Power & Light Co.
417
Hughestown Electric Co.
418
Hughesville Borough, Lycoming County
105
social conditions
105
Hughesville Furniture Co.
105, 682
Humes, Samuel
441
Hummels Wharf Village, Snyder County
586
The Hummelstown Consolidated Water Co.
419, 420
Hummelstown Borough Council
419
Hummelstown Borough, Dauphin County
419, 420, 421
The Hummelstown Electric Light Heat and Power Co.
419
The Hummelstown Water Co.
419
Hummelstown Water & Power Co.
419, 420, 421, 929
Hummelstown Water Supply Co.
420, 421
Hydraulic testing
721
Hydroelectric furnaces
822
Hydroelectric power companies
41, 94, 105, 118, 142, 365, 409, 419, 420, 428, 446, 448, 467, 471, 494, 519, 529, 558, 566, 571, 579, 586, 595, 632, 637, 681, 703, 713, 721, 727, 729, 779, 807, 829, 831, 837, 983, 987, 1015, 1038
construction costs
721, 780
historical information
721

(continued)

Susquehanna River
721, 889
Hydrographical and hydrological research
721

I

Ice companies
892
Ice plants
987
Ilgen, Samuel D.
879
Illinois
Rockford
1047
Inactive companies
39, 59, 60, 61, 84, 135, 840, 905
Incandescent lighting
8, 49, 104, 105, 108, 270, 271, 272, 273, 274, 275, 277, 280, 282, 290, 298, 303, 364, 373, 374, 412, 445, 459, 511, 571, 576, 586, 610, 613, 671, 714, 774, 804, 823, 837, 856, 863, 875, 945, 996, 1021, 1047
candlepower
105
competition with arc lighting
856
efficiency
105, 536
Independent Electric Light, Heat & Power Co.
414
Indiana
Muncie
1047
Industrial Coal Co.
424
Industrial customers
see customers, industrial

Industrial Electric Light and Power Co. of Upper Macungie
422
Industrial Electric Light and Power Co. of Upper Milford
423
Industrial Fuel Co.
347, 424
Industrial Power Co.
7, 225, 369, 425, 484, 551, 572, 664, 876, 979
Insurance
claims
210, 426, 800
funds
2
payments
365
Intercourse Electric Co.
426, 427
Intercourse Electric Light, Heat and Power Co.
426, 427
Intercourse Village, Lancaster County
426, 427
Interlocking directorates and stock control
see also Holding companies
8, 13, 16, 41, 49, 81, 82, 89, 90, 106, 111, 112, 192, 210, 226, 227, 235, 261, 272, 283, 341, 347, 348, 371, 382, 393, 408, 419, 420, 421, 424, 440, 441, 447, 460, 473, 512, 548, 576, 597, 603, 668, 670, 688, 721, 754, 774, 775, 779, 800, 802, 861, 896, 918, 922, 941, 962, 1048
Interurban electric railway companies
74, 80, 126, 168, 176, 210, 226, 235, 260, 261, 371, 372, 470, 472, 546, 657, 747, 752, 756, 803, 896, 897, 922, 966, 967, 997, 1016
Iron and steel mills
electrification of
363, 472, 486, 601, 728
Irondale Electric Light, Heat and Power Co.
45, 428
Irving Trust Co.
808

J

J. E. Aldred & Co. J E
721
Jackson-Columbia Power & Light Co.
429
Jackson-Herndon Electric Co.
430
Jackson Power & Light Co.
431
Jackson-Snyder Power & Light Co.
432
Jackson Township, Columbia County
429
Jackson Township, Dauphin County
433
Jackson Township Electric Co.
433
Jackson Township, Monroe County
431
Jackson Township, Northumberland County
430
Jackson Township, Snyder County
432
Jamestown Electric Co.
434
Jamestown Village, Lehighton Borough, Carbon County
434
Jarrad, O.O.
571
Jeddo Borough, Luzerne County
435
Jeddo-Luzerne Power & Light Co.
435
Jefferson Power & Light Co.
436
Jefferson Township, Dauphin County
437
Jefferson Township Electric Corp.
437
Jefferson Township, Lackawanna County
436
Jenkins-Luzerne Power & Light Co.
438
Jenkins Township Electric Light, Heat and Power Co.
439
Jenkins Township, Luzerne County
438, 439
Jermyn Borough Council
440
Jermyn Borough, Lackawanna County
414, 440
Jermyn Electric Light Co.
462
Jermyn Electric Light, Heat & Power Co.
440
Jersey Shore Electric Co.
441, 537
Jersey Shore Electric Street Railway Co.
441, 442
Jersey Shore, Lycoming County
441, 442
John G. White & Co., Inc.
210, 235, 261, 280, 896, 1022, 1023
Jordan-Lycoming Power & Light Co.
443
Jordan Township, Lycoming County
443
Junction Passenger Railway Co.
444, 961, 962
The Juniata No. 1
445
The Juniata No. 2
445
Juniata County
210
Fayette Township
326
McAlisterville Village
578
Mifflintown Borough
445
Monroe Township
609
Patterson Borough
445
Juniata Furnace and Foundry Co.
728
Juniata Land Co.
446
Juniata Public Service Co.
3, 326, 445, 447, 453, 567, 578, 585, 595, 642, 728
Juniata River
446, 447, 448, 567, 585, 983
Juniata River Water Power Co.
446, 448, 983

K

Keefer's Station
347
Kelly Township Electric Co.
449
Kelly Township, Union County
449
Kent Electric Co.
450
Keystone Electric Construction Co.
856
Keystone Electric Service Corp.
451
Keystone Power Corp.
451
Keystone Power & Light Co.
451
Kidder Power & Light Co.
452

Kidder Township, Carbon County
452
Killinger Electric Co.
453
Kingston Borough, Luzerne County
1023
L.C. Kinsey & Co.
412
Kizer family
969
Kline Township Electric Co.
454
Kline Township, Schuylkill County
454
Knitting mills
electrification of
105, 843
Kreamer Electric Co.
455
Krick Electric Co.
456
Kulpmont Borough, Northumberland County
457
Kulpmont Electric Co.
457
Kulpmont Steam Electric Station
890
Kunkle, Bert E.
396

L

Labor
see employees
Labor relations
81, 210, 226, 227, 261, 271, 272, 382, 470, 486, 570, 721, 774, 808, 1046
World War I
496
World War II
721
Lackawanna-Archbald Power & Light Co.
458
Lackawanna County
462, 807, 808
Abington Township
1
Archbald Township
458
Blakely Borough
55
Carbondale Borough
807
Carbondale City
78, 290, 462
Carbondale Township
79
Clifton Borough
117
Dickson Borough
807
Dunmore Borough
184, 185, 679, 807, 877
Elmhurst Borough
292
Fell Township
328
Gouldsborough Borough
351
Greenfield Township
356
Harding City
807
Jefferson Township
436
Jermyn Borough
414, 440
Lackawanna Township
461
Lehigh Township
491
Madison Township
545
Mayfield Borough
414, 576
Moosic Borough
616
Scott Township
806
Scranton City
134, 160, 264, 807, 808, 809, 877, 960, 984, 1011
Spring Brook Township
852
Taylor Borough
459
Taylor Township
902
Throop Borough
807
Vandling Borough
968
West Abington Township
1034
Winton Township
463
Lackawanna Electric Light, Heat & Power Co.
459, 462
Lackawanna Light Co.
460, 1011
Lackawanna Township Electric Co.
461
Lackawanna Township, Lackawanna County
461
Lackawanna Valley Electric Light & Power Supply Co.
290, 440, 462, 807
Lackawanna-Winton Power & Light Co.
463
Lackawaxen Power & Light Co.
464
Lackawaxen Township, Pike County
464
Laflin Borough, Luzerne County
465, 466
Laflin Borough-Luzerne Power & Light Co.
465
Laflin Electric Co.
466
Lake Ariel Village, Lake Township, Wayne County
19
Lake Hall Land Co.
467
Lake Power & Light Co.
468
Lake Township, Wayne County
468
Lakes, artificial
467, 637
Lamar-Clinton Power & Light Co.
469
Lamar Township, Clinton County
469
Lamps
see also Incandescent lighting
270, 271, 1047
cost of operation
412
sales statistics
8, 49, 81, 105, 272, 275, 303, 364, 412, 586, 716, 1019
servicing of
1019
Lancaster City Council
273
Lancaster City, Lancaster County
42, 107, 135, 136, 138, 139, 140, 176, 267, 268, 269, 270, 273, 313, 470, 471, 472, 473, 566, 737, 1039
social conditions
138, 140, 270, 273
Lancaster County
138, 140, 267, 270, 273, 470, 658, 737, 871, 872, 873, 915
Akron Borough
4
Bart Township
30
Caernarvon Township
70, 72
Christiana Borough
100, 101
Churchtown Village
915
Clay Township
319
Columbia Borough
128, 129, 131, 132, 566
Conestoga Township
137, 314
Conoy Township
145, 964
Earl Township
193
East Donegal Township
200
East Earl Township
201, 202
East Hempfield Township
206
East Lampeter Township
207, 208, 315, 426
Eden Township
265, 266
Edisonville Town
871, 872, 873
Elizabeth Township
480
Elizabethtown Borough
291
Ephrata Borough
141, 176, 296, 472
Holtwood Borough
408, 409, 410, 579, 580
integration of public utilities in
270

(continued)

Intercourse Village
426, 427
Lancaster City
42, 107, 135, 136, 138, 139, 140, 176, 267, 268, 269, 270, 273, 313, 470, 471, 472, 473, 566, 737, 1039
Lancaster Township
474
Leacock Township
426, 427, 479
Lincoln Borough
915
Lititz Borough
505, 506
Manheim Borough
498, 506, 554, 555
Manheim Township
316, 556
Manor Township
317, 557, 558
Marietta Township
559
Martic Township
139, 318, 564, 565, 629, 724, 727, 889, 894
Mount Joy Borough
554, 868
Mount Joy Township
179, 628
Paradise Township
426
Penn Township
320
Pequea Township
321
Quarryville Borough
871
Sadsbury Township
791
Salisbury Township
426
Strasburg Borough
870, 871, 872, 873
Strasburg Township
874
street lighting contracts negotiations
470
Upper Leacock Township
322, 950
Warwick Township
323, 972
Washington Borough
324
West Cocalico Township
993
West Donegal Township
994
West Hempfield Township
325, 998
West Lampeter Township
999
Wheathead Town
871
Wheatland Mills
872
The Lancaster County Electric Light, Heat and Power Co.
564
The Lancaster County Railway and light Co.
128, 129, 132, 138, 470, 471, 473, 505, 506, 554, 652, 658, 915, 1049, 1050
The Lancaster Electric Light, Heat and Power Co.
470, 471
Lancaster, Ephrata and Lebanon Street Railway Co.
472
Lancaster Gas Light and Fuel Co.
470, 473
Lancaster Township Electric Co.
474
Lancaster Township, Lancaster County
474
Lancaster Trust Co.
270
Lancaster Valley Electric Light Co.
554
Landingville Borough, Schuylkill County
249
Landisburg Borough, Perry County
475, 828
Landisburg Light, Heat and Power Co.
475
Lansford Borough, Carbon County
896
Lansford Borough Council
896
Laporte Borough, Sullivan County
881
Lattimer Borough, Luzerne County
386
Laurel Park Power & Light Co.
381, 476
Laurel Park Village, Hartleton Borough, Union County
476
Laurel Run Borough, Luzerne County
477
Laurel Run Electric Co.
477, 761
Lausanne Township, Carbon County
478
Lausanne Township Electric Co.
478
Laws and legislation
governing rivers and waterways
721, 888
governing Susquehanna River projects
579, 721, 888, 889
interpretation of
24, 1027
legislative lobbying
49, 210, 226, 261, 282, 496, 721, 808, 888, 889
regulating sale of electricity
3, 8, 24, 49, 262, 434
Lawsuits
273, 374, 800, 861, 889, 1046, 1048
Leacock Township Electric Co.
479
Leacock Township, Lancaster County
426, 427, 479
Leaman Place
427
Lebanon City, Lebanon County
472
Lebanon County
Bethel Township
48
East Hanover Township
204, 205
Lebanon City
472
Swatara Township
895
Union Township
930, 931
Lebanon Township, Wayne County
481
Lebanon Valley Light and Power Co.
480, 652
Lebanon-Wayne Power & Light Co.
481
Lee, Robert E.
922
Legislation
see Laws and legislation
Lehigh and Northampton Light, Heat and Power Co.
86, 89, 482, 483, 638
Lehigh Coal and Navigation Co.
108, 112, 118, 382, 485, 486, 571, 697, 896, 905, 954, 987, 1015, 1026
Lehigh County
484, 487, 492, 494, 495
Alburtis Borough
6
Allentown City
8, 382, 417, 422, 425, 484, 486, 492, 495, 719, 729, 1046
Catasauqua Borough
11, 86, 87, 482, 495
Coplay Borough
295, 483
Emans Borough
294
Fountain Hill Borough
332, 364
Hanover Township
367, 369, 392
Heidelberg Township
399
Lower Macungie Township
520
Lower Milford Township
523
Lowhill Township
531
Macungie Borough
542
North Whitehall Township
662
Salisbury Township
794
Siegfried
486
Slatington Borough
108, 494, 495, 836, 837
South Whitehall Township
848, 849
Upper Macungie Township
951
Upper Milford Township
423, 955
Upper Saucon Township
93, 958
Washington Township
178, 835
Whitehall Township
89, 284, 297, 493, 494
Lehigh County Electric Co.
86, 89, 295, 483, 487

Lehigh Industrial Power Co.
169, 199, 425, 484, 501, 552, 598, 790, 876, 924, 965, 992
Lehigh Navigation Electric Co., No. 1
270, 385, 485, 571, 655, 696, 742, 778, 821, 840, 857, 862, 876, 901, 905, 954, 1026, 1049
Lehigh Navigation Electric Co., No. 2
5, 38, 54, 59, 60, 178, 188, 194, 285, 297, 299, 327, 350, 357, 392, 450, 485, 486, 492, 495, 507, 509, 522, 524, 525, 526, 563, 607, 615, 640, 662, 676, 682, 695, 717, 759, 834, 849, 900, 946, 951, 955, 956, 957, 958
Lehigh-Northampton Gas and Electric Co.
482, 483, 487
Lehigh-Northampton Light, Heat & Power Co.
284, 487
Lehigh Power & Light Co.
341, 434, 488
Lehigh Power Securities Corp.
41, 81, 105, 132, 138, 157, 203, 226, 261, 270, 283, 313, 341, 349, 362, 365, 377, 380, 411, 415, 426, 441, 442, 447, 470, 473, 476, 486, 495, 496, 506, 510, 535, 537, 542, 568, 570, 573, 587, 596, 613, 614, 629, 632, 637, 645, 646, 648, 667, 668, 696, 702, 703, 713, 722, 724, 737, 760, 761, 779, 799, 802, 828, 888, 901, 941, 962, 964, 969, 987, 1015, 1019, 1031, 1038, 1046, 1048, 1049, 1050
stock acquisition procedures
283, 1046, 1048, 1049
Lehigh River
570, 1050
Lehigh Township, Carbon County
489
Lehigh Township Electric Co.
489
Lehigh Township Electric Light and Power Co.
490
Lehigh Township, Lackawanna County
491
Lehigh Township, Northampton County
5, 490
Lehigh Township Power & Light Co.
491
Lehigh Township, Wayne County
488
Lehigh Valley Coal Co.
382, 384
The Lehigh Valley Light and Power Co.
422, 486, 492, 495, 597, 717, 718, 742, 977, 1046
Lehigh Valley Light and Power Co., No. 1
493, 495, 848, 975, 1049
Lehigh Valley Light and Power Co., No. 2
6, 108, 294, 364, 367, 493, 494, 495, 593, 663, 666, 794, 798, 835, 971, 976
Lehigh Valley Light and Power Co., No. 3
8, 11, 39, 50, 89, 93, 181, 229, 284, 338, 345, 389, 401, 405, 483, 486, 490, 492, 494, 495, 520, 523, 593, 636, 641, 665, 776, 777, 843, 854, 907, 917, 1008
Lehigh Valley Railroad Co.
571
The Lehigh Valley Traction Co.
835
Lehigh Valley Transit Co.
8, 283, 295, 303, 361, 363, 482, 484, 486, 494, 495, 542, 776, 837, 887, 917, 942, 1049
Lehighton Borough, Carbon County
496, 987
Lehighton Borough Council
496
Lehighton Electric Light and Power Co.
496, 702, 987
Lehman-Pike Power & Light Co.
497
Lehman Township, Pike County
497
Leland, C. Taylor
554
Leland Electric Light Co.
498, 868
Lemoyne Borough, Cumberland County
941, 964
Lentz, L.F.
571
Lewis Township Electric Co.
499
Lewis Township, Northumberland County
499
Lewis Township, Union County
365
Lewisburg Borough, Union County
500, 936, 944
Lewisburg Light, Heat and Power Co.
936, 944
Lewisburg Light & Power Co.
500
Liberty Bonds
261, 382, 385, 486, 495, 496, 716
Liberty Township, Montour County
501
Liberty Township Montour Electric Co.
501
Light Commission of Pennsburg
262
Lighting service
see also Arc lighting, Gas lighting, Incandescent lighting, Lamps, Street lighting
811, 1019, 1021, 1022
commercial
272, 313, 1029
domestic
313, 936
Limestone-Lycoming Power & Light Co.
502
Limestone-Montour Power & Light Co.
503
Limestone Township Electric Service Co.
504
Limestone Township, Lycoming County
502
Limestone Township, Montour County
503
Limestone Township, Union County
504
Limited partnership associations
3, 629, 686, 771
Lincoln Borough, Lancaster County
915
Lithia Water
918, 919, 920, 921
Litigation
see Lawsuits
Lititz Borough, Lancaster County
505, 506
The Lititz Electric Light, Heat and Power Co.
505
Lititz Gas Co.
506
Lititz, Mannheim & Ephrata Gas Co.
506
Little Lehigh Electric Co.
507
Little Mahanoy, Northumberland County
508
Little Mahanoy-Northumberland Power & Light Co.
508
Liverpool Borough, Perry County
585, 595
Lizard Creek Electric Co.
509
Load factor analyses
270, 486, 512, 721, 1047
Lobbying
see Laws and legislation—legislative lobbying by companies
261
Local entrepreneurs
role in organizing and financing utilities
8, 18, 61, 271, 273, 274, 275, 277, 282, 385, 386, 412, 415, 442, 445, 578, 645, 835, 843, 865, 879, 901
Local governments, relations with
see also Franchises, efforts to acquire, and street lighting
1, 3, 8, 16, 18, 37, 49, 81, 82, 108, 111, 112, 128, 210, 272, 273, 275, 282, 290, 298, 303, 385, 411, 445, 495, 505, 536, 570, 571, 600, 610, 686, 697, 761, 799, 843, 863, 876, 885, 901, 915, 945, 987, 996, 1021, 1022, 1023, 1024, 1029
Lock Haven City, Clinton County
510, 511, 512
Lock Haven Electric Light and Power Co.
85, 186, 510, 511, 512
The Lock Haven Electric Light and Power Co.
510, 511, 512
Lock Haven Gas Co.
511, 512
Locust-Columbia Power & Light Co.
513
Locust Township, Columbia County
513
Logan-Clinton Power & Light Co.
514
Logan Township, Clinton County
514

Loganton Borough, Clinton County
515, 879
Loganton-Clinton Power & Light Co.
515, 879
Logging companies
888
Londonderry-Dauphin Power & Light Co.
516
Londonderry Township, Dauphin County
516
Longswamp Township, Berks County
507
Lowe water gas process
672, 754, 1023
Lower Augusta-Northumberland Power & Light Co.
517
Lower Augusta Township, Northumberland County
517
Lower Chanceford Township Transmission Co.
518, 707
Lower Chanceford Township, York County
404, 518, 519
Lower Chanceford Water and Power Co.
519
Lower Macungie Township Electric Light and Power Co.
520
Lower Macungie Township, Lehigh County
520
Lower Mahanoy Power Co.
521
Lower Mahanoy Township, Northumberland County
521
Lower Makefield Township, Bucks County
522
Lower Makefield Township Electric Co.
522
Lower Milford Township Electric Light and Power Co.
523
Lower Milford Township, Lehigh County
523
Lower Mount Bethel Electric Co.
524
Lower Mount Bethel Township, Northampton County
524
Lower Nazareth Electric Co.
525
Lower Nazareth Township, Northampton County
525
Lower Paxtang Township, Dauphin County
377
Lower Saucon Electric Co.
526
Lower Swarata Township, Dauphin County
377
Lower Towamensing-Carbon Power & Light Co.
527
Lower Towamensing Township, Carbon County
527
Lower Township, Cumberland County
370
Lower Windsor Township Public Service Co.
528
Lower Windsor Township, York County
528, 529, 530, 1038
Lower Windsor Water and Power Co.
529
Lower Windsor-York Power & Light Co.
530
Lowhill Power & Light Co.
531
Lowhill Township, Lehigh County
531
Loyalsock Power & Light Co.
532
Loyalsock Township, Lycoming County
532, 613
Loysville Town, Perry County
829
Lumber industry in southeastern Pa.
888
Luzerne County
130, 133, 189, 890
Ashley Borough
22
Avoca Borough
859
Bear Creek Township
34
Black Creek Township
53
Briar Creek Township
46
Buck Township
64
Butler Township
68
Conyngham Borough
155
Denison Township
174, 175, 1015
Dorrance Township
180
Dupont Township
187
Duryea Borough
189
Duryea Township
190
East Pittston Borough
1023
Exeter Borough
148, 304
Exeter Township
289, 306, 308, 861, 1007
Fairview Township
311
Foster Township
331
Freeland Borough
146, 344, 384
Green Ridge Village
996
Hanover Township
17, 368
Harwood Village
387
Hazle Township
383, 384, 386, 393
Hazleton City
151, 272, 384, 385, 386, 387, 394, 395, 396
Hollenback Township
407
Hughestown Borough
147, 417
Jeddo Borough
435
Jenkins Township
438, 439
Kingston Borough
1023
Laflin Borough
465, 466
Lattimer Borough
386
Laurel Run Borough
477
Milnesville Village
597
Miners Mills Borough
602, 932
Parsons Borough
932
Pittston Borough
104, 418, 1006
Pittston City
150, 305, 307, 308, 738
Salem Township
46
Slocum Township
838
Sugar Loaf Township
878
West Hazleton Borough
996
West Pittston Borough
149, 1007
White Haven Borough
1015
Wilkes-Barre City
153, 348, 932, 1017, 1018, 1019, 1020, 1021, 1022, 1023, 1041
Wilkes-Barre Township
1025
Wright Township
1037
Wyoming Borough
1023
Luzerne County Board of Commissioners
1024
Lybrand, Ross Bros. & Montgomery
86, 87, 89, 382, 387, 393, 396, 597, 826
Lycoming Apartments
537
Lycoming Consolidated Fuel Gas Co.
533
Lycoming Consolidated Gas Co.
534
Lycoming County
210, 394, 533, 534, 535, 537, 668, 890

(continued)

Anthony Township
14
Armstrong Township
20
Bastress Township
31
Brady Township
58
Clinton Township
33, 600, 610
Du Boistown Borough
183
Eldred Township
287
Fairfield Township
10, 309
Franklin Township
339
Hepburn Township
402
Hughesville Borough
105
Jersey Shore
441, 442
Jordan Township
443
Limestone Township
502
Loyalsock Township
532, 613
Lycoming Township
538
Mifflin Towhship
589
Mill Creek Township
594
Montgomery Borough
533, 534, 600, 610, 611
Montoursville Borough
613, 614
Moreland Township
618
Muncie Borough
610
Muncy Creek Township
610
Picture Rocks Borough
105, 731
Salladsburg Township
796
South Williamsport Borough
847, 850, 1029, 1032
Susquehanna Township
893
Upper Fairfield Township
948
Washington Township
973
Watsontown Borough
610
Williamsport City
2, 91, 102, 113, 203, 282, 441, 442, 444, 535, 536, 537, 614, 648, 649, 656, 847, 888, 891, 934, 961, 962, 1028, 1029, 1030, 1031, 1032
Wolf Township
1035
Woodward Township
1036
Lycoming-Edison Co.
282, 535, 536, 537, 1028
Lycoming Electric Co.
102, 282, 536
Lycoming Gas and Water Co.
1029
Lycoming Improvement Co.
2, 441, 442, 536, 537, 648, 847, 888, 962, 1030
Lycoming Township, Lycoming County
538
Lycoming Township-Lycoming County Power & Light Co.
538
Lykens Borough, Dauphin County
864, 1027, 1033
Lykens Steam Electric Station
890
Lykens Township, Dauphin County
539, 540
Lykens Township Electric Co.
539
Lykens Township Electric Co. (Dauphin)
540
Lykens Valley Consolidated Gas Co.
1033
Lykens Valley Light and Power Co.
864
Lyndon, Lamar
378

M

Machinery malfunctions
49, 571
Macungie Borough Council
542
Macungie Borough, Lehigh County
542
Macungie Electric Light, Heat and Power Co.
542
Madison-Columbia Power & Light Co.
543
Madison-Perry Power & Light Co.
544
Madison Power & Light Co.
545
Madison Township, Columbia County
543
Madison Township, Lackawanna County
545
Madison Township, Perry County
544
Mahanoy City and Tamaqua Street Railway Co.
546
Mahanoy City Borough, Schuylkill County
547, 548, 802, 945
Mahanoy City Gas Co.
547
Mahanoy City Light, Heat and Power Co.
548, 723, 826
Mahanoy City, Schuylkill County
546
Mahanoy Light Co.
549
Mahanoy Township, Carbon County
551
Mahanoy Township Electric Co.
550, 801
Mahanoy Township, Schuylkill County
63, 549, 550, 607, 723, 801
Mahonoy Plane Village, Schuylkill County
334
Mahoning Township, Carbon County
434
Mahoning Township Carbon Electric Co.
551
Mahoning Township, Montour County
552
Mahoning Township Montour Electric Co.
552
Main-Columbia Power & Light Co.
553
Main Township, Columbia County
553
Manheim and Mount Joy Electric Light Co.
498, 554, 555
Manheim Borough, Lancaster County
498, 506, 554, 555
Manheim Suburban Electric Co. No. 1
555
Manheim Suburban Electric Co., No. 2
554, 555
Manheim Township Electric Co.
556
Manheim Township, Lancaster County
316, 556
Manila Grove Park
922
Manor Township Electric Co.
557
Manor Township, Lancaster County
317, 557, 558
Manor Water and Power Co.
558
Manufactured gas
13, 112, 818, 819, 824, 851, 860, 885, 886, 1019, 1049
Maps
18, 270, 385, 447, 632, 657, 1031, 1046
Marietta Electric Co.
559
Marietta Township, Lancaster County
559
Marion Heights Borough, Northumberland County
560
Marion Heights Electric Co.
560
Marketing strategies
see also competition
621, 81, 105, 112, 210, 279, 303, 377, 426, 486, 496, 505, 511, 536, 547, 571, 696, 721, 799, 802, 885, 886, 1019
Marlboro Power & Light Co.
561
Marlborough-Montgomery Power & Light Co.
562
Marlborough Township, Montgomery County
561, 562
Marshall, Edward
728

Marshall Electric Co.
563
Martic-Drumore Electric Light, Heat and Power Co.
564
Martic Township Electric Co.
565
Martic Township, Lancaster County
139, 318, 564, 565, 629, 724, 727, 889, 894
Martic Water and Power Co.
566
Maryland
894
Baltimore County
Baltimore City
26, 720, 822, 894
Peach Bottom
888
Washington County
Hagerstown City
362
Maryland Public Service Commission
721
The Marysville Electric Light, Heat and Power Co.
567
Marysville Borough Council
447
Marysville Borough, Perry County
567, 997
Marysville Water Co.
567
Mauch Chunk Borough, Carbon County
77, 485, 568, 569, 570, 571, 573, 574, 755, 896
industry
571
Mauch Chunk Borough Council
571
Mauch Chunk Canal
571
Mauch Chunk-Carbon Gas Co.
569, 570
Mauch Chunk Gas Co.
569, 570, 571
The Mauch Chunk Heat, Power & Electric Light Co.
570, 571, 1046
Mauch Chunk & Lehighton Transit Co.
77, 568, 573
Mauch Chunk Light, Heat and Power Co.
496
Mauch Chunk Silk Co.
571
Mauch Chunk Township, Carbon County
486, 572
Mauch Chunk Township Carbon Electric Co.
572
Mauch Chunk Transit Co.
568, 573, 574, 1049
Mauch Chunk Transportation Co.
573, 574
Mauch Chunk Trust Co.
77
Maximum peak demand and connected load
52, 235, 260, 270, 271, 373, 374, 385, 412, 486, 535, 716, 721, 1047
Mayberry Township Electric Co.
575
Mayberry Township, Montour County
575
The Mayfield Electric Light, Heat & Power Co.
576
Mayfield Borough, Lackawanna County
414, 576
McAdoo Borough Council
996
McAdoo Borough, Schuylkill County
384, 386, 577
McAdoo Electric Co.
384, 386, 577
The McAlisterville Electric Light Co.
578
McAlisterville Village, Juniata County
578
McCall Ferry Power Co.
404, 566, 579, 889
McCormick Water Wheels
571
McEwensville Borough, Northumberland County
581
McEwensville Electric Co.
581
McGinty, John F.
546
McKean County
451
Mechanicsburg Borough, Cumberland County
80, 161, 163, 941, 964, 1016
Medical care
see Employees—medical services
Messinger family
901
Messinnger Manufacturing Co.
901
Metals, sale of
26
Meters
see also Electric meters, and Gas meters
Metropolitan Edison Co.
283
Middaugh, A.B.
1030
Middle Creek Township, Snyder County
455
Middle Paxtang Township, Dauphin County
377
Middle Smithfield-Monroe Power & Light Co.
582
Middle Smithfield Township, Monroe County
582, 583
Middle Smithfield Township-Monroe County Power & Light Co.
583
Middleburg Borough, Snyder County
584, 585
The Middleburg Electric Co.
584, 671
Middleburg Light, Heat and Power Co.
37, 44, 92, 96, 166, 430, 447, 455, 504, 521, 585, 588, 609, 916, 940, 963, 1005
Middlecreek Electric Co.
584, 586, 669, 883
Middleport Borough, Schuylkill County
333
Middlesex Electric Light, Heat and Power Co.
587
Middlesex Township, Cumberland County
587
Mifflin Electric Service Co.
588
Mifflin-Lycoming Power & Light Co.
589
Mifflin Towhship, Lycoming County
589
Mifflin Township, Dauphin County
588, 590
Mifflin Township Electric Co.
590
Mifflinburg Borough Council
447
Mifflinburg Borough, Union County
365
Mifflintown Borough, Juniata County
445
Mifflintown Electric Light Co.
445
Miles-Centre Power & Light Co.
591
Miles Township, Centre County
591
Milford Electric Light & Power Co.
592
Milford Township, Bucks County
592, 593
Milford Township Electric Light & Power Co.
592, 593
Mill Creek-Lycoming Power & Light Co.
594
Mill Creek Township, Lycoming County
594
The Millersburg Electric Light Heat and Power Co.
595
Millersburg Borough, Dauphin County
447, 595
Mills
electrification of
see also Grist, Knitting, Planing, Silk, and Woollen mills
595, 596
Millville Borough, Columbia County
596
Millville Electric Light Co.
596
The Milnesville Water Co.
393, 597
Milnesville Village, Luzerne County
597
Milton Borough Electric Co.
598
Milton Borough, Northumberland County
424, 598, 599, 600, 601, 918, 919, 920, 921, 944
Milton Electric Light and Power Co.
599, 944

Milton Gas Co.
600, 668
The Milton Manufacturing Co.
424, 601
Mineral springs
918, 919, 920, 921
Miners Mills Borough, Luzerne County
602, 932
Miners Mills Electric Co.
602
Minersville Borough Council
111, 603
Minersville Borough, Schuylkill County
111, 603, 604, 605, 606
The Minersville Electric Light Co., No. 1
111, 603, 604, 605
The Minersville Electric Light Co., No. 2
111, 603, 604, 605
The Minersville Fuel Gas Co.
111, 603, 605
Minersville-Schuylkill Power & Light Co.
606
Mining companies
See also Coal mining companies, and Slate quarries—electrification of
134
Mitchell Electric Co.
607
Mitchell, S.Z.
1048
Monroe County
Barrett Township
28
Chesnuthill Township
99
East Stroudsburg Borough
109, 110, 484
East Stroudsburg Township
797
Eldred Township
288
Hamilton Township
366
Jackson Township
431
Middle Smithfield Township
582, 583
Ross Township
785
Smithfield Township
450
Stroud Township
54, 110
Stroudsburg Borough
109, 110, 484, 875, 876
Tunkhannock Township
923
Monroe Township
Tobyhanna Township
906
Monroe Township, Juniata County
609
Monroe Township Light Co.
608
Monroe Township Power Co.
609
Monroe Township, Snyder County
608
Montgomery and Muncy Electric Light, Heat and Power Co.
610, 611, 634, 635
Montgomery Borough, Lycoming County
533, 534, 600, 610, 611
Montgomery County
301, 302, 303
East Greenville Borough
262, 714
Franconia Township
337, 338
Hatfield Borough
388
Hatfield Township
389, 390
Marlborough Township
561, 562
Salford Township
793
Souderton Borough
841, 842
Towamencin Township
908
Upper Dublin Township
887
Upper Gwynedd Township
361
Upper Hanover Township
949
West Telford Borough
1012
Whitpain Township
975
Montgomery Electric Light and Power Co.
610, 611
Montour County
130, 133, 385, 484, 612, 668
Anthony Township
15
Danville Borough
126, 152, 169, 467, 612, 657, 858, 860
Derry Township
177
Liberty Township
501
Limestone Township
503
Mahoning Township
552
Mayberry Township
575
Valley Township
965
Washingtonville Borough
980, 981
Montour County Gas Co.
612
Montoursville Borough, Lycoming County
613, 614
Montoursville Electric Light Co.
613, 614
Montoursville Passenger Railway Co.
10, 613, 614
Moore Township Electric Co.
615
Moore Township, Northampton County
615
Moosic Borough, Lackawanna County
616
Moosic Electric Co.
616
Moosic Powder Co.
440, 576
Moravia Electric Light, Heat & Power Co.
617
Moreland Land Co.
81
Moreland-Lycoming Power & Light Co.
618
Moreland Township, Lycoming County
618
Moscow and Covington Electric Co.
619
Moscow and Roaring Brook Electric Co.
620
Moscow Electric Co.
621, 292
Motor coach routes
see Bus transportation companies
Mount Carbon Electric Co.
622
Mount Carmel Borough, Northumberland County
274, 716
Mount Carmel Citizens Gas Co.
623
Mount Carmel Light Co.
624
Mount Carmel Township Electric Co., No. 1
625
Mount Carmel Township Electric Co., No. 2
626
Mount Carmel Township, Northumberland County
890
Mount Holly Light, Heat and Power Co.
162, 627
Mount Joy Borough, Lancaster County
554, 868
Mount Joy Electric Light Co.
868
Mount Joy Gas Co.
179
Mount Joy Township Electric Light Co.
628
Mount Joy Township, Lancaster County
179, 628
The Mount Nebo Electric Light Co.
629
Mount Pleasant Power & Light Co.
630
Mount Pleasant-Wayne Power & Light Co.
631
Mount Pocono Light and Improvement Co.
632

Mountville Electric Light Co.
633
Muncie Borough, Lycoming County
610
Muncie, Indiana
1047
Muncy Creek Township, Lycoming County
610
The Muncy Electric Light Heat and Power Co.
610, 634
The Muncy Township Lycoming County Electric Co.
635
Municipally-owned utilities
420
electric companies
3, 81, 82, 105, 577, 697, 714, 715, 744
gas companies
81
water supply companies
81, 420, 421
Myers Electric Co.
636

N

Naomi Pines Electric Co.
637
National Committee on Gas and Electric Service
613, 614
National Electric Defense Association
1, 721
National Electric Light and Power Co.
638
National Electric Light Association
105, 426, 721
National Industrial Recovery Act
721, 774, 808
National Industrial Recovery Administration
808
National Labor Relations Act(Wagner Act)
721
National Power & Light Co.
283, 1048, 1049
National Recovery Administration Codes of Fair Competition
808
National War Labor Board
721
National War Manpower Commission
721
Natural gas
competition with electricity for customers
547
drilling and transmission
891
efficiency
1022
for street lighting
272, 534, 547, 570, 600, 612, 623, 646, 716, 745, 811, 932, 1023, 1029, 1033
gas pipe line installation
547, 1023
manufacturing and distribution costs
600
plant construction
959, 1023
supply companies
13, 21, 46, 81, 82, 87, 109, 110, 111, 112, 127, 130, 131, 132, 152, 153, 179, 210, 224, 234, 348, 362, 470, 473, 487, 506, 512, 569, 605, 612, 623, 646, 656, 660, 668, 669, 716, 754, 810, 825, 826, 943, 1019, 1022, 1023, 1033, 1049
Nescopeck Borough, Luzerna County
46
Nescopeck Township Electric Co.
639
Nesquehoning Electric Co.
640
New Albany Borough, Bradford County
881
New Britain Electric Light and Power Co.
641
New Buffalo Power Co.
642
New Castle Township, Schuylkill County
216, 250
New Cumberland Borough, Cumberland County
941
New Hanover Power & Light Co.
643
New Holland Electric Co.
644
New Jersey
132, 134, 138, 283, 295, 470, 483, 487, 536, 537, 571, 665, 780, 807, 808, 815, 817, 820
Atlantic City
1047
New Jersey Zinc Co.
363
New Kingston Electric Light, Heat and Power Co.
645
New Parryville Consolidated Gas Co.
646
New Ringgold Borough Electric Co.
647
New York
New York City
267, 270, 283, 378, 667, 669, 831, 889, 1047, 1048, 1049, 1050
New York Central Railroad
442
New York City, New York
267, 270, 283, 378, 667, 669, 831, 889, 1047, 1048, 1049, 1050
Newberry Bridge Co.
648
Newberry Passenger Railway Co.
649
Newberry-York Power & Light Co.
650
Newmanstown Electric Light and Power Co. No. 1
651
Newmanstown Electric Light and Power Co. No. 2
651, 652
Newport Borough, Perry County
446, 448, 983
Newton Township Electric Corp.
653
Newville Borough, Cumberland County
51, 52
Niagara Falls
721
Nippenose Power & Light Co.
654
Nockamixon Township Electric Co.
655
North Branch Development Co.
656, 891
North Branch Transit Co.
126, 657
North Catasauqua Borough, Northampton County
487
North Lancaster County Electric Co.
658, 993
North Manheim Township, Schuylkill County
217, 659, 922
North-Point Gas Co.
349, 660
North Susquehanna Transit Co.
126
North Union Township Electric Co.
661
North Whitehall Electric Co.
662
North Whitehall Township, Lehigh County
662
North Whitehall Township Lehigh Electric Co.
664
Northampton Borough, Northampton County
487
Northampton County
484, 487, 492, 494, 495, 1026
Allen Township
7, 665, 682, 942
Bethelehem City
492, 495, 617
Bethlehem Borough
49
Bethlehem Township
50, 759
Bushkill Township
862
East Allen Township
194
Emmaus Borough
495
Forks Township
357
Freemansburg Borough
345
Hanover Township
834
Hellerton Borough
401
Lehigh Township
5, 490
Lower Mount Bethel Township
524
Lower Nazareth Township
525
Moore Township
615
North Catasauqua Borough
487

(continued)

Northampton Borough
487
Palmer Township
38
Plainfield Township
299
Saucon Township
526
South Bethlehem Borough
49, 363, 364, 495, 843
Stockertown Borough
901
Tatamy Borough
901
Upper Mount Bethel Township
956
Upper Nazareth
957
Walnutport Borough
971
Washington Township
857
West Bethlehem Borough
49
Williams Borough
118
Williams Township
1026
Northampton County Electric Co.
487, 638, 665
Northampton Heights Electric Light, Heat and Power Co.
659, 666
Northern Central Co.
667, 668, 669, 1049
Northern Central Gas Co.
127, 362, 533, 534, 600, 612, 667, 668, 673, 851, 1029, 1046
Northumberland Borough, Northumberland County
349, 586, 882
Northumberland County
130, 274, 385, 394, 484, 585, 668, 890, 918, 920
Chillisquaque Township
851
Coal Township
120, 121, 122, 813
Dalmatia Village
166, 963
Delaware Township
173, 600
East Cameron Township
198
East Chillisquaque Township
199, 668, 851
Easton City
283
Herndon Borough
963
Jackson Township
430
Kulpmont Borough
457
Lewis Township
499
Little Mahanoy
508
Lower Augusta Township
517
Lower Mahanoy Township
521
Marion Heights Borough
560
McEwensville Borough
581
Milton Borough
424, 598, 599, 600, 601, 918, 919, 920, 921, 944
Mount Carmel Borough
274, 716
Mount Carmel Township
890
Northumberland Borough
349, 586, 882
Rockefeller Township
783
Rush Township
788, 790
Shamokin Borough
276, 424, 716, 813, 814, 815, 817, 819, 820
Shamokin Township
816
Snyder City
586
Snydertown Borough
839
Sunbury Borough
277, 278, 279, 347, 667, 669, 882, 883, 884, 885, 944
Trevorton Village
914
Turbot Township
600, 924, 926
Turbotville Borough
925
Upper Augusta Township
424, 885, 886, 947
Upper Mahanoy Township
952
Washington Township
974
Watsontown Borough
982
West Cameron Township
73, 990
West Chillisquaque Township
991, 992
Zerbe Township
1045
Northumberland County Gas & Electric Co.
33, 499, 581, 586, 608, 667, 669, 673, 712, 744, 810, 811, 884, 920, 925, 926, 991, 1046
Northumberland County Railway and LIght Co.
918, 920, 921
Northumberland County Railway Co.
882
The Northumberland Electric Illuminating Co.
670, 884
Northumberland Gas Co.
349, 672, 959
Northumberland Gas Heat and Fuel Co.
672, 673, 745, 959
Norwegian Township, Schuylkill County
251, 270
Noyes Electric Light Co.
674
Nuangola-Luzerne Power & Light Co.
675

O

Oakdale Electric Co.
676
Ohio
Canton
1047
Old Lycoming Power & Light Co.
677
Old Port Power Co.
678
Olyphant and Winton Traction Street Railway Co.
679
Orange-Columbia Power & Light Co.
680
Orangeville-Columbia Power & Light Co.
681
Oregon-Wayne Power & Light Co.
683
Organization charts, corporate
210, 226, 227, 261, 349, 721, 1046
Orphanages, electrification of
829
Orwigsburg Borough, Schuylkill County
803
Orwigsburg Electric Light, Heat and Power Co.
684

P

Packer Township Electric Co.
685
Palm Electric Light & Power Co., Ltd.
686
Palmer Township, Northampton County
38
Palmerton-Carbon Power & Light Co.
687
The Palmerton Co.
688, 689, 690, 691
Palmerton Disposal Co.
688, 689
Palmerton Lighting Co.
690, 691
Palmerton Telephone Co.
688, 691
Palmyra Power & Light Co.
692
Palmyra Township Power & Light Co.
693
Palo Alto Borough, Schuylkill County
235, 261, 694
social conditions
210, 260, 261, 922
Palo Alto Heat, Light and Power Co.
16, 275, 281, 334, 604, 684, 694, 756, 898
Panther Creek Electric Co.
695
Panther Valley Electric Co.
123, 696, 697
The Panther Valley Electric Light Heat and Power Co.
123, 696, 697

'Paper companies'
158, 189, 340, 361, 522, 655, 717, 718, 761, 778, 840, 901, 905, 954, 977, 1006, 1018, 1026, 1033
Paradise Electric Light, Heat and Power Co.
698
Paradise Power & Light Co.
699
Paradise Township Electric Co.
700
Paradise Township, Lancaster County
426
Pardee, Alfred D.
802
Pardee Brothers & Co., Inc.
597, 701
Pardee, Calvin
106, 385, 386, 625, 723, 802, 945
Calvin Pardee & Co.
382
Pardee Mill
571
Parks
see Amusement parks
Parryville Electric Co.
702
Parsons Borough, Luzerne County
932
Partnership associations for supplying electricity
97, 105, 771
Passenger railways
see Railway companies
Patent infringement litigation
374, 412
Patterson Borough, Juniata County
445
Paupack Electric Co.
703
Paupack Power & Light Co., No. 1
704
Paupack Power & Light Co., No. 2
28, 34, 56, 64, 99, 117, 182, 288, 355, 431, 436, 452, 464, 468, 488, 491, 545, 692, 693, 699, 704, 705, 709, 743, 746, 751, 757, 792, 852, 865, 906, 909, 923
Paxtang Electric Co.
378, 706
Peach Bottom Electric Transmission Co.
518, 707
Peach Bottom, Maryland
888
Pen Argyl Electric Light & Power Co.
708
Penn Forest Power & Light Co.
709
Penn Harris Hotel
377
Penn-Lycoming Power & Light Co.
710
Penn-Perry Electric Co.
3
Penn Township Electric Light Co.
711
Penn Township, Lancaster County
320
Penn Township Light Co.
712
Penn Township, Perry County
3, 447
Penns Creek Hydro Electric Co.
713
Pennsburg Electric Light Commission
714, 715, 771
Pennsburg Power & Light Co.
714, 715
Pennsylvania Public Service Commission
1, 3, 18, 61, 235, 261, 295, 377, 426, 486, 496, 632, 643, 721, 766, 781, 964, 1031
Public Utilities Commission
18, 656, 721, 808, 861, 890, 1034, 1046
Pennsylvania Diamond Drill Co.
16
Pennsylvania Electric Association
105, 261, 721
Pennsylvania Giant Power Board
electric industry opposition to
1, 721, 808
Pennsylvania Lighting Co.
122, 688, 716, 814, 818, 914, 1046
Pennsylvania Manufacturing Light & Power Co.
809
Pennsylvania-New Jersey-Maryland Power Pool
721, 808
Pennsylvania Power & Light Co.
1046, 1048, 1049
and World War II
1046
capitalization
1046
formation of
125, 385, 492, 493, 668, 669, 716, 802, 1046, 1048, 1049
origins of the name
718, 977
Railways Division
210
rate schedules
1046
takeover and integration tactics
18, 21, 32, 97, 110, 192, 415, 451, 718, 977, 1046
Pennsylvania Power & Light Co., No. 1
19, 155, 423, 717
Pennsylvania Railroad
electrification of Safe Harbor-Washington, D.C. line
721
Pennsylvania Railroad Co.
128, 721, 885, 983
Pennsylvania Realty & Investment Co.
227, 380, 446, 448, 614, 719, 964, 1007
Pennsylvania, state of
Attorney-General
579, 721
Governor
18
Highway Dept.
571
Internal Affairs Dept.
18, 162, 542
Labor and Industry Dept.
18
Legislature
570, 754, 889, 1023
office buildings, utility service to
373, 379
taxes
568
Workman's Compensation Insurance Fund
427
Pennsylvania Steel Co.
863
Pennsylvania Street Railway Association
1031
Pennsylvania Transmission Co.
720
Pennsylvania Utilities Co.
283

(continued)

Pennsylvania Water & Power Co.
26, 408, 409, 410, 566, 579, 580, 720, 721, 737, 822, 889, 894, 1046
Pensions
see employees, pensions
People's Gas Co. of Lehigh County
87
Peoples Bridge Co.
722, 964
The Peoples Light, Heat and Power Co. of Shenandoah and Mahanoy County, Schuylki
723, 945
Pequea Electric Co.
629, 724
Pequea Electric Light, Heat and Power Co.
725
Pequea Township Electric Co.
726
Pequea Township, Lancaster County
321
Pequea Water and Power Co.
727
Perdix Village, Perry County
567
The Perry Electric Light, Heat and Power Co.
728
Perry County
210, 728, 966, 967
Landisburg Borough
475, 828
Liverpool Borough
585, 595
Loysville Town
829
Madison Township
544
Marysville Borough
567, 997
Newport Borough
446, 448, 983
Penn Township
3, 447
Perdix Village
567
Spring Township
853
Tyron Township
829
Wheatfield Township
3, 447
Philadelphia Electric Co.
39, 59, 60, 522
blockage of expansion
39, 59, 60, 522
Philadelphia, Pa.
investment banking firms
1022, 1023, 1030, 1041
power supply to
579
Philadelphia & Reading Coal & Iron Co.
922
Philadelphia Suburban Gas and Electric Co.
224
Phoenix Utility Co.
729
Photographs
138, 613
Piatt Power & Light Co.
730
Picture Rocks Borough, Lycoming County
105, 731
Picture Rocks Power & Light Co.
731
Pike County
Blooming Grove Township
56
Greene Township
355
Lackawaxen Township
464
Lehman Township
497
Shohola Township
830, 831
Pine-Columbia Power & Light Co.
732
Pine Creek Power & Light Co.
733
Pine Grove Borough, Schuylkill County
467, 912
Pine Grove Electric Light, Heat & Power Co.
734
Pine Grove-Schuylkill Power & Light Co.
735
Pine Grove Township, Schuylkill County
252, 734, 735, 736
Pine Grove Township-Schuylkill County Power & Light Co.
736
Pine Hill Coal Co.
electrification of
1046
Pioneer Electric Light Co.
737
Pittston Borough, Luzerne County
104, 418, 1006
religious and civic organizations
104
Pittston City Electric Co.
738
Pittston City, Luzerne County
150, 305, 307, 308, 738
Pittston Electric Co.
739
Pittston-Luzerne Power & Light Co.
740
Plainfield Township, Northampton County
299
Plains Electric Co.
741
Planing mills
987
Plumstead Township Electric Co.
742
Pocono Power & Light Co.
743
Point Township Electric Co.
744
Point Township Gas Co.
745
Police relations
8
Political patronage
see also Laws and legislation, legislative lobbying
282, 496
Polk Power & Light Co.
746
Population descriptions and statistics
Allentown
495
Harrisburg
378
Sellersville
570, 571
Sunbury
303, 374
Population mobility
808
The Port Carbon & Middleport Electric Railway Co.
747
Port Carbon Borough, Schuylkill County
897
The Port Clinton Light, Heat and Power Co.
749
The Port Electric Light Heat and Power Co.
748
Porter-Lycoming Power & Light Co.
750
Porter Power & Light Co.
751
Porter Township, Schuylkill County
253
Pottsville and Reading Railway Co.
752, 803
Pottsville Borough Council
16
Pottsville Borough, Schuylkill County
social conditions
210, 226, 227, 261, 275, 922
Pottsville City Council
210, 275, 753
Pottsville City, Schuylkill County
16, 210, 226, 227, 260, 275, 747, 748, 752, 754, 756, 800, 805, 897
Pottsville Gas Co.
754
Pottsville-Mauch Chunk Bus Line
755
Pottsville & St. Clair Electric Railway Co.
753
Pottsville Union Traction Co.
119, 260, 261, 747, 752, 753, 756, 800, 897
Powder works
576

Power plant construction
505, 807, 1021
Power station operations records
535, 721, 808
Price Power & Light Co.
757
Price, Waterhouse & Co.
826
Priceburg Electric Light Co.
758
Primrose Electric Co.
759
Prompton Electric Co.
760
Property valuation
42
Prospect Rock Electric Light, Heat and Power Co.
477, 761
Providence Electric Light, Heat and Power Co.
762
Providence Township Electric Co.
763
Public health
81
Public relations
226, 282, 721, 808, 1046, 1047
Public Utility Holding Co. Act of 1935
808, 1046, 1048, 1049
Publicly-owned utilities
see Municipally-owned utilities
Pump House (water) construction
419

Q

Quarries
electrification of
486, 871
Quarryville Borough Council
871
Quarryville Borough, Lancaster County
871
Quarryville Electric Light, Heat and Power Co.
764

R

Rahn Township Electric Co.
765
Rahn Township, Schuylkill County
234, 254, 285, 765
Railroad bridges
construction of
648
Railway companies
8, 10, 18, 74, 75, 80, 91, 113, 119, 126, 133, 135, 138, 140, 162, 163, 164, 168, 176, 185, 203, 210, 226, 227, 235, 260, 261, 310, 370, 372, 424, 442, 444, 470, 472, 495, 537, 546, 568, 573, 599, 613, 614, 627, 648, 649, 657, 679, 694, 708, 722, 747, 752, 753, 756, 800, 817, 845, 847, 882, 884, 889, 964, 966, 997, 1007, 1016, 1030, 1031, 1048, 1049
and subsidiary electric companies
8, 18, 275, 385, 627, 684, 721, 799, 817, 837, 884, 941
automobile and bus competition
1031
construction
803
earnings
847
electrification
721
fare rates
1031
growth of passenger traffic
3, 210, 226, 800, 966, 967, 1030, 1031
horse-drawn
1030
passenger statistics
8, 138, 210, 226, 227, 261, 371, 470, 756, 922, 966, 967, 1030, 1031, 1048, 1049
power supply
303, 385, 542, 567, 581, 599, 627, 721, 756, 796, 799, 804, 835, 837, 882, 884, 941, 967
repairs and improvements
966
right-of-way agreements
119, 196, 987, 1007
rolling stock
138
routes
371, 964, 997
ticket sales
8, 1030
Railway Electric Light & Power Co.
766
Railway terminals
380
Ralpho Electric Co.
767
Ransom-Lackawanna Power & Light Co.
769
Ransom Township Electric Co.
770
Rapho Township Electric Light Co.
768
Raskob, John J.
884
Rate abatements for non-profit organizations
271, 863
Rate schedules
disputes with customers
261, 1039
electric companies
621, 3, 37, 52, 81, 103, 106, 210, 235, 271, 273, 274, 277, 282, 303, 385, 395, 445, 447, 486, 570, 571, 595, 600, 610, 632, 686, 713, 714, 721, 748, 779, 802, 808, 825, 826, 830, 831, 856, 863, 864, 873, 875, 876, 901, 914, 915, 941, 987, 1015, 1019, 1021, 1022, 1034, 1046
gas companies
81, 349, 570, 600, 646, 716, 825, 885, 886, 1019, 1022, 1023, 1029
standardization of
280
steam heating
379, 396, 825, 826, 1019, 1024
water supply companies
81, 82, 202, 1039
Real estate companies
135, 136, 410, 446, 719
Real estate transactions
380
Rebates
825
Receivership
see Bankrupt companies
Red Hill Power & Light Co.
771, 772
Reed Township, Dauphin County
3, 447, 773
Reed Township Electric Co.
3, 773
Regulations
see Rules and regulations
49
Reilly Township, Schuylkill County
218, 255
Reinerton Village, Schuylkill County
541, 864
Religious organizations
104, 774
Renovo Borough, Clinton County
892
Renovo Edison Light, Heat and Power Co.
95, 674, 774, 775, 846, 1046
Renovo Edison Light, Heat and Power Co., No. 2
892, 1046
Renovo Heating Co.
775
Republic Service Corp.
1, 571, 774, 892
Research and development
721
Reservoirs
721, 1039
Residential Customers
see Customers, residential
Resorts
electrification of
632, 637
Rhoads, Hiram R.
1030
Richland Electric Light and Power Co.
776
Richland Township Electric Light and Power Co.
777
Ridgway Borough, Elk County
451
Riegelsville Electric Co.
778
Right-of-way agreements, railway
119, 997, 1007
Ringtown Light, Heat and Power Co.
779
Rishel Furniture Co.
105
River tolls
888
Rivers and Streams Company
780
Riverton Town, Cumberland County
372
Roaring Brook Power & Light Co.
781
Roaring Creek-Columbia Power & Light Co.
782
Roaring Creek Township, Columbia County
782
Rock Hill Township, Bucks County
229, 230

Rockefeller-Northumberland Power & Light Co.
783
Rockefeller Township, Northumberland County
783
Rockford, Illinois
1047
Rockland Light and Power Co.
831
Rockland Township, Berks County
784
Rockland Township Electric Co.
784
Roosevelt, Franklin D.
808
Ross, Harry C.
419, 420
Ross-Monroe Power & Light Co.
785
Ross Township, Monroe County
785
Rules and regulations
governing electric service
49, 81, 271, 274, 283, 385, 411, 419, 447, 808, 987, 1029
governing gas service
81, 570, 1029
governing steam heating service
1024
governing water heating service
81, 82, 419
Rural Electric Distributing Association
3
Rural electrification
1, 3, 32, 37, 105, 141, 426, 476, 626, 632, 637, 644, 714, 771, 831, 871, 873, 915, 1034, 1046
Ruscombmanor Township, Berks County
786
Ruscombmanor Township Electric Co.
786
Rush Township, Dauphin County
787
Rush Township Electric Co. (Dauphin)
787
Rush Township Electric Co. (Northumberland)
788
Rush Township Electric Co. (Schuylkill)
789
Rush Township, Northumberland County
788, 790
Rush Township-Northumberland Electric Co.
790
Rush Township, Schuylkill County
789
Ryan Township, Schuylkill County
256, 350

S

Sacramento Village, Hubly Township, Schuylkill County
415
Sadsbury Township Electric Co.
791
Sadsbury Township, Lancaster County
791
Safe Harbor Water Power Corp.
721
Safety equipment
138, 210, 721, 825, 1031
Safety policies and procedures
210, 721, 1031
St. Clair Borough, Schuylkill County
897
Salaries
see Payrolls
Salem Power & Light Co.
792
Salem Township, Luzerne County
46
Salem Township, Wayne County
792
Salford-Montgomery Power & Light Co.
793
Salford Township, Montgomery County
793
Salisbury Electric Light and Power Co.
794
Salisbury Township Electric Co.
795
Salisbury Township, Lancaster County
426
Salisbury Township, Lehigh County
794
Salladsburg-Lycoming Power & Light Co.
796
Salladsburg Township, Lycoming County
796
Sambo Electric Light and Power Co.
797, 875, 876
Sanitation
81
Saucon Township, Northampton County
526
Saucona Electric Light, Heat and Power Co.
798
Sawmills
888
Scherer, L. Edward
442
Schmunk, John F.
51
Schools
Harrisburg
378
Hughesville
105
Lancaster
273
Lansford
696
Mauch Chunk
571
Pottsville
275
Williamsport
282
Schuylkill Borough, Schuylkill County
119
Schuylkill County
227, 235, 260, 261, 271, 275, 384, 385, 394, 541, 694, 799
Ashland Borough
21, 271
Auburn Borough
24
Barry Township
29, 211, 236
Blythe Township
563
Branch Township
212, 237
Butler Township
67, 69, 238
Cass Township
213, 239
Coaldale Borough
123
Cressona Township
242
Delano Township
171, 172
Donaldson Village
912
East Brunswick Township
195
East Norwegian Township
243, 900
East Union Township
232, 233
Eldred Township
286
Foster Township
214, 244
Frackville Borough
334
Frailey Township
215, 335, 336
Gilberton Borough
245, 334
Girardville Borough
246, 334, 799, 804
Gordon Borough
247
Hegins Township
248, 397, 398
Hubly Township
415, 416
Sacramento Village
415
Kline Township
454
Landingville Borough
249
Mahanoy City
546
Mahanoy City Borough
547, 548, 802, 945
Mahanoy Township
63, 549, 550, 607, 723, 801
Mahonoy Plane Village
334
McAdoo Borough
384, 386, 577
Middleport Borough
333
Minersville Borough
111, 603, 604, 605, 606
New Castle Township
216, 250
North Manheim Township
217, 659, 922
Norwegian Township
251, 270

(continued)

Orwigsburg Borough
803
Palo Alto Borough
235, 261, 694
Pine Grove Borough
467, 912
Pine Grove Township
252, 734, 735, 736
Port Carbon Borough
897
Porter Township
253
Pottsville City
16, 210, 226, 227, 260, 275, 747, 748, 752, 754, 756, 800, 805, 897
Rahn Township
234, 254, 285, 765
Reilly Township
218, 255
Reinerton Village
541, 864
Rush Township
789
Ryan Township
256, 350
St. Clair Borough
897
Schuylkill Borough
119
Schuylkill Haven Borough
803
Schuylkill Township
327
Shenandoah Borough
106, 723, 823, 824, 825, 826, 827, 897
South Manheim Township
219
Tamaqua Borough
112, 280, 281, 546, 747, 896, 898, 899
Tower City Borough
541, 864, 910
Tremont Borough
911, 912
Tremont Township
220, 257, 913
Union Township
933, 938
Upper Mahantongo Township
953
Valley View Township
415
Walker Township
970
Washington Township
221
Wayne Township
222, 258
West Brunswick Township
223, 988
West Mahanoy Township
259, 1001, 1002
West Penn Township
1004
Schuylkill Electric Co.
694, 799, 804
Schuylkill Electric Railway Co.
752, 756, 800, 803, 897
Schuylkill Gas and Electric Co.
547, 548, 550, 625, 801, 802
The Schuylkill Gas and Electric Co.
63, 69, 106, 121, 156, 172, 233, 550, 625, 723, 779, 799, 801, 802, 826, 938, 945, 1002, 1046
The Schuylkill Haven & Orwigsburg Street Railway Co.
803
Schuylkill Haven Borough, Schuylkill County
803
Schuylkill Light, Heat and Power Co.
799, 804
Schuylkill Railway Co.
804
Schuylkill Subway Co.
805
Schuylkill Telephone Co.
271
Schuylkill Township, Schuylkill County
327
Scott Township Electric Corp.
806
Scott Township, Lackawanna County
806
Scranton Chamber of Commerce
808
Scranton City, Lackawanna County
134, 160, 264, 807, 808, 809, 877, 960, 984, 1011
effects of Great Depression
808
social and economic conditions
808
The scranton electric c1 Scranton
308, 807, 808
Scranton Electric Co.
621, 1, 55, 62, 76, 78, 79, 104, 134, 147, 148, 149, 150, 184, 264, 289, 290, 307, 328, 330, 414, 439, 440, 459, 460, 461, 462, 576, 616, 739, 758, 807, 808, 809, 877, 902, 960, 968, 984, 1006, 1047
Scranton Electric Light and Heat Co.
809
Scranton Railway Co.
185, 679
Securities and Exchange Commission
283, 571, 721, 774, 892, 1046, 1048, 1049
and utility holding companies
1, 571, 774, 808, 892, 1046, 1048, 1049
Selinsgrove Borough, Snyder County
810, 811
Selinsgrove Gas Co.
810
Selinsgrove Gas Light Co.
811
Sellersville Borough, Bucks County
300, 301, 302, 303, 812
marketing surveys
303
social conditions
303, 863
Sellersville Power & Light Co.
812
Service complaints
see Customers, complaints
Sewage service
688, 689
Sexton, Samuel, III
721
Shamokin and Coal Township Light and Power Co.
813, 814, 820
Shamokin and Coal Township Light, Heat and Power Co.
276, 716, 813, 814, 815, 817, 819, 820
The Shamokin Arc Light Co.
815
Shamokin Borough, Northumberland County
276, 424, 716, 813, 814, 815, 817, 819, 820
Shamokin Creek
424
Shamokin Electric Co.
816
Shamokin Electric Light and Power Co.
817
Shamokin Gas Co.
818
The Shamokin Gas Light Co.
819
Shamokin Light, Heat and Power Co.
813, 814, 815, 817, 819, 820
Shamokin Street Railway Co.
817
Shamokin Township, Northumberland County
816
Shamokin Valley Coal Co.
347, 424
Shamokin Valley Creek
347
Sharswood Electric Co.
821
Shaw, P.B.
273, 274, 277, 282, 774, 884
The Shawinigan Electro Products Co.
26, 822
Shenandoah Borough, Schuylkill County
106, 723, 823, 824, 825, 826, 827, 897
The Shenandoah Electric Illuminating Co. of Shenandoah, Pa.
823, 824, 825, 826
Shenandoah Gas Light Co.
824, 825, 826
Shenandoah Heat and Power Co.
823, 824, 825, 826
Shenandoah Light, Heat and Power Co.
385, 548, 824, 825, 826
Shenandoah Valley, Pennsylvania
802
Shepp, E.M.B.
546
Sherman Valley Electric Light, Heat and Power Co.
475, 544, 828, 829, 853
Valley Light, Heat & Power Co.
828, 829
Shohola-Pike Light & Power Co.
830, 831
Shohola Power Co.
831
Shohola Township, Pike County
830, 831
Shortline Railway Co.
800
Shrewsbury-Lycoming Power & Light Co.
832

Shrewsbury Township, Lycoming County
832
Siegfried, Lehigh County
486
Silk mills
electrification of
596, 703, 713, 963
Silverdale Borough, Bucks County
833
Silverdale Electric Light and Power Co.
833
Sinking Spring Electric Light, Heat and Power Co.
42
Sinking Springs Borough, Berks County
42
Skidmore Electric Co.
834
Slate quarries
electrification of
486
The Slatedale Electric Light, Heat and Power Co.
494, 835
Slatington Borough, Lehigh County
108, 494, 495, 836, 837
Slatington Light and Power Co.
827, 836
Slatington Power Co.
108, 495, 837
Slocum-Luzerne Power & Light Co.
838
Slocum Township, Luzerne County
838
Smithfield Township, Monroe County
450
Snyder City, Northumberland County
586
Snyder County
210, 585
Adams Township
916
Beavertown Borough
37
Centre Township
92
Chapman Township
96
Freeburg Borough
343
Hummels Wharf Village
586
Jackson Township
432
Middle Creek Township
455
Middleburg Borough
584, 585
Monroe Township
608
Selinsgrove Borough
810, 811
Union Township
937
Washington Township
977
West Perry Township
1005
Snydertown Borough, Northumberland County
839
Snydertown Power & Light Co.
839
Solebury Township, Bucks County
840
Solebury Township Electric Co.
840
Souderton Borough, Montgomery County
841, 842
Souderton Electric Light and Power Co.
841
Souderton Power & Light Co.
842
The South Bethlehem Electric Light Co.
843
South Bethlehem Borough, Northampton County
49, 363, 364, 495, 843
South Canaan Township, Wayne County
969
South Hanover-Dauphin Power & Light Co.
844
South Hanover Township, Dauphin County
420, 844
South Manheim Township, Schuylkill County
219
South Middleton Street Railway Co.
845, 966
South Middleton Township, Cumberland County
845
South Renovo Electric Light Co.
846
South Renovo Township, Clinton County
846
South Side Passenger Railway Co.
847
South Varden Village, Wayne County
969
South Whitehall Electric Light and Power Co.
848
South Whitehall Electric Light Co.
849
South Whitehall Township, Lehigh County
848, 849
South Williamsport Borough, Lycoming County
847, 850, 1029, 1032
South Williamsport Power & Light Co.
850
Southern Light Co.
851
Southwark Foundry
280
Spaulding, G.W.
721
Sponster, W.H.
133
Sports and recreation
see also Amusement parks, and Resorts, electrification of
922
Sprague Electric Railway and Motor Co.
374
Spring Brook Power & Light Co.
852
Spring Brook Township, Lackawanna County
852
Spring Township, Berks County
456
Spring Township Light, Heat and Power Co.
853
Spring Township, Perry County
853
Spring water
918, 919, 920, 921
Springfield Township, Bucks County
854
Springfield Township Electric Light and Power Co.
854
St. Johns Village, Butler Township, Luzerne County
18
Standard Construction Co. of Bloomsburg
855
The Standard Electric Co. of Parsons, Pa.
856, 1019
Standard Electric Co. of Washington Township
857
Standard Electric Light Co.
45, 152, 858
Standard Electric Light, Heat and Power Co. of Avoca, Pa.
459, 859
Standard Gas Co.
45, 152, 860
Standardization
of auditing procedures
1046, 1048, 1049
of electric generating and distribution apparatus
105, 721, 996, 1046
Stanley Electric Manufacturing Co.
996
Stanton Operating Co.
861
Stanton Steam Electric Station
280, 307, 308, 419, 571, 595, 669, 671, 714, 813, 837, 861, 875
Star Electric Co.
862
State Centre Electric Co.
451
Steam electric generating stations
307, 409, 505, 554, 567, 571, 585, 586, 601, 611, 706, 728, 779, 856, 858, 861, 863, 890, 914, 944, 966, 982, 995
Steam engines
Corliss
282, 460
Davies & Thomas
49
Erie City Iron Works
813
Weston
105, 363, 365, 412, 440, 446, 596, 601, 610, 843, 871, 872, 960, 982

Steam heating
264, 377, 379, 396, 775, 802, 808, 825, 826, 1019, 1024
Steam power
379, 825, 826, 1019, 1024, 1030
Steel industries
486
Steelton Borough, Dauphin County
863
social and civic organizations
863
social conditions
863
Steelton Light, Heat and Power Co.
863
Sterling Consolidated Electric Co.
541, 864, 1027
The Sterling Electric Light Heat and Power Co.
864
Sterling Power & Light Co.
865
Sterling Township, Wayne County
865
Stillwater Borough, Columbia County
866
Stillwater-Columbia Power & Light Co.
866
Stillwell, L.B.
485, 486
Stock issues
826, 1048
Stockertown Borough, Northampton County
901
Stockertown Light, Heat & Power Co.
867, 901
Stockholders
dividends
334, 808, 826
lists of
162, 210, 363, 380, 385, 386, 387, 395, 419, 426, 427, 587, 696, 721, 756, 808, 1046
Stoever Electric Light Co.
498, 868
Stoever, Henry V.H.
554
Stone & Webster
109
Stores, company
387
Story Electric Co.
270
Strasburg Borough Council
871
Strasburg Borough Electric Light, Heat and Power Co.
870
Strasburg Borough, Lancaster County
870, 871, 872, 873
Strasburg Electric Light, Heat and Power Co. No. 1
871, 872
Strasburg Electric Light, Heat and Power Co. No. 2
265, 698, 762, 871, 872, 873, 999
Strasburg Electric Light, Heat and Power Co. No. 3
207, 725, 764, 870, 872, 873
Strasburg Township Electric Co.
874
Strasburg Township, Lancaster County
874
Street lighting
see also Arc lighting, and Incandescent lighting
102, 105, 106, 280, 284, 440, 445, 447, 536, 571, 600, 603, 610, 613, 863, 876, 885, 886
contracts
16, 37, 106, 112, 275, 284, 470, 505, 571, 614, 696, 807, 815, 843, 871, 875, 876, 901, 915, 936, 996, 1021, 1022, 1029
conversion from carbon arc to tungsten
863, 871
conversion from gas to electric
8, 49, 273, 871
installation
427, 1015
Street lighting contracts
competition for
81, 102, 104, 106, 107, 112, 272, 273, 279, 280, 298, 363, 373, 374, 815
Street railway companies
see also Freight railways, electric, and Interurban electric railway companies, and Railway
77, 80, 91, 113, 119, 133, 138, 140, 162, 163, 168, 185, 203, 210, 226, 227, 235, 260, 261, 310, 370, 371, 372, 442, 444, 470, 472, 495, 537, 573, 614, 649, 752, 753, 756, 799, 800, 803, 845, 847, 934, 961, 962, 964, 966, 967, 1030, 1031, 1048, 1050
Strikes
226, 382, 496
Stroud Realty Co.
110
Stroud Township, Monroe County
54, 110
Stroudsburg Borough, Monroe County
109, 110, 484, 875, 876
Stroudsburg Electric Light and Power Co.
484
The Stroudsburg Electric Light and Power Co., No. 1
109, 797, 875, 876
The Stroudsburg Electric Light and Power Co., No. 2
425, 797, 875, 876
Stroudsburg Passenger Railway Co.
875
Suburban Electric Light Co.
877
Subway companies
805
Sugar Loaf Township Electric Co.
878
Sugar Loaf Township, Luzerne County
878
Sugar Valley Light, Power & Heat Co.
879
Sugarloaf-Columbia Power & Light Co.
880
Sugarloaf Township, Columbia County
880
Sullivan County
881
Dushore Borough
881
Eagles Mere Borough
192
Laporte Borough
881
Sullivan County Electric Co., No. 1
881
Sullivan County Electric Co., No. 2
881
The Sunbury and Northumberland Electric Railway Co.
670, 882, 884
Sunbury Borough Council
279, 884, 885, 886
Sunbury Borough, Northumberland County
277, 278, 279, 347, 667, 669, 882, 883, 884, 885, 944
business and industries
277, 279, 885, 886
ethnic composition
885
social and economic conditions
277, 279, 885, 886
The Sunbury Electric Co.
883
Sunbury Electric Light and Power Co.
882, 884
Sunbury Gas and Light Co.
885
Sunbury Gas Co., No. 2
885, 886
Sunbury Gas Co., No. 3
885, 886
Sunbury Gas Fuel and Power Co.
885, 886
Superior Electric Light & Power Co.
887
Surcharges
235, 260
Susquehanna Boom Co.
888
Susquehanna Canal and Power Co.
889
Susquehanna Coal Co.
890
Susquehanna Collieries Co.
890
Susquehanna County
808
Clifford Borough
115, 116
Forest City
330
Herrick Township
403
Uniondale Borough
939
Susquehanna Dye Works
885, 886
Susquehanna Falls Power Co.
566, 727, 889
Susquehanna Gas Co.
656, 891
Susquehanna Ice Co.
892
Susquehanna Light Co.
1020
Susquehanna Power & Light Co.
893
Susquehanna River
307, 409, 447, 566, 567, 580, 585, 601, 721, 722, 728, 822, 861, 888, 889, 964
Susquehanna Silk Factory
885, 886

Susquehanna Storage Lake and Power Co.
94, 142, 529, 558, 889
Susquehanna Township, Dauphin County
377
Susquehanna Township, Lycoming County
893
Susquehanna Transmission Co. of Pennsylvania
518, 707, 894
Susquehanna Water and Power Co.
404
Swatara-Lebanon Power & Light Co.
895
Swatara Township, Lebanon County
895

T

Tamaqua & Lansford Street Railroad Co.
261, 896, 922
The Tamaqua and Pottsville Electric Railroad
897
The Tamaqua Boot and Shoe Manufacturing Co.
280
Tamaqua Borough Council
112, 280, 896
Tamaqua Borough, Schuylkill County
112, 280, 281, 546, 747, 896, 898, 899
Tamaqua Light, Heat and Power Co.
546, 898
Tamaqua-Schuylkill Gas Co.
899
Taney Electric Co.
900
Tariffs
see Rate schedules
Tatamy Borough Council
901
Tatamy Borough, Northampton County
901
Tatamy Light Heat and Power Co.
901
Tatamy Silk Mill
901
Tax-exempt customers
see Rate abatements for non-profit
571
Taxes
365, 542, 568, 571, 613, 686, 831
Taylor Borough, Lackawanna County
459
Taylor Electric Co.
902
Taylor, F.E.
125
Taylor Township, Lackawanna County
902
Telephone and telegraph service and companies
271, 688, 691, 894
Telford Borough, Bucks County
903
Telford Power & Light Co.
903
Tenants
see Apartment buildings and tenants
Texas Power & Light Co.
904
Texas Township, Wayne County
904
The Scranton Electric Co. No. 2
79, 116, 356, 460, 466, 653, 770, 806, 807, 808, 859, 861, 1046, 1048
Thomson-Houston arc lighting
511
Thomson-Houston Electric Co.
8, 49, 81, 106, 298, 548, 799, 800
arc lighting equipment
511
electric street railway system
799, 800
licensing arragements
8, 49, 106
Throop Borough, Lackawanna County
807
Tidd, George N.
861
Tide Water and Susquehanna River Railroad Co.
889
Tidewater Canal
889
Tinicum Township, Bucks County
905
Tinicum Township Electric Co.
905
Tioga County
891
Covington Borough
158
Tobyhanna Power & Light Co.
906
Tobyhanna Township, Monroe Township
906
Toll bridge companies
537
Topton Borough, Berks County
907
Topton Electric Co.
907
Towamencin-Montgomery Power & Light Co.
908
Towamencin Township, Montgomery County
908
Towamensing Power & Light Co.
909
Towamensing Township, Carbon County
909
Tower City Borough, Dauphin County
1027, 1033
Tower City Borough, Schuylkill County
541, 864, 910
Tower City Electric Co.
910
Traction companies
see Bus transportation companies, Railway companies, and Street railway companies
Trade associations
721
Traffic congestion
964
Transit companies
see Bus transportation companies, Railway companies, and Street railway companies
Transmission companies, electric
139, 518, 720, 894
Tremont and Pine Grove Electric Light Heat and Power Co.
912
Tremont & Donaldson Electric Light Co.
911
Tremont Borough, Schuylkill County
911, 912
Tremont-Schuylkill Power & Light Co.
913
Tremont Township, Schuylkill County
220, 257, 913
Trenton and Princeton Traction Co. (N.J.)
65
The Trevorton Electric Light and Power Co.
716, 914
Trevorton Village, Northumberland County
914
Tri-County Electric Co.
71, 72, 202, 293, 413, 915, 1003
Triumph Electric Co.
generators
613
Troxelville Power Co.
916
Trumbauersville Borough, Bucks County
917
Trumbauersville Electric Light and Power Co.
917
Tuckahoe Lithia Water Co.
918
Tuckahoe Mineral Springs Co., No. 1
919, 921
Tuckahoe Mineral Springs Co., No. 2
918, 920, 921
Tuckahoe Mineral Springs Co., of Northumberland, Northumberland County, Pennsylv
919, 921
Tumbling Run Lake
922
Tumbling Run Opera Co.
922
Tumbling Run Park Association
261, 922
Tunkhannock Power & Light Co.
923
Tunkhannock Township, Monroe County
923
Turbines
efficiency of
721
Turbogenerators
8, 105, 382, 383, 384, 447, 484, 485, 486, 548, 595, 721
Turbot Township Electric Co.
926
Turbot Township, Northumberland County
600, 924, 926

Turbot Township Northumberland Electric Co.
924
Turbotville Borough, Northumberland County
925
Turbotville Electric Co.
925
Turnpike construction
75
Tustin, E.B.
943
Tyron Township, Perry County
829

U

Union-Buffalo Power & Light Co.
927
Union County
Buffalo Township
66, 927
East Buffalo Township
196, 197, 928
Gregg Township
359
Hartleton Borough
381
Kelly Township
449
Lewis Township
365
Lewisburg Borough
500, 936, 944
Limestone Township
504
Mifflinburg Borough
365
Union Township
935
West Buffalo Township
989
West Milton Village
944
White Deer Township
1014
Union Deposit Mill
419
Union-East Buffalo Power & Light Co.
928
Union Electric Power Co.
929
Union-Lebanon Light & Power Co.
930
Union-Lebanon Power & Light Co.
931
Union Light and Power Co.
932
Union Light Co.
933
Union organizing campaigns
721, 756
Union Passenger Railway Co.
934
Union Power & Light Co.
935
Union Power Co.
936
Union Township, Lebanon County
930, 931
Union Township Power Co.
938
Union Township Power & Light Co.
937
Union Township, Schuylkill County
933, 938
Union Township, Snyder County
937
Union Township, Union County
935
Uniondale Borough, Susquehanna County
939
Uniondale-Susquehanna Power & Light Co.
939
Unions
721, 756, 774
Uniontown Borough, Dauphin County
940
Uniontown Public Service Corp.
940
United Edison Manufacturing Co.
113, 748
The United Electric Co.
161, 567, 587, 645, 941, 964, 966, 1042
United Electric Light & Power Co.
942
United Gas and Electric Co.
267, 270, 313, 378, 426, 470, 737, 910, 1038
United Gas and Electric Co. of Bloomsburg
45, 179, 943
United Gas and Electric Corp.
1050
United Gas and Electrical Engineering Corp.
420, 471, 473, 1019
United Light and Power Co.
449, 599, 936, 944
The United Light, Heat and Power Co. of Mahanoy City, Pa.
723, 945
United Mine Workers of America
261
United States Commerce Dept.
226
United States Housing Corp.
492
United States Liberty Bonds
382, 396
United States National War Labor Board
721
United States Postmaster General
496
United States Supreme Court
1046, 1048
United Securities Corp.
1050
United States Electric Co.
49
Upper Alsace Township, Berks County
946
Upper Alsace Township Electric Co.
946
Upper Augusta Power & Light Co.
947
Upper Augusta Township, Northumberland County
424, 885, 886, 947
Upper Dublin Township, Montgomery County
887
Upper Fairfield-Lycoming Power & Light Co.
948
Upper Fairfield Township, Lycoming County
948
Upper Gwynedd Township, Montgomery County
361
Upper Hanover Power & Light Co.
949
Upper Hanover Township, Montgomery County
949
Upper Leacock Township Electric Co.
950
Upper Leacock Township, Lancaster County
322, 950
Upper Macungie Electric Co.
951
Upper Macungie Township, Lehigh County
951
Upper Mahanoy-Northumberland Power & Light Co.
952
Upper Mahanoy Township, Northumberland County
952
Upper Mahantongo Township Electric Co.
953
Upper Mahantongo Township, Schuylkill County
953
Upper Makefield Township, Bucks County
954
Upper Makefield Township Electric Co.
954
Upper Milford Electric Co.
955
Upper Milford Township, Lehigh County
423, 955
Upper Mount Bethel Electric Co.
956
Upper Mount Bethel Township, Northampton County
956
Upper Nazareth Electric Co.
957
Upper Nazareth, Northampton County
957
Upper Paxton Township, Dauphin County
1033
Upper Saucon Electric Co.
958
Upper Saucon Township, Lehigh County
93, 958
Utilities Construction Co.
959
Utilities Supply Co.
960
Utility monopolies
see also Holding companies

(continued)

13, 106, 133, 179, 210, 260, 267, 270, 348, 385, 411, 447, 495, 536, 537, 567, 667, 669, 718, 802, 807, 808, 918, 920

V

Vallamont Park
961
Vallamont Passenger Railway Co.
961, 962
Vallamont Traction Co.
91, 113, 444, 961, 962, 1031
Valley Electric Service Co.
963
Valley Railways
380, 537, 722, 941, 964, 966, 967, 1048, 1050
Valley Township, Montour County
965
Valley Township Montour Electric Co.
965
Valley Traction Co.
371, 372, 845, 941, 964, 966, 997, 1016
Valley Transportation Co.
964, 967
Valley View Township, Schuylkill County
415
Valley View Village, Hegins Township, Schuylkill County
103
Vandling Borough, Lackawanna County
968
Vandling Electric Co.
968
Varden and Lake Ariel Light, Heat and Power Co.
19, 969
Varden Village, Lake Township, Wayne County
19
Virginia
571

W

Walbridge, H.D., & Co.
1029
Walker Power & Light Co.
970
Walker Township, Schuylkill County
970
Walnutport Borough, Northampton County
971
Walnutport Electric Light and Power Co.
971
War Labor Board
261
Warren Electric Co.
603
Warwick Township Electric Co.
972
Warwick Township, Lancaster County
323, 972
Washington Borough, Lancaster County
324
Washington-Lycoming Power & Light Co.
973
Washington-Northumberland Power & Light Co.
974
Washington Square Electric Light & Power Co.
975
Washington Township, Dauphin County
987
Washington Township Electric Light and Power Co.
976
Washington Township Electric Light Co.
977
Washington Township Electric Light, Heat and Power Co.
987
Washington Township, Lehigh County
178, 835
Washington Township Lehigh Electric Co.
979
Washington Township, Lycoming County
973
Washington Township, Northampton County
857
Washington Township, Northumberland County
974
Washington Township, Schuylkill County
221
Washington Township, Snyder County
977
Washingtonville Borough, Montour County
980, 981
Washingtonville Power & Light Co.
980
Water filtration plant
419
Water filtration systems
81, 82, 419
Water heating service
313
Water mains, construction of
81, 82, 419
Water power companies
see also Hydroelectric power companies
142, 365, 404, 419, 420, 519, 529, 558, 566, 571, 579, 595, 632, 703, 713, 721, 727, 837, 1038
Water supply companies
81, 82, 84, 393, 419, 420, 421, 512, 558, 597, 727, 888, 918, 919, 920, 921, 1039
Waterworks
81, 82, 393, 419, 1039
Watson-Lycoming Power & Light Co.
981
Watsontown Borough, Lycoming County
610
Watsontown Borough, Northumberland County
982
Watsontown Door & Sash Co.
610, 982
Watts Water and Power Co.
448, 983
The Waverly Light, Heat & Power Co.
1
Waymart Borough, Wayne County
984
Waymart Electric Co.
984
Wayne County
808
Berlin Township
32
Bethany Borough
47
Canaan Township
76
Cherry Ridge Township
97, 98
Clinton Township
62
Damascus Township
167
Dreher Township
182
Dyberry Township
191
Honesdale Borough
411, 412
Lake Township
468
Lebanon Township
481
Lehigh Township
488
Salem Township
792
South Canaan Township
969
South Varden Village
969
Sterling Township
865
Texas Township
904
Waymart Borough
984
Wayne Power & Light Co.
985
Wayne Township, Clinton County
985
Wayne Township, Dauphin County
986
Wayne Township Electric Corp.
986
Wayne Township, Schuylkill County
222, 258
Weaver, Jacob S.
915
Weissport Borough, Carbon County
341, 987
Weissport Electric Co.
702, 987
Welfare work
210, 800
West Abington Township, Lackawanna County
1034
West Berwick Light, Heat and Power Co.
45
West Bethlehem Borough, Northampton County
49

The West Brunswick Township Light, Heat and Power Co.
988
West Brunswick Township, Schuylkill County
223, 988
West Buffalo Township, Union County
989
West Buffalo-Union Power & Light Co.
989
West Cameron-Northumberland Power & Light Co.
990
West Cameron Township, Northumberland County
73, 990
West Chillisquaque Township Electric Co.
991
West Chillisquaque Township, Northumberland County
991, 992
West Chillisquaque Township-Northumberland Electric Co.
992
West Cocalico Township Electric Co.
993
West Cocalico Township, Lancaster County
993
West Donegal Township Electric Light Co.
994
West Donegal Township, Lancaster County
994
West Earl Township Electric Co.
995
West End Electric Light and Power Co.
395, 996
West Fairview and Marysville Electric Street Railway Co.
567, 966, 997
West Fairwiew Borough, Cumberland County
310, 997
West Hanover Township, Dauphin County
377
West Hazleton Borough, Luzerne County
996
West Hempfield Township Electric Co.
998
West Hempfield Township, Lancaster County
325, 998
West Lampeter Electric Light, Heat and Power Co.
999
West Lampeter Township, Lancaster County
999
West Mahanoy Light Co.
1001
West Mahanoy Township Electric Co.
1002
West Mahanoy Township, Schuylkill County
259, 1001, 1002
West Milton Village, Union County
944
West Nantmeal Electric Co.
1003
West Nantmeal Township, Chester County
1003
West Penn Township Electric Co.
1004
West Penn Township, Schuylkill County
1004
West Perry Power Co.
1005
West Perry Township, Snyder County
1005
West Pittston Borough, Luzerne County
149, 1007
West Pittston Electric Co.
1006
West Pittston-Exeter Railroad Co.
1007
West Rockhill Township, Bucks County
1008, 1009
West Rockhill Township Electric Light and Power Co., No. 1
1008
West Rockhill Township Electric Light and Power Co., No. 2
1009
West Sadsbury Township, Chester County
1010, 1013
West Sadsbury Township Electric Co.
1010
The West Scranton Light Heat & Power Co.
460, 1011
West Telford Borough, Montgomery County
1012
West Telford Power & Light Co.
1012
West Virginia
Consholing
1047
Wheeling
1047
Western Chester County Electric Co.
1013
Western Electric Co.
arc lighting dynamos
107, 996
Westinghouse, Church, Kerr & Co.
290, 823
Westinghouse Electric & Manufacturing Co.
see also Alternating current
8, 24, 49, 107, 290, 298, 706, 813, 966
alternating current system
290, 298, 966
incandescent dynamos
571
licensing arrangements
107, 290
turbo-generators
548, 813, 966
Westinghouse, George
290
Westinghouse Manufacturing & Supply Co.
8, 49, 706
Weston Electric Light Co.
996
Wheatfield Township, Perry County
3, 447
Wheathead Town, Lancaster County
871
Wheatland Mills, Lancaster County
872
Wheeling, West Virginia
1047
White Deer Power & Light Co.
1014
White Deer Township, Union County
1014
White Haven Borough, Luzerne County
1015
White Haven Electric Illuminating Plant
1015
White Haven Light, Heat & Power Co.
231, 1015
White Hill Borough, Cumberland County
1016
White Hill & Mechanicsburg Passenger Railway Co.
966, 1016
Whitehall Township Board of Commissioners
284
Whitehall Township, Lehigh County
89, 284, 297, 493, 494
Whitpain Township, Montgomery County
975
Wiconisco Village, Dauphin County
1027
Wilkes Barre and Hazleton Railway
18
Wilkes Barre City Council
1023
Wilkes-Barre City, Luzerne County
153, 348, 932, 1017, 1018, 1019, 1020, 1021, 1022, 1023, 1041
social and economic conditions
1019, 1021, 1022, 1023, 1024
street lighting contracts
1021, 1022, 1023
The Wilkes Barre Co., No. 1
17, 1017, 1018, 1019, 1022
The Wilkes Barre Co., No. 2
856, 932, 1017, 1018
The Wilkes Barre Co., No. 3
1017, 1019, 1022
Wilkes Barre Electric Co.
1020, 1021, 1022, 1041
The Wilkes-Barre Electric Light Co.
1020, 1021, 1041
Wilkes Barre Gas and Electric Co.
22, 153, 348, 761, 1017, 1018, 1019, 1020, 1022, 1023
Wilkes-Barre Gas Co.
348, 1022, 1023
The Wilkes Barre Heat, Light and Motor Co.
1017, 1018
Wilkes-Barre Township Electric Co.
1025

Wilkes-Barre Township, Luzerne County
1025
Williams Borough, Northampton County
118
Williams Township Electric Co.
1026
Williams Township, Northampton County
1026
Williams Valley Light Heat and Power Co.
541, 864, 1027
Williamsport City Council
113, 536, 1029, 1030, 1031, 1032
Williamsport City, Luzerne County
street lighting contracts
282, 535, 536
Williamsport City, Lycoming County
2, 91, 102, 113, 203, 282, 441, 442, 444, 535, 536, 537, 614, 648, 649, 656, 847, 888, 891, 934, 961, 962, 1028, 1029, 1030, 1031, 1032
electric street railway system
1030
Williamsport Electric Co.
1028
Williamsport Gas Co.
668, 1029
Williamsport Passenger Railway Co.
442, 648, 649, 847, 888, 934, 961, 1030, 1031
Williamsport Railways Co.
203, 847, 962, 1030, 1031, 1032
Williamsport Transportation Co.
1031, 1032
Williamstown Borough, Dauphin County
541, 1027
Williamstown Gas Co.
1033
Wilmington City, New Castle County, Delaware
347
Wilmot Engineering Co.
385
Winola Electric Co.
1034
Winton Township, Lackawanna County
463
Wiring
of residential properties
81, 282, 482, 734, 758, 875, 917
Wise, J.S., Jr.
385, 861
Wolf Township, Lycoming County
1035
Wolf Township Lycoming County Electric Co.
1035
Womelsdorf Borough, Berks County
42
Womelsdorf Electric Co.
42
Wood suppliers
888
Woodward Power & Light Co.
1036
Woodward Township, Lycoming County
1036
Woollen mills
electrification of
105, 843
Workers
see Employees
Workmen's Compensation Act of 1915
51
Workmen's Compensation Insurance Fund
51, 382, 486, 542
World War I
81, 261, 496, 613, 614, 646, 901, 964
conservation of fuel supplies
486
defense contracts
26, 721, 822
Federal Government regulations affecting utilities
81, 226, 385, 496, 581, 646, 721, 901
strikes
261, 496
War Labor Board
261
World War II
blackouts, effect of on electric companies
721, 1046
defense contracts
721, 1034, 1046
Federal Government regulations affecting utilities
1, 721, 774, 808, 1034, 1046
National Electric Defense Association
1, 721
National War Labor Board
721
National War Manpower Commission
721
United States Federal Defense Power Administration
1, 721, 1034
Wright Township Electric Co.
1037
Wright Township, Luzerne County
1037
Wrightsville Borough, York County
566, 1038, 1039
Wrightsville Light and Power Co.
228, 528, 1038, 1049
Wrightsville Water Supply Co.
1039, 1049
Wyoming Borough, Luzerne County
1023
Wyoming Borough-Luzerne Power & Light Co.
1040
Wyoming County
808
Wyoming Valley Electric Light, Heat and Power Co.
1020, 1021, 1041
Wyoming Valley Water Supply Co.
393

Y

Yagel, L.E.
476
York Borough, York County
566
York County
721, 941
Chanceford Township
94
Conewago Township
144
East Manchester Borough
1043
East Manchester Township
269
East Prospect Borough
228, 1038
Fairview Township
1042
Hellam Township
400
Lower Chanceford Township
404, 518, 519
Lower Windsor Township
528, 529, 530, 1038
Wrightsville Borough
566, 1038, 1039
York Borough
566
York Haven Borough
1044
York County Electric Co.
1042
York-East Manchester Power & Light Co.
1043
York Haven Borough, York County
1044
York Haven Water & Power Co.
966
York-York Haven Power & Light Co.
1044
Young Men's Christian Association
800, 808
Young, Owen D.
1048

Z

Zeiders, T.M.
379
Zerbe Electric Co.
1045
Zerbe Township, Northumberland County
1045
Zimmerman, S.R.
42